VOLUME TWO

bake
FROM SCRATCH™

ARTISAN RECIPES
FOR THE HOME BAKER

Brian Hart Hoffman

PRESS™

83Press
1900 International Park Drive, Suite 50
Birmingham, Alabama 35243

ISBN: 978-1-940772-48-6
Printed in China

VOLUME TWO

bake
FROM SCRATCH™

ARTISAN RECIPES
FOR THE HOME BAKER

Brian Hart Hoffman

10
CAKES

12 LAYER CAKES

30 BUNDT CAKES

42 ONE-LAYER CAKES

110
BREADS

112 QUICK BREADS

132 YEAST BREADS

170
PIES
AND TARTS

172 PIES

220 TARTS

240
PASTRIES

264
COOKIES
AND BARS

266 COOKIES

352 BARS

368
MISCELLANEOUS

BAKING IS MY PASSION AND MY THERAPY. THIS COLLECTION OF RECIPES FROM THE SECOND YEAR OF *BAKE FROM SCRATCH* MAGAZINE WILL BE YOUR GO-TO BAKING RESOURCE, AS IT IS MINE.

My love for baking is what inspired *Bake from Scratch* magazine, and it's what I look forward to most in my free time. Every weekend, I tie on my apron and head to the kitchen to bake. I enjoy embracing each season's best ingredients and trying recipes from bakers I admire from around the world.

This gorgeous cookbook offers endless ideas for cakes, pies, breads, pastries, and more. From nostalgic classics to contemporary showstoppers, each recipe is as dependable and delicious as the next.

You won't need a special occasion to dive deep into our vault of recipes—only a love for this craft. Whether you are a novice baker or an experienced professional, you'll gain expertise on both simple and challenging baking projects, from rolling out cookie dough to shaping wreath breads and weaving the perfect pie lattice. With visual tutorials, incisive pro tips, and easy-to-follow instructions, we guide you every step of the way.

Whether it's your first bake or your thousandth, settle in and celebrate scratch baking.

After you pull a warm cake from your oven, watch it cool on your countertop, and serve it to family and friends, enjoy the moment of sharing—that's really what baking is all about. Bake. Love. Share.

CAKES

LAYER
CAKES

Our stunning layer cakes were designed for the spotlight.
From a towering showstopper topped with fresh berries to
a subtle yet sophisticated two-layer treat brimming with
caramel and dates, these cakes don't require a reason to be
made, only a will to be baked.

BANANA CAKE WITH BROWN SUGAR HAZELNUT BUTTERCREAM

Makes 1 (8-inch) cake

Frozen bananas in a cake? Heck yes. Reducing the juice from these frozen fruits adds a nutty, caramelized flavor that takes this banana cake to the next level. Top with a buttercream inspired by penuche, a brown sugar-based fudge reminiscent of Southern pralines, and this cake is downright irresistible.

3　large frozen overripe bananas (525 grams), unpeeled
¼　cup (57 grams) unsalted butter, softened
1⅓　cups (267 grams) granulated sugar
2　large eggs (100 grams)
2　cups (250 grams) all-purpose flour
1　teaspoon (5 grams) baking soda
½　teaspoon (1.5 grams) kosher salt
1　cup (240 grams) sour cream
2　teaspoons (8 grams) vanilla extract
Chocolate-Hazelnut Filling (recipe follows)
Brown Sugar Hazelnut Buttercream (recipe follows)
Praline Hazelnuts (recipe follows)

1. Thaw frozen unpeeled bananas in a medium bowl, reserving any juices during thawing process. Peel bananas, and place fruit in a fine-mesh sieve over bowl. Mash bananas, and press gently to collect juices but do not push fruit through sieve. Reserve 1½ cups (341 grams) mashed banana. Squeeze banana peel firmly over sieve to collect any remaining juice. In a stainless steel saucepan, heat banana juice over medium heat. Cook until reduced to 3 tablespoons (45 grams); set aside.
2. Preheat oven to 350°F (180°C). Butter and flour 2 (8-inch) square tall-sided cake pans. Line bottom of pans with parchment paper.
3. In the bowl of a stand mixer fitted with the paddle attachment, beat butter and sugar at medium speed until fluffy, 3 to 4 minutes, stopping to scrape sides of bowl. Add eggs, one at a time, beating well after each addition.

4. In a medium bowl, whisk together flour, baking soda, and salt. With mixer on low speed, gradually add flour mixture to butter mixture alternately with sour cream, beginning and ending with flour mixture, beating just until combined after each addition. Fold in reserved 1½ cups (341 grams) mashed banana, reserved 3 tablespoons (45 grams) banana juice reduction, and vanilla. Divide batter between prepared pans, smoothing tops with an offset spatula.
5. Bake until a wooden pick inserted in center comes out clean, about 25 minutes. Let cool in pans for 10 minutes. Remove from pans, and let cool completely on wire racks.
6. Spread Chocolate-Hazelnut Filling between layers, and spread Brown Sugar Hazelnut Buttercream on top of cake. Top with Praline Hazelnuts.

CHOCOLATE-HAZELNUT FILLING
Makes 1½ to 2 cups

½　cup (113 grams) unsalted butter, softened
3　cups (360 grams) confectioners' sugar
2½　tablespoons (37.5 grams) heavy whipping cream
½　cup (43 grams) unsweetened cocoa powder
¼　cup (64 grams) chocolate-hazelnut spread*

1. In the bowl of a stand mixer fitted with the paddle attachment, beat butter at medium speed until creamy. Gradually add confectioners' sugar and cream, beating until smooth. Add cocoa and chocolate-hazelnut spread, beating to combine. (Do not overmix.)

BROWN SUGAR HAZELNUT BUTTERCREAM
Makes 2 cups

1　cup (220 grams) firmly packed dark brown sugar
½　cup (113 grams) unsalted butter
¼　cup (60 grams) warm whole milk (105°F/40°C to 110°F/43°C)

3　cups (360 grams) confectioners' sugar
3　tablespoons (48 grams) chocolate-hazelnut spread*
1　teaspoon (3 grams) kosher salt

1. In a small saucepan, bring brown sugar and butter to a boil over medium-high heat. Boil for 1 minute. Remove from heat, and let cool for 15 minutes. Stir in warm milk.
2. In the bowl of a stand mixer fitted with the whisk attachment, beat brown sugar mixture, confectioners' sugar, chocolate-hazelnut spread, and salt at medium speed until lightened in color, about 2 minutes. Use immediately.

*We used Nutella.

PRALINE HAZELNUTS
Makes 3 cups

2　cups (226 grams) chopped raw hazelnuts
¼　cup (50 grams) granulated sugar
1　teaspoon egg white (3 grams)

1. Preheat oven to 200°F (93°C). Line a baking sheet with parchment paper.
2. In a medium bowl, whisk together hazelnuts, sugar, and egg white. Pour hazelnuts onto prepared pan.
3. Bake for 12 minutes. Let cool completely.

PRO TIPS
Resist the urge to add more chocolate-hazelnut spread to filling. It can cause the mixture to seize up.

Store cooled Praline Hazelnuts in a plastic bag, preferably out of sight. They are the perfect salty-sweet snack and far too easy to finish off before completing your cake!

BERRY BUTTERMILK CAKE WITH MASCARPONE CRÈME FRAÎCHE

Makes 1 (6-inch) cake

Buttermilk adds moisture and a slight tang while fresh berries add a punch of sweetness to this spring-inspired confection. Using creamy mascarpone and crème fraîche in the topping is just the icing—or should we say frosting—on the naked cake.

¾   cup (170 grams) unsalted butter, softened
½   cup (100 grams) granulated sugar
2   large eggs (100 grams)
2   cups (250 grams) all-purpose flour
1   tablespoon (15 grams) baking powder
½   teaspoon (1.5 grams) kosher salt
1   cup (240 grams) whole buttermilk
⅓   cup (57 grams) sliced blackberries
⅓   cup (57 grams) chopped strawberries
⅓   cup (57 grams) whole blueberries
½   teaspoon (2 grams) vanilla extract
Mascarpone Crème Fraîche Frosting (recipe follows)
Garnish: Sugared Flowers and Berries (recipe follows)

1. Preheat oven to 350°F (180°C). Butter and flour 4 (6-inch) round tall-sided cake pans. Line bottom of pans with parchment paper. (Batter is too heavy and dense to bake in 2 [6-inch] pans, so be sure to use 4 pans.)
2. In the bowl of a stand mixer fitted with the paddle attachment, beat butter and sugar at medium speed until creamy, 3 to 4 minutes, stopping to scrape sides of bowl. Add eggs, one at a time, beating well after each addition.
3. In a medium bowl, whisk together flour, baking powder, and salt. With mixer on low speed, gradually add flour mixture to butter mixture alternately with buttermilk, beginning and ending with flour mixture, beating just until combined after each addition. Fold in berries and vanilla. Divide batter among prepared pans, smoothing tops with an offset spatula.
4. Bake until a wooden pick inserted in center comes out clean, about 25 minutes. Let cool in pans for 10 minutes. Remove from pans, and let cool completely on wire racks.

5. Spread Mascarpone Crème Fraîche Frosting between layers and on top of cake. Garnish with Sugared Flowers and Berries, if desired. Cover and refrigerate for up to 3 days.

MASCARPONE CRÈME FRAÎCHE FROSTING
Makes 2 cups

8   ounces (225 grams) cold mascarpone cheese
4   cups (480 grams) confectioners' sugar
½   cup (120 grams) cold crème fraîche
1   teaspoon (4 grams) vanilla extract
½   teaspoon (1.5 grams) kosher salt

1. In the bowl of a stand mixer fitted with the paddle attachment, beat mascarpone at medium speed until creamy. Add confectioners' sugar, 1 cup (120 grams) at a time, beating until smooth. Add crème fraîche, vanilla, and salt, beating to combine. Cover and refrigerate until ready to use.

SUGARED FLOWERS AND BERRIES
Makes 12 flowers and 12 berries

1   large egg white (30 grams)
Organic food-safe small flowers
Fresh berries
Fine granulated sugar

1. In a small bowl, whisk egg white until frothy. Using a paintbrush, brush egg white onto flowers and berries just until wet. Sprinkle with sugar. Place on a wire rack to let dry. Store in an airtight container at room temperature until ready to use.

Note: *You can use only berries or only flowers, if you prefer.*

PRO TIP
Fight the instinct to bring the mascarpone cheese and crème fraîche to room temperature as that will make your frosting too soft. For the best results, keep both ingredients in the refrigerator until ready to use.

TROPICAL HUMMINGBIRD LAYER CAKE

Makes 1 (9-inch) cake

We swapped out pecans for macadamia nuts and reconstituted dried apricots in pineapple juice for a unique spin on this timeless treat blanketed in rich, swoopy frosting.

1 cup (128 grams) chopped dried apricots
1 (20-ounce) can (567 grams) pineapple slices, juice reserved
3½ cups (438 grams) all-purpose flour
1½ cups (300 grams) granulated sugar
1 teaspoon (5 grams) baking soda
1 teaspoon (2 grams) ground cinnamon
¼ teaspoon ground nutmeg
¾ cup (85 grams) chopped roasted macadamia nuts
1½ cups (341 grams) mashed ripe banana
1¼ cups (280 grams) canola oil
4 large eggs (200 grams)
1 teaspoon (4 grams) vanilla extract
Cream Cheese Frosting (recipe follows)
Garnish: chopped macadamia nuts

1. In a medium saucepan, bring apricots and reserved pineapple juice to a boil over medium-high heat. Boil for 5 minutes; remove from heat. Cover and let stand for at least 30 minutes. Finely dice 4 rings of pineapple; set aside. Reserve remaining pineapple for another use.
2. Preheat oven to 350°F (180°C). Butter and flour 3 (9-inch) round cake pans, and line bottom of pans with parchment paper.
3. In a large bowl, sift together flour, sugar, baking soda, cinnamon, and nutmeg. Stir in macadamia nuts. In a small bowl, stir together banana, oil, eggs, and vanilla. Make a well in center of dry ingredients; add banana mixture, stirring just until moistened. Fold in pineapple and apricots. Divide batter among prepared pans.
4. Bake until a wooden pick inserted in center comes out clean, 20 to 25 minutes. Let cool in pans for 10 minutes. Remove from pans, and let cool completely on wire racks. Spread Cream Cheese Frosting

between layers and on top and sides of cake. Press macadamia nuts into sides of cake, if desired. Refrigerate for at least 3 hours before serving.

CREAM CHEESE FROSTING
Makes 6 cups

8 ounces (225 grams) cream cheese, softened
1 cup (227 grams) unsalted butter, softened
5 to 6 cups (600 to 720 grams) confectioners' sugar
1 teaspoon (4 grams) vanilla extract

1. In the bowl of a stand mixer fitted with the paddle attachment, beat cream cheese and butter at medium speed until creamy. Reduce mixer speed to low. Gradually add enough confectioners' sugar until a spreadable consistency is reached. Beat in vanilla. Use immediately.

NATURAL STRAWBERRY CAKE WITH BROWNED BUTTER FROSTING

Makes 1 (8-inch) cake

If there were a cake that embodied springtime, the strawberry layer cake would be it: pretty (in pink) and perfect for any special occasion or just a day when you need a little something sweet. In our version, you'll find chunks of fresh strawberries nestled among fluffy cake layers slathered in a rich Browned Butter Frosting.

4¾   cups (807.5 grams) sliced fresh strawberries, divided
2¼   cups (450 grams) plus 3 tablespoons (36 grams) granulated
       sugar, divided
3½   tablespoons (52.5 grams) fresh lemon juice, divided
¾   cup (170 grams) unsalted butter, softened
6   large egg whites (180 grams)
1½   teaspoons (6 grams) vanilla extract
1½   cups (28 grams) freeze-dried strawberries
3   cups (375 grams) all-purpose flour
1   cup (125 grams) cake flour
1   tablespoon (15 grams) baking powder
1½   teaspoons (4.5 grams) kosher salt
1½   cups (360 grams) whole milk, room temperature
Browned Butter Frosting (recipe follows)

1. In a medium saucepan, cook 2¼ cups (382.5 grams) sliced strawberries, 3 tablespoons (36 grams) sugar, and 3 tablespoons (45 grams) lemon juice over medium heat until slightly thickened, 5 to 7 minutes. Remove from heat, and let cool completely.
2. Preheat oven to 350°F (180°C). Butter and flour 3 (8-inch) round cake pans.
3. In the bowl of a stand mixer fitted with the paddle attachment, beat butter and remaining 2¼ cups (450 grams) sugar at medium speed until fluffy, 3 to 4 minutes, stopping to scrape sides of bowl. Add egg whites, one at a time, beating well after each addition. Beat in vanilla.

4. In the work bowl of a food processor, pulse freeze-dried strawberries until powdered, 5 to 6 times.
5. In a medium bowl, whisk together flours, baking powder, salt, and strawberry powder. With mixer on low speed, gradually add flour mixture to butter mixture alternately with milk, beginning and ending with flour mixture, beating just until combined after each addition.
6. In a small bowl, toss together 1½ cups (255 grams) sliced strawberries and remaining ½ tablespoon (7.5 grams) lemon juice. Stir sliced strawberries and cooled strawberry mixture into batter. Pour batter into prepared pans, smoothing tops if necessary.
7. Bake until a wooden pick inserted in center comes out clean, 25 to 30 minutes. Let cool in pans for 10 minutes. Remove from pans, and let cool completely on wire racks. Spread Browned Butter Frosting on 2 cake layers, and top each with half of remaining 1 cup (170 grams) strawberries. Stack layers, and spread frosting on top and sides of cake.

BROWNED BUTTER FROSTING
Makes 5 cups

2   cups (454 grams) unsalted butter
5   cups (600 grams) confectioners' sugar
¼   cup (60 grams) whole milk, room temperature
1   teaspoon (4 grams) vanilla extract
¼   teaspoon kosher salt

1. In a medium saucepan, melt butter over medium heat. Cook until butter turns a medium-brown color and has a nutty aroma, about 10 minutes. Remove from heat, and let cool completely.
2. In the bowl of a stand mixer fitted with the paddle attachment, beat browned butter at medium speed until fluffy, about 2 minutes. Gradually add remaining ingredients, and beat until combined, about 2 minutes. Refrigerate in an airtight container for up to 1 week.

PRO TIP
Add lemon or other citrus juice to strawberries to help maintain their bright color during baking.

BLACK VELVET LAYER CAKE

Makes 1 (9-inch) cake

Everyone knows that cream cheese frosting is the secret to red velvet cake's stardom, and chocolate is universally beloved. By topping layers of rich chocolate cake with this favored frosting, we've created the best of both worlds.

2½ cups (313 grams) all-purpose flour
1½ cups (300 grams) granulated sugar
½ cup (110 grams) firmly packed light brown sugar
1 cup (85 grams) unsweetened dark cocoa powder
1½ teaspoons (7.5 grams) baking soda
1 teaspoon (5 grams) baking powder
½ teaspoon (1.5 grams) kosher salt
1 cup (240 grams) coffee
1 cup (224 grams) vegetable oil
3 large eggs (150 grams)
1 cup (240 grams) sour cream
½ teaspoon (2 grams) vanilla extract
Sweet Cream Cheese Frosting (recipe follows)
1 cup (240 grams) Caramel (recipe follows)

1. Preheat oven to 350°F (180°C). Butter and flour 3 (9-inch) round cake pans.
2. In the bowl of a stand mixer fitted with the paddle attachment, combine flour, sugars, cocoa, baking soda, baking powder, and salt. In a medium bowl, whisk together coffee, oil, and eggs. With mixer on medium speed, add coffee mixture to flour mixture, beating until smooth. Stir in sour cream and vanilla until combined. Divide batter among prepared pans.
3. Bake until a wooden pick inserted in center comes out clean, 20 to 25 minutes. Let cool in pans for 10 minutes. Remove from pans, and let cool completely on wire racks. Using a serrated knife, remove rounded tops from cake layers. Crumble tops, and set aside.
4. Pipe a ring of Sweet Cream Cheese Frosting around inside edge of bottom cake layer to create a border. Fill center with ⅛ cup (30 grams) Caramel. Repeat with remaining cake layers and Caramel. Spread a thin layer of frosting on top and sides of cake. Spread remaining frosting on top of cake, and swirl with a spatula. Top with reserved cake crumbs. Cover and refrigerate for up to 3 days.

SWEET CREAM CHEESE FROSTING
Makes 2½ cups

8 ounces (225 grams) cream cheese, softened
¼ cup (57 grams) unsalted butter, softened
4 cups (480 grams) confectioners' sugar
2 tablespoons (30 grams) heavy whipping cream, chilled
1 teaspoon (4 grams) vanilla extract

1. In the bowl of a stand mixer fitted with the paddle attachment, beat cream cheese and butter at medium speed until creamy. Reduce mixer speed to low. Add confectioners' sugar, 1 cup (120 grams) at a time, beating until smooth. Beat in cream, 1 tablespoon (15 grams) at a time, until frosting reaches a spreadable consistency. Beat in vanilla. Refrigerate leftover frosting for up to 2 weeks, or freeze for up to 3 months.

CARAMEL
Makes 3 cups

1½ cups (300 grams) granulated sugar
¼ cup (60 grams) water
2 tablespoons (42 grams) light corn syrup
½ cup (113 grams) unsalted butter, cubed
1 cup (240 grams) heavy whipping cream
1 teaspoon (3 grams) kosher salt

1. In a large heavy saucepan, place sugar, ¼ cup (60 grams) water, and corn syrup; swirl to combine. Cook over medium-high heat, without stirring, until mixture is amber colored, 10 to 14 minutes. Remove from heat. Add butter, stirring until melted (mixture will foam).
2. In a microwave-safe bowl, heat cream on high until warm, 30 to 40 seconds. Slowly add cream to caramel mixture, whisking until smooth (mixture will foam). Stir in salt. Let cool completely. Refrigerate in an airtight container until ready to use. (It is much easier to work with cold.) Refrigerate remaining Caramel in an airtight container for up to 2 months.

SPUMONI CAKE

Makes 1 (9-inch) cake

In our baked take on Italian Spumoni, we stacked layers of sweet strawberry, silky chocolate, and nutty pistachio cake to achieve a tasty trifecta.

1   cup (227 grams) unsalted butter, softened
2   cups (400 grams) granulated sugar
3   large eggs (150 grams)
2¾ cups (344 grams) cake flour
½   cup (63 grams) all-purpose flour, divided
1   tablespoon (15 grams) baking powder
1   teaspoon (3 grams) kosher salt
1   cup (240 grams) whole milk
1   teaspoon (4 grams) vanilla extract
1   cup (320 grams) strawberry preserves, divided
¼   cup (21 grams) unsweetened cocoa powder
¼   cup (60 grams) boiling water
½   teaspoon (2.5 grams) baking soda
Pistachio Paste (recipe follows), divided
Vanilla Buttercream (recipe follows)
Garnish: chopped roasted pistachios, chopped freeze-dried strawberries

1. Preheat oven to 350°F (180°C). Butter and flour 3 (9-inch) round tall-sided cake pans. Line bottom of pans with parchment paper.
2. In the bowl of a stand mixer fitted with the paddle attachment, beat butter and sugar at medium speed until fluffy, 3 to 4 minutes, stopping to scrape sides of bowl. Add eggs, one at a time, beating well after each addition.
3. In a medium bowl, whisk together cake flour, ¼ cup (31.5 grams) all-purpose flour, baking powder, and salt. With mixer on low speed, gradually add flour mixture to butter mixture alternately with milk, beginning and ending with flour mixture, beating just until combined after each addition. Beat in vanilla.
4. Divide batter among three separate bowls. In first bowl, fold in ½ cup (160 grams) strawberry preserves and remaining ¼ cup (31.5 grams) all-purpose flour. In a small bowl, combine cocoa, ¼ cup (60 grams) boiling water, and baking soda. Fold cocoa mixture into second bowl. In third bowl, fold in ½ cup Pistachio Paste. Spoon batters into prepared pans, and smooth tops with an offset spatula.
5. Bake until a wooden pick inserted in center comes out clean, 20 to 25 minutes. Let cool in pans for 10 minutes. Remove from pans, and let cool completely on wire racks.

6. Pipe a ring of Vanilla Buttercream around inside edge of strawberry cake layer to create a border. Spread with remaining ½ cup (160 grams) strawberry preserves. Place chocolate cake layer on top, and pipe a ring of Vanilla Buttercream around inside edge to create a border. In a small bowl, stir together ½ cup Vanilla Buttercream and remaining ½ cup Pistachio Paste; spread onto chocolate cake layer. Top with pistachio cake layer. Spread remaining Vanilla Buttercream on top and lightly on sides of cake. Garnish with pistachios and strawberries, if desired.

PISTACHIO PASTE
Makes 1 cup

2   cups (284 grams) roasted pistachios
2   tablespoons (42 grams) honey
¼   cup (60 grams) water

1. In a coffee or spice grinder, grind pistachios to a fine powder. In a small bowl, stir together pistachio powder and honey. Add ¼ cup (60 grams) water, 1 tablespoon (15 grams) at a time, until paste reaches a peanut butter consistency. Store in an airtight container at room temperature until ready to use, up to 1 week.

VANILLA BUTTERCREAM
Makes 4 cups

1½ cups (340 grams) unsalted butter, softened
2   teaspoons (8 grams) vanilla extract
½   teaspoon (1.5 grams) kosher salt
9   cups (1,080 grams) confectioners' sugar
6   tablespoons (90 grams) whole milk

1. In the bowl of a stand mixer fitted with the paddle attachment, beat butter at medium speed until creamy. Beat in vanilla and salt. Reduce mixer to low, and gradually add confectioners' sugar. Increase mixer speed to medium, and beat until smooth. Beat in milk, 1 tablespoon (15 grams) at a time, until frosting reaches a spreadable consistency.

SPICED PERSIMMON COCONUT CAKE

Makes 1 (8-inch) cake

Recipe by Rebecca Firth

This cake hints of a tropical vacation with the coconut and lime, but the persimmons and spices make it a decidedly holiday cake. Use either firm Fuyu or cinnamon persimmons for this recipe.

½   cup (113 grams) unsalted butter, softened
2   cups (400 grams) granulated sugar
½   cup (112 grams) sunflower seed or other neutral oil
4   large eggs (200 grams), room temperature
1   large egg yolk (19 grams), room temperature
1   tablespoon (6 grams) lime zest
1   tablespoon (15 grams) fresh lime juice
1   teaspoon (4 grams) coconut extract
3¼ cups (406 grams) all-purpose flour
2   teaspoons (4 grams) Chinese five-spice powder
1½ teaspoons (7.5 grams) baking powder
1½ teaspoons (7.5 grams) baking soda
1   teaspoon (2 grams) ground cinnamon
1   teaspoon (2 grams) ground ginger
1   teaspoon (3 grams) sea salt
1   cup (240 grams) whole buttermilk, room temperature
    and shaken
3   cups (510 grams) stemmed, peeled, and finely diced Fuyu
    or cinnamon persimmons, divided
2   cups (168 grams) unsweetened fine flaked coconut,
    toasted and divided
Spiced Buttercream (recipe follows)
Garnish: fresh sage leaves

1. Preheat oven to 350°F (180°C). Butter and flour 3 (8-inch) round cake pans.
2. In the bowl of a stand mixer fitted with the paddle attachment, beat butter and sugar at medium speed until fluffy, 3 to 4 minutes, stopping to scrape sides of bowl. Add oil, and beat until well combined. With mixer on low speed, add eggs and egg yolk, one at a time, beating well after each addition. Beat in lime zest and juice and coconut extract.
3. In a large bowl, whisk together flour, five-spice powder, baking powder, baking soda, cinnamon, ginger, and salt. Gradually add flour mixture to butter mixture alternately with buttermilk, beginning and ending with flour mixture, beating just until combined after each addition. Fold in three-fourths of persimmons and 1½ cups (126 grams) coconut. Divide batter among prepared pans, smoothing tops with an offset spatula. Gently tap pans on counter to release any air bubbles.
4. Bake until a wooden pick inserted in center comes out clean, 24 to 27 minutes. Let cool in pans for 10 minutes. Remove from pans, and let cool completely on wire racks. Spread Spiced Buttercream between layers and on top and sides of cake. Sprinkle with remaining one-fourth of persimmons and remaining ½ cup (42 grams) coconut. Garnish with sage, if desired.

SPICED BUTTERCREAM
Makes about 4 cups

8   ounces (225 grams) cream cheese, softened
½   cup (113 grams) unsalted butter, softened
1   tablespoon (14 grams) all-vegetable shortening
5   cups (600 grams) confectioners' sugar
1   tablespoon (6 grams) lime zest
1   tablespoon (15 grams) fresh lime juice
1   teaspoon (2 grams) Chinese five-spice powder
1   teaspoon (2 grams) ground cinnamon

1. In the bowl of a stand mixer fitted with the paddle attachment, beat cream cheese, butter, and shortening at medium speed until smooth. Add confectioners' sugar, lime zest and juice, five-spice powder, and cinnamon, beating until combined.

Photo by Joe Schmelzer

DATE AND HAZELNUT CARAMEL CAKE

Makes 1 (9-inch) cake

For this modern take on caramel cake, we simmer dates, water, and Frangelico into a rich, nutty Date Caramel to create a decadent base for the frosting.

¼	cup (57 grams) unsalted butter, softened
1½	cups (300 grams) granulated sugar
⅓	cup (75 grams) vegetable oil
2	teaspoons (10 grams) Frangelico
2	teaspoons (8 grams) vanilla extract
1	teaspoon (3 grams) kosher salt
2	large eggs (100 grams)
3	large egg yolks (56 grams)
2	cups (200 grams) cake flour
2	teaspoons (10 grams) baking powder
⅓	cup (80 grams) whole buttermilk
½	cup (120 grams) heavy whipping cream

Date Caramel Buttercream (recipe follows)
Caramel and Date Filling (recipe follows)
Caramelized Hazelnuts (recipe follows)

1. Preheat oven to 325°F (170°C). Butter and flour an 9-inch springform pan. Line bottom of pan with parchment paper.

2. In the bowl of a stand mixer fitted with the paddle attachment, beat butter and sugar at medium speed until combined, 3 to 4 minutes, stopping to scrape sides of bowl. Add oil, Frangelico, vanilla, and salt, beating just until combined. Add eggs and egg yolks, one at a time, beating just until combined after each addition.

3. In a medium bowl, whisk together flour and baking powder. With mixer on low speed, gradually add flour mixture to butter mixture alternately with buttermilk, beginning and ending with flour mixture, beating just until combined after each addition. Transfer batter to a large bowl; set aside.

4. Clean bowl of stand mixer. Using the whisk attachment, beat cream at high speed until soft peaks form, about 3 minutes. Fold whipped cream into batter. Pour batter into prepared pan.

5. Bake until light golden brown and a wooden pick inserted in center comes out clean, about 1 hour, covering with foil halfway through baking to prevent excess browning. Let cool in pan for 10 minutes. Remove from pan, and let cool completely on a wire rack.

6. Using a serrated knife, cut cake in half horizontally. Place ½ cup Date Caramel Buttercream in a piping bag fitted with a medium round tip. Pipe Date Caramel Buttercream around edge of one cake layer. Spoon Caramel and Date Filling onto cake layer, and spread within buttercream circle. Top with remaining cake layer. Spread remaining Date Caramel Buttercream on top and sides of cake. Garnish with Caramelized Hazelnuts, if desired. Cover and refrigerate for up to 4 days.

DATE CARAMEL BUTTERCREAM

Makes about 5 cups

1	cup (227 grams) unsalted butter, softened

Date Caramel (recipe follows)

5	cups (600 grams) confectioners' sugar

1. In the bowl of a stand mixer fitted with the paddle attachment, beat butter and Date Caramel at medium speed until light and fluffy, 2 to 3 minutes. Gradually add confectioners' sugar, beating until smooth. Refrigerate in an airtight container for up to 1 week.

DATE CARAMEL

Makes about ½ cup

½	cup (64 grams) dried whole pitted dates
½	cup (120 grams) water
½	cup (120 grams) Frangelico
1	cinnamon stick
1	vanilla bean, split lengthwise, seeds scraped and reserved
1	tablespoon (21 grams) maple syrup

1. In a small saucepan, bring dates, ½ cup (120 grams) water, Frangelico, cinnamon stick, and vanilla bean and reserved seeds to a boil over medium heat. Reduce heat to medium-low, and simmer until dates are softened, 15 to 20 minutes. Remove cinnamon stick and vanilla bean.

2. Transfer mixture to the container of a blender, and purée until smooth, about 3 minutes. Stir in maple syrup. Let cool completely. Refrigerate in an airtight container for up to 1 week.

CARAMEL AND DATE FILLING

Makes about 1½ cups

1	cup (200 grams) granulated sugar
6	tablespoons (84 grams) unsalted butter, softened and cubed
½	cup (120 grams) warm heavy whipping cream (105°F/40°C to 110°F/43°C)
2	teaspoons (8 grams) vanilla extract
1	teaspoon (5 grams) Frangelico
½	teaspoon (1.5 grams) kosher salt
1	cup (128 grams) chopped pitted dates

1. In a medium saucepan, cook sugar over medium heat, stirring occasionally, until melted and amber colored, about 3 minutes. (Clumps may form but will eventually melt. Be careful not to burn.) Carefully add butter, and cook, stirring constantly, until completely melted, about 2 minutes. Slowly pour in warm cream, stirring constantly. Remove from heat, and stir in vanilla, Frangelico, and salt. Let cool completely. Stir in dates. Refrigerate in an airtight container for up to 1 week.

CARAMELIZED HAZELNUTS

Makes ½ cup

½	cup (71 grams) hazelnuts
¼	cup (50 grams) granulated sugar
1	tablespoon (14 grams) unsalted butter, softened

1. Preheat oven to 350°F (180°C). Line a baking sheet with parchment paper.

2. Place hazelnuts on prepared pan. Bake for 5 minutes. Wrap nuts in a kitchen towel, and rub nuts in towel to remove loose skins. Keep warm.

3. In a small saucepan, cook sugar over medium heat, stirring occasionally, until amber colored. Add warm nuts. Cook, stirring constantly, until well coated, about 1 minute. Add butter, and stir, separating nuts.

4. Transfer to a parchment paper–lined baking sheet. Working quickly, use 2 forks to separate nuts. Let cool completely. Store in an airtight container at room temperature for up to 5 days.

10-LAYER SPICED RUSSIAN HONEY CAKE

Makes 1 (8-inch) cake

With the texture of soft, spongy gingerbread, this honey-infused cake feels more like a cookie. Although some versions do not include spices, we couldn't help but throw in a little ginger, cloves, and allspice for enhanced flavor. To balance out the spice and sweeten things up, we increased the sugar in the traditional whipped sour cream filling—think cream cheese frosting with a subtle tang. This baking process may be laborious, but it is also forgiving. Expect the assembly to be messy, and remember you can smooth over any filling overflow on the sides of the cake during the final frosting.

¾   cup (150 grams) granulated sugar
½   cup (113 grams) unsalted butter
¼   cup (85 grams) honey
1   teaspoon (5 grams) baking soda
3   large eggs (150 grams), lightly beaten
3½ cups (438 grams) all-purpose flour, divided
½   teaspoon (1 gram) ground allspice
½   teaspoon (1 gram) ground cloves
½   teaspoon (1 gram) ground ginger
¼   teaspoon kosher salt
1   teaspoon (4 grams) vanilla extract
Sour Cream Frosting (recipe follows)
Garnish: fresh currants, White Chocolate Honeycomb
    (recipe follows)

1. Preheat oven to 350°F (180°C).
2. In a medium saucepan, bring sugar, butter, and honey to a simmer over medium heat. Simmer for 4 minutes; remove from heat. Whisk in baking soda. (The mixture will violently bubble up and drastically change in color. Keep whisking until a dark amber color is achieved and mixture is no longer bubbling.) Whisking vigorously, gradually add eggs in a slow, steady stream until combined.
3. In a large bowl, whisk together 3 cups (375 grams) flour, allspice, cloves, ginger, and salt. Using a wooden spoon, stir flour mixture and vanilla into honey mixture until well combined. Add remaining ½ cup (63 grams) flour, stirring gently just until combined.
4. Transfer dough to a sheet of parchment paper, and divide into 10 equal portions. Cover with a towel to keep warm. Working with 1 piece of dough at a time, lightly sprinkle top with flour, and place on another sheet of parchment paper. Roll into an 8-inch circle, using an 8-inch round cake pan as a guide. Trim edges, reserving scraps. Transfer dough circle on parchment to a rimmed baking sheet. (If dough becomes cold while working with it, you can microwave it for 5 seconds to warm back up. When cold, dough is difficult to roll out and prone to forming a skin.)
5. Bake for 6 minutes. Remove from oven, and place on a wire rack. Repeat procedure with remaining dough circles.
6. Bake scraps for 7 minutes; let cool. Transfer to the work bowl of a food processor; pulse until finely ground. Reserve 1 cup (100 grams) cake crumbs for White Chocolate Honeycomb.

7. Place one cake layer on a serving plate, and spread with ½ cup (120 grams) Sour Cream Frosting. Repeat with remaining layers, pressing down gently as you go to keep layers from having air gaps. Refrigerate for at least 10 hours.
8. Spread remaining Sour Cream Frosting on top and sides of cake. Sprinkle remaining cake crumbs in a circle on top of cake. Garnish with currants and White Chocolate Honeycomb, if desired. Cover and refrigerate for up to 3 days.

SOUR CREAM FROSTING
Makes about 8 cups

1   cup (240 grams) heavy whipping cream
4   cups (960 grams) sour cream
3   cups (360 grams) confectioners' sugar

1. In the bowl of a stand mixer fitted with the whisk attachment, beat cream at high speed until stiff peaks form, 1 to 2 minutes.
2. In a large bowl, whisk together sour cream and confectioners' sugar. Fold whipped cream into sour cream mixture. Refrigerate until ready to use.

WHITE CHOCOLATE HONEYCOMB
Makes about 2 cups

½   cup (85 grams) white chocolate melting wafers*
1   cup (100 grams) reserved cake crumbs

1. In the top of a double boiler, melt chocolate baking wafers over simmering water. (Alternatively, in a medium microwave-safe bowl, melt chocolate on medium in 30-second intervals, stirring between each, until chocolate is melted and smooth.) Spread a thin layer of melted chocolate over a food-grade honeycomb mold. Let dry at room temperature overnight, or refrigerate until set. Gently remove mold, and break honeycomb into small pieces. Sprinkle with reserved cake crumbs.

We used Godiva.

Note: *We used a PME Honeycomb Design Impression Mat, available on amazon.com.*

PRO TIP
The overnight refrigeration is crucial, allowing the ample amounts of creamy filling slathered between each layer to soak into and help soften the cake. The cake is prone to leaning after assembly, so be sure it is on a level shelf when refrigerating. To ensure that the layers don't shift, stick a wooden skewer through the center of the cake after assembling. Remove skewer before frosting top and sides of cake.

LEMON SEMOLINA CAKE

Makes 1 (9-inch) cake

Cling to the flavors of summer with this light citrus layer cake that's ideal for entertaining. Fluffy whipped mascarpone frosting works as a creamy counterpoint to acidic and savory flavors of fresh lemon and bright olive oil. For an extra dose of citrus, we top our cake with crisp, caramelized lemon slices.

6   large eggs (300 grams)
1½   cups (300 grams) granulated sugar
1   cup (224 grams) extra-virgin olive oil
1   cup (240 grams) whole milk
1   tablespoon (6 grams) lemon zest
1   tablespoon (15 grams) fresh lemon
     juice
½   teaspoon (2 grams) vanilla extract
2½   cups (313 grams) all-purpose flour
½   cup (75 grams) semolina flour
1   tablespoon (15 grams) baking powder
1   teaspoon (3 grams) kosher salt
Garnish: Caramelized Lemons (recipe follows)
Whipped Mascarpone (recipe follows)

1. Preheat oven to 350°F (180°C). Butter and flour 2 (9-inch) round cake pans, and line bottom of pans with parchment paper.
2. In the bowl of a stand mixer fitted with the whisk attachment, beat eggs and sugar at high speed for 30 seconds. Add oil in a slow, steady stream, beating until combined. Add milk, beating until combined. Reduce mixer speed to low. Beat in lemon zest and juice and vanilla.
3. In a medium bowl, whisk together flours, baking powder, and salt. Gradually add flour mixture to egg mixture, beating until combined, stopping to scrape sides of bowl. Divide batter between prepared pans.
4. Bake until a wooden pick inserted in center comes out clean, 25 to 30 minutes. Let cool in pans for 5 minutes. Remove from pans, and let cool completely on a wire rack. Brush top of cake layers with reserved lemon simple syrup from Caramelized Lemons. Spread half of

Whipped Mascarpone onto one layer. Top with remaining cake layer, and spread with remaining Whipped Mascarpone. Garnish with Caramelized Lemons, if desired. Refrigerate in an airtight container for up to 3 days.

CARAMELIZED LEMONS
Makes 6 slices

1   cup (200 grams) granulated sugar, plus
     more for dusting
1   cup (240 grams) water
1   lemon (99 grams), sliced ⅛ inch thick

1. Line a rimmed baking sheet with parchment paper.
2. In a medium skillet, bring sugar and 1 cup (240 grams) water to a boil over medium-high heat. Reduce heat to medium-low. Add lemon slices in a single layer. Cook until slices begin to turn translucent, 10 to 12 minutes. Remove from skillet, and place on prepared pan. Reserve ½ cup lemon simple syrup to brush on cake layers.
3. Generously coat each lemon slice with additional sugar. Turn slices, and repeat. Cover with plastic wrap, and let stand overnight.

4. Dust excess sugar off slices, and place on a large sheet of foil. Using a handheld kitchen torch or broiler, carefully brown one side of each slice. Let stand for 5 minutes before placing on cake.

WHIPPED MASCARPONE
Makes about 5 cups

1   cup (225 grams) mascarpone cheese,
     chilled
1   cup (120 grams) confectioners' sugar
2   cups (480 grams) heavy whipping
     cream

1. In the bowl of a stand mixer fitted with the whisk attachment, beat mascarpone and confectioners' sugar at medium speed until smooth. Reduce mixer speed to low. Add cream, beating until combined. Increase mixer speed to medium-high, and beat until soft peaks form, 3 to 4 minutes. If mixture is too soft, continue beating in 10-second intervals until desired consistency is reached.

GINGER CAKE WITH MANGO CURD AND KEY LIME BUTTERCREAM

Makes 1 (9-inch) cake

Spicy ginger, mango, and tangy Key lime are a triple threat in this tropical layer cake.

1½   cups (340 grams) unsalted butter, softened and divided
3   cups (600 grams) granulated sugar, divided
4   large eggs (200 grams)
3   cups (375 grams) cake flour
1   tablespoon (15 grams) baking powder
1   cup (240 grams) whole milk
⅓   cup (123 grams) finely chopped crystallized ginger
2   teaspoons (8 grams) vanilla extract
6   large egg yolks (112 grams)
½   cup (120 grams) mango juice*
3   tablespoons (45 grams) fresh Key lime juice
Ginger Simple Syrup (recipe follows)
Key Lime Buttercream (recipe follows)

1. Preheat oven to 350°F (180°C). Butter and flour 2 (9-inch) round tall-sided cake pans. Line bottom of pans with parchment paper.
2. In the bowl of a stand mixer fitted with the paddle attachment, beat 1 cup (227 grams) butter and 2 cups (400 grams) sugar at medium speed until fluffy, 3 to 4 minutes, stopping to scrape sides of bowl. Add eggs, one at a time, beating well after each addition.
3. In a medium bowl, whisk together flour and baking powder. With mixer on low speed, gradually add flour mixture to butter mixture alternately with milk, beginning and ending with flour mixture, beating just until combined after each addition. Fold in ginger and vanilla. Divide batter between prepared pans, smoothing tops with an offset spatula.
4. Bake until a wooden pick inserted in center comes out clean, about 25 minutes. Let cool in pans for 10 minutes. Remove from pans, and let cool completely on wire racks. Using a serrated knife, remove rounded tops from cake layers.
5. In a medium saucepan, stir together egg yolks, mango juice, Key lime juice, and remaining 1 cup (200 grams) sugar. Cook over medium heat until mixture is slightly thickened and coats the back of a wooden spoon. Strain through a fine-mesh sieve into a bowl, discarding solids. Add remaining ½ cup (113 grams) butter, and stir to combine. Cover with plastic wrap, and refrigerate until cold, at least 3 hours.
6. Brush Ginger Simple Syrup generously onto cake layers. Pipe a ring of Key Lime Buttercream around inside edge of bottom cake layer to create a border. Fill center with ½ cup mango curd. Top with remaining cake layer. Spread a thin layer of Key Lime Buttercream on top and sides of cake. Top with remaining mango curd.

We used Lakewood Organic Mango Juice.

GINGER SIMPLE SYRUP
Makes 2 cups

1   cup (200 grams) granulated sugar
½   cup (120 grams) water
½   cup (120 grams) ginger juice*

1. In a small saucepan, bring sugar, ½ cup (120 grams) water, and ginger juice to a boil over medium-high heat. Remove from heat, and let cool.

We used Ginger People Ginger Juice.

KEY LIME BUTTERCREAM
Makes about 3 cups

¾   cup (170 grams) unsalted butter, softened
4½   cups (540 grams) confectioners' sugar
1   teaspoon (4 grams) vanilla extract
½   teaspoon (1.5 grams) kosher salt
3   tablespoons (15 grams) fresh Key lime juice
1 to 3 tablespoons (15 to 45 grams) whole milk

1. In the bowl of a stand mixer fitted with the paddle attachment, beat butter at medium speed until creamy. Gradually add confectioners' sugar, vanilla, and salt, beating to combine. Add Key lime juice, beating until combined. Add milk, 1 tablespoon (15 grams) at a time, beating until a spreadable consistency is reached.

BUNDT
CAKES

The shape that launched a thousand cakes, the Bundt pan offers the perfect mold for decadent, dense cakes destined for thick glazes and syrup soaks. Whether you're looking for an exciting update or a steadfast standard, we have a ring-shaped delight for you.

CRANBERRY STREUSEL BUNDT CAKE

Makes 1 (10-cup) Bundt cake

Recipe by Rebecca Firth

The tartness of cranberries, ribbons of streusel, and rich, buttery crumb coupled with the fresh nutmeg and fragrant five-spice blend will both surprise and delight your holiday guests. Without being too obvious, the addition of five-spice adds warmth and pizzazz to the cake and streusel. One of my favorite things about this cake is its versatility because it could just as easily grace a holiday brunch table as it could finish an elegant dinner. Fresh cranberries are ideal, but frozen will work in a pinch. If using frozen, don't defrost before folding into the batter.

4   large eggs (200 grams), room temperature
1   large egg yolk (19 grams), room temperature
1½   cups (300 grams) granulated sugar
1½   cups (360 grams) sour cream, room temperature
¾   cup (168 grams) vegetable oil
1½   tablespoons (9 grams) orange zest
1½   tablespoons (19.5 grams) pure vanilla extract
2⅔   cups (333 grams) all-purpose flour
1   tablespoon (15 grams) baking powder
1½   teaspoons (3 grams) ground cinnamon
1   teaspoon (2 grams) Chinese five-spice powder
¾   teaspoon (2.25 grams) kosher salt
½   teaspoon grated fresh nutmeg
½   cup (120 grams) 1% low-fat milk
2¼   cups (382.5 grams) fresh or frozen cranberries
Spiced Streusel (recipe follows)
Citrus Glaze (recipe follows)
Garnish: Cranberry Powder (recipe follows)

1. Preheat oven to 350°F (180°C). Heavily butter and flour a 10-cup Bundt pan*.
2. In the bowl of a stand mixer fitted with the paddle attachment, beat eggs, egg yolk, and sugar at medium speed until light and fluffy, about 4 minutes, stopping to scrape sides of bowl, if necessary. With mixer on low speed, add sour cream, oil, zest, and vanilla. Increase mixer speed to medium, and beat until combined.
3. In a medium bowl, whisk together flour, baking powder, cinnamon, five-spice powder, salt, and nutmeg. With mixer on low speed, gradually add flour mixture to egg mixture alternately with milk, beginning and ending with flour mixture, beating just until combined after each addition. Fold in cranberries.
4. Pour one-third of batter into prepared pan. Sprinkle with half of Spiced Streusel. Add another one-third of batter, and sprinkle with remaining Spiced Streusel. Pour remaining batter on top, using a

spatula to spread over Spiced Streusel. (Pan will be very full.) Gently tap pan on counter several times to release any air bubbles.
5. Bake until a wooden pick inserted near center comes out clean, 1 hour and 10 minutes to 1 hour and 15 minutes. Let cool in pan for 30 minutes. Remove from pan, and let cool completely on a wire rack. Pour Citrus Glaze over cooled cake, letting glaze drizzle down sides. Dust with Cranberry Powder, if desired.

We used the Nordic Ware Heritage Bundt Pan.

SPICED STREUSEL
Makes about ⅓ cup

⅓   cup (42 grams) all-purpose flour
⅓   cup (67 grams) granulated sugar
1½   tablespoons (21 grams) firmly packed
          light brown sugar
1   tablespoon (6 grams) ground cinnamon
1½   teaspoons (3 grams) Chinese five-spice powder
1½   tablespoons (21 grams) unsalted butter, softened

1. In a small bowl, whisk together flour, sugars, cinnamon, and five-spice powder. Use your fingers to work butter into flour mixture until it has the texture of dry sand.

CITRUS GLAZE
Makes about 1 cup

2¼   cups (270 grams) confectioners' sugar
1 to 3 teaspoons (2 to 6 grams) orange zest
1   teaspoon (5 grams) fresh orange juice
1 to 3 tablespoons (15 to 45 grams) whole milk

1. In a small bowl, whisk together confectioners' sugar and orange zest and juice until smooth. Add milk, 1 teaspoon (5 grams) at a time, until desired consistency is reached.

CRANBERRY POWDER
Makes about ¼ cup

½   cup (7 grams) freeze-dried cranberries
1   teaspoon (3 grams) cornstarch

1. Place cranberries and cornstarch in the work bowl of a food processor; pulse until powdered.

HONEY CASHEW BUNDT CAKE

Makes 1 (8- to 10-cup) Bundt cake

This ring-shaped delight is crowned with a warm cashew and honey caramel baked into the top like a traditional upside-down cake. For the ultimate decadent and gooey experience, serve this cake warm before the caramel completely sets.

¾   cup (150 grams) plus ⅔ cup (133 grams) granulated sugar, divided
¼   cup (57 grams) unsalted butter
¼   cup (85 grams) honey
1   cup (113 grams) cashew halves
3   large eggs (150 grams)
½   cup (112 grams) extra-virgin olive oil
½   cup (120 grams) whole milk
½   teaspoon (2 grams) vanilla extract
¼   teaspoon (1 gram) almond extract
1½ cups (188 grams) all-purpose flour
1½ teaspoons (7.5 grams) baking powder
½   teaspoon (1.5 grams) kosher salt

1. Preheat oven to 350°F (180°C). Butter and flour an 8- to 10-cup Bundt pan.
2. In a small saucepan, bring ⅓ cup (66.5 grams) sugar, butter, and honey to a boil over medium heat. Add ⅓ cup (66.5 grams) sugar, and boil for 2 minutes. Stir in cashews. Pour two-thirds of mixture into prepared pan. Spread remaining mixture in a single layer on a sheet of parchment paper. Let cool, and reserve for serving.
3. In the bowl of a stand mixer fitted with the whisk attachment, beat eggs and remaining ¾ cup (150 grams) sugar at high speed for 30 seconds. Add oil in a slow, steady stream, beating until combined. Add milk, beating until combined. Reduce mixer speed to low. Beat in extracts.
4. In a medium bowl, whisk together flour, baking powder, and salt. Gradually add flour mixture to egg mixture, beating until combined, stopping to scrape sides of bowl. Pour batter over honey cashew mixture in pan.
5. Bake until a wooden pick inserted near center comes out clean, 35 to 45 minutes. Let cool in pan for 5 minutes. Invert cake onto a serving plate, and replace any cashews on top that may have fallen into center. Serve warm with remaining honey cashew mixture.

ITALIAN CREAM BUNDT CAKE

Makes 1 (15-cup) Bundt cake

This cake delivers the same flavors as its three-layered cousin in a super moist, sugar-dusted package. It's Italian Cream Cake simplified.

1½ cups (340 grams) unsalted butter, softened
8   ounces (225 grams) cream cheese, softened
2   cups (400 grams) granulated sugar
1   cup (220 grams) firmly packed light brown sugar
1½ teaspoons (4.5 grams) kosher salt
5   large eggs (250 grams)
1   tablespoon (13 grams) vanilla extract
3   cups (375 grams) all-purpose flour
½   teaspoon (2.5 grams) baking powder
1   cup (113 grams) finely chopped toasted pecans
1   cup (84 grams) sweetened flaked coconut, toasted
Garnish: confectioners' sugar

1. Butter and flour a 15-cup Bundt pan.
2. In the bowl of a stand mixer fitted with the paddle attachment, beat butter and cream cheese at medium speed until creamy, 3 to 4 minutes. Increase mixer speed to high. Add granulated sugar, brown sugar, and salt; beat for 10 minutes, stopping to scrape sides of bowl. Add eggs, one at a time, beating well after each addition. Beat in vanilla.
3. In a medium bowl, whisk together flour and baking powder. With mixer on low speed, gradually add flour mixture to butter mixture, beating until combined. Beat in pecans and coconut. Spoon batter into prepared pan.
4. Place pan in a cold oven. Bake at 300°F (150°C) until a wooden pick inserted near center comes out clean, about 1 hour and 20 minutes. Let cool in pan for 10 minutes. Remove from pan, and let cool completely on a wire rack. Garnish with confectioners' sugar, if desired.

BUTTER PECAN ANGEL FOOD CAKE

Makes 1 (10-cup) tube cake

A browned butter glaze and toasted pecans add a dose of decadence to this light and fluffy cake.

12	large egg whites (360 grams), room temperature
1½	teaspoons (3 grams) cream of tartar
2	tablespoons (26 grams) butter flavoring
1	tablespoon (13 grams) vanilla, butter, and nut flavoring*
1	tablespoon (13 grams) vanilla extract
1	cup (200 grams) granulated sugar
1½	cups (180 grams) confectioners' sugar
1	cup (125 grams) cake flour
½	teaspoon (1.5 grams) kosher salt
¾	cup (72 grams) finely ground pecans

Browned Butter Glaze (recipe follows)

1. Preheat oven to 375°F (190°C).
2. In the bowl of a stand mixer fitted with the whisk attachment, beat egg whites, cream of tartar, flavorings, and vanilla at high speed until frothy. Gradually add granulated sugar, beating until stiff peaks form.
3. In a medium bowl, whisk together confectioners' sugar, flour, and salt. Stir in pecans. Using a rubber spatula, gently fold flour mixture into egg white mixture in thirds, folding just until combined. Spoon batter into an ungreased 10-cup tube pan.
4. Bake until golden brown, about 35 minutes. Immediately invert pan onto the top of a bottle. Let cool completely. Remove from pan. Drizzle with Browned Butter Glaze just before serving.

We used McCormick's Vanilla, Butter, and Nut Flavoring.

BROWNED BUTTER GLAZE
Makes about 2 cups

1	cup (120 grams) confectioners' sugar, sifted
⅛	teaspoon kosher salt
10	tablespoons (140 grams) unsalted butter, cubed

1. In a medium bowl, whisk together confectioners' sugar and salt.
2. In a medium saucepan, melt butter over medium heat. Cook until butter turns a medium-brown color and has a nutty aroma, about 8 minutes. Strain butter through a fine-mesh sieve over sugar mixture; whisk until smooth. Use immediately.

VANILLA BUNDT CAKE WITH BOURBON-VANILLA CARAMEL SAUCE

Makes 1 (12- to 15-cup) Bundt cake

Buttery caramel drizzled over a tender vanilla cake—it's a match made in confectionary heaven. With the added hint of bourbon, there's no beating this indulgent treat.

1½ cups (340 grams) unsalted butter, softened
2   cups (400 grams) granulated sugar
1   cup (220 grams) firmly packed dark brown sugar
5   large eggs (250 grams)
1   tablespoon (13 grams) vanilla extract
3   cups (375 grams) all-purpose flour
1   teaspoon (5 grams) baking powder
½   teaspoon (1.5 grams) kosher salt
1   cup (240 grams) whole milk
Bourbon-Vanilla Caramel Sauce (recipe follows)

1. Preheat oven to 325°F (170°C). Butter and flour a 12- to 15-cup Bundt pan.
2. In the bowl of a stand mixer fitted with the paddle attachment, beat butter and sugars at medium speed until fluffy, 3 to 4 minutes, stopping to scrape sides of bowl. Add eggs, one at a time, beating well after each addition. Beat in vanilla.
3. In a medium bowl, whisk together flour, baking powder, and salt. With mixer on low speed, gradually add flour mixture to butter mixture alternately with milk, beginning and ending with flour mixture, beating just until combined after each addition. Spoon batter into prepared pan.
4. Bake until a wooden pick inserted near center comes out clean, about 1 hour and 5 minutes. Let cool in pan for 10 minutes. Remove from pan, and let cool completely on a wire rack. Drizzle with Bourbon-Vanilla Caramel Sauce just before serving.

BOURBON-VANILLA CARAMEL SAUCE
Makes about 2 cups

2   cups (400 grams) granulated sugar
¼   cup (60 grams) water
½   cup (120 grams) heavy whipping cream, warmed
2   tablespoons (30 grams) bourbon
1   teaspoon (3 grams) kosher salt
½   teaspoon (2 grams) vanilla extract

1. In a medium saucepan, place sugar and ¼ cup (60 grams) water, swirling to combine. Cook over medium-high heat, without stirring, until mixture is amber colored, about 10 minutes. Remove from heat. Carefully stir in cream (mixture will bubble). Stir in bourbon, salt, and vanilla. Let cool in pan for 10 minutes, stirring frequently.
2. Pour into a heatproof container. Cover and refrigerate for up to 3 weeks. To reheat before serving, microwave on high in 30-second intervals, stirring between each, until pourable.

DOUBLE CHOCOLATE SPICE BUNDT CAKE

Makes 1 (12- to 15-cup) Bundt cake

This chocolate-on-chocolate Bundt gets an undertone of warm, cozy spice from chai tea-infused milk. Just one slice will have the chocolate lover in your life begging for more!

1   cup (240 grams) whole milk
2   chai tea bags (6 grams)
1   cup (227 grams) unsalted butter, softened
1½   cups (330 grams) firmly packed dark brown sugar
3   large eggs (150 grams)
3   cups (375 grams) all-purpose flour
¾   teaspoon (3.75 grams) baking powder
½   teaspoon (2.5 grams) baking soda
½   teaspoon (1.5 grams) kosher salt
1   cup (240 grams) whole buttermilk
8   ounces (225 grams) 70% cacao dark chocolate, finely chopped
1   cup (170 grams) semisweet chocolate morsels, melted and slightly cooled
1   teaspoon (4 grams) vanilla extract
Bittersweet Chocolate Glaze (recipe follows)

1. Preheat oven to 300°F (150°C). Butter and flour a 12- to 15-cup Bundt pan.
2. In a small saucepan, bring milk to a simmer over medium heat. Remove from heat. Add tea bags; cover and let stand for 10 minutes. Discard tea bags. Reserve ½ cup (120 grams) chai milk for batter and 5 tablespoons (75 grams) chai milk for Bittersweet Chocolate Glaze.
3. In the bowl of a stand mixer fitted with the paddle attachment, beat butter and brown sugar at medium speed until fluffy, 3 to 4 minutes, stopping to scrape sides of bowl. Add eggs, one at a time, beating well after each addition.
4. In a medium bowl, whisk together flour, baking powder, baking soda, and salt. In a small bowl, whisk together buttermilk and reserved ½ cup (120 grams) chai milk. With mixer on low speed, gradually add flour mixture to butter mixture alternately with buttermilk mixture, beginning and ending with flour mixture, beating just until combined after each addition. Beat in chopped chocolate, melted chocolate, and vanilla. Spoon batter into prepared pan, smoothing top with an offset spatula.
5. Bake until a wooden pick inserted near

center comes out clean, about 1 hour. Let cool in pan for 10 minutes. Remove from pan, and let cool completely on a wire rack. Drizzle with Bittersweet Chocolate Glaze just before serving.

BITTERSWEET CHOCOLATE GLAZE
Makes about 1 cup

1½   cups (180 grams) confectioners' sugar
3   ounces (86 grams) 70% cacao bittersweet chocolate, melted
1   tablespoon (14 grams) unsalted butter, melted
Reserved 5 tablespoons (75 grams) chai milk from Double Chocolate Spice Bundt Cake

1. In a medium bowl, whisk together confectioners' sugar, melted chocolate, and melted butter. Add reserved chai milk, 1 tablespoon (15 grams) at a time, whisking until a smooth consistency is reached. Use immediately.

GERMAN CHOCOLATE POUND CAKE

Makes 1 (10-cup) Bundt cake

This confection gets its name from the brand of chocolate it uses, not its country of origin. Our Bundt version ditches the traditional layers, but keeps the coconut, pecan, and caramel flavor notes that made this chocolate cake a classic.

1   cup (227 grams) unsalted butter, softened
2   cups (400 grams) granulated sugar
4   large eggs (200 grams)
1   cup (240 grams) sour cream
1   teaspoon (4 grams) vanilla extract
2   cups (250 grams) all-purpose flour
2   tablespoons (10 grams) unsweetened cocoa powder
½   teaspoon (2.5 grams) baking soda
¼   teaspoon kosher salt
4   ounces (115 grams) German's sweet chocolate, melted and slightly cooled
Coconut-Pecan Frosting (recipe follows)

1. Preheat oven to 325°F (170°C). Butter and flour a 10-cup Bundt pan.
2. In the bowl of a stand mixer fitted with the paddle attachment, beat butter and sugar at medium speed until fluffy, 3 to 4 minutes, stopping to scrape sides of bowl. Add eggs, one at a time, beating well after each addition. Beat in sour cream and vanilla until smooth.
3. In a medium bowl, whisk together flour, cocoa, baking soda, and salt. With mixer on low speed, gradually add flour mixture to butter mixture, beating until combined. Beat in melted chocolate until smooth. Spoon batter into prepared pan.
4. Bake until a wooden pick inserted near center comes out clean, about 1 hour. Let cool in pan for 10 minutes. Remove from pan, and let cool completely on a wire rack. Spoon Coconut-Pecan Frosting on top of cooled cake.

COCONUT-PECAN FROSTING
Makes about 2 cups

1   (5-ounce) can (150 grams) evaporated milk
¾   cup (150 grams) granulated sugar
⅓   cup (76 grams) unsalted butter
2   large eggs yolks (37 grams)
2   cups (168 grams) sweetened flaked coconut
¾   cup (85 grams) chopped pecans

1. In a medium saucepan, combine evaporated milk, sugar, butter, and egg yolks. Cook over medium heat, stirring constantly, until mixture is thickened, about 5 minutes. Stir in coconut and pecans; cook, stirring constantly, until mixture is golden brown, about 5 minutes more.

PEAR-ROSEMARY BUNDT CAKE

Makes 1 (10-cup) Bundt cake

Recipe by Allison Kave and Keavy Landreth

This recipe combines fresh pear, pear eau de vie, the delicate pine aroma of fresh rosemary, floral honey, and rich browned butter in an addictive, perfectly moist cake that you'll find yourself digging into first thing in the morning and late at night when that sweet tooth starts to beckon. Double up on the pear purée. It's delicious on pancakes, roast pork, and yes, slathered on a slice of this Bundt cake!

4	pounds (1,820 grams) ripe Anjou pears (about 8 medium pears)
1	teaspoon (2 grams) lemon zest
3	tablespoons (45 grams) fresh lemon juice
½	cup (170 grams) plus 2 tablespoons (42 grams) honey, divided
1	tablespoon (2 grams) fresh rosemary sprigs
½	cup (113 grams) unsalted butter, softened
1	cup (220 grams) firmly packed dark brown sugar
½	cup (112 grams) canola oil
2	large eggs (100 grams)
⅓	cup (80 grams) full-fat Greek yogurt
1	teaspoon (4 grams) vanilla extract
3	cups (375 grams) all-purpose flour
2	teaspoons (10 grams) baking soda
2	teaspoons (4 grams) ground cinnamon
1½	teaspoons (4.5 grams) kosher salt

Browned Butter-Pear Glaze (recipe follows)

1. Preheat oven to 375°F (190°C). Line a large rimmed baking sheet with parchment paper.
2. Peel, core, and chop pears into 1-inch pieces. Place on prepared pan. Add lemon zest and juice, 2 tablespoons (42 grams) honey, and rosemary, tossing to coat.
3. Roast until lightly caramelized and fragrant, about 40 minutes, rotating pan once. Let cool completely. Reserve 1 cup (225 grams) chopped pears. Transfer remaining pears to the container of a blender; purée until smooth. (Pear purée

can be made up to 5 days ahead and refrigerated until ready to use. It's also incredibly delicious, and remember, a double batch is a good idea.)
4. Reduce oven temperature to 350°F (180°C). Butter and flour a 10-cup Bundt pan.
5. In the bowl of a stand mixer fitted with the paddle attachment, beat butter, brown sugar, and oil at medium-high speed until fluffy, 3 to 4 minutes, stopping to scrape sides of bowl. Add eggs, one at a time, beating well after each addition. Beat in 1 cup (182 grams) pear purée, yogurt, vanilla, and remaining ½ cup (170 grams) honey.
6. In a large bowl, whisk together flour, baking soda, cinnamon, and salt. With mixer on low speed, gradually add flour mixture to butter mixture, beating just until combined. Fold in reserved 1 cup (225 grams) chopped pears. Pour batter into prepared pan. Firmly tap pan on counter a few times to release any air bubbles.
7. Bake until a wooden pick inserted near center comes out clean, 45 to 55 minutes. Let cool in pan for 10 minutes. Remove from pan, and let cool completely on a wire rack. Spoon Browned Butter-Pear Glaze over cake, letting glaze run down sides of cake. Let glaze set before slicing.

BROWNED BUTTER-PEAR GLAZE
Makes ¾ cup

¼	cup (57 grams) unsalted butter*
1	cup (120 grams) confectioners' sugar
2	tablespoons (32 grams) pear purée reserved from Pear-Rosemary Bundt Cake
1	tablespoon (21 grams) honey
¼	teaspoon kosher salt
1 to 2	tablespoons (15 to 30 grams) pear eau de vie

1. In a small saucepan, melt butter over medium heat. Cook until butter turns a medium-brown color and has a nutty aroma, about 10 minutes. Remove from heat.
2. In a medium bowl, combine confectioners' sugar, pear purée, honey, and salt. Add browned butter to sugar mixture, whisking until combined. Whisk in just enough eau de vie to make a pourable glaze.

*Whenever we make browned butter, we like to double up the batch and keep some in the refrigerator. Nothing elevates a humble slice of toast like browned butter, and it's also fantastic for mounting sauces and drizzling on popcorn.

CHOCOLATE KUGELHOPF

Makes 1 (10-cup) Bundt cake

Hailing from the Germanic region of Europe, this light, yeast-leavened cake is known for its signature tall, ringed shape. We replaced the usual raisins with chocolate chips because a little chocolate makes everything better.

2   tablespoons (30 grams) warm water (105°F/40°C to 110°F/43°C)
1½ teaspoons (4.5 grams) active dry yeast
½   cup (113 grams) unsalted butter, softened
½   cup (100 grams) granulated sugar
1   tablespoon (6 grams) orange zest
3   large eggs (150 grams)
4   cups (500 grams) all-purpose flour
1   teaspoon (3 grams) kosher salt
1   cup (240 grams) whole milk
1½ cups (255 grams) semisweet chocolate morsels
Garnish: confectioners' sugar, Candied Orange Rind (recipe follows)

1. Butter and flour a 10-cup kugelhopf pan.
2. In a small bowl, combine 2 tablespoons (30 grams) warm water and yeast. Let stand until mixture is foamy, about 5 minutes.
3. In the bowl of a stand mixer fitted with the paddle attachment, beat butter, granulated sugar, and zest at medium speed until creamy, 3 to 4 minutes, stopping to scrape sides of bowl. Add eggs, one at a time, beating well after each addition. Add yeast mixture, beating until combined.
4. In a medium bowl, whisk together flour and salt. With mixer on low speed, gradually add flour mixture to butter mixture alternately with milk, beginning and ending with flour mixture, beating just until combined after each addition. Beat in chocolate morsels. Spoon batter into prepared pan. Cover with plastic wrap, and let stand in a warm, draft-free place (75°F/24°C) until batter has risen by 1 inch, about 2 hours.
5. Preheat oven to 350°F (180°C).
6. Bake until a wooden pick inserted near center comes out clean, about 30 minutes.

Let cool in pan for 10 minutes. Remove from pan, and let cool completely on a wire rack. Garnish with confectioners' sugar and Candied Orange Rind, if desired.

Note: *A 10-cup Bundt pan may be substituted.*

CANDIED ORANGE RIND
Makes 8 strips

1   navel orange (131 grams)
½   cup (120 grams) water
1⅔ cups (333 grams) granulated sugar, divided

1. Using a channel knife, cut 8 (6-inch) strips of peel from orange. Place strips in a small saucepan; add ½ cup (120 grams) water and 1 cup (200 grams) sugar. Bring to a boil over medium heat; reduce heat, and simmer for 30 minutes. Remove from heat, and let stand for 30 minutes. Remove orange peel, and drain well. Toss peel with remaining ⅔ cup (133 grams) sugar.

ONE-LAYER
CAKES

The single-layer cake makes up in simplicity and elegance
what it lacks in height. Running the gamut from rich,
caramelized skillet cake to crunchy crumb-topped coffee
cake, find a cake for every craving and occasion.

TARTE TROPÉZIENNE

Makes 1 (11-inch) cake

This sizable French cake could be a movie star itself. A generous swoop of rich Crème Diplomat rests between two layers of buttery brioche, and a sprinkling of pearl sugar provides the slightest delicate crunch on top.

⅓ cup (80 grams) warm whole milk (105°F/40°C to 110°F/43°C)
1 tablespoon (9 grams) active dry yeast
2¼ cups (281 grams) all-purpose flour
¼ cup (50 grams) granulated sugar
3 large eggs (150 grams), divided
1 tablespoon (15 grams) dark rum
1 teaspoon (4 grams) vanilla extract
½ teaspoon (1.5 grams) kosher salt
7 tablespoons (98 grams) unsalted butter, softened and cubed
1 teaspoon (5 grams) water
Sugar Topping (recipe follows)
Crème Diplomat (recipe follows)

1. In the bowl of a stand mixer fitted with the paddle attachment, combine warm milk and yeast; let stand for 2 minutes.
2. In a medium bowl, whisk together flour and sugar. Add flour mixture to yeast mixture, and beat at low speed until combined and shaggy, about 3 minutes. Add 2 eggs (100 grams), one at a time, beating well after each addition. Beat in rum, vanilla, and salt. Increase mixer speed to medium, and beat until dough forms a smooth ball, 5 to 8 minutes. Increase mixer speed to medium-high. Add butter, a few cubes at a time, beating until dough forms a ball around paddle, 8 to 10 minutes.
3. Shape dough into a ball, and transfer to a medium bowl. Cover tightly with plastic wrap, and let stand in a warm, draft-free place (75°F/24°C) until doubled in size, 2 to 3 hours.
4. Press dough down, and reshape into a ball. Cover bowl with plastic wrap, and freeze for 30 minutes. Refrigerate for at least 2 hours or up to 2 days.
5. Line a baking sheet with parchment paper.
6. Turn out dough onto a lightly floured surface, and gently pat dough down. Lightly flour top of dough, and roll into a 9-inch circle. Transfer to prepared pan. Cover lightly with plastic wrap, and let rest in a warm, draft-free place (75°F/24°C) for 1 hour.
7. Preheat oven to 400°F (200°C).
8. In a small bowl, whisk together 1 teaspoon (5 grams) water and remaining 1 egg (50 grams). Lightly brush brioche with egg wash, and sprinkle with Sugar Topping. Transfer to oven, and immediately reduce oven temperature to 350°F (180°C).
9. Bake until golden brown, 20 to 25 minutes, rotating pan after 10 minutes. Let cool completely on a wire rack. Using a serrated knife, cut brioche in half horizontally. Spread Crème Diplomat onto bottom layer, and gently cover with top layer. Refrigerate for at least 1 hour or up to 8 hours. Serve cold.

SUGAR TOPPING
Makes about ½ cup

2 tablespoons (16 grams) all-purpose flour
2 tablespoons (12 grams) almond meal
1 tablespoon (14 grams) firmly packed light brown sugar
1 tablespoon (12 grams) turbinado sugar
1 tablespoon (8 grams) Swedish pearl sugar
1 tablespoon (14 grams) unsalted butter, cubed

1. In a medium bowl, stir together flour, almond meal, and sugars. Using your hands, work in butter until mixture is crumbly. Refrigerate for up to 1 week.

CRÈME DIPLOMAT
Makes about 2½ cups

1½ cups (360 grams) whole milk
4 large egg yolks (74 grams)
½ cup (100 grams) granulated sugar
¼ cup (32 grams) cornstarch
¼ teaspoon kosher salt
1 tablespoon (15 grams) orange blossom water
2 teaspoons (10 grams) dark rum
6 tablespoons (84 grams) unsalted butter, softened and cubed
¼ cup (60 grams) heavy whipping cream

1. In a medium saucepan, bring milk to a boil over medium heat.
2. In a medium bowl, whisk together egg yolks, sugar, cornstarch, and salt. Pour half of hot milk into egg mixture, whisking constantly. Pour egg mixture into remaining hot milk in saucepan; cook, whisking constantly, until thickened, 2 to 3 minutes.
3. Pour pastry cream into a medium bowl. Add orange blossom water and rum. Let cool for 10 minutes. Add butter; whisk to combine. Cover surface of cream directly with a piece of plastic wrap, and refrigerate for at least 2 hours or up to 3 days.
4. In the bowl of a stand mixer fitted with the whisk attachment, beat cream at high speed until stiff peaks form, 1 to 2 minutes. Remove pastry cream from refrigerator, and whisk by hand to loosen. Gently fold half of whipped cream into pastry cream until combined. Fold in remaining whipped cream. Use immediately.

CINNAMON ROLL CAKE

Makes 6 to 8 servings

This cake is the perfect hybrid of breakfast and dessert. The sweet cinnamon-sugar delight of a warm cinnamon roll comes shining through each slice, but takes half the time and effort of making a yeasted dough.

½	cup (113 grams) unsalted butter, softened
1½	cups (300 grams) granulated sugar
3	large eggs (150 grams)
2	cups (250 grams) all-purpose flour
1	teaspoon (2 grams) ground cinnamon
1	teaspoon (5 grams) baking powder
½	teaspoon (2.5 grams) baking soda
½	teaspoon (1.5 grams) kosher salt
¾	cup (180 grams) whole buttermilk
½	cup (120 grams) sour cream
2	teaspoons (8 grams) vanilla extract

Cinnamon-Pecan Streusel (recipe follows)
Cream Cheese Glaze (recipe follows)
Garnish: chopped pecans

1. Preheat oven to 350°F (180°C). Butter and flour a Nordic Ware Cinnamon Bun Pull-Aparts Pan.
2. In the bowl of a stand mixer fitted with the paddle attachment, beat butter and sugar at medium speed until fluffy, 3 to 4 minutes, stopping to scrape sides of bowl. Add eggs, one at a time, beating well after each addition.
3. In a medium bowl, whisk together flour, cinnamon, baking powder, baking soda, and salt. In a small bowl, whisk together buttermilk and sour cream. With mixer on low speed, gradually add flour mixture to butter mixture alternately with buttermilk mixture, beginning and ending with flour mixture, beating just until combined after each addition. Beat in vanilla.
4. Spoon three-fourths of batter into prepared pan, smoothing top with an offset spatula. Sprinkle with Cinnamon-Pecan Streusel; top with remaining batter. Using a knife, pull blade back and forth through batter to swirl streusel layer. Smooth top with an offset spatula.
5. Bake until a wooden pick inserted in center comes out clean, about 35 minutes. Let cool in pan for 10 minutes. Remove from pan, and let cool completely on a wire rack. Drizzle Cream Cheese Glaze over cake. Garnish with pecans, if desired.

CINNAMON-PECAN STREUSEL
Makes about ½ cup

⅓	cup (73 grams) firmly packed light brown sugar
⅓	cup (38 grams) finely chopped pecans
1	tablespoon (6 grams) ground cinnamon
¼	teaspoon kosher salt

1. In a small bowl, stir together brown sugar, pecans, cinnamon, and salt until combined.

CREAM CHEESE GLAZE
Makes about 1 cup

2	ounces (55 grams) cream cheese, softened
2	tablespoons (28 grams) unsalted butter, softened
1	cup (120 grams) confectioners' sugar
2	tablespoons (30 grams) whole milk
½	teaspoon (2 grams) vanilla extract

1. In a medium bowl, whisk together cream cheese and butter until smooth. Add confectioners' sugar, milk, and vanilla, stirring until smooth. Use immediately.

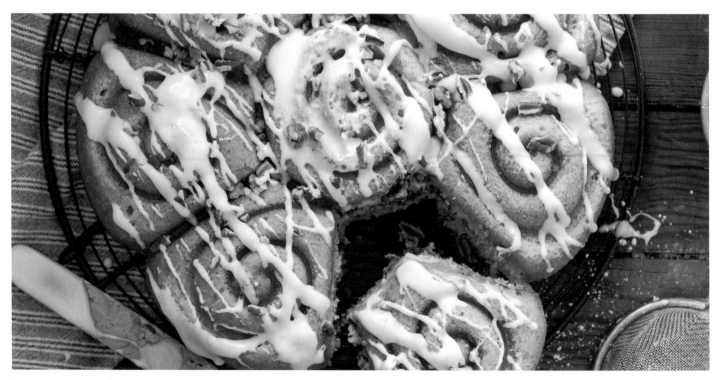

QUEEN ELIZABETH CAKE

Makes 1 (9-inch) cake

Recipe by Emily Turner

The first Canadian version of the Queen Elizabeth Cake recipe published claimed it "was created specifically for the Queen's Coronation." True or not, its toasted Coconut Cream Topping and dense fruity layers make this cake truly fit for a queen.

1   cup (240 grams) boiling water
1   cup (128 grams) chopped dates
1   teaspoon (5 grams) baking soda
½   cup (113 grams) unsalted butter, softened
½   cup (100 grams) granulated sugar
½   cup (110 grams) firmly packed light brown sugar
1   large egg (50 grams)
1   teaspoon (6 grams) vanilla bean paste
2   cups (250 grams) all-purpose flour
1   teaspoon (5 grams) baking powder
1   teaspoon (3 grams) kosher salt
½   teaspoon (1 gram) ground cinnamon
½   cup (57 grams) chopped pecans
Coconut Cream Topping (recipe follows)

1. Preheat oven to 350°F (180°C). Butter and flour a 9-inch springform pan.
2. In a medium bowl, pour 1 cup (240 grams) boiling water over dates. Stir in baking soda, and let stand until cooled to room temperature. (Soaking dates with baking soda will help cut their astringency and start to break down the dates prior to baking.)
3. In the bowl of a stand mixer fitted with the paddle attachment, beat butter and sugars at medium speed until fluffy, 3 to 4 minutes, stopping to scrape sides of bowl. Add egg, beating just until combined. Stir in vanilla bean paste.
4. In a medium bowl, whisk together flour, baking powder, salt, and cinnamon. With mixer on low speed, gradually add flour mixture to butter mixture alternately with date mixture, beginning and ending with flour mixture, beating just until combined after each addition. Stir in pecans. Pour batter into prepared pan, smoothing top with an offset spatula.
5. Bake until a wooden pick inserted in center comes out clean, 30 to 35 minutes. Increase oven temperature to broil. Spread Coconut Cream Topping onto warm cake.

Broil, checking every 30 seconds, until golden brown, about 2 minutes. Let cool in pan for 30 minutes. Run a sharp knife around edges of cake. Loosen side of springform, and let cool completely on base of pan.

COCONUT CREAM TOPPING
Makes 1⅓ cups

½   cup (110 grams) firmly packed light brown sugar
2   tablespoons (28 grams) unsalted butter
1¾   cups (147 grams) sweetened flaked coconut
¼   cup (60 grams) heavy whipping cream
⅛   teaspoon kosher salt

1. In a small saucepan, heat brown sugar and butter over medium-high heat until butter is melted. Stir in coconut, cream, and salt. Cook for 3 minutes, stirring constantly. Remove from heat, and let cool for 5 minutes.

Photo by Maya Visnyei

FRENCH APPLE-ALMOND CAKE

Makes 1 (8-inch) cake

From the dense, custardy bottom to the crisp top layer, almond flour amplifies the textures that are characteristic of this classic French cake. Additional egg yolks in the cake's base also boost its custard-like consistency.

2 Granny Smith apples (370 grams) peeled, cored, and thinly sliced
1 Gala apple (185 grams) peeled, cored, and thinly sliced
1 large egg (50 grams)
1 cup (200 grams) plus 2 tablespoons (24 grams) granulated sugar, divided
½ cup (113 grams) unsalted butter, melted
1 tablespoon (15 grams) apple brandy
1 teaspoon (6 grams) vanilla bean paste
¾ cup (94 grams) all-purpose flour
¾ cup (72 grams) almond flour (see Pro Tip)
2 teaspoons (10 grams) baking powder
½ teaspoon (1.5 grams) kosher salt
¼ cup (60 grams) whole milk
2 large egg yolks (37 grams)
1½ tablespoons (10.5 grams) sliced almonds

1. Preheat oven to 350°F (180°C). Butter and flour an 8-inch springform pan.
2. In a medium bowl, combine Granny Smith and Gala apples. Microwave on high until apples are softened but not translucent, about 2 minutes. Let cool; strain excess liquid.
3. In the bowl of a stand mixer fitted with the paddle attachment, beat egg and 2 tablespoons (24 grams) sugar at medium speed until pale in color, about 2 minutes. Stir in melted butter, brandy, and vanilla bean paste.
4. In a medium bowl, whisk together flours, baking powder, salt, and remaining 1 cup (200 grams) sugar. With mixer on low speed, gradually add flour mixture to egg mixture alternately with milk, beginning and ending with flour mixture, beating just until combined after each addition.
5. In a large bowl, whisk together 1 cup batter and egg yolks. Reserve ¼ cup (46 grams) apples. Stir remaining apples into egg yolk batter until combined. Spread egg yolk batter into prepared pan. Top with remaining batter, smoothing with an offset spatula. Press reserved ¼ cup (46 grams) apples into top of batter, and sprinkle with almonds. Place springform pan on a rimmed baking sheet to catch any drips.

6. Bake in bottom third of oven for 30 minutes. Raise springform pan to middle of oven, and bake until a wooden pick inserted in center comes out clean, about 35 minutes more, loosely covering with foil to prevent excess browning, if necessary. Let cool in pan for 15 minutes. Run a knife around edges of cake to loosen before removing from pan. Let cool completely on base of pan before serving.

Note: *The traditional French apple cake calls for the use of a variety of different apples. We went with the slightly tart Granny Smith and the sweeter Gala.*

> **PRO TIPS**
> Use almond flour made from blanched whole almonds. Flour made with unblanched almonds will give your baked good a slightly grainier texture and darker color.
>
> Microwaving the apples before stirring them into the batter removes the excess water content, which ensures your cake doesn't become soggy while baking.

CHARRED SQUASH POUND CAKE WITH BLACK PEPPER AND PARMESAN

Makes 6 to 8 servings

Recipe by Chadwick Boyd

Butternut squash takes center stage in this savory pound cake, the perfect addition to your wine and cheese board. Long, charred pieces of roasted squash are embedded within the top of this dense yet moist bread. Blending a bit of cornmeal with black pepper, fragrant rosemary, and salty Parmesan brings out the wonderful richness of the squash, and you won't miss the sugar. Sweet potatoes, large carrots, and other squash varietals, like delicata or acorn, would work fantastically well with this bread, too. Get creative with produce and have some fun!

1   peeled butternut squash (453 grams)
⅔   cup (149 grams) plus 1 tablespoon (14 grams) extra-virgin olive oil, divided
3   tablespoons (63 grams) honey, divided
2   teaspoons (6 grams) kosher salt, plus more for seasoning squash
5   large eggs (250 grams), room temperature
2¼ cups (281 grams) cake flour
1   cup (100 grams) plus 2 tablespoons (12.5 grams) freshly grated Parmesan cheese, divided
¼   cup (38 grams) cornmeal
1   tablespoon (2 grams) finely chopped fresh rosemary
2½ teaspoons (5 grams) ground black pepper
1½ teaspoons (7.5 grams) baking powder
½   cup (120 grams) whole milk
2   sprigs fresh rosemary

1. Preheat oven to 425°F (220°C). Butter and flour a 9x5-inch loaf pan; line pan with parchment paper.
2. Using a heavy-duty chef's knife, slice squash in half lengthwise. Place squash cut side up on a rimmed baking sheet.
3. In a small bowl, whisk together 1 tablespoon (14 grams) oil and 1 tablespoon (21 grams) honey. Drizzle over squash. (Make sure the oil and honey are fully mixed before drizzling over the squash. The honey can bubble up and slightly burn while roasting.) Season with salt.
4. Roast until soft and tops and edges are slightly charred, 30 to 35 minutes. Let cool for 15 minutes. Reduce oven temperature to 350°F (180°C).
5. Slice each squash in half lengthwise. Place one squash piece in the bowl of a stand mixer fitted with the paddle attachment, and mash with a fork to break it up into pieces. Add eggs, remaining ⅔ cup (149 grams) oil, and remaining 2 tablespoons (42 grams) honey; beat at medium speed until combined, 1 to 2 minutes.
6. In a medium bowl, whisk together flour, 1 cup (100 grams) cheese, cornmeal, chopped rosemary, pepper, baking powder, and remaining 2 teaspoons (6 grams) salt. With mixer on low speed, gradually add flour mixture to squash mixture alternately with milk, beginning and ending with flour mixture, beating just until combined after each addition.
7. Lay 1 squash piece in bottom of prepared pan. Pour batter over top. Nestle remaining 2 squash pieces side by side in top of batter (just enough so it peeks through). Dust with remaining 2 tablespoons (12.5 grams) cheese, and top with rosemary sprigs.
8. Bake until a wooden pick inserted in center comes out clean, about 1 hour and 10 minutes, covering with foil halfway through baking to prevent excess browning, if necessary. Let cool in pan for 10 minutes. Remove from pan, and let cool completely on a wire rack.

TAHINI SHORTCAKES WITH APRICOT JAM AND ORANGE BLOSSOM WHIPPED CREAM

Makes 9

Recipe by Ben Mims

Shortcakes haven't evolved much since they met strawberries and whipped cream, but this recipe offers a Middle Eastern version just as sophisticated as the original. The tahini and buttermilk in the shortcake dough lend a light sourness to the shortcakes that is countered by the sharp sweetness of the apricot jam and perfumed with the citrusy scent of orange blossom water. Serve these shortcakes individually for teatime, or crumble and layer them with the jam and whipped cream for an elegant, unique trifle.

1¾   cups (219 grams) all-purpose flour
1   tablespoon plus 2 teaspoons (25 grams) baking powder
1   tablespoon (12 grams) granulated sugar
1   teaspoon (3 grams) kosher salt
½   cup (113 grams) unsalted butter, frozen
1   cup (240 grams) whole buttermilk, chilled
⅓   cup (75 grams) tahini
1   cup (240 grams) heavy whipping cream, chilled
¼   cup (30 grams) confectioners' sugar, sifted
1¾   cups (560 grams) apricot preserves
1   tablespoon (15 grams) orange blossom water

1. In a large bowl, whisk together flour, baking powder, granulated sugar, and salt. Using the large holes of a box grater, grate frozen butter into flour mixture, and toss to coat.

2. In a small bowl, stir together buttermilk and tahini. Add buttermilk mixture to flour mixture, stirring until a dough forms. Refrigerate for 30 minutes.

3. Preheat oven to 350°F (180°C). Line 2 baking sheets with parchment paper.

4. Using a 2-ounce ice cream scoop or ¼-cup measuring cup, scoop dough, and drop onto prepared pans.

5. Bake until lightly browned, about 30 minutes, rotating pans front to back and top to bottom halfway through baking. Let cool completely on a wire rack.

6. In the bowl of a stand mixer fitted with the paddle attachment, beat cream and confectioners' sugar at medium speed until stiff peaks form.

7. In a medium bowl, stir together preserves and orange blossom water until combined. Split shortcakes in half, and spread preserves mixture onto bottom halves. Top with a dollop of whipped cream, and cover with top halves.

Photo by Mason + Dixon

BANANA-SESAME CAKE WITH TAHINI-CREAM CHEESE SWIRL FROSTING

Makes 12 to 16 servings

Recipe by Ben Mims

The bitterness of tahini is suited to sweet, tropical flavors like the banana in this sheet cake. Exceptionally moist, this cake will keep in the refrigerator without drying out for one week.

2½   cups (313 grams) all-purpose flour
¼   cup (36 grams) toasted sesame seeds
1½   teaspoons (7.5 grams) baking soda
1½   teaspoons (4.5 grams) kosher salt, divided
2   cups (440 grams) firmly packed light brown sugar
1   cup (224 grams) toasted sesame oil
⅔   cup (160 grams) whole buttermilk, room temperature
2   teaspoons (8 grams) vanilla extract, divided
4   large eggs (200 grams)
2   cups (454 grams) mashed banana (from about 6 very ripe bananas)
8   ounces (225 grams) cream cheese, softened
½   cup (113 grams) unsalted butter, softened
3   cups (360 grams) confectioners' sugar, sifted
¼   cup (56 grams) tahini

1. Preheat oven to 350°F (180°C). Butter and flour a 13x9-inch baking pan.
2. In a medium bowl, whisk together flour, sesame seeds, baking soda, and 1 teaspoon (3 grams) salt.
3. In a large bowl, whisk together brown sugar, oil, buttermilk, 1 teaspoon (4 grams) vanilla, and eggs until smooth. Add flour mixture to sugar mixture, and whisk just until combined. Stir in banana until smooth. Spoon batter into prepared pan, smoothing top with an offset spatula.
4. Bake until golden brown and a wooden pick inserted in center comes out clean, 40 to 45 minutes. Let cool completely on a wire rack.
5. In the bowl of a stand mixer fitted with the paddle attachment, beat cream cheese and butter at medium speed until smooth, about 1 minute. Add confectioners' sugar, remaining 1 teaspoon (4 grams) vanilla, and remaining ½ teaspoon (1.5 grams) salt, and beat until fluffy, about 1 minute. Spread three-fourths of frosting onto cake, leaving a 1-inch border on all sides. Add tahini to remaining frosting in bowl, and beat at medium speed until smooth. Dollop tahini frosting over plain frosting, and using the blade of a table knife, swirl frostings together. Cut into squares to serve.

Photo by Mason + Dixon

COCONUT BUTTERMILK POUND CAKE

Makes 2 (9x5-inch) loaves

Fluffy, moist, and filled with all kinds of coconut, this loaf is a true crowd-pleaser. Don't skip the toasted flakes on top—the subtle crunch makes this cake absolutely irresistible.

1½ cups (340 grams) unsalted butter, softened
3 cups (600 grams) granulated sugar
5 large eggs (250 grams)
3 cups (375 grams) all-purpose flour
2 teaspoons (6 grams) kosher salt
1 teaspoon (5 grams) baking powder
1 cup (240 grams) whole buttermilk
2 cups (168 grams) sweetened flaked coconut, toasted and divided
2 teaspoons (8 grams) vanilla extract
3 cups (360 grams) confectioners' sugar
¼ cup (60 grams) unsweetened coconut milk
1 tablespoon (15 grams) fresh lemon juice

1. Butter and flour 2 (9x5-inch) loaf pans. Line pans with parchment paper, letting excess extend over sides of pan. Butter and flour pans again.
2. In the bowl of a stand mixer fitted with the paddle attachment, beat butter and granulated sugar at medium speed until fluffy, 3 to 4 minutes, stopping to scrape sides of bowl. Add eggs, one at a time, beating well after each addition.
3. In a medium bowl, whisk together flour, salt, and baking powder. With mixer on low speed, gradually add flour mixture to butter mixture alternately with buttermilk, beginning and ending with flour mixture, beating just until combined after each addition. Beat in 1¼ cups (105 grams) coconut and vanilla. Divide batter between prepared pans.
4. Place pans in a cold oven. Bake at 300°F (150°C) until a wooden pick inserted in center comes out clean, about 1 hour and 15 minutes. Let cool in pans for 10 minutes. Remove from pans, and let cool completely on wire racks.
5. In a medium bowl, whisk together confectioners' sugar, coconut milk, and lemon juice. Drizzle glaze over loaves; sprinkle with remaining ¾ cup (63 grams) coconut.

GRILLED BROWNED BUTTER POUND CAKE WITH BERRIES

Makes 2 (9x5-inch) loaves

Grilled cake? Oh, yes. Lightly toasting slices of this browned butter-scented confection adds a sweet caramelized crunch.

⅔ cup (150 grams) unsalted butter, softened
⅔ cup (150 grams) Browned Butter (recipe follows), softened
2½ cups (500 grams) granulated sugar, divided
½ cup (110 grams) firmly packed light brown sugar
6 large eggs (300 grams)
3 teaspoons (12 grams) vanilla extract, divided
1 teaspoon (4 grams) almond extract
3 cups (375 grams) all-purpose flour
1 teaspoon (3 grams) kosher salt
1 cup (240 grams) whole buttermilk
4 cups (680 grams) quartered fresh strawberries
1 cup (170 grams) halved fresh blackberries
1 tablespoon (15 grams) fresh lemon juice
Vanilla ice cream, to serve

1. Preheat oven to 350°F (180°C). Butter and flour 2 (9x5-inch) loaf pans. Line pans with parchment paper, letting excess extend over sides of pan. Butter and flour pans again.
2. In the bowl of a stand mixer fitted with the paddle attachment, beat butter, Browned Butter, 2 cups (400 grams) granulated sugar, and brown sugar at medium speed until fluffy, about 5 minutes, stopping to scrape sides of bowl. Add eggs, one at a time, beating well after each addition. Beat in 2 teaspoons (8 grams) vanilla and almond extract.
3. In a medium bowl, whisk together flour and salt. With mixer on low speed, gradually add flour mixture to butter mixture alternately with buttermilk, beginning and ending with flour mixture, beating just until combined after each addition. Divide batter between prepared pans.
4. Bake until a wooden pick inserted in center comes out clean, about 45 minutes. Let cool in pans for 10 minutes. Remove from pans, and let cool completely on wire racks.
5. In a medium bowl, combine strawberries, blackberries, lemon juice, remaining ½ cup

(100 grams) granulated sugar, and remaining 1 teaspoon (4 grams) vanilla. Let stand for 15 minutes.
6. Spray a cast-iron grill pan with cooking spray. Heat pan over medium heat.
7. Slice pound cake, and cook until lightly toasted, about 1 minute per side. Serve warm with berry mixture and ice cream.

BROWNED BUTTER
Makes about ¾ cup

1 cup (227 grams) unsalted butter

1. In a medium saucepan, melt butter over medium heat. Cook until butter turns a medium-brown color and has a nutty aroma, about 10 minutes. Remove from heat, and let cool to room temperature before using.

PRO TIP
Let Browned Butter solidify slightly before using.

FIG PRESERVES CAKE

Makes 1 (9-inch) cake

Sweet fig preserves deepen the flavor of this simple buttermilk batter while a tart lemon glaze brightens up each slice. Top with halved figs for a dramatic presentation.

- ⅔   cup (160 grams) whole buttermilk
- ½   cup (160 grams) fig preserves
- ½   cup (113 grams) unsalted butter, softened
- 1   cup (200 grams) granulated sugar
- 2   large eggs (100 grams)
- 1½ cups (188 grams) all-purpose flour
- ½   teaspoon (2.5 grams) baking soda
- ¼   teaspoon kosher salt
- ¼   teaspoon ground cinnamon
- ½   cup (57 grams) chopped toasted pecans
- Lemon Cream Glaze (recipe follows)
- Garnish: fresh figs

1. Preheat oven to 350°F (180°C). Butter and flour a 9-inch round cake pan.
2. In the container of a blender, place buttermilk and preserves; process until combined. Set aside.
3. In the bowl of a stand mixer fitted with the paddle attachment, beat butter and sugar at medium speed until fluffy, 3 to 4 minutes, stopping to scrape sides of bowl. Add eggs, one at a time, beating well after each addition.
4. In a medium bowl, whisk together flour, baking soda, salt, and cinnamon. With mixer on low speed, gradually add flour mixture to butter mixture alternately with buttermilk mixture, beginning and ending with flour mixture, beating just until combined after each addition. Stir in pecans. Spoon batter into prepared pan.
5. Bake until a wooden pick inserted in center comes out clean, about 35 minutes.

Let cool in pan for 10 minutes. Remove from pan, and let cool completely on a wire rack. Spread Lemon Cream Glaze onto cake. Garnish with figs, if desired.

LEMON CREAM GLAZE
Makes about 1 cup

- 2   cups (240 grams) confectioners' sugar
- 6   tablespoons (90 grams) heavy whipping cream
- 2   tablespoons (30 grams) fresh lemon juice

1. In a medium bowl, whisk together confectioners' sugar, cream, and lemon juice until smooth. Use immediately.

BIENENSTICH

Makes 1 (9-inch) cake

German for "Bee Sting Cake," the Bienenstich is honey rich and topped with a savory/sweet blend of caramelized almonds.

1½   cups (360 grams) whole milk
¾   cup (255 grams) plus ⅓ cup (113 grams) honey, divided
3   tablespoons (24 grams) cornstarch
¼   teaspoon sea salt
5   large egg yolks (93 grams), divided
2   tablespoons (28 grams) cold unsalted butter
1   teaspoon (4 grams) vanilla extract
¾   cup (180 grams) warm whole milk (105°F/40°C to 110°F/43°C)
¼   cup (57 grams) unsalted butter, melted
2¼   cups (281 grams) all-purpose flour
⅓   cup (67 grams) plus ¼ cup (50 grams) granulated sugar, divided
2¼   teaspoons (4.5 grams) instant yeast*
1   teaspoon (3 grams) kosher salt
6   tablespoons (84 grams) unsalted butter
2   tablespoons (30 grams) heavy whipping cream
2   cups (226 grams) sliced almonds

1. In a medium saucepan, whisk together milk, ½ cup (170 grams) honey, cornstarch, and sea salt until smooth. Heat over medium heat until hot.

2. In a medium bowl, whisk 3 egg yolks (56 grams) until smooth. Pour hot milk mixture over egg yolks; whisk until smooth. Reduce heat to low. Pour egg mixture back into saucepan, and cook, whisking constantly, until mixture thickens and comes together. Whisk in cold butter and vanilla. Transfer to a medium glass bowl. Cover with a piece of plastic wrap, pressing wrap directly onto surface of custard. Refrigerate until chilled, about 2 hours.

3. Butter and flour a 9-inch round cake pan.

4. In a large glass bowl, whisk together warm milk, ⅓ cup (113 grams) honey, melted butter, and remaining 2 egg yolks (37 grams) until smooth. Whisk in flour, ¼ cup (50 grams) sugar, yeast, and salt until smooth. Pour batter into prepared pan. Cover with plastic wrap, and let stand in a warm, draft-free place (75°F/24°C) until doubled in size, 1½ to 2 hours.

5. Preheat oven 350°F (180°C).

6. In a medium saucepan, bring butter, cream, remaining ⅓ cup (67 grams) sugar, and remaining ¼ cup (85 grams) honey to a boil over medium heat. Cook for 1 minute. Remove from heat, and stir in almonds. Spoon almond mixture gently over batter.

7. Bake until golden brown and a wooden pick inserted in center comes out clean, 35 to 40 minutes. Let cool in pan for 10 minutes. Invert cake onto a wire rack, and turn cake back over, almond side up. Let cool completely.

8. Using a serrated knife, cut cake into 2 layers. Place bottom layer on a cake plate, and spread with custard. Place top layer over custard, almond side up.

We used Fleischmann's Rapid Rise Instant Yeast.

ORANGE-CARDAMOM LOAVES

Makes 2 (8½x4½-inch) loaves

Dripping with sweet orange glaze and scented with warm cardamom and vanilla, these loaves are absolutely mouthwatering. They're the perfect bright finale to your next brunch.

3   cups (375 grams) all-purpose flour
2½ cups (500 grams) granulated sugar
1½ teaspoons (4.5 grams) kosher salt
1½ teaspoons (7.5 grams) baking powder
¼   teaspoon ground cardamom
1½ cups (360 grams) whole milk
1   cup (224 grams) vegetable oil
3   large eggs (150 grams)
2   tablespoons (12 grams) orange zest
1½ teaspoons (6 grams) vanilla extract
Orange Glaze (recipe follows)

1. Preheat oven to 350°F (180°C). Butter and flour 2 (8½x4½-inch) loaf pans.
2. In a large bowl, whisk together flour, sugar, salt, baking powder, and cardamom; make a well in center of mixture. Add milk, oil, eggs, zest, and vanilla, whisking until smooth. Divide batter between prepared pans.
3. Bake until a wooden pick inserted in center comes out clean, about 55 minutes. Let cool in pans for 10 minutes. Remove from pans, and let cool completely on wire racks. Drizzle with Orange Glaze.

ORANGE GLAZE

Makes about 1⅓ cups

2   cups (240 grams) confectioners' sugar
1   teaspoon (2 grams) orange zest
⅓   cup (80 grams) fresh orange juice

1. In a medium bowl, whisk together confectioners' sugar and orange zest and juice until smooth. Use immediately.

STRAWBERRY CREAM CHEESE POUND CAKE LOAVES

Makes 2 (8½x4½-inch) loaves

These cakes bring the ever-popular combination of strawberries and cream to each decadent slice. With homemade strawberry sauce swirled into each loaf, they're just as beautiful as they are delicious.

1   cup (227 grams) unsalted butter, softened
8   ounces (225 grams) cream cheese, softened
3   cups (600 grams) granulated sugar
1   tablespoon (13 grams) vanilla extract
6   large eggs (300 grams)
3½ cups (438 grams) all-purpose flour
½   teaspoon (1.5 grams) kosher salt
¼   teaspoon (1.25 grams) baking powder
1   cup (240 grams) heavy whipping cream
Strawberry Sauce (recipe follows)
Strawberry preserves, to serve

1. Preheat oven to 325°F (170°C). Butter and flour 2 (8½x4½-inch) loaf pans. Line pans with parchment paper, letting excess extend over sides of pan. Butter and flour pans again.

2. In the bowl of a stand mixer fitted with the paddle attachment, beat butter and cream cheese at medium speed until creamy. Add sugar and vanilla; beat until fluffy, 3 to 4 minutes, stopping to scrape sides of bowl. Add eggs, one at a time, beating well after each addition.

3. In a medium bowl, whisk together flour, salt, and baking powder. With mixer on low speed, gradually add flour mixture to butter mixture alternately with cream, beginning and ending with flour mixture, beating just until combined after each addition. Transfer half of batter to a medium bowl; set aside.

4. Spoon one-third of remaining batter into 1 prepared pan. Spread ¼ cup (67 grams) Strawberry Sauce onto batter. Repeat layers once; top with remaining one-third batter. Using a wooden skewer, gently swirl batter. Repeat procedure with remaining batter and remaining Strawberry Sauce. Tap pans on counter twice to release air bubbles.

5. Bake until a wooden pick inserted in center comes out clean, about 1 hour and 10 minutes. Let cool in pans for 10 minutes.

Remove from pans, and let cool completely on wire racks. Serve with strawberry preserves, if desired.

STRAWBERRY SAUCE

Makes about 1 cup

½   pound (225 grams) fresh strawberries, hulled
2   tablespoons (30 grams) water
1   tablespoon (8 grams) cornstarch
3   tablespoons (36 grams) granulated sugar

1. In the work bowl of a food processor, pulse strawberries until smooth, about 1 minute.

2. In a small bowl, whisk together 2 tablespoons (30 grams) water and cornstarch until smooth.

3. In a medium saucepan, stir together puréed strawberries and sugar over medium-high heat. Whisk in cornstarch mixture. Bring to a boil; cook, stirring constantly, until thickened, about 1 minute.

STRAWBERRY SHEET CAKE

Makes 12 servings

This simple sheet cake is the trusty Old Reliable in our recipe box. With fresh strawberries and a light and fluffy frosting, this moist confection is quick to throw together and disappears even quicker.

2¼ cups (281 grams) self-rising flour
⅔ cup (133 grams) granulated sugar
⅔ cup (160 grams) whole buttermilk
½ cup (160 grams) strawberry preserves
½ cup (113 grams) unsalted butter, melted
3 large eggs (150 grams)
1 teaspoon (4 grams) vanilla extract
⅔ cup (113 grams) chopped fresh strawberries
Strawberry Cream Cheese Frosting (recipe follows)
Garnish: sliced fresh strawberries

1. Preheat oven to 350°F (180°C). Butter and flour a 13x9-inch baking pan.
2. In a large bowl, whisk together flour and sugar; make a well in center of mixture.
3. In a medium bowl, whisk together buttermilk, preserves, melted butter, eggs, and vanilla. Add buttermilk mixture to flour mixture, whisking to combine. Stir in strawberries. Pour batter into prepared pan.

4. Bake until a wooden pick inserted in center comes out clean, about 27 minutes. Let cool completely on a wire rack. Spread Strawberry Cream Cheese Frosting onto cake. Refrigerate for at least 1 hour before serving. Garnish with strawberries, if desired.

STRAWBERRY CREAM CHEESE FROSTING
Makes 5 cups

8 ounces (225 grams) cream cheese, softened
½ cup (113 grams) unsalted butter, softened
1 cup (170 grams) chopped fresh strawberries
4½ cups (540 grams) confectioners' sugar

1. In the bowl of a stand mixer fitted with the paddle attachment, beat cream cheese and butter at medium speed until creamy, stopping to scrape sides of bowl. Add strawberries, and beat until combined. Reduce mixer speed to low. Gradually add confectioners' sugar, beating until smooth. Use immediately.

ITALIAN CREAM SHEET CAKE

Makes 12 servings

This sheet cake is our answer to those Italian Cream Cake cravings when time is short. Each bite crunches with buttery pecans and sweet coconut flakes, complemented by a swooping layer of whipped cream on top.

1½	cups (340 grams) unsalted butter, softened
2	cups (400 grams) granulated sugar
5	large eggs (250 grams), separated
2	cups (250 grams) all-purpose flour
1½	teaspoons (4.5 grams) kosher salt
1	teaspoon (5 grams) baking soda
1	cup (240 grams) whole buttermilk
1	cup (113 grams) finely chopped pecans
1	cup (84 grams) sweetened flaked coconut, toasted
1	teaspoon (4 grams) vanilla extract
14	ounces (400 grams) sweetened condensed milk
1	tablespoon (15 grams) almond liqueur

Sweetened Whipped Cream (recipe follows)
Garnish: chopped pecans, toasted flaked coconut

1. Preheat oven to 350°F (180°C). Butter and flour a 13x9-inch baking pan.
2. In the bowl of a stand mixer fitted with the paddle attachment, beat butter and sugar at medium speed until fluffy, 3 to 4 minutes, stopping to scrape sides of bowl. Add egg yolks, one at a time, beating well after each addition.
3. In a medium bowl, whisk together flour, salt, and baking soda.

With mixer on low speed, gradually add flour mixture to butter mixture alternately with buttermilk, beginning and ending with flour mixture, beating just until combined after each addition. Stir in pecans, coconut, and vanilla. Transfer batter to a large bowl.
4. Clean bowl of stand mixer. Using the whisk attachment, beat egg whites at high speed until stiff peaks form. Gently fold egg whites into batter. Spread batter into prepared pan, smoothing top with an offset spatula.
5. Bake until a wooden pick inserted in center comes out clean, about 45 minutes, loosely covering with foil halfway through baking to prevent excess browning.
6. In a small bowl, stir together condensed milk and almond liqueur. Using a fork, poke holes in top of warm cake. Pour mixture over cake. Let cool completely. Top with Sweetened Whipped Cream. Garnish with pecans and coconut, if desired. Cover and refrigerate for up to 3 days.

SWEETENED WHIPPED CREAM
Makes 6 cups

2½	cups (600 grams) heavy whipping cream
½	cup (60 grams) confectioners' sugar
1	teaspoon (4 grams) vanilla extract

1. In the bowl of a stand mixer fitted with the whisk attachment, beat cream at medium speed until slightly thickened. Increase mixer speed to medium-high. Gradually add confectioners' sugar and vanilla, beating until stiff peaks form.

ORANGE SPICE SHEET CAKE

Makes 12 servings

The beloved flavors of orange cream and spice cake collide in this one-layer delight. Packing a punch of fresh citrus flavor and a hint of warm spice, it will have your guests running back for seconds.

¾   cup (170 grams) unsalted butter, softened
1½ cups (300 grams) granulated sugar
3   large eggs (150 grams)
1   teaspoon (4 grams) vanilla extract
2½ cups (313 grams) all-purpose flour
1½ teaspoons (7.5 grams) baking powder
1   teaspoon (2 grams) ground cinnamon
1   teaspoon (2 grams) ground ginger
1   teaspoon (2 grams) ground nutmeg
¼   teaspoon kosher salt
1¼ cups (300 grams) half-and-half
Orange Frosting (recipe follows)

1. Preheat oven to 350°F (180°C). Butter and flour a 13x9-inch baking pan.
2. In the bowl of a stand mixer fitted with the paddle attachment, beat butter and sugar at medium speed until fluffy, 3 to 4 minutes, stopping to scrape sides of bowl. Add eggs, one at a time, beating well after each addition. Beat in vanilla.

3. In a medium bowl, whisk together flour, baking powder, cinnamon, ginger, nutmeg, and salt. With mixer on low speed, gradually add flour mixture to butter mixture alternately with half-and-half, beginning and ending with flour mixture, beating just until combined after each addition. Spoon batter into prepared pan.
4. Bake until a wooden pick inserted in center comes out clean, about 25 minutes. Let cool completely on a wire rack. Spread Orange Frosting onto cake. Cover and refrigerate for up to 3 days.

ORANGE FROSTING
Makes about 3 cups

1½ cups (340 grams) unsalted butter, softened
½   cup (160 grams) orange marmalade
1   tablespoon (6 grams) orange zest
4   cups (480 grams) confectioners' sugar

1. In the bowl of a stand mixer fitted with the paddle attachment, beat butter, marmalade, and zest at medium speed until creamy. Reduce mixer speed to low. Gradually add confectioners' sugar, beating until smooth.

TEXAS SHEET CAKE

Makes 1 (15x10-inch) cake

The reigning king of all sheet cakes, this easy treat is a chocoholic's dream. A rich, fudgy cake cloaked in warm chocolate frosting with a sprinkling of pecans for added crunch? Yes, please!

2	cups (400 grams) granulated sugar
1	cup (240 grams) water
½	cup (112 grams) canola oil
½	cup (120 grams) whole buttermilk
½	cup (113 grams) unsalted butter, melted
2	large eggs (100 grams), lightly beaten
1	teaspoon (4 grams) vanilla extract
2	cups (250 grams) all-purpose flour
⅓	cup (25 grams) unsweetened cocoa powder
1	teaspoon (2 grams) ground cinnamon
1	teaspoon (5 grams) baking soda
¼	teaspoon kosher salt

Warm Chocolate Frosting (recipe follows)

1 cup (113 grams) chopped toasted pecans

1. Preheat oven to 400°F (200°C). Butter and flour a 15x10-inch jelly-roll pan.

2. In a large bowl, whisk together sugar, 1 cup (240 grams) water, oil, buttermilk, melted butter, eggs, and vanilla until smooth.

3. In a medium bowl, whisk together flour, cocoa, cinnamon, baking soda, and salt. Gradually add flour mixture to sugar mixture, whisking until smooth. Pour batter into prepared pan.

4. Bake until cake springs back when lightly touched in center, about 20 minutes. Let cool in pan for 5 minutes. Pour Warm Chocolate Frosting over cake, spreading with an offset spatula. Sprinkle with pecans. Let cool completely before serving.

WARM CHOCOLATE FROSTING

Makes about 2 cups

½	cup (113 grams) unsalted butter
⅓	cup (80 grams) whole milk
1	pound (455 grams) confectioners' sugar
⅓	cup (25 grams) unsweetened cocoa powder
1	teaspoon (4 grams) vanilla extract
¼	teaspoon kosher salt
¼	teaspoon ground cinnamon

1. In a medium saucepan, combine butter and milk. Cook over medium-low heat, stirring occasionally, until butter is melted. Whisk in confectioners' sugar, cocoa, vanilla, salt, and cinnamon until smooth. Use immediately.

CHERRY CRUMB CAKE

Makes 1 (8-inch) cake

Ditch the extravagant garnishes and towering layers for this simple and sophisticated one-layer cake that is guaranteed to impress. With a layer of cherries baked beneath the Ginger-Lime Crumb Topping, our elevated take on the cherry-limeade cake (a summertime classic) is even more beautiful after you cut into it. You'll get a juicy burst of cherry in every bite.

½	cup (113 grams) unsalted butter, softened
½	cup (100 grams) granulated sugar
¼	cup (55 grams) firmly packed light brown sugar
2	large eggs (100 grams)
1	teaspoon (4 grams) vanilla extract
1	teaspoon (4 grams) almond extract
1½	cups (188 grams) all-purpose flour
1	teaspoon (5 grams) baking powder
¼	teaspoon kosher salt
¼	cup (60 grams) whole buttermilk
1	pound (455 grams) cherries, pitted

Ginger-Lime Crumb Topping (recipe follows)

1. Preheat oven to 350°F (180°C). Butter and flour an 8-inch springform pan. Line pan with parchment paper; butter and flour pan again.

2. In the bowl of a stand mixer fitted with the paddle attachment, beat butter and sugars at medium speed until fluffy, 3 to 4 minutes, stopping to scrape sides of bowl. Add eggs, one at a time, beating well after each addition. Beat in extracts.

3. In a medium bowl, whisk together flour, baking powder, and salt. With mixer on low speed, gradually add flour mixture to butter mixture alternately with buttermilk, beginning and ending with flour mixture, beating just until combined after each addition. Pour batter into prepared pan, smoothing top with an offset spatula. Top with an even layer of cherries. Sprinkle with Ginger-Lime Crumb Topping.

4. Bake until a wooden pick inserted in center comes out clean, about 1 hour. Let cool in pan for 15 minutes. Remove from pan, and let cool completely on a wire rack. Cover and store at room temperature for up to 2 days, or refrigerate for up to 6 days.

GINGER-LIME CRUMB TOPPING
Makes about 1 cup

¾	cup (94 grams) all-purpose flour
½	cup (100 grams) granulated sugar
⅓	cup (76 grams) unsalted butter, melted
¼	cup (28 grams) chopped pecans
2	teaspoons (4 grams) lime zest
1	teaspoon grated fresh ginger
½	teaspoon (1.5 grams) kosher salt
¼	teaspoon ground cinnamon

1. In a small bowl, stir together all ingredients until mixture is crumbly. Use immediately, or refrigerate for up to 5 days.

RHUBARB BROWN SUGAR CAKE

Makes 1 (9-inch) cake

With both diced rhubarb inside and ample slices baked into the top, this cake has a one of a kind texture and taste. Brown sugar and buttermilk give it a moist crumb and wholesome sweetness that make it perfect for breakfast or dessert.

¾ cup (170 grams) unsalted butter, softened
1½ cups (330 grams) firmly packed dark brown sugar
1 tablespoon (6 grams) orange zest
2 large eggs (100 grams)
1 teaspoon (6 grams) vanilla bean paste
1½ cups (188 grams) all-purpose flour
¾ teaspoon (3.75 grams) baking powder
½ teaspoon (1.5 grams) kosher salt
¾ cup (180 grams) whole buttermilk
1 cup (100 grams) diced rhubarb
½ cup (50 grams) sliced rhubarb
2 tablespoons (24 grams) granulated sugar

1. Preheat oven to 350°F (180°C). Butter and flour a 9-inch round cake pan.

2. In the bowl of a stand mixer fitted with the paddle attachment, beat butter, brown sugar, and zest at medium-high speed until fluffy, 3 to 4 minutes, stopping to scrape sides of bowl. Add eggs, one at a time, beating well after each addition. Beat in vanilla bean paste.

3. In a medium bowl, whisk together flour, baking powder, and salt. With mixer on low speed, gradually add flour mixture to butter mixture alternately with buttermilk, beginning and ending with flour mixture, beating just until combined after each addition. Fold in diced rhubarb. Pour batter into prepared pan. Top with sliced rhubarb, and sprinkle with granulated sugar.

4. Bake until a wooden pick inserted in center comes out clean, 35 to 40 minutes. Let cool in pan for 10 minutes. Remove from pan, and let cool completely on a wire rack.

> **PRO TIP**
> When buying rhubarb, look for stalks that are firm, crisp, and blemish-free with taut, shiny skin. Store rhubarb unwashed in the refrigerator for up to 1 week.

PLUM ICEBOX CAKE

Make 1 (10-inch) cake

Recipe by Allison Kave and Keavy Landreth

Icebox cakes let you use your refrigerator as an oven, and in the height of summer, that's pretty much the best way to bake. For this recipe, we like to make the Tarragon Vanilla Wafers in the cool of the evening, and then have them ready to layer when it's time to make our cake. In fact, nearly all the elements of this recipe can be made ahead, so it's an easy one to whip together when you're expecting guests. Just make sure you give the layers enough time to come together and soften. Plums are a surprisingly underutilized fruit in most summer dessert recipes. We're not sure why. Peaches seem to always be the star of the show, but we're happy to give these juicy stone fruits a little time in the spotlight. The delicate flavor of the tarragon in the wafers, combined with lightly spiced (and the easiest ever) honey caramel, toasted pine nuts, and whipped cream, brings this retro concoction firmly into the 21st century.

⅓   cup (45 grams) pine nuts
2   cups (480 grams) heavy whipping cream
4   tablespoons (48 grams) granulated sugar, divided
1   tablespoon (13 grams) vanilla extract
Tarragon Vanilla Wafers (recipe follows)
9   ripe plums (810 grams), pitted and cut into ¼-inch slices
     (do not peel)
Spiced Honey Caramel (recipe follows)

1. In a small heavy saucepan, toast pine nuts over low heat until golden and fragrant, 2 to 5 minutes, watching carefully as they can burn quickly. Set aside to let cool.
2. In the bowl of a stand mixer fitted with the whisk attachment, beat cream, 2 tablespoons (24 grams) sugar, and vanilla at medium-high speed until soft peaks form. Spread one-third of whipped cream in bottom of a 10-inch pie dish. Arrange half of Tarragon Vanilla Wafers in a single layer over cream.
3. In a medium bowl, toss together plum slices and remaining 2 tablespoons (24 grams) sugar. Arrange half of plum slices in an even layer over Tarragon Vanilla Wafers.
4. Pour half of Spiced Honey Caramel over plums. Top with about half of toasted pine nuts. Cover with another thick layer of whipped cream. Layer with remaining Tarragon Vanilla Wafers, plums, Spiced Honey Caramel, and all but 1 tablespoon pine nuts. Finish with a dollop of remaining whipped cream in the center, leaving outer edges of layers underneath exposed. Sprinkle with remaining 1 tablespoon pine nuts. Refrigerate for at least 1 hour or overnight to allow wafers underneath to soften.

TARRAGON VANILLA WAFERS
Makes 60 to 65

½   cup (113 grams) unsalted butter, softened
½   cup (110 grams) firmly packed dark brown sugar
1   large egg (50 grams)
2   tablespoons (26 grams) vanilla extract
1   tablespoon (15 grams) whole milk
1¼   cups (156 grams) all-purpose flour
2   tablespoons (4 grams) finely chopped fresh tarragon leaves
¾   teaspoon (3.75 grams) baking powder
¾   teaspoon (2.25 grams) kosher salt

1. In the bowl of a stand mixer fitted with the paddle attachment, beat butter and brown sugar at medium-high speed until creamy, about 2 minutes, stopping to scrape sides of bowl. Add egg, and beat for 1 minute. Add vanilla and milk; beat until combined, about 1 minute, stopping to scrape sides of bowl.
2. In a medium bowl, stir together flour, tarragon, baking powder, and salt. With mixer on low speed, gradually add flour mixture to butter mixture, beating just until combined. Refrigerate for at least 30 minutes or up to 5 days.
3. Preheat oven to 350°F (180°C). Line 2 half-sheet trays with parchment paper.
4. Using a small (1-teaspoon) spring-loaded scoop, scoop dough into balls, and place on prepared pans. Using the heel of your hand, gently press down on dough to flatten.
5. Bake until golden brown around the edges, 10 to 12 minutes, rotating pans halfway through baking. Let cool completely on pans.

SPICED HONEY CARAMEL
Makes about 1½ cups

1½   cups (360 grams) heavy whipping cream, divided
½   cup (170 grams) mild honey (like clover or orange blossom)
2   tablespoons (28 grams) unsalted butter
¼   teaspoon sea salt
¼   teaspoon ground ginger
⅛   teaspoon ground cinnamon

1. In a small saucepan, bring 1 cup (240 grams) cream, honey, and butter to a boil over medium-high heat. Reduce heat, and simmer, stirring occasionally, until thickened and honey colored, 10 to 12 minutes. Remove from heat; whisk in salt, ginger, cinnamon, and remaining ½ cup (120 grams) cream. Let cool to room temperature before using.

CLASSIC OLIVE OIL CAKE

Makes 1 (8-inch) cake

A staple in most Mediterranean kitchens, this light and barely sweet cake is perfect for an afternoon snack or late morning tea. A final brush of olive oil just before serving brings the fruity flavor to the front of your palate as soon as you take a bite.

3   large eggs (150 grams)
¾   cup (150 grams) granulated sugar
½   cup (112 grams) extra-virgin olive oil
½   cup (120 grams) whole milk
½   teaspoon (2 grams) vanilla extract
¼   teaspoon (1 gram) almond extract
1½ cups (188 grams) all-purpose flour
1½ teaspoons (7.5 grams) baking powder
½   teaspoon (1.5 grams) kosher salt

1. Preheat oven to 350°F (180°C). Butter and flour an 8-inch round cake pan; line bottom of pan with parchment paper.
2. In the bowl of a stand mixer fitted with the whisk attachment, beat eggs and sugar at high speed for 30 seconds. Add oil in a slow, steady stream, beating until combined. Add milk, beating until combined. Reduce mixer speed to low. Beat in extracts.
3. In a medium bowl, whisk together flour, baking powder, and salt. Gradually add flour mixture to egg mixture, beating until combined, stopping to scrape sides of bowl. Pour batter into prepared pan.
4. Bake until a wooden pick inserted in center comes out clean, 30 to 33 minutes. Let cool in pan for 5 minutes. Remove from pan, and let cool completely on a wire rack. Brush with fresh olive oil just before serving. Store at room temperature wrapped loosely in foil or plastic wrap.

BANANA UPSIDE-DOWN CAKE WITH WALNUTS AND COCONUT

Makes 1 (9-inch) cake

If you're a fan of Bananas Foster, then this ultra-moist cake will be your upside-down dream come true. Coconut flakes and cream of coconut lend a tropical vibe and subtle nutty flavor.

½ cup (71 grams) walnuts
¼ cup (28 grams) finely chopped walnuts
¾ cup (170 grams) unsalted butter, softened and divided
½ cup (110 grams) plus ⅓ cup (73 grams) firmly packed light brown sugar, divided
2 tablespoons (30 grams) cream of coconut
½ tablespoon (7.5 grams) water
2½ teaspoons (10 grams) vanilla extract, divided
3 bananas (372 grams), halved lengthwise
½ cup (100 grams) granulated sugar
2 large eggs (100 grams)
1¾ cups (219 grams) all-purpose flour
1½ teaspoons (7.5 grams) baking powder
¾ teaspoon (2.25 grams) kosher salt
¼ teaspoon ground cinnamon
¾ cup (180 grams) whole milk
⅓ cup (28 grams) sweetened flaked coconut
¼ cup (60 grams) sour cream

1. Preheat oven to 350° (180°C). Butter and flour a 9-inch square cake pan.
2. Sprinkle whole walnuts and chopped walnuts around edges of prepared pan.
3. In a large saucepan, melt ¼ cup (57 grams) butter over medium-high heat. Stir in ⅓ cup (73 grams) brown sugar and cream of coconut; bring to a boil. Stir in ½ tablespoon (7.5 grams) water and 1 teaspoon (4 grams) vanilla; cook for 1 minute. Pour mixture into pan. Arranged halved bananas on syrup in bottom of pan, cut side down.
4. In the bowl of a stand mixer fitted with the paddle attachment, beat granulated sugar, remaining ½ cup (110 grams) brown sugar, and remaining ½ cup (113 grams) butter at medium speed until fluffy, 3 to 4 minutes, stopping to scrape sides of bowl. Add eggs, one at a time, beating well after each addition. Stir in remaining 1½ teaspoons (6 grams) vanilla.
5. In a medium bowl, whisk together flour, baking powder, salt, and cinnamon. With mixer on low speed, gradually add flour mixture to butter mixture alternately with milk, beginning and ending with flour mixture, beating just until combined after each addition. Fold in coconut and sour cream. Carefully spread batter onto bananas.
6. Bake until a wooden pick inserted in center comes out clean, 50 to 55 minutes. Let cool in pan for 10 minutes. Invert onto a wire rack, and let cool completely. Refrigerate in an airtight container for up to 3 days.

KAHLÚA ESPRESSO CAKE

Makes 1 (9x5-inch) loaf

This cake comes packed with espresso, Kahlúa, and a latte glaze. After-dinner cocktails never tasted so good.

1   cup (227 grams) unsalted butter, melted
1   cup (200 grams) granulated sugar
2   teaspoons (12 grams) vanilla bean paste
½   cup (120 grams) whole milk
½   cup (120 grams) plus 1 tablespoon (15 grams) Kahlúa, divided
2   tablespoons (12 grams) plus 1 teaspoon (2 grams) espresso powder, divided
3   large eggs (150 grams), lightly beaten
3   cups (375 grams) all-purpose flour
2   teaspoons (10 grams) baking powder
¼   teaspoon kosher salt
1   cup plus 4 tablespoons (148 grams) confectioners' sugar, divided
2   tablespoons (30 grams) heavy whipping cream

1. Preheat oven to 325°F (170°C). Butter and flour a 9x5-inch loaf pan. Line pan with parchment paper, letting excess extend over sides of pan.
2. In a large bowl, stir together melted butter, granulated sugar, and vanilla bean paste. Add milk, ½ cup (120 grams) Kahlúa, and 2 tablespoons (12 grams) espresso powder, stirring until coffee is dissolved. Whisk in eggs, flour, baking powder, and salt. Pour batter into prepared pan.
3. Bake until a wooden pick inserted in center comes out clean, about 1 hour, covering with foil halfway through baking to prevent excess browning, if necessary. Let cool in pan for 10 minutes. Using excess parchment as handles, remove from pan, and let cool completely on a wire rack.
4. In a small bowl, stir together ½ cup plus 2 tablespoons (74 grams) confectioners' sugar, remaining 1 tablespoon (15 grams) Kahlúa, and remaining 1 teaspoon (2 grams) espresso powder. In another small bowl, stir together cream and remaining ½ cup plus 2 tablespoons (74 grams) confectioners' sugar. Pour glazes over cooled cake, and swirl.

GRAND MARNIER POPPY SEED CAKE

Make 1 (9x5-inch) loaf

Candied oranges add a layer of decadence to this sweet-tart cake.

2½ cups (500 grams) granulated sugar, divided
1¼ cups (300 grams) water
32 (¼-inch-thick) slices clementine (about 8 whole clementines)
¼ cup (60 grams) plus 2 tablespoons (15 grams) Grand Marnier, divided
1 cup (227 grams) unsalted butter, melted
3 tablespoons (27 grams) poppy seeds
1 tablespoon (6 grams) grated orange rind
½ cup (120 grams) whole milk
3 large eggs (150 grams), lightly beaten
3⅓ cups (417 grams) all-purpose flour
2 teaspoons (10 grams) baking powder
½ teaspoon (1.5 grams) kosher salt

1. In a large skillet, combine 1 cup (200 grams) sugar and 1¼ cups (300 grams) water. Cook over medium heat until sugar is dissolved. Add orange slices, and simmer for 10 minutes. Remove from heat, and let cool. Lightly spray a sheet of parchment paper with cooking spray. Remove orange slices using a fork, and place on parchment. In a small bowl, stir together orange syrup and 2 tablespoons (15 grams) Grand Marnier. Set aside.

2. Preheat oven to 325°F (170°C). Butter and flour a 9x5-inch loaf pan. Line pan with parchment paper, letting excess extend over sides of pan.

3. In a large bowl, whisk together melted butter, poppy seeds, orange rind, remaining 1½ cups (300 grams) sugar, and remaining ¼ cup (60 grams) Grand Marnier. Add milk and eggs, whisking until combined. Add flour, baking powder, and salt, whisking until combined. Pour batter into prepared pan. Place candied orange slices over batter, overlapping. When removing orange slices from the sheet of parchment paper, be sure to let excess syrup drain off before adding to loaf.

4. Bake for 30 minutes. Cover with foil, and bake until a wooden pick inserted in center comes out clean, about 1 hour and 15 minutes more. Let cool in pan for 10 minutes. Using excess parchment as handles, remove from pan. Drizzle cake with half of orange syrup, and let cool completely. Serve with remaining syrup.

MULLED WINE CAKE

Make 1 (9x5-inch) loaf

A rich combination of Merlot, cinnamon, and fig preserves—this Mulled Wine Cake is its own standard.

3	cups (720 grams) Merlot
2	(4-inch) cinnamon sticks
6	whole cloves
4	whole star anise (8 grams)
⅓	cup (107 grams) fig preserves
3	cups (375 grams) all-purpose flour, divided
½	cup (57 grams) chopped almonds
1⅓	cups (267 grams) granulated sugar, divided
¾	teaspoon (2.25 grams) kosher salt, divided
¼	cup (57 grams) unsalted butter, melted
1	cup (227 grams) unsalted butter
⅔	cup (160 grams) whole milk
3	large eggs (150 grams)
2	teaspoons (10 grams) baking powder

1. In a large Dutch oven, bring wine, cinnamon, cloves, and anise to a boil over medium-high heat. Boil until wine is reduced to ¼ cup (60 grams), 20 to 30 minutes, stirring frequently during last 5 minutes of cooking. (The mixture will be thick and syrupy.) Let cool completely; discard spices. Stir in preserves. Set aside.

2. In a medium bowl, stir together ¾ cup (94 grams) flour, almonds, ⅓ cup (67 grams) sugar, and ½ teaspoon (1.5 grams) salt. Drizzle with melted butter, and stir with a wooden spoon until combined. Crumble with your fingertips until desired consistency is reached. Set aside.

3. Preheat oven to 325°F (170°C). Butter and flour a 9x5-inch loaf pan. Line pan with parchment paper, letting excess extend over sides of pan.

4. In a large bowl, stir together butter and remaining 1 cup (200 grams) sugar until almost smooth. Whisk in milk and eggs. Stir in baking powder, remaining 2¼ cups (281 grams) flour, and remaining ¼ teaspoon salt until smooth. Place 1 cup batter in a small bowl, and stir in mulled wine. Pour half of plain batter into prepared pan. Pour wine batter on top. Pour remaining plain batter on top. Swirl batters together with a knife. Sprinkle with streusel.

5. Bake until a wooden pick inserted in center comes out clean, 1 hour and 10 minutes to 1 hour and 20 minutes, covering with foil after 30 minutes of baking to prevent excess browning, if necessary. Let cool completely in pan. Using excess parchment as handles, remove from pan.

BRANDY ALEXANDER MARBLE CAKE

Makes 1 (9x5-inch) loaf

Made with melted ice cream, this rich marble cake is as close as you can come to actually eating a Brandy Alexander. Tip: Make sure you use a good sipping brandy because quality counts when it comes to flavor.

1   cup (227 grams) unsalted butter, melted
½   cup (100 grams) granulated sugar
4   tablespoons (60 grams) brandy, divided
2½   cups (360 grams) vanilla ice cream*, melted and divided
2   large eggs (100 grams), lightly beaten
3⅓   cups (417 grams) all-purpose flour
1   tablespoon (15 grams) baking powder
1   teaspoon (3 grams) kosher salt
2   tablespoons (10 grams) unsweetened cocoa powder
¼   teaspoon ground nutmeg
Garnish: confectioners' sugar

1. Preheat oven to 325°F (170°C). Butter and flour a 9x5-inch loaf pan. Line pan with parchment paper, letting excess extend over sides of pan.
2. In a large bowl, whisk together melted butter, granulated sugar, and 3 tablespoons (45 grams) brandy. Whisk in 2 cups (288 grams) melted ice cream and eggs. Whisk in flour, baking powder, and salt.
3. Place 1 cup batter in a small bowl, and whisk in cocoa and remaining ½ cup (72 grams) melted ice cream. Whisk nutmeg into remaining batter. Pour half of nutmeg batter into prepared pan. Pour cocoa batter on top. Pour remaining nutmeg batter on top. Swirl batters together with a knife.
4. Bake until a wooden pick inserted in center comes out clean, 50 to 60 minutes. Let cool in pan for 10 minutes. Poke holes in warm cake with a wooden pick, and drizzle with remaining 1 tablespoon (15 grams) brandy. Using excess parchment as handles, remove from pan. Dust with confectioners' sugar, if desired.

We used Häagen-Dazs Vanilla Ice Cream.

BOURBON CHOCOLATE-COVERED CHERRY CAKE

Makes 1 (9x5-inch) loaf

Chocolate-covered cherries and a warm kick of bourbon make this an instant liquor-infused classic.

7   tablespoons (105 grams) bourbon, divided
1   (6-ounce) package (175 grams) dried cherries
12 ounces (340 grams) 60% cacao bittersweet chocolate, chopped and divided
1   cup (227 grams) unsalted butter, melted
1½ cups (300 grams) granulated sugar
4   large eggs (200 grams), lightly beaten
¼   cup (60 grams) whole milk
3⅓ cups (417 grams) all-purpose flour
2   teaspoons (10 grams) baking powder
¼   teaspoon kosher salt
½   cup (120 grams) heavy whipping cream
2   tablespoons (28 grams) unsalted butter
Garnish: cocktail Bing cherries

1. Preheat oven to 325°F (170°C). Butter and flour a 9x5-inch loaf pan.
2. In a small skillet, heat 3 tablespoons (45 grams) bourbon over medium heat until bubbles begin to form. Remove from heat, and add cherries. Let stand for 30 minutes.
3. In a medium microwave-safe bowl, combine 8 ounces (225 grams) chopped chocolate and melted butter. Microwave on high in 30-second intervals, stirring between each, until chocolate is melted and smooth (about 1½ minutes total). Add sugar and cherry mixture, stirring until sugar is almost dissolved. Let cool for 10 minutes. Whisk in eggs and milk until smooth. Stir in flour, baking powder, and salt. Pour batter into prepared pan.
4. Bake until a wooden pick inserted in center comes out clean, about 1 hour and 15 minutes. Let cool in pan for 10 minutes. Poke holes in warm cake. Pour 3 tablespoons (45 grams) bourbon over cake. Let cool in pan for 30 minutes. Remove from pan, and let cool completely.
5. In a small microwave-safe bowl, combine cream, butter, and remaining 4 ounces (115 grams) chopped chocolate. Microwave on high in 30-second intervals, stirring between each, until chocolate is melted and smooth (about 1 minute total). Let stand for 30 seconds; stir until smooth. Stir in remaining 1 tablespoon (15 grams) bourbon. (Glaze will thicken as it sets.) Spread glaze over cooled cake. Garnish with cherries, if desired.

RUM APPLE CIDER ROSEMARY CRUMB CAKE

Makes 1 (9x5-inch) loaf

Combining the taste of rosemary with the tart punch of reduced apple cider and black spiced rum, this cake is as smooth as it is rich in flavor.

4	cups (960 grams) apple cider
1	sprig fresh rosemary
6	tablespoons (90 grams) black spiced rum, divided
3⅓	cups (417 grams) plus ¾ cup (94 grams) all-purpose flour, divided
½	cup (57 grams) roughly chopped shelled pistachios
1½	cups (330 grams) plus ⅓ cup (73 grams) firmly packed dark brown sugar, divided
1	teaspoon (3 grams) kosher salt, divided
1¼	cups (284 grams) unsalted butter, melted and divided
⅓	cup (80 grams) whole milk
3	large eggs (150 grams), lightly beaten
2	teaspoons (4 grams) chopped fresh rosemary
1	teaspoon (2 grams) lemon zest
2	teaspoons (10 grams) baking powder

1. In a large saucepan, bring apple cider to a boil over medium-high heat. Boil until cider is reduced to ½ cup (120 grams), about 30 minutes, stirring frequently during last 5 minutes of cooking. Remove from heat, and add rosemary and 2 tablespoons (30 grams) rum. Let cool completely.

2. In a medium bowl, stir together ¾ cup (94 grams) flour, pistachios, ⅓ cup (73 grams) brown sugar, and ½ teaspoon (1.5 grams) salt. Drizzle with ¼ cup (57 grams) melted butter, and stir with a wooden spoon until combined. Crumble with your fingertips until desired consistency is reached. Set aside.

3. Preheat oven to 325°F (170°C). Butter and flour a 9x5-inch loaf pan. Line pan with parchment paper, letting excess extend over sides of pan.

4. In a large bowl, whisk together remaining 1 cup (227 grams) melted butter, remaining 1½ cups (330 grams) brown sugar, and remaining 4 tablespoons (60 grams) rum until sugar is almost dissolved. Remove rosemary sprig, and whisk in apple cider reduction. Whisk in milk, eggs, chopped rosemary, and zest. Gently whisk in baking powder, remaining 3⅓ cups (417 grams) flour, and remaining ½ teaspoon (1.5 grams) salt until smooth. Pour batter into prepared pan. Sprinkle with streusel.

5. Bake until a wooden pick inserted in center comes out clean, about 1½ hours, covering with foil halfway through baking to prevent excess browning, if necessary. Let cool in pan for 10 minutes. Using excess parchment as handles, remove from pan, and let cool completely.

ONE-LAYER APPLESAUCE CAKE

Makes 1 (8-inch) cake

Burnt honey adds depth to the spicy ginger and rich mascarpone and cream cheese in this cake's frosting. As the honey cooks and caramelizes, it takes on a distinct nutty flavor and slight bitterness.

½   cup (113 grams) unsalted butter, melted
⅓   cup plus 1 tablespoon (95 grams) whole milk
⅓   cup (80 grams) sour cream
2   large eggs (100 grams)
2   tablespoons (42 grams) honey
1   tablespoon (15 grams) fresh lemon juice
2   teaspoons (1 gram) freshly grated ginger root
1¼ cups (250 grams) granulated sugar
1¼ cups (156 grams) all-purpose flour
¾   cup (72 grams) almond flour, toasted
2   teaspoons (6 grams) kosher salt
1½ teaspoons (7.5 grams) baking powder
¾   cup (180 grams) McIntosh Applesauce (recipe below), divided
Burnt Honey & Ginger Cream Frosting (recipe follows)

1. Preheat oven to 350°F (180°C). Butter and flour an 8-inch round tall-sided cake pan; line pan with parchment paper, and butter and flour pan again.
2. In a large bowl, whisk together melted butter, milk, sour cream, eggs, honey, lemon juice, and ginger. In a medium bowl, sift together sugar, flours, salt, and baking powder. Gradually whisk sugar mixture into butter mixture until combined.
3. Pour half of batter into prepared pan. Stir in ¼ cup (60 grams) McIntosh Applesauce. Top with remaining batter, and stir in remaining ½ cup (120 grams) McIntosh Applesauce.

4. Bake for 35 minutes. Cover with foil, and bake until a wooden pick inserted in center comes out clean, 30 to 40 minutes more. Let cool in pan for 15 minutes. Remove from pan, and let cool completely on a wire rack. Spread Burnt Honey & Ginger Cream Frosting on top and lightly on sides of cake. Serve immediately. Wrap tightly in plastic wrap, and refrigerate for up to 1 week, or freeze for up to 1 month.

BURNT HONEY & GINGER CREAM FROSTING
Makes 2 cups

¼   cup (85 grams) light corn syrup
3   tablespoons (63 grams) honey
8   ounces (225 grams) cream cheese, softened
½   cup (112 grams) mascarpone cheese
1   tablespoon (2 grams) grated fresh ginger
1   cup (120 grams) confectioners' sugar

1. In a small saucepan, bring corn syrup and honey to a boil over medium heat. Cook, stirring with a rubber spatula, until honey is fragrant, 2 to 3 minutes. Transfer to a glass measuring cup, and let cool slightly.
2. In the bowl of a stand mixer fitted with the paddle attachment, beat cream cheese and mascarpone at medium speed until creamy. Increase mixer speed to medium-high. Add honey mixture in a slow, steady stream, beating just until combined. Scrape sides of bowl, and beat in ginger. Reduce mixer speed to low. Gradually add confectioners' sugar, beating until fluffy. Refrigerate in an airtight container for up to 1 week.

MCINTOSH APPLESAUCE
Makes 3 cups

One of the most well-known varieties of apples, McIntosh apples are exceptionally juicy with a mellow sweet-tart flavor. This versatile sauce works in a wide range of recipes and blends beautifully with spices without being overpowering.

2   pounds (910 grams) McIntosh apples, unpeeled, cored, and chopped
1   cup (240 grams) apple brandy
½   cup (110 grams) firmly packed light brown sugar
2   tablespoons (30 grams) fresh lemon juice
1   tablespoon (9 grams) fruit pectin*
1   teaspoon (6 grams) vanilla bean paste
1   teaspoon (2 grams) ground cinnamon

1   teaspoon (2 grams) ground allspice
6 to 7 cinnamon sticks (20 grams)

1. In a large stockpot, bring all ingredients to a simmer over medium-low heat. Simmer until apples are tender, 20 to 30 minutes. Let cool to room temperature.
2. Using an immersion blender, blend until smooth**. Strain mixture through a fine-mesh sieve, discarding apple skin. Cover and refrigerate for at least 2 hours before using. Refrigerate in an airtight container for up to 2 weeks.

We used Sure-Jell Premium Fruit Pectin.

**You can also blend in the container of a blender or the work bowl of a food processor.*

PEACH ALMOND CAKE

Makes 8 servings

Fresh, juicy peaches give this vanilla and buttermilk cake bursts of color and concentrated sweet-tart flavor while the addition of brandy to the homemade marzipan lends just the right amount of kick.

6   medium fresh peaches (900 grams)
1   cup (227 grams) unsalted butter, softened
1   cup (200 grams) granulated sugar
1   cup (286 grams) Brandy Almond Marzipan (recipe follows), room temperature
3   large eggs (150 grams)
1   tablespoon (18 grams) vanilla bean paste
2½   cups (313 grams) all-purpose flour
2   teaspoons (10 grams) baking powder
½   teaspoon (1.5 grams) kosher salt
1   cup (240 grams) whole buttermilk
½   cup (57 grams) sliced almonds

1. Preheat oven to 350°F (180°C). Line a 13x9-inch baking pan with parchment paper, letting excess extend over sides of pan. Butter and flour pan.

2. Peel and cut peaches in half, removing pit. Cut each peach half into 5 slices. Set aside.

3. In the bowl of a stand mixer fitted with the paddle attachment, beat butter, sugar, and Brandy Almond Marzipan at medium speed until creamy, 3 to 4 minutes, stopping to scrape sides of bowl. Add eggs, one at a time, beating well after each addition. Beat in vanilla bean paste.

4. In a medium bowl, whisk together flour, baking powder, and salt. With mixer on low speed, gradually add flour mixture to butter mixture alternately with buttermilk, beginning and ending with flour mixture, beating just until combined after each addition. Spoon batter into prepared pan. Place peaches cut side down on top of batter. Sprinkle with almonds.

5. Bake until a wooden pick inserted in center comes out clean, 40 to 50 minutes. Using excess parchment as handles, remove from pan. Serve warm or at room temperature.

BRANDY ALMOND MARZIPAN
Makes about 1¾ cups

2   cups (240 grams) confectioners' sugar
2   cups (192 grams) superfine bleached almond flour
3   tablespoons (45 grams) brandy
2½   tablespoons (35 grams) cold unsalted butter, cubed
1   large egg white (30 grams)
1½   teaspoons (9 grams) vanilla bean paste

1. In the work bowl of a food processor, place confectioners' sugar and almond flour; process until combined. Add brandy, cold butter, egg white, and vanilla bean paste; process until mixture comes together. (Mixture will be softer than a typical marzipan.) Brandy Almond Marzipan will keep refrigerated for up to 1 week.

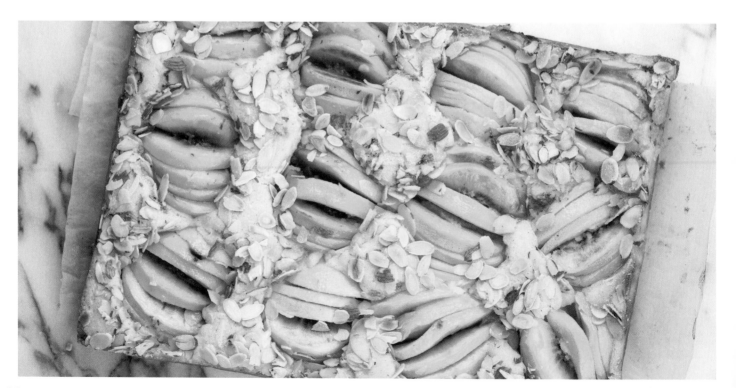

LIMONCELLO MERINGUE CAKE

Makes 10 to 12 servings

Like a grand shortcake, this meringue-topped split cake looks decadent but is simple to make. The cake's soft texture absorbs the juices from the layer of strawberries and raspberries that have been macerated in limoncello. Watch the crowd go wild over this one.

4	cups (680 grams) chopped fresh strawberries
2	cups (340 grams) fresh raspberries
1¾	cups (350 grams) granulated sugar, divided
½	cup (120 grams) limoncello
4	ounces (115 grams) cream cheese, softened
1	cup (227 grams) unsalted butter, softened
3	large eggs (150 grams)
1	tablespoon (6 grams) lemon zest
2	tablespoons (30 grams) fresh lemon juice
2	teaspoons (8 grams) vanilla extract
3½	cups (438 grams) all-purpose flour
1	tablespoon (15 grams) baking powder
1	teaspoon (3 grams) kosher salt
1½	cups (360 grams) whole milk

Vanilla Meringue Topping (recipe follows)

1. In a large glass bowl, combine strawberries, raspberries, ¼ cup (50 grams) sugar, and limoncello. Refrigerate for at least 2 hours.
2. Preheat oven to 350°F (180°C). Butter and flour a 13x9-inch baking pan.
3. In the bowl of a stand mixer fitted with the paddle attachment, beat cream cheese at medium speed until smooth and creamy, 1 to 2 minutes. Add butter and remaining 1½ cups (300 grams) sugar, and beat until fluffy, 3 to 4 minutes, stopping to scrape sides of bowl. Add eggs, one at a time, beating well after each addition. Beat in lemon zest and juice and vanilla.
4. In a large bowl, whisk together flour, baking powder, and salt. With mixer on low speed, gradually add flour mixture to cream cheese mixture alternately with milk, beginning and ending with flour mixture, beating just until combined after each addition. Pour batter into prepared pan, smoothing top if necessary.
5. Bake until a wooden pick inserted in center comes out clean, 30 to 35 minutes. Let cool in pan for 10 minutes. Remove from pan, and let cool completely on a wire rack.
6. Cut cake in half horizontally. Drain berries well, reserving juices for another use. Top

bottom of cake with macerated berries, and cover with top of cake. Spread with Vanilla Meringue Topping. Using a kitchen torch, brown meringue. Serve immediately.

VANILLA MERINGUE TOPPING
Makes 5 cups

6	large egg whites (180 grams)
¼	teaspoon cream of tartar
2	cups (400 grams) granulated sugar
½	cup (120 grams) water
½	teaspoon (2 grams) vanilla extract

1. In the bowl of a stand mixer fitted with the whisk attachment, beat egg whites and cream of tartar at high speed until tripled in volume, 2 to 3 minutes.
2. In a medium saucepan, cook sugar and ½ cup (120 grams) water over medium-high heat until a candy thermometer registers 240°F (116°C).
3. Reduce mixer speed to low. Slowly pour hot sugar mixture into egg whites, beating until combined. Increase mixer speed to high. Add vanilla, and beat until mixture is thick, white, and holds its shape. Use immediately.

PUMPKIN CAKE ROLL WITH ORANGE BLOSSOM CRÈME FRAÎCHE AND PISTACHIOS

Makes 1 (15-inch) cake roll

Recipe by Nik Sharma

A popular flavor in Moroccan, Persian, and Indian cuisines, orange blossom water's perfume-like quality pairs well with the mild flavor of pumpkin and salty pistachios in this rolled cake.

3 large eggs (150 grams), room temperature
1 cup (200 grams) granulated sugar
⅔ cup (162 grams) pumpkin purée
1 tablespoon (21 grams) maple syrup
1 teaspoon (5 grams) orange blossom water
¾ cup (94 grams) all-purpose flour
1 teaspoon (5 grams) baking powder
1 teaspoon (2 grams) freshly grated orange zest
¼ teaspoon sea salt
Confectioners' sugar, for dusting
Orange Blossom Crème Fraîche Filling (recipe follows)
Garnish: coarsely chopped toasted salted pistachios

1. Preheat to 350°F (180°C). Butter a 15x10-inch baking sheet, and line pan with parchment paper.
2. In the bowl of a stand mixer fitted with the whisk attachment, beat eggs at high speed until pale yellow, 5 to 6 minutes. Reduce mixer speed to medium. Slowly add granulated sugar, beating until combined. Add pumpkin purée, maple syrup, and orange blossom water, beating until combined, about 1 minute.
3. In a medium bowl, whisk together flour, baking powder, zest, and salt. Gradually add flour mixture to egg mixture, whisking until combined. Spoon batter into prepared pan, smoothing top with an offset spatula.
4. Bake until surface of cake is firm, soft, and spongy to the touch, about 15 minutes. Remove from oven, and immediately run a knife around edges of cake to loosen sides. Immediately turn cake onto a clean kitchen towel dusted with confectioners' sugar. Carefully peel parchment paper off hot cake. Starting with one short side, carefully roll up cake with towel. Transfer to a wire rack, and let cool completely.
5. Carefully unroll cake, and spread

Orange Blossom Crème Fraîche Filling onto cake. Reroll cake without towel. Dust with confectioners' sugar, and garnish with pistachios, if desired.

ORANGE BLOSSOM CRÈME FRAÎCHE FILLING
Makes about 1¾ cups

3 tablespoons (42 grams) cream cheese, softened
1½ cups (360 grams) crème fraîche
¼ cup (30 grams) confectioners' sugar
1 to 1½ teaspoons (5 to 7.5 grams) orange blossom water

1. In a medium bowl, whisk cream cheese until smooth. Using a silicone spatula, slowly fold in crème fraîche and confectioners' sugar until smooth. Fold in enough orange blossom water to make filling spreadable. Refrigerate in an airtight container for up to 1 day. Warm mixture to room temperature before using.

Photo by Nik Sharma

BLACKBERRY-ALMOND UPSIDE-DOWN CAKE

Makes 1 (9-inch) cake

A finishing touch of sugar-coated sliced almonds gives this sweet berry-topped cake a tempting crunch.

½   cup (113 grams) unsalted butter, softened
1   cup plus 2 tablespoons (224 grams) granulated sugar
3   large eggs (150 grams)
½   teaspoon (2 grams) almond extract
1½   cups (187 grams) cake flour
1   teaspoon (5 grams) baking powder
¼   teaspoon kosher salt
½   cup plus 2 tablespoons (150 grams) whole buttermilk
1⅓   cups (151 grams) sliced toasted almonds, divided
½   cup (113 grams) unsalted butter, melted and divided
1¼   cups (275 grams) firmly packed light brown sugar, divided
4 to 5 cups (680 to 850 grams) fresh blackberries

1. Preheat oven to 350°F (180°C). Butter and flour a 9-inch round cake pan.
2. In the bowl of a stand mixer fitted with the paddle attachment, beat butter and granulated sugar at medium speed until fluffy, 3 to 4 minutes, stopping to scrape sides of bowl. Add eggs, one at a time, beating well after each addition. Beat in almond extract.
3. In a medium bowl, whisk together flour, baking powder, and salt. With mixer on low speed, gradually add flour mixture to butter mixture alternately with buttermilk, beginning and ending with flour mixture, beating just until combined after each addition. Fold in ⅔ cup (75 grams) almonds.
4. Pour ¼ cup (56.5 grams) melted butter into prepared pan. Sprinkle with ¾ cup (165 grams) brown sugar. Arrange enough blackberries in a single layer over brown sugar to completely cover bottom of pan. Pour batter over blackberries, smoothing top with an offset spatula.
5. Bake until a wooden pick inserted in center comes out clean, 40 to 45 minutes. Let cool in pan for 10 minutes. Run a knife around edges of pan to release sides of cake; carefully invert onto a flat serving plate.
6. In a medium bowl, stir together remaining ¼ cup (56.5 grams) melted butter, remaining ½ cup (110 grams) brown sugar, and remaining ⅔ cup (75 grams) almonds. Sprinkle over top of cake. Top with remaining blackberries. Serve warm or at room temperature.

CITRUS UPSIDE-DOWN CAKE

Makes 1 (10-inch) cake

Orange, grapefruit, and lemon slices add bright flavor and undeniable appeal to this sweet, showstopping cake. Serve it at your next brunch and get ready to take a bow.

6   tablespoons (84 grams) unsalted butter, melted
¾   cup (165 grams) firmly packed light brown sugar
1   grapefruit (510 grams), peeled and thinly sliced
1   orange (131 grams), peeled and thinly sliced
½   lemon (49.5 grams), thinly sliced
1⅓ cups (167 grams) all-purpose flour
1   cup (150 grams) yellow cornmeal
½   cup plus 2 tablespoons (124 grams) granulated sugar
1   tablespoon (15 grams) baking powder
½   teaspoon (1.5 grams) kosher salt
2   large eggs (100 grams)
⅔   cup (160 grams) whole buttermilk
½   teaspoon (1 gram) orange zest

1. Preheat oven to 350°F (180°C). Butter and flour a 10-inch round cake pan.
2. Pour melted butter into prepared pan; sprinkle with brown sugar. Arrange citrus slices over brown sugar. Set aside.
3. In a large bowl, whisk together flour, cornmeal, granulated sugar, baking powder, and salt. Add eggs, buttermilk, and zest, whisking until smooth. Pour batter over citrus slices. (Batter will be thick.)
4. Bake until a wooden pick inserted in center comes out clean, about 30 minutes. Let cool in pan for 10 minutes. Carefully invert cake onto a flat serving plate. Serve warm or at room temperature.

CHOCOLATE-CHESTNUT MOUSSE CAKE

Makes 1 (8-inch) cake

This s'mores-inspired cake features a thick, velvety layer of chocolate mousse enriched with Roasted Chestnuts.

½   cup (113 grams) unsalted butter, softened
½   cup (100 grams) granulated sugar
2   large eggs (100 grams)
½   cup (170 grams) unsulphured molasses
2   teaspoons (4 grams) lemon zest
2   teaspoons (1 gram) grated fresh ginger
1½   cups (188 grams) all-purpose flour
1   teaspoon (2 grams) ground ginger
¾   teaspoon (3.75 grams) baking soda
¾   teaspoon (2.25 grams) kosher salt
½   teaspoon (1 gram) ground cloves
½   cup (120 grams) whole milk
⅓   cup (123 grams) diced crystallized ginger
Chocolate-Chestnut Mousse (recipe follows)
Salty Brown Sugar Swiss Meringue (recipe follows)

1. Preheat oven to 350°F (180°C). Butter and flour an 8-inch springform pan. Line bottom of pan with parchment paper, and butter and flour pan again.
2. In the bowl of a stand mixer fitted with the paddle attachment, beat butter and sugar at medium speed until creamy, 3 to 4 minutes, stopping to scrape sides of bowl. Add eggs, one at a time, beating well after each addition. Add molasses, zest, and grated ginger, beating until combined.
3. In a medium bowl, whisk together flour, ground ginger, baking soda, salt, and cloves. With mixer on low speed, gradually add flour mixture to butter mixture alternately with milk, beginning and ending with flour mixture, beating just until combined after each addition. Fold in crystallized ginger. Pour batter into prepared pan, smoothing top with an offset spatula.
4. Bake until a wooden pick inserted in center comes out clean, about 35 minutes. Let cool in pan for 15 minutes. Remove sides of pan, and invert cake onto a wire rack. Remove parchment, and invert cake back onto bottom of pan to let cool completely.
5. Cut parchment into a 25x5-inch strip. Wrap parchment strip around cake, and secure with tape. Place springform sides around cake and parchment, and secure. Top with Chocolate-Chestnut Mousse, smoothing with an offset spatula. Refrigerate for at least 2 hours or up to 24 hours.
6. Remove sides of springform pan and parchment. Top with Salty Brown Sugar Swiss Meringue. Using a kitchen torch, toast meringue. Freeze for 20 to 30 minutes before serving.

CHOCOLATE-CHESTNUT MOUSSE
Makes about 8 cups

2   cups (312 grams) Roasted Chestnuts (recipe on page 253)
2   cups (480 grams) whole milk
½   cup (110 grams) firmly packed light brown sugar
1   tablespoon (13 grams) vanilla extract
½   teaspoon (1.5 grams) kosher salt
½   teaspoon (1 gram) ground cinnamon
4   ounces (115 grams) bittersweet chocolate, chopped
1   tablespoon (15 grams) dark rum
2   cups (480 grams) heavy whipping cream

1. In a small saucepan, bring Roasted Chestnuts, milk, brown sugar, vanilla, salt, and cinnamon to a boil over medium heat. Reduce heat, and simmer, stirring occasionally, until milk is reduced by one-fourth and chestnuts are tender, 15 to 20 minutes. Transfer mixture to the container of a blender, and purée on high until smooth, 2 to 3 minutes, stopping to scrape sides of container. Add chocolate and rum; blend until chocolate is melted, about 2 minutes. Transfer to a large bowl, and let cool completely, stirring occasionally.
2. In the bowl of a stand mixer fitted with the whisk attachment, beat cream at medium-high speed until stiff peaks form, about 5 minutes. Fold one-third of whipped cream into cooled chestnut mixture. Fold in remaining whipped cream until just combined. Cover and refrigerate for up to 24 hours.

SALTY BROWN SUGAR SWISS MERINGUE
Makes about 3 cups

3   large egg whites (90 grams)
⅔   cup (147 grams) firmly packed light brown sugar
½   teaspoon (1.5 grams) kosher salt

1. In the bowl of a stand mixer fitted with the whisk attachment, whisk together all ingredients by hand. Set bowl over a saucepan of simmering water, and cook, whisking constantly, until sugar is dissolved and a candy thermometer registers 140°F (60°C), 5 to 7 minutes. Return bowl to stand mixer, and beat at high speed until stiff peaks form, about 10 minutes. Beat until cooled to room temperature. Use immediately.

BROWNED BUTTER AND ORANGE SKILLET CAKE

Makes 1 (12-inch) cake

Nutty browned butter and orange liqueur add an amazing depth of flavor to this ultra-moist skillet cake. Make sure the candied orange slices are completely dry before arranging on top to avoid crossing the line between perfectly moist and unpleasantly soggy.

½ cup (113 grams) Browned Butter (see Pro Tip), softened
1 cup (220 grams) firmly packed light brown sugar
1 teaspoon (4 grams) vanilla extract
1 teaspoon (4 grams) orange extract
4 large eggs (200 grams)
1 teaspoon (2 grams) orange zest
¼ cup (60 grams) fresh orange juice
2 cups (250 grams) all-purpose flour
1½ teaspoons (7.5 grams) baking powder
½ teaspoon (2.5 grams) baking soda
½ teaspoon (1.5 grams) kosher salt
Candied Orange Slices (recipe follows)
¼ cup (80 grams) apple jelly
¼ cup (60 grams) orange liqueur*

1. Preheat oven to 350°F (180°C). Butter and flour a 12-inch cast-iron skillet.
2. In the bowl of a stand mixer fitted with the paddle attachment, beat Browned Butter, brown sugar, and extracts at medium speed until fluffy, 3 to 4 minutes, stopping to scrape sides of bowl. Add eggs, one at a time, beating well after each addition. Beat in orange zest and juice.
3. In a medium bowl, whisk together flour, baking powder, baking soda, and salt. With mixer on low speed, gradually add flour mixture to butter mixture, beating just until combined. Spoon batter into prepared skillet, smoothing top with an offset spatula. Arrange Candied Orange Slices over batter.
4. Bake until a wooden pick inserted in center comes out clean, about 45 minutes. Let cool in pan for 10 minutes.
5. In a small saucepan, stir together apple jelly and orange liqueur. Cook over medium

heat, stirring constantly, until mixture is smooth. Brush over cake and oranges. Let cool for 1 hour before serving.

We used Grand Marnier.

CANDIED ORANGE SLICES
Makes about 16

2 navel oranges (262 grams), cut into ⅛-inch-thick slices
3 cups (720 grams) cold water, divided
1¾ cups (350 grams) granulated sugar, divided

1. Preheat oven to 250°F (130°C). Line a rimmed baking sheet with parchment paper; top with a wire rack.
2. In a large cast-iron skillet, bring orange slices and 2 cups (480 grams) cold water to a simmer over medium heat. Cook, without stirring, for 6 minutes; drain.
3. Return orange slices to skillet. Sprinkle with 1 cup (200 grams) sugar. Pour remaining 1 cup (240 grams) cold water over sugar, stirring to combine. Bring to a simmer over medium-low heat; cook for

15 minutes. Carefully remove orange slices from sugar water; arrange in a single layer on prepared rack.
4. Bake for 30 minutes. Place remaining ¾ cup (150 grams) sugar in a shallow dish. Dredge orange slices in sugar, turning to coat both sides. Return to rack; let dry for at least 2 hours.

PRO TIP

To make **Browned Butter**, heat ¾ cup (170 grams) unsalted butter in a medium saucepan over medium heat until butter turns a medium-brown color and has a nutty aroma, about 10 minutes. Remove from heat, and let cool to room temperature before using. Weigh out ½ cup (113 grams) Browned Butter to use in this recipe.

PEAR UPSIDE-DOWN LOAF CAKE

Makes 1 (10x5-inch) cake

This simple loaf comes together in about an hour, but packs the flavor and presentation to wow any crowd. We used Forelle pears, but small Bosc or Anjou pears will work, too.

½   cup (110 grams) firmly packed dark brown sugar
2   tablespoons (28 grams) unsalted butter, cubed
2   miniature pears (Forelle pears) (360 grams), peeled, cored, and halved lengthwise
½   cup (113 grams) unsalted butter, softened
⅔   cup (133 grams) granulated sugar
2   large eggs (100 grams)
1   teaspoon (4 grams) vanilla extract

1¼   cups (156 grams) self-rising flour
¼   teaspoon (1.25 grams) baking soda
½   cup (120 grams) whole buttermilk

1. Preheat oven to 350°F (180°C). Line a 10x5-inch loaf pan with parchment paper, letting excess extend over sides of pan. Butter and flour pan.

2. Sprinkle brown sugar and cubed butter in prepared pan. Place pan in oven until butter is melted, about 5 minutes. Remove from oven.

3. Cut a ½-inch-thick slice off rounded side of each pear half. Arrange pears crosswise in pan, placing cored side down and alternating narrow ends.

4. In the bowl of a stand mixer fitted with the paddle attachment, beat softened butter and granulated sugar at medium speed until fluffy, 3 to 4 minutes, stopping to scrape sides of bowl. Add eggs, one at a time, beating well after each addition. Beat in vanilla.

5. In a medium bowl, whisk together flour and baking soda. With mixer on low speed, gradually add flour mixture to butter mixture alternately with buttermilk, beginning and ending with flour mixture, beating just until combined after each addition. Spread batter over pears.

6. Bake until a wooden pick inserted in center comes out clean, about 30 minutes. Let cool in pan for 2 minutes. Run a sharp knife around edges of cake to loosen. Carefully invert cake onto a serving platter. Serve immediately.

AMARETTO BOSTON CREAM PIE

Makes 1 (9-inch) cake

We put an almond twist on this classic dessert with rich Amaretto Pastry Cream. Fold whipped cream into the batter to achieve a light, spongy cake (yes, the "pie" name is a long-held misnomer).

¼   cup (57 grams) unsalted butter, softened
1½   cups (300 grams) granulated sugar
⅓   cup (75 grams) vegetable oil
1   tablespoon (13 grams) vanilla extract
1   teaspoon (4 grams) almond extract
1   teaspoon (3 grams) kosher salt
2   large eggs (100 grams)
3   large egg yolks (56 grams)
2   cups (250 grams) cake flour
2   teaspoons (10 grams) baking powder
⅓   cup (80 grams) whole buttermilk
½   cup (120 grams) heavy whipping cream
Amaretto Pastry Cream (recipe follows)
1   cup (113 grams) sliced almonds, toasted
Ganache (recipe follows)

1. Preheat oven to 325°F (170°C). Butter and flour a 9-inch springform pan. Line bottom of pan with parchment paper.
2. In the bowl of a stand mixer fitted with the paddle attachment, beat butter and sugar at medium speed until fluffy, 3 to 4 minutes, stopping to scrape sides of bowl. Add oil, extracts, and salt, beating just until combined. Add eggs and egg yolks, one at a time, beating just until combined after each addition.
3. In a medium bowl, whisk together flour and baking powder. With mixer on low speed, gradually add flour mixture to butter mixture alternately with buttermilk, beginning and ending with flour mixture, beating just until combined after each addition. Transfer batter to a large bowl; set aside.
4. Clean bowl of stand mixer. Using the whisk attachment, beat cream at high speed until soft peaks form, about 3 minutes. Fold whipped cream into batter. Pour batter into prepared pan.
5. Bake until light golden brown and a wooden pick inserted in center comes out clean, about 40 minutes. Let cool in pan for 10 minutes. Remove from pan, and let cool completely on a wire rack.
6. Using a serrated knife, cut cake in half horizontally. Spread all but ¼ cup Amaretto Pastry Cream onto one cake layer. Top with remaining cake layer. Coat sides of cake with an even layer of remaining Amaretto Pastry Cream, and press sliced almonds into sides of cake. Pour Chocolate Ganache over top of cake. Refrigerate until chocolate is set, about 15 minutes. Serve at room temperature. Cover and refrigerate for up to 5 days.

AMARETTO PASTRY CREAM
Makes about 2¼ cups

Vanilla bean and amaretto add warmth to this full-bodied pastry cream. Make it a couple of days ahead to save time.

1½   cups (360 grams) whole milk
⅔   cup (160 grams) heavy whipping cream
1   vanilla bean, split lengthwise, seeds scraped and reserved
7   large egg yolks (130 grams)
½   cup (100 grams) granulated sugar
¼   cup (32 grams) cornstarch
1   teaspoon (3 grams) kosher salt
2   tablespoons (30 grams) amaretto

1. In a medium saucepan, bring milk, cream, and vanilla bean and reserved seeds to a boil over medium heat.
2. In a medium bowl, whisk together egg yolks, sugar, cornstarch, and salt. Gradually add hot milk mixture to egg mixture, whisking constantly. Strain mixture back into saucepan, and cook over medium heat, whisking constantly, until thickened.
3. Pour into a medium bowl, and stir in amaretto. Cover surface of cream directly with a piece of plastic wrap, and refrigerate for 1 hour. Cover and refrigerate for up to 4 days.

GANACHE
Makes about 1½ cups

As rich as it is lustrous, this ganache has just the right balance of bitterness.

1⅓   cups (227 grams) chopped bittersweet chocolate
¾   cup (170 grams) unsalted butter
4   teaspoons (28 grams) corn syrup
1   tablespoon (15 grams) water

1. In a small saucepan, melt chocolate and butter over medium-low heat. Remove from heat; stir in corn syrup and 1 tablespoon (15 grams) water. Let stand until slightly thickened, about 15 minutes. Use immediately, or cover and refrigerate for up to 4 days. Reheat over low heat before using.

COCONUT SKILLET CAKE

Makes 1 (10-inch) cake

Perfumed with coconut extract, swirled with silky whipped cream, and studded with sweetened coconut flakes, this cake is the perfect finale to any meal. The coconut lover in your life is about to be your biggest fan.

¾   cup (170 grams) unsalted butter, softened
1   cup (200 grams) granulated sugar
4   large egg yolks (74 grams)
½   teaspoon (2 grams) coconut extract
2   cups (250 grams) all-purpose flour
½   teaspoon (2.5 grams) baking powder
½   teaspoon (2.5 grams) baking soda
¼   teaspoon kosher salt
⅔   cup (160 grams) sour cream
1½   cups (126 grams) sweetened flaked coconut

Sweetened Whipped Cream (recipe follows)
Garnish: toasted coconut flakes

1. Preheat oven to 375°F (190°C). Butter and flour a 10-inch cast-iron skillet.
2. In the bowl of a stand mixer fitted with the paddle attachment, beat butter and sugar at medium speed until fluffy, 3 to 4 minutes, stopping to scrape sides of bowl. Add egg yolks, one at a time, beating well after each addition. Beat in coconut extract.
3. In a medium bowl, whisk together flour, baking powder, baking soda, and salt. With mixer on low speed, gradually add flour mixture to butter mixture alternately with sour cream, beginning and ending with flour mixture, beating just until combined after each addition. Stir in coconut. Spoon batter into prepared skillet.
4. Bake until a wooden pick inserted in center comes out clean, 30 to 35 minutes.

Let cool completely. Spread Sweetened Whipped Cream onto cooled cake. Garnish with coconut, if desired. Cover and refrigerate for up to 5 days.

SWEETENED WHIPPED CREAM
Makes 6 cups

2½   cups (600 grams) heavy whipping cream
½   cup (60 grams) confectioners' sugar
1   teaspoon (4 grams) vanilla extract

1. In the bowl of a stand mixer fitted with the whisk attachment, beat cream at medium speed until slightly thickened. Increase mixer speed to medium-high. Gradually add confectioners' sugar and vanilla, beating until stiff peaks form.

UPSIDE-DOWN APPLE CRISP CAKE

Makes 1 (10-inch) cake

This cake turns up the volume on two old-school classics. We combined the flavor and crunch of apple crisp with the gorgeous presentation of upside-down cake, plus added a hearty dose of caramel for good measure. You're welcome.

½ cup (113 grams) plus ⅓ cup (76 grams) unsalted butter, softened and divided
1¾ cups (385 grams) firmly packed light brown sugar, divided
¾ teaspoon (1.5 grams) ground cinnamon, divided
¾ teaspoon (1.5 grams) ground nutmeg, divided
2 large Gala apples (370 grams), peeled and thinly sliced
1 large egg (50 grams)
1 teaspoon (4 grams) vanilla extract
1⅓ cups (167 grams) all-purpose flour
2 teaspoons (10 grams) baking powder
½ teaspoon (1.5 grams) kosher salt
⅓ cup (80 grams) whole milk
Brown Sugar Crumble (recipe follows)
Sweetened Whipped Cream (recipe follows), to serve

1. Preheat oven to 350°F (180°C).
2. In a 10-inch cast iron skillet, melt ⅓ cup (76 grams) butter over medium heat. Add ¾ cup (165 grams) brown sugar, ¼ teaspoon cinnamon, and ¼ teaspoon nutmeg, stirring to combine. Cook, stirring occasionally, until thickened, about 5 minutes. Remove from heat. Arrange apple slices over caramel in skillet. Set aside.
3. In the bowl of a stand mixer fitted with the paddle attachment, beat remaining ½ cup (113 grams) butter and remaining 1 cup (220 grams) brown sugar at medium speed until fluffy, 3 to 4 minutes, stopping to scrape sides of bowl. Add egg, beating until combined. Beat in vanilla.
4. In a medium bowl, whisk together flour, baking powder, salt, remaining ½ teaspoon (1 gram) cinnamon, and remaining ½ teaspoon (1 gram) nutmeg. With mixer on low speed, gradually add flour mixture to butter mixture alternately with milk, beginning and ending with flour mixture, beating just until combined after each addition. Spoon batter over apples in skillet, smoothing top with an offset spatula. Sprinkle with Brown Sugar Crumble.
5. Bake until a wooden pick inserted in center comes out clean, about 40 minutes. Let cool in pan for 10 minutes. Carefully invert cake onto a flat serving plate. Serve with Sweetened Whipped Cream.

BROWN SUGAR CRUMBLE
Makes about ⅔ cup

¼ cup (55 grams) firmly packed light brown sugar
¼ cup (20 grams) old-fashioned oats
3 tablespoons (42 grams) unsalted butter, softened
1 tablespoon (8 grams) all-purpose flour
⅛ teaspoon kosher salt

1. In a small bowl, stir together brown sugar, oats, butter, flour, and salt until mixture is crumbly.

SWEETENED WHIPPED CREAM
Makes 6 cups

2½ cups (600 grams) heavy whipping cream
½ cup (60 grams) confectioners' sugar
1 teaspoon (4 grams) vanilla extract

1. In the bowl of a stand mixer fitted with the whisk attachment, beat cream at medium speed until slightly thickened. Increase mixer speed to medium-high. Gradually add confectioners' sugar and vanilla, beating until stiff peaks form.

STRAWBERRY SKILLET CAKE

Makes 1 (9-inch) cake

Sweet strawberries shine in this simple yet stunning skillet cake. It's quick enough to bake up any day of the week, and so tasty you'll want to eat it every day of the week. Go ahead; we won't judge.

½ cup (113 grams) unsalted butter, softened
1¼ cups (250 grams) granulated sugar, divided
2 large eggs (100 grams)
½ teaspoon (2 grams) vanilla extract
1⅓ cups (167 grams) all-purpose flour
1¼ teaspoons (6.25 grams) baking powder
¼ teaspoon kosher salt
½ cup (120 grams) sour cream
1 pound (455 grams) fresh strawberries, halved

1. Preheat oven to 350°F (180°C). Butter and flour a 9-inch enamel-coated cast-iron skillet.

2. In the bowl of a stand mixer fitted with the paddle attachment, beat butter and 1 cup (200 grams) sugar at medium speed until fluffy, 3 to 4 minutes, stopping to scrape sides of bowl. Add eggs, one at a time, beating well after each addition. Beat in vanilla.

3. In a medium bowl, whisk together flour, baking powder, and salt. With mixer on low speed, gradually add flour mixture to butter mixture alternately with sour cream, beginning and ending with flour mixture, beating just until combined after each addition. Fold in strawberries. Spread batter into prepared skillet. Sprinkle with remaining ¼ cup (50 grams) sugar.

4. Bake until a wooden pick inserted in center comes out clean, 35 to 40 minutes. Let cool completely on a wire rack. Serve immediately.

PRO TIP
Add lemon or other citrus juice to strawberries to help maintain their bright color during baking.

BLUEBERRY BROWNED BUTTER BUCKLE

Makes 1 (9-inch) cake

Think of the buckle as the dense, low-maintenance version of coffee cake. Popular in the Northeastern United States, buckles always have a crumbly streusel topping that is said to look "buckled" after the batter rises up between the fruit during the baking process.

¼   cup (57 grams) unsalted butter
¾   cup (150 grams) granulated sugar
1   large egg (50 grams)
2   cups (250 grams) cake flour
1   teaspoon (5 grams) baking powder
¾   teaspoon (1.5 grams) ground ginger
½   teaspoon (1.5 grams) kosher salt
½   teaspoon (1 gram) ground black pepper
½   cup (120 grams) whole milk
¾   pound (340 grams) fresh blueberries
1   tablespoon (15 grams) fresh lemon juice
Brown Rice Crumb Topping (recipe follows)

1. Preheat oven to 350°F (180°C). Butter and flour a 9-inch square baking pan.
2. In a medium saucepan, melt butter over medium heat. Cook until butter turns a medium-brown color and has a nutty aroma, about 10 minutes. Remove from heat, and let cool to room temperature.

3. In the bowl of a stand mixer fitted with the paddle attachment, beat browned butter and sugar at medium speed until fluffy, 3 to 4 minutes, stopping to scrape sides of bowl. Add egg, beating well.
4. In a medium bowl, whisk together flour, baking powder, ginger, salt, and pepper. With mixer on low speed, gradually add flour mixture to browned butter mixture alternately with milk, beginning and ending with flour mixture, beating just until combined after each addition.
5. In a small bowl, toss blueberries with lemon juice. Gently stir blueberries into batter. Pour batter into prepared pan. Sprinkle with Brown Rice Crumb Topping.
6. Bake until golden brown, 35 to 45 minutes. Let cool in pan for 10 minutes. Remove from pan, and serve warm, or let cool completely on a wire rack. Cover and refrigerate for up to 5 days.

BROWN RICE CRUMB TOPPING
Makes about 1 cup

½   cup (100 grams) granulated sugar
⅓   cup (42 grams) cake flour
2   tablespoons (18 grams) brown rice flour
1   teaspoon (2 grams) ground nutmeg
½   teaspoon (1.5 grams) kosher salt
¼   cup (57 grams) cold unsalted butter, cubed

1. In a small bowl, combine sugar, flours, nutmeg, and salt. Using a pastry blender, cut in cold butter until mixture is crumbly. Cover and refrigerate for up to 5 days.

Note: *To save time, you can brown the butter and make the Brown Rice Crumb Topping several days before you bake.*

PRO TIP
For a colorful top, try adding the blueberries to the buckle batter after it's in the baking dish to ensure more berries stay near the buckle's surface. Gently mix about half of the berries into the batter making sure some stay on top. More blueberries will bubble up over the crumb while baking.

SACHER S'MORES TORTE

Makes 1 (9-inch) cake

Inspired by the classic Sacher Torte of Vienna, Austria, this beauty boasts a soft graham cracker base layered with apricot preserves, Sacher cake, and a giant marshmallow before being iced with rich chocolate frosting and coated in a dark chocolate glaze.

1   9-inch round Homemade Graham Cracker (recipe on page 337)
1   (8-ounce) jar (225 grams) apricot preserves
Sacher Cake Layer (recipe follows)
Vanilla Bean Marshmallow (recipe on page 91)
Ganache Frosting (recipe follows)
Chocolate Glaze (recipe follows)
Garnish: edible gold flake*

1. Prepare Homemade Graham Crackers recipe through step 1. Roll dough between 2 sheets of parchment paper. Place a 9-inch round cake pan upside down over dough and parchment. Press to make an indention. Remove pan and parchment. Cut out round, and place on a baking sheet. Use a wooden skewer to poke holes in concentric circles from edge to middle. Freeze for 30 minutes. Bake as directed.
2. Place Homemade Graham Cracker layer on an 8-inch cardboard cake board. Spread a thin layer of apricot preserves onto graham cracker. Top with Sacher Cake Layer. Spread a thin layer of apricot preserves onto Sacher Cake Layer. Top with Vanilla Bean Marshmallow layer. Line up all edges, and trim any overhang to make smooth sides. Apply a thin layer of Ganache Frosting for a crumb coat. Apply a second thicker layer of Ganache Frosting, and refrigerate until set.
3. Place a wire rack over a baking sheet or large bowl. Place cake on wire rack. Pour Chocolate Glaze over cake starting in the middle, and working to the edge in a spiral motion. Let stand for 10 minutes. Garnish with edible gold flake, if desired.

*Edible gold leaf may be purchased at goldleaffactory.com.

SACHER CAKE LAYER
Makes 2 (9-inch) layers

1   cup (227 grams) unsalted butter, softened
1   cup (200 grams) granulated sugar
2   tablespoons (26 grams) vanilla extract
8   ounces (225 grams) bittersweet chocolate, chopped and melted
4   large eggs (200 grams), separated
1   cup (125 grams) cake flour

1. Preheat oven to 325°F (170°C). Butter and flour 2 (9-inch) round cake pans.
2. In the bowl of a stand mixer fitted with the paddle attachment, beat butter, sugar, and vanilla at medium speed until creamy, 3 to 4 minutes, stopping to scrape sides of bowl. Pour in melted chocolate. Beat in egg yolks. Transfer to a large bowl; set aside.
3. Clean bowl of stand mixer. Using the whisk attachment, beat egg whites at medium-high speed until soft peaks form. Fold egg whites into chocolate mixture alternately with flour until combined. Pour batter into prepared pans.
4. Bake until a wooden pick inserted in center comes out clean, 15 to 20 minutes. Let cool in pans for 10 minutes. Remove from pans, and let cool completely on wire racks.

GANACHE FROSTING
Makes 3 cups

12 ounces (345 grams) bittersweet chocolate, chopped
1   cup (240 grams) heavy whipping cream
⅓   cup (76 grams) unsalted butter, softened
⅓   cup (40 grams) confectioners' sugar
3   tablespoons (63 grams) light corn syrup

1. Place chocolate in a medium heatproof bowl.
2. In a small saucepan, bring cream, butter, confectioners' sugar, and corn syrup to a boil over medium-high heat. Remove from heat. Pour hot cream mixture over chocolate, and whisk until smooth. Refrigerate until a spreadable consistency is reached, about 1 hour.

CHOCOLATE GLAZE
Makes 2 cups

1   cup plus 2 tablespoons (224 grams) granulated sugar
½   cup (120 grams) plus 1 tablespoon (15 grams) cold water, divided
½   cup (120 grams) heavy whipping cream
¼   cup (21 grams) unsweetened cocoa powder
1   (0.25-ounce) envelope unflavored gelatin (7 grams)

1. In a medium saucepan, heat sugar, ½ cup (120 grams) cold water, cream, and cocoa over medium-low heat. Simmer until mixture slightly thickens, about 20 minutes.
2. Place remaining 1 tablespoon (15 grams) cold water in a small bowl. Sprinkle gelatin over top, and let stand until softened, about 5 minutes. Remove chocolate mixture from heat, and whisk in gelatin mixture until combined. Set over an ice bath, and whisk until glaze thickens, about 1 minute.

Vanilla Bean Marshmallow

Makes 1 (9-inch) round

After one taste of this fluffy, vanilla-infused marshmallow, you'll vow to never buy them from the store again.

⅔ cup (160 grams) water, divided
2 (0.25-ounce) envelopes unflavored gelatin (14 grams)
1¼ cups (250 grams) granulated sugar
⅔ cup (226 grams) light corn syrup
2 teaspoons (4 grams) vanilla bean powder
½ cup (60 grams) confectioners' sugar
¼ cup (32 grams) cornstarch

1. Line a 9-inch round cake pan with parchment paper. Spray with cooking spray, and generously dust with confectioners' sugar.

2. In the bowl of a stand mixer fitted with the whisk attachment, place ⅓ cup (80 grams) water. Sprinkle gelatin over water, and let stand for 10 minutes.

3. In a large saucepan, combine granulated sugar, corn syrup, and remaining ⅓ cup (80 grams) water. Cook over medium-high heat until sugar is dissolved and a candy thermometer registers 240°F (116°C), about 6 minutes. With mixer on low speed, slowly drizzle sugar mixture into gelatin mixture, beating just until combined. Increase mixer speed to medium, and beat until mixture begins to thicken, about 1 minute. Increase mixer speed to high, and beat until mixture turns very thick, white, and fluffy, about 10 minutes. Beat in vanilla bean powder. Spoon marshmallow into prepared pan.

4. In a medium bowl, sift together confectioners' sugar and cornstarch. Dust top of marshmallow with confectioners' sugar mixture, and flatten with hands. Wrap in plastic wrap, and let stand overnight.

5. Remove marshmallow from pan, and dust off excess confectioners' sugar. Store in an airtight container for up to 2 weeks.

CARAMEL PECAN BANANA COFFEE CAKE

Makes 1 (9-inch) cake

In this delicious coffee cake, praline pecans meet Bananas Foster, a decadent dessert created at New Orleans' Brennan's Restaurant in 1951.

½ cup (113 grams) unsalted butter, softened
1 cup (200 grams) granulated sugar
2 large eggs (100 grams)
1 cup (227 grams) mashed ripe banana
½ cup (120 grams) sour cream
1 teaspoon (4 grams) vanilla extract
1½ cups (188 grams) all-purpose flour
1 teaspoon (5 grams) baking powder
½ teaspoon (1.5 grams) kosher salt
Caramel (recipe follows), divided
½ cup (57 grams) chopped pecans
Brown Sugar Cinnamon Topping (recipe follows)

1. Preheat oven to 350°F (180°C). Butter and flour a 9-inch round cake pan.
2. In the bowl of a stand mixer fitted with the paddle attachment, beat butter and sugar at medium speed until fluffy, 3 to 4 minutes, stopping to scrape sides of bowl.

Add eggs, one at a time, beating well after each addition. Beat in banana, sour cream, and vanilla.
3. In a medium bowl, whisk together flour, baking powder, and salt. With mixer on low speed, gradually add flour mixture to banana mixture, beating just until combined. Spread half of batter into prepared pan. Drizzle with ¾ cup (246 grams) warm Caramel, and sprinkle with pecans. Top with remaining batter, and swirl in ¼ cup (82 grams) Caramel. Sprinkle with Brown Sugar Cinnamon Topping.
4. Bake for 50 minutes. Let cool in pan for 10 minutes. Remove from pan, and let cool completely on a wire rack. Drizzle with remaining Caramel before serving, if desired.

CARAMEL
Makes about 1½ cups

1½ cups (300 grams) granulated sugar
¼ cup (60 grams) water
½ cup (120 grams) warm whipping cream (105°F/10°C to 110°F/48°C)
¼ cup (57 grams) unsalted butter, softened

1. In a large skillet, stir together sugar and ¼ cup (60 grams) water. Cook over medium-high heat, without stirring, until mixture is amber colored, about 10 minutes. Remove from heat; stir in warm cream and butter. Let cool in skillet, stirring frequently.

BROWN SUGAR CINNAMON TOPPING
Makes about ½ cup

⅓ cup (73 grams) firmly packed light brown sugar
3 tablespoons (24 grams) all-purpose flour
¼ teaspoon ground cinnamon
2 tablespoons (28 grams) unsalted butter, melted
½ cup (57 grams) chopped pecans

1. In a medium bowl, whisk together brown sugar, flour, and cinnamon. Using a wooden spoon, stir in melted butter until mixture is crumbly. Stir in pecans.

RASPBERRY-BUTTERMILK COFFEE CAKE

Makes 1 (9-inch) cake

A layer of sweet raspberry jam ribbons through this tender buttermilk cake. Don't be surprised if the scent draws a crowd before it's even out of the oven.

½ cup (113 grams) unsalted butter, softened
1 cup (200 grams) granulated sugar
2 large eggs (100 grams)
1 teaspoon (4 grams) vanilla extract
1½ cups (188 grams) all-purpose flour
1½ teaspoons (7.5 grams) baking powder
½ teaspoon (1.5 grams) kosher salt
½ cup (120 grams) whole buttermilk
½ cup (85 grams) fresh raspberries
¾ cup (240 grams) seedless raspberry preserves
Cinnamon-Pecan Crumble (recipe follows)

1. Preheat oven to 350°F (180°C). Butter and flour a 9-inch round cake pan.
2. In the bowl of a stand mixer fitted with the paddle attachment, beat butter and sugar at medium speed until fluffy, 3 to 4 minutes, stopping to scrape sides of bowl. Add eggs, one at a time, beating well after each addition. Beat in vanilla.
3. In a medium bowl, whisk together flour, baking powder, and salt. With mixer on low speed, gradually add flour mixture to butter mixture alternately with buttermilk, beginning and ending with flour mixture, beating just until combined after each addition.
4. In a small bowl, lightly mash raspberries. Stir in raspberry preserves.
5. Spread three-fourths of batter into prepared pan. Gently spread raspberry mixture onto batter. Top with remaining batter, spreading to edges of pan. Sprinkle with Cinnamon-Pecan Crumble.
6. Bake until a wooden pick inserted in

center comes out clean, about 40 minutes, loosely covering with foil to prevent excess browning, if necessary. Let cool in pan for 10 minutes. Remove from pan, and let cool on a wire rack. Serve warm or at room temperature.

CINNAMON-PECAN CRUMBLE
Makes about ¾ cup

⅓ cup (42 grams) all-purpose flour
¼ cup (50 grams) granulated sugar
¼ teaspoon kosher salt
¼ teaspoon ground cinnamon
¼ cup (57 grams) unsalted butter, softened
⅓ cup (38 grams) chopped pecans

1. In a medium bowl, whisk together flour, sugar, salt, and cinnamon. Using a wooden spoon, stir in butter until mixture is crumbly. Stir in pecans.

CARROT COFFEE CAKE

Makes 1 (9-inch) cake

Buttermilk Whipped Cream complements our tropical spin on this Southern classic brimming with pecans, carrots, and crushed pineapple.

¾ cup (168 grams) vegetable oil
½ cup (110 grams) firmly packed light brown sugar
½ cup (100 grams) granulated sugar
2 large eggs (100 grams)
1 teaspoon (4 grams) vanilla extract
1 cup (125 grams) all-purpose flour
1½ teaspoons (3 grams) ground cinnamon
½ teaspoon (2.5 grams) baking powder
¼ teaspoon kosher salt
1 cup (99 grams) shredded carrot
½ cup (100 grams) drained crushed pineapple
½ cup (57 grams) chopped pecans
½ cup (42 grams) sweetened flaked coconut
Coconut-Pecan Crumble (recipe follows)
Buttermilk Whipped Cream (recipe follows)

1. Preheat oven to 350°F (180°C). Butter and flour a 9-inch round cake pan.

2. In the bowl of a stand mixer fitted with the paddle attachment, beat oil, sugars, eggs, and vanilla at medium speed until combined.

3. In a medium bowl, whisk together flour, cinnamon, baking powder, and salt. With mixer on low speed, gradually add flour mixture to oil mixture, beating just until combined. Stir in carrot, pineapple, pecans, and coconut. Spread batter into prepared pan.

4. Bake for 25 minutes. Sprinkle with Coconut-Pecan Crumble, and bake until a wooden pick inserted in center comes out clean, about 10 minutes more. Let cool in pan for 10 minutes. Remove from pan, and let cool on a wire rack. Serve warm or at room temperature with Buttermilk Whipped Cream.

COCONUT-PECAN CRUMBLE
Makes about ⅔ cup

½ cup (42 grams) sweetened flaked coconut
⅓ cup (38 grams) chopped pecans
1½ tablespoons (21 grams) firmly packed light brown sugar
1 tablespoon (8 grams) all-purpose flour
1 tablespoon (14 grams) unsalted butter, melted

1. In a medium bowl, stir together coconut, pecans, brown sugar, and flour. Using a wooden spoon, stir in melted butter until mixture is crumbly.

BUTTERMILK WHIPPED CREAM
Makes about 2½ cups

1 cup (240 grams) heavy whipping cream
½ cup (120 grams) whole buttermilk
2½ tablespoons (30 grams) granulated sugar

1. In the bowl of a stand mixer fitted with the whisk attachment, beat cream and buttermilk at high speed until foamy. Gradually add sugar, beating until stiff peaks form. Serve immediately.

PEANUT BUTTER-NUTELLA COFFEE CAKE

Makes 1 (9-inch) cake

Roasted peanuts add a salty crunch to this delectable combination of peanut butter and chocolate. We love a slice alongside a steaming mug of coffee, but a scoop of vanilla ice cream never hurt anyone!

- ½ cup (113 grams) unsalted butter, softened
- ½ cup (128 grams) creamy peanut butter
- 1 cup (200 grams) granulated sugar
- 2 large eggs (100 grams)
- ¼ cup (60 grams) sour cream
- 1½ teaspoons (6 grams) vanilla extract
- 1½ cups (188 grams) all-purpose flour
- 1 teaspoon (5 grams) baking powder
- ½ teaspoon (1.5 grams) kosher salt
- ½ cup (120 grams) whole milk
- ¾ cup (192 grams) chocolate-hazelnut spread*, warmed
- Peanut Butter Crumble (recipe follows)
- Garnish: melted dark chocolate

1. Preheat oven to 350°F (180°C). Butter and flour a 9-inch round cake pan.
2. In the bowl of a stand mixer fitted with the paddle attachment, beat butter, peanut butter, and sugar at medium speed until creamy, 3 to 4 minutes, stopping to scrape sides of bowl. Add eggs, one at a time, beating well after each addition. Beat in sour cream and vanilla.
3. In a medium bowl, whisk together flour, baking powder, and salt. With mixer on low speed, gradually add flour mixture to butter mixture alternately with milk, beginning and ending with flour mixture, beating just until combined after each addition. Pour half of batter into prepared pan. Spoon chocolate-hazelnut spread over batter, spreading to edges of pan. Top with remaining batter, smoothing top with an offset spatula. Sprinkle with Peanut Butter Crumble.
4. Bake until a wooden pick inserted in center comes out clean, 45 to 50 minutes, loosely covering with foil to prevent excess browning, if necessary. Let cool in pan for 10 minutes. Remove from pan, and let cool on a wire rack. Serve warm or at room temperature. Garnish with melted chocolate, if desired.

*We used Nutella.

PEANUT BUTTER CRUMBLE
Makes about 1 cup

- ⅓ cup (42 grams) all-purpose flour
- ¼ cup (55 grams) firmly packed light brown sugar
- 2 tablespoons (28 grams) unsalted butter, softened
- 1 tablespoon (16 grams) creamy peanut butter
- ½ cup (57 grams) chopped roasted salted peanuts

1. In a medium bowl, whisk together flour and brown sugar. Using a wooden spoon, stir in butter and peanut butter until mixture is crumbly. Stir in peanuts.

RUM RAISIN COFFEE CAKE

Makes 1 (10-inch) cake

If you like your coffee cake with a little kick, try this rum-soaked raisin-studded treat.

1 cup (227 grams) unsalted butter, softened
1½ cups (300 grams) granulated sugar
½ cup (110 grams) firmly packed light brown sugar
2 large eggs (100 grams)
1 cup (240 grams) sour cream
1½ teaspoons (6 grams) vanilla extract
1 teaspoon (5 grams) spiced rum, room temperature
2 cups (250 grams) all-purpose flour
1 teaspoon (5 grams) baking powder
¼ teaspoon kosher salt
Spiced Rum Raisins (recipe follows)
Cinnamon-Walnut Crumble (recipe follows)
¼ cup (32 grams) golden raisins
Rum Glaze (recipe follows)

1. Preheat oven to 350°F (180°C). Butter and flour a 10-inch round cake pan.
2. In the bowl of a stand mixer fitted with the paddle attachment, beat butter and sugars at medium speed until fluffy, 3 to 4 minutes, stopping to scrape sides of bowl. Add eggs, one at a time, beating well after each addition. Beat in sour cream, vanilla, and rum.

3. In a medium bowl, whisk together flour, baking powder, and salt. With mixer on low speed, gradually add flour mixture to butter mixture, beating just until combined. Spread half of batter into prepared pan. Sprinkle with Spiced Rum Raisins, and top with remaining batter, spreading to edges of pan. Sprinkle with Cinnamon-Walnut Crumble.
4. Bake until a wooden pick inserted in center comes out clean, 50 to 55 minutes, loosely covering with foil to prevent excess browning, if necessary. Let cool in pan for 10 minutes. Remove from pan, and let cool on a wire rack. Sprinkle with golden raisins, and drizzle with Rum Glaze. Serve warm or at room temperature.

Spiced Rum Raisins
Makes about 1 cup

½ cup (120 grams) spiced rum, warmed
½ cup (64 grams) raisins
½ cup (64 grams) golden raisins
⅓ cup (73 grams) firmly packed light brown sugar

1. In a small bowl, stir together warm rum, raisins, and golden raisins. Cover and let stand for 30 minutes. Drain, and reserve 2 teaspoons (10 grams) liquid. Stir reserved 2 teaspoons (10 grams) liquid and brown sugar into raisins.

Cinnamon-Walnut Crumble
Makes about ¾ cup

½ cup (63 grams) all-purpose flour
¼ cup (55 grams) firmly packed light brown sugar
1 teaspoon (2 grams) ground cinnamon
¼ teaspoon kosher salt
¼ cup (57 grams) unsalted butter, softened
⅓ cup (38 grams) chopped walnuts

1. In a medium bowl, whisk together flour, brown sugar, cinnamon, and salt. Using a wooden spoon, stir in butter until mixture is crumbly. Stir in walnuts.

Rum Glaze
Makes about ⅓ cup

1½ cups (180 grams) confectioners' sugar
1½ tablespoons (22.5 grams) whole milk
1½ tablespoons (22.5 grams) aged rum

1. In a small bowl, whisk together confectioners' sugar, milk, and rum until combined.

RIGHT-SIDE UP PINEAPPLE CRUMB CAKE

Makes 1 (10-inch) cake

Inspired by the upside-down classic, we flipped the script on this golden beauty. A brown sugar crumb topping and warm lemon glaze pair with pineapple rings to give this moist cake a sweet caramelized flavor.

1 tablespoon (14 grams) canola oil
8 (½-inch-thick) fresh pineapple rings (418 grams)
1½ cups (188 grams) all-purpose flour
¾ cup (150 grams) granulated sugar
¾ teaspoon (3.75 grams) baking powder
¼ teaspoon kosher salt
¾ cup (180 grams) whole milk
6 tablespoons (84 grams) unsalted butter, softened
½ teaspoon (2 grams) vanilla extract
3 large egg yolks (56 grams)
Brown Sugar Crumble (recipe follows)
Brown Sugar-Lemon Glaze (recipe follows)

1. Preheat oven to 350°F (180°C).
2. In a 10-inch cast-iron skillet, heat oil over medium-high heat. Add half of pineapple; cook until lightly browned, about 1 minute per side (reduce heat to medium, if necessary). Remove from skillet. Add remaining pineapple, and repeat procedure. Remove skillet from heat; let cool for 20 minutes. Wipe skillet clean.
3. In a medium bowl, whisk together flour, sugar, baking powder, and salt. Pour flour mixture into the bowl of a stand mixer fitted with the paddle attachment. Add milk, butter, and vanilla; beat at low speed until combined, about 1 minute. Increase mixer speed to high. Beat for 2 minutes, stopping to scrape sides of bowl. Reduce mixer speed to low. Add egg yolks, one at a time, beating well after each addition. Spread batter into cooled skillet. Arrange pineapple over batter, overlapping slices. Sprinkle with Brown Sugar Crumble.
4. Bake until golden brown, 35 to 40 minutes. Let cool for 30 minutes. Drizzle with Brown Sugar-Lemon Glaze before serving.

BROWN SUGAR CRUMBLE

Makes about ½ cup

⅓ cup (42 grams) all-purpose flour
¼ cup (55 grams) firmly packed dark brown sugar
⅛ teaspoon kosher salt
2 tablespoons (28 grams) unsalted butter, softened

1. In a medium bowl, whisk together flour, brown sugar, and salt. Using a wooden spoon, stir in butter until mixture is crumbly. Cover and refrigerate until ready to use.

BROWN SUGAR-LEMON GLAZE

Makes about ¼ cup

¼ cup (55 grams) firmly packed dark brown sugar
1 tablespoon (21 grams) dark corn syrup
1 tablespoon (14 grams) unsalted butter
1 tablespoon (15 grams) fresh lemon juice
⅛ teaspoon kosher salt

1. In a small saucepan, bring brown sugar, corn syrup, butter, lemon juice, and salt to a simmer over medium heat, stirring frequently. Cook until smooth, about 1 minute.

RASPBERRY JAM COFFEE CAKE WITH PISTACHIO STREUSEL

Makes 1 (8-inch) cake

A layer of raspberry jam and crunchy pistachio topping give this morning treat a lovely balance of sweet and nutty flavors. Try it with strawberry jam, too.

½ cup (113 grams) unsalted butter, softened
1 cup (200 grams) granulated sugar
2 large eggs (100 grams)
½ teaspoon (2 grams) vanilla extract
1⅓ cups (167 grams) all-purpose flour
¾ teaspoon (3.75 grams) baking powder
¼ teaspoon kosher salt
½ cup (120 grams) whole buttermilk
½ cup (160 grams) seedless raspberry jam
Pistachio Streusel (recipe follows)
Sweetened Whipped Cream (recipe follows)

1. Preheat oven to 350°F (180°C). Butter and flour an 8-inch round cake pan.
2. In the bowl of a stand mixer fitted with the paddle attachment, beat butter and sugar at medium speed until fluffy, 3 to 4 minutes, stopping to scrape sides of bowl. Add eggs, one at a time, beating well after each addition. Beat in vanilla.

3. In a medium bowl, whisk together flour, baking powder, and salt. With mixer on low speed, gradually add flour mixture to butter mixture alternately with buttermilk, beginning and ending with flour mixture, beating just until combined after each addition. Spread half of batter into prepared pan. Spoon raspberry jam over batter, spreading to edges of pan. Top with remaining batter, smoothing top with an offset spatula. Sprinkle with Pistachio Streusel.
4. Bake until a wooden pick inserted in center comes out clean, 40 to 45 minutes, loosely covering with foil to prevent excess browning, if necessary. Let cool in pan for 10 minutes. Remove from pan, and let cool on a wire rack. Serve warm or at room temperature with Sweetened Whipped Cream.

PISTACHIO STREUSEL

Makes about ¾ cup

¼ cup (31 grams) all-purpose flour
¼ cup (55 grams) firmly packed light brown sugar
2 teaspoons (4 grams) ground cinnamon
1 teaspoon (2 grams) ground cardamom
¼ teaspoon kosher salt

2 tablespoons (28 grams) unsalted butter, softened
¼ cup (28 grams) finely chopped pistachios

1. In a medium bowl, stir together flour, brown sugar, cinnamon, cardamom, and salt. Using a wooden spoon, stir in butter until mixture is crumbly. Stir in pistachios.

SWEETENED WHIPPED CREAM

Makes 6 cups

2½ cups (600 grams) heavy whipping cream
½ cup (60 grams) confectioners' sugar
1 teaspoon (4 grams) vanilla extract

1. In the bowl of a stand mixer fitted with the whisk attachment, beat cream at medium speed until slightly thickened. Increase mixer speed to medium-high. Gradually add confectioners' sugar and vanilla, beating until stiff peaks form.

BROWNED BUTTER HUMMINGBIRD COFFEE CAKE

Makes 1 (8-inch) cake

This is your best excuse for having cake for breakfast. Browned butter adds depth to this unexpected twist on the classic Southern banana-pineapple confection. Pecan streusel is just, well, the icing on the cake.

½ cup (113 grams) plus 3½ tablespoons (49 grams) unsalted butter, softened and divided

1½ cups (188 grams) plus ⅓ cup (42 grams) all-purpose flour, divided

½ cup (110 grams) firmly packed light brown sugar, divided

1½ teaspoons (3 gram) ground cinnamon, divided

1 teaspoon (3 grams) kosher salt, divided

½ cup (57 grams) pecan halves, chopped

2 large eggs (100 grams)

1 large banana (124 grams), mashed

½ cup (100 grams) drained crushed pineapple

1 teaspoon (4 grams) vanilla extract

¾ cup (150 grams) plus 1 tablespoon (12 grams) granulated sugar, divided

¾ teaspoon (3.75 grams) baking powder

½ cup (60 grams) confectioners' sugar

2 tablespoons (30 grams) sour cream

1½ teaspoons (7.5 grams) whole milk

1. Preheat oven to 350°F (180°C). Butter and flour an 8-inch round tall-sided cake pan.

2. In a medium saucepan, melt ½ cup (113 grams) butter over medium heat. Cook until butter turns a medium-brown color and has a nutty aroma, about 10 minutes. Remove from heat, and let cool to room temperature.

3. In a medium bowl, whisk together ⅓ cup (42 grams) flour, ¼ cup (55 grams) brown sugar, ½ teaspoon (1 gram) cinnamon, and ¼ teaspoon salt. Stir in remaining 3½ tablespoons (49 grams) butter until mixture is crumbly. Crumble with your fingertips until desired consistency is reached. Stir in pecans. Set aside.

4. In the bowl of a stand mixer fitted with the paddle attachment, beat eggs, banana, pineapple, and vanilla at medium speed until combined, 1 to 2 minutes. Stir in cooled browned butter.

5. In a medium bowl, whisk together ¾ cup (150 grams) granulated sugar, baking powder, ½ teaspoon (1 gram) cinnamon, remaining 1½ cups (188 grams) flour, remaining ¼ cup (55 grams) brown sugar, and remaining ¾ teaspoon (2.25 grams) salt. With mixer on low speed, gradually add flour mixture to browned butter mixture, beating just until combined.

6. In a small bowl, stir together remaining 1 tablespoon (12 grams) granulated sugar and remaining ½ teaspoon (1 gram) cinnamon. Spread half of batter into prepared pan. Sprinkle with one-third of streusel and cinnamon-sugar mixture. Top with remaining batter, smoothing top with an offset spatula. Sprinkle with remaining streusel.

7. Bake until a wooden pick inserted in center comes out clean, 45 to 50 minutes, loosely covering with foil to prevent excess browning, if necessary. Let cool in pan for 15 minutes. Run a sharp knife around edges of cake to loosen sides. Invert onto a plate, and then invert again onto a wire rack.

8. In a small bowl, whisk together confectioners' sugar, sour cream, and milk. Pour over warm cake.

ALMOND FINANCIERS

Makes 12

These bite-size beauties are your next excuse for bringing out the mini brioche à tête molds. In our take on the classic French teacake, toasted almond flour and browned butter imbue a nuttiness that balances the sweet tartness of the dried cranberries and applesauce.

¼ cup (57 grams) unsalted butter, melted
1¼ cups (284 grams) unsalted butter
1½ cups (144 grams) almond flour, toasted
1¼ cups (150 grams) confectioners' sugar
½ cup (63 grams) all-purpose flour
¼ teaspoon kosher salt
4 large egg whites (120 grams), room temperature
3 tablespoons (45 grams) fresh lemon juice
⅓ cup (80 grams) McIntosh Applesauce (recipe on page 108)
⅓ cup (43 grams) dried cranberries
1 tablespoon (6 grams) lemon zest
1 McIntosh apple (185 grams), thinly sliced
Spiced Simple Syrup (recipe follows)

1. Preheat oven to 375°F (190°C). Brush melted butter into 12 (3-inch) brioche à tête molds.
2. In a medium saucepan, melt butter over medium heat. Cook until butter turns a medium-brown color and has a nutty aroma, about 10 minutes. Remove from heat, and let cool to room temperature. Reserve ¾ cup (170 grams) browned butter. Refrigerate any leftovers for up to 1 week.
3. In the bowl of a stand mixer fitted with the paddle attachment, sift together almond flour, confectioners' sugar, all-purpose flour, and salt. With mixer on low speed, add egg whites, one at a time, beating well after each addition. Increase mixer speed to medium. Gradually add reserved ¾ cup (170 grams) browned butter and lemon juice, beating until combined, stopping to scrape sides of bowl. Fold in McIntosh Applesauce, cranberries, and zest.
4. Pipe batter into prepared molds, filling each about three-fourths full. Layer apple slices across top of batter.
5. Bake for 20 minutes. Cover with foil, and bake 10 minutes more. Brush with warm

Spiced Simple Syrup, and let stand for 10 minutes. Remove from molds, and serve warm. Refrigerate in an airtight container for up to 3 days. Freeze in an airtight container for up to 2 weeks.

SPICED SIMPLE SYRUP
Makes ¼ cup

¼ cup (60 grams) water
¼ cup (50 grams) granulated sugar
½ teaspoon (1 gram) ground cinnamon
¼ teaspoon ground allspice

1. In a medium saucepan, heat ¼ cup (60 grams) water and sugar over medium heat until sugar is dissolved. Remove from heat, and whisk in cinnamon and allspice. Use immediately, or cover and refrigerate for up to 1 week. Freeze in an airtight container for up to 2 weeks.

VANILLA BUTTERMILK CAKE WITH CHOCOLATE-BUTTERMILK FROSTING

Makes 1 (9-inch) cake

We infused our classic birthday cake with buttermilk to add a little tang and a lot of moisture. The best part? It's so simple to make, you don't have to wait for a birthday to savor this tender-crumbed treat.

½   cup (113 grams) unsalted butter, softened
1   cup (200 grams) granulated sugar
2   large eggs (100 grams)
½   teaspoon (2 grams) vanilla extract
1⅓   cups (167 grams) all-purpose flour
1¼   teaspoons (6.25 grams) baking powder
¼   teaspoon kosher salt
½   cup (120 grams) whole buttermilk
Chocolate-Buttermilk Frosting (recipe follows)
Garnish: multicolored sprinkles

1. Preheat oven to 350°F (180°C). Butter and flour a 9-inch round cake pan.
2. In the bowl of a stand mixer fitted with the paddle attachment, beat butter and sugar at medium speed until fluffy, 3 to 4 minutes, stopping to scrape sides of bowl. Add eggs, one at a time, beating well after each addition. Beat in vanilla.
3. In a medium bowl, whisk together flour, baking powder, and salt. With mixer on low speed, gradually add flour mixture to butter mixture alternately with buttermilk, beginning and ending with flour mixture, beating just until combined after each addition. Spoon batter into prepared pan.
4. Bake until a wooden pick inserted in center comes out clean, 30 to 35 minutes. Let cool in pan for 10 minutes. Remove from pan, and let cool completely on a wire rack. Spread Chocolate-Buttermilk Frosting onto cake. Garnish with sprinkles, if desired.

CHOCOLATE-BUTTERMILK FROSTING
Makes about 1½ cups

½   cup (113 grams) unsalted butter, softened
2   cups (240 grams) confectioners' sugar
¼   cup (21 grams) unsweetened cocoa powder
½   teaspoon (1.5 grams) kosher salt
3   tablespoons (45 grams) whole buttermilk

1. In the bowl of a stand mixer fitted with the paddle attachment, beat butter at medium speed until creamy.
2. In a medium bowl, sift together confectioners' sugar, cocoa, and salt. Reduce mixer speed to low. Add cocoa mixture to butter, beating until combined. Stir in buttermilk until mixture reaches a spreadable consistency.

MEYER LEMON-OLIVE OIL COFFEE CAKE

Makes 1 (8-inch) cake

If you love lemon bars, you will LOVE this cake. Meyer lemons are less acidic and slightly sweeter than the standard lemons found in the grocery store, and provide a perfect balance against the tart lemon curd swirled into this silky batter.

2   cups (250 grams) all-purpose flour, divided
3   tablespoons (42 grams) firmly packed light brown sugar
½   cup (100 grams) plus 1½ tablespoons (18 grams) granulated sugar, divided
2½   teaspoons (5 grams) Meyer lemon zest, divided
5   teaspoons (25 grams) fresh Meyer lemon juice, divided
1   teaspoon (3 grams) kosher salt, divided
9   tablespoons (126 grams) unsalted butter, melted and divided
2   large eggs (100 grams)
⅓   cup (75 grams) extra-virgin olive oil
1   teaspoon (5 grams) baking powder
2   tablespoons (30 grams) sour cream
¼   cup (80 grams) prepared lemon curd
Garnish: confectioners' sugar

1. Preheat oven to 350°F (180°C). Butter and flour an 8-inch round tall-sided cake pan.
2. In a medium bowl, whisk together ¾ cup (94 grams) flour, brown sugar, 1½ tablespoons (18 grams) granulated sugar, 1 teaspoon (2 grams) lemon zest, 1 teaspoon (5 grams) lemon juice, and ½ teaspoon (1.5 grams) salt. Drizzle with 5 tablespoons (70 grams) melted butter, and stir with a wooden spoon until combined. Crumble with your fingertips until desired consistency is reached. Set aside.
3. In the bowl of a stand mixer fitted with the paddle attachment, beat eggs, oil, and remaining ½ cup (100 grams) granulated sugar at medium-high speed until thick and pale yellow, 5 to 6 minutes. Stir in remaining 4 tablespoons (56 grams) melted butter, remaining 1½ teaspoons (3 grams) lemon zest, and remaining 4 teaspoons (20 grams) lemon juice until combined.
4. In a medium bowl, whisk together baking powder, remaining 1¼ cups (156 grams) flour, and remaining ½ teaspoon (1.5 grams) salt. With mixer on low speed, gradually add flour mixture to egg mixture, beating just until combined. Stir in sour cream. Pour three-fourths of batter into prepared pan. Spread with lemon curd, and top with remaining batter, smoothing top with an offset spatula. Sprinkle with streusel.
5. Bake until a wooden pick inserted in center comes out clean, 30 to 35 minutes. Let cool in pan for 15 minutes. Run a sharp knife around edges of cake to loosen sides. Invert onto a plate, and then invert again onto a wire rack. Let cool completely. Garnish with confectioners' sugar, if desired.

PB&J COFFEE CAKE

Makes 2 (6-inch) cakes

This cake combines salty peanuts, sweet raspberry preserves, and a drizzle of peanut butter for an all-new version of our favorite lunch box staple.

1½ cups (188 grams) plus ⅓ cup (42 grams) all-purpose flour, divided
¼ cup (55 grams) firmly packed light brown sugar
¼ cup (64 grams) creamy peanut butter
½ cup (113 grams) plus 1 tablespoon (14 grams) unsalted butter, softened and divided
⅓ cup (38 grams) dry roasted salted chopped peanuts
1 cup (200 grams) granulated sugar
2 large eggs (100 grams)
1 teaspoon (4 grams) vanilla extract
1 teaspoon (5 grams) baking powder
½ teaspoon (1.5 grams) kosher salt
½ cup (120 grams) whole buttermilk
¾ cup (240 grams) raspberry preserves
Garnish: warmed peanut butter

1. Preheat oven to 350°F (180°C). Butter and flour 2 (6-inch) round tall-sided cake pans.
2. In a medium bowl, whisk together ⅓ cup (42 grams) flour and brown sugar. Stir in peanut butter and 1 tablespoon (14 grams) butter until mixture is crumbly. Crumble with your fingertips until desired consistency is reached. Stir in peanuts. Set aside.
3. In the bowl of a stand mixer fitted with the paddle attachment, beat granulated sugar and remaining ½ cup (113 grams) butter at medium speed until fluffy, 3 to 4 minutes, stopping to scrape sides of bowl. Add eggs, one at a time, beating well after each addition. Stir in vanilla.
4. In a medium bowl, whisk together baking powder, salt, and remaining 1½ cups (188 grams) flour. With mixer on low speed, gradually add flour mixture to butter mixture alternately with buttermilk, beginning and ending with flour mixture, beating just until combined after each addition. Divide three-fourths of batter between prepared pans. Spread with raspberry preserves, and top with remaining batter, smoothing tops with an offset spatula. Sprinkle with streusel.
5. Bake until a wooden pick inserted in center comes out clean, 40 to 45 minutes, loosely covering with foil to prevent excess browning, if necessary. Let cool in pans for 15 minutes. Run a sharp knife around edges of cakes to loosen sides. Invert onto a plate, and then invert again onto a wire rack. Let cool completely. Garnish with warmed peanut butter, if desired.

MAPLE DATE WALNUT COFFEE CAKE

Makes 1 (8-inch) cake

With hints of orange essence and maple complemented by a cinnamon-laced crumble, this recipe practically screams, "Winter is here!"

2 cups (250 grams) all-purpose flour, divided
¾ cup (165 grams) plus ⅓ cup (73 grams) firmly packed light brown sugar, divided
½ teaspoon (1 gram) ground cinnamon
1¼ teaspoons (3 grams) kosher salt, divided
¾ cup (170 grams) plus 2½ tablespoons (35 grams) unsalted butter, softened and divided
6 tablespoons (126 grams) pure maple syrup, divided
½ cup (57 grams) chopped walnuts
1 cup (128 grams) chopped pitted dates
1 cup (240 grams) boiling water
½ teaspoon (2.5 grams) baking soda
⅓ cup (67 grams) granulated sugar
2 large eggs (100 grams)
2 teaspoons (4 grams) orange zest
¾ teaspoon (3 grams) maple extract
1 teaspoon (5 grams) baking powder
½ cup (120 grams) whole milk
¼ cup (60 grams) fresh orange juice
⅓ cup (80 grams) heavy whipping cream
3 tablespoons (21 grams) confectioners' sugar

1. Preheat oven to 350°F (180°C). Butter and flour an 8-inch square baking pan.
2. In a medium bowl, whisk together ½ cup (63 grams) flour, ¼ cup (55 grams) brown sugar, cinnamon, and ¼ teaspoon salt. Stir in 2½ tablespoons (35 grams) butter and 2 tablespoons (42 grams) maple syrup until combined. Crumble with your fingertips until desired consistency is reached. Stir in walnuts. Set aside.
3. In a medium bowl, combine dates, 1 cup (240 grams) boiling water, and baking soda. Let stand until just tender, about 5 minutes. Drain, discarding any excess liquid.
4. In the bowl of a stand mixer fitted with the paddle attachment, beat ½ cup (113 grams) butter, granulated sugar, and ⅓ cup (73 grams) brown sugar at medium speed until fluffy, 3 to 4 minutes, stopping to scrape sides of bowl. Add eggs, one at a time, beating well after each addition. Stir in zest, maple extract, and remaining 4 tablespoons (84 grams) maple syrup.
5. In a medium bowl, whisk together baking powder, remaining 1½ cups (188 grams) flour, and remaining 1 teaspoon (3 grams) salt. With mixer on low speed, gradually add flour mixture to butter mixture alternately with milk and orange juice, beginning and ending with flour mixture, beating just until combined after each addition. (Batter will be thin.) Fold in dates. Pour batter into prepared pan, smoothing top with an offset spatula. Sprinkle with streusel.
6. Bake until a wooden pick inserted in center comes out clean, 45 to 50 minutes, loosely covering with foil to prevent excess browning, if necessary. Let cool in pan for 15 minutes. Run a sharp knife around edges of cake to loosen sides. Invert onto a plate, and then invert again onto a wire rack. Let cool completely.
7. In a medium saucepan, heat cream, remaining ½ cup (110 grams) brown sugar, and remaining ¼ cup (57 grams) butter over medium-high heat. Bring to a boil, and cook for 1½ minutes, stirring constantly. Remove from heat, and let cool to room temperature. Whisk in confectioners' sugar, and drizzle over cooled cake.

ALMOND-BLUEBERRY COFFEE CAKE

Makes 1 (9-inch) cake

Almond flour gives this crumbly cake a complex, slightly nutty flavor while slivered almonds and a sprinkling of coarse sugar add an extra sweet crunch.

1¼ cups (156 grams) plus ⅓ cup (42 grams) all-purpose flour, divided

1¼ cups (250 grams) granulated sugar, divided

¾ teaspoon (2.25 grams) kosher salt, divided

½ cup (113 grams) plus 3 tablespoons (42 grams) unsalted butter, softened and divided

⅓ cup (38 grams) sliced almonds

2 large eggs (100 grams)

1 teaspoon (4 grams) vanilla extract

½ teaspoon (2 grams) almond extract

¼ cup (24 grams) almond flour

1½ teaspoons (7.5 grams) baking powder

¼ cup (60 grams) whole milk

½ cup (120 grams) sour cream

1½ cups (255 grams) fresh blueberries, divided

2 teaspoons (10 grams) coarse sugar

1. Preheat oven to 350°F (180°C). Butter and flour a 9-inch round tall-sided cake pan.

2. In a medium bowl, whisk together ⅓ cup (42 grams) all-purpose flour, ¼ cup (50 grams) granulated sugar, and ¼ teaspoon salt. Stir in 3 tablespoons (42 grams) butter until mixture is crumbly. Crumble with your fingertips until desired consistency is reached. Stir in almonds. Set aside.

3. In the bowl of a stand mixer fitted with the paddle attachment, beat remaining ½ cup (113 grams) butter and remaining 1 cup (200 grams) granulated sugar at medium speed until fluffy, 3 to 4 minutes, stopping to scrape sides of bowl. Add eggs, one at a time, beating well after each addition. Stir in extracts.

4. In a medium bowl, whisk together almond flour, baking powder, remaining 1¼ cups (156 grams) all-purpose flour, and remaining ½ teaspoon (1.5 grams) salt. With mixer on low speed, gradually add flour mixture to butter mixture alternately with milk, beginning and ending with flour mixture, beating just until combined after each addition. Stir in sour cream. Pour half of batter into prepared pan. Sprinkle with 1¼ cups (212.5 grams) blueberries, and top with remaining batter, smoothing top with an offset spatula. Top with remaining ¼ cup (42.5 grams) blueberries, and sprinkle with streusel and coarse sugar.

5. Bake until a wooden pick inserted in center comes out clean, 50 to 55 minutes. Let cool in pan for 15 minutes. Run a knife around edges of cake to loosen sides. Invert onto a plate, and then invert again onto a wire rack. Let cool completely.

CRÈME FRAÎCHE CHEESECAKE

Makes 1 (9-inch) cake

Recipe by Yossy Arefi

A bit of almond meal and browned butter give the crust of this cheesecake a unique toasty flavor that pairs beautifully with the tangy crème fraîche filling. Cheesecake can be tricky to get right, but Yossy's top tips are to make sure all of the ingredients are at room temperature, mix the filling carefully and thoroughly so it is silky smooth, and in lieu of a messy water bath, just set a pan of hot water on the bottom of your oven—something she learned from author and baking blogger Sarah Keiffer. Serve this with a bit of seasonal fruit macerated with sugar.

5   tablespoons (70 grams) unsalted butter
1   cup (130 grams) graham cracker crumbs
½   cup (48 grams) almond meal
1¼ cups (250 grams) plus 3 tablespoons (36 grams) granulated sugar, divided
1⅛ teaspoons (3 grams) kosher salt, divided
2   pounds (910 grams) cream cheese, softened
1   vanilla bean, split lengthwise, seeds scraped and reserved, or 1 tablespoon (13 grams) vanilla extract
2   cups (480 grams) crème fraîche, room temperature
4   large eggs (200 grams), room temperature and lightly beaten
1   tablespoon (15 grams) fresh lemon juice
Macerated seasonal fruit, to serve

1. Preheat oven to 325°F (170°C). Wrap the sides of a 9-inch springform pan with foil. Place a 13x9-inch baking dish in bottom of oven, and fill with hot water. (This will create a moist environment, which will help prevent cracks in your cheesecake.)
2. In a medium saucepan, heat butter over medium heat. Cook, stirring constantly, until butter turns a medium-brown color and has a nutty aroma, about 10 minutes. Remove from heat, and let cool slightly.
3. In a large bowl, stir together graham cracker crumbs, almond meal, 3 tablespoons (36 grams) sugar, and ⅛ teaspoon salt. Add cooled browned butter, and stir until combined. Press mixture into bottom of prepared pan.
4. Bake until golden brown, 9 to 11 minutes. Let cool slightly.
5. In the bowl of a stand mixer fitted with the paddle attachment, beat cream cheese at medium-high speed until smooth, 4 to 5 minutes, stopping to scrape sides of bowl. Add vanilla bean seeds (if using) and remaining 1¼ cups (250 grams) sugar; beat until combined, about 2 minutes, stopping to scrape sides of bowl. Add crème fraîche, beating until combined.
6. With mixer running, slowly add eggs, beating until combined. Add vanilla extract (if using), lemon juice, and remaining 1 teaspoon (3 grams) salt, beating just until combined. Pour filling onto prepared crust. Firmly tap pan on counter about 10 times to release any air bubbles.
7. Bake until edges are set and center is jiggly, about 1 hour. Turn oven off, and leave cheesecake in oven with door cracked with a wooden spoon for 4 hours. Remove from oven. Run a knife around edges of cheesecake to release sides. (As cheesecake cools, it shrinks, which is why you run a knife around sides before you refrigerate it so it doesn't crack during cooling.) Loosely cover, and refrigerate for at least 4 hours or up to 2 days. Remove ring; slice, and serve with fruit.

Photo by Yossy Arefi

SWEET CHERRY AND CORNMEAL UPSIDE-DOWN CAKE

Makes 1 (9-inch) cake

Recipe by Yossy Arefi

Upside-down cakes are one of the very best ways to use just about any seasonal fruit, and this version with juicy sweet cherries and a light and fluffy cornmeal-flecked cake batter is a stunner. The cornmeal cake pairs well with just about any fruit—try peaches or nectarines later in the season. Don't forget to serve it with a bit of vanilla ice cream or whipped cream.

⅓   cup (73 grams) firmly packed brown sugar

½   cup (113 grams) plus 3 tablespoons (42 grams) unsalted butter, softened

¾   teaspoon (2.25 grams) plus ⅛ teaspoon kosher salt, divided

1¼   pounds (570 grams) sweet cherries, pitted

¾   cup (150 grams) granulated sugar

1   teaspoon (2 grams) finely grated lemon zest

2   large eggs (100 grams)

1½   cups (187 grams) cake flour

6   tablespoons (54 grams) cornmeal

1½   teaspoons (7.5 grams) baking powder

¼   teaspoon (1.25 grams) baking soda

¾   cup (180 grams) whole buttermilk

1   teaspoon (4 grams) vanilla extract

Vanilla ice cream or whipped cream, to serve

1. Preheat oven to 350°F (180°C). Line a 9-inch springform pan with parchment paper, and butter pan and parchment.

2. In a medium saucepan, heat brown sugar, 3 tablespoons (42 grams) butter, and ⅛ teaspoon salt over medium heat. Cook, whisking occasionally, until butter is melted and sugar is dissolved. Pour mixture into prepared pan. Arrange cherries in a single layer on top of butter mixture.

3. In the bowl of a stand mixer fitted with the paddle attachment, beat granulated sugar, zest, and remaining ½ cup (113 grams) butter at medium speed until fluffy, 3 to 4 minutes, stopping to scrape sides of bowl. Add eggs, one at a time, beating well after each addition.

4. In a medium bowl, whisk together flour, cornmeal, baking powder, baking soda, and remaining ¾ teaspoon (2.25 grams) salt. In a small bowl, stir together buttermilk and vanilla. With mixer on low speed, gradually add flour mixture to butter mixture alternately with buttermilk mixture, beginning and ending with flour mixture, beating just until combined after each addition. Spread batter onto cherries. Firmly tap pan on counter to settle batter between cherries and release air bubbles. Place pan on a baking sheet lined with parchment paper.

5. Bake until golden and puffed, and a wooden pick inserted in center comes out clean, 40 to 50 minutes, rotating pan and covering with foil halfway through baking to prevent excess browning. Let cool on a wire rack for 15 minutes. Carefully remove ring; invert cake onto a serving board or platter. Carefully remove parchment. Serve warm with ice cream or whipped cream.

Photo by Yossy Arefi

PUMPKIN APPLE LOAF

Makes 1 (9x5-inch) loaf

This spiced loaf gets its magic from the McIntosh apple. The subtly sweet applesauce fuses flawlessly with the pumpkin while fresh pieces of apple give an unmistakable, straight-from-the-orchard flavor.

1⅔ cups (217 grams) whole wheat flour
1 cup (125 grams) all-purpose flour
1 teaspoon (5 grams) baking powder
1 teaspoon (5 grams) baking soda
1 teaspoon (2 grams) ground cinnamon
½ teaspoon (1.5 grams) kosher salt
½ teaspoon (1 gram) ground allspice
¼ teaspoon ground nutmeg
1 cup (244 grams) canned pumpkin
¾ cup (165 grams) firmly packed light brown sugar
½ cup (120 grams) McIntosh Applesauce (recipe below)
¼ cup (50 grams) granulated sugar
2 large eggs (100 grams)
½ cup (93 grams) grated unpeeled McIntosh apple, squeezed dry
½ cup (93 grams) chopped unpeeled McIntosh apple
1 large McIntosh apple (185 grams)
Crumble Topping (recipe follows)

1. Preheat oven to 350°F (180°C). Butter and flour a 9x5-inch loaf pan; line pan with parchment paper.
2. In a large bowl, whisk together flours, baking powder, baking soda, cinnamon, salt, allspice, and nutmeg.
3. In a medium bowl, stir together pumpkin, brown sugar, McIntosh Applesauce, granulated sugar, and eggs. Make a well in center of dry ingredients; add pumpkin mixture, stirring just until combined. Fold in grated and chopped apple.
4. Using a mandoline, thinly slice whole apple at the cross section. Line 3 slices along each long side of prepared pan.
5. Fill a 16-inch piping bag with batter, and pipe into perimeter of pan to ensure apple slices stay in place. Pipe remaining batter into pan, filling three-fourths full. Sprinkle with Crumble Topping.
6. Bake until a wooden pick inserted in center comes out clean, 50 to 60 minutes. Let cool completely on a wire rack. Wrap tightly in plastic wrap, and refrigerate for up to 4 days. To freeze, wrap tightly in plastic wrap, and store in a heavy-duty resealable plastic bag. Freeze for up to 2 months.

CRUMBLE TOPPING
Makes 1 cup

¼ cup (50 grams) granulated sugar
¼ cup (31 grams) all-purpose flour
¼ cup (24 grams) almond flour
¼ cup (20 grams) old-fashioned oats
2 tablespoons (28 grams) cold unsalted butter, cubed
¼ teaspoon kosher salt
¼ teaspoon ground cinnamon
¼ teaspoon ground allspice
⅛ teaspoon baking powder

1. In the bowl of a stand mixer fitted with the paddle attachment, beat all ingredients at medium speed just until combined, 3 to 4 minutes. Refrigerate in an airtight container for up to 1 week.

MCINTOSH APPLESAUCE
Makes 3 cups

One of the most well-known varieties of apples, McIntosh apples are exceptionally juicy with a mellow sweet-tart flavor. This versatile sauce works in a wide range of recipes and blends beautifully with spices without being overpowering.

2 pounds (910 grams) McIntosh apples, unpeeled, cored, and chopped
1 cup (240 grams) apple brandy
½ cup (110 grams) firmly packed light brown sugar
2 tablespoons (30 grams) fresh lemon juice
1 tablespoon (9 grams) fruit pectin*
1 teaspoon (6 grams) vanilla bean paste
1 teaspoon (2 grams) ground cinnamon
1 teaspoon (2 grams) ground allspice
6 to 7 cinnamon sticks (20 grams)

1. In a large stockpot, bring all ingredients to a simmer over medium-low heat. Simmer until apples are tender, 20 to 30 minutes. Let cool to room temperature.
2. Using an immersion blender, blend until smooth**. Strain mixture through a fine-mesh sieve, discarding apple skin. Cover and refrigerate for at least 2 hours before using. Refrigerate in an airtight container for up to 2 weeks.

*We used Sure-Jell Premium Fruit Pectin.

**You can also blend in the container of a blender or the work bowl of a food processor.

BREADS

QUICK
BREADS

These no-fuss bread recipes always rise to the occasion—no yeast required. Indulge in comforting classics like tender banana bread and streusel-laced muffins as well as rustic staples like Irish soda bread.

RHUBARB-GINGER MUFFINS WITH RHUBARB-VANILLA BEAN STREUSEL

Makes 18

We love the tiny bursts of red that diced rhubarb brings to this tender treat's batter. Ginger lends just the right amount of kick, and a vanilla bean streusel topping packs the perfect crunch.

2   cups (250 grams) all-purpose flour
1   cup (200 grams) granulated sugar
1   teaspoon (5 grams) baking powder
1   teaspoon (2 grams) ground ginger
1   teaspoon grated fresh nutmeg
½   teaspoon (2.5 grams) baking soda
½   teaspoon (1.5 grams) kosher salt
1½   cups (150 grams) diced rhubarb
3   large eggs (150 grams)
1   cup (240 grams) sour cream
½   cup (120 grams) whole buttermilk
¼   cup (57 grams) unsalted butter, melted and slightly cooled
1   teaspoon (6 grams) vanilla bean paste
Zest of 1 lemon
Rhubarb-Vanilla Bean Streusel (recipe follows)

1. Preheat oven to 375°F (190°C). Butter and flour 18 muffin cups, or line with paper liners.

2. In a large bowl, whisk together flour, sugar, baking powder, ginger, nutmeg, baking soda, and salt. Stir in rhubarb.

3. In a medium bowl, whisk together eggs, sour cream, buttermilk, melted butter, vanilla bean paste, and zest. Fold egg mixture into flour mixture, stirring just until combined. Divide batter among prepared muffin cups. Top with Rhubarb-Vanilla Bean Streusel.

4. Bake until a wooden pick inserted in center comes out clean, 20 to 30 minutes.

RHUBARB-VANILLA BEAN STREUSEL
Makes 2 cups

¾   cup (94 grams) all-purpose flour
¼   cup (55 grams) firmly packed light brown sugar
¼   cup (50 grams) granulated sugar
½   teaspoon (1.5 grams) kosher salt
½   teaspoon (1 gram) ground ginger
1   vanilla bean, split lengthwise, seeds scraped and reserved
¼   cup (57 grams) unsalted butter, melted
½   cup (50 grams) finely diced rhubarb

1. In a medium bowl, whisk together flour, sugars, salt, ginger, and reserved vanilla bean seeds. Drizzle with melted butter. Using a wooden spoon, stir to combine. Crumble with your fingertips until desired consistency is reached. Fold in rhubarb.

COCONUT POPOVERS
WITH MANGO CHUTNEY

Makes 6

Recipe by Ben Mims

The coconut in these popovers lends a sweetness that pairs well with curries and other spicy dishes. Use the mango chutney as a spread on sandwiches with thick slices of Cheddar cheese, or mix it into mayonnaise as a dip for chicken fingers or a spread for deli sandwiches.

1¼ cups (300 grams) coconut water (fresh or bottled)
1   tablespoon (14 grams) unrefined coconut oil, melted
1   teaspoon (4 grams) coconut extract
3   large eggs (150 grams)
1   cup (125 grams) all-purpose flour
1   teaspoon (3 grams) kosher salt
2   tablespoons (28 grams) vegetable oil
Mango Chutney (recipe follows)

1. In a medium bowl, whisk together coconut water, melted coconut oil, coconut extract, and eggs until smooth. Add flour and salt; whisk until just combined (there will be some lumps). Cover with plastic wrap, and let stand at room temperature for at least 2 hours.
2. Preheat oven to 400°F (200°C). Pour 1 teaspoon (5 grams) vegetable oil into each cup of a 6-cup nonstick popover pan. Place popover pan on a rimmed baking sheet (to catch oil drips), and preheat in oven for 15 minutes. Remove pan from oven, and quickly pour batter into prepared cups, filling each about two-thirds full.
3. Bake until risen and golden brown, 30 to 35 minutes. Using a fork, poke holes in top of popovers to release steam. Unmold popovers, and serve hot with Mango Chutney.

MANGO CHUTNEY
Makes about 3 cups

1   pound (455 grams) ripe mango flesh, finely chopped
½   cup (75 grams) coconut sugar
½   cup (110 grams) firmly packed light brown sugar
½   cup (64 grams) raisins
½   cup (120 grams) apple cider vinegar
¼   cup (21 grams) finely shredded dried (desiccated) coconut
¼   cup (8 grams) minced peeled ginger
1½   tablespoons (22.5 grams) fresh lime juice
½   teaspoon (1 gram) chili powder
½   teaspoon (1.5 grams) kosher salt
¼   teaspoon ground black pepper
1   clove garlic (5 grams), minced
1   small red onion (30 grams), finely chopped

1. In medium saucepan, bring all ingredients to a boil over medium-high heat. Reduce heat to medium-low, and cook, stirring occasionally, until reduced and thickened to a relish, 45 minutes to 1 hour. Remove from heat. Transfer chutney to glass jars, and seal while hot, or refrigerate in an airtight container for up to 2 weeks.

Photo by Mason + Dixon

COCONUT AND EARL GREY SCONES

Makes 8

Recipe by Ben Mims

Floral notes of orange and bitter black tea pair well with the rich aroma of coconut in these scones with the tea blended right inside. Even though pieces of coconut, its milk, and oil are used here, the subtle flavor of coconut needs the boost of extract for its full flavor to come through. The coconut sugar sprinkled on top is too savory to use as the sweetener in the scones, but it offers the perfect amount of crunch and toasted coconut aroma when sprinkled on top. If you can't find coconut sugar, you can use granulated or light brown sugar instead.

2   cups (480 grams) unsweetened canned coconut milk
2   tablespoons (12 grams) finely ground Earl Grey tea
1   teaspoon (4 grams) coconut extract
1   cup (84 grams) unsweetened flaked coconut
5   cups (625 grams) all-purpose flour
½   cup (100 grams) granulated sugar
1   tablespoon plus 2 teaspoons (25 grams) baking powder
2½   teaspoons (7.5 grams) kosher salt
⅓   cup (75 grams) unrefined coconut oil, frozen
½   cup (113 grams) cold unsalted butter, cubed
Heavy whipping cream, for brushing
Garnish: coconut sugar

1. In a small saucepan, bring coconut milk and tea to a boil over medium-high heat. Remove from heat, and stir in coconut extract. Let cool completely. Refrigerate tea-infused milk until chilled; strain, discarding solids.
2. Preheat oven to 350°F (180°C). Spread coconut flakes on a baking sheet, and bake until lightly golden brown, about 8 minutes. Transfer coconut to a bowl, and let cool completely.
3. In a large bowl, whisk together flour, granulated sugar, baking powder, and salt. Finely grate frozen coconut oil with a serrated knife into ¼-inch pieces; add to dry ingredients along with cold butter, and rub into dry ingredients quickly with your fingers until butter looks like pea-size crumbles. Stir in toasted coconut; add chilled tea milk, and stir with a fork until a dough forms. Transfer dough to a lightly floured surface, and pat into a 9-inch circle, about 1 inch thick. Cut into 8 wedges, and transfer to a parchment paper-lined baking sheet. Freeze for at least 1 hour or up to 1 week.
4. Preheat oven to 350°F (180°C).
5. Brush top of frozen scones with cream, and sprinkle each with a hefty pinch of coconut sugar, if desired.
6. Bake until risen and deep golden brown, 25 to 35 minutes.

Photo by Mason + Dixon

CLASSIC SODA BREAD

Makes 1 (8-inch) boule

A traditional take on quick bread, this recipe is brought to life by buttermilk and baking soda. These two ingredients combine to create a crunchy crust and a subtle tartness that's definitely mouthwatering.

6   cups (750 grams) plus 1 teaspoon (3 grams) all-purpose flour, divided
¼   cup (50 grams) granulated sugar
2   teaspoons (10 grams) baking soda
1½   teaspoons (4.5 grams) kosher salt
2   cups (256 grams) raisins
2⅓   cups (560 grams) whole buttermilk
¼   cup (57 grams) unsalted butter, melted

1. Preheat oven to 425°F (220°C). Butter and flour an 8-inch round tall-sided cake pan.

2. In a large bowl, whisk together 6 cups (750 grams) flour, sugar, baking soda, and salt. Stir in raisins. Gradually add buttermilk and melted butter, stirring just until dry ingredients are moistened. Knead dough just until ingredients are combined.

3. On a lightly floured surface, shape dough into a ball. Press into prepared pan. Sprinkle with remaining 1 teaspoon (3 grams) flour. With a sharp knife, score a shallow "X" on top of dough.

4. Bake until golden brown and a wooden pick inserted in center comes out clean, 45 to 50 minutes, loosely covering with foil halfway through baking to prevent excess browning, if necessary. Let cool in pan for 10 minutes.

Note: *Dough will rise 1 to 1½ inches above the rim of the cake pan while baking.*

WALNUT GOLDEN RAISIN SODA BREAD

Makes 1 (10-inch) boule

Earthy walnuts and sweet golden raisins add texture and a hint of sweetness to this classic, which gets extra depth from whole wheat flour as well as sunflower and pumpkin seeds.

4½ cups (563 grams) plus 1 teaspoon (3 grams)
    all-purpose flour, divided
1½ cups (195 grams) whole wheat flour
½ cup (100 grams) granulated sugar
1 tablespoon (15 grams) baking soda
2 teaspoons (6 grams) kosher salt
1½ cups (192 grams) golden raisins
1 cup (113 grams) chopped walnuts
2 cups plus 2 tablespoons (510 grams) whole buttermilk
6 tablespoons (84 grams) unsalted butter, melted
1 tablespoon (9 grams) sunflower seeds
1 teaspoon (3 grams) pumpkin seeds

1. Preheat oven to 425°F (220°C). Butter and flour a 10-inch cast-iron skillet.
2. In a large bowl, whisk together 4½ cups (563 grams) all-purpose flour, whole wheat flour, sugar, baking soda, and salt. Stir in raisins and walnuts. Gradually add buttermilk and melted butter, stirring just until dry ingredients are moistened. Gently knead dough 3 to 4 times until ingredients are combined.
3. On a lightly floured surface, shape dough into a ball. Press into prepared pan. Sprinkle with sunflower seeds, pumpkin seeds, and remaining 1 teaspoon (3 grams) all-purpose flour. With a sharp knife, score a shallow "X" on top of dough.
4. Bake until golden brown and a wooden pick inserted in center comes out clean, 35 to 40 minutes, loosely covering with foil to prevent excess browning, if necessary. Let cool in pan for 10 minutes.

ROSEMARY PARMESAN SODA BREAD

Makes 1 (8-inch) boule

The divine pairing of fresh Parmesan and rosemary strikes a perfect balance between the simple ingredients and deliciously complex flavors in this savory take on tradition.

4½ cups (563 grams) all-purpose flour
2 tablespoons (24 grams) granulated sugar
4 teaspoons (2.5 grams) chopped fresh rosemary
2 teaspoons (6 grams) kosher salt
1½ teaspoons (7.5 grams) baking soda
¼ teaspoon ground black pepper
1¼ cups (125 grams) grated Parmesan cheese
1¾ cups (420 grams) whole buttermilk
¼ cup (57 grams) unsalted butter, melted
1 large egg (50 grams)
1½ teaspoons (4.5 grams) flaked sea salt

1. Preheat oven to 425°F (220°C). Line a rimmed baking sheet with parchment paper.
2. In a large bowl, whisk together flour, sugar, rosemary, salt, baking soda, and pepper. Stir in cheese.
3. In a medium bowl, whisk together buttermilk, melted butter, and egg. Gradually add buttermilk mixture to flour mixture, stirring just until dry ingredients are moistened. Knead dough just until ingredients are combined.
4. On a lightly floured surface, shape dough into a ball. Place on prepared pan, pressing to flatten dough into a 7-inch circle, 1½ inches thick. With a sharp knife, score a shallow "X" on top of dough. Sprinkle with flaked salt.
5. Bake until golden brown and a wooden pick inserted in center comes out clean, 35 to 40 minutes, loosely covering with foil to prevent excess browning, if necessary. Let cool on pan for 10 minutes.

APPLE GUINNESS CHEDDAR SODA BREAD

Makes 1 (10x5-inch) loaf

It's a given: You can't have Irish soda bread without Guinness. Along with incorporating the signature dry stout, this recipe pairs the earthy tang of sharp Cheddar cheese with the tart crunch of Granny Smith apples.

½	cup (110 grams) plus 2 tablespoons (28 grams) firmly packed light brown sugar, divided
1½	tablespoons (22.5 grams) apple cider vinegar
1¾	cups (324 grams) finely chopped Granny Smith apple
4	cups (500 grams) plus 1 teaspoon (3 grams) all-purpose flour, divided
2¼	teaspoons (11.25 grams) baking soda
1½	teaspoons (4.5 grams) kosher salt
1½	cups (150 grams) finely shredded sharp Cheddar cheese
1	cup (240 grams) Guinness beer
⅓	cup (76 grams) unsalted butter, melted
¼	cup (60 grams) whole buttermilk
2	teaspoons (4 grams) old-fashioned oats

1. Preheat oven to 425°F (220°C). Butter and flour a 10x5-inch loaf pan.

2. In a medium bowl, whisk together 2 tablespoons (28 grams) brown sugar and vinegar. Stir in apple, and let stand for 5 minutes.

3. In a large bowl, whisk together 4 cups (500 grams) flour, baking soda, salt, and remaining ½ cup (110 grams) brown sugar. Stir in apple mixture and cheese. Gradually add beer and melted butter. Stir in buttermilk just until dry ingredients are moistened. Gently knead dough 3 to 4 times until ingredients are combined.

4. Shape dough into a log, and press into prepared pan. With a sharp knife, score a shallow line on top of dough. Sprinkle with oats and remaining 1 teaspoon (3 grams) flour.

5. Bake until golden brown and a wooden pick inserted in center comes out clean, 45 to 50 minutes, loosely covering with foil halfway through baking to prevent excess browning, if necessary. Let cool in pan for 10 minutes.

PRO TIP

The apple cider vinegar keeps your apples from turning red during the baking process. It also reacts with baking soda, creating carbon dioxide and giving your bread extra rise.

BIRTHDAY CAKE SCONES WITH VANILLA GLAZE

Makes 8

Recipe by Kevin Masse

This scone recipe combines all the flavors of a traditional vanilla birthday cake into a form that is completely socially acceptable to eat in the morning. These scones come together rather quickly. Cutting the butter into the dry ingredients provides a flakier structure than your typical scone. Prefer a less sweet scone? Omit the glaze, and serve warm.

3 cups (375 grams) all-purpose flour
¼ cup (50 grams) plus 1 teaspoon (4 grams) granulated sugar, divided
2½ teaspoons (12.5 grams) baking powder
1 teaspoon (3 grams) kosher salt
1 cup (227 grams) cold unsalted butter, cubed
1 cup (240 grams) plus 1 tablespoon (15 grams) whole milk, divided
1 tablespoon (13 grams) clear vanilla extract
1 teaspoon (4 grams) almond extract
½ cup (90 grams) rainbow sprinkles
Vanilla Glaze (recipe follows)
Garnish: rainbow sprinkles

1. Preheat oven to 375°F (190°C). Line a rimmed baking sheet with parchment paper.
2. In a large bowl, whisk together flour, ¼ cup (50 grams) sugar, baking powder, and salt. Using a pastry blender, cut in cold butter until mixture is crumbly. Make a well in center of flour mixture; add 1 cup (240 grams) milk and extracts. Using a wooden spoon, stir until a shaggy dough forms. Add sprinkles, and stir to combine.
3. Turn out dough onto a heavily floured surface, and knead for 1 minute. Pat dough into a 9-inch circle, about 1 inch thick. Cut into 8 wedges. Transfer to prepared pan. Brush with remaining 1 tablespoon (15 grams) milk, and sprinkle with remaining 1 teaspoon (4 grams) sugar.
4. Bake until lightly golden, about 30 minutes. Let cool on pan for 10 minutes. Remove from pan, and let cool completely on a wire rack. Drizzle with Vanilla Glaze, and garnish with extra sprinkles, if desired.

VANILLA GLAZE
Makes ¼ cup

½ cup (60 grams) confectioners' sugar
1 tablespoon (15 grams) whole milk
½ teaspoon (2 grams) clear vanilla extract
¼ teaspoon kosher salt

1. In a small bowl, whisk together all ingredients until smooth. Glaze should form a sturdy ribbon when drizzled from a spoon.

RAINBOW SPRINKLE BREAD WITH BIRTHDAY CAKE CRUMB TOPPING

Makes 1 (9x5-inch) loaf

Recipe by Kevin Masse

To say that I love cake is an understatement—I could eat it every day. Baked in a loaf pan like banana bread, this Rainbow Sprinkle Bread will bring to life all the flavors you remember from childhood birthday parties. You may not need to use all the crumb topping, but I'll let you in on a little secret: It keeps well in the refrigerator for a few days and makes a tremendous topping for vanilla ice cream.

1	cup (227 grams) unsalted butter, softened
1½	cups (300 grams) granulated sugar
4	large eggs (200 grams)
1	large egg yolk (19 grams)
1	tablespoon (13 grams) clear vanilla extract*
2	cups (250 grams) all-purpose flour
½	teaspoon (1.5 grams) kosher salt
⅓	cup (60 grams) rainbow sprinkles**
	Birthday Cake Crumb Topping (recipe follows)

1. Preheat oven to 325°F (170°C). Butter and flour a 9x5-inch loaf pan; line with parchment paper, letting excess extend over sides of pan. Butter and flour again.
2. In the bowl of a stand mixer fitted with the paddle attachment, beat butter and sugar at medium speed until fluffy, 3 to 4 minutes, stopping to scrape sides of bowl. Add eggs and egg yolk, one at a time, beating well after each addition. Beat in vanilla.
3. In a medium bowl, whisk together flour and salt. With mixer on low speed, gradually add flour mixture to butter mixture, beating just until combined. Stir in sprinkles. Pour batter into prepared pan. Sprinkle with half (90 grams) of Birthday Cake Crumb Topping.
4. Bake until golden brown and a wooden pick inserted in center comes out clean, about 1 hour and 10 minutes. Let cool in pan for 10 minutes. Using excess parchment as handles, remove loaf from pan, and let cool completely on a wire rack. Store in an airtight container for up to 3 days.

*Clear vanilla extract actually makes a difference in the color of the bread.

**We used Betty Crocker Rainbow Sprinkles (10.5-ounce container). These sprinkles' colors don't bleed when stirred into the cake batter.

BIRTHDAY CAKE CRUMB TOPPING
Makes about ¾ cup

¼	cup (31 grams) all-purpose flour
¼	cup (50 grams) granulated sugar
⅛	teaspoon kosher salt
2	tablespoons (28 grams) cold unsalted butter, cubed
⅓	cup (60 grams) rainbow sprinkles**
½	teaspoon (2 grams) clear vanilla extract

1. In a large bowl, whisk together flour, sugar, and salt. Using your fingers, work in cold butter until mixture has a sandy texture. Add sprinkles and vanilla, and mix with your fingers until small pebble-size crumbs remain. Refrigerate for up to 3 days.

ZUCCHINI BANANA BREAD

Makes 1 (9x5-inch) loaf

Zucchini brings extra moisture to this classic quick bread, making for a more tender crumb than you'd find in standard banana bread. A medley of warm spices complement both the banana and summer squash beautifully.

½   cup (113 grams) unsalted butter, softened
¾   cup (150 grams) granulated sugar
2   large eggs (100 grams)
2   cups (250 grams) all-purpose flour
1   teaspoon (5 grams) baking powder
1   teaspoon (5 grams) baking soda
1   teaspoon (3 grams) kosher salt
½   teaspoon (1 gram) ground cinnamon
¼   teaspoon ground nutmeg
1½   cups (341 grams) mashed ripe banana (about 3 medium bananas)
1   cup (110 grams) grated zucchini
1   teaspoon (4 grams) vanilla extract
1   banana (124 grams), halved lengthwise
1   teaspoon (5 grams) produce protector*
1   teaspoon (5 grams) water

1. Preheat oven to 350°F (180°C). Butter and flour bottom of a 9x5-inch loaf pan.
2. In the bowl of a stand mixer fitted with the paddle attachment, beat butter and sugar at medium speed until fluffy, 3 to 4 minutes, stopping to scrape sides of bowl. Add eggs, one at a time, beating well after each addition.
3. In a medium bowl, whisk together flour, baking powder, baking soda, salt, cinnamon, and nutmeg. With mixer on low speed, gradually add flour mixture to butter mixture, beating just until combined. Beat in mashed banana, zucchini, and vanilla. Spoon batter into prepared pan, smoothing top with an offset spatula. Place banana halves, cut side up, on top of batter.
4. In a small bowl, combine produce protector and 1 teaspoon (5 grams) water. Brush mixture on cut side of bananas to retain color.
5. Bake until a wooden pick inserted in center comes out clean, about 1 hour and 10 minutes. Let cool in pan for 10 minutes. Remove from pan, and let cool completely on a wire rack. Store in an airtight container at room temperature for up to 3 days.

*We used Ball Fruit-Fresh Produce Protector.

PRO TIP
If using zucchini out of season, gently press grated zucchini with paper towels to soak up excess moisture before using.

PUMPKIN BREAD WITH CONCORD GRAPE JAM AND DRUNKEN FIGS

Makes 8 to 10 servings

Recipe by Kate Jacoby

In the Philadelphia region, figs and grapes are the strawberry-rhubarb bedfellows of the early fall. Kate revisits the flavor combination every year in this vegan treat of warm, moist pumpkin bread made with vegan butter and vegetable shortening. Cooking the figs down with Madeira creates a syrupy compote that contrasts perfectly with the Concords' zingy acid.

1   cup (175 grams) whole pitted dried dates
1   cup (240 grams) warm water (105°F/40°C to 110°F/43°C)
3   cups (375 grams) all-purpose flour
2   teaspoons (10 grams) baking powder
½   teaspoon (1.5 grams) kosher salt
½   teaspoon (1 gram) ground cinnamon
¼   teaspoon ground allspice
¼   teaspoon ground cloves
1   cup (200 grams) granulated sugar
½   cup (110 grams) firmly packed light brown sugar
¼   cup plus 2 tablespoons (85 grams) vegan butter, softened
¼   cup (57 grams) all-vegetable shortening, softened
1   cup (244 grams) canned pumpkin
Concord Grape Jam (recipe follows)
Drunken Figs (recipe follows)

1. Preheat oven to 350°F (180°C). Line a 13x9-inch baking pan with parchment paper.
2. In a medium bowl, soak dates in 1 cup (240 grams) warm water for 5 minutes.
3. In a large bowl, whisk together flour, baking powder, salt, cinnamon, allspice, and cloves. Set aside.
4. In the work bowl of a food processor, place sugars, vegan butter, and shortening; pulse until combined. Add pumpkin, dates, and soaking water; pulse until well combined. (Some chunks of dates will remain.) Add pumpkin mixture to flour mixture, whisking until combined. Spoon batter into prepared pan.
5. Bake until a wooden pick inserted in center comes out clean, 30 to 45 minutes. Let cool completely. To serve, place slices of pumpkin bread on top of a generous smear of Concord Grape Jam. Top with Drunken Figs.

> **PRO TIP**
> Just like when working with regular butter, it's important to start with softened vegan butter. This helps it incorporate more easily in the dry ingredients, preventing overmixing.

CONCORD GRAPE JAM

Makes 1½ cups

2   cups (180 grams) Concord grapes
½   cup (100 grams) granulated sugar
½   cup (120 grams) Concord grape juice
1   teaspoon (1 gram) agar powder
1   teaspoon (5 grams) sherry vinegar
½   teaspoon (2 grams) vanilla extract
⅛   teaspoon kosher salt

1. In the container of a blender, purée grapes. Strain into a medium saucepan, discarding solids. Add all remaining ingredients, and bring to a boil over medium heat. Cook for 5 minutes, whisking frequently. Let cool completely before serving.

DRUNKEN FIGS

Makes 2 pints

2   pints (600 to 700 grams) ripe or preserved figs, stemmed, quartered, and drained (if preserved)
¼   cup (55 grams) firmly packed brown sugar
¼   cup (85 grams) agave syrup
¼   cup (60 grams) Madeira wine
1   teaspoon (4 grams) vanilla extract
¼   teaspoon kosher salt

1. Preheat oven to 400°F (200°C).
2. In a medium bowl, gently toss figs with all remaining ingredients. Arrange on a baking sheet.
3. Bake until figs start to caramelize, 12 to 15 minutes. Let cool slightly.

STRAWBERRY CUCUMBER BREAD

Makes 1 (9x5-inch) loaf

Ripe strawberries and fresh cucumbers are stirred into the batter to create a bread that's light enough for a morning snack but sweet enough to be an afternoon treat.

½ cup (160 grams) strawberry preserves
1 tablespoon (8 grams) cornstarch
1 tablespoon (15 grams) fresh lemon juice
½ cup (113 grams) clarified butter, softened
1 cup (200 grams) granulated sugar
2 large eggs (100 grams)
1 teaspoon (4 grams) vanilla extract
¼ teaspoon (1 gram) almond extract
2 cups (250 grams) all-purpose flour
1 teaspoon (5 grams) baking powder
½ teaspoon (2.5 grams) baking soda
½ teaspoon (1.5 grams) kosher salt
2 cups (250 grams) grated and well-drained cucumber
½ cup (57 grams) chopped walnuts
½ cup (85 grams) sliced fresh strawberries, divided

1. In a small saucepan, cook strawberry preserves, cornstarch, and lemon juice over medium heat until slightly thickened, about 5 minutes. Let cool completely.

2. Preheat oven to 325°F (170°C). Butter and flour a 9x5-inch loaf pan.

3. In the bowl of a stand mixer fitted with the paddle attachment, beat clarified butter and sugar at medium speed until fluffy, 3 to 4 minutes, stopping to scrape sides of bowl. Add eggs, one at a time, beating well after each addition. Beat in extracts.

4. In a medium bowl, whisk together flour, baking powder, baking soda, and salt. With mixer on low speed, gradually add flour mixture to butter mixture, beating just until combined. Stir in cucumber, walnuts, and ¼ cup (42.5 grams) strawberries. Spoon half of batter into prepared pan; top with strawberry preserves mixture. Add remaining batter, and top with remaining ¼ cup (42.5 grams) strawberries.

5. Bake until a wooden pick inserted in center comes out clean, 1 hour to 1 hour and 15 minutes. Let cool in pan for 10 minutes. Remove from pan, and let cool completely on a wire rack. Wrap and store at room temperature for up to 1 week.

ITALIAN PLUM-AND-PARMESAN SCONES

Makes 8

Recipe by Marian Cooper Cairns

Italian plums are most commonly associated with their dried counterpart prunes, but they are great for baking thanks to a concentrated sweetness and easy-to-remove pit. Prepare for some magic as these scones bake—the yellow-fleshed plums turn a hot fuchsia.

2½ cups (313 grams) all-purpose flour
¾ cup (75 grams) freshly grated Parmigiano-Reggiano cheese
3 tablespoons (36 grams) granulated sugar
1 tablespoon (15 grams) baking powder
1 teaspoon (3 grams) kosher salt
½ teaspoon (1 gram) ground black pepper
½ cup (113 grams) cold unsalted butter, cubed
1¼ cups (219 grams) finely chopped Italian plums
½ cup (120 grams) heavy whipping cream
½ cup (120 grams) whole buttermilk
1 large egg (50 grams), well beaten
½ cup (113 grams) unsalted butter, softened
3 tablespoons (63 grams) honey

1. Preheat oven to 425°F (220°C). Line a baking sheet with parchment paper.
2. In a large bowl, stir together flour, cheese, sugar, baking powder, salt, and pepper. Using a pastry blender, cut in cold butter until mixture is crumbly. Freeze for 15 minutes.
3. Fold plums into flour mixture. Add cream and buttermilk, stirring with a fork just until dry ingredients are moistened. Gather mixture together, and gently knead into a ball.
4. Turn out dough onto prepared pan, and pat into an 8-inch circle. Cut into 8 wedges; gently separate wedges about ½ inch apart. Brush with egg. Sprinkle with additional cheese and pepper, if desired.
5. Bake until golden and centers are firm, 22 to 25 minutes. Let cool on a wire rack for 10 minutes.
6. In a small bowl, stir together butter and honey. Season with salt and pepper to taste. Serve scones warm with butter mixture.

Photo by Matt Armendariz

CARAMELIZED ONION, POLENTA, AND FRESH HERB OLIVE OIL LOAF

Makes 1 (9x5-inch) loaf

This savory edition of our olive oil cake uses polenta to create a distinctly chewy texture similar to cornbread. Sweet caramelized onions and a bouquet of fresh herbs—rosemary, sage, and thyme—make this aromatic loaf a perfect accompaniment to dinner.

1	tablespoon (14 grams) unsalted butter
1	pound (455 grams) sweet yellow onions, sliced ¼ inch thick
1	tablespoon (15 grams) white balsamic vinegar
4	large eggs (200 grams)
¾	cup (168 grams) extra-virgin olive oil
¾	cup (180 grams) whole milk
2¼	cups (281 grams) all-purpose flour
⅓	cup (50 grams) fine-ground polenta
1	tablespoon (2 grams) chopped fresh thyme
1	tablespoon (2 grams) chopped fresh rosemary
1	tablespoon (2 grams) chopped fresh sage
2¼	teaspoons (11.25 grams) baking powder
1	teaspoon (3 grams) kosher salt
½	teaspoon (1 gram) ground black pepper

Crème fraîche, to serve
Garnish: extra-virgin olive oil, ground black pepper

1. Preheat oven to 350°F (180°C). Butter and flour a 9x5-inch loaf pan.

2. In a medium skillet, heat butter over medium heat. Add onions; cook until translucent and softened, about 10 minutes. Reduce heat to low, and cook until onions turn a very dark golden-brown color, about 2 hours, stirring every 10 minutes the first hour and every 5 minutes the second hour. (Be careful not to let onions burn.) When nearing the end of the second hour, stir and scrape any browned bits from bottom of pan. Increase heat to medium, and stir in vinegar, scraping browned bits from bottom of pan. Stir onions, and set aside to let cool.

3. Place eggs in the bowl of a stand mixer fitted with the whisk attachment. With mixer on high speed, add oil in a slow, steady stream until combined. Add milk, beating until combined.

4. In a medium bowl, whisk together flour, polenta, thyme, rosemary, sage, baking powder, salt, and pepper. With mixer on low speed, gradually add flour mixture to egg mixture, beating until combined. Fold in caramelized onions. Pour batter into prepared pan.

5. Bake until a wooden pick inserted in center comes out clean, 50 to 55 minutes. Let cool in pan for 5 minutes. Remove from pan, and let cool completely on a wire rack. Serve with crème fraîche, and garnish with a drizzle of olive oil and a sprinkle of pepper, if desired. Store at room temperature wrapped in foil.

SPICED CRANBERRY SCONES

Makes 16

Recipe by Rebecca Firth

These moist, tender scones are a great make-ahead holiday breakfast. Simply prepare all the way up until pre-bake, freeze for 1 hour, wrap tightly in plastic wrap, and store in a resealable plastic bag in the freezer. When ready to brunch, take directly from the freezer to the oven, and bake as instructed, adding a few extra minutes of bake time.

1   cup (170 grams) fresh or frozen cranberries*, chopped
3   tablespoons (32 grams) minced candied ginger
½   cup (100 grams) plus 2 tablespoons (24 grams) granulated sugar, divided
1   teaspoon (2 grams) Chinese five-spice powder
½   teaspoon (1 gram) ground cinnamon
2½   cups (313 grams) all-purpose flour
2   tablespoons (30 grams) baking powder
½   teaspoon (1.5 grams) kosher salt
½   cup (113 grams) cold unsalted butter, cubed
¾   cup (180 grams) heavy whipping cream, chilled
1   large egg (50 grams)
1   tablespoon (6 grams) tangerine zest
Tangerine Glaze (recipe follows)

1. In a small bowl, toss together cranberries, ginger, 2 tablespoons (24 grams) sugar, five-spice powder, and cinnamon. Set aside.
2. In a large bowl, whisk together flour, baking powder, salt, and remaining ½ cup (100 grams) sugar. Using a pastry blender, cut in cold butter until mixture is crumbly.
3. In a small bowl, whisk together cream, egg, and zest. Drizzle cream mixture over dough, and stir with a fork until a craggy ball forms. Add cranberry mixture, gently folding and pressing until distributed throughout. (If it's dry outside, you'll have some flour remaining in the bottom of the bowl; conversely, if it's humid, you may need a touch extra flour to keep the dough from being too sticky.)
4. On a lightly floured surface, turn out dough, and cut into quarters. With lightly floured hands, pat each quarter into a disk, about ¾ inch thick. Make sure sides of each disk are straight, forming 90-degree angles. Place disks on 2 large parchment-covered baking sheets, and freeze for 20 minutes.

5. Preheat oven to 400°F (200°C), and place rack in top third of oven.
6. Using a very sharp knife, cut each disk into 4 petite scones. Place 2 inches apart on baking sheets.
7. Bake for 13 to 16 minutes. Let cool on pans for 5 minutes. Drizzle cooled scones with Tangerine Glaze.

*If using frozen cranberries, thaw and drain well before folding into batter.

TANGERINE GLAZE
Makes about ¾ cup

1½   cups (180 grams) confectioners' sugar
1   tablespoon (6 grams) tangerine zest
2   tablespoons (30 grams) fresh tangerine juice
1 to 2 tablespoons (15 to 30 grams) whole milk

1. In a small bowl, whisk together confectioners' sugar and tangerine zest and juice until smooth. Add milk, 1 tablespoon (15 grams) at a time, until desired consistency is reached.

Photo by Joe Schmelzer

HONEY TEA LOAVES

Makes 4 mini loaves

This wholesome bread packs a subtle sweetness, making it perfect for breakfast or an afternoon snack. Substitute apple cider for bourbon for an even richer flavor.

2 cups (350) chopped dried Calimyrna figs
1⅓ cups (449 grams) honey, divided
⅓ cup (80 grams) plus ¼ cup (60 grams) bourbon, divided
½ cup (113 grams) unsalted butter
⅓ cup (67 grams) granulated sugar
3 large eggs (150 grams)
5 cups (625 grams) cake flour
2 teaspoons (10 grams) baking powder
½ teaspoon (1.5 grams) kosher salt
¾ cup (180 grams) whole milk, divided
1¼ cups (150 grams) confectioners' sugar, sifted
1 cup (175 grams) sliced dried Calimyrna figs

1. In a medium saucepan, heat chopped figs, ⅓ cup (113 grams) honey, and ⅓ cup (80 grams) bourbon over medium heat until mixture begins to simmer. Remove from heat. Let stand until cool, about 30 minutes.
2. Preheat oven to 350°F (180°C). Butter and flour 4 (4½x2½-inch) mini loaf pans.
3. In the bowl of a stand mixer fitted with the paddle attachment, beat butter and granulated sugar at medium speed for 5 to 10 seconds. With mixer running, slowly add remaining 1 cup (336 grams) honey, beating until combined. Add eggs, one at a time, beating just until combined after each addition.
4. In a large bowl, whisk together flour, baking powder, and salt. With mixer on low speed, gradually add flour mixture to butter mixture alternately with ½ cup (120 grams) milk, beginning and ending with flour mixture, beating just until combined after each addition. Spoon half of batter into prepared

pans; top with fig mixture. Spoon remaining batter over fig mixture.
5. Bake until golden brown and a wooden pick inserted in center comes out clean, about 35 minutes. Let cool in pans for 10 minutes. Run a knife around edges of loaves to loosen. Remove from pans, and let cool completely on a wire rack.
6. In a medium bowl, whisk together confectioners' sugar and remaining ¼ cup (60 grams) milk until smooth. Drizzle glaze over loaves.
7. In a small bowl, place sliced figs. In a small saucepan, heat remaining ¼ cup (60 grams) bourbon over medium heat until hot. Pour hot bourbon over sliced figs. Cover and let cool. Garnish cakes with bourbon figs, if desired. Wrap and freeze loaves for up to 2 weeks.

YEAST BREADS

Yeast-raised breads harken back to the baking of our ancestors. Featuring holiday wreath breads, voluminous cinnamon rolls, and hot cross buns, our recipes made with the timeless leavening agent merge ancient practice with modern technique.

CLASSIC HOT CROSS BUNS

Makes 12

Soft and pillowy with just the right amount of sweetness and spice—one bite into this classic and it will be in heavy rotation at your house, no matter what time of year.

1⅔ cups (213 grams) raisins
¾   cup (180 grams) warm apple juice (180°F/82°C to 185°F/85°C)
Hot Cross Buns Dough (recipe below)
1   large egg (50 grams)
1   tablespoon (15 grams) whole milk
1   cup (125 grams) all-purpose flour
6   tablespoons (90 grams) water
Golden Syrup (recipe follows)

1. In a large bowl, combine raisins and warm apple juice. Cover with plastic wrap, and let stand for 20 minutes. Strain, discarding excess liquid.
2. Prepare Hot Cross Buns Dough as directed through Step 2. Stir in raisins, and continue as directed.

3. Spray a 13x9-inch rimmed baking sheet with cooking spray. Lightly punch down dough, and let rest for 5 minutes. On a lightly floured surface, turn out dough. Divide dough into 12 pieces, and roll each piece into a ball. Place on prepared pan. Cover and let stand in a warm, draft-free place (75°F/24°C) until puffed and rolls are touching, about 30 minutes.
4. Preheat oven to 375°F (190°C).
5. In a small bowl, whisk together egg and milk. Brush tops of rolls with egg mixture.
6. In a medium bowl, stir together flour and 6 tablespoons (90 grams) water, 2 tablespoons (30 grams) at a time, until a thick paste forms. Using a pastry bag fitted with a Wilton #10 piping tip, pipe paste over top of buns to form a cross over each.
7. Bake until golden brown, 20 to 25 minutes. Brush warm rolls with Golden Syrup.

GOLDEN SYRUP
Makes 2 cups

2½ cups (500 grams) granulated sugar, divided
2   tablespoons (30 grams) room temperature water
1⅓ cups (320 grams) boiling water

1. In a medium saucepan, stir together ½ cup (100 grams) sugar and 2 tablespoons (30 grams) room temperature water. Cook over medium-high heat, without stirring, until deep amber colored. Remove from heat, and stir in 1⅓ cups (320 grams) boiling water and remaining 2 cups (400 grams) sugar. Return to medium-low heat, and simmer, without stirring, until thickened, 20 to 30 minutes. Let cool to room temperature.

Note: *This recipe makes enough syrup to use for multiple recipes. Cover and refrigerate for up to 6 months.*

HOT CROSS BUNS DOUGH
Makes 12 buns, 12 jumbo individuals, 2 (9½x5½-inch) loaves, or 1 (15-inch) round

Cinnamon, nutmeg, and allspice are the ingredient all-stars of this rich yeast dough. Soft but not sticky, sweet but not too much, this dough's best friends are flour and time.

1¼ cups (300 grams) warm whole milk (105°F/40°C to 110°F/43°C)
4½ teaspoons (14 grams) active dry yeast
½   cup (100 grams) granulated sugar, divided
5⅔ cups (709 grams) all-purpose flour, divided
1   teaspoon (3 grams) kosher salt
1   teaspoon (2 grams) ground cinnamon
¼   teaspoon ground nutmeg
¼   teaspoon ground allspice
⅓   cup (76 grams) unsalted butter, melted
2   large eggs (100 grams)

1. In the bowl of a stand mixer fitted with the paddle attachment, combine warm milk, yeast, and ¼ cup (50 grams) sugar. Let stand until mixture is foamy, about 10 minutes.
2. In a large bowl, whisk together 5⅓ cups (667 grams) flour, salt, cinnamon, nutmeg, allspice, and remaining ¼ cup (50 grams) sugar.
3. With mixer on low speed, add half of flour mixture to yeast mixture, beating just until combined. Beat in melted butter and eggs. Gradually add remaining flour mixture, beating until a soft dough forms.
4. Switch to the dough hook attachment. Beat at medium speed until smooth, about 4 minutes, adding remaining ⅓ cup (42 grams) flour as needed. (Dough should not be sticky.)
5. Spray a large bowl with cooking spray. Place dough in bowl, turning to grease top. Loosely cover and let rise in a warm, draft-free place (75°F/24°C) until doubled in size, about 1 hour.

HOW TO PIPE IT LIKE A PRO
It's time for the final touch. You want your flour paste to be stiff enough to be able to pipe in a clean line but still manageable. If the mixture is too hard to pipe, try adding a bit more water. When piping, try to keep your movements fluid to evenly pipe the lines.

RUM RAISIN HOT CROSS BUNS

Makes 12 jumbo individuals

For a more spirited take on tradition, we subbed in a punchy spiced Rum Glaze for the Golden Syrup. The aged rum and sweet almond marzipan center make this edition extra decadent.

1⅔   cups (213 grams) raisins
¾   cup (180 grams) aged rum, warmed
1   tablespoon (12 grams) granulated sugar
Hot Cross Buns Dough (recipe on page 134)
6   tablespoons (96 grams) Marzipan (recipe on page 147)
½   teaspoon (2 grams) rum extract
1   large egg (50 grams)
2   tablespoons plus 2 teaspoons (40 grams) whole milk, divided
Rum Glaze (recipe follows)
1½   cups (180 grams) confectioners' sugar

1. In a large bowl, combine raisins, warm rum, and granulated sugar. Cover with plastic wrap, and let stand for at least 40 minutes. Strain, discarding excess liquid.
2. Prepare Hot Cross Buns Dough as directed through step 2. Stir in raisins, and continue as directed.
3. Line 2 (6-cup) jumbo muffin pans with parchment paper. Lightly punch down dough, and let rest for 5 minutes.
4. In a small bowl, combine Marzipan and rum extract, kneading until smooth. Roll Marzipan into 12 (1½-teaspoon) balls. Divide dough into 12 pieces. Place one ball of Marzipan in center of each piece of dough, pinching to seal seam. Roll each piece of dough into a ball, and place in prepared muffin cups. Cover and let stand in a warm, draft-free place (75°F/24°C) until puffed, about 20 minutes.
5. Preheat oven to 375°F (190°C).
6. In a small bowl, whisk together egg and 1 tablespoon (15 grams) milk. Brush buns with egg mixture.

7. Bake until golden brown, about 20 minutes. Brush warm rolls with Rum Glaze.
8. In a medium bowl, whisk together confectioners' sugar and remaining 1 tablespoon plus 2 teaspoons (25 grams) milk, 2 teaspoons (10 grams) at a time, until a thick paste forms. Using a pastry bag fitted with a Wilton #10 piping tip, pipe paste over top of cooled buns to form a cross.

Rum Glaze
Makes ⅓ cup

⅓   cup Golden Syrup (recipe on page 134)
1   tablespoon (15 grams) spiced rum

1. In a medium saucepan, heat Golden Syrup over medium-high heat until warmed. Remove from heat, and stir in rum. Return to heat, and cook for 2 minutes, stirring constantly. Let cool to room temperature.

PRO TIP
Glazes can be made a week in advance and refrigerated in an airtight container.

CHOCOLATE CHERRY HOT CROSS BUNS

Makes 2 (9½x5½-inch) loaves

This recipe supports the claim that chocolate does, in fact, make everything better. Add in tangy dried cherries, apple juice, and a finishing touch of our just-tart-enough apricot glaze, and this chocolate twist on the hot cross bun gives a whole new meaning to the word "irresistible."

1½ cups (192 grams) dried sour cherries
⅔ cup (160 grams) apple juice
Hot Cross Buns Dough (recipe on page 134)
10 ounces (300 grams) 60% cacao chocolate, chopped
1 large egg (50 grams)
1 tablespoon (15 grams) whole milk
¾ cup (94 grams) all-purpose flour
2 tablespoons (10 grams) unsweetened cocoa powder
6 tablespoons (90 grams) water
Apricot Glaze (recipe follows)

1. In a large bowl, combine cherries and apple juice. Cover with plastic wrap, and let stand for 20 minutes. Strain, discarding excess liquid.
2. Prepare Hot Cross Buns Dough as directed through step 2. Stir in cherries, and continue as directed.
3. Preheat oven to 375°F (190°C). Butter and flour 2 (9½x5½-inch) loaf pans.
4. Lightly punch down dough, and let rest for 5 minutes. On a lightly floured surface, turn out dough. Pat dough into a 16x8-inch rectangle. Sprinkle with chocolate. Starting with one long side, roll dough into a log, pinching seam to seal. Using a serrated knife, cut log into 12 pieces. Roll each piece into a ball, concealing as much chocolate inside roll as possible. Arrange 6 rolls in each prepared pan. Cover and let stand in a warm, draft-free place (75°F/24°C) until puffed and rolls have risen three-fourths of the way up pan, about 25 minutes.
5. In a small bowl, whisk together egg and milk. Brush tops of rolls with egg mixture.

6. In a medium bowl, whisk together flour, cocoa, and 6 tablespoons (90 grams) water, 1 tablespoon (15 grams) at a time, until a thick paste forms. Using a pastry bag fitted with a Wilton #10 tip, pipe paste over top of buns to form a cross.
7. Bake until golden brown, 25 to 30 minutes. Brush warm rolls with Apricot Glaze.

APRICOT GLAZE
Makes ⅓ cup

⅓ cup (107 grams) apricot preserves
2 tablespoons (30 grams) water

1. In a small saucepan, bring preserves and 2 tablespoons (30 grams) water to a boil over medium-high heat. Reduce heat to medium-low, and cook for 2 minutes. Remove from heat, and strain, discarding solids. Let cool to room temperature.

ORANGE CURRANT HOT CROSS BUNS

Makes 1 (15-inch) round

If you love orange breakfast rolls, these tender buns are for you. Studded with tangy orange juice-soaked currants and slathered with a Honey-Orange Glaze, it's pure citrus delight.

2¼ cups (288 grams) dried currants
1¼ cups (300 grams) warm no-pulp orange juice (180°F/82°C to 185°F/85°C)
1½ cups (360 grams) warm whole milk (105°F/40°C to 110°F/43°C)
6¾ teaspoons (21 grams) active dry yeast
¾   cup (150 grams) granulated sugar, divided
10 cups (1,250 grams) all-purpose flour, divided
1½ teaspoons (4.5 grams) kosher salt
1½ teaspoons (3 grams) ground cinnamon
½   teaspoon (1 gram) ground nutmeg
½   teaspoon (1 gram) ground allspice
½   cup (113 grams) unsalted butter, melted
6   tablespoons (90 grams) freshly squeezed orange juice, strained
4   large eggs (200 grams), divided
1¾ teaspoons (3.5 grams) orange zest
1   tablespoon (15 grams) whole milk
3   tablespoons (45 grams) rose water
½   cup (120 grams) water
Honey-Orange Glaze (recipe follows)

1. In a large bowl, combine currants and warm orange juice. Cover with plastic wrap, and let stand for 20 minutes. Strain, discarding excess liquid.
2. In the bowl of a stand mixer fitted with the paddle attachment, combine warm milk, yeast, and ¼ cup (50 grams) sugar. Let stand until mixture is foamy, about 10 minutes.
3. In a large bowl, whisk together 8 cups (1,000 grams) flour, salt, cinnamon, nutmeg, allspice, and remaining ½ cup (100 grams) sugar.

4. With mixer on low speed, add half of flour mixture to yeast mixture, beating just until combined. Beat in melted butter, freshly squeezed orange juice, and 3 eggs (150 grams). Transfer dough to a large bowl, and gradually add remaining flour mixture, stirring with a spatula or a wooden spoon until a soft dough forms. (Because this is such a large amount of dough, you will need to incorporate ingredients in a larger bowl.) Stir in drained currants and zest.
5. Knead until smooth, about 8 minutes, adding up to ½ cup (63 grams) more flour as needed. (Dough should not be sticky.)
6. Spray a large bowl with cooking spray. Place dough in bowl, turning to grease top. Loosely cover and let rise in a warm, draft-free place (75°F/24°C) until doubled in size, about 1½ hours.
7. Preheat oven to 375°F (190°C). Line a 15-inch round pizza pan or stone with parchment paper, and spray with cooking spray.
8. Lightly punch down dough, and let rest for 5 minutes. On a lightly floured surface, turn out dough. Divide dough into 18 pieces, and roll each piece into a ball. Arrange balls on prepared pan in a circular pattern, leaving little space between pieces. Cover and let stand in a warm, draft-free place (75°F/24°C) until puffed and rolls are

touching, about 25 minutes. (Rolls will rise to edge of pizza stone, but will not spill over during baking.)
9. In a small bowl, whisk together milk and remaining 1 egg (50 grams). Brush tops of rolls with egg mixture.
10. In a medium bowl, stir together rose water and remaining 1½ cups (188 grams) flour. Add ½ cup (120 grams) water, 2 tablespoons (30 grams) at a time, until a thick paste forms. Using a pastry bag fitted with a Wilton #10 tip, pipe paste over top of buns to form a cross pattern.
11. Bake until golden brown, about 25 minutes. Brush warm rolls with Honey-Orange Glaze.

HONEY-ORANGE GLAZE
Makes ½ cup

½   cup (170 grams) clover honey
¼   cup (60 grams) freshly squeezed orange juice, strained

1. In a small saucepan, bring honey and orange juice to a boil over medium-high heat. Reduce heat to medium-low, and cook, stirring constantly, until slightly thickened, about 2 minutes. Let cool completely.

STRAWBERRIES AND CREAM KING CAKE

Makes about 12 servings

Strawberries and white chocolate are rolled into and spread atop this ring that you don't have to wait until Carnival season to enjoy.

King Cake Dough (recipe follows)
6   ounces (175 grams) cream cheese, softened
¼   cup (50 grams) granulated sugar
½   teaspoon (2 grams) vanilla extract
2   tablespoons (34 grams) beaten egg
½   cup (85 grams) chopped fresh strawberries
2   ounces (57.5 grams) white chocolate, chopped
¼   cup (60 grams) heavy whipping cream
¾   cup (90 grams) confectioners' sugar
2   teaspoons (10 grams) fresh lemon juice
Garnish: sliced fresh strawberries, chopped white chocolate

1. Line a large baking sheet with parchment paper.
2. On a lightly floured surface, roll King Cake Dough into a 17x16-inch rectangle.
3. In the bowl of a stand mixer fitted with the paddle attachment, beat cream cheese, granulated sugar, and vanilla at medium speed until creamy. Beat in egg until mixture is smooth. Spread cream cheese mixture in a thin layer onto dough, leaving a 1-inch border on all sides. Sprinkle with strawberries.
4. Starting with one short side, roll up dough, jelly-roll style, pinching seam to seal. Place on prepared pan, seam side down, and form into a ring, pinching ends together to seal. Cover and let rise in a warm, draft-free place (75°F/24°C) until doubled in size, about 1 hour.
5. Preheat oven to 325°F (170°C).
6. Using kitchen shears, make 8 (¼-inch-deep) cuts in top of dough.
7. Bake until golden brown, about 30 minutes, covering with foil during last 5 minutes of baking to prevent excess browning, if necessary. Remove from pan, and let cool completely on a wire rack.
8. In a small saucepan, combine chopped chocolate and cream. Cook over low heat, stirring frequently, until chocolate is melted and mixture is smooth. Remove from heat. Add confectioners' sugar and lemon juice, whisking until smooth. Drizzle over cooled cake. Garnish with strawberries and chocolate, if desired.

KING CAKE DOUGH
Makes dough for 1 king cake

⅓   cup (80 grams) warm water (105°F/40°C to 110°F/43°C)
⅓   cup (67 grams) plus ½ teaspoon (2 grams) granulated sugar, divided
1½   teaspoons (4.5 grams) active dry yeast
½   cup (120 grams) sour cream
2   large eggs (100 grams)
1   large egg yolk (19 grams)
1   teaspoon (4 grams) vanilla extract
3¼   cups (406 grams) all-purpose flour
½   teaspoon (1.5 grams) kosher salt
6   tablespoons (84 grams) unsalted butter, softened and cubed

1. In the bowl of a stand mixer fitted with the dough hook attachment, combine ⅓ cup (80 grams) warm water, ½ teaspoon (2 grams) sugar, and yeast. Let stand until mixture is foamy, about 7 minutes.
2. In a small bowl, whisk together sour cream, eggs, egg yolk, and vanilla. Add sour cream mixture to yeast mixture, and beat at low speed until combined, about 1 minute.
3. In a large bowl, whisk together flour, salt, and remaining ⅓ cup (67 grams) sugar. Add flour mixture to sour cream mixture, and beat at medium-low speed until most of dry ingredients are moistened. Increase mixer speed to medium; beat for 2 minutes. Add butter; beat until combined, about 2 minutes. Turn out dough onto a lightly floured surface (dough will be sticky), and gently knead 4 or 5 times.
4. Spray a large bowl with cooking spray. Place dough in bowl, turning to grease top. Cover and let stand in a warm, draft-free place (75°F/24°C) until doubled in size, about 1 hour and 15 minutes.

PRO TIP
To prevent dough from spreading inward, place a ball of foil coated with baking spray with flour in the center of the dough circle before baking.

CLASSIC CINNAMON ROLLS

Makes 10 to 12

The stickier, the better with this timeless treat. One of our favorite comfort foods, the recipe originated in Sweden, where they actually observe a Cinnamon Roll Day (Kanelbullens dag) on October 4, but we recommend celebrating these rolls every chance you get.

Cinnamon Roll Dough (recipe below)
¾   cup (165 grams) firmly packed light brown sugar
1   tablespoon plus 1 teaspoon (8 grams) ground cinnamon
½   cup plus 2 tablespoons (141 grams) unsalted butter, softened
1   large egg (50 grams), lightly beaten
½   cup (112 grams) cream cheese, softened
1½   tablespoons (21 grams) unsalted butter, softened
1½   cups (180 grams) confectioners' sugar
1   tablespoon (15 grams) whole milk

1. Spray a 10-inch round cake pan or a 13x9-inch sheet pan with cooking spray.
2. Lightly punch down Cinnamon Roll Dough. Cover and let stand for 5 minutes. Turn out dough onto a lightly floured surface, and roll into an 18x12-inch rectangle.
3. In a small bowl, combine brown sugar and cinnamon. Spread butter onto dough, and sprinkle with sugar mixture, leaving a ½-inch border on one long side. Brush egg over side of dough without filling.
4. Starting with one long side, roll dough into a log, pinching seam to seal. Trim ends. For round cake pan, slice into 10 rolls; for sheet pan, slice into 12 rolls. Place in prepared pan. Let rise in a warm, draft-free place (75°F/24°C) until puffed and rolls are touching, about 30 minutes.
5. Place a sheet of foil on bottom rack of oven, and preheat oven to 350°F (180°C).
6. Bake until a wooden pick inserted in center comes out clean, about 25 minutes. Let cool in pan for 10 minutes. Remove from pan.
7. In the bowl of a stand mixer fitted with the paddle attachment, beat cream cheese and butter at medium speed until creamy, 4 to 5 minutes. With mixer on low speed, gradually add confectioners' sugar, beating until fluffy. Stir in milk until combined. Spread frosting onto warm rolls.

Photo by Stephen DeVries

CINNAMON ROLL DOUGH
Makes dough for 10 to 12 rolls, 12 jumbo individual rolls, or 1 (9-inch) twist

If there were one go-with-the-flow dough, this would be it. Customize this adaptable dough to your personal preference. Simple yet forgiving, this one will become a staple in your recipe box.

1   cup (240 grams) warm whole milk (105°F/40°C to 110°F /43°C), divided
2¼   teaspoons (7 grams) active dry yeast
⅓   cup (76 grams) unsalted butter, melted
⅓   cup (67 grams) granulated sugar
¼   cup (60 grams) sour cream
1   large egg (50 grams)
4   cups (500 grams) all-purpose flour, divided
1   teaspoon (3 grams) kosher salt

1. In a medium bowl, combine ¾ cup (180 grams) warm milk and yeast. Let stand until mixture is foamy, about 10 minutes.
2. In the bowl of a stand mixer fitted with the paddle attachment, stir together melted butter, sugar, sour cream, egg, and remaining ¼ cup (60 grams) milk.
3. In a large bowl, whisk together 3⅔ cups (458 grams) flour and salt. Stir half of flour mixture into butter mixture. With mixer on low speed, add yeast mixture, beating just until combined. Beat in remaining flour mixture. Switch to the dough hook attachment. Beat at medium speed until smooth and elastic, about 4 minutes. Add remaining ⅓ cup (42 grams) flour, if needed. (Dough should not be sticky.)
4. Spray a large bowl with cooking spray. Place dough in bowl, turning to grease top. Loosely cover and let rise in a warm, draft-free place (75°F/24°C) until doubled in size, about 1 hour.

CINNAMON TWIST

Makes 1 (9-inch) twist

We gave one giant roll a showstopping twist. Using granulated sugar in place of brown sugar creates a crispier exterior while the tender interior has an elegant cinnamon swirl. Serve in slices or pull apart.

Cinnamon Roll Dough (recipe on page 140)
⅔ cup (133 grams) granulated sugar
2½ teaspoons (5 grams) ground cinnamon
½ cup (113 grams) unsalted butter, softened
1 large egg (50 grams), lightly beaten
Garnish: cinnamon sugar

1. Spray a 9-inch round cake pan with cooking spray.
2. Lightly punch down Cinnamon Roll Dough. Cover and let stand for 5 minutes. Turn out dough onto a lightly floured surface, and roll into a 21x12-inch rectangle.

3. In a small bowl, combine granulated sugar and cinnamon. Spread butter onto dough, and sprinkle with sugar mixture, leaving a ½-inch border on one long side. Brush egg over side of dough without filling.
4. Starting with one long side, roll dough into a log, pinching seam to seal. Place log seam side down on a cutting board, and cut in half lengthwise, leaving 1½ inches at top. Carefully twist dough pieces around each other, and form into a circle. Place in prepared pan, cut sides up. Let rise in a warm, draft-free place (75°F/24°C) until dough has puffed, about 30 minutes.
5. Preheat oven to 350°F (180°C).
6. Bake until a wooden pick inserted in center comes out clean, 50 to 55 minutes, covering with foil halfway through baking to prevent excess browning. Let cool in pan for 20 minutes. Remove from pan. Garnish with cinnamon sugar, if desired.

PECAN CARAMEL CINNAMON ROLLS

Makes 12 jumbo rolls

The slight saltiness of the caramel drizzle and nuttiness of the pecans complement these sweet rolls perfectly for melt-in-your-mouth, ooey-gooey goodness. Toasting the pecans adds to their crunch and deepens their flavor.

Cinnamon Roll Dough (recipe on page 140)
½ cup (110 grams) firmly packed light brown sugar
1 tablespoon (6 grams) ground cinnamon
½ cup (113 grams) unsalted butter, softened
1 cup (113 grams) pecan halves, lightly toasted and chopped
1 large egg (50 grams), lightly beaten
1 cup (200 grams) granulated sugar
¼ cup (60 grams) water
⅓ cup (80 grams) heavy whipping cream
¼ cup (57 grams) unsalted butter
1 teaspoon (4 grams) vanilla extract
½ teaspoon (1.5 grams) kosher salt

1. Spray 2 (6-cup) jumbo muffin pans with cooking spray.
2. Lightly punch down Cinnamon Roll Dough. Cover and let stand for 5 minutes. Turn out dough onto a lightly floured surface, and roll into a 20x10½-inch rectangle.
3. In a small bowl, combine brown sugar and cinnamon. Spread butter onto dough, and sprinkle with sugar mixture and pecans, leaving a ½-inch border on one long side. Brush egg over side of dough without filling.
4. Starting with one long side, roll dough into a log, pinching seam to seal. Trim ends, and slice into 12 rolls. Place in prepared muffin cups. Let rise in a warm, draft-free place (75°F/24°C) until dough has risen to just below rim of muffin cups, about 30 minutes.
5. Preheat oven to 350°F (180°C).
6. Bake until a wooden pick inserted in center comes out clean, about 25 minutes. Let cool in pans for 15 minutes. Remove from pans.
7. In a large saucepan, stir together sugar and ¼ cup (60 grams) water. Cook over medium-high heat, without stirring, until mixture is amber colored. Remove from heat, and stir in cream, butter, vanilla, and salt. (Mixture will foam.) Let cool for 5 minutes. Drizzle over warm rolls.

GREEK TSOUREKI

Makes 1 (17-inch) braid

Sharp, soft, and slightly sweet, our Tsoureki calls for mahleb—*a spice derived from ground black cherry pits. A common ingredient in many Greek breads, mahleb's distinct flavor (think slightly bitter almond and cherry) provides a perfect flavor complement to the tender, sweet dough and soft, oven-cooked eggs braided in.*

Sweet Bread Dough (recipe follows)
¼ teaspoon (1 gram) almond extract
1 tablespoon (6 grams) mahleb spice
3 cups (720 grams) boiling water
1 (1-ounce) bottle (30 grams) liquid red food coloring
1 tablespoon (15 grams) distilled white vinegar
4 large eggs (224 grams), in shell
1 teaspoon (5 grams) whole milk
1 large egg (50 grams), lightly beaten
1 teaspoon (3 grams) cumin seeds

1. Prepare Sweet Bread Dough as directed, but in step 2, beat in almond extract with eggs, and beat in mahleb spice with flour. Continue as directed.
2. Place a wire rack on top of a sheet tray lined with paper towels.

3. In a medium bowl, whisk together 3 cups (720 grams) boiling water and food coloring. Stir in vinegar. Gently lower 4 eggs (224 grams) in shell into water mixture until desired color is reached, about 2 minutes. Let dry completely on prepared rack, and refrigerate until ready to use.
4. Preheat oven to 350°F (180°C). Line a baking sheet with parchment paper, and spray with cooking spray.
5. Lightly punch down dough. Cover and let stand for 5 minutes. On a lightly floured surface, turn out dough. Divide dough into 3 equal pieces. Roll each piece into a rope about 20 inches long. Place strands vertically in front of you. Pinch 3 ends together at top. Braid ropes together until you've reached end of strands. Pinch ends together to seal. Transfer to prepared pan. Gently tuck dyed eggs between strands of dough. Cover and let stand in a warm, draft-free place (75°F/24°C) until puffed, about 30 minutes.
6. In a small bowl, whisk together milk and remaining 1 egg (50 grams). Brush dough with egg wash, avoiding eggs. Sprinkle with cumin seeds.
7. Bake until golden brown and an instant-read thermometer inserted in center registers 190°F (88°C), 40 to 45 minutes, loosely covering with foil after 30 minutes to prevent excess browning, if necessary.

SWEET BREAD DOUGH

Makes 1 (12-inch) wreath, 8 individual twists, or 1 (17-inch) braid

Raw eggs are dyed and tucked into the braids of this easily adaptable sweet bread recipe, which can be used to create many different shapes and sizes of Easter breads from around the world.

1½ cups (360 grams) warm whole milk (105°F/40°C to 110°F/43°C)
4½ teaspoons (14 grams) active dry yeast
4 large eggs (200 grams), lightly beaten
⅔ cup (133 grams) granulated sugar
2 teaspoons (6 grams) kosher salt
8¾ cups (1,094 grams) all-purpose flour, divided
1 cup (227 grams) unsalted butter, softened

1. In the bowl of a stand mixer fitted with the paddle attachment, combine warm milk and yeast. Let stand until mixture is foamy, about 10 minutes.
2. With mixer on medium speed, add eggs, sugar, and salt, beating until combined. With mixer on low speed, add 4 cups (500 grams) flour, beating until combined. Add butter, 1 tablespoon (14 grams) at a time, beating until combined. Transfer dough to a large bowl, and stir in 4 cups (500 grams) flour with a spatula or wooden spoon until combined. (Because this is such a large amount of dough, you will need to incorporate remaining flour into dough in a larger bowl.)
3. Transfer dough to a lightly floured surface, and knead until smooth and elastic, about 8 minutes, adding remaining ¾ cup (94 grams) flour as needed. (Dough should not be sticky.)
4. Spray a large bowl with cooking spray. Place dough in bowl, turning to grease top. Loosely cover and let rise in a warm, draft-free place (75°F/24°C) until doubled in size, about 1 hour.

Note: *Although some prefer to cook the eggs ahead of this process, using them raw will give a more even, vibrant color and result in a perfectly cooked egg by the time the bread is finished baking.*

KULICH

Makes 3

This tall, cylindrical Easter bread brims with flavors of cardamom, apricots, and the tang of sour cream, all topped with our lemon-tinged, made-from-scratch icing and garnished with multicolored sprinkles.

2¼ cups (540 grams) warm whole milk (105°F/40°C to 110°F/43°C)
4½ teaspoons (14 grams) active dry yeast
2¼ cups (450 grams) granulated sugar
9 large egg yolks (167 grams)
1 large egg (50 grams)
2 teaspoons (6 grams) kosher salt
1½ teaspoons (3 grams) ground cardamom
1½ teaspoons (9 grams) vanilla bean paste
12½ cups (1,563 grams) all-purpose flour, divided
2 cups (256 grams) dried apricots, finely chopped
1 cup (227 grams) unsalted butter, melted
¼ cup (60 grams) sour cream
Lemon Icing (recipe follows)
Garnish: multicolored nonpareil sprinkles

1. In the bowl of a stand mixer fitted with the paddle attachment, combine warm milk and yeast. Let stand until mixture is foamy, about 10 minutes.

2. With mixer on medium speed, add sugar, egg yolks, egg, salt, cardamom, and vanilla bean paste, beating until combined. With mixer on low speed, gradually add 6 cups (750 grams) flour, beating just until combined. Beat in apricots, melted butter, and sour cream. Transfer dough to a large bowl, and stir in 6 cups (750 grams) flour with a spatula or wooden spoon until combined. (Because this is such a large amount of dough, you will need to incorporate remaining flour into dough in a larger bowl.)

3. Transfer dough to a lightly floured surface, and knead until smooth and elastic, about 8 minutes, adding remaining ½ cup (63 grams) flour as needed. (Dough will be slightly soft and sticky, but not unmanageable.)

4. Spray a large bowl with cooking spray. Place dough in bowl, turning to grease top. Loosely cover and let stand in a warm, draft-free place (75°F/24°C) until puffed, about 2 hours.

5. Preheat oven to 350°F (180°C). Spray 3 (5¼-inch) panettone molds with cooking spray.

6. On a lightly floured surface, turn out dough. Divide dough into 3 equal pieces. Shape each piece into a ball by folding the corners of the dough into the center. Place dough, seam side down, in prepared molds. Cover and let stand in a warm, draft-free place (75°F/24°C) until slightly puffed, about 30 minutes (remaining rising will happen as it gradually bakes).

7. Cover with foil and bake until a wooden pick inserted in center comes out clean and an instant-read thermometer registers 190°F (88°C), 1 hour to 1 hour and 10 minutes. Let cool completely.

8. Spoon Lemon Icing over cooled kulichs. Garnish with sprinkles, if desired.

LEMON ICING
Makes 1⅔ cups

4 cups (480 grams) confectioners' sugar
1 teaspoon (5 grams) fresh lemon juice, strained
½ cup (120 grams) whole milk

1. In a large bowl, whisk together confectioners' sugar and lemon juice. Stir in milk, 2 tablespoons (30 grams) at a time, until desired consistency is reached.

PRO TIP
Wrap in a paper bag or loosely wrap in foil at room temperature for up to 2 days. Freezing bread is the best way to keep homemade bread fresh for longer. Wrap cooled bread tightly in plastic wrap, and freeze for up to 2 months. The same applies for our Braided Mazanec on page 147.

BRAIDED MAZANEC

Makes 2 (12-inch) braids

With amaretto-soaked golden raisins and marzipan, the Czech Republic's mazanec is an Easter bread all-star.

½	cup (120 grams) amaretto
¼	cup (60 grams) water
2	cups (256 grams) golden raisins
1¼	cups (300 grams) warm whole milk (105°F/40°C to 110°F/43°C)
4½	teaspoons (14 grams) active dry yeast
½	cup (120 grams) heavy whipping cream
¼	cup (60 grams) freshly squeezed orange juice, strained
1	cup (200 grams) granulated sugar
3	large eggs (150 grams), divided
2	large egg yolks (37 grams)
2½	teaspoons (7.5 grams) kosher salt
1½	teaspoons (3 grams) orange zest
½	teaspoon (2 grams) almond extract
9¾	cups (1,220 grams) all-purpose flour, divided
1	cup (227 grams) butter, softened
⅓	cup (87 grams) Marzipan (recipe follows), frozen and grated
1	teaspoon (5 grams) whole milk
3	tablespoons (21 grams) sliced almonds

1. In a medium saucepan, bring amaretto and ¼ cup (60 grams) water to a boil over medium-high heat. Stir in raisins; remove from heat. Cover with plastic wrap, and let stand for 30 minutes. Strain, discarding excess liquid.

2. In the bowl of a stand mixer fitted with the paddle attachment, combine warm milk and yeast. Let stand until mixture is foamy, about 10 minutes. Stir in cream and orange juice.

3. With mixer on medium speed, add sugar, 2 eggs (100 grams), egg yolks, salt, zest, and almond extract, beating until combined. With mixer on low speed, gradually add 4½ cups (563 grams) flour, beating until combined. Add butter, 1 tablespoon (14 grams) at a time, beating until combined. Stir in raisins and Marzipan. Transfer dough to a large bowl, and stir in 4½ cups (563 grams) flour with a spatula or wooden spoon until combined. (Because this is such a large amount of dough, you will need to incorporate remaining flour into dough in a larger bowl.)

4. Transfer dough to a lightly floured surface, and knead until smooth and elastic, about 8 minutes, adding remaining ¾ cup (94 grams) flour as needed. (Dough should not be sticky.)

5. Spray a large bowl with cooking spray. Place dough in bowl, turning to grease top.

Loosely cover and let rise in a warm, draft-free place (75°F/24°C) until doubled in size, about 2 hours.

6. Preheat oven to 350°F (180°C). Line 2 baking sheets with parchment paper, and spray with cooking spray.

7. Lightly punch down dough. Cover and let stand for 5 minutes. On a lightly floured surface, turn out dough. Divide dough in half. Divide one half of dough into 4 equal pieces. Roll each piece into a rope about 15 inches long. Place strands vertically in front of you. Pinch 4 ends together at top. Cross the fourth strand over the second strand, the first strand over the third strand, and the second strand over the third strand. Repeat pattern until you've reached end of strands; pinch ends together to seal. Repeat with remaining dough. Place braided loaves on prepared pans. Cover and let stand in a warm, draft-free place (75°F/24°C) until puffed, about 30 minutes.

8. In a small bowl, whisk together milk and remaining 1 egg (50 grams). Brush dough with egg wash, and sprinkle with almonds.

9. Bake until golden brown and an instant-read thermometer inserted in center registers 190°F (88°C), 45 to 50 minutes, loosely covering with foil halfway through baking to prevent excess browning, if necessary.

MARZIPAN
Makes about 1 cup

1½	cups (144 grams) almond flour
1½	cups (180 grams) confectioners' sugar
1	large egg white (30 grams)
1	teaspoon (4 grams) rum extract
3	teaspoons (12 grams) almond extract

1. In the work bowl of a food processor, combine almond flour and confectioners' sugar; pulse until combined. Add egg white, rum extract, and almond extract; process until mixture holds together. If mixture is too dry, add water, 1 teaspoon (5 grams) at a time. Refrigerate Marzipan wrapped tightly in plastic wrap for up to 1 month.

PANE DI PASQUA

Makes 1 (12-inch) wreath or 8 individual twists

This soft, slightly sweet bread with its iconic brightly colored eggs (we used blue) can be found well beyond the borders of Italy as a symbol of the season.

3 cups (720 grams) boiling water
½ teaspoon (2.5 grams) liquid royal blue food coloring
1 tablespoon (15 grams) distilled white vinegar
5 to 8 large eggs (280 to 448 grams), in shell
Sweet Bread Dough (recipe on page 145)
1 teaspoon (5 grams) whole milk
1 large egg (50 grams), lightly beaten
1½ tablespoons (13.5 grams) sesame seeds

1. Place a wire rack on top of a sheet tray lined with paper towels.
2. In a medium bowl, whisk together 3 cups (720 grams) boiling water and food coloring. Stir in vinegar. Gently lower eggs (5 [280 grams] for wreath or 8 [448 grams] for individuals) into water mixture until desired color is reached, about 1 minute. Let dry completely on prepared rack, and refrigerate until ready to use.
3. Preheat oven to 350°F (180°C).
4. Lightly punch down Sweet Bread Dough.

Cover and let stand for 5 minutes. On a lightly floured surface, turn out dough.
5. For wreath: Line a baking sheet with parchment paper, and spray with cooking spray.
6. Divide dough into 3 equal pieces. Roll each piece into a rope about 26 inches long. Place strands vertically in front of you. Pinch 3 ends together at top. Braid ropes together until you've reached end of strands. Join two ends together forming a circle, pinching ends to seal. Transfer to prepared pan. Gently tuck 5 dyed eggs between strands of dough. Cover and let stand in a warm, draft-free place (75°F/24°C) until puffed, about 30 minutes.
7. In a small bowl, whisk together milk and remaining 1 egg (50 grams). Brush dough with egg wash, avoiding eggs.
8. Bake until golden brown and an instant-read thermometer inserted in center registers 190°F (88°C), 30 to 35 minutes, loosely covering with foil to prevent excess browning, if necessary.
9. For individuals: Line 2 baking sheets with parchment paper, and spray with cooking spray.
10. Divide dough into 8 equal pieces. Divide each piece in half. Roll each piece into a rope about 12 inches long. Place 2 strands vertically in front of you. Pinch ends together at top.

Twist 2 pieces together until you've reached end of strands. Join two ends together forming a circle, pinching ends to seal. Transfer to prepared pans. Repeat with remaining dough. Place 1 dyed egg in center of each circle. Cover and let stand in a warm, draft-free place (75°F/24°C) until puffed, about 30 minutes.
11. In a small bowl, whisk together milk and remaining 1 egg (50 grams). Brush dough with egg wash, avoiding eggs. Sprinkle with sesame seeds.
12. Bake until golden brown and an instant-read thermometer inserted in center registers 190°F (88°C), 20 to 25 minutes.

PRO TIP
This bread is best eaten fresh, but to extend its shelf life, wrap in a breathable material, such as a cotton towel or brown paper bag, and store at room temperature for up to 2 days. After baking, leave dyed eggs out at room temperature for no longer than 2 hours before refrigerating or discarding. The same applies to our Greek Tsoureki on page 145.

CHEESY SCALLION PULL-APART ROLLS

Makes 16

Recipe by Yossy Arefi

These rolls are admittedly a little bit over the top and are jam-packed with cheese and springy scallions. They'd make an ideal partner to just about any soup or stew, or even your scrambled eggs in the morning. Serve these warm the day they are baked for maximum cheesy enjoyment.

¼ cup (60 grams) warm water (105°F/40°C to 110°F/43°C)
2 tablespoons (24 grams) granulated sugar
2¼ teaspoons (7 grams) active dry yeast
¾ cup (180 grams) warm whole milk (105°F/40°C to 110°F/43°C)
2 large eggs (100 grams)
4 cups (500 grams) all-purpose flour
2 teaspoons (6 grams) kosher salt
¾ cup (75 grams) sliced green onion, divided
½ cup (50 grams) (¼-inch-cubed) Cheddar cheese, divided
½ cup (50 grams) (¼-inch-cubed) Gruyère cheese, divided
5 tablespoons (70 grams) unsalted butter, softened
¼ cup (57 grams) unsalted butter, melted and cooled
½ teaspoon (1.5 grams) flaked salt
¼ teaspoon crushed red pepper

1. In the bowl of a stand mixer fitted with the dough hook attachment, combine ¼ cup (60 grams) warm water, sugar, and yeast. Let stand until mixture is foamy, about 5 minutes.

2. With mixer on medium-low speed, add warm milk and eggs to yeast mixture, beating until combined. Add flour and salt, beating until a dough forms. Add ½ cup (50 grams) green onion, ¼ cup (25 grams) Cheddar, and ¼ cup (25 grams) Gruyère, beating just until combined. Add butter, 1 tablespoon (14 grams) at a time, making sure each piece is well incorporated before adding the next. Knead until smooth and elastic, about 5 minutes. (The dough will be soft and may stick to the bowl a bit. Add a bit more flour if the dough seems very sticky.)

3. Spray a large bowl with cooking spray. Place dough in bowl, turning to grease top. Let rise in a warm, draft-free place (75°F/24°C) until doubled in size, about 1½ hours.

4. Preheat oven to 350°F (180°C). Line a baking sheet with parchment paper; place a 9-inch springform pan on baking sheet.

5. Turn out dough onto a lightly floured surface, and cut into 16 equal pieces (about 2 ounces/55 grams each). Gather corners of each piece together, and roll tightly to shape into a ball. Roll each ball in melted butter, and place in springform pan, seam side down. Loosely cover pan with a clean towel or plastic wrap, and let rise for 30 minutes. Sprinkle with remaining ¼ cup (25 grams) green onion. Top with remaining ¼ cup (25 grams) Cheddar and remaining ¼ cup (25 grams) Gruyère. Sprinkle with flaked salt and red pepper.

6. Bake until golden brown and puffed, 30 to 40 minutes. Serve warm.

Photo by Yossy Arefi

PICKLED CHERRY BOMBS

Makes 16

These little pockets of dough pack explosive flavor. Inspired by Milk Bar founder Christina Tosi's famous Bagel Bomb creation, each savory orb offers all the chew and salty, crusty goodness of a regular bagel, but with an epic epicenter: a sour pickled cherry thickly coated in rich mascarpone, cream cheese, and fried garlic.

4	cups (508 grams) bread flour
1½	cups (360 grams) warm water (105°F/40°C to 110°F/43°C)
1	tablespoon (6 grams) instant yeast
1	tablespoon (21 grams) molasses
2	teaspoons (6 grams) kosher salt
8	cups (1,920 grams) plus 1 teaspoon (5 grams) water, divided
¼	cup (60 grams) baking soda
2	tablespoons (42 grams) honey
1	tablespoon (12 grams) granulated sugar
	Pickled Cherry Cheese Balls (recipe follows)
1½	teaspoons (4.5 grams) sesame seeds
1½	teaspoons (4.5 grams) poppy seeds
1	teaspoon (3 grams) fennel seeds
1	teaspoon (2 grams) garlic salt
1	teaspoon (2 grams) diced onion flakes
½	teaspoon (1.5 gram) sea salt
1	large egg (50 grams)

1. In the bowl of a stand mixer fitted with the dough hook attachment, beat flour, 1½ cups (360 grams) warm water, yeast, molasses, and salt at medium-low speed for 10 minutes. Spray a large bowl with cooking spray. Place dough in bowl, turning to grease top. Cover with plastic wrap, and let stand in warm, draft-free place (75°F/24°C) until almost doubled in size, 1 to 1½ hours.

2. Divide dough into 16 (2-ounce) pieces, and shape into balls. Cover loosely with plastic wrap, and let rest for 30 minutes.

3. Preheat oven to 350°F (180°C). Line 2 baking sheets with parchment paper.

4. In a large stockpot, bring 8 cups (1,920 grams) water, baking soda, honey, and sugar to a boil over medium-high heat. Pull and shape dough balls into 3½-inch disks, like a pizza. Place a frozen Pickled Cherry Cheese Ball in center of each disk; bring edges up, and pinch together. Roll dough between hands to smooth out ball and ensure edges are sealed. Working with 4 balls at a time, lower balls into poaching liquid. Boil for 1 minute, turning halfway through. Transfer to prepared pans.

5. In a small bowl, whisk together sesame seeds, poppy seeds, fennel seeds, garlic salt, onion flakes, and sea salt. In another small bowl, whisk together egg and remaining 1 teaspoon (5 grams) water. Brush top of each ball with egg wash, and sprinkle with topping.

6. Bake until light golden, 20 to 25 minutes. Let cool slightly; serve warm.

PICKLED CHERRY CHEESE BALLS
Makes 16

1	tablespoon (14 grams) olive oil
½	cup (112 grams) cream cheese, softened
½	cup (112 grams) mascarpone cheese, softened
1	tablespoon (10 grams) minced garlic
½	teaspoon chopped fresh basil
½	teaspoon chopped fresh oregano
½	teaspoon chopped fresh thyme
½	teaspoon (1.5 grams) kosher salt
16	Pickled Cherries (recipe follows)

1. In a small saucepan, heat oil over medium heat. Add garlic; cook until golden, 2 to 3 minutes. Remove from heat, and let cool completely.

2. In the bowl of a stand mixer fitted with the paddle attachment, beat cream cheese, mascarpone, garlic, basil, oregano, thyme, and salt at medium speed until combined.

3. Pat Pickled Cherries dry with a paper towel. Working with one at a time, coat Pickled Cherries with cheese mixture, rolling between hands to create well-rounded balls. Freeze in an airtight container for at least 2 hours or up to 1 week.

PICKLED CHERRIES
Makes 1 quart

½	pound (225 grams) cherries, pitted
¾	cup (180 grams) distilled white vinegar
⅓	cup (67 grams) granulated sugar
½	tablespoon (4.5 grams) kosher salt
1	strip orange zest
1	cinnamon stick
½	teaspoon (1.5 gram) black peppercorns
½	teaspoon (1 gram) crushed red pepper

1. Place cherries in a 1-quart jar.

2. In a small saucepan, bring vinegar and all remaining ingredients to a boil over medium heat. Reduce heat to medium-low, and simmer for 10 minutes. Remove from heat, and let cool for 10 minutes.

3. Strain mixture through a fine-mesh sieve over cherries, discarding solids. Cherries should be completely submerged under liquid. If not completely submerged, top off with more vinegar. Let cool completely. Cover and refrigerate for at least 30 minutes and up to 1 month.

SWEET POTATO BISCUITS

Makes 9

With a hint of aromatic sage and a generous coating of honey butter, these tender biscuits will warm your soul with every bite.

2¼   cups (281 grams) all-purpose flour
1   tablespoon (15 grams) baking powder
2   teaspoons (6 grams) kosher salt
1   teaspoon (3 grams) rapid rise yeast
½   teaspoon (2.5 grams) baking soda
6   tablespoons (84 grams) cold unsalted butter, cubed
¼   cup (8 grams) chopped fresh sage
½   cup (120 grams) cold whole buttermilk
¼   cup (85 grams) golden honey
1   cup (244 grams) mashed baked sweet potato, chilled

¼   cup (55 grams) unsalted butter, melted
Honey Butter (see Pro Tip)

1. Preheat oven to 425°F (220°C). Line a baking sheet with parchment paper.
2. In a large bowl, whisk together flour, baking powder, salt, yeast, and baking soda. Using a pastry blender, cut in cold butter until mixture is crumbly. Stir in sage. In a small bowl, whisk together buttermilk and honey; stir quickly into flour mixture until combined (do not overmix). Stir in sweet potato.
3. Turn out dough onto a lightly floured surface, and knead very gently 5 or 6 times until dough comes together but is still slightly lumpy. (If dough is too sticky, work in up to ¼ cup [31 grams] more flour.)

Shape dough into a disk, and pat to 1-inch thickness. Using a 2-inch round cutter dipped in flour, cut dough, rerolling scraps as necessary. Place biscuits on prepared pan. Brush with melted butter.
4. Bake until golden brown, 12 to 15 minutes, rotating pan halfway through baking. Serve with Honey Butter.

> **PRO TIP**
> To make **Honey Butter**, in a medium bowl, stir together ½ cup (113 grams) softened unsalted butter and ¼ cup (85 grams) honey until combined. Cover and refrigerate for up to 1 week.

BISCUIT STIR-INS:

Ginger and Thyme: Substitute chopped fresh sage with 3 tablespoons (32 grams) chopped candied ginger and 1 tablespoon (2 grams) fresh thyme leaves. Proceed as directed.

Rosemary and Parmesan: Substitute chopped fresh sage with 1 tablespoon (2 grams) chopped fresh rosemary and ¼ cup (25 grams) freshly grated Parmesan cheese.

Orange and Rosemary: Substitute chopped fresh sage with 1 tablespoon (6 grams) orange zest and 1 tablespoon (2 grams) chopped fresh rosemary.

CHESTNUT, CRANBERRY, AND ROSEMARY-LAMINATED PAIN D'EPI

Makes 2 loaves

This laminated loaf will have you ditching the dinner rolls for good. Fresh rosemary and fragrant chestnuts lend warm savory notes to the buttery bread studded with sweet cranberries. The traditional Pain d'Epi shape resembles a stalk of wheat, perfect for tearing and sharing.

3⅔	cups (466 grams) plus 1¼ cups (159 grams) bread flour, divided
1¾	cups (420 grams) plus 2 teaspoons (10 grams) warm water (105°F/40°C to 110°F/43°C), divided
2⅛	teaspoons (4 grams) instant yeast, divided
6	teaspoons (18 grams) kosher salt, divided
1	teaspoon (4 grams) granulated sugar
1¼	cups (195 grams) Roasted Chestnuts (recipe on page 253), chopped
¾	cup (96 grams) dried cranberries
¾	cup (170 grams) unsalted butter, softened
2	tablespoons (4 grams) chopped fresh rosemary
1	large egg (50 grams)
2	cups (480 grams) ice water
¼	cup (56 grams) olive oil

1. In a medium bowl, combine 1¼ cups (159 grams) flour, ½ cup (120 grams) warm water, and ⅛ teaspoon yeast. Cover with plastic wrap, and let stand at room temperature for 16 hours.
2. In the bowl of a stand mixer fitted with the dough hook attachment, beat yeast mixture, 1¼ cups (300 grams) warm water, 4 teaspoons (12 grams) salt, sugar, remaining 3⅔ cups (466 grams) flour, and remaining 2 teaspoons (4 grams) yeast at medium-low speed for 6 minutes. Increase mixer speed to medium, and beat for 2 minutes. Add Roasted Chestnuts and cranberries, beating just until combined, about 1 minute. Shape dough into a ball.
3. Spray a large bowl with cooking spray. Place dough in bowl, turning to grease top. Cover with plastic wrap, and let stand in a warm, draft-free place (75°F/24°C) until doubled in size, about 1 hour.
4. Between 2 sheets of plastic wrap, shape butter into a 10x8-inch rectangle. Sprinkle with rosemary, and wrap in plastic wrap. Refrigerate for at least 20 minutes or up to 24 hours. Let stand at room temperature for 10 minutes before using.
5. Preheat oven to 400°F (200°C).

Position oven rack to lowest level, and place a large cast-iron skillet on rack. Line a baking sheet with parchment paper.
6. Freeze dough for 10 minutes. On a lightly floured surface, roll dough into a 16x10-inch rectangle. Unwrap butter block, and place in center of rectangle. Fold dough edges over to enclose butter block. Roll dough into a 24x8-inch rectangle. Fold one short side over 3 inches. Fold other short side over 9 inches, making ends meet. Fold dough in half, creating an 8x6-inch rectangle. Roll into an 18x8-inch rectangle. Fold dough into thirds, like a letter, creating an 8x6-inch rectangle. Cover with plastic wrap, and let rest for 10 minutes.
7. Roll dough into a 19x11-inch rectangle. Trim ½ inch off all sides of dough. Cut dough in half lengthwise, creating 2 (18x5-inch) rectangles. Starting at one long side, roll up 1 rectangle, pinching seam to seal. Transfer to prepared pan. Repeat with remaining dough.
8. Using kitchen scissors, make a 45-degree cut into dough 1 inch from end, leaving about ¼ inch of dough uncut. (Be careful not to cut all the way through the dough.) Lay dough piece over to one side. Make another 1-inch cut, and lay to the other side. Repeat process until you reach end of dough. Repeat with remaining loaf.
9. In a small bowl, whisk together egg and remaining 2 teaspoons (10 grams) warm water. Brush dough with egg wash. Pour 2 cups (480 grams) ice water in cast-iron skillet, and place loaves in hot oven.
10. Bake until deep golden brown, 25 to 30 minutes. Brush with oil, and sprinkle with remaining 2 teaspoons (6 grams) salt. Let cool slightly on a wire rack. Serve warm. Store in airtight container at room temperature for up to 4 days.

WHITE CHOCOLATE-TAHINI BABKA

Makes 2 (9x5-inch) loaves

Recipe by Ben Mims

Tahini and babka hail from the same area of the globe, so it's only natural to marry them together in this sweet bread, perfect for breakfast or drenched in custard for a rich bread pudding. White chocolate doesn't compete with the tahini but offers a smooth sweetness to balance the flavor while orange zest delivers brightness to the heavy, sweet dough.

4¼ cups (531 grams) all-purpose flour
½   cup (110 grams) firmly packed dark brown sugar
3½ teaspoons (7 grams) instant yeast
1   teaspoon (3 grams) kosher salt
1   teaspoon (2 grams) finely grated orange zest
½   cup (112 grams) tahini
½   cup (120 grams) warm water (120°F/49°C to 130°F/54°C)
3   large eggs (150 grams)
¾   cup (170 grams) unsalted butter, softened
Ganache Filling (recipe follows)
9   ounces (250 grams) white chocolate, cut into ½-inch pieces
Brown Sugar Syrup (recipe follows)

1. In the bowl of a stand mixer fitted with the dough hook attachment, combine flour, brown sugar, yeast, salt, and zest.
2. In a small bowl, whisk together tahini, ½ cup (120 grams) warm water, and eggs until smooth. With mixer on low speed, add tahini mixture to flour mixture, beating until dough comes together. Add butter, 1 tablespoon (14 grams) at a time, letting each tablespoon incorporate into dough before adding the next. Increase mixer speed to medium, and beat until smooth and elastic, about 10 minutes. Cover bowl with plastic wrap, and let stand in a warm, draft-free place (75°F/24°C) until doubled in size, 1½ to 2 hours.
3. Divide dough in half, and shape each half into a ball. Roll each ball into a 12x10-inch rectangle. Spread half of Ganache Filling onto each rectangle, leaving a ½-inch border on one short side. Sprinkle chocolate over Ganache Filling. Brush unfilled short side of each rectangle with water. Starting with opposite short side, roll up dough, jelly-roll style, and press edges to seal. Place logs, seam side down, on a foil-lined baking sheet. Freeze for 15 minutes.
4. Spray 2 (9x5-inch) loaf pans with cooking spray. Line pans with parchment paper.
5. Transfer 1 log to a cutting board, and cut in half lengthwise. Place 2 halves cut side up, and carefully twist dough pieces around each other, leaving cut sides up. Nestle dough twist in one prepared pan, tucking ends under if necessary. Repeat with remaining dough. Cover each loaf pan with a kitchen towel, and let stand at room temperature until dough rises to top of pans, 45 to 60 minutes.
6. Preheat oven to 350°F (180°C). Line a baking sheet with foil. Remove towels, and place loaf pans on prepared baking sheet.
7. Bake until deep golden brown on top and an instant-read thermometer inserted in center registers 190°F (88°C), 50 to 60 minutes, covering with foil to prevent excess browning after 20 minutes of baking, if necessary. Lightly drizzle warm Brown Sugar Syrup over each loaf. Let cool for 30 minutes to allow syrup to soak in completely. Remove from pans, and let cool completely on a wire rack.

GANACHE FILLING
Makes about 1½ cups

½   cup (120 grams) heavy whipping cream
⅓   cup (76 grams) unsalted butter
3   tablespoons (36 grams) granulated sugar
¼   teaspoon kosher salt
1   cup (170 grams) white chocolate morsels

1. In a small saucepan, bring cream, butter, sugar, and salt to a simmer over medium heat. Place white chocolate morsels in a medium bowl; pour hot cream over morsels. Let stand for 1 minute. Slowly whisk chocolate mixture, starting in center and working your way to edges, until smooth. Refrigerate until chilled and spreadable, at least 2 hours.

BROWN SUGAR SYRUP
Makes ⅓ cup

⅓   cup (73 grams) firmly packed light brown sugar
⅓   cup (80 grams) water

1. In a small saucepan, bring brown sugar and ⅓ cup (80 grams) water to a boil over medium heat, stirring until sugar is dissolved. Reduce heat to low, and keep warm until ready to use.

Photo by Mason + Dixon

APRICOT SWEET BUNS

Makes 12

Once a precious commodity traded on the Silk Road, jewel-hued dried apricots offer a chance to enjoy the delicately tart fruit after their notoriously short season has come and gone. We use dried apricots as the sweet golden filling of our almond-flecked sweet buns and top them off with a sticky drizzle of Brown Sugar Glaze.

1 cup (240 grams) warm whole milk (105°F/40°C to 110°F/43°C), divided
2¼ teaspoons (7 grams) active dry yeast
⅓ cup (67 grams) granulated sugar
⅓ cup (76 grams) unsalted butter, melted
¼ cup (60 grams) sour cream
1 large egg (50 grams)
1½ teaspoons (6 grams) almond extract
4 cups (500 grams) all-purpose flour, divided
1 teaspoon (3 grams) kosher salt
Apricot-Almond Filling (recipe follows)
Brown Sugar Glaze (recipe follows)

1. In a medium bowl, combine ¾ cup (180 grams) warm milk and yeast. Let stand until mixture is foamy, about 10 minutes.
2. In the bowl of a stand mixer fitted with the paddle attachment, stir together sugar, melted butter, sour cream, egg, almond extract, and remaining ¼ cup (60 grams) warm milk.
3. In a large bowl, whisk together 3⅔ cups (458 grams) flour and salt. Stir half of flour mixture into sugar mixture. With mixer on low speed, add yeast mixture, beating just until combined. Beat in remaining flour mixture. Switch to the dough hook attachment. Beat at medium speed until smooth and elastic, about 4 minutes. Add remaining ⅓ cup (42 grams) flour, if needed. (Dough should not be sticky.) Spray a large bowl with cooking spray. Place dough in bowl, turning to grease top. Loosely cover and let rise in a warm, draft-free place (75°F/24°C) until doubled in size, about 1 hour.
4. Line 2 rimmed baking sheets with parchment paper.
5. Lightly punch down dough. Cover and let stand for 5 minutes. Turn out dough onto a lightly floured surface, and roll into a 21x13-inch rectangle. Spread Apricot-Almond Filling onto dough. Fold dough in thirds, like a letter, creating a 13x7-inch rectangle. Roll dough into a 13x8-inch rectangle. Cut ½ inch off each short end of rectangle. Cut dough into 12 (1-inch) strips. Twist each strip, and tie in a knot, tucking ends under. Place on prepared pans. Cover and let rise in a warm, draft-free place (75°F/24°C) until puffed, about 30 minutes.
6. Preheat oven to 350°F (180°C).
7. Bake buns, one batch at a time, until golden brown and a wooden pick inserted in center comes out clean, 15 to 20 minutes, covering with foil halfway through baking to prevent excess browning. Brush buns with Brown Sugar Glaze. Let cool on pans for 10 minutes. Serve warm. Store in an airtight container at room temperature for up to 3 days.

APRICOT-ALMOND FILLING
Makes about 1½ cups

1 cup (128 grams) dried apricots
⅓ cup (67 grams) granulated sugar
1 tablespoon (14 grams) unsalted butter, cubed
¼ teaspoon ground cinnamon
½ cup (57 grams) sliced almonds

1. In a small saucepan, bring apricots and water to cover by 1 inch to a boil over high heat. Reduce heat to low; cook until apricots are softened, about 20 minutes. Drain apricots, reserving 2 tablespoons (30 grams) cooking liquid.
2. In the work bowl of a food processor, place warm apricots, reserved 2 tablespoons (30 grams) cooking liquid, sugar, butter, and cinnamon; pulse until mixture has the texture of jam. Stir in almonds; let cool completely. Refrigerate in an airtight container for up to 1 week.

BROWN SUGAR GLAZE
Makes about ½ cup

¼ cup (60 grams) water
¼ cup (55 grams) firmly packed light brown sugar
1 vanilla bean, split lengthwise, seeds scraped and reserved

1. In a small saucepan, bring ¼ cup (60 grams) water, brown sugar, and vanilla bean and reserved seeds to a boil over medium heat. Remove vanilla bean, and let cool completely. Refrigerate in an airtight container for up to 3 weeks.

SWISS HEFEKRANZ

Makes 1 (12-inch) wreath

For an update on this braided beauty, we turned the almond flavor up a few notches by rehydrating golden raisins and cherries in amaretto before mixing them in with the dough. We love the sour-sweetness the cherries bring and how the final dusting of confectioners' sugar looks like new fallen snow.

1   cup (240 grams) plus 1 teaspoon (5 grams) water, divided
¾   cup (96 grams) golden raisins
¾   cup (96 grams) dried cherries
½   cup (120 grams) plus 2 tablespoons (30 grams) amaretto liqueur, divided
1   tablespoon (15 grams) fresh lemon juice
6½   cups (813 grams) all-purpose flour, divided
1   cup (240 grams) warm water (115°F/46°C to 120°F/49°C)
½   cup (120 grams) warm whole milk (115°F/46°C to 120°F/49°C)
3   large eggs (150 grams), divided
¼   cup (50 grams) granulated sugar
1   tablespoon (6 grams) instant yeast
1   tablespoon (6 grams) lemon zest
2   teaspoons (6 grams) kosher salt
½   cup (113 grams) unsalted butter, softened and cubed
2   tablespoons (14 grams) sliced almonds
Garnish: confectioners' sugar

1. In a small saucepan, bring 1 cup (240 grams) water, raisins, cherries, ½ cup (120 grams) amaretto, and lemon juice to a boil over medium heat. Reduce heat, and simmer until liquid is reduced by three-fourths and fruit is plump, about 20 minutes. Drain, and let cool completely.

2. In the bowl of a stand mixer fitted with the dough hook attachment, stir together

3 cups (375 grams) flour, 1 cup (240 grams) warm water, warm milk, 2 eggs (100 grams), granulated sugar, yeast, and remaining 2 tablespoons (30 grams) amaretto. Let rest until slightly bubbly, 15 to 20 minutes.

3. With mixer on medium-low speed, add fruit mixture, zest, salt, and remaining 3½ cups (438 grams) flour, beating until combined. Add butter, a few pieces at a time, beating until combined. Increase mixer speed to medium, and beat until smooth and elastic, about 7 minutes. Spray a large bowl with cooking spray. Place dough in bowl, turning to grease top. Cover directly with plastic wrap, and let rise in a warm, draft-free place (75°F/24°C) until doubled in size, about 1 hour.

4. Line a large baking sheet with parchment paper.

5. On a lightly floured surface, divide dough into 3 equal pieces. Roll each piece into a 24-inch-long rope, and place on prepared pan. Pinch ropes together at one end to seal, and braid. Form into a circle, pinching ends to seal. Cover loosely with plastic wrap, and let stand in a warm, draft-free place (75°F/24°C) for 30 minutes.

6. Preheat oven to 350°F (180°C).

7. In a small bowl, whisk together remaining 1 teaspoon (5 grams) water and remaining 1 egg (50 grams). Brush wreath with egg wash. Sprinkle with almonds.

8. Bake until golden brown and internal temperature registers 190°F (88°C), about 40 minutes, covering with foil after 30 minutes of baking to prevent excess browning, if necessary. Let cool completely on a wire rack. Dust with confectioners' sugar, if desired. Store in an airtight container at room temperature for up to 4 days.

1. Roll each piece of dough into a 24-inch-long rope. Pinch ropes together at one end to seal. To braid, cross left strand over middle strand. Cross right strand over strand that is now in the middle.

2. Form into a circle, pinching ends to seal.

NORWEGIAN JULEKAKE

Makes 1 (12-inch) wreath

In our babka-inspired take on Julekake, we replaced the raisins with rehydrated cranberries. Instead of mixing the cranberries in with the dough, we created a sweet jam-like filling flavored with cardamom and cinnamon. The Vanilla Glaze falls over every ridge and seeps into each crevice of this updated shape.

¾ cup (180 grams) whole milk
½ cup (100 grams) granulated sugar
¼ cup (57 grams) unsalted butter, cubed and softened
1½ teaspoons (4.5 grams) kosher salt
½ cup (120 grams) warm water (105°F/40°C to 110°F/43°C)
1 tablespoon (6 grams) instant yeast
2 large eggs (100 grams)
5½ cups (688 grams) all-purpose flour
1 teaspoon (2 grams) ground cardamom
Cranberry Filling (recipe follows)
Candied Lemon Peel (recipe follows), diced
Vanilla Glaze (recipe follows)

1. In a small saucepan, bring milk to a boil over medium heat. Remove from heat; add sugar, butter, and salt, stirring until completely incorporated. Set aside until cooled to 120°F (49°C) to 130°F (54°C).
2. In the bowl of a stand mixer fitted with the dough hook attachment, combine ½ cup (120 grams) warm water and yeast. Add warm milk mixture. Stir in eggs. With mixer on low speed, add flour and cardamom, beating until combined. Increase mixer speed to medium-low, and beat until smooth and elastic, 5 to 7 minutes. Spray a large bowl with cooking spray. Place dough in bowl, turning to grease top. Cover directly with plastic wrap, and let rise in a warm, draft-free place (75°F/24°C) until doubled in size, about 1 hour.
3. Line a large baking sheet with parchment paper.
4. On a lightly floured surface, roll dough into a 24x12-inch rectangle. Spread Cranberry Filling onto dough, leaving a ½-inch border on all sides. Sprinkle with diced Candied Lemon Peel. Starting at one long side, roll up dough, jelly-roll style; press edge to seal. Place on prepared pan.

5. Using a serrated knife, cut roll in half lengthwise. With cut sides facing up, carefully twist dough pieces around each other. Form into a circle, pinching ends to seal. Cover loosely with plastic wrap, and let stand in a warm, draft-free place (75°F/24°C) for 30 minutes.
6. Preheat oven to 350°F (180°C).
7. Bake until golden brown and internal temperature registers 190°F (88°C), about 40 minutes. Let cool completely on a wire rack. Drizzle with Vanilla Glaze. Store in an airtight container at room temperature for up to 4 days.

CRANBERRY FILLING
Makes about 1½ cups

1⅓ cups (171 grams) dried cranberries
⅓ cup (67 grams) granulated sugar
1 tablespoon (14 grams) unsalted butter, cubed
½ teaspoon (1 gram) ground cardamom
¼ teaspoon ground cinnamon

1. In a small saucepan, bring cranberries and water to cover by 1 inch to a boil over high heat. Reduce heat to low, and cook until cranberries are softened, about 20 minutes. Drain cranberries, reserving 2 tablespoons (30 grams) cooking liquid.
2. In the work bowl of a food processor, place warm cranberries, reserved 2 tablespoons (30 grams) cooking liquid, sugar, butter, cardamom, and cinnamon; pulse until mixture has the texture of jam. Let cool completely.

CANDIED LEMON PEEL
Makes about ½ cup

1 lemon (99 grams)
¾ cup (180 grams) water
1¼ cups (250 grams) granulated sugar, divided

1. Peel lemon, and slice peel into ¼-inch-thick strips.
2. In a small saucepan, bring peel and water to cover by 1 inch to a boil over medium heat. Boil for 15 minutes. Drain, and rinse with cold water.
3. In same pan, bring ¾ cup (180 grams)

water and ¾ cup (150 grams) sugar to a boil over medium heat. Add peel. Reduce heat to medium-low, and simmer until peel is softened, 25 to 30 minutes. Drain.
4. Line a rimmed baking sheet with parchment paper.
5. Toss peel with remaining ½ cup (100 grams) sugar, and place on prepared pan. Let stand until dry, 1 to 2 days. Freeze in an airtight container for up to 2 months.

VANILLA GLAZE
Makes about ½ cup

1 cup (120 grams) confectioners' sugar, sifted
¼ cup (60 grams) heavy whipping cream
1 teaspoon (4 grams) vanilla extract
½ teaspoon (1.5 grams) kosher salt

1. In a small bowl, whisk together all ingredients until smooth. Use immediately.

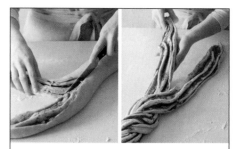

1. Using a serrated knife, cut roll in half lengthwise. With cut sides facing up, twist dough pieces around each other.

2. Form into a circle, pinching ends to seal.

FINNISH JOULULIMPPU

In our wreath-shaped pain d'epi Joululimppu, we used Grand Marnier-rehydrated raisins and molasses in place of the treacle that the traditional recipe calls for. You'll go crazy for the sweet crust brushed with our sticky orange-molasses glaze after baking. We suggest serving warm with some softened salted butter.

¾   cup (96 grams) dark raisins
⅓   cup (80 grams) water
⅓   cup (80 grams) Grand Marnier
2   tablespoons (30 grams) plus 1 teaspoon
       (5 grams) fresh orange juice, divided
¼   cup (85 grams) plus 2 tablespoons
       (42 grams) molasses, divided
1   teaspoon (3 grams) fennel seeds,
       crushed
½   teaspoon (1.5 grams) caraway seeds,
       crushed
1¼ cups (300 grams) whole milk
2¾ cups (344 grams) all-purpose flour
1½ cups (153 grams) rye flour
1   tablespoon (6 grams) instant yeast
1   teaspoon (3 grams) kosher salt
¼   cup (57 grams) unsalted butter,
       softened and cubed
½   cup (85 grams) diced Candied Orange
       Peel (recipe on page 162)

1. In a small saucepan, bring raisins, ⅓ cup (80 grams) water, Grand Marnier, and 1 teaspoon (5 grams) orange juice to a boil over medium heat. Reduce heat, and simmer until liquid is reduced by three-fourths and raisins are plump, about 20 minutes. Drain, and let cool completely.
2. In another small saucepan, bring ¼ cup (85 grams) molasses, fennel seeds, and caraway seeds to a boil over medium heat. Remove from heat; stir in milk. Set aside until cooled to 120°F (49°C) to 130°F (54°C).

3. In the bowl of a stand mixer fitted with the dough hook attachment, stir together flours, yeast, and salt. With mixer on low speed, gradually add milk mixture. Increase mixer speed to medium-low, and beat until well combined. Add butter, a few pieces at a time, beating until combined. Add raisins and diced Candied Orange Peel. Increase mixer speed to medium, and beat until smooth and elastic, about 7 minutes. Spray a large bowl with cooking spray. Place dough in bowl, turning to grease top. Cover directly with plastic wrap, and let rise in a warm, draft-free place (75°F/24°C) until doubled in size, about 1 hour.
4. Line a large baking sheet with parchment paper.
5. On a lightly floured surface, roll dough into an 18-inch-long log. Place on prepared pan, and form into a circle; pinch ends to seal.
6. Using kitchen scissors, make a 45-degree cut into dough, leaving about ¼ inch of dough uncut. (Be careful not to cut all the way through dough.) Make a second cut 1 inch from first. Make another cut 1 inch from the second. Repeat process until you reach first cut. Gently pull each cut dough piece away from the center of the wreath. Cover loosely with plastic wrap, and let stand in a warm, draft-free place (75°F/24°C) for 30 minutes.
7. Preheat oven to 350°F (180°C).
8. Bake until golden brown and internal temperature registers 190°F (88°C), about 40 minutes. Let cool completely on a wire rack.
9. In a small bowl, whisk together remaining 2 tablespoons (42 grams) molasses and remaining 2 tablespoons (30 grams) orange juice. Brush wreath with molasses glaze. Store in an airtight container at room temperature for up to 4 days.

1. On a lightly floured surface, roll dough into an 18-inch-long log.

2. Make 45-degree cuts into dough, leaving about ¼ inch of dough uncut.

3. Gently pull each cut dough piece away from the center of the wreath.

SWEDISH SAFFRANSKRANS

Makes 1 (12-inch) wreath

This bread will brighten your holiday table. While baking, our orange-and-cardamom marmalade filling oozes out of the dough to caramelize on the crust. Swedish pearl sugar and almond slices deliver the perfect crunch. We suggest sprinkling on more of both before serving for added texture.

1	teaspoon saffron threads
½	teaspoon (1.5 grams) kosher salt
1	tablespoon (15 grams) vodka
1¼	cups (300 grams) warm whole milk (115°F/46°C to 120°F/49°C)
2	large eggs (100 grams), divided
4	cups (508 grams) bread flour
½	cup (100 grams) granulated sugar
1	tablespoon (6 grams) instant yeast
⅓	cup (76 grams) unsalted butter, softened and cubed
	Orange Marmalade Filling (recipe follows)
½	cup (64 grams) golden raisins
½	cup (85 grams) diced Candied Orange Peel (recipe follows)
1	teaspoon (5 grams) water
1	tablespoon (7 grams) sliced almonds
2	teaspoons (8 grams) Swedish pearl sugar

1. In a mortar, grind saffron threads and salt with a pestle. Add vodka, and let stand for 30 minutes.

2. In a small bowl, whisk together warm milk, 1 egg (50 grams), and saffron mixture.

3. In the bowl of a stand mixer fitted with the dough hook attachment, stir together flour, granulated sugar, and yeast. With mixer on low speed, gradually add milk mixture. Increase mixer speed to medium-low, and beat until well combined. Add butter, a few pieces at a time, beating until combined. Increase mixer speed to medium, and beat until smooth and elastic, about 7 minutes. Spray a large bowl with cooking spray. Place dough in bowl, turning to grease top. Cover directly with plastic wrap, and let rise in a warm, draft-free place (75°F/24°C) until doubled in size, about 1 hour.

4. Line a large baking sheet with parchment paper.

5. On a lightly floured surface, roll dough into an 18x12-inch rectangle. Spread Orange Marmalade Filling onto dough, leaving a ½-inch border on all sides. Sprinkle

with golden raisins and diced Candied Orange Peel. Starting at one long side, roll up dough, jelly-roll style; press edge to seal. Place on prepared pan. Form into a circle, pinching ends to seal.

6. Using kitchen scissors, make a 45-degree cut into dough, leaving about ¼ inch of dough uncut. (Be careful not to cut all the way through dough.) Make a second cut ½ inch from first cut. Repeat process around the circle until you reach first cut.

7. Using your hands, gently pull and lay alternating pieces in opposite directions, either pulling toward the center of the circle or pulling toward the outside of the circle. (Make sure not to tear pieces completely off.) Cover loosely with plastic wrap, and let stand in a warm, draft-free place (75°F/24°C) for 30 minutes.

8. Preheat oven to 350°F (180°C).

9. In a small bowl, whisk together 1 teaspoon (5 grams) water and remaining 1 egg (50 grams). Brush wreath with egg wash. Sprinkle with almonds and pearl sugar.

10. Bake until golden brown and internal temperature registers 190°F (88°C), about 40 minutes, covering with foil to prevent excess browning, if necessary. Let cool completely on a wire rack. Store in an airtight container at room temperature for up to 4 days.

ORANGE MARMALADE FILLING
Makes about ½ cup

⅓	cup (107 grams) sweet orange marmalade
3	tablespoons (42 grams) unsalted butter, melted
1	teaspoon (2 grams) ground cardamom

1. In a small bowl, whisk together marmalade, melted butter, and cardamom. Use immediately, or refrigerate for up to 5 days.

CANDIED ORANGE PEEL
Makes about 1 cup

1	large orange (131 grams)
1½	cups (360 grams) water
2	cups (400 grams) granulated sugar, divided

1. Peel orange, and slice peel into ¼-inch-thick strips.

2. In a small saucepan, bring peel and water to cover by 1 inch to a boil over medium heat. Cook for 15 minutes. Drain, and rinse with cold water.

3. In same pan, bring 1½ cups (360 grams) water and 1½ cups (300 grams) sugar to a boil over medium heat. Add peel. Reduce heat to medium-low, and simmer until peel is softened, 25 to 30 minutes. Drain.

4. Line a rimmed baking sheet with parchment paper.

5. Toss peel with remaining ½ cup (100 grams) sugar, and place on prepared pan. Let stand until dry, 1 to 2 days. Freeze in an airtight container for up to 2 months.

1. Starting at one long side, roll up dough, jelly-roll style.

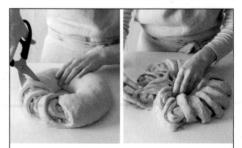

2. Make 45-degree cuts into dough, leaving about ¼ inch of dough uncut. Gently arrange alternating pieces toward or away from the wreath's center.

COCONUT BUNS

Makes 12

Recipe by Ben Mims

Forget cinnamon—these buns are the best breakfast treat around. Enriched with coconut milk and oil in the dough and filled with a sweetened, toasted coconut butter, this recipe is for the serious coconut lover. Make the dough and assemble buns the night before you plan to bake them for breakfast. Their flavor deepens with a long, slow rise in the refrigerator, but if you don't have the spare hours to wait, you can let them rise at room temperature for an hour and a half.

1¼ cups (300 grams) warm unsweetened canned coconut milk (120°F/49°C to 130°F/54°C)
⅓ cup (67 grams) granulated sugar
2 tablespoons (28 grams) unrefined coconut oil, melted
1 teaspoon (3 grams) kosher salt
1 large egg (50 grams), lightly beaten
4 cups (500 grams) all-purpose flour
3½ teaspoons (7 grams) instant yeast
½ cup (42 grams) unsweetened flaked coconut
Coconut Filling (recipe follows)
Coconut Icing (recipe follows)

1. In the bowl of a stand mixer fitted with the dough hook attachment, combine warm coconut milk, sugar, melted coconut oil, salt, and egg. Add flour and yeast, and beat at low speed until a dough forms. Increase mixer speed to medium, and knead until smooth, about 8 minutes. Cover with plastic wrap, and let rise in a warm, draft-free place (75°F/24°C) until doubled in size, about 1½ hours.
2. Preheat oven to 350°F (180°C). Spread coconut on a baking sheet, and bake, stirring halfway through, until lightly golden brown, about 8 minutes. Transfer coconut to a bowl, and let cool completely. Lightly grease a 13x9-inch baking pan with butter.
3. Transfer dough to a lightly floured surface. Roll into an 18x12-inch rectangle. Spread Coconut Filling over dough, leaving a ½-inch border on one long side. Starting with opposite long side, roll dough into a

tight log. Trim ends, and cut into 12 rounds. Transfer rounds, cut side up, to prepared pan, and cover with plastic wrap. Refrigerate for at least 8 hours or overnight (or let rolls rise at room temperature for 1½ hours).
4. Preheat oven to 375°F (190°C).
5. Bake until puffed and golden brown throughout, about 35 minutes. Let cool for 10 minutes. Drizzle with Coconut Icing while still warm, and sprinkle with toasted coconut before serving.

COCONUT FILLING
Makes 4 cups

1 cup (84 grams) finely shredded dried (desiccated) coconut
1 cup (227 grams) unsalted butter, softened
½ cup (110 grams) firmly packed light brown sugar
3 cups (360 grams) confectioners' sugar, sifted
1 teaspoon (4 grams) coconut extract
1 teaspoon (4 grams) vanilla extract
½ teaspoon (1.5 grams) kosher salt

1. Preheat oven to 350°F (180°C). Spread coconut on a baking sheet, and bake, stirring halfway through, until lightly golden brown,

about 8 minutes. Transfer to a bowl, and let cool completely.
2. In the bowl of a stand mixer fitted with the paddle attachment, beat butter and brown sugar at medium speed until smooth, about 2 minutes. Add confectioners' sugar, extracts, and salt; beat until smooth. Reserve ½ cup filling for Coconut Icing. Stir toasted coconut into remaining filling. Cover with plastic wrap until ready to use.

COCONUT ICING
Makes ½ cup

½ cup Coconut Filling (recipe precedes)
2 tablespoons (30 grams) unsweetened canned coconut milk

1. In a small bowl, stir together Coconut Filling and coconut milk. Cover with plastic wrap until ready to use.

Photo by Mason + Dixon

HONEY PEAR SWIRL BREAD

Makes 2 (9x5-inch) loaves

For this bread, we combined honey with pear preserves to create a silky filling that packs every bite with layers of fruit and spice.

2 cups (480 grams) warm whole milk (105°F/40°C to 110°F/43°C),
1 tablespoon plus 1 teaspoon (12 grams) active dry yeast
¾ cup (255 grams) honey, divided
2 large eggs (100 grams)
6 tablespoons (84 grams) unsalted butter, melted
1 tablespoon (9 grams) kosher salt
1 tablespoon (5 grams) fresh lemon juice
7½ cups (953 grams) bread flour, divided
1 (11.5-ounce) jar (325 grams) pear preserves
2 tablespoons (16 grams) cornstarch
2 teaspoons (4 grams) ground ginger
1 large egg white (30 grams), lightly beaten
¾ cup (60 grams) old-fashioned oats

1. In the bowl of a stand mixer fitted with the paddle attachment, combine warm milk and yeast. Let stand until mixture is foamy, about 5 minutes. Add ¼ cup (85 grams) honey, eggs, melted butter, salt, and lemon juice; beat at medium speed until combined. Gradually add 3 cups (381 grams) flour, beating until smooth. Gradually add 4 cups (508 grams) flour, beating until a soft dough forms. (If dough is too sticky, add remaining ½ cup [64 grams] flour.)

2. Turn out dough onto a heavily floured surface, and knead until smooth and elastic, 4 to 5 minutes, sprinkling work surface with more flour as needed. Spray a large bowl with cooking spray. Place dough in bowl, turning to grease top. Cover and let rise in a warm, draft-free place (75°F/24°C) until doubled in size, about 2 hours.

3. In a medium saucepan, bring pear preserves, cornstarch, ginger, and remaining ½ cup (170 grams) honey to a boil over medium heat. Cook for 1 minute, stirring constantly. Remove from heat, and let cool for 30 minutes.

4. Spray 2 (9x5-inch) loaf pans with cooking spray. Divide dough in half. On a lightly floured surface, roll each half into an 18x9-inch rectangle. Spread half of filling onto one rectangle, leaving a ½-inch border. Starting at one short side, roll up dough, jelly-roll style, and press edge to seal. Place roll, seam side down, in prepared pan. Repeat with remaining dough and filling. Cover and let rise in a warm, draft-free place (75°F/24°C) until doubled in size, about 45 minutes.

5. Preheat oven to 350°F (190°C).

6. Brush tops of dough with egg white, and sprinkle with oats.

7. Bake for 45 to 50 minutes, covering with foil 30 minutes into baking to prevent excess browning, if necessary. Let cool on a wire rack.

TRADITIONAL ROOSTERKOEK

Makes 16

Roosterkoek, *which roughly translates to "griddle cake," starts with a sticky, yeasted dough and ends with puffy, grill-branded bread. Serve hot off the grill and with a generous spread of our Peach Mango Chutney.*

¾ cup (180 grams) plus 2 tablespoons (30 grams) warm water (105°F/40°C to 110°F/43°C), divided
1 tablespoon (6 grams) instant yeast
2 teaspoons (8 grams) granulated sugar
2½ cups (313 grams) all-purpose flour*
2 teaspoons (6 grams) kosher salt
2 tablespoons (28 grams) sunflower oil
Peach Mango Chutney (recipe follows)

1. In a small bowl, combine 2 tablespoons (30 grams) warm water, yeast, and sugar. Let stand until mixture is foamy, about 2 minutes.
2. In the bowl of a stand mixer fitted with the dough hook attachment, combine flour and salt. With mixer on medium-low speed, gradually add oil and remaining ¾ cup (180 grams) warm water. Beat until a shaggy dough forms, 1 to 2 minutes. Scrape sides of bowl, and add yeast mixture. Increase mixer speed to medium, and beat until dough is smooth, 4 to 5 minutes.
3. Turn out dough onto a lightly floured surface, and shape into a ball. Spray a large bowl with cooking spray. Place dough in bowl, turning to grease top. Cover with plastic wrap, and let stand in a warm, draft-free place (75°F/24°C) until doubled in size, about 1 hour.
4. Preheat grill to medium-high heat (375°F/190°C).
5. Divide dough into 16 equal pieces, and shape into balls. Cover and let rest for 15 minutes.

6. Spray a braai grid or grill basket with cooking spray, and heat on grill for 5 minutes. Stretch dough into 3-inch disks.
7. Working in batches, if necessary, grill disks in braai grid or grill basket, covered, until top of bread begins to puff and bottom is golden brown, 5 to 6 minutes. Turn, and grill 5 to 6 minutes more. Serve warm with Peach Mango Chutney. Store in an airtight container for up to 4 days.

For a darker bread, substitute ¼ cup (31 grams) all-purpose flour with whole wheat or buckwheat flour.

PEACH MANGO CHUTNEY
Makes 1 quart

Based on the famous Mrs. H.S. Ball's Original Recipe Chutney—a classic South African condiment that is one of the country's culinary icons—this homemade chutney also pairs perfectly with our Caramelized Garlic Roosterkoek and the Cornmeal and Golden Raisin Roosterkoek.

3 medium peaches (450 grams), peeled, pitted, and cut into ½-inch slices
2 Granny Smith apples (370 grams), cored and chopped*

1 mango (360 grams), peeled, pitted, and cut into ½-inch slices
2 jalapeños (90 grams), seeded and diced
1 small yellow onion (170 grams), diced
¾ cup (150 grams) granulated sugar
½ cup (64 grams) golden raisins
½ cup (120 grams) apple cider vinegar
2 teaspoons grated fresh ginger
1 teaspoon (2 grams) mustard seed
½ teaspoon (1.5 grams) kosher salt

1. In a medium saucepan, cook all ingredients over medium heat until mixture has darkened and thickened, 45 minutes to 1 hour. Chutney should be thick enough that when a spoon passes through it, the bottom of the pan can be seen for a few seconds.
2. Using a potato masher, mash mixture to desired consistency. Remove from heat.
3. Transfer chutney to sterile glass jars, and seal while hot, or store in an airtight container in refrigerator for up to 2 weeks.

Do not peel the apples. The skins release natural pectin essential to the thick consistency of your chutney.

SPICY SWEET POTATO ROOSTERKOEK

Makes 6

Enterprising South African chefs would often use potatoes to supplement or replace flour in their baked goods, such as patatkoekie, a sweet potato fritter. Sweet with a little kick, this variation of roosterkoek uses mashed sweet potatoes to give it an extra pillowy texture.

¾ cup (180 grams) warm water (105°F/40°C to 110°F/43°C)
½ cup (122 grams) mashed sweet potato
⅓ cup (76 grams) unsalted butter, softened
¼ cup (55 grams) firmly packed light brown sugar
1 large egg (50 grams)
3½ cups (438 grams) all-purpose flour
1 tablespoon (6 grams) instant yeast
2 teaspoons (6 grams) kosher salt
1 teaspoon (2 grams) ground red pepper
1 teaspoon (2 grams) turmeric
½ teaspoon (1 gram) smoked paprika
½ teaspoon (1 gram) onion powder
Chakalaka Relish (recipe follows)

1. In the bowl of a stand mixer fitted with the paddle attachment, combine ¾ cup (180 grams) warm water, sweet potato, butter, brown sugar, and egg.

2. In a large bowl, whisk together flour, yeast, salt, red pepper, turmeric, paprika, and onion powder. With mixer on medium-low speed, add flour mixture to sweet potato mixture, beating until smooth, about 5 minutes, stopping to scrape sides of bowl. Switch to the dough hook attachment. With mixer on medium speed, beat for 10 minutes, stopping to scrape sides of bowl.

3. Turn out dough onto a lightly floured surface, and shape into a ball. (Dough may be sticky; use additional flour if needed.) Spray a large bowl with cooking spray. Place dough in bowl, turning to grease top. Cover with plastic wrap, and let stand in a warm, draft-free place (75°F/24°C) until doubled in size, about 1 hour.

4. Spray grill rack with nonflammable cooking spray. Preheat grill to medium-high heat (375°F/190°C).

5. Divide dough into 6 equal pieces, and shape each into a 4-inch log. Cover and let rest for 15 minutes. Stretch dough into 4x2½-inch rectangles, about 1 inch thick.

6. Grill, covered, until top of bread begins to puff and bottom is golden brown, 5 to 6 minutes. Turn, and grill 5 to 6 minutes more. Serve warm with Chakalaka Relish. Store in an airtight container for up to 4 days.

CHAKALAKA RELISH

Makes about 2 quarts

Just as fun to say as it is to eat, this South African vegetable relish is usually served with bread or amasi, thick fermented milk akin to yogurt, to cut the jalapeño and red pepper. It complements our Cornmeal and Golden Raisin Roosterkoek or Spicy Sweet Potato Roosterkoek.

¼ cup (56 grams) olive oil
1 medium onion (241 grams), diced
2 teaspoons (6 grams) minced garlic
1 teaspoon (2 grams) curry powder
1 teaspoon (2 grams) ground red pepper
½ teaspoon (1 gram) smoked paprika
½ teaspoon grated fresh ginger
½ teaspoon chopped fresh thyme
3 cups (144 grams) chopped cabbage
2 large tomatoes (528 grams), seeded and diced
1 medium carrot (84 grams), diced
1 green bell pepper (244 grams), seeded and chopped
1 jalapeño (45 grams), seeded and diced
2 cups (336 grams) cooked white Northern beans
½ cup (128 grams) barbecue sauce

1. In a large saucepan, heat oil over medium heat. Add onion; cook until almost translucent, about 2 minutes. Stir in garlic, curry powder, red pepper, paprika, ginger, and thyme; cook for 1 minute, stirring constantly. Add cabbage, tomatoes, carrot, bell pepper, and jalapeño; cook for 5 minutes, stirring occasionally. Add beans and barbecue sauce; cook for 2 minutes, stirring constantly. Serve warm. Refrigerate in an airtight container for up to 5 days.

CARAMELIZED GARLIC ROOSTERKOEK

Makes 1 (10-inch) loaf

Taking inspiration from the heavy Indian influence on South African food, this bread is reminiscent of curry-dipped garlic naan. The addition of coconut water, freshly grated ginger, and curry gives this grill cake a heady taste of India.

¾   cup (180 grams) plus 2 tablespoons (30 grams) warm coconut water (105°F/40°C to 110°F/43°C), divided
1   tablespoon (6 grams) instant yeast
2   teaspoons (8 grams) granulated sugar
2½   cups (313 grams) all-purpose flour
1   tablespoon (2 grams) grated fresh ginger
2   teaspoons (6 grams) kosher salt
1½   teaspoons (3 grams) curry powder
2   tablespoons (28 grams) sunflower oil
Caramelized Garlic (recipe follows)

1. In a small bowl, combine 2 tablespoons (30 grams) warm coconut water, yeast, and sugar. Let stand until mixture is foamy, about 2 minutes.
2. In the bowl of a stand mixer fitted with the dough hook attachment, combine flour, ginger, salt, and curry powder. With mixer on medium-low speed, gradually add oil and remaining ¾ cup (180 grams) warm coconut water. Beat until a shaggy dough forms, 1 to 2 minutes. Scrape sides of bowl, and add yeast mixture. Increase mixer speed to medium, and beat until dough is smooth, 4 to 5 minutes. Reduce mixer speed to medium-low. Add Caramelized Garlic, and beat until combined, about 2 minutes.
3. Turn out dough onto a lightly floured surface, and shape into a ball. (Dough may be sticky; use additional flour if needed.) Spray a large bowl with cooking spray. Place dough in bowl, turning to grease top. Cover with plastic wrap, and let stand in a warm, draft-free place (75°F/24°C) until doubled in size, about 1 hour.
4. Preheat grill to medium-high heat (375°F/190°C).
5. Turn out dough onto a lightly floured surface, and shape into a 10-inch disk. Cover and let rest for 15 minutes.
6. Spray a braai grid or grill basket with cooking spray, and heat on grill for 5 minutes.
7. Grill disk in braai grid or grill basket, covered, until top of bread begins to puff and bottom is golden brown, 6 to 7 minutes.

Turn, and grill 6 to 7 minutes more. Serve warm. Store in an airtight container for up to 4 days.

CARAMELIZED GARLIC

Makes about ¼ cup

6   cloves garlic (30 grams)
1   tablespoon (14 grams) olive oil
1   cup (240 grams) water
1   teaspoon (5 grams) balsamic vinegar
1   tablespoon (12 grams) granulated sugar

1. In a small saucepan, bring garlic and water to cover by 1 inch to a simmer over medium heat. Simmer for 3 minutes. Drain, and return cloves to pan. Increase heat to medium-high, and add oil; cook until cloves are golden, about 2 minutes. Remove from heat, and let cool for 5 minutes.
2. Slowly add 1 cup (240 grams) water and vinegar, and bring to a simmer over medium heat; simmer for 5 minutes. Add sugar, and cook, stirring constantly, until garlic is coated in a dark caramelized syrup, 3 to 5 minutes. Let cool completely. Refrigerate in an airtight container for up to 1 week.

CORNMEAL AND GOLDEN RAISIN ROOSTERKOEK

Makes 16

With a nod to the popular South African dish pap, a ground white corn-based porridge similar to polenta, we used a blend of white cornmeal and all-purpose flour as the base for this version of roosterkoek. Cornmeal gives this peppery bread a unique, grainy texture, and coriander balances out the sweetness from the golden raisins. Shape the dough into bite-size triangles, dollop with chutney and chakalaka, and watch as they're the first appetizer to go at your next cookout.

¾   cup (180 grams) plus 2 tablespoons (30 grams) warm water (105°F/40°C to 110°F/43°C), divided
1   tablespoon (6 grams) instant yeast
2   teaspoons (8 grams) granulated sugar
2   cups (250 grams) all-purpose flour
½   cup (75 grams) fine white cornmeal
1   tablespoon (9 grams) crushed coriander seeds

2   teaspoons (6 grams) kosher salt
½   teaspoon (1 gram) ground black pepper
2   tablespoons (28 grams) sunflower oil
½   cup (64 grams) golden raisins

1. In a small bowl, combine 2 tablespoons (30 grams) warm water, yeast, and sugar. Let stand until mixture is foamy, about 2 minutes.

2. In the bowl of a stand mixer fitted with the dough hook attachment, combine flour, cornmeal, coriander seeds, salt, and pepper. With mixer on medium-low speed, gradually add oil and remaining ¾ cup (180 grams) warm water. Beat until a shaggy dough forms, 1 to 2 minutes. Scrape sides of bowl, and add yeast mixture. Increase mixer speed to medium, and beat until dough is smooth, 4 to 5 minutes. Reduce mixer speed to medium-low. Add raisins, and beat until combined, about 2 minutes.

3. Turn out dough onto a lightly floured surface, and shape into a ball. Spray a large bowl with cooking spray. Place dough in bowl, turning to grease top. Cover with plastic wrap, and let stand in a warm, draft-free place (75°F/24°C) until doubled in size, about 1 hour.

4. Preheat grill to medium-high heat (375°F/190°C).

5. Turn out dough onto a lightly floured surface, and shape into a 10-inch disk. Cut into 16 pieces; cover and let rest for 15 minutes.

6. Spray a braai grid or grill basket with cooking spray, and heat on grill for 5 minutes.

7. Working in batches, if necessary, grill disks in braai grid or grill basket, covered, until top of bread begins to puff and bottom is golden brown, 5 to 6 minutes. Turn, and grill 5 to 6 minutes more. Serve warm. Store in an airtight container for up to 4 days.

PIES AND TARTS

PIES

Few desserts can outshine a slice of homemade pie. Take your pick from lattice-topped pies, cobblers, and hand pies bursting with fresh berries and stone fruit. Indulge in our custardy and creamy pies with decadent, velvety fillings. We have the recipe you need to build the pie of your dreams from the crust up.

BLACK FOREST PIE

Makes 1 (9-inch) pie

The secret to this dessert is Kirsch liqueur (also known as kirschwasser), a unique cherry spirit that uses the flavoring from both cherries and their stones, imparting a delicious almond aftertaste.

1¼ cups (156 grams) all-purpose flour
3   tablespoons (15 grams) Dutch process cocoa powder
2   teaspoons (6 grams) kosher salt
1½ teaspoons (6 grams) granulated sugar
½   cup (113 grams) cold unsalted butter, cubed
6   tablespoons (90 grams) ice water
Bittersweet Cherry Ganache (recipe follows)
Cherry Mousse (recipe follows)
Garnish: fresh cherries

1. In the work bowl of a food processor, place flour, cocoa, salt, and sugar; pulse until combined. Add cold butter, pulsing until mixture is crumbly. With processor running, add ice water, 1 tablespoon (15 grams) at a time, just until a dough forms. Turn out dough, and shape into a disk. Wrap tightly in plastic wrap, and refrigerate for at least 30 minutes.
2. Let dough stand at room temperature until slightly softened, about 5 minutes. On a lightly floured surface, roll dough into a 12-inch circle. Transfer to a 9-inch pie plate, pressing into bottom and up sides. Trim excess dough to ½ inch beyond edge of plate. Fold edges under, and crimp as desired. Prick bottom of dough with a fork. Refrigerate for 30 minutes.
3. Preheat oven to 350°F (180°C).
4. Top dough with a piece of parchment paper, letting ends extend over edges of plate. Add pie weights.
5. Bake for 15 minutes. Carefully remove paper and weights. Bake 10 minutes more. Let cool completely on a wire rack.
6. Spoon Bittersweet Cherry Ganache into prepared crust, smoothing with an offset spatula. Refrigerate until set, about 15 minutes. Pour Cherry Mousse over ganache, and refrigerate until set, about 45 minutes. Garnish with cherries, if desired.

BITTERSWEET CHERRY GANACHE
Makes about ¾ cup

7   ounces (200 grams) 60% cacao bittersweet chocolate, chopped
1   tablespoon (15 grams) kirschwasser cherry liqueur
¼   cup (60 grams) heavy whipping cream
¼   cup (60 grams) Cherry Purée (see Pro Tip)

1. In a medium bowl, combine chocolate and cherry liqueur.
2. In a small saucepan, bring cream and Cherry Purée to a boil over medium heat. Pour hot cream mixture over chocolate mixture, and whisk until smooth and shiny. Use immediately.

CHERRY MOUSSE
Makes about 2½ cups

1⅓ cups (320 grams) heavy whipping cream, divided
⅓   cup (80 grams) plus 3 tablespoons (45 grams) cold whole milk, divided
5   large egg yolks (93 grams)
3   tablespoons (36 grams) granulated sugar
2   tablespoons (16 grams) cornstarch
2   teaspoons (8 grams) unflavored gelatin
⅓   cup plus 1 tablespoon (95 grams) Cherry Purée (see Pro Tip)
6   ounces (175 grams) white chocolate morsels
2   tablespoons (30 grams) kirschwasser cherry liqueur

1. In a medium saucepan, bring ⅔ cup (160 grams) cream and ⅓ cup (80 grams) milk to a boil over medium heat.
2. In a medium bowl, whisk together egg yolks, sugar, cornstarch, gelatin, and remaining 3 tablespoons (45 grams) cold milk. Whisking constantly, slowly pour hot cream mixture into yolk mixture. Return cream mixture to saucepan, and cook, whisking constantly, until mixture has thickened, about 1 minute.
3. In another medium bowl, combine Cherry Purée, chocolate morsels, and cherry liqueur. Strain cream mixture over cherry mixture, and whisk until smooth. Place bowl in a larger bowl filled with ice. Let cool to room temperature over ice bath, whisking constantly to ensure even cooling and to prevent mousse from creating lumps. (If mousse cools any further than room temperature, it will become too thick.)
4. In the bowl of a stand mixer fitted with the whisk attachment, beat remaining ⅔ cup (160 grams) cream at high speed until soft peaks form. Fold whipped cream into mousse until smooth.

PRO TIP
To make **Cherry Purée**, place 1 pound (455 grams) fresh pitted cherries in the work bowl of a food processor. Purée until smooth. Strain mixture, discarding solids. This will yield about 1 cup Cherry Purée.

SATSUMA MARMALADE HAND PIES

Makes 8

Recipe by Rebecca Firth

This combination of slightly bitter marmalade, aromatic five-spice, and buttery crust is spine-tingling. Most marmalade is comprised of the entire fruit. Here, I use only one satsuma in its entirety and utilize the zest and meat of the remaining fruit for a less bitter filling.

⅓   cup (80 grams) cold water
¼   cup (60 grams) cold vodka
3   cups (375 grams) all-purpose flour
2   tablespoons (24 grams) granulated sugar
1   teaspoon (3 grams) kosher salt
1   cup (227 grams) cold unsalted butter, cubed
¼   cup (57 grams) cold all-vegetable shortening
Satsuma Marmalade (recipe follows)
1   large egg yolk (19 grams)
2   tablespoons (30 grams) heavy whipping cream or whole milk

1. In a measuring cup, stir together ⅓ cup (80 grams) cold water and vodka. Freeze for 5 minutes.
2. In a large bowl, whisk together flour, sugar, and salt until combined. Using a pastry blender, cut in cold butter and shortening until mixture is crumbly. (Do not overmix.) Drizzle vodka mixture over flour mixture, and press with the back of a spatula to bring dough together. Using your hands, gently press dough together.
3. Turn out dough, and divide in half. Shape each half into a disk, and wrap tightly in plastic wrap. Refrigerate for at least 1 hour.
4. Preheat oven to 400°F (200°C). Line a baking sheet with parchment paper.
5. Let dough stand at room temperature until slightly softened, about 15 minutes. On a lightly floured surface, roll dough to ¼-inch thickness. Using a 3¾-inch round cutter, cut 16 rounds. Using a small star-shaped cutter, cut centers from half of rounds.
6. Spoon about 1½ tablespoons (30 grams) Satsuma Marmalade onto center of each solid round, leaving a ½-inch border. Lightly moisten border of each pie, and top with rounds with cutouts. Using the tines of a fork, press down edges to crimp. Place pies on prepared pan, and freeze for 15 minutes.
7. In a small bowl, whisk together egg yolk and cream. Lightly brush egg wash over pies.
8. Bake for 20 to 25 minutes. Let cool before serving.

SATSUMA MARMALADE
Makes about 1½ cups

¾   pound (340 grams) satsumas or tangerines
1   lemon (99 grams)
1½   cups (360 grams) water
1½   cups (300 grams) granulated sugar
2   tablespoons (30 grams) minced peeled apple
1   (1-inch) piece ginger (8 grams), peeled
½   teaspoon (1 gram) Chinese five-spice powder

1. Clean and scrub fruit. Thinly slice 1 whole satsuma (peel plus fruit). Cut slices into quarters, and place in a medium saucepan. Zest remaining satsumas and lemon directly into pan. Remove and discard remaining white satsuma skin, and place fruit in pan. For lemon, remove outer skin, and place residual fruit in pan. Discard any excess pith and seeds.
2. Add 1½ cups (360 grams) water, sugar, apple, ginger, and five-spice powder, and bring to a boil over medium-high heat. Boil until mixture has darkened and thickened, about 35 minutes. Using kitchen shears, cut up any large chunks of fruit into bite-size pieces. Discard ginger. Let cool completely. Refrigerate until chilled.

Photo by Joe Schmelzer

SUGAR PIE

Makes 1 (9-inch) pie

Recipe by Emily Turner

For Quebecers, sugar pie, or tarte au sucre, is synonymous with Christmas indulgence. Brought to Quebec by French immigrants, this sweet pie combines brown sugar and maple syrup, a sugar combo that slowly caramelizes while baking, creating a light crunchy top and a custard-like silky interior.

Butter Piecrust (recipe follows)
1½ cups (330 grams) firmly packed light brown sugar
¼   cup (85 grams) maple syrup
3   tablespoons (24 grams) all-purpose flour
2   large egg yolks (37 grams)
1   large egg (50 grams)
1   cup (240 grams) heavy whipping cream
3   tablespoons (42 grams) unsalted butter
1   teaspoon (4 grams) vanilla extract
¼   teaspoon kosher salt
Garnish: confectioners' sugar

1. On a lightly floured surface, roll Butter Piecrust to ¼-inch thickness. Transfer to a 9-inch pie plate, pressing into bottom and up sides. Trim excess dough. Fold edges under, and crimp as desired. Freeze for 10 minutes.
2. Preheat oven to 400°F (200°C).
3. Top dough with a piece of parchment paper, letting ends extend over edges of plate. Add pie weights.
4. Bake until edges are set, about 10 minutes. Carefully remove paper and weights. Bake until bottom of crust is set, about 2 minutes more. Reduce oven temperature to 350°F (180°C).
5. In a large bowl, whisk together brown sugar, maple syrup, flour, egg yolks, and egg until smooth.
6. In a small saucepan, bring cream and butter to a simmer over medium-high heat. Whisking constantly, slowly pour hot cream mixture into sugar mixture. Whisk in vanilla and salt. Strain mixture through a fine-mesh sieve, discarding solids. Pour filling into prepared crust. Loosely cover with foil.
7. Bake in bottom third of oven until crust is golden brown and filling is set (center should still jiggle slightly), 50 to 55 minutes. Let cool completely. Garnish with confectioners' sugar, if desired.

BUTTER PIECRUST
Makes 1 (9-inch) crust

2½ cups (313 grams) all-purpose flour
2   tablespoons (24 grams) granulated sugar
1½ teaspoons (4.5 grams) kosher salt
¾   cup (170 grams) cold unsalted butter, cubed
½   cup (120 grams) ice water

1. In the work bowl of a food processor, place flour, sugar, and salt; pulse until combined. Add cold butter, and pulse until mixture is crumbly. Add ice water, 2 tablespoons (30 grams) at a time, just until dough comes together (you may not need all of the water). Shape dough into a disk, and wrap tightly in plastic wrap. Refrigerate until chilled, about 2 hours.

Photo by Maya Visnyei

PINEAPPLE BROWN BETTY

Makes 6 servings

A Brown Betty is a baked pudding with alternating layers of spiced and sugared fruit and buttered bread crumbs. We took the classic version on a tropical vacation and packed it with pineapple, passion fruit, and lime. Shredded coconut, sourdough bread crumbs, and almond meal create textural contrast between the bread and the soft fruit.

2   cups (113 grams) sourdough bread crumbs, toasted
1   cup (96 grams) almond meal
⅓   cup (28 grams) shredded (desiccated) coconut, toasted
½   cup (113 grams) unsalted butter, melted
⅔   cup (147 grams) firmly packed light brown sugar
¼   cup (60 grams) fresh passion fruit juice*
1   teaspoon (2 grams) lime zest
2   tablespoons (30 grams) fresh lime juice
1½   teaspoons (6 grams) almond extract
½   teaspoon (1.5 grams) kosher salt
2½   pounds (1,134 grams) peeled and cored pineapple, cut into ½-inch-thick slices

1. Preheat oven to 375°F (190°C).
2. In a medium bowl, combine bread crumbs, almond meal, and coconut. Stir in melted butter.
3. In a large bowl, combine brown sugar, passion fruit juice, lime zest and juice, almond extract, and salt. Stir in half of bread crumbs mixture. Add pineapple slices, and toss to coat. Transfer to an ungreased 9-inch square baking pan. Sprinkle with remaining bread crumbs mixture. Cover tightly with foil.
4. Bake until fruit is bubbly, about 30 minutes.

Uncover and bake until top is golden brown, about 10 minutes more. Let cool in pan for 15 minutes; serve warm. Cover and refrigerate for up to 3 days.

For an easy way to get passion fruit juice and pulp from passion fruit, use a mesh strainer and spoon to push and scrape all the excess pulp off the passion fruit seeds.

PRO TIP

For even more tropical flavor, substitute macadamia nut meal for the almond meal.

PEACH AND BLUEBERRY BUCKWHEAT SONKER

Makes 12 servings

A larger, even deeper version of the American cobbler that pairs fruit or sweet potatoes with unshaped dough, the sonker is native to North Carolina. Our crust is like a hybrid between a biscuit and a crust.

Buckwheat Black Pepper Crust (recipe follows)
2 pounds (910 grams) fresh peaches, peeled, pitted, and cut into ½-inch-thick slices
½ pound (225 grams) fresh blueberries
½ cup (110 grams) firmly packed light brown sugar
¼ cup (50 grams) granulated sugar
2 tablespoons (16 grams) cornstarch
2 teaspoons (4 grams) orange zest
1 tablespoon (15 grams) fresh orange juice
½ teaspoon (1 gram) ground cinnamon
¼ teaspoon ground nutmeg
3 tablespoons (42 grams) unsalted butter, cubed
2 tablespoons (30 grams) heavy whipping cream
2 tablespoons (24 grams) turbinado sugar
Vanilla ice cream, to serve

1. Preheat oven to 375°F (190°C). Butter a 13x9-inch baking dish.
2. On a heavily floured surface, roll two-thirds of Buckwheat Black Pepper Crust into an 18x14-inch rectangle. (This dough is tender.) Transfer to prepared pan, pressing into bottom and up sides.
3. In a large bowl, combine peaches, blueberries, sugars, cornstarch, orange zest and juice, cinnamon, and nutmeg, tossing to coat. Pour mixture into prepared crust. Place butter over fruit mixture.
4. Divide remaining dough in half. Roll one half into a 13x4-inch rectangle. Cut dough lengthwise into 4 strips. Roll remaining dough into a 9x5-inch rectangle. Cut dough lengthwise into 5 strips. Arrange dough strips in a lattice pattern on top of filling. Press edges to seal, and trim excess dough. Brush dough with cream, and sprinkle with turbinado sugar.
5. Bake until crust is golden brown and fruit is bubbly, 40 to 50 minutes, covering with foil to prevent excess browning, if necessary. Let cool for 15 minutes; serve with ice cream.

Note: *If shielding the sonker from heat, try cutting an 11x7-inch rectangular hole in a piece of foil to cover just the edges of the dish, as these tend to brown first.*

BUCKWHEAT BLACK PEPPER CRUST
Makes 1 (13x9-inch) lattice-topped crust

4 cups (500 grams) all-purpose flour
½ cup (60 grams) buckwheat flour
⅓ cup (67 grams) granulated sugar
4 teaspoons (20 grams) baking powder
1 teaspoon (3 grams) kosher salt
½ teaspoon (1 gram) ground black pepper
½ cup (113 grams) cold unsalted butter, cubed
2 large eggs (100 grams)
1½ cups (360 grams) whole milk

1. In the work bowl of a food processor, place flours, sugar, baking powder, salt, and pepper; pulse until combined. Add cold butter, and pulse until mixture is crumbly, 6 to 8 pulses. Transfer mixture to a large bowl.
2. In a small bowl, whisk together eggs and milk. Add egg mixture to flour mixture, stirring until a sticky dough begins to form.
3. Turn out dough onto a heavily floured surface; sprinkle with flour, and knead until dough is soft and workable. Shape into a disk, and wrap in plastic wrap. Refrigerate for 1 hour.

HONEY PIE

Makes 1 (9-inch) pie

This honey pie offers all the sweetness and creaminess of buttermilk pie, but with heaps of honey flavor.

1¾ cups (219 grams) all-purpose flour
1   tablespoon (12 grams) granulated sugar
1   teaspoon (3 grams) kosher salt
½   cup (113 grams) cold unsalted butter, cubed
2   tablespoons (30 grams) apple cider vinegar
2 to 4 tablespoons (30 to 60 grams) ice water
1   large egg (50 grams), lightly beaten
Honey Filling (recipe follows)

1. In the work bowl of a food processor, place flour, sugar, and salt; pulse until combined. Add cold butter, and pulse until mixture is crumbly. Add vinegar, pulsing until combined. Add ice water, 1 tablespoon (15 grams) at time, just until dough comes together. Turn out dough, and shape into a disk. Wrap tightly in plastic wrap, and refrigerate for at least 2 hours.
2. On a lightly floured surface, roll dough into a 12-inch circle. Transfer to a 9-inch pie plate, pressing into bottom and up sides. Trim excess dough to ½ inch beyond edge of plate. Roll excess dough to ¼-inch thickness. Using a 1-inch leaf cutter, cut leaf shapes. Brush edges of crust with egg wash, and adhere leaves around crust. Brush tops of leaves with egg wash. Refrigerate for 15 minutes.
3. Position oven rack in lowest position, and preheat oven to 350°F (180°C).
4. Pour Honey Filling into prepared crust.
5. Bake until center is set, about 45 minutes, covering with foil halfway through baking to prevent excess browning, if necessary. Serve warm, or refrigerate overnight.

HONEY FILLING
Makes about 2½ cups

¾   cup (255 grams) honey
¾   cup (180 grams) heavy whipping cream
½   cup (100 grams) granulated sugar
½   cup (113 grams) unsalted butter, melted
3   large eggs (150 grams)
1   tablespoon (9 grams) finely ground yellow cornmeal
1   tablespoon (15 grams) apple cider vinegar
1   teaspoon (4 grams) vanilla extract
½   teaspoon (1.5 grams) kosher salt

1. In a large bowl, whisk together honey, cream, sugar, melted butter, eggs, cornmeal, vinegar, vanilla, and salt until combined. Use immediately.

SHOOFLY PIE

Makes 1 (9-inch) pie

Recipe by Brett Braley

Traditionally consisting of a basic piecrust with a cake-like molasses-flavored filling and a crumbled flour, sugar, and butter topping, this humble pie originated in Pennsylvania Dutch Country. Pennsylvania-based food blogger Brett Braley's updated take on this classic has a punch of orange to accent the underlying molasses.

1¾   cups (219 grams) all-purpose flour
5   tablespoons (70 grams) cold unsalted butter
3   tablespoons (42 grams) cold all-vegetable shortening
2   tablespoons (28 grams) firmly packed dark brown sugar
½   tablespoon (6.5 grams) vanilla extract
¼   teaspoon kosher salt
¼   cup (60 grams) ice water
Orange Molasses Filling (recipe follows)
Crumb Topping (recipe follows)

1. In the work bowl of a food processor, combine flour, butter, shortening, brown sugar, vanilla, and salt; pulse until mixture is crumbly. With processor running, add ¼ cup (60 grams) ice water in a slow, steady stream just until dough comes together. Turn out dough, and shape into a disk. Wrap in plastic wrap, and refrigerate for at least 30 minutes.
2. Preheat oven to 400°F (200°C).
3. On a lightly floured surface, roll dough into a 10-inch circle. Transfer to a 9-inch pie plate, pressing into bottom and up sides. Fold edges under, and crimp as desired. Pour Orange Molasses Filling into prepared crust. Gently sprinkle Crumb Topping over filling.
4. Bake for 15 minutes. Reduce oven temperature to 375°F (190°C), and bake until topping is golden brown and filling is set, 30 to 40 minutes more, covering with foil during last 10 minutes of baking to prevent excess browning. Let cool completely on a wire rack.

ORANGE MOLASSES FILLING
Makes about 3 cups

¾   cup (180 grams) water
¾   cup (180 grams) fresh orange juice
1   teaspoon (5 grams) baking soda
½   teaspoon (1.5 grams) kosher salt
1   cup (336 grams) dark molasses
¼   cup (55 grams) firmly packed dark brown sugar
2   tablespoons (26 grams) vanilla extract
1   tablespoon (6 grams) orange zest
1   large egg (50 grams)

1. In a small saucepan, bring ¾ cup (180 grams) water and orange juice to a boil over medium-high heat. Cook, stirring occasionally, until reduced to ½ cup (120 grams), 20 to 25 minutes. Remove from heat, and immediately stir in baking soda and salt. Let stand until slightly warm to the touch, about 15 minutes.
2. In a large bowl, whisk together molasses, brown sugar, vanilla, zest, and egg. Pour orange juice mixture into molasses mixture in a slow, steady stream, stirring constantly, until combined. Use immediately.

CRUMB TOPPING
Makes about 2 cups

1   cup (125 grams) all-purpose flour
½   cup (110 grams) firmly packed light brown sugar
¼   cup (57 grams) cold unsalted butter, cubed
1   tablespoon (6 grams) orange zest

1. Place flour, brown sugar, cold butter, and zest in a small bowl. Crumble with your fingertips until desired consistency is reached.

CHERRY-HAZELNUT SHEKERBURAS

Makes 14

Shekerbura is a traditional sweet pastry hailing from Azerbaijan, a country located at the crossroads of Southwest Asia and Southeastern Europe. We added cherry and Frangelico to the dessert's standard filling of ground nuts and sugar. Yeasted dough lets the pastry's surface serve as a palette for intricate, textured patterns. We love how the thin, elevated ridges turn a deep golden brown while baking for even more visual contrast.

- 2⅔ cups (334 grams) all-purpose flour
- ⅔ cup (150 grams) unsalted butter, softened
- ½ cup (48 grams) hazelnut meal
- ¼ teaspoon ground cinnamon
- ¼ teaspoon ground black pepper
- ½ cup (120 grams) sour cream
- 2 large egg yolks (37 grams)
- 1½ teaspoons (4.5 grams) kosher salt
- 2 tablespoons (30 grams) warm whole milk (105°F/40°C to 110°F/43°C)
- 1 tablespoon (12 grams) granulated sugar
- ½ teaspoon (1 gram) instant yeast
- 1 large egg (50 grams)
- 1 teaspoon (5 grams) water

Cherry Frangelico Filling (recipe follows)

1. In a large bowl, combine flour, butter, hazelnut meal, cinnamon, and pepper. Rub with fingertips until well combined. Set aside.
2. In a small bowl, stir together sour cream, egg yolks, and salt. In another small bowl, combine warm milk, sugar, and yeast. Let stand until slightly bubbly, about 2 minutes.
3. Add yolk mixture and yeast mixture to flour mixture; stir until combined. Turn out dough onto a lightly floured surface, and knead until smooth, about 2 minutes. Return to bowl; cover with plastic wrap, and let rest for 30 minutes.
4. Preheat oven to 350°F (180°C). Line 2 baking sheets with parchment paper.
5. In a small bowl, whisk together egg and 1 teaspoon (5 grams) water. Divide dough into 14 equal pieces. Working with one piece at a time, shape each piece into a 4½-inch

round. Brush edges with egg wash. Spoon Cherry Frangelico Filling into center of each round, dividing evenly among rounds. Fold dough over filling, and crimp edges as desired. Place on prepared pans.
6. Using a straight fondant crimper, pinch a row of lines ¼ inch apart into top of crust at a 45-degree angle. Repeat rows 2 more times, rotating direction of lines by 180 degrees each time. Using a paring knife, cut 2 small vents in top of each shekerbura, and brush lightly with egg wash.
7. Bake until crust is lightly golden and fruit is bubbly, 20 to 25 minutes. Let cool completely. Store in an airtight container for up to 1 day.

CHERRY FRANGELICO FILLING
Makes about 1¾ cups

- ⅔ pound (302 grams) cherries, pitted
- ⅔ cup (147 grams) firmly packed light brown sugar
- ½ cup (64 grams) dried cherries
- 2 tablespoons (16 grams) cornstarch
- 1 tablespoon (6 grams) lemon zest
- 1 tablespoon (15 grams) fresh lemon juice
- 1 tablespoon (15 grams) Frangelico
- ½ teaspoon (1.5 grams) kosher salt
- ¼ teaspoon ground black pepper
- ¼ teaspoon ground cinnamon

1. In a medium saucepan, combine all ingredients. Cook over medium-low heat until cherries have released their juices, about 2 minutes. Increase heat to medium, and cook, stirring occasionally, until juices have thickened, 5 to 7 minutes. Remove from heat, and let cool completely. Refrigerate in an airtight container for up to 3 days.

PRO TIP

A maqqash, a pastry tong with serrated tips, is traditionally used to create the designs in the dough before baking. We used a fondant crimper, which can be found at most craft stores or large online retailers.

ALMOND-BROWNED BUTTER PLUM PIE

Makes 10 to 12 servings

Recipe by Marian Cooper Cairns

If you are a crust addict, this pie is your dream come true. We added super-fine almond flour to the dough for subtle crunch—the perfect contrast to the juicy, sugared plum slices inside.

2 recipes Almond-Browned Butter Pie Dough (recipe follows)
½ cup (100 grams) granulated sugar
½ cup (110 grams) firmly packed light brown sugar
¼ cup (32 grams) cornstarch
1 teaspoon (2 grams) finely grated lemon zest
½ teaspoon (1.5 grams) kosher salt
3½ pounds (1,590 grams) plums, pitted and cut into ¼-inch-thick slices
2 teaspoons (8 grams) vanilla extract
½ teaspoon (2 grams) almond extract
1 large egg (50 grams)
1 teaspoon (5 grams) water
3 tablespoons (36 grams) turbinado sugar

1. Position oven rack in lowest position, and preheat oven to 400°F (200°C).
2. On a lightly floured surface, roll one Almond-Browned Butter Pie Dough disk into an 18x12-inch rectangle. Transfer to a 15x10-inch jelly-roll pan, pressing into bottom and up sides. Trim excess dough. Refrigerate for 15 minutes.
3. In large bowl, whisk together granulated sugar, brown sugar, cornstarch, zest, and salt. Add plums, vanilla, and almond extract, tossing to coat. Spoon plum mixture into prepared crust.
4. On a lightly floured surface, roll remaining Almond-Browned Butter Pie Dough disk into an 18x12-inch rectangle. Cut dough diagonally into 2-inch-wide strips. Arrange strips diagonally over plum mixture, pressing edges to seal. Freeze for 15 minutes.
5. In a small bowl, whisk together egg and 1 teaspoon (5 grams) water. Brush dough with egg wash, and sprinkle with turbinado sugar. Place pie on a foil-lined baking sheet.
6. Bake until crust is golden brown and filling is bubbly, 55 minutes to 1 hour. Let cool on a wire rack for 30 minutes. Serve warm or at room temperature.

ALMOND-BROWNED BUTTER PIE DOUGH
Makes 1 piecrust

1 cup (227 grams) unsalted butter
2¼ cups (281 grams) all-purpose flour
¾ cup (72 grams) super-fine almond flour
1 tablespoon (12 grams) granulated sugar
1½ teaspoons (4.5 grams) kosher salt
1 large egg (50 grams)
¼ cup (60 grams) cold water

1. Line a small bowl with foil, letting excess extend over sides of bowl.
2. In a small heavy-bottomed saucepan, heat butter over medium heat. Cook, stirring frequently, until butter turns a medium-brown color and has a nutty aroma, 6 to 8 minutes. Remove from heat, and pour butter into prepared bowl. Freeze for 1 hour.
3. Using excess foil as handles, remove butter, and cut into small cubes.
4. In the work bowl of a food processor, pulse together flours, sugar, and salt until combined. Add browned butter, and pulse until mixture is crumbly. With processor running, gradually add egg and ¼ cup (60 grams) cold water until dough begins to come together.
5. Turn out dough onto a lightly floured surface. Knead until dough comes together, and shape into a disk. Wrap in plastic wrap, and refrigerate for at least 30 minutes or up to 2 days.

Photo by Matt Armendariz

PLUM-AND-PRETZEL CHEESECAKE PIE

Makes 1 (9-inch) pie

Recipe by Marian Cooper Cairns

Salty pretzels are an excellent base for this slightly sweet mascarpone cheesecake. The plums macerate in a mixture of brown sugar and nutmeg and then bake directly on the cheesecake batter. Finish this dessert with an orange-scented glaze for a pretty presentation.

4	large plums (360 grams), pitted and cut into ¼-inch-thick slices
6	tablespoons (84 grams) firmly packed light brown sugar, divided
½	teaspoon (1.5 grams) kosher salt
¼	teaspoon ground nutmeg
2	cups (186 grams) finely ground pretzels
10	tablespoons (140 grams) unsalted butter, melted
¼	cup (50 grams) granulated sugar
8	ounces (225 grams) mascarpone cheese, softened
4	ounces (115 grams) cream cheese, softened
1	large egg (50 grams)
2	teaspoons (8 grams) vanilla extract
1	teaspoon (2 grams) orange zest
1	tablespoon (15 grams) orange liqueur*
½	teaspoon (1.5 grams) cornstarch

1. In a large bowl, toss together plums, 4 tablespoons (56 grams) brown sugar, salt, and nutmeg. Let stand for 45 minutes, stirring every 15 minutes.

2. Preheat oven to 350°F (180°C).

3. In a large bowl, stir together pretzels, melted butter, and granulated sugar until combined. Press pretzel mixture firmly into a 9-inch pie plate.

4. Bake until golden around the edges, 10 to 12 minutes. Let cool completely. Reduce oven temperature to 325°F (170°C).

5. In the bowl of a stand mixer fitted with the paddle attachment, beat mascarpone, cream cheese, and remaining 2 tablespoons (28 grams) brown sugar at medium speed until smooth. Add egg, vanilla, and zest, beating until combined. Spoon into prepared crust.

6. Drain plums, reserving ¼ cup (60 grams) juice. Arrange plums on top of mascarpone mixture in a circular pattern, slightly overlapping (you may have a few leftover plum slices).

7. Bake until filling is set, 45 to 55 minutes. Let cool completely on a wire rack.

8. In a small saucepan, whisk together reserved ¼ cup (60 grams) plum juice, orange liqueur, and cornstarch. Bring to a boil over medium heat, and cook until thickened. Brush over pie. Refrigerate for at least 3 hours or overnight.

We used Grand Marnier.

Photo by Matt Armendariz

STRAWBERRY RASPBERRY COBBLER

Makes 6 servings

Traditional only in method, this berry cobbler has a Middle Eastern flair with cardamom and rose water. This cobbler made with cake batter soaks up the fruit's flavorful juices as it bakes and develops a light, spongy crumb. Pistachios create a slightly crunchy texture that pairs well with the tender baked fruit.

½	pound (227 grams) sliced fresh strawberries
½	pound (227 grams) fresh raspberries
¾	cup (150 grams) granulated sugar
1	tablespoon (15 grams) fresh lemon juice
1	cup (125 grams) all-purpose flour
1	cup (240 grams) whole milk
½	cup (48 grams) pistachio meal
2	teaspoons (10 grams) baking powder
1	teaspoon (2 grams) ground cardamom
1	teaspoon (4 grams) rose water
½	teaspoon (1.5 grams) kosher salt
½	cup (113 grams) unsalted butter, melted

1. In a medium bowl, stir together strawberries, raspberries, sugar, and lemon juice. Let stand until a fruit syrup forms, about 20 minutes.

2. Preheat oven to 375°F (190°C).

3. In a large bowl, stir together flour, milk, pistachio meal, baking powder, cardamom, rose water, and salt. Stir in melted butter until well combined. Pour into an ungreased 8-inch square baking pan, smoothing top. Spoon berry mixture over batter. (Make sure to pour the fruit mixture over the batter quickly. If the batter cools too much, the fruit won't sink as well.)

4. Bake until golden brown, 35 to 45 minutes, loosely covering with foil halfway through baking to prevent excess browning. Cover and refrigerate for up to 3 days.

Note: *To make pistachio nut meal, grind roasted salted pistachios in a food processor.*

PEAR, HONEY, AND LIME PIE

Makes 1 (9-inch) pie

For this rosette-style pie, pears poached in a Sauvignon Blanc and honey bath sit atop a creamy vanilla bean custard and lime-scented piecrust.

1¼ cups (156 grams) all-purpose flour
1½ teaspoons (6 grams) granulated sugar
1 teaspoon (3 grams) kosher salt
½ cup (113 grams) cold unsalted butter, cubed
3 tablespoons (45 grams) ice water
2 teaspoons (4 grams) lime zest
1 tablespoon (15 grams) fresh lime juice
Vanilla Custard (recipe follows)
Poached Pears (recipe follows)

1. In the work bowl of a food processor, place flour, sugar, and salt; pulse until combined. Add cold butter, pulsing until mixture is crumbly. Add 3 tablespoons (45 grams) ice water and lime zest and juice, pulsing until dough just comes together. Refrigerate for 30 minutes.
2. Preheat oven to 350°F (180°C).
3. On a lightly floured surface, roll dough into a 12-inch circle. Transfer to a 9-inch pie plate, pressing into bottom and up sides. Trim excess dough to ½ inch beyond edge of plate. Fold edges under, and crimp as desired. Prick bottom and sides of dough with a fork. Refrigerate for at least 30 minutes.
4. Top dough with a piece of parchment paper, letting ends extend over edges of plate. Add pie weights.
5. Bake for 15 minutes. Carefully remove paper and weights. Bake until golden brown, 10 to 15 minutes more. Let cool for 10 minutes. Pour Vanilla Custard into warm crust. Place pie in a roasting pan. Fill roasting pan with enough water to come halfway up sides of pie plate. (This is to prevent custard from curdling.)
6. Bake for 30 minutes. Arrange Poached Pears in a spiral pattern on top of Vanilla Custard. Bake 30 minutes more, covering with foil during last 15 minutes of baking to prevent excess browning.

VANILLA CUSTARD

Makes about 1 cup

1 cup (240 grams) heavy whipping cream
¼ cup (50 grams) granulated sugar
2 large eggs (100 grams)
1 large egg yolk (19 grams)
1 teaspoon (6 grams) vanilla bean paste
¼ teaspoon kosher salt

1. In a medium bowl, whisk together cream, sugar, eggs, egg yolk, vanilla bean paste, and salt until smooth.

POACHED PEARS

Makes about 5 cups

1⅔ cups (400 grams) Sauvignon Blanc
1⅔ cups (400 grams) water
½ cup (100 grams) granulated sugar
⅓ cup (113 grams) honey
2 pounds (908 grams) Anjou pears, peeled and thinly sliced

1. In a large saucepan, bring wine, 1⅔ cups (400 grams) water, sugar, and honey to a boil over medium-high heat. Reduce heat, and add pears. Cover pears with a cheesecloth, and simmer until pears are pliable but not mushy, about 10 minutes. Strain liquid before using.

MANGO FRANGIPANE PIE

Makes 1 (9-inch) pie

Soft slices of mango are baked into a frangipane filling while a sweet basil crust rounds out the fruity-nutty flavor.

½	cup (120 grams) plus 1 teaspoon (5 grams) water, divided
5	fresh basil leaves (4 grams)
3	cups (375 grams) all-purpose flour
1	tablespoon (12 grams) granulated sugar
1⅛	teaspoons (3 grams) kosher salt
1	cup (227 grams) cold unsalted butter, cubed
⅓	cup plus 2 teaspoons (90 grams) ice water
2	tablespoons (4 grams) chopped fresh basil
1½	pounds (765 grams) mangoes, peeled and diced

Frangipane (recipe follows)
1	large egg (50 grams)

1. In a small saucepan, bring ½ cup (120 grams) water to a boil over medium-high heat. Remove from heat, and add basil leaves. Let basil steep for 5 minutes. Strain basil juice, discarding solids. Refrigerate until chilled.
2. In the work bowl of a food processor, place flour, sugar, and salt; pulse until combined. Add cold butter, pulsing until mixture is crumbly. Add ⅓ cup plus 2 teaspoons (90 grams) ice water, chopped basil, and basil juice, pulsing until dough just comes together. Divide dough in half, and shape each half into a disk. Wrap tightly in plastic wrap, and refrigerate for 30 minutes.
3. Preheat oven to 350°F (180°C).
4. On a lightly floured surface, roll half of dough into a 12-inch circle. Transfer to a 9-inch pie plate, pressing into bottom and up sides. Trim excess dough to ½ inch beyond edge of plate. Fold edges under. Refrigerate for at least 30 minutes.
5. Top dough with a piece of parchment paper, letting ends extend over edges of plate. Add pie weights.
6. Bake for 15 minutes. Carefully remove paper and weights. Bake until golden brown, about 10 minutes more. Let cool for 10 minutes.
7. Fold mangoes into Frangipane, and pour mixture into prepared crust.
8. On a lightly floured surface, roll remaining dough into a 9½-inch circle. Using a sharp knife, cut ¼-inch-wide strips. Reserve 3 strips. Arrange remaining strips over filling in a lattice design.
9. Brush water on rim of prepared dough in plate. Place reserved 3 dough strips along brushed rim, and crimp as desired. In a small bowl, whisk together egg and remaining 1 teaspoon (5 grams) water; lightly brush over dough.
10. Bake until golden brown, 35 to 45 minutes.

FRANGIPANE
Makes about 1 cup

¾	cup plus 1 tablespoon (211 grams) almond paste
⅔	cup (150 grams) unsalted butter, softened
3	large eggs (150 grams)
⅓	cup (42 grams) all-purpose flour

1. In the bowl of a stand mixer fitted with the paddle attachment, beat almond paste at medium speed until smooth. In a small bowl, beat butter with a mixer at medium speed until creamy. Add butter to almond paste, beating until combined. Add eggs, one at a time, beating well after each addition. Scrape sides of bowl, and beat in flour.

FRENCH SILK PIE

Makes 1 (9-inch) pie

Bergamot-scented Earl Grey tea in this piecrust brings a citrusy, floral finish and balances the richness of our bittersweet chocolate mousse.

1¼   cups (156 grams) all-purpose flour
1½   teaspoons (6 grams) granulated sugar
1¼   teaspoons (3 grams) kosher salt
1   teaspoon (2 grams) loose-leaf Earl Grey tea
½   cup (113 grams) cold unsalted butter, cubed
3   tablespoons (45 grams) ice-cold Earl Grey tea
French Silk Filling (recipe follows)
Garnish: fresh raspberries

1. In the work bowl of a food processor, place flour, sugar, salt, and loose-leaf tea; pulse until combined. Add cold butter, pulsing until mixture is crumbly. Gradually add ice-cold tea, pulsing until a dough forms. Turn out dough, and shape into a disk. Wrap tightly in plastic wrap, and refrigerate for at least 30 minutes.
2. Let dough stand at room temperature until slightly softened, about 5 minutes. On a lightly floured surface, roll dough into a 12-inch circle. Transfer to a 9-inch pie plate, pressing into bottom and up sides. Trim excess dough to ½ inch beyond edge of plate. Fold edges under. Prick bottom of dough with a fork. Refrigerate for 30 minutes.
3. On a lightly floured surface, roll excess dough to ¼-inch thickness. Using a small triangle cutter, cut dough, rerolling scraps as necessary. Brush water on rim of prepared dough in plate. Place triangles along brushed rim, alternating direction of the points. Freeze for 30 minutes.
4. Preheat oven to 350°F (180°C).
5. Top dough with a piece of parchment paper, letting ends extend over edges of plate. Add pie weights.
6. Bake for 15 minutes. Carefully remove paper and weights. Bake until golden brown, about 20 minutes more. Let cool completely on a wire rack.
7. Pour French Silk Filling into prepared crust. Refrigerate until set, about 30 minutes. Garnish with raspberries, if desired.

FRENCH SILK FILLING
Makes about 2 cups

1½   cups plus 4 teaspoons (380 grams) heavy whipping cream, divided
1   tablespoon (12 grams) granulated sugar, divided
2   large egg yolks (37 grams)
8   ounces (227 grams) 60% cacao bittersweet chocolate, chopped

1. In a small saucepan, heat ½ cup plus 1 teaspoon (125 grams) cream and ½ tablespoon (6 grams) sugar over medium heat.
2. In a medium bowl, whisk together egg yolks and remaining ½ tablespoon (6 grams) sugar. Whisking constantly, slowly pour hot cream mixture into yolk mixture. Return cream mixture to saucepan, and cook until a candy thermometer registers 180°F (82°C).
3. Place chocolate in a medium bowl. Strain hot cream mixture over chocolate, and let stand for 5 minutes. Whisk until ganache is smooth and shiny.
4. In the bowl of a stand mixer fitted with the whisk attachment, beat remaining 1 cup plus 3 teaspoons (255 grams) cream at high speed until soft peaks form. Fold whipped cream into ganache until combined.

PEACH-PLUM CRUMBLE PIE

Makes 1 (9-inch) pie

Nutty browned butter adds another dimension of flavor to the crumbly, crunchy topping for this stone fruit-filled pie.

1½   pounds (681 grams) fresh peaches, peeled, pitted, and sliced (3 to 4 medium peaches)
1½   pounds (681 grams) fresh plums, pitted and sliced (4 to 6 plums)
1   cup (200 grams) plus 2 tablespoons (24 grams) granulated sugar, divided
1   lemon (99 grams), zested and juiced
½   teaspoon (1.5 grams) kosher salt
Basic Pie Dough (recipe on page 192)
1   large egg (50 grams)
1   teaspoon (5 grams) water
1   tablespoon (8 grams) cornstarch
2   tablespoons (18 grams) low-sugar fruit pectin
1   teaspoon (2 grams) ground nutmeg
Browned Butter Pecan Streusel (recipe follows)

1. In a large bowl, stir together peaches, plums, 1 cup (200 grams) sugar, lemon zest and juice, and salt. Let stand for 30 minutes.
2. Let Basic Pie Dough stand at room temperature until slightly softened, about 5 minutes. On a lightly floured surface, roll dough into a 12-inch circle. Transfer to a 9-inch pie plate, pressing into bottom and up sides. Trim excess dough to ½ inch beyond edge of plate. Fold edges under.
3. On a lightly floured surface, roll excess dough to ¼-inch thickness. Using a sharp knife, cut dough into 8 (½-inch-wide) strips. Line up 4 strips vertically. Lightly hold strips together at center. Use the thumb and forefinger to twist the bottom half of the dough to the left. Pinch the end to hold the shape. Twist the top half of the dough to the right, pinching the end to hold the shape. Repeat with remaining 4 strips.
4. Brush water on rim of prepared dough in plate. Place dough ropes along brushed rim. Overlap end pieces, and pinch together to seal. Freeze for 30 minutes. In a small bowl, whisk together egg and 1 teaspoon (5 grams) water; lightly brush over dough.
5. Transfer 1 cup (188 grams) fruit mixture to a small bowl, and mash with a fork. Strain remaining fruit mixture through a colander into a large bowl. Reserve ½ cup (120 grams) fruit juice; discard remainder. Return drained fruit to large bowl, and toss with cornstarch.

6. Preheat oven to 400°F (200°C).
7. In a small skillet, whisk together reserved ½ cup (120 grams) fruit juice, pectin, nutmeg, and remaining 2 tablespoons (24 grams) sugar. Cook over medium heat until pectin is dissolved and mixture thickens slightly, 3 to 4 minutes.
8. Toss together fruit mixture and reserved 1 cup (188 grams) mashed fruit; pour into prepared crust. Drizzle with pectin mixture. Top with Browned Butter Pecan Streusel. Place pie on a baking sheet.
9. Bake for 20 minutes. Reduce oven temperature to 375°F (190°C), and cover pie loosely with foil. Bake until golden brown and bubbly, 30 to 40 minutes more.

BROWNED BUTTER PECAN STREUSEL

Makes 1½ cups

½   cup (57 grams) unsalted butter
½   cup plus 1 tablespoon (71 grams) all-purpose flour
½   cup (40 grams) old-fashioned oats
⅓   cups (38 grams) toasted chopped pecans
¼   cup (50 grams) granulated sugar
2   tablespoons (28 grams) firmly packed dark brown sugar
1   teaspoon (3 grams) kosher salt

1. In a small saucepan, melt butter over medium heat. Cook until butter turns a medium-brown color and has a nutty aroma, about 10 minutes. Remove from heat, and let cool slightly.
2. In a medium bowl, whisk together flour, oats, pecans, sugars, and salt. Drizzle with browned butter, and stir with a wooden spoon until combined. Crumble with your fingertips until desired consistency is reached.

PINEAPPLE & COCONUT PIE

Makes 1 (9-inch) pie

Think of this tropical dish as a Piña Colada in pie form, minus the paper umbrella and rum.

3   cups (375 grams) all-purpose flour
1   tablespoon (12 grams) granulated sugar
2   teaspoons (6 grams) kosher salt
1   cup (227 grams) cold unsalted butter, cubed
⅓   cup plus 2 teaspoons (90 grams) ice water
2   tablespoons (12 grams) orange zest
2   tablespoons (30 grams) fresh orange juice
1   large egg (50 grams)
1   teaspoon (5 grams) water
4   cups (800 grams) fresh pineapple, peeled, cored, sliced ¼-inch-thick, and divided

Toasted Coconut Pastry Cream (recipe follows)
Garnish: toasted flaked coconut

1. In the work bowl of a food processor, place flour, sugar, and salt; pulse until combined. Add cold butter, pulsing until mixture is crumbly. Add ⅓ cup plus 2 teaspoons (90 grams) ice water and orange zest and juice, pulsing until dough just comes together. Divide dough in half, and shape each half into a disk. Wrap tightly in plastic wrap, and refrigerate for 30 minutes.
2. Preheat oven to 350°F (180°C).

3. On a lightly floured surface, roll half of dough into a 12-inch circle. Transfer to a 9-inch pie plate, pressing into bottom and up sides. Trim excess dough to ½ inch beyond edge of plate. Fold edges under. Prick bottom and sides of dough with a fork. Refrigerate for at least 30 minutes.
4. On a lightly floured surface, roll remaining dough into a 10-inch circle. Using a sharp knife, cut ¼-inch-wide strips. Braid dough strips, pinching ends to seal.
5. Brush water on rim of prepared dough in plate. Place braided dough along brushed rim. Overlap end pieces, and pinch together to seal. In a small bowl, whisk together egg and 1 teaspoon (5 grams) water; lightly brush over dough.
6. Top dough with a piece of parchment paper, letting ends extend over edges of plate. Add pie weights.
7. Bake for 15 minutes. Carefully remove paper and weights. Bake until golden brown, about 15 minutes more. Let cool for 10 minutes.
8. Arrange 1 cup (200 grams) pineapple in bottom of prepared crust. Top with Toasted Coconut Pastry Cream. Top with remaining 3 cups (600 grams) pineapple. Garnish with coconut, if desired.

TOASTED COCONUT PASTRY CREAM

Makes about 2 cups

1   cup (240 grams) whole milk
1   cup (240 grams) unsweetened coconut milk
⅔   cup (133 grams) granulated sugar, divided
4½ tablespoons (36 grams) cornstarch
5   large egg yolks (93 grams)
2   tablespoons (28 grams) unsalted butter, softened
⅔   cup (56 grams) unsweetened flaked coconut, toasted

1. In a medium saucepan, bring milk, coconut milk, and ⅓ cup (66.5 grams) sugar to a boil over medium heat.
2. In a medium bowl, whisk together cornstarch, egg yolks, and remaining ⅓ cup (66.5 grams) sugar until combined. Whisking constantly, add 1 cup (240 grams) hot milk mixture to yolk mixture. Pour warm yolk mixture into remaining hot milk mixture in saucepan. Cook, whisking constantly, until thickened, 1 to 2 minutes. Remove from heat, and add butter. Fold in coconut.
3. Pour mixture onto a rimmed half-sheet pan, and cover with a piece of plastic wrap, pressing wrap directly onto surface. Let cool to room temperature before using.

MEYER LEMON & BLUEBERRY PIE

Makes 1 (9-inch) pie

Fragrant Meyer lemons are the heart and soul of our tart lemon curd, brightening the natural sweetness of ripe blueberries.

2½ cups (313 grams) all-purpose flour
2 teaspoons (8 grams) granulated sugar
2 teaspoons (6 grams) kosher salt
1 cup (227 grams) cold unsalted butter, cubed
½ cup (120 grams) whole buttermilk, chilled
Blueberry Jam (recipe follows)
Meyer Lemon Curd (recipe follows)
Garnish: Glazed Blueberries (see Pro Tip)

1. In the work bowl of a food processor, place flour, sugar, and salt; pulse until combined. Add cold butter, pulsing until mixture is crumbly. Add buttermilk, 1 tablespoon (15 grams) at a time, just until a dough forms. Turn out dough, and shape into a disk. Wrap in plastic wrap, and refrigerate for at least 30 minutes.
2. Let dough stand at room temperature until slightly softened, about 5 minutes. On a lightly floured surface, roll dough into a 12-inch circle. Transfer to a 9-inch pie plate, pressing into bottom and up sides. Prick bottom of dough with a fork. Trim excess dough to ½ inch beyond edge of plate. Fold edges under.
3. Create a fluted crust by using thumb and forefinger on one hand as spacers, and pushing dough in with other thumb. Freeze for 30 minutes.
4. Preheat oven to 350°F (180°C).
5. Top dough with a piece of parchment paper, letting ends extend over edges of plate. Add pie weights.
6. Bake for 15 minutes. Carefully remove paper and weights. Bake until golden brown, about 15 minutes more. Let cool completely on a wire rack.
7. Spoon room temperature Blueberry Jam into prepared crust. Refrigerate for at least 35 minutes. Top with Meyer Lemon Curd, smoothing with an offset spatula. Garnish with Glazed Blueberries, if desired.

BLUEBERRY JAM
Makes about 1¼ cups

⅓ cup (67 grams) granulated sugar
¼ cup (60 grams) water

1 tablespoon (9 grams) low-sugar fruit pectin
1 teaspoon (4 grams) unflavored gelatin
1 teaspoon (5 grams) fresh Meyer lemon juice
⅛ teaspoon kosher salt
1¾ cups (298 grams) fresh blueberries

1. In a medium saucepan, whisk together sugar, ¼ cup (60 grams) water, pectin, gelatin, lemon juice, and salt. Add blueberries, and bring to a boil over medium heat. Reduce heat to low, and simmer, whisking constantly, until smooth, about 5 minutes.
2. Transfer blueberry mixture to a medium bowl, and place in a larger bowl filled with ice. Let cool in ice bath, whisking occasionally, until jam has thickened and reached room temperature.

MEYER LEMON CURD
Makes about 2¾ cups

2 cups (200 grams) granulated sugar
2 tablespoons (12 grams) Meyer lemon zest
½ cup (64 grams) cornstarch
½ teaspoon (1.5 grams) kosher salt
1½ cups (360 grams) fresh Meyer lemon juice
½ cup (120 grams) water
10 large egg yolks (186 grams)

1 teaspoon (4 grams) unflavored gelatin
¼ cup (57 grams) unsalted butter, softened

1. In a medium saucepan, rub together sugar and zest with fingertips. Whisk in cornstarch and salt. Add lemon juice and ½ cup (120 grams) water, whisking until smooth. Whisk in egg yolks and gelatin. Cook over medium-high heat until thickened, about 8 minutes. Remove from heat, and stir in butter.
2. Line a rimmed baking sheet with plastic wrap. Pour curd onto prepared pan, and press another piece of plastic wrap directly onto surface of curd. Place pan on a wire rack, and let cool to room temperature. Refrigerate until chilled.

> **PRO TIP**
> To make **Glazed Blueberries**, heat ⅓ cup (67 grams) granulated sugar, ⅓ cup (80 grams) water, and ¼ teaspoon (1.5 grams) vanilla bean paste over medium heat in a small saucepan until sugar is dissolved. Transfer to a medium bowl; fold in 6 ounces (175 grams) fresh blueberries. Let cool to room temperature, and drain. This will yield about ½ cup.

STRAWBERRY-RHUBARB PIES

Makes 3 (5-inch) pies

Strawberry and rhubarb are a classic pairing for a reason. Slightly sour rhubarb holds its own against the natural sweetness of strawberries and their complementary hues of pink and red offer a burst of warm color to this summer dessert.

2   recipes Basic Pie Dough (recipe follows)
1   pound (680 grams) quartered fresh strawberries
1¼   cups (125 grams) chopped fresh rhubarb
1   cup (200 grams) granulated sugar, divided
¼   cup plus 3 tablespoons (61 grams) tapioca flour
½   teaspoon (1.5 grams) kosher salt

1. Preheat oven to 350°F (180°C).
2. Let Basic Pie Dough stand at room temperature until slightly softened, about 5 minutes. Divide half of dough into 3 equal pieces. On a lightly floured surface, roll each piece of dough into a 6½-inch circle. Transfer each circle to a 5-inch pie plate, pressing into bottom and up sides. Fold edges under.
3. In a large saucepan, heat strawberries, rhubarb, and ½ cup (100 grams) sugar over medium heat. Cook, stirring occasionally, until berries are tender, about 8 minutes. Strain fruit through a fine-mesh sieve into a medium bowl; reserve 1 cup (221 grams) fruit juice.
4. In another medium bowl, whisk together reserved 1 cup (221 grams) fruit juice, flour, salt, and remaining ½ cup (100 grams) sugar. Add fruit to juice mixture, stirring gently to combine. Divide mixture among prepared crusts.
5. On a lightly floured surface, roll remaining dough into an 8-inch circle. Using a sharp knife, cut 7 (½-inch-wide) strips. Create a lattice design on one pie by laying 3 strips horizontally on top of filling, evenly spaced apart. Fold back top and bottom strips. Place another strip vertically over horizontal strip. Unfold folded strips. Fold back center horizontal strip. Place another strip vertically over horizontal strips, evenly spaced apart. Unfold folded strip. Repeat with remaining strips. Trim edges of strips to ½ inch beyond edge of plate. Tuck strips under bottom crust. Repeat procedure to create a lattice design for remaining two pies.
6. With remaining dough, cut 9 (1½-inch-wide) strips. Lay 3 strips on edges of each pie to form a triangle on top of lattice design. Trim edges as necessary.
7. Bake until crusts are golden brown and filling is bubbly, 30 to 40 minutes, loosely covering with foil to prevent excess browning, if necessary. Let cool to room temperature before serving.

BASIC PIE DOUGH
Makes 1 (9-inch) crust or 3 (5-inch) crusts

1¼   cups (156 grams) all-purpose flour
1½   teaspoons (6 grams) granulated sugar
1   teaspoon (3 grams) kosher salt
½   cup (113 grams) cold unsalted butter, cubed
¼   cup (60 grams) ice water

1. In the work bowl of a food processor, place flour, sugar, and salt; pulse until combined. Add cold butter, pulsing until mixture is crumbly. Gradually add ¼ cup (60 grams) ice water, pulsing until a dough forms.
2. Turn out dough onto a lightly floured surface, and shape into a disk. Wrap tightly in plastic wrap, and refrigerate for at least 30 minutes.

COCONUT CREAM PIE

Makes 1 (9-inch) pie

This creamy, tropical dessert makes use of unsweetened coconut milk in both the filling and the fluffy cloud of whipped topping.

1¼ cups (156 grams) all-purpose flour
1 teaspoon (4 grams) granulated sugar
1 teaspoon (3 grams) kosher salt
½ cup (113 grams) cold unsalted butter, cubed
3 tablespoons (45 grams) whole buttermilk, chilled
Coconut Filling (recipe follows)
Coconut Whipped Cream (recipe follows)
Garnish: toasted sweetened flaked coconut

1. In a medium bowl, stir together flour, sugar, and salt. Using a pastry blender, cut in cold butter until mixture is crumbly. Add buttermilk, 1 tablespoon (15 grams) at a time, until a dough forms. Turn out dough, and shape into a disk. Wrap tightly in plastic wrap, and refrigerate for at least 30 minutes.
2. Preheat oven to 350°F (180°C).
3. On a lightly floured surface, roll dough into a 12-inch circle. Transfer to a 9-inch pie plate, pressing into bottom and up sides. Trim excess dough to ½ inch beyond edge of plate. Fold edges under, and crimp as desired. Top with a piece of parchment paper, letting ends extend over edges of plate. Add pie weights.
4. Bake for 20 minutes. Carefully remove paper and weights. Bake until golden brown, about 10 minutes more. Let cool for 20 minutes on a wire rack.
5. Spoon warm Coconut Filling into prepared crust. Let cool for 10 minutes. Press a piece of plastic wrap directly onto surface of filling. Refrigerate until firm, about 3 hours. Top with Coconut Whipped Cream, and garnish with coconut, if desired.

COCONUT FILLING
Makes about 4 cups

½ cup (100 grams) granulated sugar
3 tablespoons (24 grams) cornstarch
⅛ teaspoon kosher salt
1 cup (240 grams) whole milk
1 cup (240 grams) unsweetened coconut milk
4 large egg yolks (74 grams)
1 cup (84 grams) sweetened flaked coconut
1 teaspoon (4 grams) vanilla extract

1. In a medium saucepan, combine sugar, cornstarch, and salt; whisk in milk, coconut milk, and egg yolks. Cook over medium heat, stirring constantly, until thickened, about 10 minutes. Remove from heat; stir in coconut and vanilla. Use immediately.

COCONUT WHIPPED CREAM
Makes about 3 cups

1½ cups (360 grams) heavy whipping cream
6 tablespoons (72 grams) granulated sugar
¼ cup (60 grams) unsweetened coconut milk

1. In the bowl of a stand mixer fitted with the whisk attachment, beat cream and sugar at high speed until soft peaks form. Add coconut milk, beating until stiff peaks form, about 1 minute.

RASPBERRY LEMON CHIFFON PIE

Makes 1 (9-inch) pie

Your favorite in-flight snack gets a starring role in this sweet-tart pie. A buttery Biscoff Cookie crust balances out the berry citrus filling while a toasty Lemon Swiss Meringue topping adds a touch of marshmallow-like decadence.

1½ cups (180 grams) crushed Biscoff Cookies
¼ cup (50 grams) granulated sugar
¼ cup (57 grams) unsalted butter, melted
¼ teaspoon kosher salt
Raspberry Lemon Filling (recipe follows)
Lemon Swiss Meringue (recipe follows)
Garnish: fresh raspberries, grated lemon zest

1. Preheat oven to 350°F (180°C).
2. In a medium bowl, stir together crushed cookies, sugar, melted butter, and salt. Press mixture into bottom and up sides of 9-inch pie plate.
3. Bake for 10 minutes. Pour Raspberry Lemon Filling into prepared crust. Top with Lemon Swiss Meringue. Using a kitchen torch, brown meringue. Garnish with raspberries and zest, if desired.

RASPBERRY LEMON FILLING
Makes about 1½ cups

1½ cups (255 grams) fresh raspberries, divided
¼ cup (50 grams) plus 1 tablespoon (12 grams) granulated sugar, divided
¼ cup (60 grams) water
2 tablespoons (12 grams) lemon zest
1 tablespoon (15 grams) fresh lemon juice
½ teaspoon (1.5 grams) kosher salt
2 tablespoons (18 grams) tapioca flour
1 tablespoon (12 grams) unflavored gelatin
4 large egg whites (120 grams)

1. In a small saucepan, bring ½ cup (85 grams) raspberries, ¼ cup (50 grams) sugar, ¼ cup (60 grams) water, lemon zest and juice, and salt to a boil over medium heat. Whisk in flour and gelatin; cook until thickened, 2 to 3 minutes. Let cool to room temperature.
2. In the bowl of a stand mixer fitted with the whisk attachment, beat egg whites and remaining 1 tablespoon (12 grams) sugar at high speed until soft peaks form. Fold into raspberry mixture. Fold in remaining 1 cup (170 grams) raspberries.

LEMON SWISS MERINGUE
Makes about 2 cups

1 cup (200 grams) granulated sugar
4 large egg whites (120 grams)
1 tablespoon (6 grams) lemon zest

1. In the top of a double boiler, whisk together all ingredients. Cook over simmering water, stirring constantly, until sugar is dissolved and a candy thermometer registers 140°F (60°C). Transfer to the bowl of a stand mixer fitted with the whisk attachment. Beat at high speed until stiff and glossy peaks form, 8 to 10 minutes.

KEY LIME PIE

Makes 1 (9-inch) pie

Our take on the beloved original features a salty-sweet crust and intense lime flavor thanks to a cup of juice from this pie's tiny namesake citrus.

1¼ cups (150grams) graham cracker crumbs
¼ cup (55 grams) firmly packed light brown sugar
¼ cup (57 grams) unsalted butter, melted
½ teaspoon (1.5 grams) kosher salt
3½ cups (840 grams) sweetened condensed milk

1 cup (240 grams) Key lime juice*
2 large eggs (100 grams)
1½ cups (360 grams) heavy whipping cream
¼ cup (30 grams) confectioners' sugar

1. Preheat oven to 350°F (180°C).
2. In a medium bowl, stir together graham cracker crumbs, brown sugar, melted butter, and salt. Using a measuring cup, press mixture into bottom and up sides of a 9-inch pie plate.
3. Bake until lightly browned, about 10 minutes. Let cool completely.
4. In a large bowl, whisk together condensed milk, lime juice, and eggs until combined. Pour into prepared crust.

5. Bake until set, about 10 minutes. Let cool completely.
6. In the bowl of a stand mixer fitted with the whisk attachment, beat cream and confectioners' sugar at high speed until stiff peaks form, 2 to 3 minutes. Spread whipped cream over pie.

Regular lime juice may be substituted.

CHESTNUT HAZELNUT CARAMEL PIE

Makes 1 (9-inch) pie

Chestnuts infuse this custard filling with a sweet, earthy flavor while a toasted hazelnut meal crust brings a warm nuttiness.

1	cup (125 grams) all-purpose flour
¼	cup (24 grams) hazelnut flour
1	teaspoon (4 grams) granulated sugar
1	teaspoon (3 grams) kosher salt
½	cup (113 grams) cold unsalted butter, cubed
4	tablespoons (60 grams) ice water

Caramel Sauce (recipe follows)
Chestnut Filling (recipe follows)
Garnish: Candied Hazelnuts (see Pro Tip)

1. In the work bowl of a food processor, place flours, sugar, and salt; pulse until combined. Add cold butter, pulsing until mixture is crumbly. Add ice water, 1 tablespoon (15 grams) at a time, just until a dough forms. Turn out dough, and shape into a disk. Wrap tightly in plastic wrap, and refrigerate for at least 30 minutes.
2. Let dough stand at room temperate until slightly softened, about 5 minutes. On a lightly floured surface, roll dough into a 12-inch circle. Transfer to a 9-inch pie plate, pressing into bottom and up sides. Trim excess dough to ½ inch beyond edge of plate. Fold edges under, and crimp as desired. Prick bottom of dough with a fork. Refrigerate for 30 minutes.
3. Preheat oven to 350°F (180°C).
4. Top dough with a piece of parchment paper, letting ends extend over edges of plate. Add pie weights.
5. Bake for 15 minutes. Carefully remove paper and weights. Bake until golden brown, about 15 minutes more. Let cool completely on a wire rack.
6. Pour Caramel Sauce into prepared crust. Freeze until set, about 30 minutes. Pour Chestnut Filling over Caramel Sauce. Refrigerate until set, about 1 hour. Garnish with Candied Hazelnuts, if desired.

CARAMEL SAUCE
Makes about 1½ cups

⅔	cup (133 grams) granulated sugar
2	tablespoons (42 grams) light corn syrup
¾	cup (180 grams) heavy whipping cream, warmed
¾	cup (180 grams) heavy whipping cream, chilled
2	large egg yolks (37 grams)
¼	cup (57 grams) unsalted butter, softened
½	teaspoon (1.5 grams) kosher salt

1. In a medium saucepan, heat sugar and corn syrup over medium heat until amber colored and a candy thermometer registers 180°F (82°C). Remove from heat, and carefully add warm cream. Transfer caramel to a medium bowl; set aside.
2. In same saucepan, bring chilled cream to a boil over medium heat.
3. Place egg yolks in a medium bowl. Whisking constantly, slowly pour hot cream into yolks. Return cream mixture to saucepan, and heat over medium heat. Add caramel, whisking until combined. Add butter and salt, whisking until smooth.

CHESTNUT FILLING
Makes about 2 cups

1½	cups (360 grams) water
1¼	cups (250 grams) plus ⅓ cup (67 grams) granulated sugar, divided
¾	cup plus 2 tablespoons (228 grams) roasted and peeled chestnuts
1⅓	cups (320 grams) heavy whipping cream
1¼	teaspoons (5 grams) unflavored gelatin
3	large eggs (150 grams)
5	large egg yolks (93 grams)
2	tablespoons (28 grams) unsalted butter

1. In a large saucepan, bring 1½ cups (360 grams) water, 1¼ cups (250 grams) sugar, and chestnuts to a boil over medium-high heat. Reduce heat to low, and simmer for 30 minutes. Strain chestnut mixture into a large bowl, reserving ⅓ cup (113 grams) chestnut syrup. Let cool completely.
2. Transfer candied chestnut mixture to the work bowl of food processor; process until finely chopped. Set aside.
3. In a medium saucepan, bring cream and reserved ⅓ cup (113 grams) chestnut syrup to a boil over medium heat. Whisk in gelatin.
4. In a medium bowl, whisk together eggs, egg yolks, and remaining ⅓ cup (67 grams) sugar. Slowly pour hot cream mixture into egg mixture. Return cream mixture to saucepan, and cook, whisking constantly, until mixture registers 180°F (82°C) on a candy thermometer. Remove from heat, and stir in butter. Strain into a medium bowl. Stir ¾ cup candied chestnut purée into cream mixture. Use immediately.

PRO TIP
To make **Candied Hazelnuts**, pierce 24 toasted and cooled hazelnuts with wooden skewers, and insert in a Styrofoam block to hold skewers up. Place a newspaper on the floor to catch drips. Fill a large bowl with ice and halfway full with cold water. Set aside. In a small saucepan, heat ½ cup (100 grams) granulated sugar and 2 tablespoons (30 grams) water over medium heat until a candy thermometer registers 223°F (106°C) to 234°F (112°C). Place pan in prepared ice bath until mixture begins to thicken, about 45 seconds. Remove pan from ice bath, and place on a heatproof surface next to Styrofoam block. Carefully dip each hazelnut in caramel. Insert skewers in side of Styrofoam block, letting caramel drip onto newspaper. Once caramelized hazelnut threads have stiffened, transfer skewers upright. Store in a cool environment with low humidity until ready to use.

BUTTERSCOTCH PIE
WITH COCONUT CURRY CRUST

Makes 1 (9-inch) pie

A bit of curry in the crust pairs perfectly with the custardy butterscotch filling in this sweet yet slightly savory dessert.

½ cup (113 grams) unsalted butter, cubed
1¾ cups (385 grams) firmly packed dark brown sugar
¾ teaspoon (2.25 grams) kosher salt
⅔ cup (160 grams) heavy whipping cream, room temperature
4 large eggs (200 grams)
2 large egg yolks (37 grams)
1 tablespoon (13 grams) vanilla extract
Coconut Curry Crust (recipe follows)
Garnish: confectioners' sugar

1. Preheat oven to 400°F (200°C).
2. In a medium saucepan, melt butter over medium heat. Add brown sugar and salt, stirring to combine. Bring to a simmer, and cook for 3 minutes, stirring constantly. Remove from heat, and carefully whisk in cream. Let cool for 20 minutes.
3. To cream mixture, add eggs and egg yolks, one at a time, whisking until well combined after each addition. Stir in vanilla. Pour into prepared Coconut Curry Crust.
4. Bake for 10 minutes. Reduce oven temperature to 300°F (150°C), and bake until set but slightly jiggly in center, 25 to 30 minutes more. Let cool completely. Garnish with confectioners' sugar, if desired. Cover and refrigerate for up to 5 days.

COCONUT CURRY CRUST
Makes 1 (9-inch) crust

1¼ cups (156 grams) all-purpose flour
¼ cup (21 grams) desiccated coconut, toasted
1½ teaspoons (6 grams) granulated sugar
1 teaspoon (2 grams) madras curry powder
½ teaspoon (1 gram) ground ginger
½ teaspoon (1.5 grams) kosher salt
½ teaspoon (1 gram) ground black pepper
¼ teaspoon turmeric
½ cup (113 grams) cold unsalted butter, cubed
4 tablespoons (60 grams) ice water

1. In the work bowl of a food processor, place flour, coconut, sugar, curry powder, ginger, salt, pepper, and turmeric; pulse until combined. Add cold butter, and pulse until mixture is crumbly. Add ice water, 1 tablespoon (15 grams) at a time, just until dough comes together. Turn out dough, and shape into a disk. Wrap tightly in plastic wrap, and refrigerate for at least 30 minutes. Dough may be refrigerated for up to 3 days or frozen for up to 2 months.
2. On a lightly floured surface, roll dough into a 12-inch circle. Transfer to a 9-inch pie plate, pressing into bottom and up sides. Trim excess dough to ½ inch beyond edge of plate. Fold edges under. Using kitchen scissors, make a ¼-inch 45-degree cut into dough, being careful not to cut all the way through dough. Lay one dough piece over to left side. Make another ¼-inch cut, and lay to right side. Repeat process around pie plate until you reach the first cut. Freeze for 20 minutes.
3. Preheat oven to 400°F (200°C).
4. Top dough with a piece of parchment paper, letting ends extend over edges of plate. Add pie weights.
5. Bake for 20 minutes. Carefully remove paper and weights. Let cool completely.

PUMPKIN PIE WITH GOAT CHEESE CRUST

Makes 1 (9-inch) pie

A modern twist on pumpkin pie, this stovetop recipe has a spicy kick as vibrant as its orange custard filling. We put our own twist on the classic pumpkin pie formula by including gorgeous ripples of a salty-sweet Brown Sugar Whipped Cream.

1½   cups (360 grams) whole milk
6   large egg yolks (112 grams)
½   cup (100 grams) granulated sugar
3   tablespoons (24 grams) cornstarch
¾   teaspoon (1.5 grams) ground cinnamon
¼   teaspoon ground red pepper
1   cup (244 grams) canned pumpkin
Goat Cheese Crust (recipe follows)
Garnish: Brown Sugar Whipped Cream
        (recipe follows)

1. In a medium saucepan, bring milk to a boil over medium heat. In a medium bowl, whisk together egg yolks, sugar, cornstarch, cinnamon, and red pepper. Slowly add hot milk, whisking to combine. Return mixture to saucepan; bring to a boil. Cook, whisking constantly, until mixture is thickened.
2. Remove from heat, and stir in pumpkin.

Spoon filling into prepared Goat Cheese Crust. Let cool for 10 minutes. Press a piece of plastic wrap directly onto surface of filling. Refrigerate until firm, about 3 hours. Top with Brown Sugar Whipped Cream, if desired.

GOAT CHEESE CRUST
Makes 1 (9-inch) crust

2   cups (250 grams) all-purpose flour
1   teaspoon (3 grams) kosher salt
½   teaspoon (2.5 grams) baking powder
¾   cup (170 grams) cold unsalted butter,
      cubed
4   ounces (115 grams) cold goat cheese
1   tablespoon (15 grams) apple cider vinegar
2   tablespoons (30 grams) ice water

1. In the work bowl of a food processor, place flour, salt, and baking powder; pulse until combined. Add cold butter and goat cheese, and pulse until mixture is crumbly. Add vinegar, pulsing until combined. With processor running, add ice water, 1 tablespoon (15 grams) at a time, just until dough comes together. Turn out dough, and shape into a disk. Wrap tightly in plastic wrap, and refrigerate for at least 30 minutes.

2. On a lightly floured surface, roll dough into a 12-inch circle. Transfer to a 9-inch pie plate, pressing into bottom and up sides. Trim excess dough to ½ inch beyond edge of plate. Fold edges under, and crimp as desired. Freeze for 20 minutes.
3. Preheat oven to 400°F (200°C).
4. Top dough with a piece of parchment paper, letting ends extend over edges of plate. Add pie weights.
5. Bake for 20 minutes. Carefully remove paper and weights. Bake until golden brown, about 10 minutes more. Let cool completely on wire rack.

BROWN SUGAR WHIPPED CREAM
Makes about 2 cups

1   cup (240 grams) heavy whipping cream
¼   cup (55 grams) firmly packed brown
      sugar
¼   teaspoon kosher salt

1. In the bowl of a stand mixer fitted with the whisk attachment, beat cream, brown sugar, and salt at high speed until stiff peaks form, 2 to 3 minutes. Cover and refrigerate for up to 24 hours.

BUTTERMILK SHEET PAN PIE

Makes 10 to 12 servings

For our tangy update on chess pie, we cut the custardy sweetness with a burst of lemon flavor and a dash of nutmeg. For the finishing touch, dust a soft, snowy layer of confectioners' sugar over the top for a simple, rustic look.

4 cups (500 grams) all-purpose flour
¾ cup (170 grams) cold unsalted butter, cubed
½ cup (100 grams) granulated sugar
2 teaspoons (6 grams) kosher salt
1 cup (240 grams) cold water
Buttermilk Filling (recipe follows)
Garnish: confectioners' sugar

1. In the work bowl of a food processor, place flour, cold butter, granulated sugar, and salt; pulse until mixture is crumbly. With processor running, add 1 cup (240 grams) cold water in a slow, steady stream until a dough forms. Divide dough in half, and shape each half into a disk. Wrap in plastic wrap, and refrigerate for at least 30 minutes.
2. Preheat oven to 350°F (180°C).
3. On a lightly floured surface, roll half of dough into a 16x12-inch rectangle. Press dough into bottom and up sides of a 12x8½-inch rimmed baking sheet. Trim excess dough to ½ inch beyond edge of pan. Fold edges under. Prick bottom of dough with a fork.
4. On a lightly floured surface, roll remaining dough to ¼-inch thickness. Using a sharp knife, cut 2 (9x2-inch) strips and 2 (13x1-inch) strips. Brush water on rim of prepared dough in pan. Place dough strips along brushed rim, pressing gently to adhere.
5. Using kitchen scissors, make ½-inch 45-degree cuts around perimeter of dough, being careful not to cut all the way through dough. Alternate folding segments left and right.
6. Pour Buttermilk Filling into prepared crust. Bake for 20 minutes. Cover loosely with foil, and bake until set and light golden brown, 20 to 30 minutes more. Let cool completely on a wire rack. Garnish with confectioners' sugar, if desired. Cover and refrigerate for up to 5 days.

BUTTERMILK FILLING
Makes about 2½ cups

1 cup (200 grams) granulated sugar
3 tablespoons (24 grams) all-purpose flour
1½ tablespoons (13.5 grams) yellow cornmeal
1 teaspoon (3 grams) kosher salt
¼ teaspoon ground nutmeg
5 large eggs (250 grams), room temperature
¾ cup (180 grams) whole buttermilk, room temperature
3 tablespoons (45 grams) plain Greek yogurt
1 tablespoon (6 grams) lemon zest
2 tablespoons (30 grams) fresh lemon juice
⅓ cup (76 grams) unsalted butter, melted and cooled
2 teaspoons (8 grams) vanilla extract

1. In a medium bowl, whisk together sugar, flour, cornmeal, salt, and nutmeg. In another medium bowl, whisk eggs until smooth. Add sugar mixture to eggs, whisking until combined.
2. In a small bowl, whisk together buttermilk, yogurt, and lemon zest and juice until smooth. Add melted butter and vanilla. Gradually add buttermilk mixture to egg mixture, whisking until smooth. Use immediately.

PEANUT BUTTER PIE

Makes 1 (9-inch) pie

Think of this as a giant, sophisticated take on a peanut butter cup. A decadent peanut butter mousse, studded with roasted, salted peanuts, tops a bittersweet ganache base and a chocolate cookie crust.

1½   cups (184 grams) crushed chocolate wafer cookies
6   tablespoons (84 grams) unsalted butter, melted
¼   cup (50 grams) granulated sugar
⅛   teaspoon kosher salt
Ganache (recipe follows)
Peanut Butter Filling (recipe follows)

1. Preheat oven to 350°F (180°C).
2. In a medium bowl, stir together crushed cookies, melted butter, sugar, and salt. Using a measuring cup, press mixture into bottom and up sides of a 9-inch pie plate.
3. Bake until set, about 10 minutes. Let cool completely on a wire rack.
4. Pour Ganache into prepared crust.

Refrigerate until ganache has set, 15 to 20 minutes. Spoon Peanut Butter Filling over Ganache, smoothing top with an offset spatula. Cover and refrigerate for at least 3 hours.

GANACHE
Makes about 2 cups

1   pound (455 grams) German or semisweet chocolate
1   cup (240 grams) heavy whipping cream

1. Place chocolate in a medium bowl.
2. In a small saucepan, bring cream to a simmer over medium-low heat; pour over chocolate. Let stand for 2 minutes. Whisk mixture, starting from the center and working outward, until smooth.

PEANUT BUTTER FILLING
Makes about 3 cups

8   ounces (225 grams) cream cheese, softened
1   cup (256 grams) creamy peanut butter

½   cup (57 grams) roasted salted peanuts, chopped
¼   cup (50 grams) granulated sugar
¼   cup (85 grams) honey
1   cup (240 grams) heavy whipping cream

1. In the bowl of a stand mixer fitted with the paddle attachment, beat cream cheese and peanut butter at high speed until smooth. Add peanuts, sugar, and honey, beating until combined. Transfer mixture to a large bowl; set aside.
2. Clean bowl of stand mixer. Using the whisk attachment, beat cream at high speed until stiff peaks form. Fold one-third of whipped cream into peanut butter mixture. Fold in remaining whipped cream. Use immediately.

STRAWBERRY SWIRL CHEESECAKE PIE

Makes 1 (9-inch) pie

For a hint of subtle heat, we added a pinch of black pepper to the crust of this rich cheesecake pie.

1½ cups (195 grams) graham cracker crumbs
7 tablespoons (98 grams) unsalted butter, melted
⅔ cup (133 grams) plus 2 tablespoons (24 grams) granulated sugar, divided
½ teaspoon (1 gram) ground black pepper
¼ teaspoon kosher salt
16 ounces (450 grams) cream cheese, softened
1 tablespoon (8 grams) all-purpose flour
2 large eggs (100 grams)
¼ cup (60 grams) sour cream, room temperature
1 teaspoon (4 grams) vanilla extract
⅔ cup (213 grams) strawberry preserves
½ cup (85 grams) chopped fresh strawberries

1. Preheat oven to 350°F (180°C). Butter and flour a 9-inch pie plate.
2. In a medium bowl, stir together graham cracker crumbs, melted butter, 2 tablespoons (24 grams) sugar, pepper, and salt. Using a measuring cup, press mixture into bottom and up sides of prepared plate.
3. Bake for 5 minutes. Let cool on a wire rack. Reduce oven temperature to 325°F (170°C).
4. In the bowl of a stand mixer fitted with the paddle attachment, beat cream cheese at medium speed until creamy, stopping to scrape sides of bowl. Add flour and remaining ⅔ cup (133 grams) sugar, beating until combined. Add eggs, one at a time, beating just until combined after each addition (do not overbeat). Reduce mixer speed to low. Add sour cream and vanilla, beating until smooth. Pour into prepared crust.
5. In the container of a blender, place preserves and strawberries; blend until smooth. Drizzle 5 tablespoons (100 grams) strawberry mixture over filling. Using the tip of a knife, gently swirl over top of pie. Refrigerate remaining strawberry mixture.
6. Bake until edges are set and slightly puffed, 35 to 45 minutes. Let cool on a wire rack for 1 hour. Refrigerate until cold, about 3 hours. Serve with remaining strawberry mixture.

CINNAMON ROLL APPLE PIE

Makes 1 (9-inch) deep-dish pie

This pie's unique cinnamon roll crust adds even more cinnamon-sugar flavor and offers just the right amount of sweetness.

6   cups (750 grams) all-purpose flour
1½ cups (300 grams) granulated sugar, divided
1   tablespoon (9 grams) kosher salt
1   cup plus 2 tablespoons (255 grams) cold unsalted butter, cubed
1¼ cups (300 grams) cold water
1½ tablespoons (9 grams) ground cinnamon
4   tablespoons (56 grams) unsalted butter, softened and divided
Apple Filling (recipe follows)
1   large egg (50 grams), lightly beaten
1   teaspoon (4 grams) coarse sugar

1. In the work bowl of a food processor, place flour, 1 cup (200 grams) granulated sugar, and salt; pulse until combined. Add cold butter, and pulse until mixture is crumbly.
2. With processor running, add 1¼ cups (300 grams) cold water in a slow, steady stream until a dough forms. Divide dough in half, and shape each half into a disk. Wrap tightly in plastic wrap, and refrigerate for at least 30 minutes.
3. On a lightly floured surface, roll half of dough into a 17x10½-inch rectangle. In a small bowl, stir together cinnamon and remaining ½ cup (100 grams) granulated sugar. Spread 2 tablespoons (28 grams) softened butter onto dough, and sprinkle with half of sugar mixture.
4. Starting with one long side, roll dough into a log, pinching seam to seal. Wrap in plastic wrap, and refrigerate for at least 1 hour. Repeat procedure with remaining dough, remaining 2 tablespoons (28 grams) softened butter, and remaining sugar mixture.
5. Slice 1 log of dough into ½-inch pieces. On a lightly floured piece of parchment paper, arrange pieces in a tight circle, making sure all edges are touching. Gently roll into a 12-inch circle. Transfer to a 9-inch deep-dish pie plate, pressing into bottom and up sides. Trim excess dough. Refrigerate for 10 minutes.
6. Slice remaining log of dough into ½-inch pieces. On a lightly floured piece of parchment paper, arrange pieces in a tight circle, making sure all edges are touching. Gently roll into a 12-inch circle. Transfer dough on parchment to a sheet pan, and refrigerate for 10 minutes.
7. Preheat oven to 375°F (190°C).
8. Spoon Apple Filling into prepared crust. Lightly brush edges with water. Place second piece of dough on top of filling, and peel off parchment. Fold edges under, and crimp as desired. Freeze for at least 15 minutes. Place pie on a rimmed half-sheet pan. Cut a vent in top of dough to release steam. Brush with egg, and sprinkle with coarse sugar.
9. Bake for 15 minutes. Reduce oven temperature to 350°F (180°C), and bake until apples are tender and crust is golden brown, 30 to 35 minutes more, covering with foil to prevent excess browning, if necessary. Let cool for 1 hour before serving.

APPLE FILLING
Makes about 8 cups

3½ pounds (1,590 grams) Granny Smith apples, peeled, cored, and sliced
¾   cup (150 grams) granulated sugar
½   cup (110 grams) firmly packed light brown sugar
1¾ teaspoons (3.5 grams) ground cinnamon
½   teaspoon (1.5 grams) kosher salt
¼   teaspoon ground ginger
¼   cup (32 grams) cornstarch

1. In a large bowl, toss together apples, sugars, cinnamon, salt, and ginger. Let stand for 30 minutes. Transfer apples to a colander; drain and discard liquid. Toss drained apples with cornstarch.

ORANGE BLOSSOM
VANILLA BROWN SUGAR PIE

Makes 1 (10-inch) pie

Orange blossom water offers light, floral flavor while a crisp brûlée topping lends a crunchy texture to the custard filling in this elegant pie.

2¾ cups (330 grams) crushed shortbread cookies
½ cup (110 grams) firmly packed light brown sugar
6 tablespoons (84 grams) unsalted butter, melted
1 teaspoon (2 grams) orange zest
⅛ teaspoon kosher salt
Orange Blossom Filling (recipe follows)
3 tablespoons (36 grams) granulated sugar
3 tablespoons (36 grams) turbinado sugar

1. Preheat oven to 350°F (180°C).
2. In a medium bowl, stir together crushed cookies, brown sugar, melted butter, zest, and salt. Using a measuring cup, press mixture into bottom and up sides of a 10-inch pie plate.
3. Bake until golden brown, about 15 minutes. Let cool completely on a wire rack.
4. Pour Orange Blossom Filling into prepared crust. Refrigerate for at least 1 hour. In a small bowl, stir together granulated sugar and turbinado sugar. Sprinkle sugar mixture over filling. Use a kitchen torch to brûlée top.

ORANGE BLOSSOM FILLING
Makes 2½ cups

1 cup (240 grams) whole milk
1¾ cups (420 grams) heavy whipping cream, divided
⅔ cup (147 grams) firmly packed light brown sugar, divided
¼ teaspoon kosher salt
4½ tablespoons (36 grams) cornstarch
5 large egg yolks (93 grams)
2 teaspoons (12 grams) vanilla bean paste, divided
2 tablespoons (28 grams) unsalted butter, softened
1 tablespoon (13 grams) orange blossom water

1. In a medium saucepan, bring milk, 1 cup (240 grams) cream, ⅓ cup (73.5 grams) brown sugar, and salt to a boil over medium heat.

2. In a medium bowl, whisk together cornstarch, egg yolks, 1 teaspoon (6 grams) vanilla bean paste, and remaining ⅓ cup (73.5 grams) brown sugar. Whisking constantly, pour hot milk mixture into egg mixture. Return milk mixture to saucepan, and cook, stirring constantly, until a candy thermometer registers 180°F (82°C). Remove from heat, and whisk in butter and orange blossom water.
3. Strain mixture over a rimmed baking sheet lined with plastic wrap. Press another piece of plastic wrap directly onto surface of pastry cream. Place baking pan on a wire rack, and let cool to room temperature.
4. Transfer pastry cream to the bowl of a stand mixer fitted with the paddle attachment, and beat at medium speed until smooth. Transfer to a large bowl; set aside.
5. Clean bowl of stand mixer. Using the whisk attachment, beat remaining ¾ cup (180 grams) cream and remaining 1 teaspoon (6 grams) vanilla bean paste at high speed until soft peaks form. Fold whipped cream into pastry cream until combined and smooth. Use immediately.

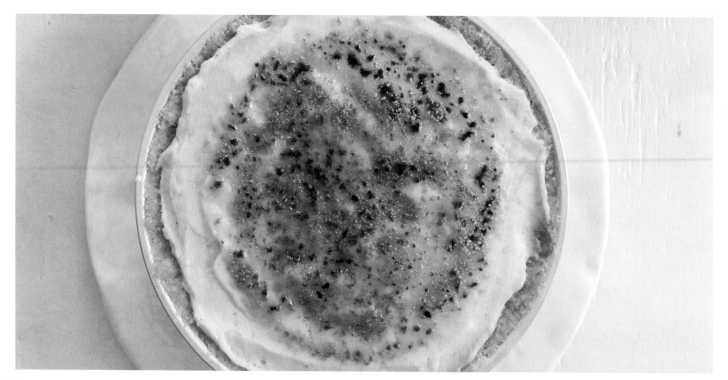

BANOFFEE PIE

Makes 1 (9-inch) pie

This British pie import has been thoroughly absorbed into American tradition. With the winning combination of ripe bananas, sticky toffee, and whipped cream, it's not hard to see why.

1½ cups (195 grams) graham cracker crumbs
4½ tablespoons (54 grams) granulated sugar
¼ teaspoon kosher salt
8 tablespoons (112 grams) unsalted butter, melted and divided
Brown Sugar Filling (recipe follows)
5 bananas (620 grams), sliced
1 tablespoon (15 grams) fresh lemon juice
Whipped Cream (recipe follows)
Garnish: chocolate shavings

1. Preheat oven to 350°F (180°C). Butter and flour a 9-inch pie plate.
2. In a medium bowl, stir together graham cracker crumbs, sugar, and salt. Add 6 tablespoons (84 grams) melted butter, and stir with a fork until moistened. Add remaining 2 tablespoons (28 grams) melted butter, if needed. Using a measuring cup, press mixture into bottom and up sides of prepared plate.
3. Bake until lightly browned, 10 to 12 minutes. Let cool on a wire rack.
4. Reserve ¼ cup Brown Sugar Filling. Pour remaining Brown Sugar Filling into prepared crust. Lightly cover with plastic wrap, and refrigerate until set, 3 to 4 hours.
5. In a medium bowl, toss together banana slices and lemon juice. Spoon bananas over chilled Brown Sugar Filling. Gently spread Whipped Cream over bananas.
6. In a small microwave-safe bowl, heat reserved ¼ cup Brown Sugar Filling on low just until pourable, about 10 seconds. Drizzle over pie. Serve immediately, or refrigerate for up to 1 hour. Garnish with chocolate shavings, if desired.

BROWN SUGAR FILLING
Makes about 2 cups

1 cup (227 grams) unsalted butter
¾ cup (165 grams) firmly packed dark brown sugar
⅔ cup (160 grams) heavy whipping cream
1 tablespoon (21 grams) light corn syrup
¼ teaspoon kosher salt

1. In a large saucepan, bring butter, brown sugar, cream, corn syrup, and salt to a boil over medium-high heat, stirring occasionally. Reduce heat to medium-low; simmer for 10 minutes. Remove from heat. Let cool for 10 minutes, stirring occasionally.

WHIPPED CREAM
Makes about 4 cups

2 cups (480 grams) heavy whipping cream
⅓ cup plus 2 tablespoons (54 grams) confectioners' sugar

1. In the bowl of a stand mixer fitted with the whisk attachment, beat cream and confectioners' sugar at high speed just until stiff peaks form.

SWEET POTATO YOGURT PIE

Makes 1 (9-inch) pie

Recipe by Nik Sharma

If there is one pie I look forward to each Thanksgiving season, it's sweet potato. Indian chefs often use yogurt as a thickener and cool counterpoint to the spice in curries. In this recipe, it enriches the pie and balances the sweetness of the potatoes with tangy acidity.

Cream Cheese Pastry Crust (recipe follows)
2   cups (488 grams) roasted sweet potato purée*
3   large eggs (150 grams), room temperature
1   cup (240 grams) full-fat unsweetened plain Greek yogurt
¾   cup (165 grams) firmly packed brown sugar
½   cup (170 grams) maple syrup
3   tablespoons (45 grams) bourbon
2   tablespoons (28 grams) unsalted butter, melted
1   tablespoon (8 grams) cornstarch
¼   teaspoon sea salt

1. Let Cream Cheese Pastry Crust stand at room temperature for 5 to 6 minutes.
2. On a lightly floured surface, roll dough into a 13-inch circle, about ⅛ inch thick. Transfer to a 9-inch pie plate, pressing into bottom and up sides. Fold edges under, and crimp as desired. Cover loosely with plastic wrap, and freeze for at least 3 hours or overnight.
3. Preheat to 350°F (180°C).
4. Top dough with a piece of parchment paper, letting ends extend over edges of plate. Add pie weights.
5. Bake for 15 minutes. Carefully remove paper and weights.
6. In the container of a blender, place sweet potato purée and all remaining ingredients; pulse on high until smooth and combined, 30 to 40 seconds. Pour filling into prepared crust.
7. Bake until filling is firm yet slightly jiggly in center, 35 to 40 minutes. Let cool on a wire rack. Cover lightly with plastic wrap, and refrigerate overnight before serving.

*To make roasted sweet potato purée, wash and scrub sweet potatoes under cold running tap water to remove any dirt. Preheat oven to 400°F (200°C), and place sweet potatoes in an ovenproof dish. (Most baking pans can't withstand temperatures beyond 400°F [200°C], so I recommend using a cast-iron baking dish.) Bake until a skewer or knife passes through center of potato easily and flesh is soft and tender, 45 minutes to 1 hour. Let cool to room temperature. Remove and discard skins. Purée until smooth using a handheld blender, food processor, or blender.

CREAM CHEESE PASTRY CRUST
(From Rose Levy Beranbaum's The Pie and Pastry Bible)

Makes 1 (9-inch) crust

1⅓ cups (173 grams) whole wheat pastry flour
2   tablespoons (14 grams) fine-grain sugar
½   teaspoon (3 grams) fine-grain salt
⅛   teaspoon baking powder
3   ounces (86 grams) cream cheese, softened
½   cup (113 grams) unsalted butter, grated or cut into small chunks and kept frozen
2   tablespoons (30 grams) heavy whipping cream
1½   teaspoons (7.5 grams) apple cider vinegar

1. In a medium bowl, whisk together flour, sugar, salt, and baking powder. Freeze in a resealable plastic bag for 30 minutes.
2. Place chilled dry ingredients in the work bowl of a food processor fitted with a dough blade. Cut cream cheese into 4 chunks, and add to dry ingredients. Pulse until mixture just starts to come together, about 20 seconds. Add frozen chunks of butter, and pulse for 20 to 30 seconds. Add cream and vinegar, and pulse until mixture is crumbly. Transfer to a plastic bag, and knead from outside of bag until mixture holds together in one piece. Remove dough from bag, and wrap in plastic wrap. Refrigerate for at least 1 hour or overnight.

Photo by Nik Sharma

APRICOT-ALMOND HAND PIES

Makes about 14

Sliced almonds and cinnamon bring a subtle nuttiness and heat to balance out the concentrated sweetness of the dried apricot filling in these fruity hand pies.

2½ cups (313 grams) all-purpose flour
1   tablespoon (2 grams) fresh thyme leaves
2   teaspoons (6 grams) kosher salt
1   teaspoon (4 grams) granulated sugar
1   cup (227 grams) cold unsalted butter, cubed
1   teaspoon (4 grams) almond extract
4 to 8 tablespoons (60 to 120 grams) ice water
Apricot-Almond Filling (recipe follows)
1   large egg (50 grams)
1   tablespoon (15 grams) water
¼   cup (28 grams) sliced almonds

1. In the work bowl of a food processor, place flour, thyme, salt, and sugar; process until combined. Add cold butter, and pulse until mixture is crumbly. Add almond extract, pulsing until combined. With processor running, add ice water, 1 tablespoon (15 grams) at a time, pulsing just until dough comes together. Turn out dough onto a lightly floured surface. Divide dough in half, and shape each half into a disk. Wrap in plastic wrap, and refrigerate for at least 2 hours.
2. Preheat oven to 350°F (180°C). Line a baking sheet with parchment paper.
3. On a lightly floured surface, roll dough to ¼-inch thickness; cut dough into 4-inch squares. Place 1 tablespoon Apricot-Almond Filling in center of each square. Brush edges of dough with water. Fold dough over filling, creating triangles, and crimp edges with a fork. Cut vents in top of dough to release steam.
4. In a small bowl, whisk together egg and 1 tablespoon (15 grams) water. Brush tops with egg wash, and sprinkle with almonds.
5. Bake until golden brown, about 30 minutes; serve warm.

APRICOT-ALMOND FILLING
Makes about 1¼ cups

6   ounces (175 grams) dried apricots
⅓   cup (67 grams) granulated sugar
1   tablespoon (14 grams) unsalted butter, cubed
¼   teaspoon ground cinnamon
½   cup (57 grams) sliced almonds

1. In a small saucepan, bring apricots and water to cover by 1 inch to a boil over high heat. Reduce heat to low; cook until apricots are softened, about 20 minutes. Drain apricots, reserving 2 tablespoons (30 grams) cooking liquid.
2. In the work bowl of a food processor, place warm apricots, reserved 2 tablespoons (30 grams) cooking liquid, sugar, butter, and cinnamon; pulse until mixture has the texture of jam. Stir in almonds; let cool completely.

APPLE CHEDDAR PIE

Makes 1 (9-inch) pie

For this modern twist on traditional apple pie, we use two crusts, our Traditional American Piecrust and a Cheddar Cheese Piecrust, to create a marbled look.

Traditional American Piecrust (recipe follows)
Cheddar Cheese Piecrust (recipe follows)

8	cups (884 grams) ¼-inch-thick sliced peeled Granny Smith apples*	
⅓	cup (73 grams) firmly packed light brown sugar	
2	tablespoons (16 grams) all-purpose flour	
1	teaspoon (2 grams) lemon zest	
2	tablespoons (30 grams) fresh lemon juice	
1	teaspoon (2 grams) ground black pepper	
½	teaspoon (1.5 grams) kosher salt	
¼	teaspoon ground nutmeg	
¼	teaspoon ground cinnamon	
1	large egg (50 grams)	
1	tablespoon (15 grams) heavy whipping cream	
1	tablespoon (12 grams) turbinado sugar	

1. Preheat oven to 375°F (190°C).
2. On a lightly floured surface, roll Traditional American Piecrust into an 18x3-inch rectangle. Repeat procedure with Cheddar Cheese Piecrust. Place Traditional American Piecrust on top of Cheddar Cheese Piecrust. Starting with one long side, roll into a log, jelly-roll style, and pinch seam to seal. Wrap in plastic wrap, and refrigerate for 20 minutes.
3. On a lightly floured surface, cut dough crosswise into 2 (1½-inch-long) logs. Stand up logs vertically. Roll half of dough into a 12-inch circle. Transfer to a 9-inch pie plate, pressing into bottom and up sides. Trim excess dough to ½ inch beyond edge of plate.
4. In a large bowl, combine apple slices, brown sugar, flour, lemon zest and juice, pepper, salt, nutmeg, and cinnamon. Spoon apple mixture into prepared crust.
5. Roll remaining dough into a 12-inch square. Cut into 6 (2-inch-wide) strips. Place 3 dough strips vertically on pie, spacing evenly apart. Fold back alternating strips, and place one dough strip horizontally across vertical strips; unfold folded strips. Fold back center vertical strip, and place another horizontal strip across first strips, spacing evenly. Unfold vertical folded strip, then fold back alternating vertical strips. Place another horizontal strip across vertical strip, spacing evenly. Unfold vertical folded strips.
6. Trim lattice until it meets inside of pan's lip. Roll excess dough from crust over so that it is even with inside lip of pan, pressing down to make it adhere. Crimp as desired.
7. In a small bowl, whisk together egg and cream. Brush dough with egg wash. Sprinkle with turbinado sugar.
8. Bake until crust is golden brown and filling is bubbly, about 1 hour, covering with foil to prevent excess browning, if necessary. Let cool slightly; serve warm.

While we prefer to use Granny Smith, it's fine to combine three to four kinds of apples in an apple pie. Be sure to use ones with low water content, such as Macoun, Cortland, Golden Delicious, York Imperial, or Pink Lady.

CHEDDAR CHEESE PIECRUST
Makes 1 (9-inch) crust

1¼	cups (156 grams) all-purpose flour	
½	teaspoon (1.5 grams) kosher salt	
½	teaspoon (1 gram) ground mustard	
½	teaspoon (1 gram) smoked paprika	
1	cup (100 grams) freshly grated extra-sharp Cheddar cheese	
¼	cup (57 grams) cold unsalted butter, cubed	
¼	cup (60 grams) ice water	

1. In the work bowl of a food processor, place flour, salt, mustard, and paprika; pulse until combined. Add Cheddar and cold butter, and pulse until mixture is crumbly. With processor running, pour ¼ cup (60 grams) ice water through food chute in a slow, steady stream just until dough comes together. (Mixture may appear crumbly. It should be moist and hold together when pinched.) Turn out dough, and shape into a disk. Wrap tightly in plastic wrap, and refrigerate for at least 30 minutes. Dough may be refrigerated for up to 3 days or frozen for up to 2 months.

TRADITIONAL AMERICAN PIECRUST
Makes 1 (9-inch) crust

Meet your new go-to pie dough. This crust's paper-thin layers will melt in your mouth while effortlessly holding the heaviest of fruit fillings. Its easy-to-handle dough makes it great for lattice designs.

1½	cups (188 grams) all-purpose flour	
½	teaspoon (1.5 grams) kosher salt	
½	cup (113 grams) cold unsalted butter, cubed	
⅓	cup (80 grams) ice water	

1. In the work bowl of a food processor, place flour and salt; pulse until combined. Add cold butter, and pulse until mixture is crumbly. With processor running, pour ⅓ cup (80 grams) ice water through food chute in a slow, steady stream just until dough comes together. (Mixture may appear crumbly. It should be moist and hold together when pinched.) Turn out dough, and shape into a disk. Wrap tightly in plastic wrap, and refrigerate for at least 30 minutes. Dough may be refrigerated for up to 3 days or frozen for up to 2 months.

Note: *Press the dough into a disk rather than shaping it into a ball to allow it to chill faster. This will also make the dough easier to roll out.*

BLUSHING PEAR PIE

Makes 1 (9-inch) pie

Roasted beets deliver subtle, earthy tones that complement the sweet pears.

Traditional American Piecrust (recipe on page 209)

½ cup (83 grams) diced roasted beet*
⅓ cup (67 grams) granulated sugar
¼ cup (55 grams) firmly packed light brown sugar
3 tablespoons (24 grams) all-purpose flour
2 teaspoons (4 grams) lemon zest
2 tablespoons (30 grams) fresh lemon juice
2 teaspoons (10 grams) apple cider vinegar
1 teaspoon grated fresh ginger
½ teaspoon (1.5 grams) kosher salt
½ teaspoon (1 gram) ground black pepper
½ teaspoon (1 gram) ground cardamom
3 to 4 dashes bitters
8 cups (928 grams) ¼-inch-thick sliced peeled Bosc pears
Almond Oat Crumble (recipe follows)

1. On a lightly floured surface, roll Traditional American Piecrust into a 12-inch circle. Transfer to a 9-inch pie plate, pressing into bottom and up sides. Trim excess dough to ½ inch beyond edge of plate. Fold edges under. Using kitchen scissors, make 2 (45-degree) cuts into folded edge ¼ inch apart, being careful not to cut all the way through the dough. Twist cut piece of dough, and tuck pointed end underneath crust. Make another ¼-inch cut, twist, and tuck under. Repeat procedure around pie until you reach the first cut. Freeze for 20 minutes.

2. Preheat oven to 375°F (190°C).

3. In the work bowl of a food processor, combine beet, sugars, flour, lemon zest and juice, vinegar, ginger, salt, pepper, cardamom, and bitters; process until puréed. Place pears in a medium bowl; pour beet mixture over pears, and stir to combine. Spoon into prepared crust.

4. Bake for 30 minutes. Top with Almond Oat Crumble, and bake until bubbly, about 30 minutes more, covering with foil to prevent excess browning, if necessary. Let cool for 1 hour; serve warm.

*To roast a beet, cut off stem, coat in 1 tablespoon (14 grams) olive oil, and wrap in foil. Roast in a 400°F (200°C) oven until soft, about 1 hour. Let cool for 15 minutes. Remove foil, and let cool 10 minutes more. Rub with a paper towel to peel. Refrigerate for up to 5 days.

ALMOND OAT CRUMBLE
Makes about 2 cups

1 cup (80 grams) old-fashioned oats
½ cup (48 grams) almond meal
⅓ cup (73 grams) firmly packed light brown sugar
¼ cup (31 grams) all-purpose flour
½ teaspoon (1.5 grams) kosher salt
¼ cup (57 grams) unsalted butter, cubed
½ cup (57 grams) chopped pecans

1. In a small bowl, whisk together oats, almond meal, brown sugar, flour, and salt. Using a pastry blender, cut in butter until mixture is crumbly. Stir in pecans. Refrigerate for up to 5 days.

PRO TIP
If your fruit pies tend to be runny, precook half your filling to ensure that it is thick enough. Take half of the fruit-sugar-starch mixture, and bring it to a boil. Simmer for 2 to 3 minutes. Remove from heat, and stir in the remaining raw fruit. The uncooked fruit will help your thickened filling retain its texture.

PEACH AND CANTALOUPE GRUNT

Makes 8 to 10 servings

The main difference between a cobbler and this messier cousin is that the grunt (sometimes called a slump) can be cooked on a stovetop in a covered skillet instead of the oven, causing the biscuit topping to steam rather than bake. We went beyond the basic biscuit topping and created dense, nutty dough brimming with fresh basil that makes for the perfect complement to the sweet cantaloupe and stone fruit filling.

2   pounds (910 grams) fresh peaches, peeled, pitted, and cut into ½-inch-thick slices
1⅓ pounds (700 grams) peeled and seeded cantaloupe, cut into ¼-inch-thick slices
1   cup (220 grams) firmly packed light brown sugar
1   teaspoon (2 grams) lemon zest
2   tablespoons (30 grams) water
1   tablespoon (8 grams) cornstarch
Macadamia Nut Basil Topping (recipe follows)
1   tablespoon (12 grams) turbinado sugar

1. Preheat oven to 375°F (190°C).
2. In a 12-inch skillet, combine peaches, cantaloupe, brown sugar, and zest. Cook over medium-high heat for 8 to 10 minutes, stirring occasionally.
3. In a small bowl, stir together 2 tablespoons (30 grams) water and cornstarch; stir into fruit mixture. (Dissolving the cornstarch in water helps to prevent clumping when it's added to the fruit mixture.) Cook, stirring frequently, until thickened, about 2 minutes. Remove from heat, and transfer to a 3-quart baking dish.
4. Using a large (¼-cup) spring-loaded cookie scoop or spoon, divide Macadamia Nut Basil Topping into 8 rounds, and flatten slightly. Place over fruit mixture; sprinkle with turbinado sugar.
5. Bake until browned and bubbly, about 30 minutes. Let cool in pan for 15 minutes. Serve warm. Cover and refrigerate for up to 3 days.

MACADAMIA NUT BASIL TOPPING
Makes 8 biscuits

1¼ cups (156 grams) all-purpose flour
½   cup (100 grams) granulated sugar
1½ teaspoons (7.5 grams) baking powder
1   teaspoon (3 grams) kosher salt
6   tablespoons (84 grams) cold unsalted butter, cubed
½   cup (48 grams) macadamia nut meal
½   cup (120 grams) heavy whipping cream
1   tablespoon (2 grams) chopped fresh basil

1. In a large bowl, stir together flour, sugar, baking powder, and salt. Using a pastry blender, cut in cold butter until mixture is crumbly. Stir in nut meal, cream, and basil just until combined. Gently shape dough into a disk. Wrap in plastic wrap, and refrigerate for at least 30 minutes.

Note: *To keep the butter as cold as possible, try freezing it for 10 to 15 minutes before using. To make macadamia nut meal, grind macadamia nuts in a food processor.*

> **PRO TIP**
> Acidic fruits and vegetables like peaches can sometimes pick up a metallic flavor when baked in cast iron. For this reason, we recommend using a regular skillet or enamel-coated cast iron.

RHUBARB PISTACHIO PIE

Makes 1 (10-inch) pie

Recipe by Allison Kave and Keavy Landreth

Rhubarb is one of our absolute favorite ingredients, perhaps because it appears so fleetingly at farmers' markets, or maybe because its pink and green stalks herald the first blush of spring and the impending arrival of summer's bounty. While many wait for strawberries to come into season before baking with rhubarb, we like to use it as much as possible for as long as we can get our hands on it. Its tart, slightly vegetal flavor is complex and beautiful when combined with the nutty richness of buttery frangipane, which is normally made with almonds and used as the base of classic French fruit tarts. Here, we swap the almonds for pistachios and layer a fluffy pillow of this creamy concoction at the bottom of an All-Butter Piecrust to absorb the sweet-tart juices of the rhubarb. It's the perfect hit of vibrant flavor you crave when the world starts to bloom again.

All-Butter Piecrust (recipe follows)
Pistachio Frangipane (recipe follows)
Rhubarb Filling (recipe follows)
Egg wash or milk, for brushing
Turbinado sugar, for sprinkling

1. Preheat oven to 425°F (220°C).
2. On a lightly floured surface, roll half of All-Butter Piecrust into a 12-inch circle, ⅛ to ¼ inch thick. Transfer to a 10-inch pie plate, pressing into bottom and up sides. Trim excess dough to 1 inch beyond edge of plate. Spread Pistachio Frangipane into prepared crust. If you're using a pie bird, place it in the center. Spread Rhubarb Filling over Pistachio Frangipane.
3. Roll remaining All-Butter Piecrust into an 11-inch circle. Place dough over filling. Trim excess dough. Fold edges under, and crimp as desired. Brush with egg wash or milk. Sprinkle with turbinado sugar. If you're not using a pie bird, cut vents in top of dough to release steam. Place pie on a baking sheet.
4. Bake for 20 minutes, rotating pan halfway through baking. Reduce oven temperature to 350°F (180°C), and bake until crust is golden and filling is set, 30 to 40 minutes more (you'll see thick juices bubbling out when it's ready). Let cool completely on a wire rack, at least 1 hour. Cover with plastic wrap, and refrigerate for up to 1 week. Let come to room temperature before serving, or warm it in a low oven. Pie can also be frozen, covered in plastic wrap and foil, for up to 2 months.

ALL-BUTTER PIECRUST

Makes 1 (10-inch) double piecrust

1   cup (227 grams) unsalted butter
½   cup (120 grams) whole milk
1   tablespoon (15 grams) apple cider vinegar
3   cups (375 grams) all-purpose flour, chilled
2   tablespoons (24 grams) granulated sugar
1   tablespoon (9 grams) kosher salt

1. Cut butter into ½-inch cubes (a bench scraper is perfect for this, but a sharp knife works well, too), and return to refrigerator or freezer to cool.
2. In a liquid-measuring cup, stir together milk and vinegar. Refrigerate until ready to use.
3. On a clean flat surface or in a large shallow bowl, toss together flour, sugar, and salt. Add butter to dry ingredients, and using a pastry blender, cut butter into flour mixture with speed and patience, until it has been reduced to small pea-sized chunks. Spread mixture out gently to expose as much surface area as possible, then gently drizzle about half of milk mixture over flour mixture, trying to cover as wide an area as you can. Using bench scrapers or a large spoon, toss flour mixture over the liquid (don't stir, just lightly toss), spread everything out again, and repeat process with second half of liquid. You should now have a dough that will just hold together when pressed against the bowl, with visible little chunks of butter. If you need to add more liquid to bind it, do so with more cold milk, adding 1 tablespoon at a time until you reach the right texture. It's not an exact science as everything from the humidity in the air to the dryness of your flour will affect the consistency of your dough. Once you've reached your goal, wrap dough tightly in plastic wrap, and refrigerate for at least 1 hour. Dough will keep refrigerated for up to 1 week, well wrapped, or frozen for up to 2 months.

PISTACHIO FRANGIPANE

Makes 1 cup

⅔   cup (75 grams) shelled pistachios, toasted
⅓   cup (67 grams) granulated sugar
6   tablespoons (84 grams) unsalted butter, softened
1   large egg (50 grams)
1   tablespoon (8 grams) all-purpose flour
¼   teaspoon (1 gram) vanilla extract

1. In the work bowl of a food processor, pulse together pistachios and sugar until sandy. Add butter, egg, flour, and vanilla; pulse until smooth.

RHUBARB FILLING

Makes about 3½ cups

¾   cup (150 grams) granulated sugar
3   tablespoons (24 grams) cornstarch
¼   teaspoon kosher salt
1½   pounds (680 grams) fresh rhubarb, tough strings removed and cut into 1-inch pieces
Zest of 1 medium orange

1. In a large bowl, stir together sugar, cornstarch, and salt. Add rhubarb and zest, tossing to coat.

BUTTERNUT SQUASH PIE

Makes 1 (9-inch) pie

Forget pumpkin and sweet potato. This bourbon-spiked squash pie is the star of your next holiday dinner. This pie embodies all that a custard pie should be, appearing firm with clean slices, but dissolving into silky deliciousness with every bite.

⅔ cup (147 grams) firmly packed light brown sugar
2 large eggs (100 grams)
1 large egg yolk (19 grams)
2 tablespoons (30 grams) bourbon
1 teaspoon (2 grams) ground ginger
1 teaspoon (4 grams) vanilla extract
¾ teaspoon (1.5 grams) ground cinnamon
½ teaspoon (1.5 grams) kosher salt
½ teaspoon (1 gram) smoked paprika
1 cup (244 grams) roasted butternut squash purée*
¾ cup (180 grams) heavy whipping cream
Rosemary Saltine Crumb Crust (recipe follows)
Garnish: Maple Whipped Cream (recipe follows)

1. Preheat oven to 325°F (170°C).
2. In a medium bowl, whisk together brown sugar, eggs, egg yolk, bourbon, ginger, vanilla, cinnamon, salt, and paprika. Add squash purée, and whisk until well combined. Whisking constantly, slowly pour in cream until well combined. Transfer mixture to prepared Rosemary Saltine Crumb Crust.
3. Bake until edges are set and center is still slightly jiggly, 45 to 55 minutes, covering crust with foil after 20 minutes of baking to prevent excess browning, if necessary. Let cool completely on a wire rack. Garnish with Maple Whipped Cream, if desired.

To make butternut squash purée, coat 1 peeled, seeded, and quartered butternut squash with 1 tablespoon (14 grams) olive oil. Place on a baking sheet lined with parchment paper. Roast in a 400°F (200°C) oven until soft, 45 minutes to 1 hour. Let cool completely. Scrape out pulp. Transfer pulp to the work bowl of a food processor; process on high until puréed. Refrigerate for up to 5 days.

ROSEMARY SALTINE CRUMB CRUST

Makes 1 (9-inch) crust

The savory herbs and salty notes in this cracker-based crumb crust complement the fragrant spices in this pie's filling. We love the brighter, gold crust that saltines create and how it makes the burnt orange in the filling pop, encircling it like a crumbly halo.

2 cups (154 grams) saltine cracker crumbs
⅓ cup (73 grams) firmly packed light brown sugar
1 tablespoon (2 grams) chopped fresh rosemary
½ cup (113 grams) unsalted butter, melted

1. Preheat oven to 350°F (180°C).
2. In a medium bowl, whisk together cracker crumbs, brown sugar, and rosemary. Add melted butter, and whisk to combine. Using the bottom of a measuring cup, gently press crumb mixture into bottom and up sides of a 9-inch pie plate.
3. Bake until lightly golden brown and set, about 15 minutes. Let cool completely.

MAPLE WHIPPED CREAM

Makes about 1½ cups

This whipped cream is the perfect sweet topping to any dessert.

½ cup (120 grams) heavy whipping cream
2 tablespoons (42 grams) maple syrup

1. In the bowl of a stand mixer fitted with the whisk attachment, beat cream and maple syrup at high speed until stiff peaks form, 2 to 3 minutes. Refrigerate for up to 24 hours.

HONEY NUT PIE

Makes 1 (9-inch) pie

If you like a pie with some crunch, this is the recipe for you. Our remix on the classic pecan pie abounds with texture. Smooth orange blossom honey and a tender Pâte Brisée crust soften the unique blend of pine nuts, hazelnuts, pecans, and walnuts.

Pâte Brisée (recipe below)
½ cup (100 grams) granulated sugar
⅓ cup (113 grams) orange blossom honey
¼ cup (85 grams) light corn syrup
1 teaspoon (3 grams) kosher salt
¾ cup (170 grams) unsalted butter, cubed
½ cup (120 grams) heavy whipping cream
1 large egg (50 grams)

1 large egg yolk (19 grams)
½ cup (57 grams) pine nuts
½ cup (57 grams) chopped pecans
½ cup (57 grams) chopped walnuts
½ cup (57 grams) chopped hazelnuts, toasted and skins removed

1. On a lightly floured surface, roll Pâte Brisée into a 12-inch circle. Transfer to a 9-inch pie plate, pressing into bottom and up sides. Trim excess dough to ½ inch beyond edge of plate. Fold edges under, and crimp as desired. Freeze for 20 minutes.
2. Preheat oven to 350°F (180°C).
3. Top dough with a piece of parchment paper, letting ends extend over edges of plate. Add pie weights.

4. Bake until edges are set and golden brown, about 12 minutes. Carefully remove paper and weights. Bake 8 minutes more. Let cool completely.
5. In a medium saucepan, bring sugar, honey, corn syrup, and salt to a boil over medium heat, stirring until sugar is dissolved. Add butter, whisking to combine. Transfer to a medium bowl, and let cool for 30 minutes.
6. Whisk cream, egg, and egg yolk into honey mixture. Arrange nuts in bottom of prepared crust. Pour honey mixture over nuts.
7. Bake until crust is golden brown and center is set, 50 minutes to 1 hour, covering crust with foil to prevent excess browning, if necessary. Let cool completely on a wire rack.

PÂTE BRISÉE
Makes 1 (9-inch) crust

Because of its mixing method and smaller amount of sugar, Pâte Brisée is sturdier and easier to handle than other forms of shortcrust, like Pâte Sucrée, which makes it perfect for pies.

1½ cups (188 grams) all-purpose flour
1½ teaspoons (6 grams) granulated sugar
½ teaspoon (1.5 grams) kosher salt

½ cup (113 grams) cold unsalted butter, cubed
¼ cup (60 grams) ice water

1. In the bowl of a stand mixer fitted with the paddle attachment, beat flour, sugar, and salt at low speed until combined. Increase mixer speed to medium-low. Add cold butter, and beat until mixture is crumbly. With mixer running, add ¼ cup (60 grams) ice water, beating until dough comes together. Turn out dough, and

shape into a disk. Wrap tightly in plastic wrap, and refrigerate for at least 30 minutes. Dough may be refrigerated for up to 3 days or frozen for up to 2 months.

Note: *Chilling the Pâte Brisée dough is crucial. The butter needs to stay cold, and the flour needs time to fully absorb water before it's rolled out. If you choose to refrigerate the dough for longer than the required 30 minutes, let it warm up on the counter for 10 minutes before rolling it out.*

MEXICAN CHOCOLATE FUDGE PIE

Makes 1 (9-inch) pie

Guajillo chili and ground red pepper give this fudge pie spicy depth and a kick. Velvety cocoa notes and a light dusting of confectioners' sugar curb the heat.

Pâte Brisée (recipe on page 216)
½   cup (120 grams) heavy whipping cream
½   cup (120 grams) whole milk
¼   cup (57 grams) unsalted butter
5   ounces (150 grams) chopped semisweet chocolate
3   ounces (86 grams) chopped Mexican chili chocolate*
1½   cups (300 grams) granulated sugar
¾   cup (64 grams) unsweetened cocoa powder
¼   cup (31 grams) all-purpose flour
2   tablespoons (18 grams) cornmeal
½   teaspoon (1.5 grams) kosher salt
¼   teaspoon ground red pepper
2   large eggs (100 grams)
3   large egg yolks (56 grams)
1   tablespoon (15 grams) apple cider vinegar
Garnish: confectioners' sugar

1. On a lightly floured surface, roll Pâte Brisée into a 12-inch circle. Transfer to a 9-inch pie plate, pressing into bottom and up sides. Trim excess dough to ½ inch beyond edge of plate. Fold edges under. Using kitchen scissors, make 2 (45-degree) cuts into folded edge ¼ inch apart, being careful not to cut all the way through the dough. Lay dough piece over to one side. Make another ¼-inch cut, and lay to the other side. Repeat procedure around pie until you reach the first cut. Freeze for 20 minutes.
2. Preheat oven to 350°F (180°C).

3. In a medium saucepan, cook cream, milk, butter, and chocolates over medium-low heat, stirring frequently, until chocolate is melted and smooth. Remove from heat. Let stand for 2 minutes.
4. In a medium bowl, whisk together granulated sugar, cocoa, flour, cornmeal, salt, and red pepper. Add sugar mixture to chocolate mixture, and whisk to combine. Add eggs, egg yolks, and vinegar, whisking until well combined. Spoon filling into prepared crust.
5. Bake until center is set, 35 to 45 minutes, covering crust with foil after 20 minutes of baking to prevent excess browning. Let cool on a wire rack for 20 minutes; serve warm. Dust with confectioners' sugar, if desired.

*We used Taza Guajillo Chili Mexican Chocolate.

CHAI SPICE CARAMEL PIE

Makes 1 (9-inch) pie

This luxurious pie offers a medley of spicy, salty, sharp, and sweet. Our crisp Gingersnap Crumb Crust is the perfect cradle for the light, velvety caramel filling topped with billowy, torched meringue.

2   cups (480 grams) whole milk
1   cinnamon stick (4 grams)
1   (3x1-inch) strip orange peel (3 grams)
1   vanilla bean (2 grams), split lengthwise, seeds scraped and reserved
½   teaspoon (1.5 gram) black peppercorns
¼   teaspoon whole cloves
¼   teaspoon green cardamom pods
1   whole star anise (2 grams)
1   cup (220 grams) firmly packed light brown sugar
½   cup (63 grams) all-purpose flour
½   teaspoon (1.5 grams) kosher salt
4   large egg yolks (74 grams)
1   cup (200 grams) granulated sugar
Gingersnap Crumb Crust (recipe below)
Salty Honey Meringue (recipe follows)
Garnish: flaked sea salt

1. In a medium saucepan, bring milk, cinnamon stick, orange peel, vanilla bean and reserved seeds, peppercorns, cloves, cardamom, and star anise to a boil over medium heat. Cover, remove from heat, and let steep for 20 minutes. Strain milk, discarding solids; return milk to saucepan. Whisk in brown sugar, flour, salt, and egg yolks. Cook, whisking constantly, until thickened. Remove from heat to keep custard from overcooking. You want custard as hot as possible, so do not give it time to cool down before adding caramel in next step.

2. In a small nonstick skillet, cook granulated sugar over medium heat, stirring occasionally, until deep amber colored. Whisking milk mixture constantly, slowly add caramel. Strain through a fine-mesh sieve into prepared Gingersnap Crumb Crust. Smooth top, and let cool for 10 minutes. Cover directly with plastic wrap, and refrigerate until set, at least 3 hours or up to 2 days. Top with Salty Honey Meringue, and toast with a kitchen torch. Garnish with sea salt, if desired.

Salty Honey Meringue
Makes about 4 cups

4   large egg whites (120 grams)
⅓   cup (73 grams) firmly packed light brown sugar
⅓   cup (113 grams) clover honey
½   teaspoon (1.5 grams) kosher salt

1. In the top of a double boiler, whisk together egg whites, brown sugar, honey, and salt. Cook over simmering water, whisking constantly, until sugar is dissolved and a candy thermometer registers 140°F (60°C), 5 to 7 minutes. Transfer to the bowl of a stand mixer fitted with the whisk attachment, and beat at high speed until stiff peaks form, about 10 minutes. Use immediately.

GINGERSNAP CRUMB CRUST
Makes 1 (9-inch) crust

Substitute any of your favorite crisp cookies for the gingersnaps. The recipe method will stay the same, but you may have to adjust the amount of butter and sugar if the cookie has a different sugar or fat content than gingersnaps. Add the sugar to taste, and add the butter gradually, mixing only until crumbs are slightly moist.

2   cups (200 grams) gingersnap crumbs
¼   cup (55 grams) firmly packed light brown sugar
½   teaspoon (1.5 grams) kosher salt
¼   cup (57 grams) unsalted butter, melted

1. Preheat oven to 350°F (180°C).
2. In a medium bowl, whisk together gingersnap crumbs, brown sugar, and salt. Add melted butter, stirring until well combined. Using the bottom of a measuring cup, gently press crumb mixture into bottom and up sides of a 9-inch pie plate.
3. Bake for 10 minutes. Let cool completely on a wire rack.

Note: *For the best results, the crumbs you use should be fine, like the texture of a nut meal. You should not see any chunks.*

TARTS

With a single tender base crust, tarts are the hallmark
of classic refinement. From a richly spiced Tarte Tatin
to a s'mores-inspired tart topped with toasted peaks of
marshmallow cream, find a showstopping recipe for any
and all seasons.

CHOCOLATE TART
WITH HONEY-GLAZED PECANS

Makes 1 (9-inch) tart

With this decadent tart, less is more. A simple graham cracker crust ensures that the bittersweet ganache and honeyed pecans remain the stars of the show.

2   cups (260 grams) crushed cinnamon graham crackers
½   cup (113 grams) unsalted butter, melted
½   teaspoon (1 gram) smoked paprika
12 ounces (340 grams) 60% cacao semisweet chocolate, chopped
1¼ cups (300 grams) heavy whipping cream
1   large egg (50 grams)
1   large egg yolk (19 grams)
1   teaspoon (4 grams) vanilla extract
¼   teaspoon kosher salt
Garnish: Honey-Glazed Pecans (recipe follows)

1. Preheat oven to 350°F (180°C).
2. In a medium bowl, stir together crushed graham crackers, melted butter, and paprika until well combined. Press mixture into bottom and up sides of a 9-inch round removable-bottom tart pan.
3. Bake until golden brown, about 10 minutes. Let cool completely. Reduce oven temperature to 250°F (130°C).
4. In a medium saucepan, heat chocolate and cream over medium heat, stirring constantly, just until chocolate is melted. Remove from heat.
5. In a large bowl, gently whisk together egg and egg yolk. Gradually add chocolate mixture, whisking constantly. Whisk in vanilla and salt. Pour filling into prepared crust.
6. Bake until center is set, 30 to 35 minutes. Let cool completely on a wire rack. Refrigerate for at least 3 hours. Garnish with Honey-Glazed Pecans, if desired. Cover and refrigerate for up to 3 days.

HONEY-GLAZED PECANS
Makes 2 cups

2   cups (284 grams) pecan halves
1   teaspoon (5 grams) canola oil
¼   teaspoon kosher salt
⅓   cup (113 grams) honey

1. Preheat oven to 350°F (180°C).
2. On a rimmed baking sheet, stir together pecans, oil, and salt until combined. Bake for 7 minutes.
3. In a medium saucepan, bring honey to a boil over medium-high heat. Add pecans, stirring to coat. Cook for 1 minute; remove from heat. Spread pecans in a single layer on parchment paper, and let cool before using.

BLACK BOTTOM COCONUT CREAM TART

Makes 1 (14x4-inch) tart

Tall peaks of toasted marshmallow fluff hide Coconut Pastry Cream and ganache.

1   cup (227 grams) unsalted butter, softened
¾   cup (165 grams) firmly packed brown sugar
2   tablespoons (42 grams) honey
1   tablespoon (21 grams) molasses
1   teaspoon (3 grams) kosher salt
1   teaspoon (2 grams) ground cinnamon
1   cup (125 grams) all-purpose flour
1   teaspoon (5 grams) baking soda
2   cups (260 grams) whole wheat flour
Ganache Filling (recipe follows)
Coconut Pastry Cream (recipe follows)
Fluffy Marshmallow Cream (recipe follows)

1. Spray a 14x4-inch removable-bottom tart pan with cooking spray.
2. In the bowl of a stand mixer fitted with the paddle attachment, beat butter, brown sugar, honey, molasses, salt, and cinnamon at medium speed until combined. In a small bowl, whisk together all-purpose flour and baking soda. Gradually add whole wheat flour to butter mixture alternately with all-purpose flour mixture, beating until combined.
3. Preheat oven to 315°F (157°C).
4. Roll dough into a 15x5-inch rectangle. Transfer to prepared pan, pressing into bottom and up sides. Prick bottom and sides of dough with a fork.
5. Bake for 15 minutes. Let cool completely.
6. Pour Ganache Filling into prepared crust; refrigerate until firm. Pour Coconut Pastry Cream over ganache layer. Using an offset spatula, swirl Fluffy Marshmallow Cream onto tart. Using a kitchen torch, brown meringue. Refrigerate for up to 2 days.

GANACHE FILLING

Makes 1 cup

⅔   cup (113 grams) 60% cacao semisweet chocolate morsels
⅓   cup (80 grams) heavy whipping cream
1   tablespoon (21 grams) light corn syrup
½   teaspoon (2 grams) vanilla extract
¼   teaspoon kosher salt

1. Place chocolate in a medium bowl, and set aside.
2. In a small saucepan, bring cream and corn syrup to a simmer over medium-low heat; pour over chocolate. Let stand for 2 minutes. Whisk mixture, starting from the center and working outward, until smooth. Add vanilla and salt, and whisk until combined.

COCONUT PASTRY CREAM

Makes 1½ cups

¼   cup (50 grams) granulated sugar
1½   tablespoons (12 grams) cornstarch
⅛   teaspoon kosher salt
½   cup (120 grams) whole milk
½   cup (120 grams) unsweetened full-fat coconut milk
2   large egg yolks (37 grams)
½   cup (25 grams) sweetened flaked coconut

1. Line a large rimmed baking sheet with plastic wrap.
2. In a medium saucepan, combine sugar, cornstarch, and salt. Whisk in milk, coconut milk, and egg yolks. Cook over medium heat, stirring constantly, until thickened, about 10 minutes. Remove from heat, and stir in coconut.
3. Pour hot coconut mixture onto prepared pan. Top with another piece of plastic wrap, making sure entire surface is touching plastic wrap. Refrigerate for at least 2 hours or overnight.

FLUFFY MARSHMALLOW CREAM

Makes 4 cups

3   large egg whites (90 grams)
½   teaspoon (1 gram) cream of tartar
⅔   cup (133 grams) plus 2 tablespoons (24 grams) granulated sugar, divided
¾   cup (255 grams) light corn syrup
⅓   cup (80 grams) water
2   teaspoons (12 grams) vanilla bean paste

1. In the bowl of a stand mixer fitted with the whisk attachment, beat egg whites and cream of tartar at medium speed until foamy. Add 2 tablespoons (24 grams) sugar, and beat until soft peaks form.
2. In a medium saucepan, combine corn syrup, ⅓ cup (80 grams) water, and remaining ⅔ cup (133 grams) sugar. Cook over medium heat, stirring constantly, until mixture registers 248°F (120°C) on a candy thermometer, about 15 minutes.
3. With mixer on medium speed, pour corn syrup mixture into egg white mixture in a slow, steady stream until combined. Increase mixer speed to high, and beat for 5 minutes. Add vanilla bean paste, and beat for 1 minute.

BLUEBERRY-ALMOND GALETTES

Makes 3 (7-inch) tarts

Almond flour is finer than standard all-purpose. It absorbs more moisture from the dough, giving the buttermilk crusts of these galettes added crispness. A hint of tart lemon zest balances out the sweetness of the blueberries.

2   cups (192 grams) almond flour
1¾   cups (219 grams) all-purpose flour
½   cup (100 grams) plus 2 tablespoons (24 grams) granulated sugar, divided
1½   teaspoons (4.5 grams) kosher salt
1   cup (227 grams) unsalted butter, softened
2   tablespoons (30 grams) whole buttermilk
2   tablespoons (30 grams) cold water
5¼   cups (893 grams) fresh blueberries, divided
3   tablespoons (24 grams) cornstarch
1   teaspoon (2 grams) lemon zest
1   tablespoon (15 grams) fresh lemon juice
1   large egg (50 grams), lightly beaten
2   tablespoons (24 grams) turbinado sugar

1. In the work bowl of a food processor, place flours, 2 tablespoons (24 grams) granulated sugar, and salt; process until combined. Add butter, and pulse until mixture is crumbly.

2. In a small bowl, stir together buttermilk and 2 tablespoons (30 grams) cold water. With processor running, add buttermilk mixture in a slow, steady stream just until dough comes together but is not sticky. Shape dough into a disk, and wrap in plastic wrap. Refrigerate for at least 30 minutes.

3. In a large bowl, combine 1 cup (170 grams) blueberries, cornstarch, lemon zest and juice, and remaining ½ cup (100 grams) granulated sugar. With a fork or potato masher, crush blueberries. Stir in remaining 4¼ cups (723 grams) blueberries.

4. Preheat oven to 400°F (200°C). Line 2 rimmed baking sheets with parchment paper.

5. Divide dough into 3 equal pieces. On a lightly floured surface, roll each piece into a 9-inch circle. Trim edges of dough, and transfer to prepared pans. Spoon one-third of blueberry mixture into center of each circle, leaving a 2-inch border. Fold up dough around filling, pinching to seal edges of folds. (Filling will spill out if not sealed properly. See Note.) Brush edges of dough with egg, and sprinkle with turbinado sugar. Freeze for 10 minutes.

6. Bake for 10 minutes. Reduce oven temperature to 350°F (180°C), and bake until crust is golden brown and fruit is bubbly, 20 to 25 minutes more, loosely covering with foil to prevent excess browning, if necessary. Let cool on pans for 25 minutes before serving.

Note: This dough is less pliable than a typical galette due to the different structure of almond flour. Folding may be more difficult, which is why it is so important to pinch the seams before baking.

PRO TIP
Use almond flour made from blanched whole almonds. Flour made with unblanched almonds will give your baked good a slightly grainier texture and darker color.

MASCARPONE PRETZEL STRAWBERRY TART

Makes 1 (9-inch) tart

By swapping the traditional cream cheese filling with vanilla bean-scented Mascarpone Cream and replacing the congealed topping with fresh strawberries, we've given this classic pastry a modern salty-sweet makeover.

1½ cups (160 grams) crushed pretzels
½ cup (113 grams) unsalted butter, melted
⅓ cup (73 grams) firmly packed light brown sugar
Mascarpone Cream (recipe follows)
4 cups (680 grams) fresh strawberries, hulled and halved

1. Preheat oven to 350°F (180°C). Butter and flour a 9x1-inch round removable-bottom tart pan.

2. In a medium bowl, stir together crushed pretzels, melted butter, and brown sugar. Transfer mixture to prepared pan, pressing into bottom and up sides.

3. Bake until set, 10 to 15 minutes. Let cool completely on a wire rack. Spoon Mascarpone Cream into prepared crust, and spread to edges. Top with strawberries before serving.

MASCARPONE CREAM
Makes about 1¾ cups

1 cup (240 grams) half-and-half
1 vanilla bean, split lengthwise, seeds scraped and reserved
1 large egg (50 grams)
1 large egg yolk (19 grams)
¼ cup (55 grams) firmly packed light brown sugar
3 tablespoons (24 grams) cornstarch
¾ cup (169 grams) mascarpone cheese, room temperature

1. In a medium saucepan, bring half-and-half and vanilla bean and reserved seeds to a boil over medium heat.

2. In a medium bowl, whisk together egg, egg yolk, brown sugar, and cornstarch. Gradually add hot milk mixture to egg mixture, whisking constantly. Return milk mixture to saucepan, and cook, whisking constantly, until thickened.

3. Place mascarpone in a large bowl. Strain pastry cream through a fine-mesh sieve over mascarpone, using a spoon to push cream through. Let stand for 30 seconds; stir to combine. Cover surface of cream directly with plastic wrap, and refrigerate for 1 hour.

ORANGE AND PISTACHIO STRAWBERRY TART

Makes 1 (9-inch) tart

Sweet strawberries and a hint of cardamom balance the classic bright and nutty combination of orange and pistachio in this tart.

1⅓ cups (167 grams) all-purpose flour
¾ cup (85 grams) roasted pistachios
½ cup (60 grams) confectioners' sugar
½ teaspoon (1.5 grams) kosher salt
½ cup (113 grams) cold unsalted butter, cubed
1 large egg (50 grams)
1 teaspoon (4 grams) orange blossom water
½ teaspoon (1 gram) orange zest
Orange Pastry Cream (recipe follows)
4 cups (680 grams) fresh strawberries, hulled and halved

1. In the work bowl of a food processor, pulse together flour, pistachios, confectioners' sugar, and salt until pistachios are ground into a meal. Add cold butter, and pulse until pea-size crumbs remain.
2. In a small bowl, whisk together egg, orange blossom water, and zest. With processor running, add egg mixture in a slow, steady stream just until dough comes together. Turn out dough, and shape into a disk. Wrap in plastic wrap, and refrigerate for at least 1 hour.
3. Butter and flour a 9x1-inch round removable-bottom tart pan.
4. On a lightly floured surface, roll dough into a 12-inch circle. Transfer to prepared pan, pressing into bottom and up sides. Trim excess dough. Prick bottom and sides of dough with a fork. Freeze for 15 minutes.
5. Preheat oven to 350°F (180°C).
6. Top dough with a piece of parchment paper, letting ends extend over edges of pan. Add pie weights.
7. Bake until edges are set, about 15 minutes. Carefully remove paper and weights. Bake until crust is golden brown, about 10 minutes more. Let cool completely on a wire rack. Spoon Orange Pastry Cream into prepared crust, and spread to edges. Top with strawberries before serving.

ORANGE PASTRY CREAM
Makes about 2 cups

1½ cups (360 grams) heavy whipping cream
¾ cup (180 grams) whole milk
2 tablespoons (12 grams) orange zest
1 teaspoon (3 grams) cardamom seeds
1 large egg (50 grams)
2 large egg yolks (37 grams)
¼ cup plus 2 tablespoons (83 grams) firmly packed light brown sugar
4½ tablespoons (36 grams) cornstarch
2 tablespoons (28 grams) unsalted butter, softened

1. In a medium saucepan, bring cream, milk, zest, and cardamom seeds to a boil over medium heat. Remove from heat; cover and steep for 20 minutes. Strain cream mixture, gently pressing on solids. Return mixture to pan, and return to a boil over medium heat.
2. In a medium bowl, whisk together egg, egg yolks, brown sugar, and cornstarch. Gradually add hot milk mixture to egg mixture, whisking constantly. Return milk mixture to saucepan, and cook, whisking constantly, until thickened. Pour through a fine-mesh sieve into a bowl, discarding solids. Stir in butter until melted. Cover surface of cream directly with plastic wrap, and refrigerate for 1 hour.

BASIL AND PINE NUT STRAWBERRY TART

Makes 1 (9-inch) tart

Sometimes, unexpected combinations just work. Fresh basil, pine nuts, and black pepper give this strawberry tart a savory twist.

6 tablespoons (84 grams) unsalted butter, softened
⅓ cup (67 grams) granulated sugar
¾ teaspoon (3 grams) vanilla extract
½ teaspoon (1.5 grams) kosher salt
½ teaspoon (1 gram) ground black pepper
1 cup plus 2 tablespoons (141 grams) all-purpose flour
½ cup (57 grams) ground pine nuts
Basil Pastry Cream (recipe follows)
Halved fresh strawberries

1. Butter and flour a 9x1-inch round removable-bottom tart pan.
2. In the bowl of a stand mixer fitted with the paddle attachment, beat butter, sugar, vanilla, salt, and pepper at medium speed until fluffy, about 2 minutes. Add flour and pine nuts, and beat at low speed until mixture is crumbly. Transfer mixture to prepared pan, pressing into bottom and up sides. Prick bottom and sides of dough with a fork. Freeze for 15 minutes.
3. Preheat oven to 350°F (180°C).
4. Top dough with a piece of parchment paper, letting ends extend over edges of pan. Add pie weights.
5. Bake until edges are set, about 15 minutes. Carefully remove paper and weights. Bake until crust is golden brown, about 10 minutes more. Let cool completely on a wire rack. Spoon Basil Pastry Cream into prepared crust, and spread to edges. Top with strawberries.

BASIL PASTRY CREAM
Makes about 2 cups

1½ cups (360 grams) heavy whipping cream
¾ cup (180 grams) whole milk
½ cup (16 grams) chopped fresh basil
1 teaspoon (3 grams) fennel seeds
1 large egg (50 grams)
2 large egg yolks (37 grams)
¼ cup plus 2 tablespoons (83 grams) firmly packed light brown sugar
4½ tablespoons (36 grams) cornstarch
2 tablespoons (28 grams) unsalted butter, softened

1. In a medium saucepan, bring cream, milk, basil, and fennel seeds to a boil over medium heat. Remove from heat; cover and steep for 20 minutes. Strain cream mixture, gently pressing on solids. Return mixture to pan, and return to a boil over medium heat.
2. In a medium bowl, whisk together egg, egg yolks, brown sugar, and cornstarch. Gradually add hot milk mixture to egg mixture, whisking constantly. Return milk mixture to saucepan, and cook, whisking constantly, until thickened. Pour mixture through a fine-mesh sieve into a medium bowl, discarding solids. Stir in butter until melted. Cover surface of cream directly with plastic wrap, and refrigerate for 1 hour.

PECAN BUTTER TARTS

Makes 12

Recipe by Emily Turner

While much of Canada's cuisine has European roots and inspiration, butter tarts, which first appeared in Ontario in the early 1900s, are uniquely Canadian. Some insist that the only authentic filling must include raisins, but we'll let you be the judge of that.

Flaky Pastry Dough (recipe follows)
¾ cup (165 grams) firmly packed light brown sugar
5 tablespoons (70 grams) unsalted butter, melted
¼ cup (85 grams) dark corn syrup
¼ cup (85 grams) Grade A amber maple syrup
2 large eggs (100 grams)
1½ teaspoons (6 grams) vanilla extract
1 teaspoon (5 grams) distilled white vinegar
¼ teaspoon kosher salt
½ cup (57 grams) chopped pecans

1. Preheat oven to 450°F (230°C). Butter and flour a 12-cup muffin pan.
2. On a lightly floured surface, roll half of Flaky Pastry Dough to ⅛-inch thickness. Using a 4½- to 5-inch round cutter, cut dough into 6 circles, rerolling scraps once. Gently press rounds into prepared muffin cups, letting edges fold up around each other and extend over sides of pan. Repeat with remaining dough. Freeze for 20 minutes.
3. In a medium bowl, whisk together brown sugar, melted butter, corn syrup, maple syrup, eggs, vanilla, vinegar, and salt. Spoon 2 to 2½ teaspoons (4 to 5 grams) pecans into each prepared crust. Pour filling on top of pecans to ½ inch below edge of cup.
4. Bake in bottom third of oven for 10 minutes. Reduce oven temperature to 400°F (200°C). Bake until filling is set and puffed, 8 to 10 minutes more, covering with foil to prevent excess browning, if necessary. (If you want a runnier texture to your butter tart, bake just until filling is set, 3 to 4 minutes less.) Let cool in pan for 10 minutes. Run a sharp knife around edges of tarts, and let cool completely in pan. (If

you have difficulty removing tarts from pan, freeze for 20 minutes before popping them out.) Bring to room temperature before serving.

FLAKY PASTRY DOUGH
Makes dough for 12 tarts

3½ cups (438 grams) all-purpose flour
1 tablespoon (12 grams) granulated sugar
1 teaspoon (3 grams) kosher salt
½ cup (113 grams) cold all-vegetable shortening, cubed
½ cup (113 grams) cold unsalted butter, cubed
⅓ to ½ cup (80 to 120 grams) cold water, divided
1 large egg yolk (19 grams)
1½ teaspoons (7.5 grams) fresh lemon juice

1. In the work bowl of a food processor, place flour, sugar, and salt; pulse until combined. Add cold shortening and butter, and pulse until mixture is crumbly.
2. In a small bowl, whisk together ⅓ cup (80 grams) cold water, egg yolk, and lemon juice. With processor running, gradually add egg yolk mixture, pulsing until dough begins to come together. (Dough will be softer than a pie dough, but you don't want it to be sticky.) Add remaining water, if necessary.
3. Turn out dough onto a lightly floured surface, and knead until dough comes together. Divide in half. On a lightly floured sheet of parchment paper, roll half of dough to ¼-inch thickness. Transfer to a rimmed baking sheet. Repeat with remaining dough. Refrigerate for 1 hour.

Photo by Maya Visnyei

TARTE TATIN

Makes 1 (8-inch) tart

This classic upside-down apple tart first appeared as a delicious accident at the Hôtel Tatin in the French village of Lamotte-Beuvron. Our modern take uses whole star anise for a boost of warm spice in a simple, refined presentation.

Tart Dough (recipe follows)
5 large apples* (925 grams)
Juice of 1 lemon (30 grams)
5 tablespoons (60 grams) granulated sugar, divided
1 tablespoon (1 gram) grated fresh ginger
¼ teaspoon ground cinnamon
¼ teaspoon ground cloves
¼ cup (57 grams) unsalted butter
9 whole star anise (8 grams)

1. On a lightly floured surface, roll Tart Dough into a 9-inch circle. Wrap in plastic wrap, and refrigerate for 20 minutes.
2. Peel, core, and quarter apples. Cut each quarter in half lengthwise. In a medium bowl, toss together apples, lemon juice, 1 tablespoon (12 grams) sugar, ginger, cinnamon, and cloves. Let stand for 20 minutes. Drain excess juice.
3. Preheat oven to 425°F (220°C).
4. In an 8-inch cast-iron skillet, melt butter over medium heat. Add remaining 4 tablespoons (48 grams) sugar; cook, stirring occasionally, until mixture becomes a light caramel color. (Mixture may look separated.)
5. Remove pan from heat, and arrange star anise and apple slices along

bottom. Place extra apple slices on top. Cook over medium-high heat, without stirring, until apples begin to turn golden brown and caramel is a dark amber color, 10 to 15 minutes. Remove from heat, and let cool for 5 minutes.
6. Cut several 1-inch vents in top of Tart Dough to release steam. Place Tart Dough on top of hot apples, tucking in along edges, being careful not to burn your fingertips.
7. Bake until golden brown, about 25 minutes. Let cool for 15 minutes before inverting onto a cake plate.

*We used Granny Smith, but Gala, Braeburn, and Golden Delicious are also great alternatives. Almost any variety of apple will do.

TART DOUGH
Makes 1 (8-inch) crust

1¼ cups (156 grams) all-purpose flour
1 teaspoon (4 grams) granulated sugar
1 teaspoon (3 grams) kosher salt
½ cup (113 grams) cold unsalted butter, cubed
4 to 8 tablespoons (60 to 120 grams) ice water

1. In the work bowl of a food processor, place flour, sugar, and salt; pulse until combined. Add cold butter, and pulse until mixture is crumbly. With processor running, add ice water, 1 tablespoon (15 grams) at a time, just until dough comes together. Turn out dough, and shape into a disk. Wrap in plastic wrap, and refrigerate for at least 1 hour before using.

CRANBERRY-CARAMEL TART

Makes 1 (9-inch) tart

Rich ripples of caramel balance out the tartness of the cranberries in this elegant holiday tart. Pecans pull double duty as the toasted base for the crust and an additional source of crunch in the filling.

Pecan Dough (recipe follows)
1   cup (200 grams) granulated sugar
1   cup (240 grams) heavy whipping cream, warmed
½   cup (113 grams) unsalted butter, softened
2   cups (226 grams) chopped pecans
2   cups (340 grams) frozen cranberries
¼   teaspoon kosher salt

1. Preheat oven to 350°F (180°C).
2. Press Pecan Dough into bottom and up sides of a 9-inch round removable-bottom tart pan. Freeze for 10 minutes. Prick bottom and sides of Pecan Dough with a fork. Top with a piece of parchment paper, letting ends extend over edges of pan. Add pie weights.
3. Bake for 20 minutes. Carefully remove paper and weights. Bake until lightly browned, about 5 minutes more. Let cool completely on a wire rack.

4. In a 10-inch skillet, sprinkle sugar in an even layer. Cook over medium heat, without stirring, until sugar is dissolved and turns amber colored, about 10 minutes. Remove from heat; carefully whisk in cream and butter until combined. Stir in pecans, cranberries, and salt. (Mixture will bubble up.) Spoon mixture into prepared crust.
5. Bake until bubbly, 20 to 25 minutes. Let cool to room temperature. Refrigerate for at least 30 minutes before slicing.

PECAN DOUGH
Makes 1 (9-inch) crust

¾   cup (94 grams) all-purpose flour
6   tablespoons (42 grams) confectioners' sugar
¼   cup (36 grams) toasted pecan halves
¼   teaspoon kosher salt
⅓   cup (76 grams) unsalted butter, softened and cubed

1. In the work bowl of a food processor, place flour, confectioners' sugar, pecans, and salt; pulse until finely ground. With processor running, gradually add butter, pulsing until dough comes together.

APRICOT FRANGIPANE TART

Makes 1 (14x4-inch) tart

We love the extra crunchy texture almond flour lends to this not-too-sweet dessert's crust. Smooth frangipane, an almond pastry cream, adds another nutty element, and is a great base for the fresh, juicy apricots in both taste and texture.

1   cup (125 grams) all-purpose flour
1¼   cups (120 grams) almond flour, divided
½   cup (100 grams) plus 1 teaspoon (4 grams) granulated sugar, divided
½   teaspoon (1.5 grams) kosher salt
7   tablespoons (98 grams) cold unsalted butter
3   tablespoons (45 grams) cold water
½   cup (113 grams) unsalted butter, softened
2   large eggs (100 grams)
1   teaspoon (5 grams) dark rum
¼   teaspoon (1 gram) almond extract
4   small apricots (250 grams), peeled and halved
3   tablespoons (60 grams) apricot jam, warmed and strained

1. In the work bowl of a food processor, place all-purpose flour, ¼ cup (24 grams) almond flour, 1 teaspoon (4 grams) sugar, and salt; process until combined. Add cold butter, and pulse until mixture is crumbly. With processor running, add 3 tablespoons (45 grams) cold water in a slow, steady stream just until dough comes together but is not sticky (you may not need all the water). Shape dough into a disk, and wrap in plastic wrap. Refrigerate for at least 30 minutes.

2. In the bowl of a stand mixer fitted with the paddle attachment, beat butter and remaining ½ cup (100 grams) sugar at medium speed until creamy, 3 to 4 minutes, stopping to scrape sides of bowl. Reduce mixer speed to low. Add eggs, one at a time, beating just until combined after each addition. Stir in rum and almond extract. Stir in remaining 1 cup (96 grams) almond flour just until combined.

3. Preheat oven to 350°F (180°C). Butter and flour a 14x4-inch tart pan.

4. On a lightly floured surface, roll dough into a 15x5-inch rectangle. Transfer to prepared pan, pressing into bottom and up sides. Trim excess dough. Freeze for 10 minutes. Top dough with a piece of parchment paper, letting ends extend over edges of pan. Add pie weights.

5. Bake just until edges are set, 10 to 12 minutes. Carefully remove paper and weights, and bake 2 minutes more. Let cool. Spread filling into prepared crust. Top with apricots, cut side down.

6. Place tart pan on a rimmed baking sheet to catch any drips. Bake until lightly browned, 40 to 45 minutes. Let cool for 20 minutes before removing from pan. Brush tops of apricots with jam before serving.

APRICOT AND HAZELNUT CRUMB TART

Makes 1 (9-inch) tart

Recipe by Yossy Arefi

This deep-dish tart is a true celebration of one of Yossy's very favorite fruits—the rosy-cheeked apricot. Apricots are one of those fruits that truly come alive with a bit of heat, and in this tart, they are wrapped in a toasty and crunchy hazelnut crust and crumble. Use Blenheim apricots if they are available where you live—their honey-sweet flavor just can't be beat.

1⅓   cups (151 grams) plus 2 tablespoons (14 grams) toasted skinned hazelnuts, divided
⅔   cup (80 grams) confectioners' sugar
2   cups (250 grams) plus 1 tablespoon (8 grams) all-purpose flour, divided
1⅛   teaspoons (3 grams) kosher salt, divided
1   cup (227 grams) cold unsalted butter, cubed
1   large egg (50 grams)
1   tablespoon (15 grams) cold water
½   cup (100 grams) granulated sugar
1   vanilla bean, split lengthwise, seeds scraped and reserved
2   pounds (910 grams) fresh apricots, quartered
Vanilla ice cream, to serve

1. In the work bowl of a food processor, pulse together 1⅓ cups (151 grams) hazelnuts and confectioners' sugar until combined. Add 2 cups (250 grams) flour and 1 teaspoon (3 grams) salt; pulse until combined. Add cold butter, and pulse until mixture is crumbly.
2. In a small bowl, whisk together egg and 1 tablespoon (15 grams) cold water. With processor running, pour egg mixture through food chute in a slow, steady stream until combined. Pulse until mixture begins to hold together, adding more water if necessary. (The dough should hold together easily when squeezed.) Reserve 1 cup (235 grams) hazelnut mixture for topping. Press remaining mixture into bottom and up sides of a 9-inch springform pan. Freeze until firm.
3. Preheat oven to 375°F (190°C).
4. In a small bowl, combine granulated sugar and vanilla bean seeds with fingertips. Stir in remaining ⅛ teaspoon salt; set aside. Roughly chop remaining 2 tablespoons (14 grams) hazelnuts; set aside.
5. Sprinkle remaining 1 tablespoon (8 grams) flour in prepared tart shell. Starting from outside edge, arrange apricots, standing upright with skins facing out, in tight concentric circles. They should be tightly packed so they stand up on their ends. Sprinkle apricots with sugar mixture. Crumble reserved 1 cup (235 grams) hazelnut mixture over apricots. Sprinkle with chopped hazelnuts.
6. Bake until topping is deep golden brown and fruit is bubbly, 50 to 60 minutes, covering with foil to prevent excess browning, if necessary. Let cool completely in pan. Remove ring, and serve at room temperature with ice cream.

Photo by Yossy Arefi

RHUBARB AND ALMOND TART

Makes 1 (12x8-inch) tart

If there were a tart that embodied springtime, this would be it. The addition of rhubarb to this delicate pastry's nutty filling energizes a classic—and that chevron lattice isn't too shabby either.

Pâte Sucrée (recipe on page 235)
1½ cups Almond Cream Filling (recipe follows)
2 cups (200 grams) sliced rhubarb
2 tablespoons (24 grams) granulated sugar

1. On a lightly floured surface, roll Pâte Sucrée into a 14x10-inch rectangle. Transfer dough to a 12x8-inch removable-bottom tart pan, pressing into bottom and up sides. Trim excess dough. Freeze for 30 minutes. Place pan on a rimmed baking sheet to catch drips.
2. Preheat oven to 375°F (190°C).
3. Bake for 10 minutes. Let cool completely.
4. Spoon Almond Cream Filling into prepared crust, using an offset spatula to smooth. Place sliced rhubarb on top of filling in a chevron pattern*. Sprinkle with sugar.
5. Bake until filling is set and crust is golden brown, 35 to 40 minutes. Let cool in pan for 15 minutes before carefully removing.

To make a chevron pattern, cut each stalk of rhubarb in half lengthwise. Keeping the two halves together, make 1-inch slices on an angle. When the top and bottom halves are placed next to each other, they will make a nice "V" shape.

Note: *If your rhubarb is very thin, it may shrink during the baking process.*

ALMOND CREAM FILLING
Makes about 2 cups

1 cup (227 grams) unsalted butter, softened
1 cup (200 grams) granulated sugar
1 tablespoon (6 grams) orange zest
1 teaspoon (6 grams) vanilla bean paste
1 teaspoon (5 grams) rum
4 large eggs (200 grams)
1¾ cups (168 grams) almond flour

1. In the bowl of a stand mixer fitted with the paddle attachment, beat butter and sugar at medium speed until creamy, 3 to 4 minutes, stopping to scrape sides of bowl. Beat in zest, vanilla bean paste, and rum. Reduce mixer speed to medium-low. Add eggs, one at a time, beating well after each addition. Gradually add flour, beating until combined. Refrigerate in an airtight container until ready to use, up to 2 weeks.

RHUBARB AND BROWNED BUTTER TARTLETS

Makes 12

Is there anything that browned butter doesn't turn into pure magic? Sweet, caramelized Browned Butter Filling in a delicate, homemade Pâte Sucrée is the perfect juxtaposition to the tangy rhubarb in these tartlets.

Pâte Sucrée (recipe follows)
Browned Butter Filling (recipe follows)
2   cups (200 grams) thinly sliced rhubarb
2   tablespoons (24 grams) granulated sugar

1. Line a baking sheet with parchment paper.
2. On a lightly floured surface, divide Pâte Sucrée into 12 equal portions. Roll each piece into a 4-inch circle. Transfer dough to 12 (2½-inch) tart pans, pressing into bottom and up sides. Trim excess dough. Transfer tart shells to prepared pan. Freeze for 30 minutes.
3. Preheat oven to 375°F (190°C).
4. Spoon 2 tablespoons Browned Butter Filling into each prepared tart shell. Shingle sliced rhubarb on top of filling, and sprinkle with sugar.
5. Bake until filling is set and crust is golden brown, 18 to 20 minutes. Let cool in pans for 10 minutes before carefully removing.

Pâte Sucrée
Makes 12 (2½-inch) tart shells or 1 (12x8-inch) tart shell

½   cup plus 3 tablespoons (155 grams) unsalted butter, softened
½   cup (60 grams) confectioners' sugar
1   teaspoon (2 grams) orange zest
1   large egg (50 grams)
2¼ cups (227 grams) pastry flour
½   teaspoon (1.5 grams) kosher salt

1. In the bowl of a stand mixer fitted with the paddle attachment, beat butter, confectioners' sugar, and zest at medium speed until creamy, 3 to 4 minutes, stopping to scrape sides of bowl. Beat in egg. Add flour and salt, beating just until mixture comes together. Shape dough into a disk, and wrap in plastic wrap. Refrigerate for at least 2 hours.

Browned Butter Filling
Makes about 1½ cups

¾   cup (170 grams) unsalted butter
½   vanilla bean, split lengthwise, seeds scraped and reserved
1   cup (200 grams) granulated sugar
2   tablespoons (16 grams) all-purpose flour
2   large eggs (100 grams)

1. In a medium saucepan, heat butter and vanilla bean and reserved seeds over medium heat. Cook until butter turns a deep amber color and has a nutty aroma, about 10 minutes. Remove from heat.
2. In a large bowl, whisk together sugar, flour, and eggs. Remove vanilla bean from saucepan; slowly drizzle hot butter mixture into egg mixture, whisking constantly. Let cool to room temperature. Once mixture is cool, whisk once more before transferring to an airtight container. Refrigerate for at least 8 hours.

JUNIPER, PEAR, AND BLUEBERRY BRETON TARTS

Makes 20

For this ode to blueberries, we paired slivers of dried pears with a dried blueberry, lemon, and gin-flavored filling.

4   large egg yolks (74 grams)
¾   cup (150 grams) granulated sugar
¾   cup (170 grams) unsalted butter, softened and cubed
¾   teaspoon (2.25 grams) kosher salt
1¾   cups (219 grams) all-purpose flour
¾   cup (94 grams) cake flour
⅓   cup (43 grams) diced dried pear
1½   tablespoons (22.5 grams) baking powder
¾   teaspoon (1.5 grams) ground juniper berries
½   teaspoon (1 gram) ground black pepper
Lemon Blueberry Filling (recipe follows)
Toasty Brown Sugar Pastry Cream (recipe follows)

1. In the bowl of a stand mixer fitted with the paddle attachment, beat egg yolks and sugar at medium speed until pale yellow, 2 to 3 minutes. Add butter and salt, beating until combined.
2. In a medium bowl, whisk together flours, pear, baking powder, juniper berries, and pepper. With mixer on low speed, gradually add flour mixture to yolk mixture, beating just until combined. Turn out dough, and divide in half. Shape each half into a disk. Wrap in plastic wrap, and refrigerate for at least 30 minutes.
3. Preheat oven to 325°F (170°C). Line a baking sheet with parchment paper. Place 5 (2½-inch) round cutters on pan; butter and flour cutters and pan.
4. On a lightly floured surface, roll half of dough to ¼-inch thickness. Using a 2½-inch round cutter, cut 5 rounds from dough. Place rounds in prepared ring molds. Reserve dough scraps, and keep refrigerated. Using a rounded teaspoon, press a slight indentation into center of each round.
5. Bake until puffed and golden brown, about 15 minutes. Let cool completely. Carefully remove ring molds; transfer pastry to wire racks, and let cool completely. Repeat procedure with remaining dough, buttering and flouring rings each time. Spoon 1½ teaspoons Lemon Blueberry Filling into

each Breton crust. Pipe Toasty Brown Sugar Pastry Cream around edges of tarts in desired pattern. Serve immediately.

LEMON BLUEBERRY FILLING
Makes ½ cup

⅓   cup (43 grams) dried blueberries
¼   cup (80 grams) blueberry preserves
¼   cup (55 grams) firmly packed light brown sugar
2   teaspoons (10 grams) unsalted butter
2   teaspoons (4 grams) lemon zest
1   teaspoon (5 grams) gin

1. In a small saucepan, bring dried blueberries and water to cover by 1 inch to a boil over high heat. Reduce heat to low; cook until blueberries are softened, about 15 minutes. Drain blueberries, reserving 2 teaspoons (10 grams) cooking liquid.
2. In the work bowl of a food processor, place warm blueberries, reserved 2 teaspoons (10 grams) cooking liquid, blueberry preserves, brown sugar, butter, zest, and gin; pulse until mixture has the texture of jam. Let cool completely. Refrigerate in an airtight container for up to 1 week.

TOASTY BROWN SUGAR PASTRY CREAM
Makes about 2¾ cups

1½   cups (360 grams) heavy whipping cream
¾   cup (180 grams) whole milk
1   large egg (50 grams)
2   large egg yolks (37 grams)
⅓   cup (73 grams) firmly packed light brown sugar
4½   tablespoons (36 grams) cornstarch
1½   tablespoons (21 grams) toasted sesame oil

1. In a medium saucepan, bring cream and milk to a boil over medium heat.
2. In a medium bowl, whisk together egg, egg yolks, brown sugar, and cornstarch. Whisking constantly, slowly add hot cream mixture to egg mixture. Return cream mixture to saucepan, and cook, whisking constantly, until thickened.
3. Transfer to a medium bowl, and stir in oil. Press a piece of plastic wrap directly onto surface of pastry cream to prevent a skin from forming. Refrigerate for 1 hour.

INDIVIDUAL PLUM LAVENDER TARTS

Makes 18

Recipe by Marian Cooper Cairns

For a range of colors and textures, we suggest using a variety of plums in these simple and fast puff pastry squares. (We like Damson, Victoria, or Satsuma.) Dress them up with our sour cream-lavender drizzle. The aromatic lavender adds floral undertones while the sour cream cuts through the fruit's sweetness.

1   (17.3-ounce) package (490 grams) frozen puff pastry, thawed
1   large egg (50 grams)
1   tablespoon (15 grams) water
4 to 5 assorted medium plums (300 to 375 grams), pitted and very thinly sliced
6   tablespoons (72 grams) granulated sugar
¾   cup (90 grams) confectioners' sugar
2½   tablespoons (37.5 grams) sour cream
¼   teaspoon lavender blossoms, crushed
⅛   teaspoon kosher salt

1. Preheat oven to 425°F (220°C). Line 2 baking sheets with parchment paper.
2. Unfold pastry on a lightly floured surface. Cut each pastry sheet into 9 (3-inch) squares, and place on prepared pans.
3. In a small bowl, whisk together egg and 1 tablespoon (15 grams) water. Brush pastry with egg wash. Arrange plums on pastry squares; sprinkle with granulated sugar.
4. Bake until pastry is golden brown, 15 to 18 minutes, rotating pans halfway through baking. Let cool on a wire rack for 5 minutes.
5. In a small bowl, whisk together confectioners' sugar, sour cream, lavender, and salt until smooth. Drizzle over tarts. Serve warm.

Photo by Matt Armendariz

CHOCOLATE-COCONUT TART WITH ALMONDS

Makes 1 (9-inch) tart

Recipe by Ben Mims

Like a grown-up version of the popular Almond Joy candy bar, this tart balances almonds and sweet chocolate with plenty of salt and toasted coconut. The tart crust needs to be dark brown to ensure that it is cooked through properly and is crunchy. For a chewier, more macaroon-like texture, simply cook the crust 5 minutes less.

2   tablespoons (28 grams) unrefined coconut oil, melted, plus more for greasing pan
2¼   cups (189 grams) finely shredded dried (desiccated) coconut
⅓   cup (67 grams) granulated sugar
½   teaspoon (1.5 grams) kosher salt
1   large egg white (30 grams), lightly beaten
1¼   cups (141 grams) roasted salted almonds, halved or roughly chopped

Ganache (recipe follows)
½   cup (17 grams) sweetened and toasted coconut "chips," such as Dang or Bare brands

1. Preheat oven to 350°F (180°C). Grease a 9x1-inch round removable-bottom tart pan with melted coconut oil.
2. In a medium bowl, combine coconut, sugar, 2 tablespoons (28 grams) melted coconut oil, salt, and egg white; mix with your hands until a moldable dough forms. Press dough into bottom and up sides of prepared pan. Place tart pan on a rimmed baking sheet to catch any drips.
3. Bake until deep golden brown and set, 23 to 25 minutes (crust should be fully brown with no white spots visible). Let cool completely on a wire rack.
4. Spread almonds over bottom of cooled crust in a single layer. Spread Ganache over almonds, and smooth top. Drop pan from a height of 5 inches a few times to settle Ganache around almonds. Sprinkle with coconut chips. Refrigerate until Ganache is set and firm, at least 6 hours. Cut into wedges to serve.

GANACHE
Makes about 2 cups

1   pound (455 grams) German or semisweet chocolate
1   cup (240 grams) heavy whipping cream

1. Place chocolate in a medium bowl.
2. In a small saucepan, bring cream to a simmer over medium-low heat; pour over chocolate. Let stand for 2 minutes. Whisk mixture, starting from the center and working outward, until smooth.

Photo by Mason + Dixon

TANGERINE TART

Makes 1 (9-inch) tart

Sweeter than the common orange, tangerine juice imparts elevated citrus flavor to this tart's creamy filling.

Basil Macadamia Dough (recipe follows)
1½ cups (360 grams) fresh tangerine juice
¼ cup (8 grams) chopped fresh basil
¾ cup (150 grams) granulated sugar
⅓ cup (42 grams) all-purpose flour
4 large eggs (200 grams)
½ cup (120 grams) whole milk
1 tablespoon (6 grams) tangerine zest
2 tablespoons (28 grams) unsalted butter
½ cup (120 grams) sour cream
1 teaspoon (4 grams) vanilla extract
Brown Sugar Whipped Cream (recipe follows)

1. Preheat oven to 325°F (170°C).
2. Press Basil Macadamia Dough into bottom and up sides of a 9-inch round removable-bottom tart pan. Top with a piece of parchment paper, letting ends extend over edges of pan. Add pie weights.
3. Bake until lightly browned, about 15 minutes. Let cool slightly. Carefully remove paper and weights. Bake until light golden brown and firm, about 10 minutes more. Let cool completely.
4. In a medium saucepan, bring tangerine juice and basil to a simmer over medium heat. Remove from heat, and let stand for 15 minutes. Strain mixture, discarding solids, and return juice to pan.
5. Add sugar and flour to pan, whisking to combine. Whisk in eggs, milk, and zest. Cook over medium heat, stirring constantly, until thickened, about 20 minutes.
6. Remove from heat, and stir in butter until melted. Stir in sour cream and vanilla. Pour into prepared crust. Cover with plastic wrap, pressing wrap directly onto surface of custard to prevent a skin from forming. Refrigerate overnight. Top with Brown Sugar Whipped Cream.

Basil Macadamia Dough
Makes 1 (9-inch) crust

1 cup (96 grams) finely ground toasted macadamia nuts
3 tablespoons (36 grams) granulated sugar
2 teaspoons (1 gram) chopped fresh basil
½ teaspoon (1.5 grams) kosher salt
1½ cups (188 grams) all-purpose flour
½ cup (113 grams) unsalted butter, softened
1 large egg yolk (19 grams)

1. In the work bowl of a food processor, place macadamia nuts, sugar, basil, and salt; pulse until combined. Add flour, and pulse until finely ground.
2. In the bowl of a stand mixer fitted with the paddle attachment, beat nut mixture, butter, and egg yolk at medium speed until combined. Shape dough into a disk, and wrap in plastic wrap. Refrigerate for at least 10 minutes before using.

Brown Sugar Whipped Cream
Makes about 1½ cups

¾ cup (180 grams) heavy whipping cream, chilled
2 tablespoons (28 grams) firmly packed light brown sugar
¼ teaspoon kosher salt

1. In the bowl of a stand mixer fitted with the whisk attachment, beat cream, brown sugar, and salt at high speed until stiff peaks form, 2 to 3 minutes. Cover and refrigerate for up to 24 hours.

PASTRIES

CHOCOLATE ALMOND MOONCAKES

Makes 15

Recipe by Rebecca Firth

These mooncakes are not difficult to make as long as you follow some key instructions. For this particular recipe, it's imperative that you use Medjool dates, as other dates won't yield the same firm and delicious texture that the filling requires. It's equally important to not only chill the dough and filling prior to assembling the cakes, but to also give them ample freezer time just before baking. This last step ensures that the intricate detail on top stays intact throughout the baking process.

4	tablespoons (60 grams) water, divided
1	tablespoon (15 grams) vodka
¾	teaspoon (3.75 grams) baking soda
⅔	cup (226 grams) honey
⅓	cup (75 grams) sunflower seed oil or other neutral-flavored oil
1½	cups (187 grams) cake flour
1	cup (125 grams) all-purpose flour
	Chocolate Almond Filling (recipe follows)
1	large egg yolk (19 grams)
1	tablespoon (15 grams) heavy whipping cream or whole milk

1. In a medium bowl, whisk together 2 tablespoons (30 grams) water, vodka, and baking soda. Add honey and oil, whisking to combine. Sift flours over honey mixture, and stir until a ball starts to form.

2. Turn out dough onto a lightly floured surface, and shape into a disk. Wrap tightly in plastic wrap, and refrigerate for at least 1 hour.

3. Line a baking sheet with parchment paper, and place on top of another baking sheet.

4. Divide dough into 15 balls (each weighing about 1.35 ounces). Cover with a lightly damp, clean towel to keep dough from drying out. Divide Chocolate Almond Filling into 15 balls (each weighing 1 ounce). Roll each dough ball into a 4-inch circle. Place one ball of Chocolate Almond Filling in center of each circle, and cover completely with dough. Pull off any excess dough, and discard it or use it to patch any thin spots. Hold dough ball in your hands for 1 minute to soften, and gently shape into a sphere.

5. Lightly dust mooncake ball and a mooncake mold with flour, shaking off excess. Place mooncake mold on top of mooncake ball, and firmly press down until you reach some resistance. Always place smoothest side of ball upright to get best design imprint. Tap mooncake mold on counter to gently release mooncake from mold. Set mooncakes on prepared pan. Freeze for 1 hour.

6. Position oven rack in top third of oven, and preheat oven to 350°F (180°C).

7. Take mooncakes from freezer, and immediately place in oven. Bake for 10 minutes. In a small bowl, whisk together egg yolk, cream, and remaining 2 tablespoons (30 grams) water. Lightly brush egg wash over mooncakes. (Don't let wash get too thick in areas, or you'll lose detail of mooncake design.) Gently brush off any excess. Bake for 4 minutes. Let cool for 10 minutes.

8. Lightly brush a final thin layer of egg wash over mooncakes, taking care not to use too much. Bake 4 minutes more. Let cool completely. Store in an airtight container at room temperature for 2 to 3 days before serving.

CHOCOLATE ALMOND FILLING
Makes about 1¾ cups

1	cup (240 grams) water
14	pitted Medjool dates (194 grams)
1½	tablespoons (21 grams) unsalted butter, softened
1	teaspoon (4 grams) vanilla extract
½	teaspoon (2 gram) almond extract
¾	cup (85 grams) chopped unsalted almonds, toasted
4	ounces (115 grams) 60% cacao dark chocolate, chopped
3	tablespoons (21 grams) confectioners' sugar
3	tablespoons (15 grams) unsweetened dark cocoa powder
½	teaspoon (1.5 grams) sea salt
½	teaspoon (1 gram) Chinese five-spice powder

1. In a medium saucepan, bring 1 cup (240 grams) water and dates to a boil over high heat. Reduce heat, and simmer until most of liquid has been absorbed by dates, about 15 minutes.

2. Place dates and any remaining liquid in the work bowl of a food processor. Add butter and extracts; process until smooth, about 3 minutes.

3. With processor running, add almonds, and process until smooth, about 3 minutes. (Mixture should be thick with only small bits of almond visible. Be sure to scrape down sides of bowl so that everything gets incorporated.)

4. Add chocolate, confectioners' sugar, cocoa, salt, and five-spice powder; process until combined. (Mixture will be sticky.) Scrape filling into a bowl, and cover tightly with plastic wrap. Refrigerate for at least 1 hour before using.

Note: *We used a KINGSO Round Mooncake 50g DIY Moon Cake Mold Cookie Cutter, available on amazon.com.*

Photo by Joe Schmelzer

CHOCOLATE RUGELACH

Makes 36

Recipe by Shiran Dickman/*feedfeed*

This classic rugelach is hard to resist after the first bite thanks to the flaky, buttery dough and sweet chocolate filling.

2¼   cups (281 grams) all-purpose flour
¼   cup (50 grams) granulated sugar
¼   teaspoon kosher salt
1   cup (227 grams) cold unsalted butter, cubed
8   ounces (225 grams) cold cream cheese, cubed
1   cup (256 grams) chocolate or chocolate-hazelnut spread
Garnish: confectioners' sugar

1. In the work bowl of a food processor, place flour, granulated sugar, and salt; process until combined. Add cold butter, and pulse until mixture is crumbly, about 15 pulses. Add cold cream cheese, and pulse until dough starts to clump together, 10 to 15 seconds.

Turn out dough onto a lightly floured surface, and shape into a disk. Wrap in plastic wrap, and refrigerate until firm, at least 2 hours.
2. Preheat oven to 350°F (180°C). Line a baking sheet with parchment paper.
3. Cut dough into 3 equal pieces. While working with one piece, keep remaining pieces in refrigerator. Roll dough into a 12x8-inch rectangle. Spread dough with one-third of chocolate spread. Starting with one long side, roll up dough, jelly-roll style. Place on prepared pan. Using a knife, make ¾-inch cuts crosswise into dough at 1-inch intervals. (Do not cut all the way through dough.) If dough is too soft to cut, refrigerate for 20 minutes. Repeat with remaining dough and remaining chocolate spread.
4. Bake until golden brown, about 30 minutes. Transfer to a wire rack. While still warm, cut slices all the way through. Let cool completely. Dust with confectioners' sugar, if desired. Store in an airtight container at room temperature for up to 1 week.

Photo by Shiran Dickman

BAKLAVA

Makes about 36 pieces

Recipe by Fanny Lam/*feedfeed*

Baklava is a decadent and highly addictive treat. With layers of crispy phyllo, crunchy chopped walnuts, and a generous pour of honey-lemon syrup, this will be the dessert that disappears the fastest.

1	cup (200 grams) granulated sugar
1	cup (240 grams) water
½	cup (170 grams) honey
2	tablespoons (30 grams) fresh lemon juice
1	(16-ounce) package (454 grams) frozen phyllo pastry, thawed
1	cup (227 grams) unsalted butter, melted
3	cups (339 grams) roughly chopped walnuts
1	teaspoon (2 grams) ground cinnamon

1. In a medium saucepan, bring sugar, 1 cup (240 grams) water, honey, and lemon juice to a boil over medium-high heat. Reduce heat to low, and cook, without stirring, for 5 minutes. Remove from heat, and let cool completely.
2. Preheat oven to 350°F (180°C). Butter a 13x9-inch baking pan.
3. Trim pastry dough to fit baking pan. Keep phyllo covered with a damp towel at all times to keep dough from drying out. Line pan with 1 layer of phyllo, and lightly brush with melted butter. Continue lining pan with phyllo, covering bottom of pan only, to make 10 layers, brushing each layer with melted butter.
4. In a large bowl, combine walnuts and cinnamon. Sprinkle 1 cup nut mixture over top layer of phyllo. Repeat entire procedure twice. Top last layer of nuts with 10 layers of phyllo, brushing each layer with melted butter. Cut baklava diagonally into diamonds, cutting all the way through.
5. Bake until golden and crisp, 50 to 55 minutes. Remove from oven, and immediately pour honey mixture over baklava. Let stand, uncovered, at room temperature for at least 4 hours or overnight. (This helps syrup penetrate the layers.) Store at room temperature, loosely covered with a tea towel, for up to 1 week.

PRO TIPS
For the perfect cut, start in the middle with a diagonal slice and work your way to one end and then the other. This will help keep your slices uniform.

Use a light hand when brushing sheets with butter. It's not necessary to drench the sheets in butter, but mark with a few wide brush strokes. This will prevent tearing the delicate phyllo sheets and keep your baklava light and crisp.

Photo by Fanny Lam

GALETTE DES ROIS

Makes about 8 servings

Layers of buttery puff pastry wrap around orange-scented almond cream to create this heavenly treat. With a gorgeous swirling design slashed into the top, this pastry is royalty in our book.

1	cup (240 grams) plus 1 teaspoon (5 grams) whole milk, divided
3	large egg yolks (56 grams)
½	cup (100 grams) granulated sugar, divided
2	tablespoons (16 grams) cornstarch, divided
1	tablespoon (8 grams) all-purpose flour
¼	cup (57 grams) unsalted butter, softened
1	tablespoon (6 grams) orange zest
2	large eggs (100 grams), divided
1	tablespoon (15 grams) orange liqueur*
¼	cup (24 grams) almond flour
¼	teaspoon kosher salt
1	(17.3-ounce) package (490 grams) frozen puff pastry, thawed
1	almond or piece of candied fruit
¼	cup (85 grams) pure maple syrup

1. In a large saucepan, bring 1 cup (240 grams) milk to a boil over medium-high heat, whisking constantly. Remove from heat.
2. In a medium bowl, whisk together egg yolks, ¼ cup (50 grams) sugar, 1 tablespoon (8 grams) cornstarch, and all-purpose flour. Add ½ cup (120 grams) hot milk to egg mixture, whisking constantly. Add egg mixture to remaining hot milk in pan, whisking to combine. Strain mixture through a fine-mesh sieve, discarding solids. Return mixture to pan, and cook, stirring constantly, until thickened, 5 to 7 minutes. Spoon mixture into a heatproof bowl. Cover with plastic wrap, pressing wrap directly onto surface of custard. Refrigerate until cold, at least 4 hours.
3. In the bowl of a stand mixer fitted with the paddle attachment, beat butter, zest, and remaining ¼ cup (50 grams) sugar at medium speed until creamy. Add 1 egg (50 grams) and orange liqueur, beating until combined. Reduce mixer speed to medium-low. Gradually add almond flour, salt, and remaining 1 tablespoon (8 grams) cornstarch, beating until smooth. Cover and refrigerate until cool, at least 30 minutes.
4. In a medium bowl, stir together custard and almond cream. Spoon into a pastry bag fitted with a large round tip.

5. Line a baking sheet with parchment paper.
6. On a lightly floured surface, unfold puff pastry sheets, and roll lightly to remove seams. Trim each sheet of pastry into a 9-inch circle. Using a fork, lightly pierce both rounds all over. Place 1 round on prepared pan. Brush edge of round with water. Starting from center and moving outward, pipe almond cream onto round, leaving a 1-inch border. Place almond or candied fruit somewhere in the cream. Top with second round, and press with fingertips to seal edges. Carefully turn galette over, and reseal edges from opposite side. Using a sharp knife, score a design in galette, being careful not to cut through pastry. Notch edges of galette.
7. In a small bowl, whisk together remaining 1 egg (50 grams) and remaining 1 teaspoon (5 grams) milk. Brush galette with egg wash, and refrigerate for at least 1 hour.
8. Preheat oven to 400°F (200°C).
9. Bake for 15 minutes. Reduce oven temperature to 375°F (190°C), and bake until deep golden brown, 35 to 40 minutes more. Let cool completely on pan. Just before serving, brush with maple syrup.

We used Grand Marnier.

BEAR CLAWS

Makes 12

Originating in the United States in the mid-1920s, these flaky puff pastries get their name from the oversized claw-like shape.

4   cups (500 grams) all-purpose flour
2½   cups (569 grams) cold unsalted butter, cubed
2   teaspoons (6 grams) kosher salt
¾   cup (180 grams) cold water
1   large egg (50 grams)
1   teaspoon (5 grams) whole milk
Marzipan Filling (recipe follows)
½   cup (57 grams) sliced almonds
2   tablespoons (24 grams) turbinado sugar

1. In the bowl of a stand mixer fitted with the paddle attachment, beat flour, butter, and salt at low speed just until butter is coated with flour, about 30 seconds. With mixer running, add ¾ cup (180 grams) cold water in a slow, steady stream just until dough comes together, about 1 minute (there will still be large pieces of butter). Cover and refrigerate for 30 minutes.
2. On a lightly floured surface, roll dough into an 18x11-inch rectangle. Fold dough into thirds, like a letter. Rotate dough 90 degrees, and fold into thirds again. Wrap dough in plastic wrap, and refrigerate for at least 1 hour.
3. Divide dough in half. On a lightly floured surface, roll half of dough into a 15x11-inch rectangle. Trim edges of dough. Cut dough in half lengthwise; cut each half into 3 (5½x5-inch) rectangles. Repeat with remaining dough.
4. Preheat oven to 400°F (200°C). Line 2 rimmed baking sheets with parchment paper.
5. In a small bowl, whisk together egg and milk. Fill a pastry bag with Marzipan Filling, and pipe into center of each rectangle. Brush edges with egg wash, and fold dough over filling, pressing sealed edges to seal. Trim edges with a pizza wheel to further seal. Using a sharp knife, make 4 cuts on sealed edge of dough, being careful not to cut through to filling. Transfer to prepared pans, gently curving to spread out cuts. Freeze for 10 minutes. Brush tops of dough with egg wash, and sprinkle with almonds and turbinado sugar.
6. Bake until golden brown, about 20 minutes. Let cool slightly before serving. Bear Claws can be prepared days in advance and frozen for up to a week until ready to bake.

MARZIPAN FILLING
Makes about 1½ cups

2   cups (240 grams) confectioners' sugar
2   cups (192 grams) almond flour (see Pro Tip)
2½   tablespoons (35 grams) unsalted butter
2   tablespoons (30 grams) amaretto
1   large egg white (30 grams)
1½   teaspoons (6 grams) almond extract

1. In the work bowl of a food processor, place confectioners' sugar and almond flour; process until combined. Add butter, amaretto, egg white, and almond extract; process until mixture comes together. (Mixture will be softer than a typical marzipan.) Use immediately.

> **PRO TIP**
> Use almond flour made from blanched whole almonds. Flour made with unblanched almonds will give your filling a slightly grainier texture and darker color.

STRAWBERRY GINGER KOUIGN AMANN

Makes 12

A generous sprinkling of ginger sugar gives this impressive pastry an addictive crunch.

2½ tablespoons (22.5 grams) active dry yeast
1⅓ cups (320 grams) warm water
 (100°F/38°C to 105°F/40°C)
4 cups (508 grams) bread flour
2 teaspoons (6 grams) kosher salt
1¾ cups (397 grams) salted butter, softened
Ginger Sugar (recipe follows)
Strawberry Filling (recipe follows)

1. In the bowl of a stand mixer fitted with the dough hook attachment, stir together yeast and 1⅓ cups (320 grams) warm water. Add flour and salt, and beat at low speed until moistened, about 2 minutes. Increase mixer speed to medium, and beat until a smooth, elastic dough forms, 3 to 5 minutes. Cover with plastic wrap, and let rise at room temperature for 20 minutes.
2. Between 2 sheets of plastic wrap, shape butter into a 10x8-inch rectangle. Refrigerate for 5 minutes before dough has finished rising.
3. On a lightly floured surface, roll dough into a 16x10-inch rectangle. Unwrap butter block, and place in center of rectangle. Fold dough edges over to enclose butter block. Roll dough into an 18x8-inch rectangle. Fold dough into thirds, like a letter, to form an 8x6-inch rectangle. Repeat procedure once, rolling dough into an 18x8-inch rectangle and folding into thirds. Wrap in plastic wrap, and refrigerate for 1 hour.
4. Liberally coat a work surface with Ginger Sugar. Transfer dough to work surface, and bring to room temperature, about 10 minutes. Generously coat dough with Ginger Sugar. Roll dough into an 18x8-inch rectangle, and fold into thirds, like a letter, to form an 8x6-inch rectangle again. Roll dough into a 17x13-inch rectangle, continuously adding Ginger Sugar. Cut ½ inch off each side of dough. Cut dough into 4-inch squares.
5. Preheat oven to 375°F (190°C). Generously butter a 12-cup muffin pan.
6. Transfer squares to prepared muffin cups. Fill each with 1 tablespoon Strawberry Filling, and fold corners in. Let rise, covered, for 20 minutes. Place muffin pan on a rimmed baking sheet to catch any drips.
7. Bake until golden brown, 25 to 30 minutes. Carefully remove from pan, and let cool on a wire rack for 20 minutes. If kouign ammans begin to stick to pan, return to oven for a few minutes to reheat sugar coating. Store in an airtight container at room temperature for up to 2 days and or refrigerated for up to 4 days.

GINGER SUGAR
Makes 2 cups

2 cups (400 grams) granulated sugar
2 tablespoons (4 grams) fresh ginger, peeled and grated

1. Preheat oven to 200°F (93°C). Line a baking sheet with parchment paper.
2. In the work bowl of a food processor, pulse together sugar and ginger until well combined. Spread onto prepared pan.
3. Bake until dry, 10 to 15 minutes. Let cool completely.

STRAWBERRY FILLING
Makes about 1½ cups

1¼ cups (212 grams) diced fresh strawberries
2 tablespoons (28 grams) firmly packed light brown sugar
1½ tablespoons (18 grams) granulated sugar
1½ tablespoons (12 grams) cornstarch
1½ tablespoons (31.5 grams) honey
2 teaspoons (10 grams) fresh lemon juice
½ teaspoon (2 grams) vanilla extract
¼ teaspoon kosher salt
¼ teaspoon ground black pepper

1. In a medium bowl, combine all ingredients. Use immediately.

MINCEMEAT BRAID

Makes about 8 servings

Recipe by Emily Turner

A medley of dried fruits, distilled spirits, and spices, mincemeat reflects Canada's—particularly British Columbia's—English roots, where this fruity mix originated. We incorporated the boozy, jammy filling into a buttery puff pastry braid.

Quick Puff Pastry (recipe follows)
Mincemeat Filling (recipe follows)
1 large egg (50 grams), lightly beaten
2 teaspoons (10 grams) whole milk
2 tablespoons (24 grams) turbinado sugar

1. Preheat oven to 400°F (200°C).
2. On a lightly floured sheet of parchment paper, roll Quick Puff Pastry into a 16x14-inch rectangle. Trim edges of dough. Spread Mincemeat Filling down center third of dough, leaving a 1-inch border at top and bottom. Using a sharp knife, cut 1-inch diagonal strips into dough on both sides of filling. Fold top and bottom pieces over filling, and braid strips of dough over filling. Pinch last piece to seal. Transfer braid with parchment to a rimmed baking sheet. Freeze for 15 minutes.
3. In a small bowl, whisk together egg and milk. Brush top of dough with egg wash, and sprinkle with turbinado sugar.
4. Bake until golden brown, 45 to 50 minutes, loosely covering with foil to prevent excess browning, if necessary. Let cool for 30 minutes. Serve warm or at room temperature.

Quick Puff Pastry

Makes dough for 1 braid

2⅔ cups (334 grams) all-purpose flour
1⅔ cups (377 grams) cold unsalted butter, cubed
1½ teaspoons (4.5 grams) kosher salt
½ cup (120 grams) cold water

1. In the bowl of a stand mixer fitted with the paddle attachment, beat flour, cold butter, and salt at low speed just until butter is coated with flour, about 30 seconds. With mixer running, add ½ cup (120 grams) cold water in a slow, steady stream just until dough comes together, about 1 minute. (There will still be large pieces of butter.) Cover and refrigerate for 30 minutes.
2. On a lightly floured surface, roll dough into a 15x9-inch rectangle. Fold dough into thirds, like a letter. Rotate dough 90 degrees, and fold dough into thirds again. Wrap in plastic wrap, and refrigerate for at least 1 hour.

Mincemeat Filling

Makes 4 cups

⅓ cup (76 grams) unsalted butter
¾ cup (165 grams) firmly packed light brown sugar
2 medium Gala apples (280 grams), peeled and grated
1 cup (240 grams) apple cider
¾ cup (96 grams) chopped dried apricots
¾ cup (96 grams) dried figs, stems removed, and diced
¾ cup (96 grams) mixed fruit peel
¾ cup (96 grams) sour cherries
½ cup (64 grams) dried cranberries
½ cup (64 grams) dried currants
1 tablespoon (6 grams) orange zest
⅓ cup (80 grams) fresh orange juice
1 tablespoon (11 grams) chopped candied ginger
1 teaspoon (3 grams) kosher salt
1 teaspoon (2 grams) ground cinnamon
1 teaspoon (2 grams) ground nutmeg
½ teaspoon (1 gram) ground ginger
½ teaspoon (1 gram) ground cloves
½ cup (120 grams) brandy

1. In a large Dutch oven, melt butter and brown sugar over medium-high heat, stirring constantly. Add apples, apple cider, apricots, figs, mixed peel, cherries, cranberries, currants, orange zest and juice, candied ginger, salt, cinnamon, nutmeg, ground ginger, and cloves; bring to a boil, stirring frequently. Reduce heat to low, and simmer, stirring frequently, until thickened and no liquid remains, about 30 minutes. Remove from heat, and stir in brandy. Let cool completely. Transfer to an airtight container, and refrigerate for least 12 hours before using. (Letting the mincemeat stand overnight will allow flavors to marinate and fruit to soak up the brandy.)

Note: *You can make Mincemeat Filling up to 1 week ahead of time. Instead of adding ½ cup (120 grams) brandy after cooking, add only ¼ cup (60 grams) brandy, and reserve remaining brandy to stir in gradually every other day to keep the filling from drying out.*

Photo by Maya Visnyei

CHESTNUT, FIG, AND GINGER CROQUEMBOUCHE

Makes 1 tower

In this dramatic tower of deliciousness, bite-size profiteroles are stacked and bound with sweeping threads of caramel. In French, "croquembouche" means "crunch in the mouth," and you'll love the occasional crunch of the hardened caramel.

½   cup (113 grams) unsalted butter
1½ cups (360 grams) plus 2 teaspoons
     (10 grams) water, divided
½   cup (120 grams) whole milk
4   cups (800 grams) plus 1 teaspoon
     (4 grams) granulated sugar, divided
½   teaspoon (1.5 grams) kosher salt
1¼ cups (156 grams) all-purpose flour
5   large eggs (250 grams), divided
Chestnut Pastry Cream (recipe follows)
Fig Pastry Cream (recipe follows)
Ginger Pastry Cream (recipe follows)

1. Preheat oven to 375°F (190°C). Line 2 baking sheets with parchment paper.
2. In a medium saucepan, melt butter over medium heat. Add ½ cup (120 grams) water, milk, 1 teaspoon (4 grams) sugar, and salt; bring to a boil. Remove from heat, and stir in flour. Place back over medium heat, and cook, stirring constantly, until a skin forms on bottom of pan.
3. Transfer mixture to the bowl of a stand mixer fitted with the paddle attachment; let cool for 3 minutes. With mixer on medium speed, add 4 eggs (200 grams), one at a time, beating until combined. Transfer mixture to an 18-inch piping bag fitted with a ³⁄₈-inch tip. (Dough can be made up to 1 day ahead of baking. Refrigerate in a pastry bag until ready to bake.) Using even pressure, pipe 1-inch rounds onto prepared pans. Smooth pointed peaks with a moistened finger.
4. In a small bowl, whisk together 2 teaspoons (10 grams) water and remaining 1 egg (50 grams). Using a pastry brush, lightly brush puffs with egg wash.
5. Bake until puffed and golden brown, 20 to 25 minutes. Turn oven off, and carefully remove from oven. Using a knife or wooden skewer, poke holes in bottom of cream puffs to release excess moisture. Place cream puffs on pan, right side up, and return to oven. Leave in oven with door cracked for 1 hour, covering with foil to prevent excess browning, if necessary.
6. Using a ³⁄₁₆-inch tip, poke holes in bottom of cream puffs. Fit a pastry bag with a ³⁄₁₆-inch tip, and fill one-third of puffs with Chestnut Pastry Cream, one-third with Fig Pastry Cream, and one-third with Ginger Pastry Cream.
7. Line a baking sheet with parchment paper, and trace a 4½-inch circle. Prepare a large ice bath.
8. In a large saucepan, bring remaining 1 cup (240 grams) water and remaining 4 cups (800 grams) sugar to a boil over medium-high heat. Cook until mixture registers 320°F (160°C) on a candy thermometer.

Transfer pan to prepared ice bath. Carefully dip top of cream puffs into caramel, and place on an unlined baking sheet to harden.
9. Dip side of 1 puff into caramel, and place hot caramel side down onto prepared pan just outside parchment circle (top of puff should be facing out). Dip 2 sides (9 o'clock and 6 o'clock) of another puff in caramel, and position on parchment so 1 side adheres to side of first puff and other side is on parchment. Using parchment circle as your guide, repeat with 7 more puffs to complete bottom layer. Choose 8 puffs to make up second layer. Adhere puffs to croquembouche in same way as first layer, anchoring puffs in spaces between puffs on first layer. Continue building croquembouche with slightly smaller circles for each layer. The number of puffs per layer may not be consecutive numerically, due to difference of puff sizes and steepness of croquembouche. There should be about 8 layers total, with final layer being a single puff. (If caramel becomes too stiff while constructing, reheat over medium-low heat to loosen, but be careful not to overcook. You may have to reheat several times.)
10. Once assembled, let caramel cool in pan just until it begins to form a thread when a fork is lifted from it. Dip fork in caramel, and circle around croquembouche to enclose cream puffs with thin caramel strings. For additional garnish, line a baking sheet with a silicone mat, and create decorative string designs with excess caramel. Once hardened, remove decorative strings, and place around base of croquembouche. Serve immediately, or refrigerate for up to 8 hours.

Note: *Pâte à choux can be piped and frozen for up to 1 month. Leave uncovered until no longer tacky, about 1 hour, then cover. If baking from frozen, add 5 minutes to baking time.*

CHESTNUT PASTRY CREAM
Makes about 1½ cups

3   tablespoons (36 grams) granulated sugar
2   tablespoons (16 grams) cornstarch
1   large egg (50 grams)
1   cup (240 grams) whole milk
2   tablespoons (28 grams) unsalted
     butter, cubed
½   cup (130 grams) Chestnut Paste
     (recipe on page 252)

1. In a small bowl, whisk together sugar, cornstarch, and egg.
2. In a medium saucepan, bring milk to a boil over medium heat. Gradually pour hot milk into egg mixture, whisking constantly. Return mixture to saucepan, and cook, whisking constantly, until thickened.
3. Transfer cream to a small bowl, and let stand at room temperature for 10 minutes. Whisk to loosen, and add butter; stir until well combined. Cover with plastic wrap, pressing wrap directly onto surface of cream. Refrigerate for at least 2 hours. Remove from refrigerator, and stir in Chestnut Paste. Pastry cream will keep refrigerated for up to 3 days.

FIG PASTRY CREAM

Makes about 1½ cups

- 3   tablespoons (36 grams) granulated sugar
- 2   tablespoons (16 grams) cornstarch
- 1   large egg (50 grams)
- 1   cup (240 grams) whole milk
- 2   tablespoons (28 grams) unsalted butter, cubed
- ¼   cup (80 grams) fig preserves

1. In a small bowl, whisk together sugar, cornstarch, and egg.
2. In a medium saucepan, bring milk to a boil over medium heat. Gradually pour hot milk into egg mixture, whisking constantly. Return mixture to saucepan, and cook, whisking constantly, until thickened.
3. Transfer cream to a small bowl, and let stand at room temperature for 10 minutes. Whisk to loosen, and add butter; stir until well combined. Cover with plastic wrap, pressing wrap directly onto surface of cream. Refrigerate for at least 2 hours. Remove from refrigerator, and stir in fig preserves.

GINGER PASTRY CREAM

Makes about 1½ cups

- 1¼   cups (300 grams) whole milk
- 2   tablespoons (2 grams) grated fresh ginger
- 3   tablespoons (36 grams) granulated sugar
- 2   tablespoons (16 grams) cornstarch
- 1   large egg (50 grams)
- 2   tablespoons (28 grams) unsalted butter, cubed

1. In a medium saucepan, bring milk and ginger to a boil over medium heat. Remove from heat; cover and let steep for 20 minutes.
2. In a small bowl, whisk together sugar, cornstarch, and egg.
3. Strain milk mixture, and return to saucepan; bring to a boil over medium heat. Gradually pour hot milk mixture into egg mixture, whisking constantly. Return to saucepan, and cook, whisking constantly, until thickened.
4. Transfer cream to a small bowl, and let stand at room temperature for 10 minutes. Whisk to loosen; add butter, and stir until well combined. Cover with plastic wrap, pressing wrap directly onto surface of cream. Refrigerate for at least 2 hours.

PLAN AHEAD

This masterpiece is doable for even pâtisserie novices. We suggest making the pastries and pastry cream a day before you plan to serve, and assembling the croquembouche on the morning of. It can be assembled up to 8 hours before serving. Keep refrigerated.

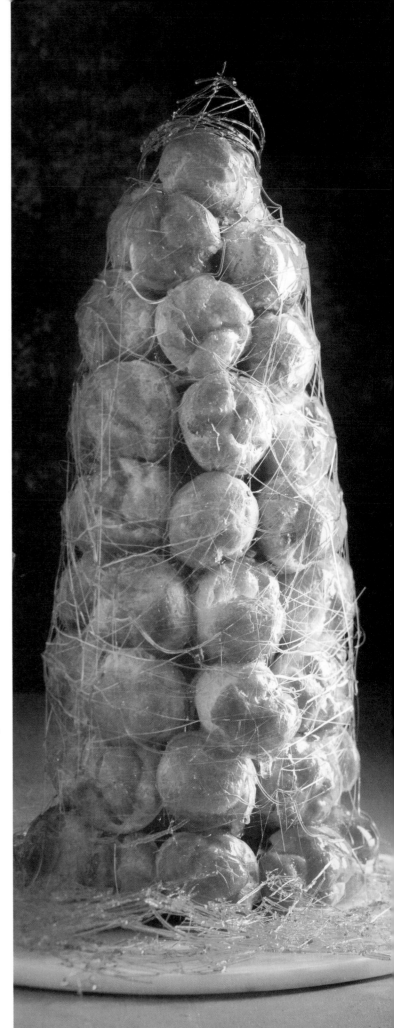

CHESTNUT MONT BLANC

Makes 12

Chestnut has always been the star of this classic Italian dessert.

Swiss Meringues (recipe follows)
Almond Tarts (recipe follows)
Whipped Cream (recipe follows)
Chestnut Paste (recipe follows)
Garnish: gold leaf

1. Place 1 Swiss Meringue in center of an Almond Tart. Place Whipped Cream in a pastry bag fitted with a 2A Wilton tip. Pipe a circle around edge of Swiss Meringue. Continue piping inward in a circular motion, finishing with a 2½-inch cone on top of Swiss Meringue. Use a small offset spatula to smooth out ridges.
2. Place 3½ cups Chestnut Paste in a piping bag fitted with a #10 piping tip. Pipe Chestnut Paste in a circular motion around Whipped Cream to create a swirled cone shape. Repeat with remaining Swiss Meringues, Almond Tarts, Whipped Cream, and Chestnut Paste. Garnish with gold leaf, if desired.

SWISS MERINGUES
Makes about 2 cups

2   large egg whites (60 grams)
½   cup (100 grams) granulated sugar
⅛   teaspoon cream of tartar

1. Preheat oven to 200°F (93°C). Line a baking sheet with parchment paper.
2. In the bowl of a stand mixer fitted with the whisk attachment, whisk together egg whites, sugar, and cream of tartar by hand. Set bowl over a saucepan of simmering water, and cook, whisking constantly, until sugar is dissolved and a candy thermometer registers 140°F (60°C), 5 to 7 minutes. Return bowl to stand mixer, and beat at high speed until stiff peaks form, about 10 minutes. Let cool to room temperature. Transfer to a pastry bag fitted with a Wilton 1M Open Star tip. Pipe 1½- to 2-inch rosettes on prepared pan.
3. Bake for 1½ hours. Turn oven off, and leave meringues in oven with door closed for 30 minutes. Store in an airtight container for up to 2 weeks.

ALMOND TARTS
Makes 12

¾   cup (170 grams) unsalted butter, softened
⅓   cup (67 grams) granulated sugar
¾   teaspoon (2.25 grams) kosher salt
1   large egg yolk (19 grams)
1¾   cups (219 grams) all-purpose flour
½   cup (48 grams) almond meal
2   tablespoons (30 grams) heavy whipping cream
Almond Filling (recipe follows)

1. In the bowl of a stand mixer fitted with the paddle attachment, beat butter, sugar, and salt at medium speed until creamy, 3 to 4 minutes, stopping to scrape sides of bowl. Stir in egg yolk. Reduce mixer speed to low. Add flour, almond meal, and cream, beating until combined. Shape dough into a disk, and wrap in plastic wrap. Refrigerate for 1 hour.
2. Preheat oven to 350°F (180°C). Butter and flour 12 (3-inch) tart pans.
3. Divide dough into 12 balls. Transfer to prepared tart pans, pressing into bottom and up sides. Refrigerate for 20 minutes. Divide Almond Filling among prepared tart shells.
4. Bake until golden brown, 20 to 25 minutes. Let cool completely on wire racks.

ALMOND FILLING
Makes 2 cups

1   cup (200 grams) granulated sugar
1   cup (142 grams) whole almonds
1   cup (227 grams) unsalted butter, softened
2   large eggs (100 grams)
1   teaspoon (4 grams) almond extract
¼   teaspoon kosher salt

1. In the work bowl of a food processor, place sugar and almonds; pulse until finely ground, 2 to 3 minutes. Add butter, and pulse until combined. Add eggs, almond extract, and salt; pulse until smooth, stopping to scrape sides of bowl. Transfer to a small bowl. Cover and refrigerate for at least 1 hour or up to 8 hours.

WHIPPED CREAM
Makes about 6 cups

3   cups (720 grams) heavy whipping cream
¾   cup (90 grams) confectioners' sugar

1. In the bowl of a stand mixer fitted with the whisk attachment, beat cream at medium speed until soft peaks form, 1 to 2 minutes. Gradually add confectioners' sugar, beating until stiff peaks form. Cover and refrigerate for up to 2 days.

CHESTNUT PASTE
Makes about 4 cups

4   cups (624 grams) Roasted Chestnuts (recipe on page 253)
1   vanilla bean, split lengthwise, seeds scraped and reserved
4   cups (960 grams) water
1½   cups (394 grams) Simple Syrup (recipe follows)

1. In a medium saucepan, bring Roasted Chestnuts, vanilla bean, and 4 cups (960 grams) water to a boil over medium heat. Reduce heat to low; cover and simmer until chestnuts are softened, about 30 minutes. Remove vanilla bean, and drain chestnuts.
2. Transfer chestnuts to the work bowl of a food processor; pulse until a smooth, thick paste forms, about 5 minutes, stopping to scrape sides of bowl. With processor running, add Simple Syrup in a slow, steady stream until a piping consistency is reached. Refrigerate in an airtight container for up to 1 week.

SIMPLE SYRUP
Makes about 1½ cups

1¼   cups (300 grams) water
1¼   cups (250 grams) granulated sugar

1. In a small saucepan, bring 1¼ cups (300 grams) water and sugar to a boil over medium-high heat, stirring occasionally, until sugar is dissolved. Remove from heat, and let cool completely.

ROASTED CHESTNUTS

Makes about 4 cups

There's a reason this treat made it into one of the most beloved Christmas carols: roasted chestnuts are classic—and delicious. Follow our foolproof method to get your chestnuts ready for the recipe. Or just eat them on their own for a warm, nutty holiday snack.

6   cups (892 grams) whole chestnuts in
    shells

1. Preheat oven to 425°F (220°C).
2. Using a sharp paring knife, cut an "X" in rounded side of chestnuts. (This lets steam escape, and will prevent them from exploding.) Place on a rimmed baking sheet, cut side up.
3. Roast until shells curl away from nutmeats, 20 to 30 minutes.
4. Wrap hot chestnuts in a kitchen towel, and squeeze gently to further loosen shells. Let stand until cool enough to handle. Peel shells from nutmeats. Use immediately, or store in a resealable plastic bag at room temperature for up to 24 hours.

Note: *Fresh chestnuts will keep refrigerated for up to 6 months in a breathable container.*

BLUEBERRY AND BITTERS STRUDELS

Makes 10

Consider these the blueberry cordials of pastry. Orange bitters, used as an aromatic flavor enhancer in many cocktails, gives the filling in this strudel a boost as the refreshing citrus notes brighten our blueberry preserves.

Fast Puff Pastry Dough (recipe below)
Blueberry and Bitters Filling (recipe follows)
1   large egg (50 grams), lightly beaten
Blueberry Bitters Glaze (recipe follows)

1. Preheat oven to 450°F (230°C). Line 2 large baking sheets with parchment paper.
2. On a lightly floured surface, roll half of Fast Puff Pastry Dough into a 26x7-inch rectangle. Using a sharp knife, cut dough into 10 (5x3-inch) rectangles, trimming dough as needed. Repeat with remaining dough. Place half of rectangles on prepared pans.
3. Fill half of each rectangle with 1 tablespoon Blueberry and Bitters Filling, leaving a ¼-inch border on all sides. (Reserve remaining filling for Blueberry Bitters Glaze.) Brush egg wash around outside edges. Top with remaining rectangles, and crimp with a floured fork to seal.
4. Bake for 15 minutes. Let cool completely. Spread 1½ tablespoons Blueberry Bitters Glaze onto each tart. Store in an airtight container at room temperature for up to 2 days.

BLUEBERRY AND BITTERS FILLING

Makes 1 cup

1   cup (320 grams) Blueberry Preserves (recipe follows)
2   teaspoons (10 grams) Angostura Orange Bitters

1. In a small bowl, whisk together Blueberry Preserves and bitters until combined. Use immediately.

BLUEBERRY PRESERVES

Makes 1½ cups

2½   cups (425 grams) fresh or frozen blueberries, roughly chopped
1½   cups (300 grams) granulated sugar
¼   cup (32 grams) cornstarch
¼   cup (60 grams) water

1. In a medium heavy-bottomed saucepan, cook blueberries and sugar over medium heat until sugar is dissolved. Increase heat to medium-high, and bring to a boil. After berries have softened, use a potato masher to press berries just enough to release some of their juices and partially break up the berries, keeping the texture chunky.
2. Continue to boil mixture, stirring frequently to prevent scorching on bottom of pan. Mixture will foam up and expand, and then shrink back as it cooks. Use a metal spoon with a thin edge to skim foam from surface and discard.
3. In a small bowl, stir together cornstarch and ¼ cup (60 grams) water.
4. Continue boiling until mixture thickens to a slow bubble and registers 215°F (102°C) on a candy thermometer. Stir in cornstarch mixture, and boil for 1 to 2 minutes, stirring constantly. Mixture will thicken. Pour preserves into jars or plastic containers, and refrigerate for at least 1 hour before using. Preserves will keep refrigerated for up to 2 months or frozen for up to 6 months in jars with tight-fitting lids.

BLUEBERRY BITTERS GLAZE

Makes 1 cup

1   cup (120 grams) confectioners' sugar
2   tablespoons (40 grams) Blueberry and Bitters Filling (recipe precedes)
2   tablespoons (30 grams) whole milk

1. In a small bowl, whisk together all ingredients until combined. Use immediately.

FAST PUFF PASTRY DOUGH

Makes dough for 10 strudels

Laminated dough often requires the arduous task of layering and folding fat—in this case, butter—into the dough in a continuous loop. We save time and sanity by giving flour, salt, and frozen butter a whirl in the food processor, producing perfect little slivers of butter that, in turn, help lift and separate the layers of dough while baking to deliver a ridiculously flaky puff pastry.

2   cups (454 grams) unsalted butter
2¾   cups (344 grams) all-purpose flour
1   tablespoon (9 grams) kosher salt
½   cup (120 grams) ice water

1. Freeze butter for 30 minutes.
2. In the work bowl of a food processor, place flour and salt; pulse until combined.
3. Cut frozen butter into cubes; add to flour mixture, and pulse until mixture is crumbly. With processor running, gradually add ½ cup (120 grams) ice water through food chute, processing just until mixture forms a ball.
4. On a lightly floured surface, turn out dough. Shape into a disk, and wrap in plastic wrap. Refrigerate for at least 30 minutes. Dough can be made up to 3 days in advance and frozen for up to 3 months.

OVERSIZED HONEY RICOTTA STRUDEL

Makes 8 to 10 servings

For this sophisticated slab, we opted for a creamy honey topping, a thicker version of honey that, unlike liquid honey, contains a crystalline structure that makes it ideal for spreading. Bonus points? The pastry's 13x9-inch shape allows you to get extravagant with the portions.

**Fast Puff Pastry Dough (recipe on
    page 255)**
Ricotta Filling (recipe follows)
1   large egg (50 grams), lightly beaten
¼   cup (95 grams) creamy honey spread*
½   teaspoon (1 gram) ground black pepper

1. Preheat oven to 450°F (230°C).
2. On a lightly floured surface, roll half of

Fast Puff Pastry Dough into a 15x12-inch rectangle. Place a quarter rimmed (13x9-inch) sheet pan upside down in center of dough. Trim dough to ½ inch around all sides of pan. Place dough in sheet pan, letting excess extend over sides of pan. Fill with Ricotta Filling. Brush egg wash along inside edges of dough.
3. Roll remaining dough into a 12x9-inch rectangle, and place on top of filling. Press dough along sides of pan to crimp.
4. Bake until golden brown, 15 to 20 minutes. Let cool completely. Spread with honey spread, and sprinkle with pepper. Store wrapped in foil at room temperature for up to 2 days.

*We used Natural American Foods Honey Original Creamy Spread.

RICOTTA FILLING
Makes 1½ cups

¾   cup (169 grams) ricotta cheese
¾   cup (169 grams) cream cheese,
     softened
¾   cup (90 grams) confectioners' sugar

1. In a medium bowl, combine ricotta, cream cheese, and confectioners' sugar. Use immediately.

NUTELLA AND MARSHMALLOW STRUDELS

Makes 10

These indulgent rounds prove that chocolate for breakfast is here to stay.

Fast Puff Pastry Dough (recipe on
  page 255)
¾ cup (192 grams) chocolate-hazelnut
  spread*
Marshmallow Filling (recipe follows)
1 large egg (50 grams), lightly beaten
Chocolate Glaze (recipe follows)
White Drizzle (recipe follows)

1. Preheat oven to 450°F (230°C). Line
2 large baking sheets with parchment paper.
2. Roll half of Fast Puff Pastry Dough to
⅛-inch thickness. Using a 4-inch round cutter,
cut dough, rerolling scraps as necessary.
Repeat with remaining dough until you have
20 rounds. Place half of rounds on prepared
pans.
3. Spread 1 tablespoon chocolate-hazelnut
spread onto half of rounds, leaving a ¼-inch
border. Place Marshmallow Filling in a piping
bag, and pipe an ⅛-inch layer on top of
chocolate-hazelnut spread. Brush egg wash
around outside edges. Top with remaining
rounds, and crimp with a floured fork to seal.

4. Bake for 15 minutes. Let cool completely.
Spread ½ tablespoon Chocolate Glaze in
center of each tart, and drizzle with White
Drizzle. Store in an airtight container at room
temperature for up to 2 days.

We used Nutella.

MARSHMALLOW FILLING
Makes 3 to 4 cups

3   large egg whites (90 grams)
½   teaspoon (1 gram) cream of tartar
⅔   cup (133 grams) plus 2 tablespoons
  (24 grams) granulated sugar, divided
¾   cup (255 grams) light corn syrup
⅓   cup (80 grams) water
2   teaspoons (12 grams) vanilla bean paste

1. In the bowl of a stand mixer fitted with the
whisk attachment, beat egg whites and cream
of tartar at low speed until foamy, about
2 minutes. Increase mixer speed to medium.
Add 2 tablespoons (24 grams) sugar, and beat
until soft peaks form, about 2 minutes.
2. In a medium saucepan, cook corn syrup,
⅓ cup (80 grams) water, and remaining ⅔ cup
(133 grams) sugar over medium heat, stirring
frequently, until mixture registers 248°F

(120°C) on a candy thermometer, about
15 minutes.
3. With mixer on medium speed, add corn syrup
mixture in a slow, steady stream. Increase mixer
speed to high, and beat for 5 minutes. Add
vanilla bean paste, and beat for 1 minute. Store
in an airtight container at room temperature for
up to 2 weeks.

CHOCOLATE GLAZE
Makes ½ cup

1   cup (120 grams) confectioners' sugar
2   tablespoons (30 grams) whole milk
1   tablespoon (5 grams) unsweetened
  cocoa powder

1. In a small bowl, whisk together all
ingredients until combined. Use immediately.

WHITE DRIZZLE
Makes ¼ cup

½   cup (60 grams) confectioners' sugar
1   tablespoon (15 grams) whole milk

1. In a small bowl, whisk together confectioners'
sugar and milk until combined. Use immediately.

STRAWBERRY MASCARPONE STRUDELS

Makes 10

While decorating these classic strawberry and mascarpone-filled pastries, we looked to strudels' nostalgic breakfast cousin, the Pop-Tart. For our version, we swap out the usual sprinkles for crushed freeze-dried strawberries for a more refined look and an extra boost of berry.

Fast Puff Pastry Dough (recipe on page 255)
8   ounces (225 grams) mascarpone cheese, softened
Strawberry Preserves (recipe follows)
1   large egg (50 grams), lightly beaten
Mascarpone Glaze (recipe follows)
Garnish: crushed freeze-dried strawberries

1. Preheat oven to 450°F (230°C). Line 2 large baking sheets with parchment paper.
2. On a lightly floured surface, roll half of Fast Puff Pastry Dough into a 26x7-inch rectangle. Using a sharp knife, cut dough into 10 (5x3-inch) rectangles, trimming dough as needed. Repeat with remaining dough. Place half of rectangles on prepared pans.
3. Place mascarpone cheese in a pastry bag, and fill half of each rectangle with about 2 teaspoons mascarpone to make an ⅛-inch layer, leaving a ¼-inch border on all sides. Top with 2 heaping teaspoons Strawberry Preserves. Brush egg wash around outside edges. Top with remaining rectangles, and crimp with a floured fork to seal.
4. Bake for 15 minutes. Let cool completely. Spread 1½ tablespoons Mascarpone Glaze onto each tart. Garnish with freeze-dried strawberries, if desired. Store in an airtight container at room temperature for up to 2 days.

STRAWBERRY PRESERVES
Makes 1½ cups

1   (16-ounce) package (455 grams) fresh or frozen strawberries, partially thawed and roughly chopped
1½ cups (300 grams) granulated sugar
¼   cup (32 grams) cornstarch
¼   cup (60 grams) water

1. In a medium heavy-bottomed saucepan, cook strawberries and sugar over medium heat until sugar is dissolved. Increase heat to medium-high, and bring to a boil. After berries have softened, use a potato masher to press berries just enough to release some of their juices and partially break up the berries, keeping the texture chunky.
2. Continue to boil mixture, stirring frequently to prevent scorching on bottom of pan. Mixture will foam up and expand, and then shrink back as it cooks. Use a metal spoon with a thin edge to skim foam from surface and discard.
3. In a small bowl, stir together cornstarch and ¼ cup (60 grams) water.
4. Continue boiling until mixture thickens to a slow bubble and registers 215°F (102°C) on a candy thermometer. Stir in cornstarch mixture, and boil for 1 to 2 minutes, stirring constantly. Mixture will thicken. Pour preserves into jars or plastic containers, and refrigerate for at least 1 hour before using. Preserves will keep refrigerated for up to 2 months or frozen for up to 6 months in jars with tight-fitting lids.

MASCARPONE GLAZE
Makes 1 cup

1   cup (120 grams) confectioners' sugar
2   tablespoons (28 grams) mascarpone cheese
2   tablespoons (30 grams) whole milk

1. In a small bowl, whisk together confectioners' sugar and mascarpone cheese. Gradually whisk in milk until combined. Use immediately.

SWEET POTATO TURNOVERS WITH SWEET KRAUT & VEGAN ORANGE SOUR CREAM

Makes 6

Recipe by Kate Jacoby

Kate grew up making pierogi with her Polish-American grandmother and recreated the memory with this dessert that honors the fall harvest.

2   cups (250 grams) all-purpose flour
2   tablespoons (28 grams) cold vegan butter
2   tablespoons (28 grams) cold all-vegetable shortening
¼   cup (50 grams) granulated sugar
2   tablespoons (28 grams) olive oil
1   teaspoon (3 grams) kosher salt
1   teaspoon (2 grams) ground cinnamon
½   teaspoon (1 gram) ground allspice
4 to 6 tablespoons (60 to 90 grams) cold water
Sweet Potato Filling (recipe follows)
Sweet Kraut (recipe follows)
Vegan Orange Sour Cream (recipe follows)

1. In the work bowl of a food processor, place flour, cold vegan butter, and cold shortening; pulse until mixture is crumbly. Add sugar, oil, salt, cinnamon, and allspice; pulse until combined. With processor running, add cold water, 1 tablespoon (15 grams) at time, just until a loose dough ball forms. Wrap dough in plastic wrap, and refrigerate for at least 10 minutes or up to 2 days.
2. Preheat oven to 400°F (200°C). Line a baking sheet with parchment paper.
3. On a lightly floured surface, roll dough to ¼-inch thickness. Using a 4½-inch round cutter, cut dough into 6 rounds. Place 1 tablespoon Sweet Potato Filling in center of each round. Fold dough over filling, and pinch seams to seal. Use a fork to crimp edges. Place on prepared pan.
4. Bake until golden brown, 10 to 12 minutes. Let cool slightly. Serve with Sweet Kraut and Vegan Orange Sour Cream.

SWEET POTATO FILLING
Makes 1 cup

1   sweet potato (200 grams), peeled and chopped into 1-inch pieces
½   cup (110 grams) firmly packed light brown sugar
3   tablespoons (42 grams) vegan butter
1½   teaspoons (6 grams) pure vanilla extract
½   teaspoon (1.5 grams) kosher salt

1. Bring a medium stockpot of salted water to a boil over high heat. Add sweet potatoes, and boil until just tender, about 10 minutes.
2. In the work bowl of a food processor, place sweet potatoes, brown sugar, vegan butter, vanilla, and salt; pulse until combined. Let cool completely.

SWEET KRAUT
Makes about 1 cup

1   tablespoon (14 grams) olive oil
2   cups (200 grams) thinly sliced red cabbage (about ¼ head, outer leaves and stem removed)
¼   cup (55 grams) firmly packed light brown sugar
½   teaspoon (1 gram) ground cinnamon
¼   teaspoon ground allspice
¼   teaspoon ground cloves
1   cup (240 grams) sweet Riesling

1. In a medium skillet, heat oil over medium heat. Add cabbage; cook for 3 minutes. Stir in brown sugar, cinnamon, allspice, and cloves; cook until sugar is dissolved, about 3 minutes. Add wine, and cook, stirring occasionally, until cabbage begins to wilt and turns a dark pink color, 8 to 10 minutes. Remove from heat, and let cool completely.

VEGAN ORANGE SOUR CREAM
Makes about ½ cup

½   cup (120 grams) vegan sour cream
½   teaspoon (1 gram) orange zest
½   tablespoon (7.5 grams) fresh orange juice
¼   teaspoon (1 gram) vanilla extract
⅛   teaspoon kosher salt

1. In a small bowl, combine all ingredients. Refrigerate until ready to use.

> **PRO TIP**
> For a little extra sugar and spice, dust turnovers in cinnamon sugar right when they come out of the oven.

DEEP-DISH QUICHE
WITH SPRING VEGETABLES

Makes 1 (9-inch) quiche

Recipe by Yossy Arefi

Quiche is such a classic brunch dish, but it's also easy to adapt to your own tastes and the season. This one is packed full of a generous amount of caramelized shallots and leeks, springy greens, and of course, some cheese. Yossy likes to serve it with a bit of herb salad made from chopped parsley, chives, and dill dressed with lemon juice, olive oil, and flaky salt for a little punch of spring flavor.

1¼ cups (128 grams) rye flour
1¼ cups (156 grams) all-purpose flour
2⅛ teaspoons (6 grams) kosher salt, divided
1   cup (227 grams) cold unsalted butter, cubed
3   tablespoons (45 grams) ice water
3   tablespoons (42 grams) olive oil
2½ cups (250 grams) thinly sliced shallot (about 10 small shallots)
1   cup (100 grams) thinly sliced leeks, white and pale green parts only (about 2 leeks)
½   cup (1-inch pieces) (53 grams) fresh asparagus
2   cups (53 grams) chopped fresh baby spinach

6   large eggs (300 grams)
2   cups (480 grams) whole milk
1   cup (240 grams) heavy whipping cream
2   teaspoons (10 grams) Dijon mustard
½   teaspoon (1 gram) ground black pepper
1   cup (100 grams) freshly grated cheese (such as aged provolone or Monterey Jack), divided

1. In the work bowl of a food processor, pulse together flours and 1 teaspoon (3 grams) salt until combined. Add cold butter, and pulse until pea-sized pieces remain.
2. With processor running, gradually pour 3 tablespoons (45 grams) ice water through food chute in a slow, steady stream until combined. Pulse until mixture begins to hold together, adding more water if necessary. (The dough should hold together easily when squeezed.)
3. Turn out dough onto a heavily floured surface, and press into a rectangle. Roll to ¼-inch thickness. Fold dough into thirds, like a letter. Rotate dough 90 degrees, and fold into thirds again. Wrap dough in plastic wrap, and refrigerate for at least 30 minutes.
4. On a lightly floured surface, roll dough into a 15-inch circle. Transfer to a 9-inch springform pan, pressing into bottom and 1½ inches up sides. (Dough is very tender—

if dough tears, you can repair any cracks with excess dough.) Trim excess dough. Freeze for at least 2 hours or overnight.
5. Preheat oven to 350°F (180°C). Line crust with foil; add pie weights. Place pan on a baking sheet.
6. Bake until lightly golden brown, about 50 minutes. Remove foil and weights. Reduce oven temperature to 325°F (170°C).
7. In a large skillet, heat oil over medium-low heat. Add shallot, leek, and ⅛ teaspoon salt; cook, stirring occasionally, until deep golden brown and caramelized, 30 to 40 minutes. Add asparagus, and cook until just green, about 2 minutes. Remove from heat, and fold in spinach, letting excess heat wilt spinach.
8. In a large bowl, whisk eggs. Add milk, cream, mustard, pepper, and remaining 1 teaspoon (3 grams) salt. Add vegetables and ½ cup (50 grams) cheese. Carefully pour mixture into prepared crust. Top with remaining ½ cup (50 grams) cheese.
9. Bake until golden brown, set at edges, and slightly jiggly in center, 1 hour and 15 minutes to 1½ hours, covering with foil to prevent excess browning, if necessary. Let cool on a wire rack for at least 30 minutes before slicing.

Photo by Yossy Arefi

CELERY GRUYÈRE GOUGÈRES

Makes about 30

Recipe by Chadwick Boyd

This recipe is inspired by one of Julia Child's favorite flavor combos—celery, butter, and cream. Here, celery and butter are cooked down until soft and turned into a traditional gougères batter swirled with rich bits of Gruyère cheese and laced with pieces of celery leaves, which provide a distinct yet delicate flavor. The glossy dough balls are sprinkled with dark celery seeds and flaky Maldon sea salt, and then placed in a hot oven to puff into airy, crusty, cheesy deliciousness.

½   cup plus 2 tablespoons (141 grams) unsalted butter
1¼ cups (125 grams) plus 2 to 4 tablespoons (12 to 24 grams) very thinly sliced celery*, divided
½   cup (120 grams) heavy whipping cream
½   cup (120 grams) water
¾   teaspoon (1.5 grams) celery salt**
1   cup (125 grams) all-purpose flour
5   large eggs (250 grams), room temperature
1½ cups (150 grams) finely grated Gruyère cheese
½   cup (20 grams) roughly chopped fresh celery leaves

1   teaspoon (2 grams) celery seeds, divided
Maldon sea salt

1. Preheat oven to 425°F (220°C). Line 2 rimmed baking sheets with parchment paper.
2. In a medium heavy saucepan, heat butter over medium heat. Stir in 1¼ cups (125 grams) celery, and cook until soft and translucent, 7 to 8 minutes. Increase heat to medium-high. Add cream, ½ cup (120 grams) water, and celery salt; bring to a boil, stirring frequently. Reduce heat to medium-low, and quickly stir in flour with a heavy-duty whisk or thick-handled wooden spoon. (Dough will quickly become smooth and have a nice shine.) Continue whisking until a skin begins to form on bottom of pan to ensure dough is dry enough to finish batter, about 1 minute.
3. Quickly transfer dough to the bowl of a stand mixer fitted with the paddle attachment, and beat at medium-low speed to release heat (you will see steam escape), about 1 minute. Add eggs, one at a time, beating well after each addition, stopping to scrape sides of bowl. (Dough will be smooth and glossy.) Add cheese, and beat for 1 minute. Scrape sides of bowl, and beat until combined, 15 to 20 seconds. Add

celery leaves and ¾ teaspoon (1.5 grams) celery seeds, and beat until combined.
4. Using a medium (1-tablespoon) spring-loaded scoop, drop dough 1 to 1½ inches apart onto prepared pans. (The gougères dough should be scooped out immediately and placed on a baking sheet. If the dough sits, it will become tough.) Sprinkle with remaining 2 to 4 tablespoons (12 to 25 grams) celery. Dust lightly with remaining ¼ teaspoon celery seeds, and sprinkle with Maldon sea salt.
5. Bake for 5 minutes. Reduce oven temperature to 350°F (180°C), and bake 12 minutes more. Rotate pans from front to back and top to bottom, and bake until gougères are golden and puffy and celery bits are lightly browned, 15 to 20 minutes more. Let cool on a wire rack for 5 minutes. Serve freshly baked or at room temperature. Store in an airtight container for 2 to 3 days.

We used a mandoline to slice celery.

**Use kosher salt if you don't have celery salt on hand. Sprinkle a few more pieces of celery on top with the Maldon flakes to garnish.*

CHESTNUT-RICOTTA SFOGLIATELLE

Makes about 16

This shell-shaped Italian pastry takes lamination to a new level. Pasta-thin dough is brushed with butter, tightly rolled into a log shape, and sliced into disks. Each disk is hand-shaped into a cone, and then filled. We added chopped chestnuts to the traditional ricotta filling for extra crunch and depth in the creamy cheese.

2¾   cups (349 grams) bread flour
1¼   cups (188 grams) semolina flour
1   cup plus 2 tablespoons (270 grams) water
4   teaspoons (28 grams) honey
1   tablespoon (9 grams) kosher salt
16   tablespoons (224 grams) unsalted butter, softened and divided
Chestnut-Ricotta Filling (recipe follows)
Garnish: confectioners' sugar

1. In the bowl of a stand mixer fitted with the paddle attachment, beat flours, 1 cup plus 2 tablespoons (270 grams) water, honey, and salt at low speed until a shaggy dough forms, about 2 minutes. Increase mixer speed to medium, and beat until cohesive, about 10 minutes. (Dough will be dry, like pasta.)
2. Turn out dough onto a lightly floured surface, and knead until smooth, about 5 times. Divide dough in half, and roll each half into a 12x5-inch rectangle. Cover with plastic wrap. With smooth rollers, set a pasta machine to widest setting. Feed one piece of dough through rollers; fold in half lengthwise, and feed through again. Repeat 5 times. Cover with plastic wrap, and repeat with remaining dough. Place pieces of dough one on top of another, and roll to ½-inch thickness. Feed dough through rollers 10 times, folding in half each time. Wrap in plastic wrap, and refrigerate for at least 2 hours or overnight.
3. Divide dough into fourths. Cover with plastic wrap. On a lightly floured surface, roll 1 piece of dough into an 8x4-inch rectangle. Feed dough through rollers of pasta machine. Lightly dust dough with flour as necessary. Make the space between rollers slightly narrower, and feed dough through again. Continue process until dough has gone

through the narrowest setting. Set aside, and cover with plastic wrap. Repeat rolling process with 3 remaining pieces of dough.
4. Place 1 piece of dough on a lightly floured surface, and trim ends. Spread 3 tablespoons (42 grams) butter onto dough. Gently stretch dough strip to 9 inches wide with fingers, working down length of dough. Starting at one short side, tightly roll up dough, jelly-roll style, leaving 1 inch of strip unrolled. Set aside, and cover loosely with plastic wrap. Place second piece of dough on a lightly floured surface, and trim ends. Spread 3 tablespoons (42 grams) butter onto dough. Gently stretch dough strip to 9 inches wide with fingers, working down length of dough. Overlap 1 inch of a short side with exposed end of first roll. Roll up first roll in second dough piece, jelly-roll style, to create a roll about 9 inches long and 2 inches in diameter. Cover with plastic wrap. Repeat process with remaining 2 dough pieces. Refrigerate for at least 3 hours or overnight.
5. Preheat oven to 400°F (200°C). Line 2 baking sheets with parchment paper.
6. Remove 1 roll from refrigerator, and trim ½ inch from each end. Cut roll into ¾-inch-thick slices. Working with 1 slice at a time, create a 4-inch round by using the heel of your hand and even pressure, pressing in all directions, starting from the center. Repeat with remaining slices. Carefully shape rounds into cones. Place thumbs in center of round to gently push upward, and use index and middle fingers to pull sides downward, keeping layers overlapping slightly. Spoon 1½ tablespoons Chestnut-Ricotta Filling into each cone. Pinch edges together to seal, and place on prepared pans. Repeat with remaining rolls.
7. In a small saucepan, melt remaining 4 tablespoons (56 grams) butter over medium heat. Brush melted butter onto sfogliatelle.
8. Bake until golden brown and crisp, 25 to 30 minutes. Let cool completely on a wire rack. Garnish with confectioners' sugar, if desired. Store in an airtight container in refrigerator for up to 4 days. Reheat in a 350°F (180°C) oven before serving.

CHESTNUT-RICOTTA FILLING
Makes about 1½ cups

½   cup (120 grams) water
¼   cup (50 grams) granulated sugar
⅓   cup (50 grams) semolina flour
1   large egg yolk (19 grams)
¾   teaspoon (3 grams) vanilla extract
½   teaspoon (1.5 grams) kosher salt
½   teaspoon (1 gram) ground cinnamon
¾   cup (169 grams) ricotta cheese
⅓   cup (52 grams) Roasted Chestnuts (recipe on page 253), chopped

1. In a small saucepan, bring ½ cup (120 grams) water and sugar to a boil over medium heat. Slowly add flour, stirring constantly; cook until thickened, about 2 minutes. Pour mixture into a small bowl. Cover and refrigerate for 30 minutes.
2. Transfer mixture to the bowl of stand mixer, and beat at low speed for 1 to 2 minutes. Add egg yolk, vanilla, salt, and cinnamon; beat at medium-low speed until smooth, 3 to 4 minutes. Reduce mixer speed to low. Add ricotta and Roasted Chestnuts; beat until combined, about 2 minutes. Transfer to a small bowl. Cover and refrigerate until ready to use, up to 24 hours.

PRO TIP
You will need 4 to 6 feet of counter space when rolling dough through the pasta rollers. An extra set of hands is helpful during this process. While one person feeds the dough into and helps it out of the pasta machine, the other can keep the dough that's been through the machine stretched out to ensure that it doesn't fold up on top of itself.

COOKIES AND BARS

COOKIES

The humble heroes of a baker's repertoire, cookies offer an unmatched homespun charm. With coffee-ready biscotti, chocolate chip cookies, and a bonanza of holiday favorites like Linzers and gingerbread, this cookie collection will keep your oven on preheat for months on end.

SOUR CHERRY SHORTBREAD LINZER COOKIES

Makes 12

These are the best sandwich cookies you'll make this summer. A tiny bit of citric acid in the cookie dough creates a zesty sour cherry flavor, which balances out the buttery shortbread cookies.

- ¾ cup (170 grams) unsalted butter, softened
- ½ cup (60 grams) confectioners' sugar
- ¼ teaspoon (1 gram) vanilla extract
- 1½ cups (188 grams) all-purpose flour
- ½ teaspoon (1.5 grams) citric acid
- ¼ teaspoon kosher salt
- 2 tablespoons (24 grams) granulated sugar
- ¼ cup (80 grams) cherry preserves

1. In the bowl of a stand mixer fitted with the paddle attachment, beat butter, confectioners' sugar, and vanilla at medium speed until creamy, 3 to 4 minutes, stopping to scrape sides of bowl.

2. In a medium bowl, sift together flour, citric acid, and salt. With mixer on low speed, gradually add flour mixture to butter mixture, beating until combined. Divide dough in half, and wrap in plastic wrap. Refrigerate for at least 2 hours or overnight.

3. Preheat oven to 350°F (180°C). Line 2 baking sheets with parchment paper.

4. On a lightly floured surface, roll half of dough to ⅛-inch thickness. Using a 2½-inch fluted round cutter, cut dough, rerolling scraps only once. Repeat with remaining dough. Using a 1-inch fluted round cutter, cut centers from half of cookies. Place 1 inch apart on prepared pans. Sprinkle cookies with granulated sugar.

5. Bake until just set, 8 to 10 minutes. (Be careful not to overbake, or cookies will look speckled.) Let cool completely on pans. Spread about 1 teaspoon cherry preserves on flat side of all solid cookies. Place cookies with cutouts, flat side down, on top of preserves. Bake 2 minutes more. Let cool completely. Store in an airtight container at room temperature for up to 5 days.

CANDIED CHERRY, DATE, AND PISTACHIO BISCOTTI

Makes 14

With a little cherry brandy and candied cherries, this twice-baked Italian treat gets a double dose of cherry flavor. Chopped pistachios and sea salt flakes offset the sweet and lend the perfect amount of crunch. Dunk these in your coffee for the ultimate biscotti experience.

1	cup (200 grams) granulated sugar
½	cup (113 grams) unsalted butter, melted and cooled
3	tablespoons (45 grams) cherry brandy
1	teaspoon (4 grams) vanilla extract
	Candied Cherries (recipe follows)
½	cup (64 grams) chopped dates
½	cup (57 grams) chopped pistachios
4	large eggs (200 grams), divided
2¾	cups (344 grams) all-purpose flour
1½	teaspoons (7.5 grams) baking powder
¼	teaspoon kosher salt
1	teaspoon (5 grams) water
2	tablespoons (24 grams) turbinado sugar
1	tablespoon (9 grams) sea salt

1. In a large bowl, stir together granulated sugar, melted butter, brandy, and vanilla. Add Candied Cherries, dates, pistachios, and 3 eggs (150 grams), stirring to combine.
2. In a medium bowl, whisk together flour, baking powder, and salt. Gradually add flour mixture to sugar mixture, stirring just until combined. Cover and refrigerate for 30 minutes.
3. Preheat oven to 350°F (180°C).
4. On a lightly floured surface, shape dough into a 14x8-inch rectangle. Place on an ungreased baking sheet.
5. In a small bowl, whisk together 1 teaspoon (5 grams) water and remaining 1 egg (50 grams). Brush egg wash onto dough. Sprinkle with turbinado sugar and sea salt.
6. Bake until pale golden, about 30 minutes. Carefully transfer loaf to a wire rack to let cool for 15 minutes. Using a serrated knife, cut loaf into 1-inch slices. Return to baking sheet, cut side down. Bake until golden, about 15 minutes more, turning slices halfway through baking. Transfer to a wire rack to let cool completely. Store in an airtight container for up to 4 days.

CANDIED CHERRIES

Makes 1 cup

½	pound (227 grams) cherries, pitted and chopped
½	cup (100 grams) granulated sugar
½	cup (120 grams) fresh lemon juice
½	cup (120 grams) water

1. In a medium saucepan, combine all ingredients. Cook over medium heat, stirring frequently, until sugar is dissolved. Continue cooking until syrup is thick enough that it takes 2 seconds for liquid to close together when a spoon is passed through it, 30 to 35 minutes.
2. Preheat oven to 200°F (93°C). Line a baking sheet with parchment paper.
3. Transfer cherries to prepared pan, spreading to edges.
4. Bake until dry but tacky, 1½ to 2 hours. Refrigerate in an airtight container for up to 1 week.

CLASSIC OR OVERSIZED CHOCOLATE CHIP COOKIES

Makes about 36 traditional or 18 oversized

Think of this as the elevated, from-scratch version of the Original Nestlé Toll House treat. If you're a "the bigger, the better" kind of baker, triple up on those scoops for our oversized version.

1   cup (227 grams) unsalted butter, softened
1   cup (220 grams) firmly packed light brown sugar
⅔   cup (133 grams) granulated sugar
2   large eggs (100 grams)
1   tablespoon (18 grams) vanilla bean paste
2⅓   cups plus 1 tablespoon (300 grams) all-purpose flour
1   teaspoon (5 grams) baking soda
¾   teaspoon (2.25 grams) kosher salt
2   cups (340 grams) semisweet chocolate morsels*

1. Preheat oven to 350°F (180°C). Line rimmed baking sheets with parchment paper.
2. In the bowl of a stand mixer fitted with the paddle attachment, beat butter and sugars at medium speed until fluffy, 3 to 4 minutes, stopping to scrape sides of bowl. Reduce mixer speed to medium-low. Add eggs, one at a time, beating well after each addition. Beat in vanilla bean paste.
3. In a medium bowl, whisk together flour, baking soda, and salt. With mixer on low speed, gradually add flour mixture to butter mixture, beating just until combined (do not overmix). Gently stir in chocolate morsels. Using a medium (1-tablespoon) spring-loaded scoop, drop dough at least 2 inches apart onto prepared pans. For Oversized Cookies, bake 2 cookies at a time. Scoop 3 tablespoons dough, and pat together.
4. For Classic Cookies: Bake until golden brown around the edges, 11 to 12 minutes,

rotating pans halfway through baking. For Oversized Cookies: Bake until golden brown around the edges, 13 to 14 minutes, rotating pans halfway through baking. Bake 1 sheet at a time for even cooking. Let cool on pans for 5 minutes. Using a thin spatula, remove from pans, and let cool completely on wire racks. Store in an airtight container at room temperature for up to 3 days.

We used Guittard.

> **PRO TIP:**
> If you chill the dough for the Oversized Cookie, it does not need to rest as long. Chilled dough will stay more compact when baking while warm dough will spread more in the oven.

CAKEY CHOCOLATE CHIP COOKIES

Makes about 36

This dough is mixed more like a cake batter so that the final cookie's texture is tender with a cake-like lift. Chilling this dough gives the ingredients time to bind together and solidifies the butter, which helps it spread less when baking.

¾   cup plus 2 tablespoons (198 grams) unsalted butter, softened
1   cup (220 grams) firmly packed light brown sugar
⅓   cup (67 grams) granulated sugar
2   large eggs (100 grams)
1   teaspoon (6 grams) vanilla bean paste
2   cups (250 grams) all-purpose flour
1   cup (125 grams) cake flour
1   teaspoon (5 grams) baking soda
½   teaspoon (2.5 grams) baking powder
¾   teaspoon (2.25 grams) kosher salt
¼   cup (60 grams) whole milk
2   cups (340 grams) semisweet chocolate morsels*

1. In the bowl of a stand mixer fitted with the paddle attachment, beat butter and sugars at medium speed until fluffy, 3 to 4 minutes, stopping to scrape sides of bowl. Reduce mixer speed to medium-low. Add eggs, one at a time, beating well after each addition. Beat in vanilla bean paste.
2. In a medium bowl, whisk together flours, baking soda, baking powder, and salt. With mixer on low speed, gradually add flour mixture to butter mixture alternately with milk, beginning and ending with flour mixture, beating just until combined after each addition. (Do not overmix. Dough will be softer than traditional cookie dough.) Gently stir in chocolate morsels. Refrigerate for at least 3 hours.
3. Preheat oven to 350°F (180°C). Line rimmed baking sheets with parchment paper.
4. Using a medium (1-tablespoon) spring-loaded scoop, drop dough at least 2 inches apart onto prepared pans. Place an additional 1½-teaspoon scoop of dough onto each cookie. Lightly press together.

5. Bake until golden brown around the edges, 11 to 12 minutes, rotating pans halfway through baking. Bake 1 sheet at a time for even cooking. Let cool on pans for 5 minutes. Using a thin spatula, remove from pans, and let cool completely on wire racks. For even softer cookies, let stand for at least 30 minutes for edges to soften. Store in an airtight container at room temperature for up to 3 days.

We used Guittard.

> **PRO TIP:**
> The longer these cookies rest post-bake, the softer they will be because they will soak up even more moisture from the air. We recommend letting them rest for 30 minutes before serving.

CRISPY CHOCOLATE CHIP COOKIES

Makes about 36

Using hand-chopped chocolate instead of morsels helps this cookie flatten out properly. We give the baking sheet a firm whack on a hard surface halfway through baking to make the final result even thinner.

1   cup (227 grams) unsalted butter, softened
1½ cups (300 grams) granulated sugar
2   large eggs (100 grams)
1   tablespoon (18 grams) vanilla bean paste
2¼ cups plus 3 tablespoons (305 grams) all-purpose flour
1   teaspoon (5 grams) baking soda
¾   teaspoon (2.25 grams) kosher salt
8   ounces (225 grams) semisweet baking chocolate*, chopped

1. Preheat oven to 375°F (190°C). Line rimmed baking sheets with parchment paper.
2. In the bowl of a stand mixer fitted with the paddle attachment, beat butter and sugar at medium speed until fluffy, 3 to 4 minutes, stopping to scrape sides of bowl. Reduce mixer speed to medium-low. Add eggs, one at a time, beating well after each addition. Beat in vanilla bean paste.
3. In a medium bowl, whisk together flour, baking soda, and salt. With mixer on low speed, gradually add flour mixture to butter mixture, beating just until combined (do not overmix). Gently stir in chopped chocolate. Using a medium (1-tablespoon) spring-loaded scoop, drop dough at least 2 inches apart onto prepared pans. Slightly press each scoop to flatten to half the original height.
4. Bake until golden brown around the edges, 12 to 13 minutes, rotating and whacking pans hard on counter halfway through baking to help cookies spread. Bake 1 sheet at a time for even cooking. Let cool on pans for 5 minutes. Using a thin spatula, remove from pans, and let cool completely on wire racks. Store in an airtight container at room temperature for up to 3 days.

We used Ghirardelli.

CHEWY CHOCOLATE CHIP COOKIES

Makes about 36

Dough lovers of the world gravitate toward this chocolate-laden, fudge-like cookie that stays soft and flexible even when cooled.

¾   cup (170 grams) unsalted butter, melted
1   cup (220 grams) firmly packed light brown sugar
⅔   cup (133 grams) granulated sugar
1   large egg (50 grams)
1   large egg yolk (19 grams)
1   tablespoon (18 grams) vanilla bean paste
2   cups (250 grams) all-purpose flour
⅓   cup (42 grams) bread flour
2   teaspoons (6 grams) cornstarch
¾   teaspoon (3.75 grams) baking soda
¾   teaspoon (2.25 grams) kosher salt
1½ cups (255 grams) semisweet chocolate morsels*

1. Preheat oven to 350°F (180°C). Line rimmed baking sheets with parchment paper.
2. In the bowl of a stand mixer fitted with the paddle attachment, beat butter and sugars at medium speed until fluffy, 3 to 4 minutes, stopping to scrape sides of bowl. Reduce mixer speed to medium-low. Add egg and egg yolk, one at a time, beating well after each addition. Beat in vanilla bean paste.
3. In a medium bowl, whisk together flours, cornstarch, baking soda, and salt. With mixer on low speed, gradually add flour mixture to butter mixture, beating just until combined (do not overmix). Gently stir in chocolate morsels. Using a medium (1-tablespoon) spring-loaded scoop, drop dough at least 2 inches apart onto prepared pans. Place an additional 1½-teaspoon scoop of dough onto each cookie. Lightly press together.
4. Bake until edges are just beginning to brown, 9 to 10 minutes, rotating pans halfway through baking. (Cookies may look under baked, but this helps achieve a soft and chewy cookie.) Bake 1 sheet at a time for even cooking. Let cool on pans for 5 minutes. Using a thin spatula, remove from pans, and let cool completely on wire racks. Store in an airtight container at room temperature for up to 3 days.

*We used Guittard.

LAVENDER SANDWICH COOKIES WITH LEMON CURD FILLING

Makes about 30 sandwich cookies

Recipe by Jenn Yee

At San Francisco's Craftsman & Wolves, Chef William Werner makes a simple cookie look like art. His lavender shortbread wreaths are topped with royal icing and adorned with dried flowers and fruit. They're available only at Christmas, so when I'm craving them, I make my own. These sandwich cookies are perfect for brunches, teas, and showers. The tangy lemon curd pairs beautifully with the lavender. Instead of royal icing, the buttery cookies are dusted with powdered sugar for a hint of sweetness. I like to prepare this recipe over the course of two days to break up the workload and ensure the dough and curd are well-chilled before baking and assembling.

¾ cup (170 grams) unsalted butter, softened
½ cup plus 2 tablespoons (124 grams) granulated sugar
1 teaspoon (2 grams) dried culinary lavender, coarsely ground or finely chopped
1 large egg yolk (19 grams)
1 teaspoon (4 grams) pure vanilla extract
2 cups (250 grams) all-purpose flour
¾ teaspoon (2.25 grams) kosher salt
Confectioners' sugar, for dusting
Lemon Curd Filling (recipe follows)

1. In the bowl of a stand mixer fitted with the paddle attachment, beat butter, granulated sugar, and lavender at medium speed until creamy, 3 to 4 minutes, stopping to scrape sides of bowl. With mixer on low speed, add egg yolk and vanilla, beating just until incorporated, 15 to 30 seconds. (It may not be completely combined, but we want to avoid overwhipping the eggs, which can make for uneven cookies.) Once again, scrape sides of bowl.
2. In a medium bowl, whisk together flour and salt. Gradually add flour mixture to butter mixture, beating just until combined. Scrape sides of bowl, and incorporate any remaining flour.

3. On your work surface, divide dough in half, and shape each half into a disk. The warmth from your hands will help the dough come together. Wrap in plastic wrap, and refrigerate until firm, at least 3 hours. I leave it overnight, and resume the process the next day.
4. Preheat oven to 350°F (180°C). Line rimmed baking sheets with parchment paper.
5. Unwrap one disk of dough, and roll to ¼-inch thickness. If dough is too firm, let it sit out until it is pliable but still cold. If dough is too soft and starts sticking while rolling, place it on a parchment-lined sheet pan, and put it back into the fridge for 5 to 10 minutes before continuing to roll it out.
6. Using a 2¼-inch fluted round cutter, cut dough, rerolling scraps as necessary. Using a ¾-inch round cutter or piping tip, cut centers from half of cookies. Use a wooden pick to remove dough from piping tip. Place cookies 1 inch apart on prepared pans. They shouldn't spread in the oven. Repeat with remaining dough. You should end up with about 30 cookie tops with centers cut out and about 30 cookie bottoms.
7. Bake each tray in middle rack of the oven until cookies are golden on the edges, 8 to 10 minutes, rotating pans halfway through baking. Let cool on pans for 5 minutes. Remove from pans, and let cool completely on wire racks.
8. To assemble, place cookie tops on a sheet pan. Dust with confectioners' sugar. Turn cookie bottoms over so they are bottom side up. Spoon 1½ teaspoons Lemon Curd Filling in center of each, leaving a ½-inch border. Be careful not to put too much or else it will splurt out when you sandwich them. You can also fill a piping bag fitted with a small round tip, and quickly pipe the filling in the center of each cookie. This is best done with cold hands to prevent the curd from warming up. Gently place powdered cookies on top of curd, and press slightly to sandwich them. Serve immediately.

LEMON CURD FILLING
Makes 1 cup

½ cup (100 grams) granulated sugar
1 tablespoon (8 grams) cornstarch
¼ teaspoon kosher salt
½ cup (120 grams) fresh lemon juice (from 3 to 4 lemons)
2 large eggs (100 grams)
2 large egg yolks (37 grams)
1 tablespoon (6 grams) finely grated lemon zest
¼ cup (57 grams) cold unsalted butter, cubed

1. Place a fine-mesh sieve over a medium bowl, and set aside.
2. In another medium bowl, whisk together sugar, cornstarch, and salt. Gradually add lemon juice, and whisk until cornstarch dissolves completely. Add eggs and egg yolks, and whisk until well combined.
3. Set the bowl over a saucepan of simmering water, making sure the bottom of the bowl does not touch the water. Cook, whisking constantly, until mixture begins to thicken, 3 to 4 minutes. Then whisk vigorously for 1 minute more. It should have a pudding-like consistency. Remove the bowl from the pot of simmering water.
4. Press curd through sieve. Whisk in zest and butter, 1 to 2 pieces at a time, letting the cubes melt before adding additional butter. Let curd cool to room temperature.
5. Once cool, press a piece of plastic wrap directly against surface of lemon curd to prevent a skin from forming, and refrigerate until well chilled and set, at least 6 hours

Photo by Kassie Borreson

TAHINI AND CRANBERRY WHOLE WHEAT SKILLET COOKIE

Makes 1 (10- or 12-inch) skillet cookie

Recipe by Dan and Julie Resnick/*feedfeed*

This recipe tells the story of our region, the local farmers, and the beauty of using local and seasonal ingredients. With wheat berries from two of our favorite farms in Amagansett, New York—Amber Waves Farm and Quail Hill Farm—we milled a beautiful whole wheat flour to elevate the taste and texture of this treat. Local cranberries, which we foraged ourselves at a bog around the corner from our house with our three children, give the cookie a hint of tartness.

¾ cup (170 grams) unsalted butter, softened
½ cup (110 grams) firmly packed light brown sugar
½ cup (100 grams) organic granulated sugar
⅓ cup (75 grams) tahini
2 large eggs (100 grams)
2 teaspoons (8 grams) vanilla extract*
2½ cups (325 grams) whole wheat flour
1 teaspoon (5 grams) baking soda
½ teaspoon (1.5 grams) kosher salt
1 cup (170 grams) high-quality dark chocolate morsels
1 cup (170 grams) fresh or 1½ cups (255 grams) frozen cranberries, thawed
Garnish: flaky sea salt
Ice cream, to serve

1. Preheat oven to 350°F (180°C). Grease a 10- to 12-inch cast-iron skillet with butter.
2. In the bowl of a stand mixer fitted with the paddle attachment, beat butter, sugars, and tahini at medium speed until fluffy, 3 to 4 minutes, stopping to scrape sides of bowl. Add eggs, one at a time, beating well after each addition. Beat in vanilla.
3. In a medium bowl, whisk together flour, baking soda, and salt. With mixer on low speed, gradually add flour mixture to butter mixture, beating until combined. Stir in chocolate morsels and cranberries. Spread dough in prepared skillet.
4. Bake for 35 to 40 minutes. Remove from oven, and let cool slightly. Sprinkle with sea salt, if desired. Serve with ice cream.

We used Rodelle Pure Vanilla Extract.

Photo by Dan & Julie Resnick

TAHINI AND MILK CHOCOLATE CHIP COOKIES

Makes about 48

Recipe by Ben Mims

Chocolate chip cookies don't need any improving, but this tahini version balances the sometimes too-sweet cookie and gives it a brittle, crunchier texture. The milk chocolate chunks are superior to dark chocolate here, offering a creamy complement to the lean-tasting tahini.

1½   cups (330 grams) firmly packed dark brown sugar
1   cup (256 grams) tahini
1   cup (227 grams) unsalted butter, melted and cooled
1   teaspoon (4 grams) vanilla extract
2   large eggs (100 grams)
2½   cups (313 grams) all-purpose flour
1   teaspoon (3 grams) kosher salt
¾   teaspoon (3.75 grams) baking soda
9   ounces (250 grams) high-quality milk chocolate, roughly chopped
Garnish: sesame seeds

1. In a large bowl, stir together brown sugar, tahini, melted butter, and vanilla with a wooden spoon until smooth. Add eggs, and stir until combined.
2. In a medium bowl, whisk together flour, salt, and baking soda. Add flour mixture to sugar mixture, stirring just until combined. Stir in chopped chocolate. Refrigerate for at least 1 hour or overnight.
3. Preheat oven to 350°F (180°C).
4. Using a 1-ounce ice cream scoop or heaping tablespoon, scoop dough, and roll into smooth balls. Place 12 balls each on 2 ungreased baking sheets. Lightly press each ball with the palm of your hand, and sprinkle with a pinch of sesame seeds, if desired.
5. Bake until set and lightly browned at the edges, 10 to 15 minutes, rotating pans front to back and top to bottom halfway through baking. Let cool on pans for 1 minute. Remove from pans, and let cool completely on wire racks. Repeat with remaining dough. Store in an airtight container for up to 5 days.

> **PRO TIP**
> Allowing this cookie dough to rest overnight isn't essential, but it dramatically improves the texture of the cookies. If you like, simply refrigerate the dough for 1 hour, and proceed to baking cookies.

Photo by Mason + Dixon

TAHINI-CARDAMOM SHORTBREADS WITH PISTACHIOS

Makes 30

Recipe by Ben Mims

Tahini is a natural match with shortbread because its slight drying effect produces a crumbly texture in baked goods, a boon to shortbread. This version adds buttery pistachios for color and crunch. A thick coating of confectioners' sugar sprinkled as soon as the cookies come out of the oven melds to the top, creating a snow-white, sweet layer to the nutty-toasty cookies.

⅔   cup (133 grams) granulated sugar
½   teaspoon (1.5 grams) kosher salt
¼   teaspoon ground cardamom
1   cup (227 grams) unsalted butter, softened
¼   cup (56 grams) tahini
3   cups (375 grams) all-purpose flour
⅓   cup (38 grams) roughly chopped pistachios
½   cup (60 grams) confectioners' sugar

1. Preheat oven to 325°F (170°C). Line a 13x9-inch baking pan with parchment paper, letting excess extend over sides of pan.
2. In the bowl of a stand mixer fitted with the paddle attachment, stir together granulated sugar, salt, and cardamom. With mixer on medium speed, add butter and tahini, beating until smooth, about 1 minute. Add flour, beating just until combined and crumbly. Reduce mixer speed to low, and beat for 10 minutes. (This amount of time helps develop some gluten, which you want to create the characteristic brittle texture of the shortbread.) Beat in pistachios.
3. Transfer dough to prepared pan, pressing into bottom. Using a paring knife, score dough into 2¼x1½-inch rectangles. Prick dough all over with a fork, being careful to stay within lines of rectangles.
4. Bake until very light golden brown at the edges, about 40 minutes. Transfer pan to a wire rack, and cut along scored lines to separate rectangles while dough is still hot. Immediately dust top with confectioners' sugar. Let cool completely in pan. Using excess parchment as handles, gently remove from pan, and break apart to serve.

Photo by Mason + Dixon

MIMI'S COOKIES

Makes about 72

Recipe by Brian Hart Hoffman

Every holiday season, I spend a day baking these decorated sugar cookies with my grandmother (Mimi). Part nostalgia, part deliciousness, it wouldn't be Christmas without these iced treats at our family gathering.

½   cup (113 grams) unsalted butter, softened
1   cup (200 grams) granulated sugar
2   large eggs (100 grams)
½   teaspoon (2 grams) vanilla extract
4   cups (500 grams) all-purpose flour
2   teaspoons (10 grams) baking powder
1   teaspoon (3 grams) kosher salt
2 to 3 tablespoons (30 to 45 grams) whole
       milk or heavy whipping cream
Food coloring (optional)
Icing (recipe follows)
Sprinkles (optional)

1. In the bowl of a stand mixer fitted with the paddle attachment, beat butter and sugar at medium speed until fluffy, 3 to 4 minutes, stopping to scrape sides of bowl. Add eggs, one at a time, beating well after each addition. Beat in vanilla.
2. In a large bowl, whisk together flour, baking powder, and salt. With mixer on low speed, gradually add flour mixture to butter mixture, beating until combined. Add 2 tablespoons (30 grams) milk or cream, beating until a moist, thick dough forms. Add remaining 1 tablespoon (15 grams) milk or cream, if necessary. (Dough should not be crumbly.) Beat in food coloring, if desired. (For multiple colors of dough, divide dough into batches, and add desired amount of food coloring.) Cover and refrigerate for at least 2 hours.
3. Preheat oven to 375°F (190°C).
4. On a lightly floured surface, roll dough to ¼-inch thickness. Using desired holiday cutters, cut dough, and place on ungreased baking sheets.

5. Bake until golden, about 12 minutes. Let cool completely. Frost cookies with Icing, adding sprinkles, if desired.

Icing
Makes about ½ cup

1½   cups (180 grams) confectioners' sugar
1   large egg white (30 grams)
1   teaspoon (4 grams) vanilla extract
Food coloring (optional)

1. In the bowl of a stand mixer fitted with the paddle attachment, beat confectioners' sugar, egg white, vanilla, and food coloring at medium speed until smooth. Icing should dry quickly and be hard to the touch.

SALTED CHOCOLATE CHIP COOKIES

Makes 24

Recipe by Allison Kave and Keavy Landreth

Chocolate chip cookies can be a polarizing subject. Some prefer crispy all the way through, others like them soft and chewy. We fall into that Goldilocks middle ground, opting for perfectly gooey insides (let's be real: under baked), with crispy, chewy edges. It's the best of both worlds. The other key to these bad boys is salt: the not-so-secret ingredient that is crucial to all desserts. It amps up flavors and provides a savory foil to all that sugar. The final, and perhaps most essential, ingredient that makes these cookies so damned stellar is time. Patience is not the virtue of most cookie cravers, but it's vital that this dough has its beauty sleep in the fridge before baking (rest assured, this doesn't prevent you from sneaking a taste or three of the dough before you bake it). Reward your willpower by gilding the lily; bake these cookies, then dunk them in the most adult version of milk we can think of: a White Russian.

1½	cups (340 grams) unsalted butter
½	cup (120 grams) plus ⅓ cup (80 grams) cold water, divided
1⅔	cups (333 grams) granulated sugar

1⅔	cups (367 grams) firmly packed dark brown sugar
8	large egg yolks (149 grams)
⅓	cup (75 grams) canola oil
2	tablespoons (26 grams) vanilla extract
6	cups (750 grams) all-purpose flour
2¾	teaspoons (13.75 grams) baking soda
1	tablespoon plus 1 teaspoon (12 grams) kosher salt
12	ounces (340 grams) bittersweet chocolate morsels

Garnish: fleur de sel*

1. In a small saucepan, bring butter to a boil over medium-high heat. You're turning this into browned butter, or *beurre noisette*. When the butter starts to foam, and you will smell a nutty aroma, immediately remove it from the heat. (Be careful, as browned butter can quickly turn to burnt butter if you let it go too far.) Let cool slightly. Whisk in ½ cup (120 grams) water.

2. In a large bowl, whisk together sugars; whisk in browned butter mixture. In a medium bowl, whisk together egg yolks, oil, vanilla, and remaining ⅓ cup (80 grams) water until combined. Whisk egg mixture into butter mixture until combined.

3. In another medium bowl, stir together flour, baking soda, and salt. Gradually add flour mixture to butter mixture, stirring until combined. Fold in chocolate morsels.

4. Cover with plastic wrap, and refrigerate overnight (this allows the dough to fully hydrate, and prevents the cookies from spreading too much during baking).

5. Preheat oven to 350°F (180°C). Line 2 baking sheets with parchment paper.

6. Using a ½-cup ice cream scoop, scoop dough onto prepared pans. (If you want to have some cookies for another time, or don't want to bake a full batch, cover the extra scooped dough with plastic wrap, and freeze for up to 1 month.)

7. Gently press down on each cookie with the palm of your hand to flatten it a bit. Sprinkle a pinch of fleur de sel on each cookie, if desired.

8. Bake until cookies are golden around the edges and light in the center, about 10 minutes, rotating pans halfway through baking. Let cool before serving. Store in an airtight container for up to 2 days.

We used Maldon sea salt flakes.

HALVA AND PISTACHIO PINWHEEL COOKIES

Makes about 54

Recipe by Amisha Gurbani/*feedfeed*

I consider pinwheels to be the quintessential Christmas cookie. Here, I swirl halva and pistachio dough into a cookie log, then roll them in dried rose petal sugar.

1¼   cups (284 grams) unsalted butter, softened
1½   cups (300 grams) granulated sugar, divided
1   large egg (50 grams), room temperature
2   teaspoons (8 grams) vanilla extract
3½   cups (438 grams) all-purpose flour
½   teaspoon (1.5 grams) kosher salt
¼   teaspoon (1.25 grams) baking soda
¾   cup (82 grams) halva
3   tablespoons (45 grams) warm whole milk (105°F/40°C to 110°F/43°C), divided
¾   cup (85 grams) pistachios
⅛   teaspoon liquid green food coloring (optional)
½   cup (10 grams) dried rose petals

1. In the bowl of a stand mixer fitted with the paddle attachment, beat butter and 1¼ cups (250 grams) sugar at medium speed until creamy, 3 to 4 minutes, stopping to scrape sides of bowl. Beat in egg and vanilla. In a medium bowl, sift together flour, salt, and baking soda. With mixer on low speed, gradually add flour mixture to butter mixture, beating just until combined. Divide dough in half.

2. For halva dough: In small bowl, whisk together halva and 2 tablespoons (30 grams) warm milk to make a smooth paste. Place half of dough back in stand mixer. With mixer on low speed, add halva mixture, beating until combined. Turn out dough onto a work surface, and divide in half. Place one portion on a piece of plastic wrap, and shape into a 6-inch square; wrap well in plastic wrap. Repeat with second portion of halva dough. Refrigerate for 1 hour.

3. For pistachio dough: Finely grind pistachios in a coffee grinder. Place remaining dough back in stand mixer. With mixer on low speed, add pistachios and remaining 1 tablespoon (15 grams) warm milk, beating until combined. Increase mixer speed to medium. If using food coloring, add it. Beat

until color is green throughout. Turn out dough onto a work surface, and divide in half. Place one portion on a piece of plastic wrap, and shape into a 6-inch square; wrap well in plastic wrap. Repeat with second portion of pistachio dough. Refrigerate for 1 hour.

4. Remove one portion of dough from refrigerator. Roll dough between two sheets of parchment paper into an 8-inch square. Place on a baking sheet, and refrigerate for 10 minutes. Repeat procedure with remaining 3 portions of dough.

5. Remove one halva sheet and one pistachio sheet from refrigerator. Peel off top sheet of parchment from each layer. Invert halva layer exactly onto pistachio layer. Place parchment back over the 2 layers, and gently roll to seal the two layers together. Peel off top sheet of parchment.

6. Roll edge facing you gently inward, and with the help of the parchment paper, gently roll, making sure to leave no gaps in pinwheel. Roll into a cylinder, making it neat and even by rolling it back and forth. Tighten edges with kitchen twine, and refrigerate for at least 2 hours. Repeat procedure with remaining halva dough and remaining pistachio dough.

7. Preheat oven to 350°F (180°C). Line 2 baking sheets with parchment paper.

8. Coarsely grind rose petals in a coffee grinder; pour into a small bowl. Add remaining ¼ cup (50 grams) sugar, and stir to combine.

9. Remove one log from refrigerator, and remove parchment. Cut two edges off cookie roll. Spread rose sugar in a small baking tray. Start rolling log in rose sugar to coat entire log. Roll back and forth a few times with slight pressure to make sure rose sugar sticks to log. Using a sharp knife, cut ¼-inch-thick slices. Place about 1 inch apart on prepared pans. Repeat with remaining log.

10. Bake in upper and middle racks of oven for about 15 minutes, rotating pans halfway through baking. Make sure cookies do not brown. Let cool on pans for 2 minutes. Remove from pans, and let cool completely on wire racks. Store in an airtight container for up to 2 weeks. Dough can be refrigerated for up to 3 days or frozen for up to 1 month.

Photo by Amisha Gurbani

THANDAI SHORTBREAD COOKIES DIPPED IN WHITE CHOCOLATE WITH PISTACHIOS AND ROSE PETALS

Makes about 45

Recipe by Amisha Gurbani/*feedfeed*

Thandai is the name of a cold Indian drink that is prepared with a mix of various nuts and spices. Here, instead of a drink, it's in the form of a shortbread cookie, which is perfect for the colder winter months.

1¼   cups (284 grams) unsalted butter, softened
1   cup (200 grams) granulated sugar
1   tablespoon (13 grams) vanilla extract
2½   cups (313 grams) all-purpose flour
½   cup plus 2 tablespoons (70 grams) Thandai Powder (recipe follows)
½   teaspoon (1.5 grams) kosher salt
2   cups (340 grams) high-quality white chocolate morsels
2   teaspoons (10 grams) coconut oil
¾   cup (85 grams) finely chopped pistachios
4   tablespoons (1 gram) powdered dried rose petals

1. In the bowl of a stand mixer fitted with the paddle attachment, beat butter and sugar at medium speed until creamy, 3 to 4 minutes, stopping to scrape sides of bowl. Beat in vanilla.
2. In a medium bowl, whisk together flour, Thandai Powder, and salt. With mixer on low speed, gradually add flour mixture to butter mixture, beating just until combined. Turn out dough, and divide in half. Shape into disks, and wrap in plastic wrap. Refrigerate for 2 hours.
3. Preheat oven to 350°F (180°C). Line 2 baking sheets with parchment paper.

4. On a lightly floured surface, roll half of dough to ¼-inch thickness. Using a 2½-inch fluted round cutter, cut dough, and place on prepared pans.
5. Bake on lower and middle racks of oven until golden brown, about 15 minutes, rotating pans halfway through baking. Let cool on pans for 5 minutes. Remove from pans, and let cool completely on wire racks. Repeat with remaining dough.
6. In a small microwave-safe bowl, combine chocolate morsels and oil. Microwave on high in 30-second intervals, stirring between each, until chocolate is melted and smooth (about 2 minutes total). In another small bowl, stir together pistachios and rose petals.
7. Line a baking sheet with parchment paper.
8. Dip one-third of each cookie in chocolate mixture, letting excess drip off. Sprinkle pistachio mixture onto chocolate, shaking off excess. Place on prepared pan. Freeze until chocolate is set, about 5 minutes. If chocolate begins to thicken while dipping cookies, microwave for 10 to 15 seconds to rewarm. Store cookies in an airtight container for up to 2 weeks.

Note: *Dough will keep refrigerated for up to 1 week or frozen for up to 1 month.*

THANDAI POWDER
Makes 1½ cups

⅓   cup (45 grams) almonds
¼   cup (36 grams) pistachios
¼   cup (36 grams) cashews
¼   cup (36 grams) poppy seeds
¼   cup (3 grams) dried rose petals
20   black peppercorns
Seeds from 8 cardamom pods
1   cinnamon stick (5 grams), crushed
6   cloves
2   tablespoons (18 grams) fennel seeds
2   star anise (4 grams)
½   teaspoon (1 gram) ground nutmeg

1. In a small bowl, roughly stir together all ingredients. Working in batches, add mixture to a coffee grinder; blend until finely ground.

Photo by Amisha Gurbani

MATCHA MACARONS WITH BAILEYS ORIGINAL IRISH CREAM BUTTERCREAM FILLING

Makes 30

Recipe by Amisha Gurbani/*feedfeed*

No holiday party is complete without good liqueur and desserts. The two are combined here in macarons sandwiched with a Baileys Original Irish Cream Buttercream Filling. The addition of earthy matcha powder gives a festive green color to the macaron shells without overpowering the taste.

2   tablespoons (12 grams) matcha powder
1⅔ cups (200 grams) plus ¼ cup (30 grams) confectioners' sugar, divided
1   cup plus 2 tablespoons (108 grams) almond flour
4   large egg whites (120 grams), room temperature
⅛   teaspoon cream of tartar
½   cup plus 1 tablespoon (112 grams) granulated sugar
1   teaspoon (4 grams) vanilla extract
Baileys Original Irish Cream Buttercream Filling (recipe follows)

1. Preheat oven to 325°F (170°C). Line baking sheets with parchment paper. Using a pencil, draw 1⅓-inch circles onto parchment; turn parchment over.
2. Place matcha in the work bowl of a food processor. Add ¼ cup (30 grams) confectioners' sugar and almond flour; pulse until a fine powder is formed. Transfer to a medium bowl, and stir in remaining 1⅔ cups (200 grams) confectioners' sugar. Sift mixture three times into a large bowl. Set aside.
3. In the bowl of a stand mixer fitted with the whisk attachment, beat egg whites and cream of tartar at medium speed until foamy. Gradually add granulated sugar, beating until combined. Scrape sides of bowl, and add vanilla. Increase mixer speed to high. Beat until stiff, firm, glossy peaks form, 5 to 10 minutes.
4. Sift almond flour mixture, one-third at a time, over egg white mixture; fold using a large spatula until mixture is smooth and shiny. Once all almond flour mixture is incorporated, check for correct consistency. (The batter should be firm, have a glossy shine, and drip smoothly from the spatula. Make sure that the entire almond mixture is incorporated. This step is very important.)
5. Transfer batter to a pastry bag fitted with a ½-inch plain round tip (#12), and pipe batter onto drawn circles on prepared pans. Gently tap pans on counter 5 to 7 times to release air bubbles. If they have a tip, gently pat it down with your finger. Let stand at room temperature for at least 30 minutes. (This is crucial for shell to form a nice crust.) Check for a slight crust to form on the macaron. Macarons should not stick to your finger when lightly touched.
6. Bake, one sheet at a time, until crisp and firm, 13 to 14 minutes, rotating pan halfway through baking. Let cool on pans for 2 to 3 minutes. Remove from pans, and let cool completely on wire racks. Pipe Baileys Original Irish Cream Buttercream Filling onto flat side of half of macarons. Place remaining macarons, flat side down, on top of filling. Refrigerate in an airtight container for up to 4 days.

Note: *When using the pastry bag to pipe the macarons, hold it absolutely vertical, center to the circles on the template and slightly above, making sure not to touch the paper when piping. You can keep the baked shells covered and fill them the next day. The shells will keep for 2 days in an airtight container.*

BAILEYS ORIGINAL IRISH CREAM BUTTERCREAM FILLING
Makes ½ cup

½   cup (113 grams) unsalted butter, softened
¼   teaspoon kosher salt
1½ cups (180 grams) confectioners' sugar
2   tablespoons (30 grams) Baileys Irish Cream
½   teaspoon (2 grams) vanilla extract

1. In the bowl of a stand mixer fitted with the whisk attachment, beat butter and salt at medium speed until light and creamy, about 2 minutes. With mixer on low speed, add confectioners' sugar, Baileys Irish Cream, and vanilla, beating until well combined and smooth, about 2 minutes.

Photo by Amisha Gurbani

SALTED CARAMEL SABLÉ SANDWICH COOKIES

Makes about 28 sandwich cookies

Recipe by Susan Spungen/*feedfeed*

These dainty cookie sandwiches are addictive thanks to their salty-sweet flavor profile. You can make them in any size or shape you want as long as you have graduated cutters so that you can cut the windows out for the top cookies.

1   cup (227 grams) unsalted butter, softened
½   cup (100 grams) granulated sugar
¼   teaspoon kosher salt
1   large egg (50 grams)
1   teaspoon (4 grams) vanilla extract
2½   cups (313 grams) all-purpose flour
Vanilla Caramel Filling (recipe follows)
Garnish: Maldon sea salt

1. In the bowl of a stand mixer fitted with the paddle attachment, beat butter, sugar, and salt at medium speed until creamy, 3 to 4 minutes, stopping to scrape sides of bowl. Beat in egg and vanilla.
2. With mixer on low speed, gradually add flour, beating just until combined. Divide dough in half, and shape into disks. Wrap in plastic wrap, and refrigerate for at least 1 hour or up to 3 days.
3. Generously flour a silicone baking mat or sheet of parchment paper. Place one disk of dough in center, and dust top and rolling pin with flour. Working quickly, roll dough to about ¼-inch thickness (you don't want the cookies to be too thick since they will be sandwiched later). Transfer baking mat or parchment with dough onto a baking sheet, and place pan in refrigerator. Repeat procedure with remaining dough.
4. Preheat oven to 350°F (180°C). Line baking sheets with parchment paper.
5. Using a 1½-inch fluted round cutter dipped in flour, cut dough, rerolling scraps and flouring cutter as necessary. Using a ¾- to 1-inch fluted round cutter dipped in flour, cut centers from half of cookies. Place on prepared pans.
6. Bake until just set, pale on top, and just golden on bottom, 9 to 11 minutes, rotating pans after 5 minutes. Let cool completely on wire racks. Spread about ½ teaspoon Vanilla Caramel Filling on flat side of all solid cookies. Place cookies with cutouts, flat side down, on top of filling. Just before serving, garnish with sea salt, if desired. Refrigerate in an airtight container.

VANILLA CARAMEL FILLING
Makes about 1 cup

You may have a bit more of this luscious filling than you need to fill the cookies. Warm it up and serve over ice cream, or add it to an apple pie or tart filling. Don't be afraid to cook it until it is quite dark as you want the flavor to come through.

1   cup (200 grams) granulated sugar
½   cup (120 grams) water
⅓   cup (80 grams) heavy whipping cream
2   tablespoons (28 grams) cold unsalted butter, cubed
½   vanilla bean, split lengthwise, seeds scraped and reserved
⅛   teaspoon kosher salt

1. In a small heavy-bottomed, tall-sided saucepan, bring sugar and ½ cup (120 grams) water to a boil over medium-high heat. Cook until sugar is dissolved, 2 to 3 minutes. Using a wet pastry brush, brush sides of pan to prevent crystals from forming. Increase heat to high. Cook, swirling pan occasionally and carefully, until mixture starts to color, 8 to 10 minutes. Reduce heat, and watch very carefully, continuing to swirl gently until it turns amber colored.
2. Turn off heat, and immediately add cream. (It will sputter and expand temporarily.) As it calms down, add butter, whisking until smooth. Add vanilla bean and reserved seeds and salt. Let cool completely before using. Store any leftover caramel in a glass jar in refrigerator for up to 1 month. Warm to a liquid consistency before using.

> **PRO TIPS**
> Roll and cut all of the cookies, returning baking sheets to refrigerator as needed before heating the oven, especially if you have a small kitchen. This will help keep the dough cool as you work.
>
> A silicone baking mat is the perfect surface for rolling out a finicky dough. If it starts to soften, just slide the mat onto a baking sheet, and chill until it is workable. Parchment paper works, too, but it will slide around on the surface more. Use a longer piece of parchment than needed, and lean against it to hold it in place while you roll.

Photo by Dave Katz

GLUTEN-FREE HOLIDAY ALMOND RAINBOW COOKIES WITH MATCHA AND CHERRY

Makes about 40

Recipe by Jill Fergus/feedfeed

Festive and scrumptious holiday cookies are steeped in memory and tradition. Rainbow cookies are a family favorite (adults and children alike) for their lovely almond flavor and cake-like quality. Commercially baked rainbow cookies are made with large amounts of artificial food coloring and flavor, which I very much wanted to avoid. Gluten-free versions are frequently made with additional sugar, masking any real flavor and assorted processed starches in place of wheat flour, not benefiting the texture. My goal was to create a delicious, flavorful, and fun holiday cookie using wholesome ingredients for everyone to enjoy!

¾ cup (170 grams) unsalted butter
1 cup (260 grams) almond paste
1 cup (200 grams) natural cane sugar
4 large eggs (200 grams), room temperature and separated
1 teaspoon (4 grams) vanilla extract
¼ teaspoon (1 gram) natural almond extract
⅔ cup (64 grams) almond flour
½ cup (68 grams) gluten-free oat flour
½ cup (68 grams) gluten-free corn flour
½ heaping teaspoon (2 grams) kosher salt
2 teaspoons (4 grams) matcha powder
4 to 5 drops natural blue food coloring (optional)
2 teaspoons (4 grams) beet root powder
½ cup plus 1 tablespoon (180 grams) sour cherry preserves
1 heaping cup (180 grams) good-quality dark chocolate, chopped
1 teaspoon (5 grams) coconut oil

1. Preheat oven to 350°F (180°C). Lightly spray 3 (9-inch) square cake pans with cooking spray. Line pans with parchment paper, letting excess extend over sides of pans.
2. In the bowl of a stand mixer fitted with the paddle attachment, beat butter, almond paste, and sugar at medium speed until creamy, 3 to 4 minutes, stopping to scrape sides of bowl. Add egg yolks and extracts, beating until combined.
3. In a medium bowl, whisk together flours and salt. By hand, stir flour mixture into butter mixture until fully combined. Transfer batter to another bowl; set aside.
4. Clean bowl of stand mixer. Using the whisk attachment, beat egg whites at high speed just until stiff peaks form. Fold egg whites into batter.

5. Divide batter into 3 equal parts. (You want the batter to be as equally distributed as possible, as each layer is quite thin, and your goal is to achieve uniform stripes.) Set one bowl aside as this is your natural "white" stripe. Add matcha and blue food coloring (if using) to second bowl, stirring until combined. Add beet powder to third bowl, stirring until combined. Spread batter into prepared pans, smoothing tops.
6. Bake until cake springs back when lightly touched in center and edges have slightly pulled away from sides, 10 to 12 minutes. Let cool in pans for 10 minutes. Using excess parchment as handles, gently remove from pans. Let cool completely on wire racks.
7. Invert red layer on a work surface lined with parchment paper. Using an offset spatula, spread with a thin and even layer of cherry preserves. Invert white layer on top, and spread with another thin and even layer of cherry preserves. Invert green layer on top. Cover top and sides of cake with plastic wrap, and top with another piece of parchment paper. Place a heavy cookbook on top to firmly but gently weight it down. Refrigerate for 3 hours.
8. Remove book and wrapping, leaving base layer of parchment. Place on a cutting surface, and using a sharp knife, trim edges of cake. Place another sheet of parchment paper on counter (to catch drips), and top with a wire rack. Gently place cake on wire rack using its parchment base layer.
9. In a microwave-safe bowl, heat chocolate on high in 30-second intervals, stirring between each, until melted and smooth. Add coconut oil, stirring to combine. Carefully pour a stream of chocolate over top of cake, and spread evenly and coat sides. Apply traditional wavy lines using the tines of a fork, or swirl as desired. Let stand at room temperature until chocolate has completely cooled. Refrigerate until set.
10. Cover with plastic wrap, and set on a solid surface or a large plate. Freeze for at least 1 hour or overnight. Using a sharp knife, cut into 1½x1-inch bars. Bring to room temperature, or serve slightly chilled.

PRO TIP

Matcha tends to be a more yellowish green. I like to add a few drops of blue food coloring to offset this, but this addition is truly optional. If you do not want to use matcha, you may substitute natural green food coloring of choice.

Photo by Dave Katz

PEPPERMINT S'MORES WITH CHOCOLATE GRAHAM CRACKERS

Makes about 20

Recipe by Erin Clarkson/*feedfeed*

When I moved to the U.S. from New Zealand three years ago, I was fascinated by s'mores, which aren't super popular in New Zealand due to the lack of "proper" ingredients. This fascination only deepened when I discovered how fun it was to make marshmallows from scratch. I wanted to capture both the magic of a toasty marshmallow campfire snack and the flavors of the holidays, so chocolate grahams with a fluffy peppermint marshmallow seemed like the perfect fit!

1¾ cups (219 grams) all-purpose flour
1 cup (130 grams) whole wheat flour
¾ cup (165 grams) firmly packed light brown sugar
½ cup (43 grams) unsweetened cocoa powder
1 teaspoon (5 grams) baking soda
½ teaspoon (1.5 grams) kosher salt
7 tablespoons (98 grams) cold unsalted butter, cubed
⅓ cup plus 2 tablespoons (110 grams) whole milk
¼ cup (85 grams) honey
1 teaspoon (4 grams) vanilla extract
Peppermint Marshmallows (recipe follows)

1. In the work bowl of a food processor, place flours, brown sugar, cocoa, baking soda, and salt; pulse until combined. Add cold butter, and pulse until mixture is crumbly.
2. In a small bowl, combine milk, honey, and vanilla. Slowly add milk mixture to flour mixture, pulsing until dough comes together. Turn out dough onto a piece of plastic wrap, and divide in half. Wrap half of dough in plastic wrap while working with the other half.
3. Roll half of dough between 2 sheets of parchment paper to about ⅛-inch thickness. (Roll thinner than you think because the crackers will rise in the oven.) Place dough, between parchment, on a baking sheet. Freeze for 1 hour. Repeat with remaining dough.
4. Preheat oven to 350°F (180°C).
5. Remove one sheet of dough from freezer, and peel off top layer of parchment. Using

a ruler and a pastry wheel or knife, score dough into 3x2-inch rectangles. (Do not separate rectangles yet.)
6. Bake until lightly puffed and set, about 20 minutes. Let cool on pan for 5 minutes. Using a pastry wheel or sharp knife, cut over scored lines. Let cool completely on pan before breaking into individual crackers. Repeat with remaining dough.
7. Place a Peppermint Marshmallow between two graham crackers. Serve immediately. Store any extra crackers and Peppermint Marshmallows separately, and assemble just before eating. Undipped marshmallows can be stored in an airtight container at room temperature. Dipped marshmallows need to be stored in refrigerator.

PRO TIP
Measure the size of the baked graham crackers before cutting the marshmallow so that you can cut the marshmallow to the same size.

PEPPERMINT MARSHMALLOWS
Makes 20

½ cup plus 2 tablespoons (150 grams) cold water
2 tablespoons plus 1 teaspoon (28 grams) gelatin
2½ cups plus 3 tablespoons (536 grams) granulated sugar
½ cup plus 2 tablespoons (150 grams) warm water
½ cup plus ⅛ cup (212 grams) light corn syrup
1 tablespoon (18 grams) vanilla paste or 1 vanilla bean, split lengthwise, seeds scraped and reserved
1 teaspoon (4 grams) peppermint extract
½ cup (64 grams) cornstarch
½ cup (60 grams) confectioners' sugar
9 ounces (250 grams) high-quality 60% to 70% cacao chocolate, melted
3 large or 6 small (125 grams) candy canes, finely crushed

1. Grease a 13x9-inch baking pan with butter.
2. In the bowl of a stand mixer fitted with the whisk attachment, stir together ½ cup plus 2 tablespoons (150 grams) cold water and gelatin; let stand until softened, about 5 minutes.
3. In a medium saucepan, heat granulated sugar, ½ cup plus 2 tablespoons (150 grams) warm water, corn syrup, and vanilla over medium-high heat. Cook, stirring occasionally, until a candy thermometer registers 240°F (116°C). Remove from heat, and let cool to 210°F (99°C).
4. With mixer on medium speed, beat gelatin mixture for 3 to 4 seconds. With mixer running, carefully add hot sugar syrup. Increase mixer speed to high, and beat until marshmallow has doubled in volume, turned white, and holds somewhat of a peak, 5 to 7 minutes. Add peppermint extract, and beat for 30 seconds.
5. Working quickly, scrape marshmallow into prepared pan using a lightly oiled rubber spatula. Smooth surface using an oiled offset spatula or the back of a spoon. Use wet fingers to help smoothing process, if necessary.
6. In a small bowl, combine cornstarch and confectioners' sugar. Liberally dust cornstarch mixture over marshmallow. Let cure for 3 to 4 hours.
7. Carefully turn marshmallow out onto a board, and dust entire surface with cornstarch mixture. Using a sharp knife dusted with cornstarch mixture, cut marshmallow into 3x2-inch rectangles. Lightly dust cut surfaces of marshmallow with cornstarch-sugar mixture to help avoid sticking.
8. Line a baking sheet with parchment paper. Dip half of each marshmallow in melted chocolate, and sprinkle with crushed candy canes. Place on prepared pan, and refrigerate until set.

PRO TIP
Prepare your baking dish and the tools you need before you begin to whip the marshmallow. Things will move quickly once it is ready, and you want to get it into the pan as quickly as possible.

Photo by Dave Katz

SNOWFLAKE SANDWICH COOKIES WITH PEPPERMINT BUTTERCREAM FILLING

Makes about 24 sandwich cookies

Recipe by Judy Kim/*feedfeed*

These cookies are sure to transport you to a winter wonderland. The buttery cookies have an unexpected crunch and a touch of saltiness from the sea salt. I like to crush the flakes by hand so there are slightly uneven bits that disperse through the dough. The cookies are filled with peppermint buttercream, and the tops are piped with delicate snowflakes that sparkle like jewels.

¾ cup (170 grams) unsalted butter, softened
¾ cup (150 grams) granulated sugar
½ teaspoon (1.5 grams) crushed flaky sea salt
1 large egg (50 grams), room temperature
½ teaspoon (2 grams) vanilla extract
2 cups (250 grams) all-purpose flour
Peppermint Buttercream Filling (recipe follows)
¾ cup (150 grams) white sanding sugar

1. In the bowl of a stand mixer fitted with the paddle attachment, beat butter, granulated sugar, and salt at medium speed until creamy, 3 to 4 minutes, stopping to scrape sides of bowl. Beat in egg and vanilla.
2. In a medium bowl, sift flour. With mixer on low speed, gradually add half of flour, beating just until barely combined, stopping to scrape sides and bottom of bowl. Add remaining flour, and beat until combined. (Do not overmix.) Divide dough in half, and wrap in plastic wrap. Refrigerate for at least 3 hours or overnight.
3. Preheat oven to 350°F (180°C). Line 2 half-sheet pans with parchment paper.
4. On a lightly floured surface, roll half of dough to ⅛-inch thickness. (To prevent dough from becoming too soft to handle, keep remaining dough in refrigerator until you are ready. Ensure surface is floured just enough to prevent dough from sticking, especially before cutting.) Using a 3½-inch snowflake cookie cutter dipped in flour, cut dough, rerolling scraps only once. Place cookies about 1 inch apart on prepared pans. (For best results, place sheet pan in freezer for a few minutes to chill dough. This will help them keep their shape.) Repeat with remaining dough.

5. Bake until lightly golden around the edges, about 10 minutes. (Be careful not to overbake, or cookies will not be tender.) Let cool completely on a wire rack.
6. Spoon half of Peppermint Buttercream Filling into a large pastry bag fitted with a large open star pastry tip (Ateco #826). Spoon remaining Peppermint Buttercream Filling into a large pastry bag fitted with a small round decorating tip (Ateco #5).
7. Using pastry bag fitted with large star tip, pipe filling in short strokes starting at the tip of each snowflake, working toward center of cookie. The bottom cookie can face up, as it will show a hint of the golden edges. Immediately place another cookie face-up and gently sandwich cookie just enough to ensure it will adhere but without deflating piped filling.
8. Using pastry bag fitted with small decorating tip, create a snowflake pattern using filling on surface of top cookie. Place cookie in a shallow bowl, and spoon sanding sugar all over it. (This way, you can use the sugar in the bowl for the next cookie.) Shake off excess sugar, and place on a wire rack. Repeat procedure with remaining cookies and filling. Let set before serving. Store in airtight container at room temperature for up to 4 days.

PEPPERMINT BUTTERCREAM FILLING
Makes 2 cups

1 cup (227 grams) unsalted butter, softened
½ teaspoon (2 grams) peppermint extract
3 cups (360 grams) confectioners' sugar

1. In the bowl of a stand mixer fitted with the paddle attachment, beat butter and peppermint extract at medium-high speed until creamy. Gradually add confectioners' sugar, beating until smooth.

PRO TIP
Delicate snowflake cutters are beautiful, but the narrow points tend to break off. To give them a sparkly delicate look, try selecting a simpler shape but concentrate on creating the snowflake pattern by using a fine decorating tip to pipe the Peppermint Buttercream Filling on top and cover in pretty white sanding sugar. To give extra definition, after applying sanding sugar, use a wooden pick to remove excess sugar to help shape the snowflake design.

Photo by Dave Katz

ESPRESSO SHORTBREAD COOKIES

Makes about 12

Recipe by Laura Kasavan/*feedfeed*

These shortbread cookies are absolutely indulgent, and the deep espresso flavor makes them the perfect match for your afternoon pick-me-up. Finished with a dip in chocolate and sparkling turbinado sugar, you'll fight for every last wedge.

1 tablespoon (6 grams) instant espresso powder*
1 tablespoon (15 grams) boiling water
¾ cup (170 grams) unsalted butter, softened
⅔ cup (133 grams) granulated sugar
1 teaspoon (4 grams) vanilla extract
⅛ teaspoon fine sea salt
1¾ cups (219 grams) all-purpose flour
4 ounces (115 grams) semisweet chocolate, chopped
2 tablespoons (24 grams) turbinado sugar
Garnish: edible gold sprinkles

1. Spray a 9-inch round removable-bottom tart pan with cooking spray.
2. In a small bowl, stir together espresso powder and 1 tablespoon (15 grams) boiling water; set aside to let cool to room temperature.
3. In the bowl of a stand mixer fitted with the paddle attachment, beat butter and granulated sugar at medium speed until creamy, 3 to 4 minutes, stopping to scrape sides of bowl. With mixer on medium-low speed, add cooled espresso mixture, vanilla, and salt, beating until combined. With mixer on low speed, add flour, beating until combined and dough starts to come together. Transfer dough to prepared pan, pressing into bottom and up sides. Cover and refrigerate until firm, about 1 hour.
4. Preheat oven to 350°F (180°C).
5. Using a sharp knife, score dough into 12 wedges, and prick all over with a wooden skewer.
6. Bake until top is light brown and set in center, 30 to 32 minutes. Remove from oven, and place on a wire rack. Use a sharp knife to recut shortbread into wedges, and let cool completely in pan.

7. Line 2 baking sheets with parchment paper.
8. In the top of a double boiler, melt chocolate over simmering water. Cook, stirring occasionally, until glossy and smooth. One by one, dip widest end of each cookie triangle in chocolate, and place on prepared pans. Sprinkle with turbinado sugar. Garnish with gold sprinkles, if desired. Refrigerate until chocolate is set, about 20 minutes.

*I used Starbucks VIA Italian Roast Coffee.

PRO TIP
Shortbread dough can be made up to 1 month in advance. After refrigerating dough for 1 hour, score dough into wedges, and prick all over with a wooden skewer. Wrap tart pan in foil, and place in a large resealable plastic bag to freeze. When you're ready to bake, you can bake the shortbread directly from the freezer, adding 2 or 3 minutes to baking time.

Photo by Laura Kasavan

PUMPKIN SPICE SHORTBREAD COOKIES

Makes about 24

Recipe by Laura Kasavan/*feedfeed*

Everyone's favorite pumpkin spice flavor infuses these soft and buttery shortbread cookies. Decorate with turbinado sugar and pecan halves for a sparkling finishing touch.

¾   cup (170 grams) unsalted butter, softened
⅔   cup (133 grams) granulated sugar
⅓   cup (81 grams) canned pumpkin
½   teaspoon (2 grams) vanilla extract
1¾ cups (219 grams) all-purpose flour
1   teaspoon (2 grams) ground cinnamon
⅛   teaspoon ground cloves
⅛   teaspoon ground ginger
⅛   teaspoon ground nutmeg
⅛   teaspoon fine sea salt
2   tablespoons (24 grams) turbinado sugar
24 pecan halves

1. In the bowl of a stand mixer fitted with the paddle attachment, beat butter and granulated sugar at medium speed until creamy, 3 to 4 minutes, stopping to scrape sides of bowl. With mixer on medium-low speed, add pumpkin and vanilla, beating until combined.

2. In a medium bowl, whisk together flour, cinnamon, cloves, ginger, nutmeg, and salt. With mixer on low speed, add flour mixture to butter mixture, beating until combined and dough starts to come together. Turn out dough, and shape into a disk. Wrap tightly in plastic wrap, and refrigerate until firm, about 2 hours.

3. Preheat oven to 350°F (180°C). Line 2 baking sheets with parchment paper.

4. On a lightly floured surface, roll dough to ¼-inch thickness. Using a 2½-inch fluted round cutter dipped in flour, cut dough, rerolling scraps as necessary. Place on prepared pans. Refrigerate for 20 minutes.

5. Sprinkle cookies with turbinado sugar, and press a pecan into center of each cookie.

6. Bake until tops and edges are set, 15 to 16 minutes, rotating pans after 8 minutes of baking. Let cool on pans for 10 minutes. Remove from pans, and let cool completely on wire racks.

Photo by Laura Kasavan

CHOCOLATE HAZELNUT SHORTBREAD COOKIES

Makes about 28

Recipe by Laura Kasavan/*feedfeed*

Dipped in rich chocolate and decked with toasted hazelnuts and gold sprinkles, these shortbread cookies are holiday perfection. A touch of hazelnut liqueur and vanilla add depth of flavor to the hazelnut dough, making these cookies a sophisticated take on shortbread.

1 cup (113 grams) toasted chopped hazelnuts, divided
⅔ cup (133 grams) plus 2 tablespoons (24 grams) granulated sugar, divided
¾ cup (170 grams) unsalted butter, softened
1 tablespoon (15 grams) hazelnut liqueur*
½ teaspoon (2 grams) vanilla extract
⅛ teaspoon fine sea salt
1¾ cups (219 grams) all-purpose flour
8 ounces (225 grams) semisweet chocolate, chopped
Garnish: edible gold sprinkles

1. In the work bowl of a food processor, place ½ cup (56.5 grams) hazelnuts and ⅔ cup (133 grams) sugar; pulse until finely ground.
2. In the bowl of a stand mixer fitted with the paddle attachment, beat butter and hazelnut-sugar at medium speed until creamy, 3 to 4 minutes, stopping to scrape sides of bowl. With mixer on medium-low speed, add hazelnut liqueur, vanilla, and salt, beating until combined. With mixer on low speed, add flour, beating until combined and dough starts to come together. Turn out dough, and shape into a disk. Wrap tightly in plastic wrap, and refrigerate until firm, about 45 minutes.
3. Preheat oven to 350°F (180°C). Line 2 baking sheets with parchment paper.
4. On a lightly floured surface, roll dough to ¼-inch thickness. Using a 2-inch fluted round cutter dipped in flour, cut dough, rerolling scraps as necessary. Place on prepared pans, and sprinkle with remaining 2 tablespoons (24 grams) sugar. Refrigerate for 20 minutes.
5. Bake until lightly golden and tops and edges are set, 14 to 16 minutes, rotating pans after 8 minutes of baking. Let cool on pans for 5 minutes. Remove from pans, and let cool completely on wire racks.
6. Line 2 baking sheets with parchment paper.
7. In the top of a double boiler, melt chocolate over simmering water. Cook, stirring occasionally, until glossy and smooth. One by one, dip half of each cookie in chocolate, and place on prepared pans. Sprinkle with remaining ½ cup (56.5 grams) hazelnuts. Garnish with gold sprinkles, if desired. Refrigerate until chocolate is set, about 20 minutes.

*I used Frangelico.

Photo by Laura Kasavan

BROWNED BUTTER MACADAMIA CRESCENT COOKIES

Makes about 16

Recipe by Laura Kasavan/*feedfeed*

Soft and buttery, these molded crescent cookies are studded with roasted macadamia nuts and drizzled with a luscious browned butter glaze. With notes of spice and vanilla, the rich crescents are perfect for holiday gifting.

½ cup (113 grams) unsalted butter, softened
½ cup (100 grams) granulated sugar
½ teaspoon (2 grams) vanilla extract
¼ teaspoon ground cinnamon
⅛ teaspoon ground ginger
¹⁄₁₆ teaspoon ground nutmeg
1¼ cups (156 grams) all-purpose flour
2 tablespoons (30 grams) 2% reduced-fat milk
½ cup (57 grams) roasted macadamia nuts, finely chopped
Browned Butter Glaze (recipe follows)
Garnish: finely chopped roasted macadamia nuts

1. In the bowl of a stand mixer fitted with the paddle attachment, beat butter and sugar at medium speed until creamy, 3 to 4 minutes, stopping to scrape sides of bowl. With mixer on medium-low speed, add vanilla, cinnamon, ginger, and nutmeg, beating until combined. With mixer on low speed, gradually add flour, beating just until combined. Add milk, and beat until dough starts to come together. Fold in macadamia nuts. Cover and refrigerate until firm, about 2 hours.
2. Line 2 baking sheets with parchment paper.
3. Shape dough into 1-inch balls, and roll each ball into a log. Place logs 2 inches apart on prepared pans, and gently curve ends to form crescents. Refrigerate for 20 minutes.
4. Preheat oven to 350°F (180°C).
5. Bake until lightly golden and tops and edges are set, 12 to 13 minutes, rotating pans after 6 minutes of baking. Let cool on pans for 10 minutes. Remove from pans, and let cool completely on wire racks. Using a small piping bag, drizzle Browned Butter Glaze over cookies. Garnish with macadamia nuts, if desired. Let glaze set before serving.

BROWNED BUTTER GLAZE
Makes about ⅔ cup

1 tablespoon (14 grams) unsalted butter
¾ cup (90 grams) confectioners' sugar, sifted
2 tablespoons (30 grams) 2% reduced-fat milk
¼ teaspoon (1 gram) vanilla extract
¹⁄₁₆ teaspoon fine sea salt
¹⁄₁₆ teaspoon ground nutmeg

1. In a medium saucepan, melt butter over medium heat. Cook until butter turns a medium-brown color and has a nutty aroma, about 5 minutes. Remove from heat, and let cool to room temperature.
2. In a small bowl, whisk together browned butter, confectioners' sugar, milk, vanilla, salt, and nutmeg until smooth.

Photo by Laura Kasavan

ROSE, WHITE CHOCOLATE, AND PISTACHIO WREATH COOKIES

Makes 18 to 20

Recipe by Amy Ho/*feedfeed*

These cookies are light and crisp yet still very buttery. A simple rose water glaze covers the topside of the cookie and is then garnished with dried rose petals, chopped pistachios, and white chocolate.

½ cup (113 grams) unsalted butter, softened
½ cup (60 grams) confectioners' sugar
½ teaspoon (1.5 grams) kosher salt
½ teaspoon (2 grams) vanilla extract
1 cup (125 grams) all-purpose flour
Rose Water Glaze (recipe follows)
Garnish: chopped pistachios, chopped white chocolate, dried rose petals, coarse sanding sugar

1. In the bowl of a stand mixer fitted with the paddle attachment, beat butter at low speed until smooth, 1 to 2 minutes. Add confectioners' sugar, salt, and vanilla, beating until well combined. Scrape sides of bowl, and add flour, beating until combined. Turn out dough, and shape into a disk. Wrap tightly in plastic wrap, and refrigerate for at least 2 hours or up to 5 days.
2. Preheat oven to 350°F (180°C). Line a baking sheet with parchment paper.
3. Using a 2½-inch round cutter, cut dough, and place at least 1 inch apart on prepared pan. Using a 1-inch round cutter, cut centers from cookies.
4. Bake until golden around the edges, about 12 minutes, rotating pan halfway through baking. Let cool on pan for 10 minutes. Remove from pan, and let cool completely on a wire rack. Dip one side of each cookie in Rose Water Glaze, and place on a wire rack. Garnish with pistachios, white chocolate, rose petals, and sanding sugar, if desired. Store in an airtight container for up to 3 days.

ROSE WATER GLAZE
Makes about ½ cup

1 cup (120 grams) confectioners' sugar
2 tablespoons (30 grams) whole milk
½ teaspoon (2 grams) rose water

1. In a shallow bowl, whisk together confectioners' sugar, milk, and rose water until combined. Use immediately.

Photo by Amy Ho

SPECULOOS COOKIES

Makes about 36

Recipe by Amy Ho/*feedfeed*

Gingerbread is the go-to choice for Christmas baking, but I never liked eating the cookies after decorating them. Speculoos is the sweeter, more buttery version of gingerbread— more fun to eat, but just as easy to decorate.

½ cup (113 grams) unsalted butter, softened
½ cup (110 grams) firmly packed brown sugar
¼ cup (50 grams) granulated sugar
2 tablespoons (42 grams) molasses
1 large egg (50 grams), room temperature
1 teaspoon (4 grams) vanilla extract
2¼ cups (281 grams) all-purpose flour
1 tablespoon (6 grams) ground cinnamon
¾ teaspoon (1.5 grams) ground ginger
½ teaspoon (1.5 grams) fine sea salt
½ teaspoon grated fresh nutmeg
⅛ teaspoon ground cloves
Royal Icing (recipe follows)

1. In the bowl of a stand mixer fitted with the paddle attachment, beat butter and sugars at medium speed until fluffy, 3 to 4 minutes, stopping to scrape sides of bowl. Add molasses, egg, and vanilla, beating until combined.
2. In a medium bowl, whisk together flour, cinnamon, ginger, salt, nutmeg, and cloves. With mixer on low speed, gradually add flour mixture to butter mixture, beating until combined. (Dough should be quite tacky at this point.) Divide dough into thirds, and shape into disks. Wrap tightly in plastic wrap, and refrigerate for at least 2 hours.
3. Preheat oven to 375°F (190°C). Line baking sheets with parchment paper.
4. On a lightly floured surface, roll one disk of dough to ⅛-inch thickness. Using desired holiday cutters, cut dough, and place on prepared pans. Freeze while rolling and cutting remaining two disks of dough. (Shape and design of cookies will retain better if frozen before baking.)
5. Bake until golden brown and centers are almost firm, 11 to 13 minutes. Let cool on pans for 5 minutes. Remove from pans, and let cool completely on wire racks. Using

a pastry bag fitted with a piping tip, pipe Royal Icing onto cookies. Let icing harden completely before stacking. Store in an airtight container at room temperature for up to 5 days.

Royal Icing
Makes about 1 cup

2 cups (240 grams) confectioners' sugar
3 tablespoons (45 grams) warm water (105°F/40°C to 110°F/43°C)
1 tablespoon plus ¼ teaspoon (10 grams) meringue powder

1. In a medium bowl, stir together all ingredients until combined. Use immediately.

Note: *The Royal Icing will be quite stiff and thick, allowing you to better control the speed of your piping but requiring quite a bit of force. If you would like a thinner Royal Icing, try adding warm water, 1 teaspoon (5 grams) at a time, until you reach your desired consistency.*

Photo by Amy Ho

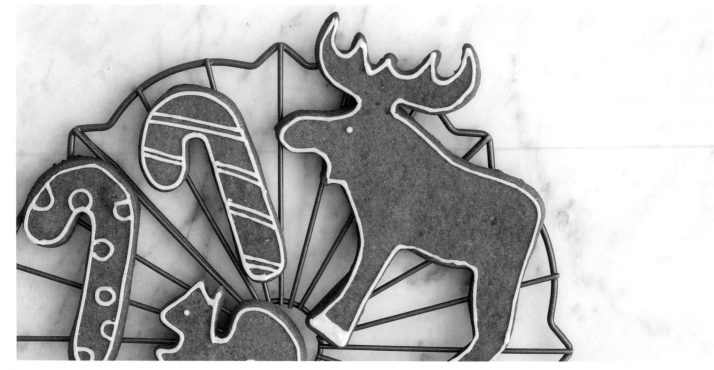

SPICY CHOCOLATE SANDWICH COOKIES WITH HORCHATA BUTTERCREAM

Makes 7 large sandwich cookies

Recipe by Amy Ho/*feedfeed*

Horchata, a sweetened, cinnamon-spiced rice drink, is the sweet secret to the buttercream filling, mellowing out the spicy, chewy chocolate cookie. Roll the cookie dough balls in coarse sanding sugar for an extra sparkly cookie.

¾ cup (170 grams) unsalted butter, softened
1 cup (200 grams) granulated sugar, plus more for rolling
1 large egg (50 grams), room temperature
¼ cup (85 grams) molasses
1¾ cups (219 grams) all-purpose flour
⅓ cup (25 grams) unsweetened cocoa powder
2 teaspoons (10 grams) baking soda
1 teaspoon (2 grams) ground cinnamon
½ teaspoon (1.5 grams) kosher salt
½ teaspoon (1 gram) ground ginger
¼ teaspoon ground red pepper
¼ teaspoon ground cloves
Horchata Buttercream (recipe follows)

1. Preheat oven to 375°F (190°C). Line a baking sheet with parchment paper.
2. In the bowl of a stand mixer fitted with the paddle attachment, beat butter and sugar at medium speed until fluffy, 3 to 4 minutes, stopping to scrape sides of bowl. With mixer on medium-low speed, add egg, beating well. Beat in molasses.
3. In a medium bowl, whisk together flour, cocoa, baking soda, cinnamon, salt, ginger, red pepper, and cloves. With mixer on low speed, gradually add flour mixture to butter mixture, beating until combined.
4. Using a large (¼-cup) spring-loaded scoop, scoop dough into balls. Fill a small bowl with sugar, and roll balls in sugar to coat. Place at least 1 inch apart on prepared pan.
5. Bake until cookies begin to slightly crack on top, 8 to 10 minutes. Let cool on pan for 2 minutes. Remove from pan, and let cool completely on wire racks. Pipe Horchata Buttercream onto flat side of half of cookies. Place remaining cookies, flat side down, on top of filling. Unfilled cookies will keep in an airtight container at room temperature for up to 5 days. Sandwich

cookies will keep in an airtight container at room temperature for up to 3 days.

HORCHATA BUTTERCREAM
Makes about 1 cup

⅓ cup (81 grams) horchata
1½ cups (180 grams) confectioners' sugar
¾ cup (170 grams) unsalted butter, softened
1 teaspoon (2 grams) ground cinnamon
1 teaspoon (4 grams) vanilla extract

1. In a small saucepan, bring horchata to a boil over medium heat. Boil until reduced to 2 tablespoons.
2. In the bowl of a stand mixer fitted with the paddle attachment, beat confectioners' sugar, butter, cinnamon, and vanilla at medium speed until combined. Add 1 tablespoon reduced horchata, beating until creamy. If mixture is too stiff to spread, add remaining 1 tablespoon reduced horchata.

Photo by Amy Ho

VANILLA SHORTBREAD WITH APPLE PIE FILLING

Makes 30 to 35

Recipe by Sarah Brunella/*feedfeed*

With the scents of apples and cinnamon wafting through your whole house, the nice, cozy feeling you get cooking your applesauce will only increase knowing there are some vanilla shortbread cookies in the oven, ready to be filled with it.

2½ cups (313 grams) all-purpose flour, sifted
2 cups (300 grams) white rice flour, sifted
1¼ cups (250 grams) granulated sugar
⅛ teaspoon kosher salt
1¼ cups (284 grams) cold unsalted butter, cubed
2 large eggs (100 grams), room temperature
1 teaspoon (4 grams) vanilla extract
Apple Pie Filling (recipe follows)
Garnish: confectioners' sugar

1. In the bowl of a stand mixer fitted with the paddle attachment, beat flours, granulated sugar, and salt at low speed for 3 to 4 seconds. Add cold butter, beating until mixture is crumbly. Stir in eggs and vanilla. Beat at medium-low speed until a dough starts to form. (Mixture may look like it is too dry, but continue mixing. It will come together and form big chunks.) Turn out dough, and knead a bit by hand to form a smooth dough. Wrap in plastic wrap, and refrigerate until firm, about 2 hours.
2. Preheat oven to 350°F (180°C). Line baking sheets with parchment paper.
3. On a heavily floured surface, roll dough to ¼-inch thickness. Using desired round cutter, cut dough, and place on prepared pans. Refrigerate for 15 minutes.
4. Bake for 10 to 12 minutes. Let cool on pans for 5 minutes. Remove from pans, and let cool completely on wire racks. Spoon about 1 teaspoon Apple Pie Filling onto flat side of half of cookies. Place remaining cookies, flat side down, on top of filling. Press gently to seal. Dust with confectioners' sugar, if desired. Store in an airtight container at room temperature for up to 1 week without Apple Pie Filling or in refrigerator if already filled.

APPLE PIE FILLING
Makes about 1 cup

½ cup (113 grams) unsalted butter, softened
⅓ cup (80 grams) Apple Pie Sauce (recipe follows)
½ cup (60 grams) confectioners' sugar

1. In the bowl of a stand mixer fitted with the whisk attachment, beat butter at medium speed until creamy and almost white in appearance. Add Apple Pie Sauce, beating until combined. Add confectioners' sugar, beating until well combined. (Add more confectioners' sugar to stiffen filling, or a bit of milk to make more spreadable.)

APPLE PIE SAUCE
Makes 2 cups

7 medium (980 grams) Golden Delicious apples, cored, peeled, and sliced
¼ cup (55 grams) firmly packed dark brown sugar
1 tablespoon (15 grams) fresh lemon juice
½ teaspoon (3 grams) vanilla bean paste
1 teaspoon (2 grams) ground cinnamon
⅛ teaspoon ground nutmeg

1. In a slow cooker, place apple slices, brown sugar, lemon juice, and vanilla bean paste. Cover and cook on low for 4 hours. Uncover and cook 2 hours more, checking and stirring once or twice. Add cinnamon and nutmeg, and carefully blend with an immersion blender. Leftover Apple Pie Sauce can be stored in a sterilized jar or an airtight container in refrigerator for up to 1 week.

Photo by Sarah Brunella

SPITZBUBEN (LINZER) COOKIES

Makes 30 to 35

Recipe by Sarah Brunella/*feedfeed*

There's no other cookie that looks more festive than these jam-packed, classic Spitzbuben. The famous buttery Austrian Linzer sandwiches literally melt in your mouth. They make a perfect cookie for the big holiday swap.

5½ cups (688 grams) all-purpose flour, sifted
1 cup (200 grams) granulated sugar
¼ teaspoon kosher salt
1½ cups (340 grams) cold unsalted butter, cubed
1 large egg (50 grams)
1 cup (320 grams) raspberry jam
Garnish: confectioners' sugar

1. In the bowl of a stand mixer fitted with the paddle attachment, beat flour, granulated sugar, and salt at low speed for 3 to 4 seconds. Add cold butter, beating until mixture is crumbly. Stir in egg. Beat at medium-low speed until a dough starts to form. (Mixture may look like it is too dry, but continue mixing. It will come together and form big chunks. If not, add 1 teaspoon [5 grams] cold water to help.) Turn out dough, and knead a bit by hand to form a smooth dough. Wrap in plastic wrap, and refrigerate until firm, about 1 hour.
2. Preheat oven to 350°F (180°C). Line baking sheets with parchment paper.
3. On a heavily floured surface, roll dough to ¼-inch thickness. Using desired round cutter, cut dough, and place on prepared pans. Using smaller patterned cutters, cut centers from half of cookies.

4. Bake for 10 to 12 minutes (they should stay pale and not brown). Let cool on pans for 5 minutes. Remove from pans, and let cool on wire racks. Before cookies are completely cool, drop about 1 teaspoon raspberry jam onto flat side of all solid cookies. Place cookies with cutouts, flat side down, on top of jam. Press gently to seal. Let cool completely. Dust with confectioners' sugar, if desired. Store in an airtight container for up to 1 week.

Photo by Sarah Brunella

FLOURLESS PEANUT BUTTER COOKIES WITH PEANUT BUTTER CREAM CHEESE FILLING

Makes 12 sandwich cookies

Recipe by Sarah Brunella/*feedfeed*

I discovered peanut butter during my honeymoon six years ago and have loved it ever since. These cookies are quick and easy to make. Packed with the classic sweet and savory peanut butter flavor, they're sure to please everyone.

1   cup (256 grams) creamy peanut butter
¾   cup (150 grams) granulated sugar
¼   cup (20 grams) old-fashioned oats
1   large egg (50 grams)
1   teaspoon (5 grams) baking soda or
     baking powder
1   teaspoon (4 grams) vanilla extract
⅛   teaspoon kosher salt
1   tablespoon (7 grams) roughly chopped
     toasted salted peanuts
1   tablespoon (11 grams) semisweet
     chocolate morsels
Peanut Butter Cream Cheese Filling (recipe
follows)

1. Preheat oven to 350°F (180°C). Line baking sheets with parchment paper.
2. In the bowl of a stand mixer fitted with the paddle attachment, beat peanut butter, sugar, oats, egg, baking soda, vanilla, and salt at medium speed until combined. Add peanuts and chocolate morsels, stirring gently with a spatula or a wooden spoon. Using a small (2-teaspoon) spring-loaded scoop, scoop dough, and shape into balls. Place dough 2 inches apart on prepared pans.
3. Bake for about 13 minutes. Let cool completely. Pipe Peanut Butter Cream Cheese Filling onto flat side of half of cookies. Place remaining cookies, flat side down, on top of filling. Refrigerate until ready to serve. Let stand at room temperature for 30 minutes before serving. Refrigerate in an airtight container for up to 1 week.

PEANUT BUTTER CREAM CHEESE FILLING
Makes 1 cup

½   cup (112 grams) cream cheese,
     softened
¼   cup (64 grams) creamy peanut butter
1   teaspoon (4 grams) vanilla extract
½   cup (60 grams) confectioners' sugar

1. In the bowl of a stand mixer fitted with the whisk attachment, beat cream cheese, peanut butter, and vanilla at low speed until creamy. Add confectioners' sugar, beating until smooth. Use immediately.

Photo by Sarah Brunella

LEMON SHORTBREAD COOKIES WITH LEMON CURD FILLING

Makes about 30

Recipe by Sarah Brunella/*feedfeed*

These cookies are for the true lemon lover. The sweet and zingy flavor of lemon cookies is combined with the tangy, silky consistency of lemon curd. To die for.

3¼ cups (406 grams) all-purpose flour, sifted
⅔ cup (133 grams) granulated sugar
⅛ teaspoon kosher salt
¾ cup plus 2 tablespoons (198 grams) cold unsalted butter, cubed
1 large egg (50 grams), room temperature
1 large egg yolk (19 grams), room temperature
1 teaspoon (2 grams) lemon zest
½ teaspoon (2 grams) lemon extract
Lemon Curd (recipe follows)
Garnish: confectioners' sugar

1. In the bowl of a stand mixer fitted with the paddle attachment, beat flour, granulated sugar, and salt at low speed for 3 to 4 seconds. Add cold butter, beating until mixture is crumbly. Stir in egg, egg yolk, lemon zest, and lemon extract. Beat at medium-low speed until a dough starts to form. Turn out dough, and wrap in plastic wrap. Refrigerate until firm, about 1 hour.
2. Preheat oven to 350°F (180°C). Line baking sheets with parchment paper.
3. On a heavily floured surface, roll dough to ¼-inch thickness. Using desired fluted round cutter, cut dough, and place on prepared pans. Using smaller patterned cutters, cut centers from half of cookies. (I sometimes like to use engraved rolling pins to print pattern on my cookies as well.)
4. Bake until lightly golden at the edges, about 10 minutes. Let cool on pans for 5 minutes. Remove from pans, and let cool on wire racks. Before cookies are completely cool, drop about 1 teaspoon Lemon Curd onto flat side of all solid cookies. Place cookies with cutouts, flat side down, on top of curd. Press gently to seal. Let cool

completely. Dust with confectioners' sugar, if desired. Store in an airtight container for up to 1 week.

PRO TIP

When chilling the dough, instead of using plastic wrap, place it in a resealable plastic bag. When ready to bake, take out of the refrigerator one bag at a time, leaving the other one to chill until the very last moment, which is a great idea when working with shortbread. You can make the dough in advance and store it in the freezer up to 1 month.

LEMON CURD

Makes 1 cup

⅓ cup (67 grams) granulated sugar
1 teaspoon (2 grams) lemon zest
¼ cup (60 grams) fresh lemon juice
1 large egg (50 grams)
2 large egg yolks (37 grams)
3 tablespoons (42 grams) cold unsalted butter, cubed

1. In the top of a double boiler, whisk together sugar, lemon zest and juice, egg, and egg yolks. Cook over simmering water, whisking constantly, until creamy and thick enough to coat the back of a spoon. Remove from heat. Add cold butter, whisking until combined. You should have a thick curd with a few lumps in it.
2. Pass curd through a fine-mesh sieve into a bowl; let cool completely. Spoon curd into sterilized jars, and seal. Refrigerate until ready to use.

PRO TIP

Leftover Lemon Curd is great on toast or in muffins, and you can even use it on a pavlova, whisked with some cream and topped with fresh fruit.

Photo by Sarah Brunella

DOUBLE CHOCOLATE PEPPERMINT SUGAR COOKIES

Makes about 36

Recipe by Mary Ann Dwyer/*feedfeed*

Rich with double the chocolate and a festive little sprinkle of crushed candy canes, these Double Chocolate Peppermint Sugar Cookies are the perfect way to ring in the holidays!

1   cup (227 grams) unsalted butter, softened
1½ cups (300 grams) granulated sugar, plus more for rolling
2   large eggs (100 grams), room temperature
1   teaspoon (4 grams) peppermint extract
2   cups (250 grams) all-purpose flour
⅔   cup (50 grams) unsweetened cocoa powder
1   teaspoon (5 grams) baking soda
½   teaspoon (1.5 grams) kosher salt
Garnish: crushed candy canes
Melted Chocolate (recipe follows)

1. In the bowl of a stand mixer fitted with the paddle attachment, beat butter and sugar at medium speed until fluffy, 3 to 4 minutes, stopping to scrape sides of bowl. Add eggs, one at a time, beating well after each addition. Beat in peppermint extract.
2. In a medium bowl, sift together flour, cocoa, baking soda, and salt. With mixer on low speed, gradually add flour mixture to butter mixture, beating until combined. Wrap dough in plastic wrap, and refrigerate for 30 minutes.
3. Preheat oven to 350°F (180°C). Line a large baking sheet with parchment paper.
4. Scoop dough into 1-tablespoon balls, and roll in sugar to coat. Place 2 inches apart on prepared pan.
5. Bake until slightly cracked, about 8 minutes. Sprinkle with crushed candy canes, if desired. Bake 2 minutes more. Let cool on pan for 5 minutes. Remove from pan, and let cool completely on wire racks.
6. Dip each cookie in Melted Chocolate, and sprinkle with additional crushed candy canes, if desired. Let set on wax paper or parchment paper before serving.

MELTED CHOCOLATE
Makes about 1 cup

1   cup (170 grams) 46% cacao semisweet chocolate morsels
1   tablespoon (14 grams) all-vegetable shortening

1. In a microwave-safe bowl, combine chocolate morsels and shortening. Microwave on high in 30-second intervals, stirring between each, until melted and smooth.

Photo by Mary Ann Dwyer

GINGERBREAD THUMBPRINT COOKIES WITH CRANBERRY ORANGE JAM

Makes 30 to 40

Recipe by Mary Ann Dwyer/*feedfeed*

It wouldn't be the holidays without the warm, cozy taste of gingerbread. These cookies made with homemade jam are just what Santa's looking for.

10 tablespoons (140 grams) unsalted butter, softened
½ cup (100 grams) granulated sugar
½ cup (110 grams) firmly packed light brown sugar
1 large egg (50 grams)
¼ cup (85 grams) unsulphured molasses
2½ cups (313 grams) all-purpose flour
1 teaspoon (2 grams) ground cinnamon
½ teaspoon (1 gram) ground ginger
½ teaspoon (1.5 grams) kosher salt
¼ teaspoon ground allspice
⅛ teaspoon ground nutmeg
½ cup (100 grams) pure cane sugar
Cranberry Orange Jam (recipe follows)

1. In the bowl of a stand mixer fitted with the paddle attachment, beat butter, granulated sugar, and brown sugar at medium speed until fluffy, 3 to 4 minutes, stopping to scrape sides of bowl. Beat in egg and molasses.
2. In a medium bowl, whisk together flour, cinnamon, ginger, salt, allspice, and nutmeg. Stir flour mixture into butter mixture just until combined. Wrap dough in plastic wrap, and refrigerate for at least 5 hours or overnight.
3. Preheat oven to 350°F (180°C). Line a large baking sheet with parchment paper.
4. Shape dough into 1-inch balls. Place cane sugar in a small bowl. Roll balls in cane sugar until well coated, and place 2 inches apart on prepared pan. Using your thumb or the back of a spoon, gently make an indentation in center of each ball. Fill centers with about ½ teaspoon (3.5 grams) Cranberry Orange Jam. Reserve remaining jam for another use.
5. Bake until edges are firm, 10 to 11 minutes. Let cool on pan for 5 minutes. Remove from pan, and let cool completely on a wire rack. Store in an airtight container for up to 2 days. Dough balls can be frozen on a baking sheet until firm, and then placed in plastic freezer bags until you're ready to finish baking.

CRANBERRY ORANGE JAM
Makes about 2 cups

1 (12-ounce) package (340 grams) fresh or frozen cranberries
1¼ cups (250 grams) granulated sugar
1½ teaspoons (3 grams) freshly grated orange zest
½ cup (120 grams) fresh orange juice
¼ cup (60 grams) water
⅛ teaspoon ground nutmeg

1. In a large heavy-bottomed saucepan, bring all ingredients to a boil over medium-high heat, stirring occasionally. Reduce heat, and simmer, stirring frequently, until mixture has thickened and coats the back of spoon and most of cranberries have popped, 10 to 15 minutes. Taste for sweetness, adding more sugar, if desired. Remove from heat. Press jam through a fine-mesh sieve into a bowl, discarding solids. Cover and refrigerate for up to 2 weeks. Jam will thicken as it cools.

Photo by Mary Ann Dwyer

MEXICAN CHOCOLATE SANDWICH COOKIES WITH DULCE DE LECHE FILLING

Makes 12 large sandwich cookies

Recipe by Mary Ann Dwyer/*feedfeed*

These Mexican Chocolate Sandwich Cookies are a decadent little holiday treat! Dark chocolate cookies with just the right amount of spice are sandwiched with indulgent dulce de leche.

½ cup (113 grams) unsalted butter, softened
1½ cups (300 grams) granulated sugar, plus more for sprinkling
2 large eggs (100 grams), room temperature
1 teaspoon (4 grams) vanilla extract
1 cup (125 grams) all-purpose flour
½ cup (43 grams) unsweetened Dutch process cocoa powder
½ teaspoon (1.5 grams) kosher salt
½ teaspoon (2.5 grams) baking soda
½ teaspoon (1 gram) ground cinnamon
⅛ teaspoon ground red pepper
1 (13.4-ounce) can (380 grams) dulce de leche

1. Preheat oven to 325°F (170°C). Line a large baking sheet with parchment paper.
2. In the bowl of a stand mixer fitted with the paddle attachment, beat butter and sugar at medium speed until fluffy, 3 to 4 minutes, stopping to scrape sides of bowl. Add eggs, one at a time, beating well after each addition. Beat in vanilla.
3. In a medium bowl, whisk together flour, cocoa, salt, baking soda, cinnamon, and red pepper. With mixer on low speed, gradually add flour mixture to butter mixture, beating until combined. Using a medium (1½-tablespoon) spring-loaded scoop, drop dough 2 inches apart on prepared pan. Sprinkle with additional sugar.
4. Bake for 13 to 15 minutes. Cookies should be on the soft side. Let cool on pan for 5 minutes. Remove from pan, and let cool completely on wire racks. Spread a heaping tablespoon of dulce de leche onto flat side of half of cookies. Place remaining cookies, flat side down, on top of filling.

Photo by Mary Ann Dwyer

SLICE 'N' BAKE VANILLA BEAN SHORTBREAD SANDWICH COOKIES WITH CHAI BUTTERCREAM FROSTING

Makes about 30 sandwich cookies

Recipe by Mary Ann Dwyer/*feedfeed*

Kick the classic Vanilla Bean Shortbread Cookie up a notch with some warm Chai Buttercream Frosting. These Slice 'n' Bake cookies are perfect for all your guests this holiday season.

1   cup (227 grams) unsalted butter, softened
⅔   cup (133 grams) granulated sugar
1   vanilla bean, split lengthwise, seeds scraped and reserved
2¼ cups (281 grams) all-purpose flour
2   tablespoons (16 grams) cornstarch
½   teaspoon (1.5 grams) sea salt
1   cup (200 grams) turbinado sugar
Chai Buttercream Frosting (recipe follows)

1. In the bowl of a stand mixer fitted with the paddle attachment, beat butter, granulated sugar, and vanilla bean seeds at medium speed until creamy, 3 to 4 minutes, stopping to scrape sides of bowl.

2. In a medium bowl, whisk together flour, cornstarch, and salt. With mixer on low speed, gradually add flour mixture to butter mixture, beating until combined. Turn out dough onto a lightly floured surface, and divide in half. Shape each half into a 12-inch-long log, about 1 inch thick. Roll logs in turbinado sugar to coat. Wrap in plastic wrap, and refrigerate for at least 3 hours or overnight.

3. Preheat oven to 325°F (170°C). Line a large baking sheet with parchment paper.

4. Using a sharp knife, cut logs into ¼-inch-thick slices. Place 1 inch apart on prepared pan.

5. Bake until golden brown around the edges and bottom, 18 to 20 minutes. Let cool on pan for 5 minutes. Remove from pan, and let cool completely on a wire rack. Using a pastry bag fitted with a large round tip (1A), pipe Chai Buttercream Frosting onto flat side of half of cookies. Place remaining cookies, flat side down, on top of frosting. Store in an airtight container at room temperature for up to 3 days.

Note: *The vanilla bean shortbread logs can be frozen for up to 2 months. Wrap logs in two layers of plastic wrap, and place in a heavy-duty resealable bag. When you're ready to bake, pop the dough out of the freezer, and let thaw in refrigerator for about 1 hour before slicing and baking.*

CHAI BUTTERCREAM FROSTING
Makes about 1¼ cups

½   cup (113 grams) unsalted butter, softened
2   cups (240 grams) confectioners' sugar, sifted
¼   teaspoon ground cinnamon
¼   teaspoon ground cardamom
⅛   teaspoon ground ginger
⅛   teaspoon ground cloves
⅛   teaspoon ground allspice
⅛   teaspoon ground nutmeg
⅛   teaspoon kosher salt
2   tablespoons (30 grams) whole milk

1. In the bowl of a stand mixer fitted with the paddle attachment, beat butter at medium speed until smooth, 3 to 5 minutes.

2. In a medium bowl, whisk together confectioners' sugar, cinnamon, cardamom, ginger, cloves, allspice, nutmeg, and salt. With mixer on low speed, gradually add sugar mixture to butter, beating just until combined. Increase mixer speed to medium, and beat until well combined. Add milk, 1 tablespoon (15 grams) at a time, until a spreadable consistency is reached (you may not use all of the milk).

Photo by Mary Ann Dwyer

GOLD LEAF BOURBON CARAMEL MILLIONAIRE BITES

Makes 28

Recipe by Rebecca Firth/*feedfeed*

Super rich, lots of bling. A very LA cookie. If you're looking for an easy cookie that dazzles, look no further. A thick, not-too-sweet cookie crust is coated in Bourbon-Vanilla Caramel, then ganache, and later topped with a single edible gold leaf flake. Best part? They are actually better when made ahead of time.

2   cups (250 grams) all-purpose flour
⅓   cup (67 grams) granulated sugar
¼   cup (32 grams) cornstarch
1   teaspoon (3 grams) sea salt
1¼ cups (284 grams) cold unsalted butter, cubed
    Bourbon-Vanilla Caramel (recipe follows)
7   ounces (200 grams) 60% to 70% cacao dark chocolate, coarsely chopped
½   cup (120 grams) heavy whipping cream, warmed
    Garnish: edible gold leaf

1. Preheat oven to 350°F (180°C). Line an 11x8-inch baking dish with parchment paper, letting excess extend over sides of pan.
2. In the bowl of a stand mixer fitted with the paddle attachment, beat flour, sugar, cornstarch, and salt at low speed for 1 minute. Add cold butter, and beat until a ball starts to form, 3 to 4 minutes. Press dough into bottom of prepared pan.
3. Bake until sides are lightly bronzed, about 35 minutes. Let cool completely. Pour three-fourths of Bourbon-Vanilla Caramel over prepared crust. Reserve remaining Bourbon-Vanilla Caramel for another use. Wrap pan in plastic wrap, and refrigerate for at least 12 hours or up to 24 hours.

4. Line a baking sheet with parchment paper; top with a wire rack.
5. Using excess parchment as handles, remove cookie from pan. Using a sharp knife, cut ½ inch off each side so that you have a nice 90-degree edge all around crust. Cut into 1-inch square cookie bites, cleaning your knife between cuts to get the cleanest cut possible. Place cookies on prepared rack.
6. Place chopped chocolate in a heatproof bowl; pour warmed cream over top. Stir until chocolate is completely melted and cool to the touch. Spoon cooled chocolate over cookie bites, covering tops completely and allowing little drips to go down sides. If your ganache is too thick, it might not properly cover the edges of the bites. For a thinner ganache, add more cream, 1 tablespoon (15 grams) at a time, until desired consistency is reached. Let set for at least 1 hour.
7. Using tweezers, grab little bits of gold leaf, and place in center of each cookie, if desired. Serve immediately, or store in an airtight container at room temperature for up to 3 days.

BOURBON-VANILLA CARAMEL
Makes about 1 cup

¾   cup (170 grams) unsalted butter
¾   cup (165 grams) firmly packed light brown sugar
½   cup (120 grams) heavy whipping cream
3   tablespoons (45 grams) good-quality bourbon
½   vanilla bean, split lengthwise, seeds scraped and reserved, or 1 teaspoon (4 grams) pure vanilla extract
½   teaspoon (1.5 grams) sea salt

1. In a medium heavy-bottomed saucepan, heat butter and brown sugar over medium heat. Cook, whisking constantly, until sugar is melted and mixture is thoroughly combined with no butter visible. Add cream; increase heat to medium-high, and bring to a boil. Reduce heat to medium, and simmer for 8 minutes, whisking frequently. Add bourbon, vanilla, and sea salt; cook for 2 minutes. Remove from heat, and let cool completely. Caramel will continue to thicken as it cools. Refrigerate until ready to use.

Photo by Matt Armendariz

MINT CHOCOLATE BISCUIT SANDWICH COOKIES

Makes about 18 sandwich cookies

Recipe by Amanda Frederickson/*feedfeed*

Growing up, my favorite cookie was the mint Milano. I couldn't get enough of that minty, chocolaty filling and those perfectly crisp cookies. Here is my version of that classic cookie. Traditional recipes call for the cookies to be piped out, but in order to make the cookies more uniform, I developed a dough that could be rolled out and stamped with a cookie cutter.

¾   cup (170 grams) unsalted butter, softened
¾   cup (90 grams) confectioners' sugar
½   cup (100 grams) granulated sugar
1   large egg (50 grams)
2   tablespoons (30 grams) whole milk
1   teaspoon (4 grams) vanilla extract
2¾   cups (344 grams) all-purpose flour
½   teaspoon (1.5 grams) kosher salt
16   ounces (455 grams) semisweet chocolate morsels, divided
2   tablespoons (30 grams) heavy whipping cream
½   teaspoon (2 grams) peppermint extract, divided
4   candy canes, crushed

1. In the bowl of a stand mixer fitted with the paddle attachment, beat butter and sugars at medium speed until fluffy, 3 to 4 minutes, stopping to scrape sides of bowl. Add egg, beating well.
2. In a small bowl, stir together milk and vanilla. Add milk mixture to butter mixture, beating until combined. In a medium bowl, whisk together flour and salt. With mixer on low speed, gradually add flour mixture to butter mixture, beating just until combined. Turn out dough onto a work surface, and divide in half. Wrap each half in plastic wrap, and refrigerate for at least 4 hours.
3. Preheat oven to 325°F (170°C). Line baking sheets with parchment paper.
4. On a lightly floured surface, roll dough to ⅛-inch thickness. Using a 3x2-inch oval cutter, cut dough, rerolling scraps as necessary. Place on prepared pans.
5. Bake until edges are lightly browned, 12 to 15 minutes, rotating pans halfway through baking. Let cool completely on a wire rack.
6. In a medium microwave-safe bowl, combine 8 ounces (227 grams) chocolate morsels and 2 tablespoons cream (30 grams). Microwave on high in 30-second intervals, stirring between each, until melted and smooth. Stir in ¼ teaspoon (1 gram) peppermint extract until smooth. Spread about 1 tablespoon melted chocolate onto flat side of half of cookies. Place remaining cookies, flat side down, on top of chocolate.
7. In a medium microwave-safe bowl, microwave remaining 8 ounces (227 grams) chocolate morsels on high in 30-second intervals, stirring between each, until melted and smooth. Stir in remaining ¼ teaspoon (1 gram) peppermint extract. Gently dip half of cookies into melted chocolate. Place on a parchment paper-lined baking sheet. Sprinkle with crushed candy canes. Let cool completely. Cover and refrigerate for up to 3 days.

Photo by Matt Armendariz

SPICED PINEAPPLE LINZER COOKIES

Makes 18

Recipe by Christine Carlson/*feedfeed*

No holiday season passed without a batch of my grandma's fragrant mini pineapple tarts. Inspired by her classic recipe, these uniquely spiced Linzer cookies are flavored with earthy sage, spicy ginger, and warm toasted coconut. These bright and buttery cookies will have you dreaming of sunny afternoons no matter how distant summer feels.

1	cup (227 grams) unsalted butter, softened
⅓	cup (67 grams) granulated sugar
⅓	cup (73 grams) firmly packed light brown sugar
1	large egg (50 grams)
1	(5-inch) vanilla bean (3 grams), split lengthwise, seeds scraped and reserved
1	teaspoon (2 grams) lemon zest
1⅔	cups (208 grams) all-purpose flour
1¼	cups (120 grams) almond flour
½	teaspoon (1.5 grams) kosher salt

Spiced Pineapple Filling (recipe follows)
Toasted Coconut Sugar (recipe follows)
Garnish: Candied Sage Leaves (recipe follows)

1. In the bowl of a stand mixer fitted with the paddle attachment, beat butter and sugars at medium speed until creamy, 3 to 4 minutes, stopping to scrape sides of bowl. Add egg, vanilla bean seeds, and zest, beating for 1 minute.
2. In a medium bowl, stir together flours and salt with a fork. With mixer on low speed, gradually add flour mixture to butter mixture, beating until combined. Divide dough in half, and wrap in plastic wrap. Refrigerate for at least 2 hours or overnight.
3. Preheat oven to 325°F (170°C).
4. Place a sheet of parchment paper on a work surface, and lightly dust with flour. (Because the dough is fragile and hard to handle, it is best to roll it directly on the parchment paper it will bake on rather than

trying to transfer it.) Place half of dough on floured surface, and sprinkle top with more flour. Cover with a second sheet of parchment paper. Carefully roll dough to ⅛-inch thickness. Remove top piece of parchment. Repeat with remaining dough.
5. Using a 2-inch square cutter, cut dough, rerolling scraps only once. Using a 1-inch square cutter, cut centers from half of cookies. Transfer cookies, on parchment, to baking sheets.
6. Bake until set, 13 to 15 minutes. (Be careful not to overbake, or cookies will brown and come out crispy.) Let cool completely on pans. Spread about 1 teaspoon Spiced Pineapple Filling on flat side of all solid cookies. Dust cookies with cutouts with Toasted Coconut Sugar. Place cookies with cutouts, flat side down, on top of filling. Garnish with Candied Sage Leaves, if desired. Store in an airtight container for up to 5 days.

SPICED PINEAPPLE FILLING
Makes about 2 cups

2	cups (400 grams) diced fresh pineapple
1	cup (200 grams) canned pineapple chunks
1	cup (240 grams) pineapple juice
¾	cup (150 grams) granulated sugar
¼	teaspoon lemon zest
2	tablespoons (30 grams) fresh lemon juice
1	tablespoon (2 grams) minced fresh sage leaves
1½	teaspoons (1 gram) grated fresh ginger
1½	teaspoons (3 grams) ground cinnamon
1	teaspoon (4 grams) vanilla extract
3	tablespoons (45 grams) water
2	teaspoons (6 grams) cornstarch

1. In the container of a blender, process fresh pineapple, canned pineapple, and pineapple juice until only small chunks remain.
2. In a medium saucepan, combine pineapple mixture, sugar, lemon zest and juice, sage, ginger, cinnamon, and vanilla. Simmer over medium-low heat, stirring

frequently, until thickened and reduced, 30 to 35 minutes.
3. In a small bowl, stir together 3 tablespoons (45 grams) water and cornstarch. Add cornstarch mixture to pineapple mixture, and simmer until filling has thickened, 1 to 2 minutes. Let cool completely before using. Spiced Pineapple Filling will keep in refrigerator for up to 5 days.

TOASTED COCONUT SUGAR
Makes about 2 cups

1	cup (200 grams) granulated sugar
1	cup (84 grams) unsweetened flaked coconut, toasted
1	tablespoon (8 grams) cornstarch

1. In the container of a blender, combine all ingredients; blend until powdered, 1 to 2 minutes, stopping to scrape sides of bowl. Store in an airtight container for up to 2 weeks.

CANDIED SAGE LEAVES
Makes 18

1	cup (200 grams) granulated sugar, divided
¾	cup (180 grams) water
18	small fresh sage leaves

1. In a small saucepan, heat ¾ cup (150 grams) sugar and ¾ cup (180 grams) water over low heat. Bring to a gentle simmer.
2. Pour remaining ¼ cup (50 grams) sugar onto a small plate. Lightly oil a wire rack.
3. Using tongs or chopsticks, carefully dip sage leaves, 2 to 3 at a time, into melted sugar mixture for about 1 minute. Dip each leaf in sugar on plate, coating both sides. Let dry on prepared rack for at least 4 hours or overnight.

Photo by Matt Armendariz

CRANBERRY ORANGE COOKIES

Makes 18 to 22

Recipe by Rachel Conners/*feedfeed*

These soft, chewy cookies are packed with some of the best winter flavors: cranberries, orange, and pecans. The cranberries and orange add hints of bright, tart flavor to the cookies, and the toasted pecans add the most delicious crunch.

3 tablespoons (45 grams) cold water
1 tablespoon (6 grams) ground flaxseed
¾ cup (114 grams) coconut sugar
½ cup (112 grams) coconut oil
2 tablespoons (12 grams) orange zest
   (from 1 large orange)
1 teaspoon (4 grams) vanilla extract
2½ cups (240 grams) blanched almond
   flour
½ teaspoon (2.5 grams) baking soda
½ teaspoon (1.5 grams) kosher salt
½ teaspoon (1 gram) ground cinnamon
½ cup (64 grams) dried cranberries
½ cup (57 grams) chopped pecans, toasted
Garnish: flaky sea salt

1. In a small bowl, whisk together 3 tablespoons (45 grams) cold water and flaxseed; let stand for 5 minutes.
2. In the bowl of a stand mixer fitted with the paddle attachment, beat coconut sugar and coconut oil at medium speed until well combined, 3 to 4 minutes. With mixer on low speed, add flaxseed mixture, zest, and vanilla. Increase mixer speed to medium, and beat until combined.
3. In a medium bowl, whisk together flour, baking soda, salt, and cinnamon. With mixer on low speed, gradually add flour mixture to sugar mixture, beating until combined. Fold in cranberries and pecans. Cover with plastic wrap, and refrigerate for at least 1 hour. Dough can be prepared up to 48 hours in advance.
4. Preheat oven to 350°F (180°C). Line a baking sheet with parchment paper.
5. Using a medium (1½-tablespoon) spring-loaded scoop, scoop dough, and place 2 inches apart on prepared pan. Press down tops slightly. Sprinkle with sea salt, if desired.
6. Bake until just beginning to turn golden brown around the edges, about 10 minutes. Let cool on pan for 5 minutes. Remove from pan, and let cool completely on wire racks. Store in an airtight container at room temperature.

Photo by Rachel Conners

DOUBLE CHOCOLATE MACAROONS

Makes 20

Recipe by Rachel Conners/*feedfeed*

These Double Chocolate Macaroons are some serious chocolate goodness. When I first took a bite of one, I was astonished at the chocolaty flavor that came through. They remind me of a fudge brownie crossed with a classic coconut macaroon. These are for the chocolate lovers!

1¾	cups (147 grams) unsweetened flaked coconut	
¼	cup (24 grams) almond flour	
¼	cup (21 grams) Dutch process cocoa powder	
½	teaspoon (1.5 grams) kosher salt	
½	cup (170 grams) pure maple syrup	
¼	cup (57 grams) coconut butter, melted	
1	ounce (30 grams) unsweetened dairy-free chocolate, melted and slightly cooled	
1	teaspoon (4 grams) vanilla extract	
3	ounces (86 grams) dairy-free dark chocolate	
1	teaspoon (5 grams) coconut oil	

Garnish: flaky sea salt

1. Preheat oven to 275°F (140°C). Line a baking sheet with parchment paper.
2. In a large bowl, stir together coconut, flour, cocoa, and salt. In a medium bowl, whisk together maple syrup, melted coconut butter, melted chocolate, and vanilla. Pour syrup mixture over coconut mixture, and stir until well combined. Using a medium (1½-tablespoon) spring-loaded scoop, scoop heaping balls, and place about 1 inch apart on prepared pan.
3. Bake for 15 minutes. Rotate pan, and bake until dry to the touch, 7 to 10 minutes more. Let cool on pan for 5 minutes. Remove from pan, and let cool completely on wire racks.
4. In a microwave-safe bowl, combine dark chocolate and coconut oil. Microwave on high in 30-second intervals, stirring between each, until melted and smooth. Dip each macaroon in melted chocolate to coat bottom, letting excess drip off. Place on a sheet of parchment paper. If desired, place excess chocolate in a resealable plastic bag, snip a corner, and drizzle over macaroons. Sprinkle with sea salt, if desired. Refrigerate until chocolate is set, about 30 minutes. Store at room temperature or refrigerate in an airtight container.

Photo by Rachel Conners

PLACE CARD COOKIES

Makes 36

Recipe by Amber Spiegel/*feedfeed*

Gingerbread Cookie Dough (recipe below)
Vanilla Royal Icing (recipe follows)
Gold pearl dust
Few drops alcohol or vanilla, lemon, or
   almond extract

1. Preheat oven to 350°F (180°C). Line baking sheets with parchment paper.
2. Using a 4-inch plaque-shaped cutter and a 1-inch triangle cutter, cut Gingerbread Cookie Dough, rerolling scraps as necessary. Place on prepared pans. Freeze until firm, about 15 minutes.
3. Bake for 10 to 12 minutes. Let cool on pans for 5 minutes. Remove from pans, and let cool completely on wire racks. Trim bottom of plaque-shaped cookies to form a straight edge.
4. Using a 12-inch pastry bag fitted with a #3 piping tip, ice cookies with flood consistency Vanilla Royal Icing. Let dry completely, about 6 hours.
5. Using a 12-inch pastry bag fitted with a #1 piping tip, pipe a filigree design around edge of plaque-shaped cookies with white soft peak Vanilla Royal Icing. Let dry completely, about 30 minutes.
6. In a small dish, stir together gold pearl dust and a few drops alcohol or extract. Paint names using a fine-tip brush.
7. Use a small amount of soft peak icing to attach triangle cookies to each plaque cookie so that it stands upright. Store in an airtight container at room temperature for up to 1 week.

Photo by Amber Spiegel

GINGERBREAD COOKIE DOUGH
Makes dough for about 36 cookies

Gingerbread cookies baking in the oven will fill your home with the delicious aroma of the holidays. Soft and chewy, these cookies are perfectly paired with the crispy texture of the Vanilla Royal Icing.

1   cup (227 grams) unsalted butter, softened
1   cup (200 grams) granulated sugar
1   cup (336 grams) molasses
2   large eggs (100 grams), room temperature
5   cups (625 grams) all-purpose flour
2   teaspoons (4 grams) ground ginger
1   teaspoon (2 grams) ground cinnamon
1   teaspoon (3 grams) kosher salt
½   teaspoon (2.5 grams) baking powder
½   teaspoon (1 gram) ground allspice
½   teaspoon (1 gram) ground cloves
½   teaspoon (1 gram) ground nutmeg

1. In the bowl of a stand mixer fitted with the paddle attachment, beat butter and sugar at medium speed until creamy, 3 to 4 minutes, stopping to scrape sides of bowl. Reduce mixer speed to low. Add molasses, beating until well combined. Increase mixer speed to medium-low. Add eggs, one at time, beating well after each addition.
2. In a large bowl, sift together flour, ginger, cinnamon, salt, baking powder, allspice, cloves, and nutmeg. With mixer on low speed, gradually add flour mixture to butter mixture, beating until combined. If dough is very sticky and difficult to handle, add more flour, 2 tablespoons (16 grams) at a time, until it stiffens up.
3. Divide dough in half, and shape into disks. Wrap tightly in plastic wrap, and refrigerate for at least 1 hour.
4. Let dough stand at room temperature until slightly softened, 15 to 20 minutes. On a lightly floured sheet of parchment or wax paper, roll dough to ³⁄₁₆-inch thickness. Place dough on baking sheets, and refrigerate for 30 minutes.

VANILLA ROYAL ICING
Makes 4½ cups

7½   cups (900 grams) confectioners' sugar
½   cup plus 2 tablespoons (104 grams) meringue powder
⅛   teaspoon kosher salt
¾   cup (180 grams) water, plus more for thinning
2   teaspoons (8 grams) vanilla extract

1. In the bowl of a stand mixer fitted with the paddle attachment, beat confectioners' sugar, meringue powder, and salt at low speed until combined. Add ¾ cup (180 grams) water and vanilla, beating until combined. Scrape sides of bowl, and increase mixer speed to medium-low. Beat until icing is light in color and holds a stiff peak, 3 to 5 minutes. Use icing as is, or add more water to thin icing to soft peaks or flood consistency. Refrigerate in an airtight container for up to 2 weeks.

Note: *Add 1 tablespoon (15 grams) water at a time to icing until it reaches medium or flood consistency. To test flood-consistency icing, scoop out a spoonful, and drop it back into bowl. It should take 15 to 20 seconds for surface of the icing to become completely smooth.*

FILIGREE TREES

Makes 36

Recipe by Amber Spiegel/*feedfeed*

Gingerbread Cookie Dough (recipe on page 312)
Vanilla Royal Icing (recipe on page 312)
Gold pearl dust
Few drops alcohol or vanilla, lemon, or almond extract

1. Preheat oven to 350°F (180°C). Line baking sheets with parchment paper.
2. Using a 2- to 4-inch pine tree-shaped cutter, cut Gingerbread Cookie Dough, rerolling scraps as necessary. Place on prepared pans. Freeze until firm, about 15 minutes.
3. Bake for 10 to 12 minutes. Let cool on pans for 5 minutes. Remove from pans, and let cool completely on wire racks.

4. Using a 12-inch pastry bag fitted with a #3 piping tip, ice cookies with pastel shades of flood-consistency Vanilla Royal Icing. Let dry.
5. To make filigree trees, use a 12-inch pastry bag fitted with a #1 piping tip. Starting from bottom and working toward top, pipe design with light brown soft-peak Vanilla Royal Icing. Let dry completely, about 30 minutes.
6. In a small dish, stir together gold pearl dust and a few drops alcohol or extract. Paint filigree using a fine-tip brush.
7. To make striped trees, use a flat brush to paint diagonal lines using gold pearl dust mixture. Store in an airtight container at room temperature for up to 1 week.

Photo by Amber Spiegel

EMBROIDERED ORNAMENTS

Makes 36

Recipe by Amber Spiegel/*feedfeed*

Gingerbread Cookie Dough (recipe on page 312)
Vanilla Royal Icing (recipe on page 312)

1. Preheat oven to 350°F (180°C). Line baking sheets with parchment paper.
2. Using a 3-inch round, heart-shaped, or star-shaped cutter, cut Gingerbread Cookie Dough, rerolling scraps as necessary. Using a #10 piping tip, cut a small hole in top of each cookie. Place on prepared pans. Freeze until firm, about 15 minutes.
3. Bake for 10 to 12 minutes. Let cool on pans for 5 minutes. Remove from pans, and let cool completely on wire racks.
4. Using a 12-inch pastry bag fitted with a #3 piping tip, ice cookies with red flood-consistency Vanilla Royal Icing. Let dry completely, about 6 hours.
5. Using a 12-inch pastry bag fitted with a #1 piping tip, create "embroidered" patterns on cookies by piping trees with a series of lines using white soft-peak Vanilla Royal Icing. Add staggered dots to top and bottom of each line to complete the embroidered look. Add "stitches" around edge by piping a series of short lines. Let icing dry completely, about 30 minutes. Thread a piece of baker's twine through hole, and tie a knot to secure. Store in an airtight container at room temperature for up to 1 week.

Photo by Amber Spiegel

1. Before baking, use a #10 piping tip to cut a small hole in the top of each cookie.

2. Ice baked cookies with red flood-consistency icing, and let dry completely, about 6 hours.

3. Create an "embroidered" pattern on the cookie by piping trees with series of lines using white soft-peak icing. Add staggered dots to the top and bottom of each line to complete the embroidered look.

4. Add "stitches" around the edge by piping a series of short lines, and let icing dry completely, about 30 minutes.

5. Thread a piece of baker's twine through hole, and tie a knot to secure.

SNOWFLAKE COOKIES

Makes 36

Recipe by Amber Spiegel/*feedfeed*

Gingerbread Cookie Dough (recipe on page 312)
Vanilla Royal Icing (recipe on page 312)

1. Preheat oven to 350°F (180°C). Line baking sheets with parchment paper.
2. Using a 3-inch snowflake-shaped cutter, cut Gingerbread Cookie Dough, rerolling scraps as necessary. Place on prepared pans. Freeze until firm, about 15 minutes.
3. Bake for 10 to 12 minutes. Let cool on pans for 5 minutes. Remove from pans, and let cool completely on wire racks.
4. Using a 12-inch pastry bag fitted with a #1 piping tip, ice snowflakes with white soft peak Vanilla Royal Icing in a variety of designs. Store in an airtight container at room temperature for up to 1 week.

Photo by Amber Spiegel

PRO TIP
Make a mark in center of the snowflake with a wooden pick. Start piping your design on outside edge of cookie, and work your way toward center, stopping every so often to make sure design looks symmetrical. If you make a mistake, just scrape icing off with a wooden pick.

SWEET AND SALTY MONSTER COOKIES

Makes about 24

Recipe by Molly Adams/*feedfeed*

I've been making a variation of these monster cookies for years. They are always a hit and are the perfect crowd-pleasing cookie to bring to any function. My family has enjoyed these at Christmas, summer cookouts, birthday parties, and every event in between. These cookies freeze beautifully; I like to freeze them fully baked in individual wax paper bags. Whenever I need a cookie, I just pop one out of the freezer, and let it thaw at room temperature for an hour or two before enjoying.

3   large eggs (150 grams), room temperature
1   cup (220 grams) firmly packed light brown sugar
½   cup (100 grams) granulated sugar
1   teaspoon (4 grams) vanilla extract*
1   vanilla bean (about 5 grams), split lengthwise, seeds scraped and reserved
½   teaspoon (1.5 grams) kosher salt
1¾ cups (448 grams) creamy peanut butter
½   cup (113 grams) unsalted butter, softened
1   cup (175 grams) candy-coated chocolate pieces
1   cup (170 grams) 70% cacao dark chocolate, chopped
4   cups (320 grams) old-fashioned oats
1   cup (35 grams) kettle-cooked potato chips

1   cup (36 grams) miniature pretzel twists, plus more for topping (optional)
½   cup (25 grams) unsweetened flaked coconut
2   teaspoons (10 grams) baking soda

1. Preheat oven to 350°F (180°C). Line 2 large baking sheets with parchment paper.
2. In the bowl of a stand mixer fitted with the paddle attachment, beat eggs and sugars at medium speed until pale yellow and fluffy, about 3 minutes. Add vanilla extract, vanilla bean seeds, and salt, beating to combine. Beat in peanut butter and butter, stopping to scrape sides of bowl.
3. Reduce mixer to low speed. Add chocolate pieces and chopped chocolate, beating until well combined. Add oats, chips, pretzels, coconut, and baking soda, beating until well combined. Using a large (¼-cup) spring-loaded scoop, drop dough at least 3 inches apart on prepared pans.
4. Bake until golden brown, 15 to 17 minutes, rotating pans halfway through baking. Let cool on pans for 2 to 3 minutes. Remove from pans, and let cool completely on wire racks. Top with pretzel twists, if desired. Store in an airtight container for up to 4 days.

I used Rodelle Pure Vanilla Extract.

Photo by Alexis Sinclair

CHOCOLATE TURTLE COOKIES

Makes about 24

Recipe by Shiran Dickman/*feedfeed*

Coated with pecans and filled with soft caramel, these festive chocolate cookies are a popular treat during the holidays.

½   cup (113 grams) unsalted butter, softened
¾   cup (150 grams) granulated sugar
1   large egg (50 grams), separated
1   teaspoon (4 grams) vanilla extract
1   cup (125 grams) all-purpose flour
½   cup (43 grams) unsweetened cocoa powder
¼   teaspoon kosher salt
2   tablespoons (30 grams) whole milk
1   cup (113 grams) finely chopped pecans
Thick Caramel Sauce (recipe follows)

1. In the bowl of a stand mixer fitted with the paddle attachment, beat butter and sugar at medium speed until fluffy, 3 to 4 minutes, stopping to scrape sides of bowl. Beat in egg yolk and vanilla.
2. In a medium bowl, sift together flour, cocoa, and salt. With mixer on low speed, gradually add flour mixture to butter mixture, beating until combined. Beat in milk. (Batter will be thick and sticky.) Cover and refrigerate for at least 1 hour.

3. Preheat oven to 350°F (180°C). Line 2 large baking sheets with parchment paper.
4. Place egg white in a small bowl. Place pecans in another small bowl. Roll dough into 1-inch balls. Roll dough balls in egg white, letting excess drip off. Roll in pecans to coat, and place 2 inches apart on prepared pans. Using your thumb or the back of a spoon, gently make an indentation in center of each ball.
5. Bake until edges are set and center is slightly soft, 10 to 12 minutes. Let cool on pans for 10 minutes. Remove from pans, and let cool completely on wire racks. Fill centers of cookies with Thick Caramel Sauce. Store in an airtight container for up to 4 days.

THICK CARAMEL SAUCE
Makes about 1 cup

14   caramel candies (about 4 ounces)
3   tablespoons (45 grams) heavy whipping cream

1. In a microwave-safe bowl, combine caramels and cream. Microwave on high in 30-second intervals, stirring between each, until melted (about 2 minutes total).

Photo by Shiran Dickman

CHOCOLATE CRINKLE COOKIES

Makes 30

Recipe by Shiran Dickman/*feedfeed*

Perfectly chewy and coated in confectioners' sugar, these are the ultimate fudgy chocolate cookies. They are so soft that they will almost melt in your mouth.

8 ounces (225 grams) 54% to 60% cacao dark chocolate, roughly chopped
¼ cup (57 grams) unsalted butter
2 large eggs (100 grams)
½ cup (100 grams) granulated sugar
2 teaspoons (8 grams) vanilla extract
¾ cup (72 grams) almond meal
½ cup (63 grams) all-purpose flour, sifted
½ teaspoon (2.5 grams) baking powder
¼ teaspoon kosher salt
1 cup (120 grams) confectioners' sugar

1. In a microwave-safe bowl, combine chocolate and butter. Microwave on high in 30-second intervals, stirring between each, until melted and smooth.

2. In the bowl of a stand mixer fitted with the whisk attachment, beat eggs and granulated sugar at high speed until fluffy and pale, about 4 minutes. Reduce mixer speed to medium. Gradually add melted chocolate and vanilla, beating until combined.

3. In a medium bowl, whisk together almond meal, flour, baking powder, and salt. With mixer on low speed, gradually add almond meal mixture to egg mixture, beating just until combined. Cover with plastic wrap, and refrigerate until firm, 1 to 2 hours.

4. Preheat oven to 350°F (180°C). Line 2 baking sheets with parchment paper.

5. Place confectioners' sugar in a small bowl. Using a medium (1½-tablespoon) spring-loaded scoop, scoop dough into balls. (You can also roll dough into 1-inch balls using your hands.) Roll each ball generously in confectioners' sugar, and place 2 inches apart on prepared pans.

6. Bake until cookies are cracked and still soft in center, 8 to 10 minutes. (Overbaking cookies will make them dry.) Let cool on pans for 10 minutes. Remove from pans, and let cool completely on wire racks. Store in an airtight container at room temperature for up to 3 days.

Photo by Shiran Dickman

DOUBLE CHOCOLATE BISCOTTI

Makes 40

Recipe by Shiran Dickman/*feedfeed*

These crisp biscuits have a deep chocolate flavor and are perfect served with coffee or hot chocolate for dipping.

3   large eggs (150 grams)
1   cup (200 grams) granulated sugar
¼   cup (57 grams) unsalted butter, melted
1   teaspoon (4 grams) vanilla extract
1¾   cups (219 grams) all-purpose flour
½   cup (43 grams) unsweetened cocoa powder
1   teaspoon (5 grams) baking powder
½   teaspoon (1.5 grams) kosher salt
¾   cup (128 grams) dark or milk chocolate morsels
¾   cup (85 grams) coarsely chopped hazelnuts, slightly toasted

1. Preheat oven to 325°F (170°C). Line a baking sheet with parchment paper.
2. In the bowl of a stand mixer fitted with the whisk attachment, beat eggs at high speed until light and pale in color, about 2 minutes. Reduce mixer speed to low. Add sugar, melted butter, and vanilla, beating just until combined.
3. In a medium bowl, sift together flour, cocoa, baking powder, and salt. Gradually add flour mixture to egg mixture, beating just until combined and a dough starts to form. Fold in chocolate morsels and hazelnuts. Refrigerate for at least 30 minutes.
4. On a lightly floured surface, with slightly wet hands, shape dough into a ball. Divide in half, and roll each half into a 14x2½-inch rectangle. Place 4 inches apart on prepared pan.
5. Bake until slightly risen, firm to the touch, and top begins to crack, 25 to 30 minutes. Let cool on a wire rack for 30 minutes.
6. Using a serrated knife, cut logs into ½-inch-thick slices. Return slices to pan, cut side up, in a single layer. Bake until crisp, about 15 minutes more. (The longer they stay in the oven, the harder they become.) Let cool completely on a wire rack. Store in an airtight container at room temperature for up to 1 week.

Photo by Shiran Dickman

PECAN-TOFFEE BITES

Makes about 30

Recipe by Lisa Tutman-Oglesby/*feedfeed*

Pecan-Toffee Bites seem more like tarts than cookies, but spread them out on a dessert tray and they'll get gobbled up just as fast. Infused with all manner of delicious goodness, every bite is a treat for your taste buds.

4	large eggs (200 grams)
1½	cups (330 grams) firmly packed light brown sugar
1	cup (113 grams) chopped pecans
½	cup (100 grams) granulated sugar
½	cup (113 grams) unsalted butter, melted and cooled
2	tablespoons (16 grams) all-purpose flour
2	tablespoons (30 grams) whole milk
1½	teaspoons (6 grams) vanilla extract
1	(14.1-ounce) package (400 grams) refrigerated piecrusts
1	cup (170 grams) chopped toffee bits
1	cup (170 grams) white chocolate melting wafers

1. Preheat oven to 350°F (180°C).

2. In a large bowl, whisk eggs until foamy. Add brown sugar, pecans, granulated sugar, melted butter, flour, milk, and vanilla, whisking to combine. Set aside.

3. On a lightly floured surface, unroll piecrusts. Using a 2½-inch fluted round cutter, cut dough, rerolling scraps as necessary. Transfer to the wells of 12-cavity miniature tart pans. Spoon egg mixture into crusts. Sprinkle with toffee.

4. Bake until browned and caramelized, 25 to 30 minutes. Let cool in pans for 2 minutes. Use a fork to gently remove each bite from pans. Let cool completely on a wire rack.

5. In a microwave-safe bowl, heat white chocolate wafers on high for about 25 seconds. Stir chocolate vigorously. Spoon chocolate into a pastry bag fitted with a #03 metal piping tip. Drizzle chocolate over bites.

Photo by Lisa Tutman-Oglesby

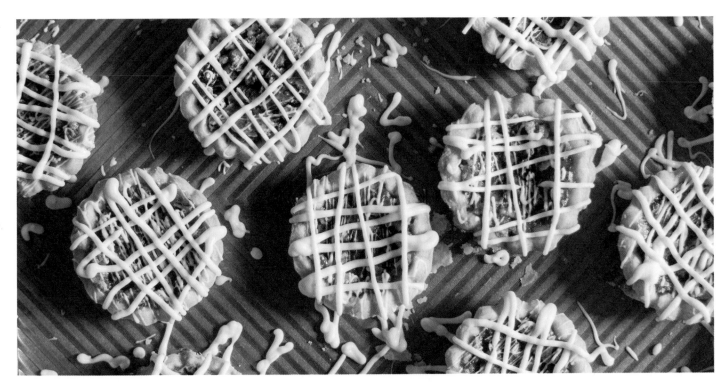

GINGERBREAD ORNAMENTS

Makes 36 to 50

Recipe by Lisa Tutman-Oglesby/*feedfeed*

The charm of these edible ornaments lies in all the varied shapes and sizes. This baking project is also a great way to finally use all those cookie cutters you've been collecting for years.

¾ cup (170 grams) unsalted butter, softened
1 cup (220 grams) firmly packed light brown sugar
1 large egg (50 grams)
¾ cup (255 grams) molasses
4 cups (500 grams) all-purpose flour
2 teaspoons (4 grams) ground ginger
2 teaspoons (4 grams) ground cinnamon
¾ teaspoon (1.5 grams) ground cloves
¼ teaspoon kosher salt
Royal Icing (recipe follows)

1. In the bowl of a stand mixer fitted with the paddle attachment, beat butter and brown sugar at medium speed until fluffy, 3 to 4 minutes, stopping to scrape sides of bowl. Add egg, beating just until combined. Beat in molasses.
2. In a large bowl, whisk together flour, ginger, cinnamon, cloves, and salt. With mixer on low speed, gradually add flour mixture to butter mixture, beating until combined. Divide dough into 4 equal portions. Roll each portion between 2 sheets of lightly floured parchment paper. Place each portion on a baking sheet. Refrigerate for at least 1 hour.
3. Preheat oven to 350° (180°C).
4. Remove one piece of dough from refrigerator. While working with one piece, keep remaining pieces in refrigerator. Roll dough to ¼-inch thickness. Using desired holiday cutters dipped in flour, cut dough, rerolling scraps as necessary. Use a straw to create a small hole in top of each cookie. Repeat with all remaining dough.
5. Bake until edges are slightly darker than rest of cookie, about 12 minutes. Let cool on pans for 3 minutes. Remove from pans, and let cool completely on wire racks.
6. Spoon Royal Icing into a piping bag fitted with #01 metal tip. Draw an outline around each cookie. Add other decorative designs onto cookies as desired. Let stand until icing is hardened, about 2 hours.
7. Cut baker's twine, decorative ribbon, or kitchen string into 8-inch strips; string through cookie hole. Tie a knot on end, and slide knot down behind cookie. Adorn tree, wreath, or holiday garland.

PRO TIP
After piercing the gingerbread dough with the straw, you'll find the end of the straw beginning to fill with dough. Use scissors to snip ½ inch or so off the straw to create a clean straw end to continue creating the loop holes.

Photo by Lisa Tutman-Oglesby

ROYAL ICING
Makes 4 cups

2 large pasteurized egg whites (60 grams)
1 teaspoon (2 grams) cream of tartar
¼ cup (60 grams) water
1 teaspoon (4 grams) vanilla extract
4 cups (480 grams) confectioners' sugar

1. In the bowl of a stand mixer fitted with the paddle attachment, beat egg whites and cream of tartar at medium-high speed until foamy. Add 1 tablespoon (15 grams) water and vanilla, beating until combined. Gradually add confectioners' sugar, beating until well combined and shiny, about 3 to 4 minutes. Royal Icing should not be thick and should not be runny at all. To determine best consistency, dip a spoon into icing, and let icing drip back into mixer. The icing should slowly drip off the spoon. If the icing is too thick, add more water, 1 teaspoon (5 grams) at a time, until desired consistency is reached.

MELTED SNOWMAN SUGAR COOKIES

Makes 32

Recipe by Lisa Tutman-Oglesby/*feedfeed*

Melted Snowman Sugar Cookies will also melt your heart. These treats have clearly succumbed to warmer temperatures, but that doesn't make them any less adorable or delicious. A combination of marshmallows and royal icing creates the illusion that these snowmen are having a bad day.

1   cup (227 grams) unsalted butter
1   cup (200 grams) granulated sugar
1   large egg (50 grams)
2   teaspoons (8 grams) vanilla extract
3   cups (375 grams) all-purpose flour
½   teaspoon (1.5 grams) kosher salt
Royal Icing (recipe on page 322)
32   marshmallows
Assorted gel food coloring
Orange sprinkles

1. In the bowl of a stand mixer fitted with the paddle attachment, beat butter and sugar at medium speed until creamy, 3 to 4 minutes, stopping to scrape sides of bowl. Add egg, beating well. Beat in vanilla.

2. In a medium bowl, whisk together flour and salt. With mixer on low speed, gradually add flour mixture to butter mixture, beating until combined. Turn out dough onto a lightly floured surface, and divide into 3 equal portions. Roll each portion between 2 sheets of parchment paper. Place each portion on a baking sheet. Refrigerate for 1 hour.

3. Preheat oven to 350°F (180°C).

4. Remove one piece of dough from refrigerator. While working with one piece, keep remaining pieces in refrigerator. Roll dough to ¼-inch thickness. Using a 3-inch round cutter dipped in flour, cut dough, rerolling scraps as necessary. Repeat with all remaining dough.

5. Bake until light golden brown, 10 to 12 minutes. Let cool completely on wire racks.

6. Place cookies on parchment paper or baking sheets. Set aside one-fourth of Royal Icing for decorating. Spoon remaining Royal Icing into a 12-inch pastry bag fitted with a #10 metal piping tip and coupler. Hold bag vertically over top of each cookie, and gently squeeze bag, depositing icing over cookie so that it puddles. (You want icing to look like melted snow. It's OK to let the icing run over edges of the cookies.) Let icing dry and harden, about 2 hours.

7. Spray a sheet of parchment paper with cooking spray. Place 4 to 5 marshmallows on parchment, and microwave for about 10 to 20 seconds. (The marshmallows will double in size.) Let stand for 10 minutes. (They will deflate during this time. They'll also harden on the bottom, which will make them easier to manage.) Gently remove marshmallows from parchment, and place on cookies. Repeat with all remaining marshmallows.

8. Place a small amount of remaining Royal Icing into multiple bowls. Add desired food coloring to each bowl, and stir together to create colors for facial features, arms, and buttons. Fit small resealable plastic bags with #01 metal piping tips and couplers, and fill with each color. Bring your cookie to life with eyes, a smile, tree branch-shaped arms, and buttons. Insert a sprinkle into each marshmallow for the nose. Let dry.

Photo by Lisa Tutman-Oglesby

THREE-DIMENSIONAL
REINDEER COOKIES

Makes about 12 assembled reindeer cookies

Recipe by Lisa Tutman-Oglesby/*feedfeed*

These fanciful reindeer cookies may look too cute to eat, but don't let that stop you. Fun to bake and assemble, these cute bites deliver a delightful three-dimensional effect that will have cookie lovers looking twice.

¾ cup (170 grams) unsalted butter, softened
1 cup (220 grams) firmly packed light brown sugar
1 large egg (50 grams)
¾ cup (255 grams) molasses
4 cups (500 grams) all-purpose flour
2 teaspoons (4 grams) ground ginger
2 teaspoons (4 grams) ground cinnamon
¾ teaspoon (1.5 grams) ground cloves
¼ teaspoon kosher salt
Royal Icing (recipe on page 322)
Assorted gel food coloring

1. In the bowl of a stand mixer fitted with the paddle attachment, beat butter and brown sugar at medium speed until fluffy, 3 to 4 minutes, stopping to scrape sides of bowl. Add egg, beating just until combined. Beat in molasses.

2. In a large bowl, whisk together flour, ginger, cinnamon, cloves, and salt. With mixer on low speed, gradually add flour mixture to butter mixture, beating until combined. Divide dough into 4 equal portions. Roll each portion between 2 sheets of lightly floured parchment paper. Place each portion on a baking sheet. Refrigerate for at least 1 hour.

3. Preheat oven to 350° (180°C).

4. Remove one piece of dough from refrigerator. While working with one piece, keep remaining pieces in refrigerator. Roll dough to ⅛-inch thickness. Using 3-D reindeer cookie cutters, cut dough, rerolling scraps as necessary. Pay close attention to number of reindeer bodies you're cutting, and cut required number of corresponding reindeer legs. Repeat with all remaining dough.

5. Bake until edges are slightly darker than rest of cookie, about 12 minutes. Let cool on pans for 3 minutes. Remove from pans, and let cool completely on wire racks.

6. Divide Royal Icing among multiple bowls, and add desired food coloring to each bowl. Spoon icing into pastry bags fitted with #01 metal piping tips and couplers.

7. Separate baked cookies by body part. Decorate body parts in assembly line fashion in order to keep all parts consistent. Do not deposit icing too close to edge of cookies. (Leave about a ¼-inch border along edges.) Let icing dry and harden. Gently assemble cookies. Display assembled cookies on a baking tray for serving.

Note: *I used Williams Sonoma Holiday Storybook Cookie Cutters kit (limited availability online), but you can find a variety of 3-D holiday cookie cutters via an online search. Most kits come with a variety of holiday shapes, such as sleighs and trees.*

Photo by Lisa Tutman-Oglesby

After cutting out the shapes, return the tray to the refrigerator for 1 hour to let cookies chill even more. This will help the cookies maintain their shape while baking so they can fit together like puzzle pieces.

Sort various cookie parts into piles, organizing by specific cut. Organizing the cookies into an assembly line fashion is the best decorating approach when you're dealing with so many cookies. It'll help keep your piping uniform.

When icing your cookies, leave about a ¼-inch border along edges so that the cookies will be able to interlock with their accompanying pieces once the icing has dried. Don't forget to select one reindeer in the group to get that famous red nose!

CHOCOLATE-DIPPED PEANUT BUTTER CRINKLE COOKIES

Makes about 24

Recipe by Maryanne Cabrera/*feedfeed*

A sweet, salty, and chocolaty cookie that will satisfy any peanut butter fan. Dipped in melted dark chocolate and topped with chopped honey-roasted peanuts, these cookies are a decadent treat.

½ cup (113 grams) unsalted butter, softened
1 cup (220 grams) firmly packed dark brown sugar
¾ cup (192 grams) creamy peanut butter
1 large egg (50 grams)
½ teaspoon (2 grams) vanilla extract
1⅓ cups (167 grams) all-purpose flour
1 teaspoon (5 grams) baking soda
½ teaspoon (2.5 grams) baking powder
½ teaspoon (1.5 grams) kosher salt
½ cup (100 grams) granulated sugar
½ cup (60 grams) confectioners' sugar
8 ounces (225 grams) 72% cacao dark chocolate, chopped
Roughly chopped honey-roasted peanuts

1. Preheat oven to 350°F (180°C). Line baking sheets with parchment paper.
2. In the bowl of a stand mixer fitted with the paddle attachment, beat butter, brown sugar, and peanut butter at medium speed until creamy, 3 to 4 minutes, stopping to scrape sides of bowl. Beat in egg and vanilla.
3. In a medium bowl, whisk together flour, baking soda, baking powder, and salt. With mixer on low speed, gradually add flour mixture to butter mixture, beating just until combined.
4. Place granulated sugar and confectioners' sugar in small bowls. Using a medium (1½-tablespoon) spring-loaded scoop, scoop dough into balls. Roll balls in granulated sugar to coat; roll in confectioners' sugar until coated. Place 2 inches apart on prepared pans.
5. Bake until edges are set and cookies are cracked on top, 15 to 18 minutes, rotating pans halfway through baking. Let cool on pans for 5 minutes. Remove from pans, and let cool completely on wire racks.
6. In a microwave-safe bowl, heat chocolate on high in 30-second intervals, stirring between each, until melted and smooth. Let cool slightly, 3 to 5 minutes. Dip half of each cookie in melted chocolate, and place on a wire rack. Immediately sprinkle with peanuts. Let stand until chocolate is set, 8 to 10 minutes. Store in an airtight container at room temperature for up to 5 days.

Photo by Maryanne Cabrera

LOADED HOLIDAY COOKIES

Makes about 28

Recipe by Maryanne Cabrera/*feedfeed*

It's your classic chewy chocolate chip cookie loaded with a medley of holiday toppings. The combination of oats, pistachios, cranberries, and chocolate with a hint of orange tastes like a Christmas party.

1	cup (227 grams) unsalted butter, softened
½	cup (100 grams) granulated sugar
¾	cup (165 grams) firmly packed dark brown sugar
1	teaspoon (2 grams) finely grated orange zest
2	large eggs (100 grams)
1	teaspoon (4 grams) vanilla extract
2½	cups (313 grams) all-purpose flour
1	teaspoon (3 grams) kosher salt
1	teaspoon (5 grams) baking powder
½	teaspoon (2.5 grams) baking soda
1	cup (80 grams) old-fashioned oats
1	cup (170 grams) white chocolate morsels
1	cup (170 grams) 46% cacao semisweet chocolate morsels
½	cup (25 grams) dried sweetened flaked coconut
½	cup (57 grams) chopped pistachios
½	cup (57 grams) chopped pecans
½	cup (64 grams) dried cranberries

1. Preheat oven to 350°F (180°C). Line baking sheets with parchment paper.

2. In the bowl of a stand mixer fitted with the paddle attachment, beat butter, sugars, and zest at medium speed until fluffy, 3 to 4 minutes, stopping to scrape sides of bowl. Add eggs, one at a time, beating well after each addition. Beat in vanilla.

3. In a medium bowl, whisk together flour, salt, baking powder, and baking soda. With mixer on low speed, gradually add flour mixture to butter mixture, beating just until combined. Fold in oats, white chocolate, semisweet chocolate, coconut, pistachios, pecans, and cranberries. Using a large (¼-cup) spring-loaded scoop, scoop dough, and place 2 inches apart on prepared pans.

4. Bake until edges are golden brown, 13 to 15 minutes, rotating pans halfway through baking. Let cool on pans for 5 minutes. Remove from pans, and let cool completely on wire racks. Store in an airtight container at room temperature for up to 5 days.

Photo by Maryanne Cabrera

PEPPERMINT CHOCOLATE-DIPPED SUGAR COOKIES

Makes about 24

Recipe by Maryanne Cabrera/*feedfeed*

These soft sugar cookies are dipped in melted dark chocolate and topped with crunchy candy cane bits—fantastic for making holiday ice cream sandwiches.

10 tablespoons (140 grams) unsalted butter, softened
1¼ cups (250 grams) granulated sugar
1   large egg (50 grams)
1   teaspoon (4 grams) vanilla extract
1¾ cups (219 grams) all-purpose flour
1   teaspoon (5 grams) baking soda
½   teaspoon (1.5 grams) kosher salt
6   ounces (175 grams) 72% cacao dark chocolate, chopped
Crushed candy canes or peppermint candies

1. Preheat oven to 350°F (180°C). Line baking sheets with parchment paper.
2. In the bowl of a stand mixer fitted with the paddle attachment, beat butter and sugar at medium speed until fluffy, 3 to 4 minutes, stopping to scrape sides of bowl. Beat in egg and vanilla.
3. In a medium bowl, whisk together flour, baking soda, and salt. With mixer on low speed, gradually add flour mixture to butter mixture, beating just until combined. Using a medium (1½-tablespoon) spring-loaded scoop, scoop dough, and place 2 inches apart on prepared pans.
4. Bake until edges are set and cookies have puffed up, 15 to 18 minutes, rotating pans halfway through baking. Let cool on pans for 5 minutes. Remove from pans, and let cool completely on wire racks.
5. In a microwave-safe bowl, heat chocolate on high in 30-second intervals, stirring between each, until melted and smooth. Let cool slightly, 3 to 5 minutes. Dip half of each cookie in melted chocolate, letting excess drip off, and place on a wire rack. Immediately sprinkle with crushed candy canes. Let stand until chocolate is set, 8 to 10 minutes. If you live in a humid area, try chilling your chocolate-dipped cookies in the refrigerator for 20 minutes to help set the chocolate. Store in an airtight container at room temperature for up to 3 days.

Photo by Maryanne Cabrera

GUAVA CREAM CHEESE COOKIES

Makes about 24 sandwich cookies

Recipe by Maryanne Cabrera/*feedfeed*

These cookies take the exotic flavors of Cuban pastelitos de guayaba and turns them into familiar-looking cookie sandwiches.

½   cup (113 grams) unsalted butter, softened
½   cup (112 grams) cream cheese, softened
⅓   cup (67 grams) granulated sugar
⅓   cup (40 grams) confectioners' sugar, plus more for dusting
3   large egg yolks (56 grams)
1   teaspoon (4 grams) vanilla extract
2¾ cups (344 grams) all-purpose flour
½   teaspoon (1.5 grams) kosher salt
½   cup (160 grams) guava jam*

1. In the bowl of a stand mixer fitted with the paddle attachment, beat butter and cream cheese at medium speed until smooth, 2 to 3 minutes. Add sugars, and beat until creamy, 2 to 3 minutes, stopping to scrape sides of bowl. Add egg yolks and vanilla, beating until well combined.

2. In a medium bowl, whisk together flour and salt. With mixer on low speed, gradually add flour mixture to butter mixture, beating just until combined. Divide dough in half, and wrap each half in plastic wrap. Refrigerate for at least 1 hour or overnight.

3. Preheat oven to 350°F (180°C). Line baking sheets with parchment paper.

4. On a lightly floured surface, roll half of dough to ¼-inch thickness. Using a 2½-inch round cutter, cut dough, rerolling scraps as necessary. Place 1 inch apart on prepared pans. Repeat with remaining dough. Using a 1-inch star-shaped cutter, cut centers from half of cookies.

5. Bake until edges are lightly golden brown, 18 to 20 minutes, rotating pans halfway through baking. Let cool completely on pans. Lightly dust cookies with cutouts with confectioners' sugar. Spread ½ teaspoon jam onto flat side of all solid cookies. Place cookies with cutouts, flat side down, on top of jam. Refrigerate in an airtight container for up to 3 days.

*While guava paste, a thick, gel-like product of guava, is readily available at many grocery stores, guava jam is harder to come by. Look for it on amazon.com or at specialty food stores.

Photo by Maryanne Cabrera

BROWNED BUTTER MOLASSES COOKIES

Makes 24

Recipe by Phillip Fryman/*feedfeed*

There is nothing more inviting than chewy, rich molasses cookies for the holidays. These spiced cookies go the extra three miles in the snow by using browned butter to keep them soft and flavorful.

¾   cup (170 grams) unsalted butter
½   cup (100 grams) granulated sugar
½   cup (110 grams) firmly packed dark brown sugar
¼   cup (85 grams) molasses
1   large egg (50 grams)
2¼   cups (281 grams) all-purpose flour
2   teaspoons (10 grams) baking soda
1   teaspoon (2 grams) ground cinnamon
½   teaspoon (1 gram) ground ginger
¼   teaspoon ground cardamom
½   cup (100 grams) turbinado sugar

1. In a small saucepan, melt butter over medium heat. Cook until butter turns a medium-brown color and has a nutty aroma, about 5 minutes. Remove from heat, and let cool to room temperature.
2. In the bowl of a stand mixer fitted with the paddle attachment, beat browned butter, granulated sugar, and brown sugar at medium speed until fluffy, 3 to 4 minutes, stopping to scrape sides of bowl. Beat in molasses and egg.
3. In a medium bowl, sift together flour, baking soda, cinnamon, ginger, and cardamom. With mixer on low speed, gradually add flour mixture to browned butter mixture, beating until combined. Wrap dough in plastic wrap, and refrigerate for at least 30 minutes.
4. Preheat oven to 350°F (180°C). Line a baking sheet with parchment paper or a silicone baking mat.
5. Place turbinado sugar in a small bowl. Using a medium (1½-tablespoon) spring-loaded scoop, scoop dough, and roll into balls. Roll balls in turbinado sugar to coat. Place at least 2 inches apart on prepared pan.
6. Bake for 12 to 15 minutes. (Be careful not to overbake as that will prevent cookies from being chewy.) Let cool completely.

Photo by Phillip Fryman

BRANDY SNAPS

Makes 20

Recipe by Phillip Fryman/*feedfeed*

Brandy Snaps are a popular UK holiday treat made from equal parts by weight of golden syrup, flour, butter, and sugar with the addition of ginger and a splash of lemon. Very crisp and quite thin, Brandy Snaps are best served with a whipped cream filling, such as the brandy honey recipe here.

5   tablespoons (70 grams) unsalted butter
4½ tablespoons (54 grams) Demerara sugar
3   tablespoons (63 grams) golden syrup
9   tablespoons (72 grams) all-purpose flour
½   teaspoon (1 gram) ground ginger
1   teaspoon (5 grams) fresh lemon juice
Brandy Honey Whipped Cream (recipe follows)

1. Preheat oven to 350°F (180°C). Line a baking sheet with parchment paper. Lightly oil a wooden spoon handle.
2. In a small saucepan, heat butter, Demerara sugar, and golden syrup over low heat. Cook, stirring and pressing sugar with a silicone spatula, until sugar is dissolved, about 15 minutes. Remove from heat.
3. In a small bowl, sift together flour and ginger. Add flour mixture and lemon juice to butter mixture, stirring until well combined. Using a teaspoon, drop hot mixture 4 to 5 inches apart onto prepared pan. If mixture is too hard to spoon onto pan, roll it into a ball, place on pan, and flatten lightly.

4. Bake until mixture spreads, forms a lace, and darkens to a rich golden color, 8 to 10 minutes. Let cool on pan for 2 to 3 minutes. Using a spatula, carefully transfer each disk to oiled spoon handle. Carefully wrap around handle, overlapping ends to form a tube. If disks are too brittle to wrap, place pan back in oven for 1 minute to soften. Let cool completely on a wire rack. Just before serving, use a piping bag to fill each snap with Brandy Honey Whipped Cream. Refrigerate unfilled Brandy Snaps in an airtight container for up to 1 week.

BRANDY HONEY WHIPPED CREAM
Makes 2 cups

1   cup (240 grams) cold heavy whipping cream
1   tablespoon (21 grams) honey
1   teaspoon (5 grams) brandy (optional)

1. In the cold bowl of a stand mixer fitted with the whisk attachment, beat cold cream at medium-high speed until it starts to thicken. Add honey, and beat until firm. Reduce mixer speed to low, and beat in brandy (if using). Refrigerate until ready to use.

Photo by Phillip Fryman

COOKIES AND CREAM MACARONS

Makes 24

Recipe by Phillip Fryman/*feedfeed*

Macarons may sound intimidating, but they aren't all that bad once you get the technique down. These nostalgic cookie-inspired macarons are rich and elegant while bringing back some old school flavors into the kitchen.

3   large egg whites (90 grams), room temperature
¼   cup (50 grams) granulated sugar
¼   teaspoon cream of tartar
1⅔   cups (200 grams) confectioners' sugar
1   cup (96 grams) almond flour
Reserved cookie crumbs from Cookies and Cream Filling (recipe follows)

1. Line 2 baking sheets with parchment paper. Using a pencil, draw 1½-inch circles 2 inches apart onto parchment; turn parchment over.
2. In the bowl of a stand mixer fitted with the whisk attachment, beat egg whites at medium speed until foamy, about 1 minute. Add granulated sugar and cream of tartar, beating until stiff peaks form.
3. In a medium bowl, sift together confectioners' sugar and flour. Sift flour mixture over egg white mixture. Using a spatula, fold in flour mixture until you can write a figure eight in it, and it sinks back into the batter in about 15 seconds.
4. Fill a pastry bag with batter, and pipe batter onto drawn circles on prepared pans. Tap pans firmly on counter to release air bubbles. Sprinkle shells with reserved cookie crumbs. Let rest for 1 hour.
5. Preheat oven to 290°F (143°C).
6. Bake for 15 to 19 minutes. Let cool completely. Pipe Cookies and Cream Filling onto flat side of half of cookies. Place remaining cookies, flat side down, on top of filling.

COOKIES AND CREAM FILLING
Makes about 1 cup

10   cream-filled chocolate sandwich cookies, cookies and filling separated
6   tablespoons (84 grams) unsalted butter, softened
1½   cups (180 grams) confectioners' sugar
¼   teaspoon (1 gram) clear vanilla extract
⅛   teaspoon kosher salt

1. In the work bowl of a food processor, place cookies; process until finely ground. Set aside ½ cup (65 grams) cookie crumbs. Reserve remaining cookie crumbs for macaron shells.
2. In the bowl of a stand mixer fitted with the paddle attachment, beat butter and confectioners' sugar at medium speed until fluffy, 3 to 4 minutes, stopping to scrape sides of bowl. Add cookie filling, vanilla, and salt, beating until smooth. Stir in reserved ½ cup (65 grams) cookie crumbs.

Photo by Phillip Fryman

OATMEAL CRANBERRY CREAM PIE COOKIES

Makes 12 sandwich cookies

Recipe by Phillip Fryman/*feedfeed*

Classic oatmeal cookies get a holiday-sweetened, dried cranberry addition. Double trouble with two cookies stuffed with a cream filling.

1¼ cups (284 grams) unsalted butter, softened
¾ cup (165 grams) firmly packed dark brown sugar
½ cup (100 grams) granulated sugar
1 large egg (50 grams)
1½ tablespoons (31.5 grams) molasses
2 teaspoons (8 grams) vanilla extract
3 cups (240 grams) quick-cooking oats
1½ cups (188 grams) all-purpose flour
1 teaspoon (5 grams) baking powder
1 teaspoon (2 grams) ground cinnamon
½ teaspoon (1.5 grams) kosher salt
1 cup (128 grams) dried sweetened cranberries
8 ounces (225 grams) cream cheese, softened
½ cup (60 grams) confectioners' sugar

1. Preheat oven to 350°F (180°C). Line a baking sheet with parchment paper.
2. In the bowl of a stand mixer fitted with the paddle attachment, beat butter, brown sugar, and granulated sugar at medium speed until creamy, 3 to 4 minutes, stopping to scrape sides of bowl. Add egg, molasses, and vanilla, beating until combined.
3. In a large bowl, whisk together oats, flour, baking powder, cinnamon, and salt. With mixer on low speed, gradually add oat mixture to butter mixture, beating until combined. Fold in cranberries. (Dough may be quite thick, but this is expected.) Using a large (¼-cup) spring-loaded scoop, scoop dough, and place at least 1 inch apart on prepared pan.
4. Bake for 12 to 14 minutes. Let cool on pan for 5 minutes. Remove from pan, and let cool completely on a wire rack.
5. In the bowl of a stand mixer fitted with the paddle attachment, beat cream cheese and confectioners' sugar at medium speed until smooth. Pipe or spoon frosting onto flat side of half of cookies. Place remaining cookies, flat side down, on top of frosting. Store in an airtight container.

Photo by Phillip Fryman

LEMON CREAM CHEESE PECAN COOKIES

Makes about 40

Recipe by Fanny Lam/*feedfeed*

Buttery, tangy, and nutty. Lemon Cream Cheese Pecan Cookies combine all the wonderful flavors and amazing textures that you crave from a holiday treat. If you're not a pecan fan, replace them with walnuts or pistachios.

1   cup (227 grams) unsalted butter, softened
3   ounces (86 grams) cream cheese, softened
¾   cup (150 grams) granulated sugar
1   tablespoon (6 grams) lemon zest
1   tablespoon (15 grams) fresh lemon juice
2   cups (250 grams) all-purpose flour
½   teaspoon (1.5 grams) kosher salt
1½   cups (170 grams) roughly chopped pecans

1. In the bowl of a stand mixer fitted with the paddle attachment, beat butter, cream cheese, and sugar at medium speed until creamy, 3 to 4 minutes, stopping to scrape sides of bowl. Beat in lemon zest and juice.
2. In a medium bowl, whisk together flour and salt. With mixer on low speed, gradually add flour mixture to butter mixture, beating until combined. Beat in pecans. Turn out dough, and shape into a disk. Wrap in plastic wrap, and refrigerate for at least 1 hour.
3. Preheat oven to 350°F (180°C). Line 2 baking sheets with parchment paper.
4. On a lightly floured surface, roll dough to ¼-inch thickness. Using 1½-inch fluted square cutter dipped in flour, cut dough, and place on prepared pans. Refrigerate for 15 minutes.
5. Bake until lightly browned, 12 to 15 minutes. Let cool on pans for 3 minutes. Remove from pans, and let cool completely on wire racks. Store in an airtight container for up to 1 week.

Photo by Fanny Lam

DRIED CRANBERRY SHORTBREAD COOKIES

Makes about 30

Recipe by Fanny Lam/*feedfeed*

Simple, delicious, and buttery shortbread cookies are your go-to edible gift during the holiday season. Dried cranberries yield the perfect balance to the creamy texture of the cookie base. The lovely ruby-red color also adds a festive touch.

1	cup (227 grams) unsalted butter, softened
½	cup (60 grams) confectioners' sugar
1	teaspoon (4 grams) vanilla extract
2	cups (250 grams) all-purpose flour
½	teaspoon (1.5 grams) kosher salt
¼	cup (32 grams) finely chopped dried cranberries

1. In the bowl of a stand mixer fitted with the paddle attachment, beat butter and confectioners' sugar at medium speed until creamy, 3 to 4 minutes, stopping to scrape sides of bowl. Beat in vanilla.
2. In a medium bowl, sift together flour and salt. With mixer on low speed, gradually add flour mixture to butter mixture, beating until combined. Fold in cranberries. Turn out dough, and shape into a disk. (Batter may be sticky.) Wrap in plastic wrap, and refrigerate for at least 30 minutes.
3. Preheat oven to 350°F (180°C). Line 2 baking sheets with parchment paper.
4. On a lightly floured surface, roll dough to ¼-inch thickness. Using a 1½-inch round cutter dipped in flour, cut dough, and place on prepared pans. Refrigerate for 15 minutes.
5. Bake until lightly browned, 10 to 15 minutes. Let cool on pans for 3 minutes. Remove from pans, and let cool completely on wire racks. Store in an airtight container for up to 1 week

Photo by Fanny Lam

BROWNED BUTTER PIZZELLES WITH CARDAMOM

Makes 96

Recipe by Kevin Masse/*feedfeed*

I grew up in a big Italian-American family, and at the holidays, my grandmother always made pizzelles—fragrant with anise and dusted with powdered sugar. I loved the texture of the cookies, but my 6-year-old self was not a fan of anise. I've updated this recipe to include some of my favorite flavors. The browned butter adds a nice caramel note while the cardamom provides just the right amount of warmth for the holidays.

½   cup (113 grams) unsalted butter, softened
3   large eggs (150 grams)
¾   cup (150 grams) granulated sugar
1½   cups (188 grams) all-purpose flour*

1   tablespoon (15 grams) baking powder
2   teaspoons (4 grams) ground cardamom
1   teaspoon (3 grams) cornstarch
½   teaspoon (1.5 grams) kosher salt
2   teaspoons (4 grams) pure vanilla extract*
Garnish: confectioners' sugar

1. Preheat pizzelle maker according to manufacturer's instructions.
2. In a small saucepan, melt butter over medium heat. Cook until butter turns a medium-brown color and has a nutty aroma, about 5 minutes. Remove from heat, and let cool slightly.
3. In a large bowl, whisk together eggs and granulated sugar until light and fluffy, about 2 minutes. Gradually add browned butter, whisking to combine.

4. In a medium bowl, stir together flour, baking powder, cardamom, cornstarch, and salt. Add flour mixture to egg mixture, stirring to combine. Stir in vanilla.
5. Spoon 1 teaspoon batter onto pizzelle maker, and bake according to manufacturer's instructions. Repeat with remaining batter. Dust with confectioners' sugar, if desired.

I used Bob's Red Mill Organic All-Purpose Flour and Rodelle Pure Vanilla Extract.

Note: *I used Chef's Choice 835 Pizzelle Pro Express Bake Pizzelle Maker, available on amazon.com.*

Photo by Alexis Sinclair

BASIC BUT BETTER: CLASSIC S'MORES

Makes 12

These are not your camp-out s'mores. We've updated the classic with vanilla bean-speckled marshmallows, homemade graham crackers, and rich orange dark chocolate. Boom.

6 (3-ounce) bars (516 grams) high-quality, orange dark chocolate, halved
Homemade Graham Crackers (recipe follows)
Vanilla Bean Marshmallows (recipe follows)

1. Place half of chocolate on half of Homemade Graham Crackers. Toast Vanilla Bean Marshmallows over a fire, or use a kitchen torch held about 6 inches away. Place marshmallows on chocolate, and top with remaining chocolate and graham crackers.

HOMEMADE GRAHAM CRACKERS
Makes 24

These crackers are softer and richer in flavor than your standard packaged graham. The best part? They hold their shape when you take a bite, saving your s'more from crumbling into a sticky heap.

1 cup (227 grams) unsalted butter, softened
¾ cup (165 grams) firmly packed brown sugar
2 tablespoons (42 grams) honey
1 tablespoon (21 grams) molasses
1 teaspoon (3 grams) kosher salt
1 teaspoon (2 grams) ground cinnamon
1 cup (125 grams) all-purpose flour
1 teaspoon (5 grams) baking soda
2 cups (260 grams) whole wheat flour

1. In the bowl of a stand mixer fitted with the paddle attachment, beat butter, brown sugar, honey, molasses, salt, and cinnamon at medium speed until combined. In a small bowl, whisk together all-purpose flour and baking soda. Gradually add whole wheat flour to butter mixture alternately with all-purpose flour mixture, beating until combined.
2. Between 2 sheets of parchment paper, roll dough into an 18x16-inch rectangle, ⅛ inch thick. Transfer to a baking sheet. Remove top sheet of paper. Using a sharp knife, score dough into 2-inch squares, being sure to cut all the way through. Using a wooden skewer, prick holes in crackers. Freeze for 30 minutes.
3. Preheat oven to 350°F (180°C).

4. Bake until crackers begin to brown, about 10 minutes. Let cool completely. Break apart into squares.

VANILLA BEAN MARSHMALLOWS
Makes 12

After trying these fluffy marshmallows, you'll vow to never buy them from the store again.

⅔ cup (160 grams) water, divided
2 (0.25-ounce) envelopes (14 grams) unflavored gelatin
1¼ cups (250 grams) granulated sugar
⅔ cup (226 grams) light corn syrup
2 teaspoons (4 grams) vanilla bean powder
½ cup (60 grams) confectioners' sugar
¼ cup (32 grams) cornstarch

1. Line a 9-inch square baking pan with parchment paper. Spray with cooking spray, and generously dust with confectioners' sugar.
2. In the bowl of a stand mixer fitted with the whisk attachment, place ⅓ cup (80 grams) water. Sprinkle gelatin over water, and let stand for 10 minutes.
3. In a large saucepan, cook granulated sugar, corn syrup, and remaining ⅓ cup (80 grams) water over medium-high heat until sugar is dissolved and a candy thermometer registers 240°F (116°C), about 6 minutes. With mixer on low speed, slowly drizzle hot sugar mixture into gelatin mixture, beating just until combined. Increase mixer speed to medium, and beat until mixture begins to thicken, about 1 minute. Increase mixer speed to high, and beat until mixture turns very thick, white, and fluffy, about 10 minutes. Beat in vanilla bean powder. Spoon marshmallow mixture into prepared pan.
4. In a medium bowl, sift together confectioners' sugar and cornstarch. Dust top of marshmallow mixture with confectioners' sugar mixture, and flatten with hands. Let set for at least 2 hours or overnight.
5. Using a wet knife, cut into pieces, and toss in confectioners' sugar mixture. Store in an airtight container for up to 2 weeks.

ROOIBOS & VANILLA BISCOTTI

Makes 32

Recipe by Dale Gray/*feedfeed*

Biscotti is very similar in texture to the South African coffee-time treat "rusks." Rooibos tea is native to the Cederberg Mountains in the Western Cape of South Africa and is high in antioxidants.

¾ cup (150 grams) granulated sugar
1   whole vanilla bean (5 grams), chopped
2   tablespoons (7 grams) rooibos tea leaves
⅓ cup (76 grams) unsalted butter, softened
2   large eggs (100 grams)
1   teaspoon (4 grams) pure vanilla extract

2½ cups (313 grams) all-purpose flour
1½ teaspoons (7.5 grams) baking powder
¼   teaspoon kosher salt
Melted white chocolate, for dipping
Garnish: ground rooibos tea leaves

1. Preheat oven to 350°F (180°C).
2. In the work bowl of a food processor, place sugar, chopped vanilla bean, and rooibos tea leaves; pulse until no large particles remain.
3. In the bowl of a stand mixer fitted with the paddle attachment, beat butter and sugar mixture at medium speed until fluffy, 3 to 4 minutes, stopping to scrape sides of bowl. Add eggs, one at a time, beating well after each addition. Beat in vanilla extract.
4. In a medium bowl, whisk together flour,

baking powder, and salt. With mixer on low speed, gradually add flour mixture to butter mixture, beating just until combined. Divide dough in half, and shape into 2 (10x2-inch) logs. Place on an ungreased baking sheet.
5. Bake until lightly browned, about 25 minutes. Let cool on a wire rack for 10 minutes. Using a serrated knife, cut into 1-inch-thick slices. Return to baking sheet, cut side down. Bake until golden, about 15 minutes more, turning halfway through baking. Let cool completely on a wire rack.
6. Dip in melted white chocolate. Garnish with ground rooibos tea leaves, if desired. Store in an airtight container for up to 5 days.

Photo by Dale Gray

FIVE-SPICE FIG SOETKOEKIES

Makes 32

Recipe by Dale Gray/*feedfeed*

In South Africa, soetkoekies are a basic cookie that no home is ever without during the holiday season. They are as popular as gingerbread here but milder in flavor because of fewer spices. Soetkoekies are often eaten for breakfast with a cup of coffee. I've added figs and five-spice powder for a pleasantly warm and fragrant cookie.

½   cup (113 grams) unsalted butter, softened
½   cup (100 grams) granulated sugar
1   large egg (50 grams)
2   teaspoons (4 grams) Chinese five-spice powder
1   teaspoon (4 grams) pure vanilla extract
1¼ cups (125 grams) cake flour
1   teaspoon (5 grams) baking powder
1   teaspoon (3 grams) kosher salt
½   cup (64 grams) finely chopped dried mission figs
Royal Icing (recipe follows)

1. In the bowl of a stand mixer fitted with the paddle attachment, beat butter and sugar at medium speed until creamy, 3 to 4 minutes, stopping to scrape sides of bowl. Add egg, five-spice powder, and vanilla, beating until combined.
2. In a medium bowl, whisk together flour, baking powder, and salt. With mixer on low speed, gradually add flour mixture to butter mixture, beating until combined. Stir in figs just until combined. Wrap in plastic wrap, and refrigerate for at least 45 minutes.
3. Preheat oven to 350°F (180°C). Line 2 baking sheets with parchment paper.
4. Turn out dough onto a lightly floured surface, and gently bring together. Roll into an 18x12-inch rectangle, about ¼ inch thick. Using a 3-inch star-shaped cutter,

cut dough, making sure to press down firmly where there are figs. Place on prepared pans.
5. Bake until edges are light golden brown, 12 to 15 minutes. Let cool on pans for 5 minutes. Remove from pans, and let cool completely on wire racks. Decorate cookies as desired with Royal Icing. Store in an airtight container for up to 6 days.

ROYAL ICING
Makes 1 cup

1½ cups (180 grams) confectioners' sugar
1   large egg white (30 grams)

1. In the bowl of a stand mixer fitted with the whisk attachment, beat confectioners' sugar and egg white at low speed for 30 seconds. Increase mixer speed to medium, and beat until smooth and glossy, about 5 minutes.

Photo by Dale Gray

MELKTERTJIES

Makes 38

Recipe by Dale Gray/*feedfeed*

A Sunday afternoon treat often served with a cup of rooibos tea. There are two versions: this one with a pastry bottom, and one that has no crust at all but is made in a larger size. Simply put, it's a mini milk tart or egg custard tart dusted with cinnamon. So many South Africans can instantly recognize the rich buttery aroma of melktert. It is the one recipe that we all seek out during the holidays, especially expats here in the United States.

2   cups (250 grams) all-purpose flour
1   teaspoon (5 grams) baking powder
1   teaspoon (2 grams) finely grated orange zest
½   teaspoon (1.5 grams) kosher salt
½   cup (113 grams) cold unsalted butter, cubed
½   cup (100 grams) granulated sugar
2   large eggs (100 grams)
1   teaspoon (4 grams) vanilla extract
Melktertjies Filling (recipe follows)
Garnish: Indonesian cinnamon powder

1. In the work bowl of a food processor, place flour, baking powder, zest, and salt; pulse just until combined. Add cold butter, and pulse until mixture is crumbly.
2. In a small bowl, whisk together sugar, eggs, and vanilla. Add sugar mixture to flour mixture, and pulse until combined. Wrap dough in plastic wrap, and refrigerate for at least 45 minutes.
3. Preheat oven to 350°F (180°C).
4. Turn out dough onto a lightly floured surface, and roll into a 13x9-inch rectangle, about ¼ inch thick. Using a 2-inch fluted round cutter, cut dough, and gently place in ungreased muffin cups, pressing into bottom and up sides.
5. Bake until golden, about 8 minutes. Use a fork to gently lift shells out of pan. Let cool completely on a wire rack. Pipe 1 tablespoon (20 grams) Melktertjies Filling into each cookie cup. Sprinkle with cinnamon, if desired. Refrigerate in an airtight container for up to 3 days.

MELKTERTJIES FILLING
Makes 4 cups

2   large eggs (100 grams)
½   cup (100 grams) granulated sugar
3   tablespoons (24 grams) cornstarch
2   cups (480 grams) whole milk
2   tablespoons (28 grams) cold unsalted butter, cubed
¼   teaspoon (1.5 grams) vanilla bean paste

1. In a small bowl, whisk together eggs, sugar, and cornstarch until smooth.
2. In a medium saucepan, heat milk and butter over medium heat, stirring frequently, just until bubbles form around edges of pan (do not boil). Remove from heat. Add ¼ cup warm milk mixture to egg mixture, whisking constantly. Add egg mixture to remaining warm milk mixture, and cook, whisking frequently, until mixture thickens, 5 to 10 minutes. Stir in vanilla bean paste. Remove from heat, and cover with plastic wrap. Let cool completely.

PRO TIP
It is not necessary to flour or line the muffin pans. These cookies come out very easily due to the high butter content. The cookies will soften as time passes, so it's best to eat them immediately.

Photo by Dale Gray

FIVE-SPICE MOLASSES COOKIES

Makes 24

Recipe by Rebecca Firth

Muscovado, an unprocessed cane sugar, is perfect for holiday baking. It lends flavors of molasses, toffee, and caramel that pair wonderfully with a little hit of Chinese five-spice. That rich trio of tastes is the perfect contrast to the spicy notes of cloves, cinnamon, and Szechuan peppercorn found in the blend. Muscovado, which has the consistency of wet sand, has a tendency to clump, so break up any large lumps when creaming it with the butter.

½   cup (113 grams) unsalted butter, softened
½   cup (110 grams) firmly packed dark muscovado sugar*
½   cup (100 grams) granulated sugar, divided
⅓   cup (75 grams) sunflower seed or other neutral oil
⅓   cup (113 grams) unsulphured molasses

2   large eggs (100 grams), room temperature
1   tablespoon (13 grams) vanilla extract
1½   cups (188 grams) all-purpose flour
1   cup (127 grams) bread flour
1   tablespoon (6 grams) ground ginger
2   teaspoons (10 grams) baking soda
2   teaspoons (4 grams) Chinese five-spice powder
1   teaspoon (2 grams) ground cinnamon
1   teaspoon (3 grams) kosher salt
½   teaspoon (1 gram) ground cloves
½   teaspoon (1 gram) ground cardamom

1. In the bowl of a stand mixer fitted with the paddle attachment, beat butter, muscovado sugar, ¼ cup (50 grams) granulated sugar, and oil at medium speed until fluffy, 3 to 4 minutes, stopping to scrape sides of bowl. With mixer on low speed, add molasses, eggs, and vanilla, beating until combined.

2. In a medium bowl, whisk together flours, ginger, baking soda, five-spice powder, cinnamon, salt, cloves, and cardamom. Fold flour mixture into butter mixture just until combined. Wrap dough tightly in plastic wrap, and refrigerate for at least 1 hour or up to 3 days. (This dough is sticky; do not skip this step.)

3. Preheat oven to 375°F (190°C), and place rack in top third of oven. Line a baking sheet with parchment paper.

4. Place remaining ¼ cup (50 grams) granulated sugar in a shallow bowl. Using a 1-tablespoon scoop, scoop dough, and roll into balls. Roll balls in granulated sugar, coating completely. Place 2 inches apart on prepared pan.

5. Bake for 10 minutes. (You want to slightly undercook these.) Let cool on pan for 5 to 10 minutes. Remove from pan, and let cool completely on wire racks.

You can easily substitute dark brown sugar for the muscovado.

Photo by Joe Schmelzer

CHEWY CHAI-SPICED CRANBERRY MOLASSES COOKIES

Makes 24

Recipe by Kristie Pryor/*feedfeed*

Full of warm spices and studded with tart dried cranberries, these Chewy Chai-Spiced Cranberry Molasses Cookies are a treat you'll want to enjoy throughout the holiday season. Cozy up with a few by the fire, or wrap a stack up with some twine to give as the perfect homemade holiday gift.

¾   cup (170 grams) unsalted butter, softened
½   cup (110 grams) firmly packed light brown sugar
½   cup (100 grams) granulated sugar
¼   cup (85 grams) fancy molasses
1   large egg (50 grams)
2   teaspoons (8 grams) vanilla extract*
2¼   cups (281 grams) all-purpose flour
2   teaspoons (10 grams) baking soda
1   teaspoon (3 grams) kosher salt
1   teaspoon (2 grams) ground cinnamon
¾   teaspoon (1.5 grams) ground ginger
½   teaspoon (1 gram) ground cardamom
¼   teaspoon ground nutmeg
⅛   teaspoon ground cloves
¾   cup (96 grams) dried cranberries
Cinnamon-Spiced Rolling Sugar (recipe follows)
Chai Tea Glaze (recipe follows)

1. Preheat oven to 325°F (170°C). Line 2 baking sheets with parchment paper.
2. In the bowl of a stand mixer fitted with the paddle attachment, beat butter and sugars at medium speed until fluffy, 3 to 4 minutes, stopping to scrape sides of bowl. Add molasses, beating to combine. Beat in egg and vanilla.
3. In a medium bowl, whisk together flour, baking soda, salt, cinnamon, ginger, cardamom, nutmeg, and cloves. With mixer on low speed, gradually add flour mixture to butter mixture, beating just until combined. Stir in cranberries.
4. Place Cinnamon-Spiced Rolling Sugar in a small bowl. Using a medium (1½-tablespoon) spring-loaded scoop, scoop dough, and roll into balls. Roll balls in Cinnamon-Spiced Rolling Sugar, coating completely. Place about 2 inches apart on prepared pans.
5. Bake until tops are crackly and edges are golden, 9 to 11 minutes. Let cool on pans for 5 minutes. Remove from pans, and place on wire racks set over sheets of parchment paper. Drizzle cookies with Chai Tea Glaze. Let set for 10 minutes before serving. Cookies are best eaten within first 3 days after baking. Store in an airtight container at room temperature.

*I used Rodelle Pure Vanilla Extract.

PRO TIP
If you don't want to bake off all the cookie dough right away, you can reserve half of the dough, wrap in plastic wrap, and refrigerate in an airtight container for up to 1 week. Use reserved dough to bake fresh cookies when desired.

CINNAMON-SPICED ROLLING SUGAR
Makes ½ cup

½   cup (100 grams) granulated sugar
½   tablespoon (3 grams) ground cinnamon

1. In a small bowl, whisk together sugar and cinnamon.

CHAI TEA GLAZE
Makes 1 cup

1¼   cups (150 grams) confectioners' sugar
2   tablespoons (30 grams) strongly brewed chai tea
½   teaspoon (2 grams) pure vanilla extract*

1. In a small bowl, whisk together confectioners' sugar, tea, and vanilla until smooth and creamy. Refrigerate in an airtight container for up to 1 week.

*I used Rodelle Pure Vanilla Extract.

Note: *You want your glaze to be a thick yet pourable consistency. If you find that your glaze is a bit too thick, start by adding a bit more chai tea, about 1 teaspoon (5 grams) at a time, whisking until smooth and desired consistency is reached. Alternatively, if you find that your glaze is too thin, add in additional confectioners' sugar, 1 tablespoon (7 grams) at a time, until it thickens up.*

PRO TIP
When drizzling the glaze over your cookies, hold your spoon a good 6 inches above each cookie as you work. Begin to slowly drizzle the Chai Tea Glaze at the top outer edge of the cookie to create the nice drizzled look, and avoid large blobs of glaze.

Photo by Kristie Pryor

GINGERBREAD HOUSE

Makes dough for 1 gingerbread house

Recipe by Bill Bowick and David Bouffard

Architects-turned-bakers and the guys behind Charleston's Sugar Bakeshop Bill Bowick and David Bouffard put a Southern twist on a beloved holiday tradition by making gingerbread houses in the style of the city's signature single house. This all-purpose gingerbread dough is tender and delicious enough to eat, but sturdy enough for construction.

½   cup (113 grams) unsalted butter, softened
1   cup (220 grams) firmly packed light brown sugar
1   large egg (50 grams)
⅔   cup (226 grams) molasses
2¾   cups (344 grams) all-purpose flour
1½   teaspoons (7.5 grams) baking powder
1¼   teaspoons (6.25 grams) baking soda
1   teaspoon (2 grams) ground cinnamon
1   teaspoon (2 grams) ground cloves
1   teaspoon (2 grams) ground ginger
½   teaspoon (1.5 grams) kosher salt
¼   teaspoon ground allspice
Royal Icing (recipe follows)

1. Visit *bakefromscratch.com/gingerbread-house* to download and print the true-to-scale template pieces for the house. Cut out each template piece, and trace the shapes onto stiff cardboard. Cut outlined template pieces from cardboard.
2. In the bowl of a stand mixer fitted with the paddle attachment, beat butter and brown sugar at medium speed until fluffy, 3 to 4 minutes, stopping to scrape sides of bowl. Add egg, beating well. Beat in molasses.
3. In a medium bowl, sift together flour, baking powder, baking soda, cinnamon, cloves, ginger, salt, and allspice. With mixer on low speed, gradually add flour mixture to butter mixture, beating until combined. Shape dough into a disk, and wrap in plastic wrap. Refrigerate for at least 8 hours or overnight.
4. Preheat oven to 350°F (180°C).
5. Divide dough in half, and return one half to refrigerator. Place other half on a lightly floured sheet of parchment paper. Top with a second sheet of parchment paper, and roll dough to ⅛-inch thickness. Remove top sheet of parchment.
6. Brush cardboard templates with flour so they do not stick to dough. Gently place 2 side elevation, front elevation, and rear elevation templates onto dough. Using a sharp knife, cut around templates. Instead of pulling knife, press directly up and down so knife doesn't pull the dough too much and the templates will stay in shape. Using a pastry brush, dust any excess flour off dough. Pull away dough scraps to be rerolled.
7. To cut out a porch door on the side of the house, choose which side elevation you want to build the porch on. Cut a 2½x1-inch rectangle out of the center of one of the long (7½-inch) edges. You will attach this edge to your base.
8. Transfer dough and parchment paper to a baking sheet. If any pieces shift during transfer, use the end of a spatula to gently reshape. Use a pastry brush to gently dust off any excess flour.
9. Roll remaining dough to ⅛-inch thickness. Use templates to cut out remaining pieces of house. Use holiday cookie cutters* to cut out a star for the roof of the house and gingerbread people to place around the house. Transfer pieces to baking sheets. Freeze for 10 minutes.
10. Bake until crisp, 15 to 20 minutes. Let cool completely, about 30 minutes. (Do not use wire rack to cool pieces. It will prevent them from drying as flat as possible.) Once pieces are removed from oven, dust again with a pastry brush so that they are as clean as possible to help them attach better when constructing the house. Gingerbread can be baked up to 2 days in advance and stored in an airtight container until ready to construct house. Dough can be frozen for up to 1 month.
11. Construct house, and decorate with Royal Icing. Your gingerbread house should last up to 2 months. You can enjoy eating your completed house for up to 1 week after you build it.

We like the Wilton Holiday Cookie Cutter Set, available on amazon.com.

ROYAL ICING

Makes 3 cups

This is basically glue you can eat. It is the mortar, paint, and most important tool in building a gingerbread house. Bill and David use less water in the icing that holds the house together, which makes it stronger, and put a little more water in the icing used to decorate the house, which makes it more pliable.

4   cups (480 grams) confectioners' sugar
5   tablespoons (35 grams) meringue powder
⅓   cup (80 grams) plus ½ tablespoon (7.5 grams) cold water, divided

1. In the bowl of a stand mixer fitted with the whisk attachment, beat confectioners' sugar and meringue powder at low speed until combined. Switch to the paddle attachment. With mixer on medium speed, add ⅓ cup (80 grams) water in a slow, steady stream, beating until thick and fluffy, about 3 minutes. Remove 1½ cups icing from bowl, and spoon into a piping bag fitted with a #10 piping tip. You will use this icing to hold the main pieces of the house together.
2. Add remaining ½ tablespoon (7.5 grams) water to remaining 1½ cups icing, and beat until combined. Spoon icing into a piping bag fitted with a #2 piping tip. You will use this icing to decorate the house. Icing will keep refrigerated for up to 24 hours. Cover with plastic wrap, pressing wrap directly onto surface of icing to prevent it from hardening. (It will become lumpy and dry if exposed to the air for too long.) Let icing come to room temperature before using.

PRO TIP
You can pipe the windows, shutters, and door on the house before you put the pieces together. This will prevent icing from dripping, which sometimes occurs while decorating the house once it's built. After templates have baked and cooled, pipe windows and shutters. Let dry for 30 minutes before constructing house.

ROSEMARY SHORTBREAD LINZER COOKIES WITH RED PEPPER JELLY

Makes about 12

Red pepper jelly brings a festive, spicy flair to these buttery rosemary-infused sandwich cookies. Skip the cheese and crackers at your next cocktail party and serve these sweet and savory Linzers with your favorite sparkling wine.

¾   cup (170 grams) unsalted butter, softened
½   cup (60 grams) confectioners' sugar
½   teaspoon (2 grams) vanilla extract
1½ cups (188 grams) all-purpose flour
2   tablespoons (4 grams) chopped fresh rosemary
½   teaspoon (1.5 grams) kosher salt
½   teaspoon (1 gram) ground black pepper
¼   cup (80 grams) red pepper jelly

1. In the bowl of a stand mixer fitted with the paddle attachment, beat butter, confectioners' sugar, and vanilla at medium speed until creamy, 3 to 4 minutes, stopping to scrape sides of bowl.

2. In a medium bowl, whisk together flour, rosemary, salt, and pepper. With mixer on low speed, gradually add flour mixture to butter mixture, beating until combined. Divide dough in half, and shape into disks. Wrap in plastic wrap, and refrigerate for at least 1 hour or overnight.

3. Preheat oven to 350°F (180°C). Line 2 baking sheets with parchment paper.

4. On a lightly floured surface, roll half of dough to ¼-inch thickness. Using a 3-inch fluted round cutter, cut dough, rerolling scraps only once. Repeat with remaining dough. Using a 1-inch fluted round cutter, cut centers from half of cookies. Place about 1 inch apart on prepared pans.

5. Bake until edges are lightly browned, 10 to 12 minutes. Let cool on pans for 1 minute. Remove from pans, and let cool completely on wire racks. Spread about 1 teaspoon pepper jelly onto flat side of all solid cookies. Place cookies with cutouts, flat side down, on top of jelly. Bake 2 to 3 minutes more. Let cool completely. Store in an airtight container at room temperature for up to 4 days.

CRANBERRY ORANGE YULE LOG COOKIES

Makes 24

We gave the classic holiday roulade also known as a bûche de Noël a mini makeover. These bite-size Yule logs have a tart and citrusy dough complemented with a sweet "bark" coating of white or semisweet chocolate. Miniature Gumdrop Mushrooms and Leaves add a precious level of detail to your small-scale masterpiece.

½   cup (113 grams) unsalted butter, softened
½   cup (60 grams) confectioners' sugar
½   teaspoon (1.5 grams) kosher salt
½   teaspoon (1 gram) ground nutmeg
1   large egg (50 grams), separated
1¼   cups (156 grams) all-purpose flour
⅓   cup (43 grams) chopped dried cranberries
1   teaspoon (2 grams) orange zest
1   teaspoon (5 grams) water
2   ounces (55 grams) white chocolate, chopped
2   ounces (55 grams) semisweet chocolate, chopped
Gumdrop Mushrooms and Leaves (recipe follows)
Garnish: confectioners' sugar

1. In the bowl of a stand mixer fitted with the paddle attachment, beat butter, confectioners' sugar, salt, and nutmeg at medium speed until creamy, 3 to 4 minutes, stopping to scrape sides of bowl. Add egg yolk, beating until combined.
2. In a medium bowl, whisk together flour, cranberries, and zest. With mixer on low speed, gradually add flour mixture to butter mixture, beating until combined. Divide dough into 4 equal portions. Shape into disks, and wrap in plastic wrap. Refrigerate for 1 hour.
3. Preheat oven to 350°F (180°C). Line 2 baking sheets with parchment paper.
4. On a lightly floured surface, roll each disk into an 18-inch-long rope. Cut each rope into 6 (3-inch-long) logs. Cut ¼ inch off ends of each log on a bias, reserving dough scraps. Place logs on prepared pans.
5. In a small bowl, whisk together egg white and 1 teaspoon (5 grams) water. Brush logs and scraps with egg wash, and adhere 2 dough scraps to each log to create stumps.
6. Bake until lightly golden, 8 to 10 minutes. Remove from oven, and let cool completely.
7. In a microwave-safe bowl, heat white chocolate on high in 30-second intervals, stirring between each, until melted and smooth. Repeat with semisweet chocolate.

Dip each log in melted chocolate, coating top and sides of cookie. Using a fork, create bark lines on chocolate-coated cookies. Adhere Gumdrop Mushrooms and Leaves to cookies as desired. Let chocolate set. Garnish with confectioners' sugar, if desired.

GUMDROP MUSHROOMS AND LEAVES
Makes 60 mushrooms and 40 leaves

5   red gumdrops
4   white gumdrops
1   ounce (30 grams) white chocolate, melted
3   green gumdrops

1. Line a baking sheet with parchment paper.
2. Roll out red gumdrops to flatten. Using the tip of a Wilton #10 round piping tip, cut out 60 circles (about 12 per gumdrop).
3. Roll out white gumdrops to flatten. Cut into very thin strips. Using melted white chocolate, adhere each strip to flat side of a red disk. Place mushrooms, strip side up, on prepared pan. Let chocolate set for 1 hour.
4. Roll out green gumdrops to flatten. Using a Wilton #104 leaf piping tip, cut out 40 teardrop leaves. Store in an airtight container at room temperature for up to 2 weeks.

PECAN GINGER LINZER COOKIES WITH ORANGE MARMALADE

Makes 12

Old-fashioned Linzer cookies use the same nutty almond and citrus-scented dough as a Linzer Torte. For our version, pecans sub in for almonds and grated fresh ginger brings a welcome dose of heat to this orange marmalade-filled sandwich cookie.

⅔ cup (75 grams) pecan halves
¼ cup (50 grams) granulated sugar
1⅓ cups (167 grams) all-purpose flour
¼ cup (55 grams) firmly packed light brown sugar
1 teaspoon (2 grams) lemon zest
1 teaspoon grated fresh ginger
½ teaspoon (1.5 grams) kosher salt
½ cup (113 grams) unsalted butter, softened
¼ cup (80 grams) orange marmalade
Garnish: confectioners' sugar

1. In the work bowl of a food processor, place pecan halves and granulated sugar; process until mixture is crumbly, about 2 minutes. Add flour, brown sugar, zest, ginger, and salt; process until finely ground.
2. In the bowl of a stand mixer fitted with the paddle attachment, beat pecan mixture and butter at medium-low speed until well combined. Shape dough into a disk, and wrap in plastic wrap. Refrigerate for 30 minutes.
3. Preheat oven to 350°F (180°C). Line 2 baking sheets with parchment paper.
4. Roll dough to ¼-inch thickness between 2 sheets of parchment paper. Remove top sheet of parchment. Using a 3-inch star cutter, cut dough, rerolling scraps as necessary. Using a 1¼-inch star cutter, cut centers from half of cookies. Place on prepared pans.
5. Bake until lightly golden, 7 to 10 minutes. Let cool on pans for 15 minutes. Spread 1 teaspoon orange marmalade onto flat side of all solid cookies. Place cookies with cutouts, flat side down, on top of marmalade. Bake 2 minutes more. Sprinkle with confectioners' sugar, if desired. Store, covered, at room temperature for up to 1 week.

CARDAMOM HONEY CUT OUT COOKIES

Makes 36

This recipe is inspired by the holiday honey bread cookies of Croatia known as Licitars. Since the 16th century, these brilliant red cookies have been displayed as ornaments and edible gifts during the Christmas season. Our warmly spiced adaptation pairs mellow honey with bold cardamom and swaps the traditional gelatin glaze with an easier-to-maneuver and tastier Vanilla-Almond Royal Icing.

½ cup (113 grams) unsalted butter, softened
⅓ cup (67 grams) granulated sugar
1 large egg yolk (19 grams)
2 tablespoons (42 grams) honey
¾ teaspoon (3 grams) vanilla extract
1½ cups (188 grams) all-purpose flour
¾ teaspoon (1.5 grams) ground cardamom
½ teaspoon (1.5 grams) kosher salt
¼ teaspoon (1.25 grams) baking soda
Vanilla-Almond Royal Icing (recipe follows)
Garnish: nonpareils

1. In the bowl of a stand mixer fitted with the paddle attachment, beat butter and sugar at medium speed until creamy, 3 to 4 minutes, stopping to scrape sides of bowl. Add egg yolk, honey, and vanilla, beating until well combined.
2. In a medium bowl, whisk together flour, cardamom, salt, and baking soda. With mixer on low speed, gradually add flour mixture to butter mixture, beating until combined. Divide dough in half, and shape into disks. Wrap in plastic wrap, and refrigerate for 1 hour.
3. Preheat oven to 350°F (180°C). Line 3 baking sheets with parchment paper.
4. Working with one disk at a time, roll dough to ¼-inch thickness on a lightly floured surface. Using desired 2½-inch holiday cutters, cut dough, rerolling scraps as necessary. Place on prepared pans. Freeze for 15 minutes.
5. Bake until lightly golden, 8 to 10 minutes. Let cool on pans for 3 minutes. Remove from pans, and let cool completely on wire racks. Decorate as desired with Vanilla-Almond Royal Icing. Garnish with nonpareils, if desired. Let dry completely. Store in airtight containers for up to 1 week.

Note: *If decorating with the traditional Licitar colors, let red icing dry completely before adding white icing on top, or colors will bleed.*

VANILLA-ALMOND ROYAL ICING
Makes about 4 cups

4½ cups (540 grams) confectioners' sugar, divided
2 large egg whites (60 grams)
2 teaspoons (8 grams) almond extract
1½ teaspoons (6 grams) clear vanilla extract
¾ teaspoon (2.25 grams) kosher salt
½ teaspoon (1 gram) cream of tartar
3 tablespoons (45 grams) heavy whipping cream
Gel food coloring

1. In the top of a double boiler, stir together 4 cups (480 grams) confectioners' sugar, egg whites, extracts, salt, and cream of tartar. Cook over simmering water, stirring occasionally, until mixture registers 140°F (60°C) on a candy thermometer. Pour mixture into the bowl of a stand mixer fitted with the paddle attachment.
2. With mixer on low speed, add remaining ½ cup (60 grams) confectioners' sugar, beating until well combined and cooled to room temperature. Add cream, 1 tablespoon (15 grams) at a time, beating until desired consistency is reached. To test consistency, dip a spoon in frosting and lift, moving it in a figure-eight pattern over bowl as icing drizzles down. The figure-eight shape should disappear in 8 seconds for a cookie glaze and in 10 seconds for a thicker icing used for detail work. Color as desired with food coloring. Use immediately, or refrigerate with a piece of plastic wrap pressed directly onto surface for up to 2 days. Bring to room temperature, and stir before using.

EGGNOG DROP COOKIES

Makes about 30

Your favorite holiday toddy gets the cookie send-up it deserves. Nutmeg, cloves, cinnamon, and spiced rum come together in these simple, tender drop cookies for a perfectly balanced eggnog flavor.

¾ cup (170 grams) unsalted butter, softened
¼ cup (50 grams) granulated sugar
¾ cup (165 grams) firmly packed light brown sugar
2 large egg yolks (37 grams)
1 teaspoon (4 grams) vanilla extract
½ teaspoon (2 grams) rum extract
½ teaspoon (2 grams) maple syrup extract
2¼ cups (281 grams) all-purpose flour
2 teaspoons (10 grams) baking powder
1 teaspoon (2 grams) ground nutmeg
½ teaspoon (1.5 grams) kosher salt
½ teaspoon (1 gram) ground cinnamon
¼ teaspoon ground cloves
¼ cup (60 grams) spiced rum
¼ cup (60 grams) heavy whipping cream
Vanilla Buttercream (recipe follows)
Garnish: grated fresh nutmeg

1. Preheat oven to 350°F (180°C). Line 3 baking sheets with parchment paper.
2. In the bowl of a stand mixer fitted with the paddle attachment, beat butter and sugars at medium speed until fluffy, 3 to 4 minutes, stopping to scrape sides of bowl. Add egg yolks, one at a time, beating just until combined after each addition. Beat in extracts.
3. In a medium bowl, whisk together flour, baking powder, nutmeg, salt, cinnamon, and cloves. In a small bowl, combine rum and cream. With mixer on low speed, gradually add flour mixture to butter mixture alternately with rum mixture, beginning and ending with flour mixture, beating just until combined after each addition. Using a medium (1½-tablespoon) scoop, drop dough 2 inches apart onto prepared pans. Press down to flatten slightly.

4. Bake until lightly golden, 10 to 12 minutes. Let cool on pans for 5 minutes. Remove from pans, and let cool completely on wire racks. Spread Vanilla Buttercream onto cooled cookies, and garnish with nutmeg, if desired. Store in an airtight container at room temperature for up to 4 days.

VANILLA BUTTERCREAM
Makes about 3 cups

½ cup (113 grams) unsalted butter, softened
3 cups (360 grams) confectioners' sugar
2 tablespoons (30 grams) heavy whipping cream
1 teaspoon (4 grams) vanilla extract

1. In the bowl of a stand mixer fitted with the paddle attachment, beat butter, confectioners' sugar, cream, and vanilla at medium-low speed until light and fluffy, 2 to 3 minutes. Use immediately.

CHOCOLATE PEPPERMINT COOKIES

Makes 24

For our sleek twist to the "stained glass" cookies from childhood, starlight peppermint candies are melted and then swirled within a dark cocoa cookie frame. A little kick of black pepper gives these chocolate cookies a hint of heat, rounding out the cool mint center.

½   cup (113 grams) unsalted butter, softened
⅔   cup (147 grams) firmly packed light brown sugar
1   tablespoon (14 grams) olive oil
1   teaspoon (4 grams) vanilla extract
¾   teaspoon (2.25 grams) kosher salt
1   large egg (50 grams)
1½   cups (188 grams) all-purpose flour
½   cup (43 grams) dark unsweetened cocoa powder
¼   cup (32 grams) cornstarch
¼   teaspoon ground black pepper
Garnish: turbinado sugar
24   peppermint candies

1. In the bowl of a stand mixer fitted with the paddle attachment, beat butter, brown sugar, oil, vanilla, and salt at medium-low speed just until combined, about 2 minutes. Add egg, beating well.
2. In a medium bowl, whisk together flour, cocoa, cornstarch, and pepper. With mixer on low speed, gradually add flour mixture to butter mixture, beating until combined. Shape dough into a disk, and wrap in plastic wrap. Refrigerate for 30 minutes.

3. Preheat oven to 350°F (180°C). Line 2 baking sheets with parchment paper.
4. On a lightly floured surface, roll dough to ¼-inch thickness. Using a 2¾-inch fluted square cutter, cut dough, rerolling scraps as necessary. Using a 1½-inch round cutter, cut centers from cookies. Place on prepared pans. Sprinkle with turbinado sugar, if desired.
5. Bake for 2 minutes. Place a peppermint in center of each cookie. Bake 6 minutes more. Using a wooden skewer and working quickly, swirl melted candy to create desired patterns. Let cool completely. Store in an airtight container at room temperature for up to 1 week.

BARS

Any way you slice it, bars are classic and convenient. From warm, fudgy brownies to jammy crumble bars and tangy custard pastry, these bars will bring on a rush of nostalgia and delight.

CARROT MASALA BARS

Makes about 32

Recipe by Chadwick Boyd

When carrots are cooked in the oven, their natural sugars become deep and rich all on their own. A not-so-sweet version of a shortbread cookie, these cookies are inspired by traditional tea cakes in India and allow the delicious sweetness of fresh carrots to shine through in a surprising yet subtle way. Finely shredded carrots are mixed into a traditional shortbread dough along with a homemade masala of turmeric, cinnamon, cardamom, and ginger for a bold pop of flavor. I am not a fan of traditionally sweet desserts, but I love how a light dusting of pink peppercorn and Indian Demerara sugar on top brings out the natural sweetness of the carrots and the depth of the spices. Be creative with the toppings! Mix in chia seeds with the Demerara sugar. I use pink peppercorns, but you can also use black pepper.

¾ cup (170 grams) unsalted butter, softened
¼ cup (50 grams) plus 1 to 2 teaspoons (4 to 8 grams) Demerara sugar*, divided
1 large egg (50 grams)
1⅓ cups (167 grams) all-purpose flour
⅔ cup (83 grams) cake flour
½ cup (75 grams) semolina flour
½ teaspoon (2.5 grams) baking powder
¾ teaspoon (2.25 grams) sea salt
¾ cup (74 grams) finely grated carrot
¼ cup (25 grams) shredded carrot
1½ teaspoons (3 grams) curry powder
1 teaspoon grated fresh ginger
2 to 3 teaspoons (6 to 9 grams) cracked pink peppercorns, divided
¾ teaspoon (1.5 grams) turmeric
¾ teaspoon (1.5 grams) ground cardamom
½ teaspoon (1 gram) ground cinnamon

1. In the bowl of a stand mixer fitted with the paddle attachment, beat butter and ¼ cup (50 grams) Demerara sugar at medium-high speed until creamy, about 1 minute. (The sugar does not dissolve, and will still look grainy.) Using a rubber scraper, scrape sides of bowl, and beat for 15 to 20 seconds. Add egg, and beat until combined.
2. In a medium bowl, whisk together flours, baking powder, and salt. Add grated and shredded carrot, and whisk until fully coated.
3. In a small bowl, stir together curry powder, ginger, 1 teaspoon (3 grams) pink peppercorns, turmeric, cardamom, and cinnamon. Add curry mixture to carrot mixture, stirring until combined.
4. Reduce mixer speed to medium. Gradually add carrot mixture to butter mixture, and beat until a dough forms, about 1 minute.
5. Turn out dough onto a lightly floured surface, and roll into a 17x2½-inch rectangle, about ¾ inch thick. Wrap tightly in plastic wrap, and refrigerate for at least 2 hours or overnight.
6. Preheat oven to 300°F (150°C). Line 2 baking sheets with parchment paper. (These bars bake at a lower oven temperature to keep their unique rectangular shape. The lower temperature ensures the butter does not melt too quickly.)
7. Using a lightly floured chef's knife, slice dough into ½-inch bars. Place bars, cut side down, on prepared pans. Dust with remaining 1 to 2 teaspoons (4 to 8 grams) Demerara sugar, and sprinkle with remaining 1 to 2 teaspoons (3 to 6 grams) peppercorns.
8. Bake until bottoms are golden brown, about 35 minutes. Let cool completely on a wire rack.

Demerara sugar can be found in higher-end grocery stores and specialty shops. Raw or coarsely granulated cane sugar would work well, also. If you like cookies a touch more sweet, add an additional tablespoon of Demerara to the butter when mixing.

Note: *We used the side of a box grater with small holes to grate the carrot finely, and the side with larger holes to shred the carrot.*

FIG BROWNIES WITH
SOUR BEER CARAMEL

Makes 9

Though fresh figs are delicious gems in their own right, there is much to be gained by baking with the dried form. We like to add them to fudgy brownies to impart an intense, caramel-like sweetness. Here, crystallized ginger and our Sour Beer Caramel add complementary spicy and tangy counter notes.

1½ cups (262.5 grams) chopped and stemmed dried figs
¼   cup (43.8 grams) chopped and pitted Medjool dates
1   tablespoon (23 grams) minced crystallized ginger
4   cups (960 grams) boiling water
6   ounces (175 grams) semisweet chocolate, chopped
⅓   cup (75 grams) canola oil
3   large eggs (150 grams)
2   teaspoons (8 grams) vanilla extract
⅓   cup (42 grams) all-purpose flour
¼   cup (21 grams) unsweetened cocoa powder
¾   teaspoon (2.25 grams) kosher salt
½   teaspoon (2.5 grams) baking powder
Sour Beer Caramel (recipe follows)
Garnish: flaked sea salt

1. Preheat oven to 350°F (180°C). Butter and flour a 9-inch square baking pan.
2. In a medium bowl, combine figs, dates, and ginger. Add 4 cups (960 grams) boiling water, and let stand until fruit is softened, about 5 minutes. Drain fruit mixture. Transfer to the work bowl of a food processor, and process until smooth, 2 to 3 minutes.
3. In a small microwave-safe bowl, heat chocolate on high in 30-second intervals, stirring between each, until chocolate is melted and smooth (about 1½ minutes total). Add melted chocolate and oil to fruit mixture; process until well combined. Add eggs and vanilla; process just until combined.
4. In a medium bowl, whisk together flour, cocoa, salt, and baking powder. Add flour mixture to chocolate mixture, and process just until combined. Pour batter into prepared pan, smoothing top with an offset spatula.
5. Bake until a wooden pick inserted in center comes out clean, 15 to 20 minutes. Let cool completely. Pour warm Sour Beer Caramel over brownies. Sprinkle with sea salt, if desired. Let stand until caramel is set. Cut into 9 squares. Store in an airtight container at room temperature for up to 4 days.

SOUR BEER CARAMEL
Makes about 2½ cups

1½ cups (330 grams) firmly packed light brown sugar
¾   cup (170 grams) unsalted butter
¾   cup (180 grams) plus 1 tablespoon (15 grams) sour beer*, divided
½   cup (170 grams) light corn syrup
1   teaspoon (4 grams) vanilla extract

1. In a medium saucepan, cook brown sugar and butter over medium heat until butter is melted. Slowly add ¾ cup (180 grams) beer and corn syrup. Cook, stirring frequently, until a candy thermometer registers 240°F (115°C). (Be careful not to let mixture bubble over.) Remove from heat; stir in vanilla and remaining 1 tablespoon (15 grams) beer. Let cool for 10 minutes. Use immediately.

We used Westbrook Brewing Gose.

TURTLE BROWNIES

Makes 8 servings

Double-chocolate brownies layered with caramel filling and topped with chocolate-covered pecans just might be the perfect indulgent dessert.

¾ cup (170 grams) unsalted butter
4 ounces (115 grams) 60% cacao bittersweet chocolate, chopped
1¼ cups (250 grams) granulated sugar
2 large eggs (100 grams)
1 cup (125 grams) all-purpose flour
¼ teaspoon (1.25 grams) baking powder
¼ teaspoon kosher salt
1 cup (170 grams) miniature semisweet chocolate morsels
1 teaspoon (4 grams) vanilla extract
Caramel Sauce (recipe follows)
Garnish: Caramel Sauce, Chocolate-Covered Pecans (recipe follows)
Vanilla ice cream, to serve

1. Preheat oven to 350°F (180°C). Line a 9-inch square baking pan with foil, letting excess extend over sides of pan; lightly spray with cooking spray.
2. In a large microwave-safe bowl, microwave butter and chopped chocolate on high in 30-second intervals, stirring between each, until melted and smooth (1½ to 2 minutes total). Whisk in sugar. Add eggs, one at a time, whisking until combined after each addition. Whisk in flour, baking powder, and salt. Gently stir in chocolate morsels and vanilla. Pour batter into prepared pan.
3. Bake until a wooden pick inserted in center comes out clean, 30 to 35 minutes. Let cool in pan for 1 hour. Using excess foil as handles, remove from pan, and cut into small triangles.
4. Layer brownie triangles and Caramel Sauce in 8 coupe glasses. Garnish with Caramel Sauce and Chocolate-Covered Pecans, if desired. Serve with ice cream.

CARAMEL SAUCE
Makes 1½ cups

¼ cup (57 grams) unsalted butter
1 cup (220 grams) firmly packed light brown sugar
½ cup (120 grams) heavy whipping cream, room temperature
2 teaspoons (8 grams) vanilla extract
⅛ teaspoon kosher salt

1. In a medium saucepan, melt butter over medium heat. Add brown sugar, and stir to combine. Cook for 5 minutes, stirring constantly (mixture will be thick). Carefully pour in cream (mixture will foam), vanilla, and salt. Remove from heat, and stir to combine. Let cool slightly. Pour into a glass jar, and refrigerate for up to 3 weeks.

CHOCOLATE-COVERED PECANS
Makes 22

½ cup (85 grams) miniature semisweet chocolate morsels
2 tablespoons (30 grams) heavy whipping cream
22 pecan halves, toasted

1. In a small microwave-safe bowl, microwave chocolate morsels and cream on high in 30-second intervals, stirring between each, until chocolate is melted and smooth (about 1 minute total). Dip pecan halves halfway into chocolate, and place on a sheet of parchment paper; let dry.

Photo by Stephen DeVries

BLACKBERRY JAM BARS

Makes 8 to 10

Grating then freezing this dough before baking creates little air pockets that give the bars a crumbly texture, which contrasts nicely with the smooth jam center. Give these a generous dusting of confectioners' sugar, and serve right out of your 13x9.

2 cups (454 grams) unsalted butter, softened
2 cups (400 grams) granulated sugar
4 large egg yolks (74 grams)
2 teaspoons (8 grams) vanilla extract
4 cups (500 grams) all-purpose flour
2 teaspoons (10 grams) baking powder
¼ teaspoon kosher salt
1 cup (320 grams) Blackberry Jam (recipe follows)
¼ cup (30 grams) confectioners' sugar

1. In the bowl of a stand mixer fitted with the paddle attachment, beat butter and granulated sugar at medium speed until creamy, 3 to 4 minutes, stopping to scrape sides of bowl. Add egg yolks, one at a time, beating well after each addition. Beat in vanilla.

2. In a large bowl, whisk together flour, baking powder, and salt. With mixer on low speed, gradually add flour mixture to butter mixture, beating just until combined. Divide dough into 4 pieces, and wrap in plastic wrap. Refrigerate for 1 hour.
3. Preheat oven to 350°F (180°C). Line a 13x9-inch baking pan with parchment paper, letting excess extend over sides of pan. Butter and flour pan.
4. Grate 2 pieces of dough using the large holes of a box grater, and spread over bottom of prepared pan in an even layer. Press down gently. Freeze for 10 minutes. Grate remaining dough, and place on a baking sheet. Freeze for 10 minutes.
5. Spread Blackberry Jam onto dough in prepared pan. Sprinkle remaining grated dough over Blackberry Jam in an even layer.
6. Bake until golden brown and set, about 40 minutes, covering with foil to prevent excess browning, if necessary. Let cool for 10 minutes, and dust with confectioners' sugar. Let cool completely. Using excess parchment as handles, remove from pan, and cut into bars. Dust with additional confectioners' sugar, if desired. Freeze in an airtight container for up to 2 weeks.

BLACKBERRY JAM
Makes 2½ cups

8 cups (1,360 grams) fresh blackberries
3 cups (600 grams) granulated sugar
2 tablespoons (30 grams) fresh lemon juice
2 tablespoons (4 grams) fresh thyme leaves

1. In a large saucepan, stir together blackberries, sugar, and lemon juice. Let stand for 2 hours.
2. Bring mixture to a boil over medium-high heat; remove from heat. Using an immersion blender, process until smooth. Strain mixture through a fine-mesh sieve, discarding solids. Pour liquid back into saucepan.
3. Cook over medium-high heat for 5 minutes, stirring frequently. Reduce heat to medium; cook, stirring frequently, until mixture thickens, 20 to 45 minutes. Remove from heat, and stir in thyme. Let cool for 1 hour. Cover and refrigerate for at least 4 hours before using.

ORANGE CUSTARD BARS

Makes 8 to 10

Sophisticated meets doable in this party go-to, a thick layer of creamy custard between two flaky sheets of homemade puff pastry. Dress it up with whipped cream and fresh fruit.

Buttery Puff Pastry (recipe follows)
3½ cups (840 grams) plus 4 tablespoons (60 grams) heavy whipping cream, divided
1½ cups (300 grams) plus 2 tablespoons (24 grams) granulated sugar, divided
¾ cup (96 grams) cornstarch
3½ cups (840 grams) whole milk
6 large egg yolks (112 grams)
1 tablespoon (6 grams) orange zest
¼ cup (57 grams) unsalted butter
3 tablespoons (45 grams) orange liqueur
¼ teaspoon kosher salt
Confectioners' sugar

1. Preheat oven to 400°F (200°C).
2. On a lightly floured piece of parchment paper, roll half of Buttery Puff Pastry into a 16x12-inch rectangle. Place on a large jelly-roll pan. Brush with 2 tablespoons (30 grams) cream, and sprinkle with 1 tablespoon (12 grams) granulated sugar. Top with parchment paper, and place another large jelly-roll pan on top of pastry.

3. Bake until golden brown, 20 to 22 minutes, pressing down on middle of top pan halfway through baking to release air from pastry. Remove from oven, and press down on pan again. Remove top pan and parchment paper; let cool completely on pan. Repeat with remaining Buttery Puff Pastry, 2 tablespoons (30 grams) cream, and 1 tablespoon (12 grams) granulated sugar.
4. In a large saucepan, whisk together cornstarch and remaining 1½ cups (300 grams) granulated sugar. Add milk and remaining 3½ cups (840 grams) cream, whisking until smooth. Bring to a low boil over medium heat.
5. In a medium bowl, whisk together egg yolks and zest. Gradually add 2 cups hot milk mixture to egg mixture, whisking constantly. Whisk egg mixture into remaining hot milk mixture in saucepan. Cook over medium heat, whisking constantly, until thickened. Remove from heat; whisk in butter, orange liqueur, and salt. Let stand at room temperature for 10 minutes. Transfer to bowl, and press a piece of plastic wrap directly onto surface of custard to prevent a skin from forming.
6. Line a 13x9-inch baking pan with parchment paper, letting excess extend over sides of pan. Using a pastry cutter, cut pastry sheets into 13x9-inch rectangles. Place one pastry sheet in prepared pan. Pour custard

over top, and cover with remaining pastry sheet, pressing down gently. Refrigerate until set, 3 to 4 hours.
7. To serve, dust with confectioners' sugar. Using excess parchment as handles, remove from pan. Using a serrated knife, gently cut into squares.

BUTTERY PUFF PASTRY
Makes 2 (16x12-inch) sheets

4 cups (500 grams) all-purpose flour
2 teaspoons (6 grams) kosher salt
2½ cups (567 grams) cold unsalted butter, cubed
¾ cup (180 grams) cold water

1. In the bowl of a stand mixer fitted with the paddle attachment, beat flour and salt at low speed to combine. Add cold butter, and beat until butter is coated with flour, about 30 seconds. With mixer running, add ¾ cup (180 grams) cold water in a slow, steady stream just until dough comes together, about 1 minute. (There will still be large pieces of butter.) Cover and refrigerate for 30 minutes.
2. On a lightly floured surface, roll dough into an 18x11-inch rectangle. Fold dough into thirds, like a letter. Rotate dough 90 degrees, and fold into thirds again. Wrap dough in plastic wrap, and refrigerate for at least 1 hour.
3. Divide dough in half, and wrap tightly in plastic wrap. Refrigerate until ready to use.

> **PRO TIP**
> With your fingers, press down on the Orange Custard Bars in the pan halfway through baking and after removing from oven to ensure the puff pastry is thin, crisp, and evenly cooked.

APPLE BUTTER BARS

Makes 9

Applesauce keeps the thick, fudgy base of these bars moist and chewy, and a generous amount of butter rounds out the tartness of the Granny Smith Applesauce. On top, crispy old-fashioned oats and slivered almonds deliver a satisfying crunch.

½   cup (63 grams) all-purpose flour
½   cup (48 grams) almond flour, toasted
½   cup (40 grams) old-fashioned oats, toasted
6   tablespoons (84 grams) unsalted butter, melted
¼   cup (55 grams) firmly packed light brown sugar
¼   cup (50 grams) granulated sugar
1   teaspoon (3 grams) kosher salt
½   teaspoon (1 gram) ground allspice
¾   cup (180 grams) Granny Smith Applesauce (recipe follows)
Almond Crumble Topping (recipe follows)

1. Preheat oven to 350°F (180°C). Butter and flour an 8-inch square baking pan; line pan with parchment paper.
2. In a medium bowl, stir together flours, oats, melted butter, sugars, salt, and allspice until crumbly. Press mixture into bottom of prepared pan. Spread Granny Smith Applesauce on top. Sprinkle with Almond Crumble Topping.
3. Bake until golden brown and bubbly, 20 to 30 minutes. Let cool on a wire rack for 30 minutes. Refrigerate for at least 1 hour before serving. Wrap in plastic wrap, and refrigerate for up to 3 days.

GRANNY SMITH APPLESAUCE

Makes 2 cups

Notorious for their bright green color and slightly sour taste, Granny Smith apples are more acidic than most apples and create a deliciously tart applesauce—perfect for upgrading your baked goods with an extra punch of flavor.

2   pounds (910 grams) Granny Smith apples, unpeeled, cored, and chopped
1   cup (240 grams) apple brandy
½   cup (110 grams) firmly packed light brown sugar
2   tablespoons (30 grams) fresh lemon juice
1   tablespoon (9 grams) fruit pectin*
1   teaspoon (6 grams) vanilla bean paste
1   teaspoon (2 grams) ground cinnamon
1   teaspoon (2 grams) ground allspice
6 to 7 cinnamon sticks (20 grams)

1. In a large stockpot, bring all ingredients to a simmer over medium-low heat. Simmer until apples are tender, 20 to 30 minutes. Let cool to room temperature.
2. Using an immersion blender, blend until smooth**. Strain mixture through a fine-mesh sieve, discarding apple skin. Cover and refrigerate for at least 2 hours before using. Refrigerate in an airtight container for up to 2 weeks.

We used Sure-Jell Premium Fruit Pectin.

**You can also blend in the container of a blender or work bowl of a food processor.*

ALMOND CRUMBLE TOPPING

Makes 2 cups

¾   cup (85 grams) slivered almonds, toasted
½   cup (63 grams) all-purpose flour
½   cup (48 grams) almond flour, toasted
½   cup (40 grams) old-fashioned oats, toasted
½   cup (113 grams) cold unsalted butter, cubed
¼   cup (55 grams) firmly packed light brown sugar
¼   cup (50 grams) granulated sugar
1   teaspoon (3 grams) kosher salt

1. In the bowl of a stand mixer fitted with the paddle attachment, beat all ingredients at medium speed just until combined, 3 to 4 minutes. Refrigerate for at least 30 minutes before using. Refrigerate in an airtight container for up to 1 week.

SCOTTISH FRUIT SLICE BARS

Makes 9

Traditional Scottish Fruit Slice is a combination of jammy dried fruit with a crumbly shortbread crust that's reminiscent of the more familiar British mincemeat pie. In our spirited take on the original, we added a generous splash of Scotch whisky to the filling.

1 cup (128 grams) raisins
1 cup (128 grams) golden raisins
1 cup (128 grams) dried currants
1 cup (220 grams) firmly packed light brown sugar
½ cup (120 grams) water
½ cup (120 grams) Scotch whisky
1 tablespoon (6 grams) lemon zest
1 tablespoon (8 grams) cornstarch
½ teaspoon (1 gram) ground allspice
Lavender Oregano Shortcrust (recipe follows)
1 large egg (50 grams)
1 tablespoon (15 grams) heavy whipping cream

1. In a medium saucepan, bring raisins, golden raisins, currants, brown sugar, ½ cup (120 grams) water, Scotch, zest, cornstarch, and allspice to a boil over medium heat. Cook, stirring frequently, until thickened, about 15 minutes. Let cool completely.
2. Preheat oven to 375°F (190°C). Butter and flour an 8-inch square baking dish; line with parchment paper, letting excess extend over sides of pan.
3. On a lightly floured surface, roll half of Lavender Oregano Shortcrust into an 8-inch square. Transfer to prepared pan. Spread fruit mixture onto crust. Roll remaining Lavender Oregano Shortcrust into 8-inch square, and place on top of fruit mixture.
4. In a small bowl, whisk together egg and cream. Brush crust with egg wash.
5. Bake until golden brown and bubbly, 20 to 25 minutes. Let cool in pan for 10 minutes. Using excess parchment as handles, remove from pan. Let cool completely before cutting into bars. Store in an airtight container at room temperature for up to 4 days.

LAVENDER OREGANO SHORTCRUST
Makes 2 (8-inch) crusts

3½ cups (438 grams) self-rising flour
1 tablespoon (2 grams) chopped fresh oregano
½ teaspoon (1 gram) ground lavender
½ teaspoon (1.5 grams) kosher salt
¾ cup (170 grams) cold unsalted butter, cubed
½ cup (120 grams) ice water

1. In the work bowl of a food processor, place flour, oregano, lavender, and salt; pulse until combined. Add cold butter, and pulse until mixture is crumbly. With processor running, add ½ cup (120 grams) ice water in a slow, steady stream until a soft dough forms. (Dough may be crumbly, but should hold together when squeezed.) Turn out dough, and divide in half. Shape each half into a disk. Wrap in plastic wrap, and refrigerate for at least 30 minutes.

NANAIMO BARS

Makes 16

Recipe by Emily Turner

Named after the city of Nanaimo on British Columbia's Vancouver Island, this chocolate wafer crumb-crusted and custard-filled treat has been an iconic staple in Canadian households since the mid-1950s.

½ cup (113 grams) unsalted butter
6 tablespoons (30 grams) unsweetened cocoa powder
⅓ cup (67 grams) granulated sugar
1 teaspoon (3 grams) kosher salt
1 large egg (50 grams), lightly beaten
½ teaspoon (3 grams) vanilla bean paste
1¾ cups (228 grams) graham cracker crumbs
1 cup (84 grams) sweetened flaked coconut
⅓ cup (38 grams) blanched slivered almonds, finely chopped
Custard Filling (recipe follows)
Grand Marnier Ganache (recipe follows)
⅓ cup (38 grams) roughly chopped almonds
2 teaspoons (6 grams) flaked salt

1. Line an 8-inch square baking pan with parchment paper, letting excess extend over sides of pan. Spray with cooking spray.

2. In the top of a double boiler, combine butter, cocoa, sugar, and salt. Cook over simmering water, stirring constantly, until butter is melted. Add egg and vanilla bean paste, stirring until thickened and smooth, about 1 minute. Remove from heat, and stir in graham cracker crumbs, coconut, and slivered almonds.

3. Press mixture into bottom of prepared pan. Spread Custard Filling onto prepared crust, smoothing top with an offset spatula. Spread Grand Marnier Ganache on top of Custard Filling, smoothing top with an offset spatula. Sprinkle with chopped whole almonds and flaked salt. Refrigerate for at least 2 hours. Using excess parchment as handles, remove from pan, and cut into bars. Serve at room temperature.

CUSTARD FILLING
Makes 1⅔ cups

½ cup plus 2 tablespoons (141 grams) unsalted butter, softened
2 tablespoons (20 grams) vanilla custard powder*
1 teaspoon (4 grams) vanilla extract
2½ cups (300 grams) confectioners' sugar, sifted
3 tablespoons (45 grams) heavy whipping cream

1. In the bowl of a stand mixer fitted with the paddle attachment, beat butter and custard powder at medium speed until creamy, 2 to 3 minutes, stopping to scrape sides of bowl. Stir in vanilla. Gradually add confectioners' sugar alternately with cream, beating until combined. Beat until fluffy, about 1 minute.

We used Bird's Custard Powder.

GRAND MARNIER GANACHE
Makes ½ cup

4 ounces (115 grams) 56% cacao semisweet chocolate, chopped
1½ tablespoons (21 grams) unsalted butter
2 tablespoons (30 grams) heavy whipping cream, warmed
1 teaspoon (5 grams) Grand Marnier

1. In the top of a double boiler, melt chocolate and butter over medium-low heat. Remove from heat; stir in warm cream until combined. Stir in Grand Marnier.

Photo by Maya Visnyei

BROWNED BUTTER CRANBERRY ORANGE BARS WITH BROWN SUGAR OAT STREUSEL

Makes 15 to 18

Recipe by Amy Ho/*feedfeed*

Browned butter is the answer for anything and everything. These bars have three parts: a rich orange browned butter shortbread base, a tart cranberry and jam filling, and a generous topping of Brown Sugar Oat Streusel.

1   cup (227 grams) unsalted butter
½   cup (100 grams) granulated sugar
1   tablespoon (6 grams) orange zest
2   teaspoons (8 grams) vanilla extract
½   teaspoon (1.5 grams) kosher salt
2   cups (250 grams) all-purpose flour
1½   cups (480 grams) strawberry preserves
1   cup (170 grams) fresh cranberries, chopped
Brown Sugar Oat Streusel (recipe follows)
Garnish: confectioners' sugar

1. Preheat oven to 300°F (150°C). Line a 13x9-inch baking pan with parchment paper, letting excess extend over sides of pan.
2. In a medium saucepan, melt butter over medium heat. Cook, swirling pan occasionally, until butter turns a medium-brown color and has a nutty aroma, about 5 minutes. Pour browned butter into a bowl; set aside.
3. In a small bowl, rub together granulated sugar and zest until fragrant.
4. In the bowl of a stand mixer fitted with the paddle attachment, beat browned butter, sugar mixture, vanilla, and salt at medium speed until combined. With mixer on low speed, gradually add flour, beating until combined. Press mixture into bottom of prepared pan.
5. Bake for 15 minutes. Remove from oven. Increase oven temperature to 350°F (180°C). Spread preserves onto warm crust. Dot preserves with cranberries, and sprinkle with Brown Sugar Oat Streusel.
6. Bake until streusel is golden brown and filling is bubbly, about 35 minutes more. Let

cool at room temperature for at least 20 minutes. Refrigerate for at least 1 hour.
7. Using excess parchment as handles, remove from pan, and cut into bars. Dust with confectioners' sugar, if desired. Refrigerate in an airtight container for up to 5 days.

BROWN SUGAR OAT STREUSEL
Makes about 2 cups

1¾   cups (140 grams) old-fashioned oats
½   cup (63 grams) all-purpose flour
⅓   cup (73 grams) firmly packed brown sugar
½   teaspoon (1 gram) ground cinnamon
½   cup (113 grams) cold unsalted butter, cubed

1. In a medium bowl, whisk together oats, flour, brown sugar, and cinnamon. Using a pastry blender, cut in cold butter until mixture is crumbly.

Photo by Amy Ho

PINK GRAPEFRUIT BARS

Makes 16

Recipe by Ryan Alvarez and Adam Merrin/
feedfeed

*Made with fresh grapefruit juice and lots of
zest, these tangy treats are filled with intense
grapefruit flavor. Resting on a crispy buttery
crust with hints of cinnamon, and lightly
dusted with powdered sugar, these irresistible
sweet squares are here to bring a little citrus
and sunshine to the holidays.*

½ cup (113 grams) unsalted butter, softened
¼ cup (50 grams) granulated sugar
¼ cup (30 grams) confectioners' sugar
1 tablespoon (6 grams) grapefruit zest
¼ teaspoon kosher salt
⅛ teaspoon ground cinnamon
1 cup (125 grams) all-purpose flour
Pink Grapefruit Filling (recipe follows)
Garnish: confectioners' sugar

1. Preheat oven to 350°F (180°C). Line an
8-inch square baking pan with parchment
paper, letting excess extend over sides of pan.

2. In the bowl of a stand mixer fitted with
the paddle attachment, beat butter at
medium speed until creamy. Add sugars,
zest, salt, and cinnamon, beating until fluffy,
3 to 4 minutes, stopping to scrape sides
of bowl. Add flour, beating to combine.
(Mixture will be sandy and crumbly.)
Transfer to prepared pan, and use your
fingers to press crust into bottom of pan.
3. Bake until edges are just beginning
to brown, 15 to 18 minutes. Pour Pink
Grapefruit Filling over warm crust, and bake
until center is set and edges are beginning
to lightly brown, 25 to 30 minutes more.
Let cool completely in pan. Cover and
refrigerate for at least 2 hours or overnight.
4. Using excess parchment as handles, remove
from pan, and cut into squares. Dust with
confectioners' sugar, if desired. Refrigerate in
an airtight container for up to 1 week.

PINK GRAPEFRUIT FILLING
Makes about 1 cup

2 cups (480 grams) fresh grapefruit juice
(from 2 to 4 grapefruits)

3 large eggs (150 grams)
¾ cup (150 grams) granulated sugar
¼ cup (30 grams) confectioners' sugar
3 tablespoons (24 grams) all-purpose flour
2 tablespoons (12 grams) grapefruit zest
1 teaspoon (4 grams) pink dragon fruit
purée or 3 drops red food coloring
(optional)

1. In a small saucepan, bring grapefruit juice
to a boil over medium-high heat. Reduce
heat, and simmer, stirring occasionally,
until juice reduces to ⅓ cup (80 grams),
40 to 45 minutes. Carefully pour reduced
juice into a heatproof measuring cup, and
refrigerate until lukewarm, 10 to 15 minutes.
2. In the bowl of a stand mixer fitted with
the whisk attachment, beat eggs and sugars
at medium speed until smooth. Add cooled
reduced grapefruit juice, flour, zest, and
dragonfruit purée or food coloring (if using),
and beat until smooth and combined. Use
immediately.

PRO TIP

Pink dragon fruit purée is an excellent
all-natural food color. Also known as
red or pink pitaya, it is available in the
frozen aisle of natural food stores as
well as in the produce section. If buying
fresh fruit, make sure you select the
red variety as many dragon fruit are
white inside but appear identical to
those with red. To make the purée,
mash a few spoonfuls of fruit through a
fine-mesh sieve into a bowl to remove
seeds. Refrigerate excess purée in an
airtight container for up to 2 weeks.

Photo by Matt Armendariz

GINGERBREAD CHEESECAKE BARS

Makes 16

Recipe by Rachel Conners/feedfeed

No need to free up oven space for these Gingerbread Cheesecake Bars. These "cheesecake" bars are made with soaked cashews to replicate cheesecake's creamy texture—no dairy or baking necessary. With an easy pecan-and-date crust and tons of warm spices, these Gingerbread Cheesecake Bars are packed with the holiday season's warm flavors. You won't miss the dairy one bit in these gluten-free and vegan bars.

1   cup (175 grams) pitted dates
1½   cups (170 grams) chopped pecans
2   teaspoons (4 grams) ground ginger, divided
1½   teaspoons (3 grams) ground cinnamon, divided
½   teaspoon (1.5 grams) kosher salt, divided
2   cups (284 grams) unsalted cashews, soaked in cold water for 4 to 10 hours
½   cup (120 grams) full-fat coconut milk, shaken
⅓   cup (113 grams) pure maple syrup
¼   cup (56 grams) refined coconut oil, melted and cooled
3   tablespoons (63 grams) unsulphured molasses
½   teaspoon (1 gram) lemon zest
2   tablespoons (30 grams) fresh lemon juice
1   tablespoon (13 grams) vanilla extract
1   teaspoon grated fresh nutmeg
¼   teaspoon ground cloves
Garnish: ground cinnamon, grated fresh nutmeg, pecan halves

1. Line an 8-inch square baking pan with parchment paper, and lightly grease with melted coconut oil.
2. In the work bowl of a food processor, place dates. Pulse until finely chopped. Add pecans, ½ teaspoon (1 gram) ginger, ½ teaspoon (1 gram) cinnamon, and ¼ teaspoon salt; pulse on medium-low speed until a sticky dough begins to form, with small pecan bits remaining. (Do not overprocess or dough will become oily.) Press dough into bottom of prepared pan.

3. Drain soaked cashews, and rinse with cold water. In the container of a blender, combine cashews, coconut milk, maple syrup, melted coconut oil, molasses, lemon zest and juice, vanilla, nutmeg, cloves, remaining 1½ teaspoons (3 grams) ginger, remaining 1 teaspoon (2 grams) cinnamon, and remaining ¼ teaspoon salt; blend until mixture is silky smooth and creamy, 2 to 3 minutes. Taste and adjust seasonings, if desired.
4. Pour filling into prepared crust, smoothing top with an offset spatula. Tap pan on counter a few times to release any air bubbles. Freeze until completely firm, at least 3 hours. Run a knife under hot water to warm it up before cutting bars with the still-hot (dried) knife. Cut into 16 squares. Let thaw at room temperature for 10 to 15 minutes before serving. Refrigerate in an airtight container for up to 2 weeks, or freeze for up to 2 months. Garnish with cinnamon, nutmeg, and pecan halves, if desired.

Photo by Rachel Conners

PALEO MAGIC COOKIE BARS

Makes 16

Recipe by Rachel Conners/*feedfeed*

Magic Cookie Bars by Eagle Brand have been a holiday tradition in my family for as long as I can remember. I used to sneak down to our outside freezer when my mom wasn't paying attention to snack on these gooey, chocolaty treats. When my sister and I started to follow a gluten-free, dairy-free diet, creating a version of Magic Cookie Bars my whole family could eat was at the top of my to-do list. This version has all the flavors I love from the original and brings me right back to my childhood.

1   cup (96 grams) blanched almond flour
¼   cup (57 grams) coconut butter, melted
½   teaspoon (1.5 grams) kosher salt
½   teaspoon (1 gram) ground cinnamon
Coconut Milk Caramel (recipe follows)
¾   cup (128 grams) 60% cacao dairy-free
       dark chocolate morsels
½   cup (42 grams) unsweetened flaked
       coconut
½   cup (57 grams) coarsely chopped
       walnuts
¼   cup (28 grams) coarsely chopped
       almonds

1. Preheat oven to 350°F (180°C). Line an 8-inch square baking pan with parchment paper, and lightly grease with coconut oil.
2. In a large bowl, stir together flour, melted coconut butter, salt, and cinnamon. Sprinkle mixture into prepared pan. Using your fingers or a spatula, press mixture down in an even layer, covering bottom of pan. (Mixture will be dry and crumbly at first, but keep pressing dough into pan until it comes together.)
3. Pour Coconut Milk Caramel into prepared crust. Sprinkle with chocolate morsels, coconut, walnuts, and almonds. Use a fork, a spatula, or your fingers to press toppings down into caramel.
4. Bake until lightly browned, 25 to 30 minutes. Refrigerate until completely chilled and set, at least 1 hour. Using a sharp knife, cut into 16 squares. Serve chilled or at room temperature. Store in an airtight container in refrigerator or freezer.

COCONUT MILK CARAMEL
Makes 1 cup

1¾   cups plus 1 tablespoon (435 grams)
       full-fat coconut milk
½   cup (75 grams) coconut sugar
2   tablespoons (28 grams) coconut butter
1   teaspoon (4 grams) vanilla extract

1. In a medium heavy-bottomed saucepan, bring coconut milk and coconut sugar to a boil over medium heat, stirring frequently. Reduce heat, and simmer, stirring frequently to prevent sugar from scorching, until mixture reduces by one-third to one-half, 40 to 45 minutes. (If thicker, caramelized sugar begins to form on sides or bottom of pan, use a whisk to reincorporate it.) Stir in coconut butter and vanilla until combined. Remove from heat. Let cool completely.

PRO TIP
You can use your favorite nuts in place of the walnuts and almonds in this recipe; just keep the amounts the same.

Photo by Rachel Conners

MISCELLANEOUS

BOURBON-BRAISED PINEAPPLE DOUGHNUTS

Makes about 18

In our adult version of a classic doughnut, we braise fresh pineapple in a brown sugar-bourbon sauce.

¼ cup (57 grams) unsalted butter
2 cups plus 3 tablespoons (525 grams) whole milk
¼ cup (56 grams) vegetable oil
3 large eggs (150 grams), lightly beaten
2 tablespoons (18 grams) plus ⅛ teaspoon active dry yeast
7⅓ cups (931 grams) bread flour
¾ cup plus 2 tablespoons (174 grams) granulated sugar
1 teaspoon (3 grams) kosher salt
Peanut oil, for frying
Bourbon-Braised Pineapple Glaze (recipe follows)

1. In a small saucepan, melt butter over medium-low heat. Whisk in milk, oil, and eggs; cook until mixture registers between 100°F (38°C) and 110°F (43°C) on an instant-read thermometer. Remove from heat, and transfer to the bowl of a stand mixer fitted with the dough hook attachment. Whisk in yeast, and let stand for 10 minutes.
2. In a large bowl, stir together flour, sugar, and salt. With mixer on medium-low speed, gradually add flour mixture to yeast mixture, beating until combined. Increase mixer speed to medium-high, and beat until dough is smooth and pulls away from sides of bowl, 10 to 15 minutes. Spray a large bowl with cooking spray. Place dough in bowl, and spray dough with cooking spray. Cover lightly with plastic wrap, and refrigerate for 1 hour.
3. Line 2 rimmed baking sheets with parchment paper, and spray with cooking spray.
4. Punch down dough. On a lightly floured surface, turn out dough. Lightly dust top of dough with flour, and roll to ½-inch thickness. Using a 3-inch doughnut cutter dipped in flour, cut dough. Lightly brush off any excess flour. Place 2 inches apart on prepared pans. Lightly spray top of doughnuts with cooking spray, and cover with plastic wrap. Let rise in a warm, draft-free place (75°F/24°C) until doubled in size, 30 to 60 minutes.
5. In a large stockpot or deep fryer, pour oil to a depth of 4 inches, and heat over medium heat until a deep-fry thermometer registers 350°F (180°C). Fry 2 doughnuts at a time for 15 seconds. Using skewers or a spider skimmer, turn doughnuts, and fry for 80 seconds per side, turning once. Remove using a slotted spoon or spider skimmer. (The oil needs to maintain a temperature of 350°F/180°C. After frying the first batch, let oil return to correct temperature before frying the second batch.) Dip doughnuts in Bourbon-Braised Pineapple Glaze. Let dry on a wire rack. These doughnuts are best eaten while fresh and warm. Store in an airtight container for up to 1 day. Reheat in the microwave for 10 seconds before eating.

BOURBON-BRAISED PINEAPPLE GLAZE
Makes 3 cups

¼ cup (55 grams) firmly packed dark brown sugar
¼ cup (60 grams) bourbon
1½ tablespoons (31.5 grams) honey
1½ cups (235 grams) peeled, cored, and diced medium-ripe pineapple
2½ cups (300 grams) confectioners' sugar

1. Preheat oven to 400°F (200°C).
2. In an ovenproof skillet, whisk together brown sugar, bourbon, and honey. Stir in pineapple.
3. Bake for 30 minutes, stirring every 10 minutes. Let cool for 5 minutes.
4. Transfer mixture to the container of a blender, and blend until smooth. Place in a large bowl, and whisk in confectioners' sugar. Use immediately, or cover and refrigerate for up to 3 days. Reheat over a double boiler before using.

TRIPLE BERRY CAKE DOUGHNUTS

Makes about 24

A cake doughnut done correctly has a tender interior—denser than a yeast-raised doughnut—with a slightly crunchy, cracked exterior. Tiny flecks of baked-in blueberry and strawberry brighten up the cakey crumb.

6½   cups (813 grams) all-purpose flour
⅔   cup (133 grams) granulated sugar
2   tablespoons (30 grams) baking powder
1   teaspoon (3 grams) kosher salt
½   cup (113 grams) unsalted butter, melted
2   cups (340 grams) frozen blueberries
1   cup (170 grams) diced fresh strawberries
¾   cup (180 grams) whole milk
2   large eggs (100 grams), lightly beaten
2   teaspoons (8 grams) vanilla extract
1   teaspoon (4 grams) almond extract
Peanut oil, for frying
Blackberry Glaze (recipe follows)
White Glaze (recipe follows)
Garnish: crushed freeze-dried strawberries

1. In a large bowl, stir together flour, sugar, baking powder, and salt. Add melted butter, stirring until mixture is crumbly.
2. In the container of a blender, combine blueberries, strawberries, milk, eggs, and extracts. Pulse a few times until berries have turned the milk purple and only small bits of berries remain. Stir berry mixture into flour mixture, bringing dough together with a spoon. (Dough will be very loose.) Shape dough into a ball.
3. Line 2 rimmed baking sheets with parchment paper, and spray with cooking spray. On a heavily floured surface, roll dough to ½-inch thickness. Using a 3-inch doughnut cutter dipped in flour, cut dough, rerolling scraps as necessary. Place on prepared pans. Lightly brush off any excess flour.
4. In a large stockpot or deep fryer, pour oil to a depth of 4 inches, and heat over medium-high heat until a deep-fry thermometer registers 375°F (190°C). Working in batches, fry doughnuts, turning each after it rises to the surface, about 80 seconds per side. Remove using a slotted spoon or spider skimmer. (The oil needs to maintain a temperature of 375°F/190°C. After frying the first batch, let oil return to correct temperature before frying the second batch.) Dip doughnuts in Blackberry Glaze. Let dry on a wire rack. Drizzle with White Glaze, and garnish with freeze-dried strawberries, if desired. Store in an airtight container at room temperature for up to 1 day.

Note: *The key to a soft cake doughnut is not overworking the dough.*

BLACKBERRY GLAZE
Makes about 2 cups

2   cups (340 grams) fresh blackberries
2   teaspoons (10 grams) fresh lemon juice
4   cups (480 grams) confectioners' sugar

1. In a small saucepan, combine blackberries and lemon juice over medium heat. Cook for 10 minutes, stirring occasionally. Remove from heat, and lightly mash berries. Strain through a fine-mesh sieve into a large bowl, pressing on berries with the back of a spoon to release juices. Add confectioners' sugar, 1 cup (120 grams) at a time, whisking until combined. If glaze starts to set, microwave in 10-second intervals until fluid. Use immediately, or cover and refrigerate for up to 5 days.

WHITE GLAZE
Makes 1 cup

1   cup (120 grams) confectioners' sugar
3   tablespoons (45 grams) whole milk

1. In a small bowl, whisk together confectioners' sugar and milk. Place in a plastic piping bag fitted with a small round tip. Use immediately, or cover and refrigerate for up to 5 days.

PRO TIP
When checking for doneness in a cake doughnut, look for a cracked top. This indicates that the doughnut has expanded while frying, which gives you that cakey crumb.

FIGGY DUFF

Makes 6 to 8 servings

Recipe by Emily Turner

Originating from Newfoundland on the Canadian East Coast, this traditional steamed bread pudding derives its eclectic name from two old Cornish colloquialisms: "figgy," a word for raisins, and "duff," another term for pudding.

1   cup (128 grams) golden raisins
1   cup (128 grams) sultana raisins
1   cup (128 grams) raisins
1½   teaspoons (3 grams) lemon zest
⅓   cup (80 grams) spiced rum
½   cup (113 grams) unsalted butter, softened
¾   cup (165 grams) firmly packed light brown sugar
2   large eggs (100 grams)
3   tablespoons (63 grams) fancy molasses
1¾   cups (228 grams) dried bread crumbs
¾   cup (94 grams) all-purpose flour
2   teaspoons (4 grams) ground cinnamon
1½   teaspoons (4.5 grams) kosher salt
1½   teaspoons (7.5 grams) baking powder
1   teaspoon (2 grams) ground allspice
½   teaspoon (1 gram) ground ginger
⅔   cup (113 grams) fresh blueberries
Maple Butter Sauce (recipe follows)

1. In a heatproof bowl, combine golden raisins, sultanas, raisins, and zest. In a small saucepan, heat rum over medium heat (do not boil). Pour hot rum over dried fruit. Cover and let stand for 30 minutes.
2. Preheat oven to 275°F (140°C). Butter and flour a 6-cup steamed pudding mold.
3. In the bowl of a stand mixer fitted with the paddle attachment, beat butter and brown sugar at medium speed until fluffy, 3 to 4 minutes, stopping to scrape sides of bowl. Add eggs, one at a time, beating just until combined after each addition. Beat in molasses.
4. In a medium bowl, whisk together bread crumbs, flour, cinnamon, salt, baking powder, allspice, and ginger. With mixer on low speed, gradually add bread crumbs mixture to butter mixture, beating just until combined. Add dried fruit mixture and blueberries, beating just until combined. (Batter with be thick.)
5. Spoon batter into prepared mold, smoothing top with an offset spatula. Cover with lid, and place in a large Dutch oven. Fill Dutch oven with enough water to come three-fourths of the way up pudding basin. (Your Dutch oven should remain uncovered.)
6. Bake until a wooden pick inserted in center comes out clean, 2 hours and 15 minutes to 2 hours and 45 minutes. (Texture of center will be closer to a pudding consistency than a cake.) Let cool in pan for 20 minutes. Invert onto a wire rack. Serve warm or at room temperature with Maple Butter Sauce.

Note: *You can substitute a 6-cup Bundt pan for the pudding steamer, if desired. In step 5, cover pan with a sheet of parchment paper, followed by a piece of foil. Fasten with twine around lip of pan, and trim overhanging edges. Continue as directed.*

Maple Butter Sauce

Makes ⅔ cup

½   cup (170 grams) Grade A amber maple syrup
2   tablespoons (28 grams) unsalted butter
1   teaspoon (5 grams) spiced rum
⅛   teaspoon kosher salt
2   tablespoons (30 grams) heavy whipping cream

1. In a small saucepan, bring maple syrup and butter to a boil over medium-high heat. Cook for 3 minutes, stirring constantly. Remove from heat, and stir in rum and salt. Let cool to room temperature. Whisk in cream.

Photo by Maya Visnyei

LEMON MERINGUE NESTS

Makes 12 to 14

There's no reinventing the lemon meringue pie, so why not reimagine it—as a meringue nest. Taking flavor cues from its classic inspiration, this recipe puts delicate, crunchy meringue in the spotlight with a sweet-tart lemon curd centerpiece.

4   large egg whites (120 grams), room temperature
½   teaspoon (2 grams) vanilla extract
¼   teaspoon cream of tartar
¾   cup (150 grams) granulated sugar
Lemon Curd (recipe follows)

1. Preheat oven to 200°F (93°C). Line baking sheets with parchment paper.
2. In the bowl of a stand mixer fitted with the whisk attachment, beat egg whites, vanilla, and cream of tartar at medium speed until foamy. Increase mixer speed to high, and beat in sugar, 1 tablespoon (12 grams) at a time, until stiff glossy peaks form, 5 to 7 minutes.
3. Spoon half of meringue into a piping bag fitted with an Open Star Tip #32 by Wilton. Pipe meringue into 3-inch round nests on prepared pans by making a flat bottom spiral, followed by 2 stacked rings on the outer edge. Pipe remaining meringue into kisses on prepared pans.
4. Bake until set and dry, about 2 hours. Turn oven off, and let meringues stand in oven with door closed for 1 hour.
5. Spoon Lemon Curd into center of each meringue nest, spreading to edges. Top with meringue kisses. Serve immediately.

LEMON CURD
Makes about 2 cups

3   large eggs (150 grams)
1   cup (200 grams) granulated sugar
⅓   cup (80 grams) fresh lemon juice, strained
½   cup (113 grams) cold unsalted butter, cubed
½   tablespoon (2 grams) lemon zest
⅛   teaspoon rose water

1. In a medium saucepan, whisk eggs until combined and a lemon-yellow color. Add sugar and lemon juice, stirring to combine. Cook over low heat, stirring constantly, until mixture thickens, 5 to 10 minutes. Remove from heat, and immediately pour through a fine-mesh sieve into a heatproof bowl, discarding solids. Add cold butter, zest, and rose water, stirring until combined. Refrigerate for at least 2 hours before using. Lemon Curd can be stored in an airtight container in refrigerator for up to 2 weeks.

LAYERED MERINGUE TERRINE

Makes 6 to 8 servings

You read that right. This recipe calls for a perfect dessert union of meringue and ice cream.

White Chocolate Cream (recipe follows)
Coffee Cream (recipe follows)
Coffee Chocolate Fudge (recipe follows)

1. Prepare White Chocolate Cream, Coffee Cream, and Coffee Chocolate Fudge.
2. Line a 9x5-inch loaf pan with parchment paper, letting excess extend over sides of pan.
3. Spread a ½-inch layer of White Chocolate Cream in bottom of prepared pan; spread a ½-inch layer of Coffee Cream on top. Swirl 3 to 4 tablespoons Coffee Chocolate Fudge into coffee layer. Repeat layers once.
4. Cover top with plastic wrap, pressing to touch surface. Wrap entire pan in plastic wrap. Freeze until solid, about 8 hours or overnight.
5. Remove plastic wrap. Using excess parchment as handles, lift terrine out of pan onto a cutting board. Cut frozen terrine into slices to serve. Leftover terrine can be stored in loaf pan wrapped tightly in plastic wrap, and frozen for up to 1 month.

WHITE CHOCOLATE CREAM

Makes 3 cups

1½   cups (360 grams) heavy whipping cream
½   cup (85 grams) finely chopped white chocolate, melted
1   tablespoon (15 grams) white chocolate liqueur*
3   cups crumbled Meringue Cookies (recipe follows)

1. In the bowl of a stand mixer fitted with the whisk attachment, beat cream until thick and soft, but not to soft peaks. (If you go too far, simply add a little more cream.) Fold in melted chocolate and white chocolate liqueur. Fold in crumbled Meringue Cookies. Refrigerate until ready to assemble terrine.

We used Godiva White Chocolate Liqueur.

MERINGUE COOKIES

Makes 72 to 84

4   large egg whites (120 grams), room temperature
½   teaspoon (2 grams) vanilla extract
¼   teaspoon cream of tartar
¾   cup (150 grams) granulated sugar

1. Preheat oven to 200°F (93°C). Line baking sheets with parchment paper.
2. In the bowl of a stand mixer fitted with the whisk attachment, beat egg whites, vanilla, and cream of tartar at medium speed until foamy. Increase mixer speed to high, and beat in sugar, 1 tablespoon (12 grams) at a time, until stiff glossy peaks form, 5 to 7 minutes. Spoon meringue into a piping bag fitted with a star or shell tip. Pipe meringue into small 1-inch cookies on prepared pans.
Bake until set and dry, about 2 hours. Turn oven off, and let meringues stand in oven with door closed for 1 hour. Cookies can be made up to 2 days ahead and stored in an airtight container in a dry, dark place.

COFFEE CREAM

Makes 3 cups

1½   cups (360 grams) heavy whipping cream
1   tablespoon (6 grams) instant espresso powder
1   teaspoon (5 grams) Irish cream liqueur*
3   cups crumbled Meringue Cookies (recipe on page 372)
2   tablespoons Coffee Chocolate Fudge (recipe follows)

1. In the bowl of a stand mixer fitted with the whisk attachment, beat cream until thick and soft, but not to soft peaks. Fold in espresso powder and coffee liqueur. Fold in crumbled Meringue Cookies and Coffee Chocolate Fudge. Refrigerate until ready to assemble terrine.

COFFEE CHOCOLATE FUDGE

Makes ¾ cup

½   cup (85 grams) finely chopped 70% cacao bittersweet chocolate
½   cup (120 grams) heavy whipping cream
1½   tablespoons (22.5 grams) Irish cream liqueur*

1. Place chocolate in a medium bowl, and set aside.
2. In a small saucepan, bring cream to a simmer over medium-low heat; pour over chocolate. Let stand for 2 minutes. Whisk mixture, starting from the center and working outward, until smooth. Add coffee liqueur, and stir to combine. Fudge can be stored in an airtight container in refrigerator for up to 2 weeks; bring to room temperature before using.

We used Baileys Irish Cream.

BELGIAN WAFFLES WITH MAPLE CRÈME FRAÎCHE & CANDIED WALNUTS

Makes 6 to 8

The yeast in these waffles guarantees volume while the addition of applesauce keeps them extra tender and fluffy. We infused Granny Smith apple peel, maple syrup, and ground spices into the milk prior to mixing the batter for a little added oomph of that signature fall flavor.

1½   cups (360 grams) whole milk
2   tablespoons (28 grams) unsalted butter
1   tablespoon (12 grams) plus ½ teaspoon (2 grams) granulated sugar, divided
1   tablespoon (21 grams) maple syrup
1   teaspoon (2 grams) ground cinnamon
½   teaspoon (1 gram) ground allspice
½   teaspoon (1 gram) ground cloves
Peel of 1 Granny Smith apple (25 grams)
1¼   teaspoons (2.5 grams) instant yeast
2⅓   cups (292 grams) all-purpose flour
¼   teaspoon (1.25 grams) baking powder
2   large egg yolks (37 grams)
¾   cup plus ⅛ cup (210 grams) Granny Smith Applesauce (recipe below)
3   large egg whites (90 grams)
¼   teaspoon kosher salt
Maple Crème Fraîche (recipe follows)
Candied Walnuts (recipe follows)

1. In a medium saucepan, heat milk, butter, 1 tablespoon (12 grams) sugar, maple syrup, cinnamon, allspice, and cloves over medium heat until butter is melted. Remove from heat, and add apple peel. Cover with plastic wrap, and let cool for 15 minutes.
2. Remove apple peel, and discard. Add yeast to milk mixture, whisking until dissolved.
3. In a large bowl, whisk together flour and baking powder. Add milk mixture and egg yolks to flour mixture, whisking to combine. Stir in Granny Smith Applesauce.
4. In the bowl of a stand mixer fitted with the whisk attachment, beat egg whites, salt, and remaining ½ teaspoon (2 grams) sugar at high speed until soft peaks form. Fold egg whites into batter. Refrigerate for 8 hours.
5. Preheat waffle press, and spray with cooking spray. Cook waffles according to manufacturer's instructions. Serve with Maple Crème Fraîche and Candied Walnuts. These waffles are best kept frozen in a heavy-duty resealable plastic bag for up to 2 months.

Maple Crème Fraîche

Makes ½ cup

½   cup (120 grams) crème fraîche
1½   tablespoons (31.5 grams) maple syrup

1. In the bowl of a stand mixer fitted with the whisk attachment, beat crème fraîche and maple syrup at medium speed until thickened. Use immediately. Refrigerate in an airtight container for up to 2 days.

Candied Walnuts

Makes ¾ cup

¾   cup (85 grams) chopped walnuts
⅓   cup (73 grams) firmly packed light brown sugar
½   teaspoon (1.5 grams) kosher salt
1   large egg white (30 grams), lightly beaten

1. Preheat oven to 350°F (180°C). Line a rimmed baking sheet with parchment paper.
2. In a large bowl, toss together walnuts, brown sugar, salt, and egg white until lightly coated. Spread in a single layer on prepared pan.
3. Bake until browned and crisp, 10 to 15 minutes. Let cool slightly before serving. In an area with low humidity at room temperature, walnuts can be stored in an airtight container for up to 5 days.

GRANNY SMITH APPLESAUCE

Makes 2 cups

Notorious for their bright green color and slightly sour taste, Granny Smith apples are more acidic than most apples and create a deliciously tart applesauce—perfect for upgrading your baked goods with an extra punch of flavor.

2   pounds (910 grams) Granny Smith apples, unpeeled, cored, and chopped
1   cup (240 grams) apple brandy
½   cup (110 grams) firmly packed light brown sugar
2   tablespoons (30 grams) fresh lemon juice
1   tablespoon (9 grams) fruit pectin*
1   teaspoon (6 grams) vanilla bean paste
1   teaspoon (2 grams) ground cinnamon
1   teaspoon (2 grams) ground allspice
6 to 7 cinnamon sticks (20 grams)

1. In a large stockpot, bring all ingredients to a simmer over medium-low heat. Simmer until apples are tender, 20 to 30 minutes. Let cool to room temperature.
2. Using an immersion blender, blend until smooth.** Strain mixture through a fine-mesh sieve, discarding apple skin. Cover and refrigerate for at least 2 hours before using. Refrigerate in an airtight container for up to 2 weeks.

*We used Sure-Jell Premium Fruit Pectin.

**You can also blend in the container of a blender or work bowl of a food processor.

GHEE-INFUSED PUMPKIN BREAD PUDDING WITH POMEGRANATE MOLASSES

Makes 6 servings

Recipe by Nik Sharma

In this bread pudding, the custard is infused with ghee, an Indian cousin of clarified butter. Ghee is simmered longer than traditional clarified butter, until the milk solids begin to brown, imparting it with an aromatic nuttiness similar to browned butter. Served with a slight drizzle of sweet and tart pomegranate molasses, this custardy bread pudding is the epitome of autumn comfort food.

¼   cup (57 grams) ghee, melted, plus more for greasing pan

1   loaf stale sweet bread (567 grams), such as challah, cut into ½-inch-thick slices
2½   cups (600 grams) whole milk
1   cup (244 grams) pumpkin purée
¾   cup (165 grams) muscovado sugar
1   whole Madagascar vanilla bean, split lengthwise, seeds scraped and reserved
4   large eggs (200 grams)
½   cup (170 grams) pomegranate molasses, room temperature

1. Grease a 13x9-inch baking dish with melted ghee. Line pan with overlapping bread slices to fit entire dish.
2. In the container of a blender, place milk, pumpkin purée, moscovado sugar, melted ghee, reserved vanilla bean seeds, and eggs; blend on low speed until combined and smooth. Pour mixture over bread, and place vanilla bean on top. Cover with plastic wrap, and refrigerate for 2 hours to allow bread to absorb liquid.
3. Preheat to 350°F (180°C).
4. Bake until top is golden brown and custard is jiggly but set, 25 to 30 minutes, covering with foil halfway through baking to prevent excess browning, if necessary. Serve warm or at room temperature. Drizzle each serving with pomegranate molasses.

Photo by Nik Sharma

BUTTERNUT SQUASH PUDDING WITH CARDAMOM CRÈME FRAÎCHE AND CARAMELIZED CASHEWS

Makes 8 servings

Recipe by Nik Sharma

Here, the rich custardy texture and sweetness of the pudding is balanced by a lightly spiced cardamom-infused crème fraîche topping and a few crunchy caramelized cashews.

1⅔ cups (400 grams) sweetened condensed milk
1¼ cups (300 grams) evaporated milk
1   cup (220 grams) roasted and mashed butternut squash
5   large eggs (250 grams)
1   cup (240 grams) whole milk
3   tablespoons (24 grams) all-purpose flour
1½   teaspoons (6 grams) Madagascar bourbon vanilla extract
1   teaspoon (2 grams) turmeric powder
Garnish: Cardamom Crème Fraîche (recipe follows), Caramelized Cashews (recipe follows)

1. Preheat to 350°F (180°C). Boil enough water to cover a large baking pan or dish that can hold 8 ramekins or Mason jars.
2. In the container of a blender, place condensed milk, evaporated milk, squash, eggs, milk, flour, vanilla, and turmeric; blend until combined. Divide mixture among 8 (6-ounce) ramekins, and place on a wire rack. Place rack in baking pan. Carefully pour boiling water in pan to about ½ inch below height of ramekins.
3. Bake until pudding is slightly firm to the touch yet jiggly in center, 20 to 30 minutes. Remove ramekins from pan, and cover with plastic wrap. Refrigerate overnight to set before serving.
4. To serve, garnish each pudding with a generous teaspoon of Cardamom Crème Fraîche and a few Caramelized Cashews, if desired.

CARDAMOM CRÈME FRAÎCHE

Makes ½ cup

½   cup (120 grams) crème fraîche
2   tablespoons (14 grams) confectioners' sugar
¼   teaspoon ground green cardamom

1. In a small bowl, stir together all ingredients until combined. Refrigerate in an airtight container until ready to use.

CARAMELIZED CASHEWS

Makes 1 cup

1   cup (113 grams) cashews
¼   cup (50 grams) granulated sugar
1   tablespoon (14 grams) unsalted butter
¼   teaspoon sea salt

1. In a medium skillet, heat all ingredients over medium-high heat, swirling until sugar starts to brown, 5 to 6 minutes. Using a silicone spatula, carefully transfer cashews to a baking sheet lined with parchment paper. Let cool completely.
2. Once cashews have cooled, separate nuts from each other if they're stuck together. Store in an airtight jar until ready to use.

Photo by Nik Sharma

BLACK SESAME AND TOASTED COCONUT MADELEINES

Makes 24

Recipe by Amisha Gurbani/*feedfeed*

The black sesame and coconut sweet buns you find in Asian bakeries inspired these delicious madeleines. The nutty flavor of black sesame seeds combines with the toasted coconut perfectly.

3   tablespoons (27 grams) black sesame seeds
¼   cup (21 grams) unsweetened flaked coconut, toasted
1¼ cups (156 grams) all-purpose flour
1   teaspoon (5 grams) baking powder
½   teaspoon (1.5 grams) kosher salt
¾   cup (150 grams) granulated sugar
3   large eggs (150 grams), room temperature
1   teaspoon (2 grams) lemon zest
1   teaspoon (4 grams) vanilla extract
11 tablespoons (154 grams) unsalted butter, melted, cooled, and divided

Garnish: confectioners' sugar

1. Place black sesame seeds and coconut in a coffee grinder; blend until finely ground. Transfer to a medium bowl; add flour, baking powder, and salt, whisking to combine. Set aside.

2. In the bowl of a stand mixer fitted with the paddle attachment, beat granulated sugar and eggs at medium speed until light and ribbon-like, about 4 minutes. Stir in zest and vanilla. Fold in flour mixture, a little bit at a time, with a spatula. Add 9 tablespoons (126 grams) melted butter, stirring just until combined. Refrigerate for at least 1 hour.

3. Preheat oven to 425°F (220°C). Grease 2 (12-well) madeleine pans with remaining 2 tablespoons (28 grams) melted butter. Place 1 tablespoon batter in each prepared well.

4. Bake until madeleines are risen and firm, 8 to 9 minutes. Let cool on a wire rack. Dust with confectioners' sugar, if desired. Store in an airtight container for up to 4 days.

Photo by Amisha Gurbani

MEYER LEMON & ALMOND MADELEINES WITH AVOCADO OIL

Makes 12 to 16

Recipe by Becky Sue Wilberding/*feedfeed*

Traditional French madeleines are made with browned butter, but this take on the original subs in avocado oil for an airy, buttery finish. The Meyer lemon, ground almonds, and signature shell shape bring a SoCal vibe to these cakey cookies.

2   large eggs (100 grams)
½   cup (100 grams) granulated sugar
1   tablespoon (21 grams) honey
1   tablespoon (15 grams) Meyer lemon juice
¾   teaspoon (3 grams) almond extract
1   cup (125 grams) all-purpose flour
1   teaspoon (5 grams) baking powder
½   teaspoon (1.5 grams) kosher salt
¼   teaspoon ground cardamom
6   tablespoons (84 grams) avocado oil
1   tablespoon (6 grams) Meyer lemon zest
Meyer Lemon Glaze (recipe follows)
1   cup (113 grams) toasted sliced almonds, finely ground

1. In the bowl of a stand mixer fitted with a whisk attachment, beat eggs at medium-high speed. Gradually add sugar, beating until combined. Increase mixer speed to high, and beat until frothy and doubled in volume, 3 to 5 minutes. Stir in honey, lemon juice, and almond extract.
2. In a medium bowl, sift together flour, baking powder, salt, and cardamom. Fold flour mixture into egg mixture.
3. In a small bowl, whisk together avocado oil and zest. Slowly stir oil mixture into egg mixture until smooth. Cover and refrigerate for at least 1½ hours or overnight.
4. Place a madeleine pan in freezer for at least 1 hour before baking.
5. Preheat oven to 400°F (200°C). Butter and flour madeleine pan, and place pan on a baking sheet.
6. Using a cookie scoop, fill each madeleine mold three-fourths full with batter. (Be careful not to overfill.)
7. Bake in upper third of oven until tops begin to brown and feel set to the touch, 8 to 10 minutes. Let cool in pan for 1 minute. Remove from pan, and let cool for 10 minutes on a wire rack. Using a pastry brush, lightly glaze top of madeleines with Meyer Lemon Glaze. Let cool on a wire rack until glaze is set, 10 to 15 minutes. Glaze one corner of each madeleine diagonally, and dip glazed corners in almonds. Let stand on wire rack until glaze is set, 10 to 15 minutes.

MEYER LEMON GLAZE
Makes about 1 cup

1½   cups (180 grams) confectioners' sugar
3   tablespoons (45 grams) Meyer lemon juice
¼   teaspoon (1 gram) almond extract

1. In a small bowl, whisk together confectioners' sugar, lemon juice, and almond extract until smooth.

Note: *Madeleines taste best fresh, so plan to enjoy them right away.*

PRO TIP
Chilling the batter in the refrigerator for at least 1½ hours and the madeleine pans in the freezer for at least 1 hour helps to create that signature bump on the bottom.

Photo by Matt Armendariz

PINK PEPPERCORN MADELEINES WITH FIVE-SPICE POMEGRANATE GLAZE

Makes 20

Recipe by Rebecca Firth

Instead of the traditional melted butter, I use softened butter to give these madeleines extra lift and a cake-like texture. You'll know your butter is perfectly softened when it's easily smeared on a plate.

⅔ cup (133 grams) granulated sugar
1 teaspoon (3 grams) pink peppercorns
2 large eggs (100 grams), room temperature
1 tablespoon (15 grams) whole milk, room temperature
1 teaspoon (4 grams) vanilla extract
⅔ cup (83 grams) all-purpose flour
1 tablespoon (8 grams) cornstarch
1 tablespoon (6 grams) orange zest
½ teaspoon (2.5 grams) baking powder
½ teaspoon (1.5 grams) sea salt
½ cup (113 grams) unsalted butter, softened and cubed
¼ cup (30 grams) confectioners' sugar
Five-Spice Pomegranate Glaze (recipe follows)

1. Preheat oven to 400°F (200°C). Butter and flour 20 madeleine pan wells. Freeze for at least 5 minutes.
2. In the work bowl of a food processor, place granulated sugar and peppercorns; process until finely ground. (The sugar will have the appearance of confectioners' sugar with flecks of peppercorns.)
3. In the bowl of a stand mixer fitted with the paddle attachment, beat sugar mixture and eggs at high speed until pale yellow and thick, about 5 minutes. With mixer on low speed, add milk and vanilla; beat for 1 minute.
4. In a small bowl, whisk together flour, cornstarch, zest, baking powder, and salt. With mixer on medium-low speed, add flour mixture and butter to sugar mixture; beat for 1 minute. (Mixture will be smooth and creamy with some small butter chunks visible.)
5. Place about 1 tablespoon batter in each prepared madeleine well. (They should be between halfway and three-fourths full. Place batter in deep end of each well, not the middle. Do not smooth or flatten.) Place madeleine pans back in freezer for 5 minutes. Move directly from freezer to center of oven.
6. Bake for 8 minutes. Rotate pans, and bake

until golden around the edges and puffed up in the middle, 3 to 4 minutes more. Let cool in pans for 1 minute. Remove from pans, and let cool completely on wire racks. Sift with confectioners' sugar. Dip top edge of each cookie in Five-Spice Pomegranate Glaze. These cookies are best eaten the day they are baked.

FIVE-SPICE POMEGRANATE GLAZE
Makes about ½ cup

1 cup (120 grams) confectioners' sugar
1 tablespoon (15 grams) pomegranate juice
¼ teaspoon Chinese five-spice powder
1 tablespoon (15 grams) whole milk (optional)

1. In a small bowl, whisk together confectioners' sugar, pomegranate juice, and five-spice powder. Add milk to thin, if necessary.

Photo by Joe Schmelzer

SWEET CORN AND PEPPER JELLY OLD-FASHIONED DOUGHNUTS

Makes about 24

Filled with fresh grated corn and dipped in a Pepper Jelly Glaze, this savory doughnut tastes like summertime. This old-fashioned doughnut is similar to the cake style, but with a bit more crunch on the outside and an irregular shape. Those ridges and nooks make the perfect vessel for soaking up the glaze.

3   tablespoons (42 grams) unsalted butter
1¼   cups (250 grams) granulated sugar
5   large egg yolks (93 grams)
1¼   cups (300 grams) sour cream
⅓   cup (80 grams) grated fresh corn
3   cups (300 grams) cake flour
2⅓   cups plus 1 tablespoon (300 grams) all-purpose flour
½   cup (75 grams) yellow cornmeal
1   tablespoon (15 grams) baking powder
1   tablespoon (9 grams) kosher salt
Peanut oil, for frying
Pepper Jelly Glaze (recipe follows)

1. In the bowl of a stand mixer fitted with the paddle attachment, beat butter, sugar, and egg yolks at high speed until fluffy and pale in color, about 2 minutes. Reduce mixer speed to medium. Add sour cream and corn, and beat until smooth, 1 to 2 minutes.

2. In a large bowl, whisk together flours, cornmeal, baking powder, and salt. With mixer on low speed, gradually add flour mixture to corn mixture, beating just until combined.

3. Line a medium bowl with plastic wrap, and lightly spray with cooking spray. Transfer dough to prepared bowl. Spray top of dough with cooking spray. Cover with plastic wrap, and refrigerate for at least 1 hour or up to 1 day.

4. Line 2 rimmed baking sheets with parchment paper, and spray with cooking spray.

5. Dust top of dough with flour, and turn out onto a lightly floured surface. Lightly dust top of dough with flour, and roll to ½-inch thickness. Using a 3-inch doughnut cutter dipped in flour, cut dough, rerolling scraps as necessary. Place 2 inches apart on prepared pans. Lightly brush off any excess flour. Lightly spray top of doughnuts with cooking spray, and cover with plastic wrap. Refrigerate for 30 minutes.

6. In a large stockpot or deep fryer, pour oil to a depth of 4 inches, and heat over medium heat until a deep-fry thermometer registers 350°F (180°C). Working in batches, fry doughnuts, turning each after it rises to the surface, about 80 seconds per side. Remove using a slotted spoon or spider skimmer. (The oil needs to maintain a temperature of 350°F/180°C. After frying the first batch, let oil return to correct temperature before frying the second batch.) Let cool for 15 minutes. Drizzle with Pepper Jelly Glaze. Let stand on a wire rack until dry.

Note: *Frying these at a lower temperature gives them the rough, cracked exterior characteristic of an old-fashioned doughnut.*

PEPPER JELLY GLAZE
Makes about 3 cups

⅔   cup (160 grams) whole milk
½   cup (160 grams) red pepper jelly
½   teaspoon (1 gram) ground red pepper
½   teaspoon (1 gram) ground white pepper
6   cups (720 grams) confectioners' sugar

1. In the top of a double boiler, whisk together milk, pepper jelly, red pepper, and white pepper until jelly is melted. Whisk in confectioners' sugar, 1 cup (120 grams) at a time. Cook over simmering water until glaze is viscous and slightly see-through. Use immediately, or cover and refrigerate for up to 5 days.

> **PRO TIP**
> Let doughnuts cool for 15 minutes before glazing. If they're too warm, the glaze will just run off the sides.

PEANUT BUTTER WAFFLES WITH GANACHE, CURRY-BANANA ICE CREAM, AND MISO CARAMEL

Makes 4 to 6 servings

Recipe by Kate Jacoby

On vacation in Hong Kong researching desserts for her second restaurant, V Street, Kate found herself surveying street food in the nearby former Portuguese colony of Macau. She found a crispy, peanut butter-enriched waffle she picked up from a vendor, loved, and recreated back at home using tapioca starch to replace the egg. It's sweet and savory, with bittersweet ganache, umami-inflected miso caramel, and banana ice cream with fragrant curry spices Kate calls a savory envelope that carries the rich fruit flavor.

1   cup (240 grams) soy milk
¼   cup (56 grams) plus 4 teaspoons
     (20 grams) sunflower oil, divided
¼   cup (64 grams) creamy peanut butter
1   tablespoon (14 grams) firmly packed light brown sugar
1   tablespoon (14 grams) sesame oil
½   teaspoon (2 grams) vanilla extract
1   cup (125 grams) all-purpose flour
2   teaspoons (10 grams) baking powder
2   teaspoons (4 grams) vegan egg replacer powder
¼   teaspoon kosher salt
Ganache (recipe follows)
Curry-Banana Ice Cream (recipe follows)
Miso Caramel (recipe follows)

1. In a large bowl, whisk together soy milk, ¼ cup (56 grams) sunflower oil, peanut butter, brown sugar, sesame oil, and vanilla.
2. In a medium bowl, sift together flour, baking powder, egg replacer, and salt. Add flour mixture to milk mixture, whisking until combined.
3. Heat a waffle iron according to manufacturer's instructions. Lightly brush iron with 1 teaspoon (5 grams) sunflower oil. Spoon batter into waffle iron, and cook according to manufacturer's instructions. Repeat with remaining batter, lightly brushing iron with 1 teaspoon (5 grams) sunflower oil before each use. Refrigerate any remaining batter for up to 24 hours. To serve, smear waffles with Ganache. Place a scoop of Curry-Banana Ice Cream on top, and drizzle with Miso Caramel.

GANACHE
Makes 1½ cups

1   cup (170 grams) 60% cacao bittersweet chocolate morsels
½   cup (120 grams) soy milk
1   teaspoon (2 grams) instant coffee powder
¼   teaspoon kosher salt

1. In the top of a double boiler, whisk together chocolate and soy milk. Cook over simmering water until chocolate is melted. Remove from heat. Add coffee and salt, whisking to combine. Let cool. Refrigerate in an airtight container for up to 1 week.

CURRY-BANANA ICE CREAM
Makes 1 quart

1   cup (240 grams) water
1   cup (200 grams) granulated sugar
2   cups (400 grams) chopped banana
1   teaspoon (2 grams) curry powder
½   teaspoon (1 gram) ground turmeric
1   cup (240 grams) soy milk
1   cup (240 grams) coconut milk
2   teaspoons (10 grams) fresh lime juice
1   teaspoon (4 grams) vanilla extract
½   teaspoon (1.5 grams) kosher salt

1. In a medium saucepan, bring 1 cup (240 grams) water and sugar to a boil over medium-high heat. Cook, stirring occasionally, until sugar is dissolved, about 5 minutes. Reduce heat to low. Add banana, curry powder, and turmeric; cover and simmer just until bananas are softened, about 4 minutes. Remove from heat. Stir in soy milk and coconut milk; let cool completely.
2. Transfer mixture to the container of a blender, and add all remaining ingredients; blend until combined. Transfer to a large bowl, and refrigerate until chilled.
3. Place mixture in an ice cream maker, and freeze according to manufacturer's instructions. Freeze in an airtight container for up to 1 week.

PRO TIP
Citrus juice is key for waking up the ice cream's flavor. All Kate's ice creams contain lemon or lime juice, but only add it when the mixture has fully cooled, otherwise it will have a flat, cooked flavor.

MISO CARAMEL
Makes ½ cup

½   cup (100 grams) granulated sugar
¼   cup (60 grams) soy milk
2   tablespoons (32 grams) white miso
1   teaspoon (4 grams) vanilla extract

1. In a small saucepan, whisk together all ingredients. Cook over medium heat, stirring occasionally, until sugar turns amber colored, about 5 minutes. Let cool completely.

HOMEMADE HALVA

Makes 30

Recipe by Ben Mims

This isn't technically how halva is made, but it gets close enough, tasting like a tahini-flavored filling of a Butterfinger candy bar. The fat and the bitter notes in the tahini create a smooth, crumbly, and less-sweet candy. Coat the halva bars in chocolate to make your own candy bars, or crumble the plain bars over chocolate ice cream for a sophisticated take on chocolate and peanut butter.

1½   cups (336 grams) tahini
¾   teaspoon (2.25 grams) kosher salt
1   cup (200 grams) granulated sugar
¾   cup (255 grams) light corn syrup
2   tablespoons (30 grams) water
1   tablespoon (14 grams) unsalted butter
1   teaspoon (4 grams) vanilla extract
½   teaspoon (2.5 grams) baking soda
1   teaspoon (3 grams) toasted sesame seeds

1. Preheat oven to 200°F (93°C). Line a 9-inch square baking pan with foil, letting excess extend over sides of pan. Spray with cooking spray.
2. In a large heatproof bowl, combine tahini and salt. Place bowl in oven, and keep warm until ready to use.
3. In a medium saucepan, stir together sugar, corn syrup, and 2 tablespoons (30 grams) water until smooth. Add butter, and bring to a boil over high heat, stirring until sugar is dissolved. Cook until a candy thermometer registers 285°F (141°C), about 10 minutes.
4. In a small bowl, whisk together vanilla and baking soda. Carefully stir vanilla mixture into sugar mixture (syrup will foam and bubble up). Immediately pour syrup into warm tahini mixture, and using a heatproof spatula, fold together as quickly as possible (mixture does not have to be completely homogenous).
5. Immediately scrape tahini mixture into prepared pan. Using the spatula, press into a flat, even layer. Immediately sprinkle with sesame seeds while tahini is still hot so they stick to the top. Let cool completely.
6. Using excess foil as handles, remove halva, and peel off foil. Cut into 2x1-inch rectangles. Store in an airtight container for up to 5 days.

Photo by Mason + Dixon

SWEET POTATO BEBINCA

Makes 1 (9-inch) bebinca

Recipe by Nik Sharma

Growing up, this was one of my favorite desserts. Traditionally from Goa, a coastal state in India, bebinca is a stunning seven-layer cake, made of egg yolks, flour, coconut milk, and sugar and topped with ghee. But since it's fall, I've added golden sweet potatoes to the batter and simplified it to one layer for a more approachable, seasonal take. For a final flourish, I like to pour a little maple syrup over a chilled slice.

6   tablespoons unsalted butter or ghee (84 grams), melted, plus more for greasing pan
1⅔ cups (406 grams) roasted sweet potato purée*

1⅔ cups (400 grams) full-fat coconut milk
5   large eggs (250 grams)
1   cup (200 grams) granulated sugar
1   cup (125 grams) all-purpose flour
½   teaspoon (1 gram) ground nutmeg
¼   teaspoon sea salt

1. Preheat to 350°F (180°C). Grease a 9-inch round baking pan melted butter or ghee, and line pan with parchment paper.
2. In a large bowl, whisk together sweet potato purée, coconut milk, eggs, sugar, and melted butter or ghee. In a medium bowl, whisk together flour, nutmeg, and salt. Add flour mixture to sweet potato mixture, whisking until combined. Pour batter into prepared pan. Gently tap pan on counter to release any air bubbles.
3. Bake for 1 hour. Let cool to room temperature. Remove from pan. Cover and refrigerate for at least 4 hours or overnight before slicing and serving. Serve chilled or at room temperature.

*To make roasted sweet potato purée, wash and scrub sweet potatoes under cold running tap water to remove any dirt. Preheat oven to 400°F (200°C), and place sweet potatoes in an ovenproof dish. (Most baking pans can't withstand temperatures beyond 400°F [200°C], so I recommend using a cast-iron baking dish.) Bake until a skewer or knife passes through center of potato easily and flesh is soft and tender, 45 minutes to 1 hour. Let cool to room temperature. Remove and discard skins. Purée until smooth using a handheld blender, food processor, or blender.

Photo by Nik Sharma

EGGNOG PANNA COTTA

Makes 4¼ cups

Recipe by Allison Kave and Keavy Landreth

When done right, panna cotta is light, creamy, and ethereal. When done wrong, it can be a soupy mess or an over-gelled rubber ball. This is a foolproof recipe, inspired by the Platonic ideal of the form: the panna cotta at Franny's in Brooklyn, which is the best we've ever had. It toes the line between rich and light, and just holds itself together. With the curds from our Clarified Eggnog, it provides classic holiday flavor in a totally unexpected form.

2 cups (450 grams) reserved curds from Clarified Eggnog (recipe follows)
2 tablespoons (30 grams) cold water
2 teaspoons (8 grams) unflavored gelatin
3 cups (720 grams) heavy whipping cream
½ cup (100 grams) granulated sugar
¼ teaspoon kosher salt
2 vanilla beans, split lengthwise, seeds scraped and reserved
Garnish: grated fresh nutmeg

1. Prepare Clarified Eggnog.
2. In a small bowl, stir together 2 tablespoons (30 grams) cold water and gelatin; let stand until softened, about 5 minutes.
3. In a large saucepan, combine cream, sugar, and salt. Add vanilla beans and reserved seeds, and bring to a simmer over medium heat. Add reserved Clarified Eggnog curds and gelatin mixture, stirring until completely dissolved. Strain through a chinois into a liquid measuring cup.
4. Pour into ramekins or small bowls. Cover with plastic wrap, pressing wrap directly onto surface to prevent a skin from forming. Refrigerate for at least 4 hours or overnight. Serve in ramekins, or if you're feeling adventurous, run a paring knife around perimeter of each ramekin, and invert onto small plates. Garnish with nutmeg, if desired.

CLARIFIED EGGNOG
Makes 16 servings

What do you get when you add and then remove the dairy from eggnog? A crystal-clear, silky-smooth cocktail with the warm spiced flavor you know and love without the thick texture that some find off-putting. This is a straightforward but time-consuming process, so we highly suggest making a big batch and using it as an excuse to throw a holiday bash!

2½ cups (600 grams) brandy
1½ cups (360 grams) aged rum
1 cup (240 grams) orange liqueur
½ cup (170 grams) mild honey
½ cup (120 grams) fresh lemon juice
½ cup (120 grams) fresh orange juice
2 teaspoons (4 grams) ground nutmeg
2 teaspoons (4 grams) ground cinnamon
1 teaspoon (2 grams) ground cloves
1 teaspoon (2 grams) ground allspice
4 cups (960 grams) whole milk
Garnish: orange twists

1. In a large bowl, whisk together brandy, rum, orange liqueur, honey, lemon juice, orange juice, nutmeg, cinnamon, cloves, and allspice. Pour into a large heatproof container.
2. In a large saucepan, heat milk over medium heat, stirring frequently, just until bubbles form around edges of pan (do not boil). Remove from heat, and pour into brandy mixture. Immediately, curds will form on surface of mixture. Using a perforated spoon (or a skimmer designed specifically for this purpose), skim larger curds off top of cocktail, and reserve for Eggnog Panna Cotta.
3. Strain remaining mixture through a straining bag, coffee filters, or a very fine-mesh chinois strainer into a large glass pitcher or plastic container. This will take a fair bit of time (the exact length of time depends on how tightly woven your strainer is), so you can leave it to strain in your refrigerator overnight if you're planning ahead.
4. After the mixture has strained, reserve the Clarified Eggnog curds, and check the cocktail for clarity. If it's crystal clear, you're good to go! If it's still a bit cloudy, you have a few options: Pour the cocktail through a coffee filter-lined chinois (this will take at least a couple of hours, and you might have to replace the filters periodically); pour it through the straining bag again if its weave is tight enough; or refrigerate it overnight (without moving it), and then siphon off the clarified cocktail, as the remaining fine milk solids will settle to the bottom.
5. At the end, you'll be left with a delicious, perfectly clear, amber-hued cocktail. Bottle it, or add it to a punch bowl. Garnish with an orange twist, if desired. This cocktail will keep in the refrigerator for up to 1 year, so feel free to make it well ahead of time!

COOKIE BUTTER TRUFFLES

Makes about 48

Cookie butter, much like peanut butter, pulverizes a good thing (Biscoff Cookies) into an addictive spread. These truffles double down on the Biscoff flavor with alternating layers of Cookie Butter Ganache and straight cookie butter. Try not to get too attached—these truffles will be the first to disappear at your holiday get-together.

18 ounces (510 grams) 66% cacao semisweet chocolate baking wafers*
Cookie Butter Ganache (recipe follows)
1 cup (256 grams) cookie butter*
Garnish: Biscoff Cookie crumbs or melted white chocolate

1. In the top of a double boiler, melt chocolate baking wafers over simmering water. (Alternatively, in a large microwave-safe bowl, microwave chocolate on medium in 30-second intervals, stirring between each, until chocolate is melted and smooth.) Fill 4 (12-cavity) silicone or plastic truffle molds** with melted chocolate. (For white chocolate garnish, pipe a small amount of white chocolate into molds before filling with melted chocolate. Let dry.) Turn over molds, emptying chocolate into a bowl. Let chocolate drip out until you can see outlines on bottoms of molds when the molds are turned over. Let truffle molds set slightly, and scrap off excess with a bench scraper. Let set completely, right side up.

2. Place Cookie Butter Ganache and cookie butter in 2 separate pastry bags fitted with medium-size round tips. Fill chocolate shells halfway full with Cookie Butter Ganache, and top with cookie butter (do not fill completely). Freeze for 10 minutes. Reheat reserved melted chocolate until smooth, if necessary. Spread melted chocolate over molds to form bottom, scraping off excess with a bench scraper. Freeze for 10 minutes.

3. Remove truffles from molds, and clean any rough edges using a sharp paring knife. Using a fork or a piping tip as a template, garnish with Biscoff Cookie crumbs, if desired. Store in an airtight container for up to 2 weeks.

We used Guittard Semisweet Chocolate Baking Wafers and Biscoff Cookie Butter.

**We used Webake Silicone Chocolate Molds and Zicome Non-Stick Silicone Molds, available on amazon.com.*

COOKIE BUTTER GANACHE

Makes 2 cups

1⅓ cups (227 grams) 62% cacao dark chocolate morsels*
⅓ cup (85 grams) cookie butter*
2 tablespoons (28 grams) unsalted butter, softened
¾ cup plus 1 tablespoon (195 grams) heavy whipping cream

1. In a medium bowl, combine chocolate, cookie butter, and butter.

2. In a small saucepan, bring cream to a boil over medium-high heat. Immediately pour hot cream over chocolate mixture; let stand for 1 minute. Whisk gently until combined and shiny. Cover and let cool to room temperature. Refrigerate for up to 2 weeks.

We used Scharffen Berger Dark Chocolate Baking Chunks and Biscoff Cookie Butter.

CHERRY, ALMOND, PISTACHIO, AND HONEY NOUGAT

Makes about 5 bars or 30 pieces

Nougat De Montélimar is a chewy nougat candy from the south of France that's included in Les Treize Desserts de Noël, the 13 desserts served during a traditional Provençal Christmas. While paying homage to the original combination of pistachios, almonds, and cherries, we included a warm note of caramelized honey. Making nougat is a team sport, so invite a second set of hands to help maneuver the sticky sweet.

1⅓ cups (187 grams) whole almonds
1⅓ cups (187 grams) whole pistachios
1 cup (336 grams) honey
1¾ cups (350 grams) granulated sugar
½ cup (170 grams) light corn syrup
½ cup (120 grams) water
1 tablespoon (15 grams) amaretto
1 teaspoon (4 grams) almond extract
3 large egg whites (90 grams), room temperature
½ teaspoon (1 gram) cream of tartar
1 cup (128 grams) dried cherries

1. Preheat oven to 300°F (150°C).
2. Place almonds and pistachios on a small baking sheet. Bake for 12 minutes. Turn oven off, and leave nuts in oven to keep warm.
3. Line an 8-inch square metal baking pan with parchment paper, letting excess extend over sides of pan.
4. In a small saucepan, bring honey to a boil over medium heat. Boil until mixture registers 252°F (122°C) on a candy thermometer.
5. In another small saucepan, heat sugar, corn syrup, and ½ cup (120 grams) water over medium heat. Cook until mixture registers 295°F (146°C) on a candy thermometer. Remove from heat; stir in amaretto and almond extract.
6. In the bowl of a stand mixer fitted with the whisk attachment, beat egg whites at medium speed until foamy. Add cream of tartar, and beat until stiff peaks form. Add hot honey in a slow, steady stream until combined, about 3 minutes. Switch to the paddle attachment. With mixer on medium-high speed, add hot sugar mixture in a slow, steady stream, and beat for 15 to 25 minutes, depending on humidity. The longer the nougat is mixed, the harder the end product will be. If you want a softer nougat, mix for only 10 to 15 minutes. Nougat is ready when you can pinch off a small amount and roll it between your fingers without it sticking once cooled. (Be careful; your nougat will still be quite hot.)
7. Add warm nuts, and stir well with a greased spatula. (Nougat should be very thick and very hard to stir.) Sprinkle half of cherries in prepared pan. Using a greased plastic bench scraper, add half of nougat. Press down with greased hands. Sprinkle with remaining cherries. Add remaining nougat, and smooth top with a greased spatula. Cover with parchment paper, and press down with bench scraper to further smooth top and square edges. Let stand overnight. Using excess parchment as handles, remove from pan. Using a sharp knife, cut into 5 equal bars or 30 square pieces. Wrap in wax paper, and tie string around the ends. Store in an airtight container for up to 1 month.

PRO TIP
The success of this nougat recipe is dependent on the humidity. It must be lower than 50 percent. To combat humidity, try blowing the nougat with a hair dryer on high heat while it is being mixed in the stand mixer. The warm heat should remove any excess moisture.

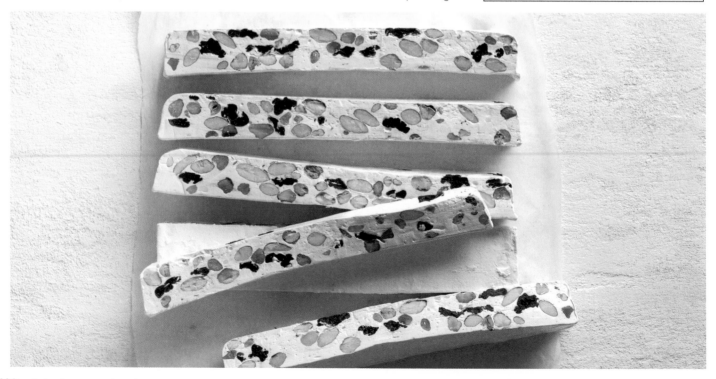

ESPRESSO AND CACAO CARAMELS

Makes about 120 pieces

Our homemade soft caramel merges luscious dark chocolate and a bite of espresso for an energized take on the chewy original. To bring a touch of crunchy texture, we added a salty-bitter topping of Maldon sea salt and coarse cacao nibs.

⅔ cup (113 grams) chopped 70% bittersweet chocolate*
1 cup plus 2 tablespoons (270 grams) heavy whipping cream
½ cup plus 1 tablespoon (135 grams) sweetened condensed milk
1 cup (200 grams) granulated sugar
½ cup (170 grams) golden syrup*
½ cup (170 grams) light corn syrup
¼ cup (60 grams) water
¼ cup (57 grams) unsalted butter, softened
1 tablespoon (6 grams) espresso powder
½ tablespoon (9 grams) vanilla bean paste
½ teaspoon (1.5 grams) Maldon sea salt
½ teaspoon (1.5 grams) cacao nibs, finely chopped

1. Line a 13x9-inch metal baking pan with parchment paper, and spray with cooking spray.
2. In a medium bowl, place chocolate. In a small saucepan, heat cream and condensed milk over low heat, stirring until combined. Pour hot cream mixture over chocolate; let stand for 1 minute. Whisk until combined; cover and keep warm.
3. In a medium saucepan, heat sugar, golden syrup, corn syrup, and ¼ cup (60 grams) water over low heat, stirring occasionally, until sugar is dissolved. Increase heat to medium, and cook, without stirring, until mixture registers 240°F (116°C) on a candy thermometer, about 10 minutes. Remove from heat, and carefully stir in cream mixture. Return to heat, and cook, stirring constantly, until mixture registers 240°F (116°C) on a candy thermometer, about 20 minutes. Remove from heat, and add butter, espresso powder, and vanilla bean paste. Immediately pour into prepared pan. Let stand for 5 minutes.
4. In a small bowl, stir together salt and cacao nibs. Sprinkle over caramel. Cover with plastic wrap, and let stand overnight.
5. Using a sharp knife, cut into 1½x½-inch pieces; wrap in wax paper. Store in an airtight container for up to 1 month.

*We used Valrhona Guanaja Feves Bitter 70% and Tate & Lyle's Golden Syrup.

CRANBERRY-PECAN DIVINITY

Makes about 40 pieces

A Southern candy classic, divinity walks the fine line between rich fudge and fluffy marshmallow. Though traditionally formed into homey spoon-drop bites, we piped the confection into a clean circle, topping with a pecan half to create a sweet sugary button hiding a surprise note of tart cranberry flavor.

2½ cups (500 grams) granulated sugar
½ cup (170 grams) light corn syrup
½ cup (120 grams) water
¼ teaspoon kosher salt
2 large egg whites (60 grams)
¼ teaspoon cream of tartar
1½ teaspoons (6 grams) vanilla extract
1 cup (128 grams) chopped dried cranberries
40 pecan halves, toasted

1. Line 2 baking sheets with parchment paper. Lightly spray with cooking spray.

2. In a large saucepan, stir together sugar, corn syrup, ½ cup (120 grams) water, and salt until combined. Cook over medium heat, without stirring, until mixture registers 258°F (126°C) on a candy thermometer.

3. Meanwhile, in the bowl of a stand mixer fitted with the whisk attachment, beat egg whites at medium high speed until foamy. Add cream of tartar, and beat until stiff peaks form. Remove sugar mixture from heat, and stir in vanilla. With mixer on high speed, add hot sugar mixture to egg whites in a slow, steady stream, avoiding whisk. Beat until mixture thickens and begins to lose its gloss, 5 to 9 minutes, depending on humidity. (The lower the humidity, the less time this step will take. Watch closely—do not overmix, or it will stiffen.)

4. Working quickly, add cranberries, stirring to combine. Spoon mixture into a pastry bag fitted with a large round tip. Pipe small rounds onto prepared pans. After every fourth or fifth row piped, place a pecan on top of each piece, and press in slightly. Let stand until dry and can be removed easily from pans. Store in an airtight container for up to 1 month.

ORANGE AND CAMPARI TURKISH DELIGHT

Makes about 30 pieces

Though inspired by the floral jelly classic of the former Ottoman empire, our Turkish Delight trades the signature rose water for a sunburst of orange flavor. A shot of Campari brings a complementary bitter citrus note that cuts through the sweetness and adds a cast of pastel pink that recalls the rosy Turkish original.

2½ cups (600 grams) cold water, divided
¾ cup (96 grams) cornstarch
3 cups (600 grams) granulated sugar
¼ cup (85 grams) light corn syrup
1 tablespoon (15 grams) Campari
2 teaspoons (8 grams) pure orange extract
Confectioners' sugar, for dusting

1. Line a 9-inch square metal baking pan with parchment paper, letting excess extend over sides of pan. Butter and flour pan.
2. In a medium bowl, whisk together ½ cup (120 grams) water and cornstarch until dissolved. Transfer to a large saucepan, and add remaining 2 cups (480 grams) water. Cook over medium heat, stirring frequently, until mixture turns opaque and has thickened. Add granulated sugar and corn syrup, and cook until mixture turns translucent. Cook, stirring constantly, until mixture becomes very gelatinous and hard to stir, 20 to 25 minutes. (To test mixture, place a small amount on a plate, and let cool. Mixture should easily hold its shape, be slightly firm to the touch, and should not be sticky.) Stir in Campari and orange extract; pour into prepared pan.
3. Cover with a piece of plastic wrap, pressing wrap directly onto surface; smooth with a spatula. Wrap pan in plastic wrap, and let cool for at least 6 hours or overnight.
4. Gently peel off plastic wrap. Using excess parchment as handles, remove candy from pan. Using a sharp knife, cut into 1½-inch squares. Toss each piece in confectioners' sugar to coat. Sprinkle equal parts confectioners' sugar and cornstarch in bottom of an airtight container (to keep candy from sticking together). Store candy in airtight container for up to 1 month.

PRO TIP
If it turns out too soft, or just too soft for your personal preference, you can simply remelt your Turkish delight and continue cooking it until it has thickened enough to your liking.

KOEKSISTERS

Makes 36

Recipe by Dale Gray/*feedfeed*

These are even better the next day since the syrup has had a chance to soak in. They can be stored in the freezer and are delicious eaten ice cold with a cup of hot tea!

2   cups (250 grams) cake flour
¼   cup (57 grams) cold unsalted butter, cubed
2   tablespoons (30 grams) baking powder
½   teaspoon (1.5 grams) kosher salt
¾   cup (180 grams) whole buttermilk
1   large egg (50 grams), lightly beaten
Vegetable oil, for frying
Ginger Syrup (recipe follows)

1. In the work bowl of a food processor, place flour, cold butter, baking powder, and salt; pulse until mixture is crumbly. Add buttermilk and egg, and pulse until mixture just comes together. Turn out dough onto a lightly floured surface, and knead gently until elastic but not sticky. Let rest in an airtight container at room temperature for at least 2 hours.

2. On a lightly floured surface, roll dough into a 13x9-inch rectangle, about ¼ inch thick. (Dough should be bouncy and not stick easily.) Trim off any uneven edges. Using a pastry cutter, cut dough into 2½x1-inch strips. Make 2 (2-inch) cuts through length of each one, leaving ½ inch at top intact. Braid strips, pinching end to secure. Fold top corners back, and pinch together to ensure an even shape.

3. In a large heavy-bottomed cast-iron stockpot, heat oil over medium-high heat until a deep-fry thermometer registers 370°F (188°C). Fry koeksisters in batches of 6 to 8 for 30 seconds, turning once to ensure an even golden brown color. Using a slotted spoon, remove koeksisters, and let drain on a paper towel very quickly. Immediately place in ice-cold Ginger Syrup for about 1 minute. Place on a wire rack, letting excess syrup drip off. Repeat with remaining koeksisters. These cookies are best eaten the next day but can be frozen for up to 1 month when stored in an airtight container.

GINGER SYRUP
Makes about 4 cups

2   cups (400 grams) granulated sugar
1¼   cups (300 grams) water
1   tablespoon (6 grams) lemon zest
2   tablespoons (30 grams) fresh lemon juice
½   teaspoon (1.5 grams) kosher salt
1   rooibos tea bag (2.5 grams)
2   slices fresh ginger (5 grams)
1   cinnamon stick
4   whole cloves

1. In a medium saucepan, stir together sugar and 1¼ cups (300 grams) water until sugar is dissolved. Add all remaining ingredients, and bring to a boil over medium-high heat; boil for 5 minutes. Reduce heat to medium-low, and cook until mixture thickens slightly, 25 to 30 minutes. Let cool completely before straining through a fine-mesh sieve and transferring to an airtight container. Refrigerate overnight or for up to 2 weeks.

Photo by Dale Gray

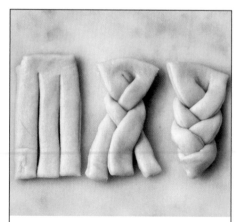

PRO TIP
1. Using a pastry cutter, cut dough into 2½x1–inch strips. Make 2 (2-inch) cuts through length of each one, leaving ½ inch at top intact.
2. Braid strips pinching end to secure.
3. Fold top corners back, and pinch together to ensure an even shape.

RASPBERRY SWIRL PISTACHIO MERINGUE COOKIES

Makes about 20

Recipe by Fanny Lam/*feedfeed*

These light and fluffy cookies, slightly swirled with a fresh raspberry syrup and sprinkled with pistachio, take traditional meringues to a whole new level.

1   cup (170 grams) fresh or frozen raspberries
¾   cup (150 grams) plus 3 tablespoons (36 grams) granulated sugar, divided
3   large egg whites (90 grams)
1   teaspoon (5 grams) fresh lemon juice
½   teaspoon (1 gram) cream of tartar
½   cup (57 grams) roughly chopped pistachios

1. In a small saucepan, heat raspberries and 3 tablespoons (36 grams) sugar over medium-high heat. Cook until raspberries have softened and released their juices, about 10 minutes. Remove from heat, and strain through a fine-mesh sieve, discarding solids. Let cool completely.
2. Preheat oven to 225°F (107°C). Line 2 baking sheets with parchment paper.
3. In the bowl of a stand mixer fitted with the whisk attachment, beat egg whites at medium speed until foamy, about 1 minute. Beat in lemon juice and cream of tartar. With mixer running, gradually add remaining ¾ cup (150 grams) sugar, stopping to scrape sides of bowl. Increase mixer speed to high, and beat until stiff glossy peaks form.
4. Using a medium (1½-tablespoon) spring-loaded scoop, scoop meringue, and place on prepared pans. Smooth tops using the back of a spoon. Drizzle about ½ teaspoon raspberry sauce over each meringue. Using a wooden pick, swirl sauce into meringue. Sprinkle with pistachios.
5. Bake until exteriors of cookies become crispy, about 1½ hours. Turn oven off, and let meringues stand in oven with door closed for 2 hours. Store in an airtight container at room temperature for up to 1 week.

Photo by Fanny Lam

CHOCOLATE POTS DE CRÈME WITH TOASTED MERINGUE

Makes 4

With its silky texture and dark chocolate flavor, this make-ahead dessert is capped off with a delectable toasted meringue.

2   cups (480 grams) half-and-half
10   ounces (300 grams) 60% bittersweet chocolate morsels
2   large egg yolks (37 grams)
Garnish: Toasted Chocolate Swirl Meringues (recipe follows), Homemade Graham Cracker pieces (recipe 337)

1. In a medium saucepan, bring half-and-half to a boil over medium-high heat.
2. Place chocolate in the container of a blender. Carefully pour hot half-and-half into blender, and let stand for 1 minute. Blend until smooth. With blender running, add egg yolks, beating until combined. Let mixture cool slightly.

3. Pour into 4 dessert glasses or jars, and cover with plastic wrap. Refrigerate until firm, 2 to 4 hours or overnight. Garnish with Toasted Chocolate Swirl Meringues and Homemade Graham Cracker pieces, if desired.

TOASTED CHOCOLATE SWIRL MERINGUES
Makes 24

3   large egg whites (90 grams), room temperature
¼   teaspoon cream of tartar
½   cup (100 grams) granulated sugar
¼   cup (30 grams) confectioners' sugar
1   teaspoon (4 grams) vanilla extract
½   cup (85 grams) semisweet chocolate morsels, melted

1. Preheat oven to 275°F (140°C). Line a baking sheet with parchment paper.

2. In the bowl of a stand mixer fitted with the whisk attachment, beat egg whites and cream of tartar at high speed until soft peaks form. Gradually add sugars and vanilla, beating until stiff peaks form, about 5 minutes.
3. Transfer mixture to a piping bag fitted with a large round tip. Pipe 1½-tablespoon mounds onto prepared pan. Using a spoon, drop about ¼ teaspoon melted chocolate into center of each meringue. Using a wooden pick, swirl chocolate into meringues.
4. Bake for 1 hour. Turn oven off, and let meringues stand in oven with door cracked for 6 hours or overnight. Store in an airtight container.

CHURRO S'MORES

Makes 6

These s'mores are a playful twist on the classic combo. Fried churro spirals are dusted with sweet cinnamon-sugar and dipped in a spicy Mexican chocolate ganache before being sandwiched with a toasty vanilla bean marshmallow.

Vanilla Bean Marshmallows (recipe on page 337)
Churro Rounds (recipe follows)
Spicy Ganache (recipe follows)

1. Prepare Vanilla Bean Marshmallows as directed, using a 2½-inch round cutter to cut marshmallows. Toast marshmallows over a fire, or use a kitchen torch.
2. Dip a hot Churro Round in melted Spicy Ganache, and place a toasted marshmallow on top of ganache. Dip another hot Churro Round in melted Spicy Ganache, and place on top. Repeat with remaining Churro Rounds, Vanilla Bean Marshmallows, and Spicy Ganache.

CHURRO ROUNDS

Makes 12

Canola oil, for frying
1   cup (240 grams) water
½   cup (113 grams) unsalted butter
½   cup (100 grams) plus 1 tablespoon (12 grams) granulated sugar, divided
¼   teaspoon kosher salt
1   cup (125 grams) all-purpose flour
3   large eggs (150 grams)
1   teaspoon (2 grams) ground cinnamon

1. In a large Dutch oven, pour oil to halfway full, and heat over medium heat until a deep-fry thermometer registers 350°F (180°C).
2. In a medium saucepan, bring 1 cup (240 grams) water, butter, 1 tablespoon (12 grams) sugar, and salt to a boil over medium heat. Reduce heat to low. Add flour, and stir well. Cook over low heat for 2 minutes. Remove from heat, and let cool for 15 minutes.
3. Transfer mixture to the bowl of a stand mixer fitted with the paddle attachment. With mixer on medium speed, add eggs, one at a time, beating well after each addition.

4. Place dough in a pastry bag fitted with a large star tip. Quickly dip a flat spatula into oil. Pipe spiral round onto spatula. Gently slide round off spatula into oil. Fry dough for 5 minutes per side.
5. In a medium bowl, stir together cinnamon and remaining ½ cup (100 grams) sugar. Toss churros in cinnamon sugar. Serve immediately.

SPICY GANACHE

Makes 3 cups

12   ounces (340 grams) spicy chocolate*, chopped
1½   cups (360 grams) heavy whipping cream

1. In a medium microwave-safe bowl, combine chocolate and cream. Microwave on high in 30-second intervals, stirring between each, until chocolate is melted and smooth (about 1½ minutes total).

We used Taza Chipotle Chili Chocolate.

RECIPE INDEX

A

All-Butter Piecrust 213
Almond-Blueberry Coffee Cake 105
Almond-Browned Butter Pie Dough 183
Almond-Browned Butter Plum Pie 183
Almond Cream Filling 234
Almond Crumble Topping 360
Almond Filling 252
Almond Financiers 100
Almond Oat Crumble 210
Almond Tarts 252
Amaretto Boston Cream Pie 85
Amaretto Pastry Cream 85
Apple Butter Bars 360
Apple Cheddar Pie 209
Apple Filling 203
Apple Guinness Cheddar Soda Bread 121
Apple Pie Filling 298
Apple Pie Sauce 298
Apricot-Almond Filling 155, 207
Apricot-Almond Hand Pies 207
Apricot and Hazelnut Crumb Tart 233
Apricot Frangipane Tart 232
Apricot Glaze 137
Apricot Sweet Buns 155

B

Baileys Original Irish Cream
    Buttercream Filling 283
Baklava 245
Banana Cake with Brown Sugar Hazelnut
    Buttercream 15
Banana-Sesame Cake with Tahini-
    Cream Cheese Swirl Frosting 51
Banana Upside-Down Cake with
    Walnuts and Coconut 67
Banoffee Pie 205
Basic but Better: Classic S'mores 337
Basic Pie Dough 192
Basil and Pine Nut Strawberry Tart 228
Basil Macadamia Dough 239
Basil Pastry Cream 228
Bear Claws 247
Belgian Waffles with Maple Crème
    Fraîche & Candied Walnuts 377
Berry Buttermilk Cake with Mascarpone
    Crème Fraîche 16
Bienenstich 55
Birthday Cake Crumb Topping 123
Birthday Cake Scones with Vanilla Glaze 122
Bittersweet Cherry Ganache 175
Bittersweet Chocolate Glaze 38
Black Bottom Coconut Cream Tart 224
Black Forest Pie 175
Black Sesame and Toasted Coconut
    Madeleines 380
Black Velvet Layer Cake 20
Blackberry-Almond Upside-Down Cake 79
Blackberry Glaze 371

Blackberry Jam 358
Blackberry Jam Bars 358
Blueberry-Almond Galettes 225
Blueberry and Bitters Filling 255
Blueberry and Bitters Strudels 255
Blueberry Bitters Glaze 255
Blueberry Browned Butter Buckle 89
Blueberry Jam 191
Blueberry Preserves 255
Blushing Pear Pie 210
Bourbon-Braised Pineapple
    Doughnuts 370
Bourbon-Braised Pineapple Glaze 370
Bourbon Chocolate-Covered Cherry
    Cake 72
Bourbon-Vanilla Caramel 306
Bourbon-Vanilla Caramel Sauce 37
Braided Mazanec 147
Brandy Alexander Marble Cake 71
Brandy Almond Marzipan 76
Brandy Honey Whipped Cream 331
Brandy Snaps 331
Brown Rice Crumb Topping 89
Brown Sugar Cinnamon Topping 92
Brown Sugar Crumble 87, 97
Brown Sugar Filling 205
Brown Sugar Glaze 155
Brown Sugar Hazelnut Buttercream 15
Brown Sugar-Lemon Glaze 97
Brown Sugar Oat Streusel 364
Brown Sugar Syrup 154
Brown Sugar Whipped Cream 199, 239
Browned Butter 53, 82
Browned Butter and Orange Skillet
    Cake 82
Browned Butter Cranberry Orange Bars
    with Brown Sugar Oat Streusel 364
Browned Butter Filling 235
Browned Butter Frosting 19
Browned Butter Glaze 36, 294
Browned Butter Hummingbird Coffee
    Cake 99
Browned Butter Macadamia Crescent
    Cookies 294
Browned Butter Molasses Cookies 330
Browned Butter-Pear Glaze 40
Browned Butter Pecan Streusel 189
Browned Butter Pizzelles with
    Cardamom 336
Buckwheat Black Pepper Crust 179
Burnt Honey and Ginger Cream
    Frosting 75
Butter Pecan Angel Food Cake 36
Butter Piecrust 177
Buttermilk Filling 200
Buttermilk Sheet Pan Pie 200
Buttermilk Whipped Cream 94
Butternut Squash Pie 215
Butternut Squash Pudding with
    Cardamom Crème Fraîche and
    Caramelized Cashews 379

Butterscotch Pie with Coconut Curry
    Crust 198
Buttery Puff Pastry 359

C

Cakey Chocolate Chip Cookies 271
Candied Cherries 269
Candied Cherry, Date, and Pistachio
    Biscotti 269
Candied Hazelnuts 197
Candied Lemon Peel 158
Candied Orange Peel 162
Candied Orange Rind 41
Candied Orange Slices 82
Candied Sage Leaves 308
Candied Walnuts 377
Caramel 20, 92
Caramel and Date Filling 25
Caramel Pecan Banana Coffee Cake 92
Caramel Sauce 197, 357
Caramelized Cashews 379
Caramelized Garlic 168
Caramelized Garlic Roosterkoek 168
Caramelized Hazelnuts 25
Caramelized Lemons 28
Caramelized Onion, Polenta, and Fresh
    Herb Olive Oil Loaf 128
Cardamom Crème Fraîche 379
Cardamom Honey Cutout Cookies 349
Carrot Coffee Cake 94
Carrot Masala Bars 354
Celery Gruyère Gougères 261
Chai Buttercream Frosting 305
Chai Spice Caramel Pie 219
Chai Tea Glaze 342
Chakalaka Relish 167
Charred Squash Pound Cake with Black
    Pepper and Parmesan 49
Cheddar Cheese Piecrust 209
Cheesy Scallion Pull-Apart Rolls 149
Cherry Crumb Cake 62
Cherry Frangelico Filling 182
Cherry-Hazelnut Shekerburas 182
Cherry Mousse 175
Cherry Purée 175
Cherry, Almond, Pistachio, and Honey
    Nougat 390
Chestnut Filling 197
Chestnut Hazelnut Caramel Pie 197
Chestnut Mont Blanc 252
Chestnut Paste 252
Chestnut Pastry Cream 250
Chestnut-Ricotta Filling 263
Chestnut-Ricotta Sfogliatelle 263
Chestnut, Cranberry, and Rosemary-
    Laminated Pain d' Epi 153
Chestnut, Fig, and Ginger
    Croquembouche 250
Chewy Chai-Spiced Cranberry Molasses
    Cookies 342

Chewy Chocolate Chip Cookies 273
Chocolate Almond Filling 243
Chocolate Almond Mooncakes 243
Chocolate-Buttermilk Frosting 101
Chocolate Cherry Hot Cross Buns 137
Chocolate-Chestnut Mousse 81
Chocolate-Chestnut Mousse Cake 81
Chocolate-Coconut Tart with Almonds 238
Chocolate-Covered Pecans 357
Chocolate Crinkle Cookies 319
Chocolate-Dipped Peanut Butter
    Crinkle Cookies 326
Chocolate Glaze 90, 257
Chocolate-Hazelnut Filling 15
Chocolate Hazelnut Shortbread
    Cookies 293
Chocolate Kugelhopf 41
Chocolate Peppermint Cookies 351
Chocolate Pots de Crème with Toasted
    Meringue 396
Chocolate Rugelach 244
Chocolate Tart with Honey-Glazed
    Pecans 223
Chocolate Turtle Cookies 318
Churro Rounds 397
Churro S'mores 397
Cinnamon-Pecan Crumble 93
Cinnamon-Pecan Streusel 46
Cinnamon Roll Apple Pie 203
Cinnamon Roll Cake 46
Cinnamon Roll Dough 140
Cinnamon-Spiced Rolling Sugar 342
Cinnamon Twist 142
Cinnamon-Walnut Crumble 96
Citrus Glaze 32
Citrus Upside-Down Cake 80
Clarified Eggnog 388
Classic Cinnamon Rolls 140
Classic Hot Cross Buns 134
Classic Olive Oil Cake 66
Classic or Oversized Chocolate Chip
    Cookies 270
Classic Soda Bread 118
Coconut and Earl Grey Scones 117
Coconut Buns 164
Coconut Buttermilk Pound Cake 52
Coconut Cream Pie 193
Coconut Cream Topping 47
Coconut Curry Crust 198
Coconut Filling 164, 193
Coconut Icing 164
Coconut Milk Caramel 367
Coconut Pastry Cream 224
Coconut-Pecan Crumble 94
Coconut-Pecan Frosting 39
Coconut Popovers with Mango
    Chutney 116
Coconut Skillet Cake 86
Coconut Whipped Cream 193
Coffee Chocolate Fudge 374
Coffee Cream 374

Concord Grape Jam **125**
Cookie Butter Ganache **389**
Cookie Butter Truffles **389**
Cookies and Cream Filling **332**
Cookies and Cream Macarons **332**
Cornmeal and Golden Raisin
    Roosterkoek **169**
Cranberry-Caramel Tart **231**
Cranberry Filling **158**
Cranberry Orange Cookies **310**
Cranberry Orange Jam **303**
Cranberry Orange Yule Log Cookies **347**
Cranberry Powder **32**
Cranberry Streusel Bundt Cake **32**
Cranberry Pecan Divinity **392**
Cream Cheese Frosting **17**
Cream Cheese Glaze **46**
Cream Cheese Pastry Crust **206**
Crème Diplomat **45**
Crème Fraîche Cheesecake **106**
Crispy Chocolate Chip Cookies **272**
Crumb Topping **181**
Crumble Topping **108**
Curry-Banana Ice Cream **385**
Custard Filling **363**

D

Date and Hazelnut Caramel Cake **25**
Date Caramel **25**
Date Caramel Buttercream **25**
Deep-Dish Quiche with Spring
    Vegetables **260**
Double Chocolate Biscotti **320**
Double Chocolate Macaroons **311**
Double Chocolate Peppermint Sugar
    Cookies **302**
Double Chocolate Spice Bundt Cake **38**
Dried Cranberry Shortbread
    Cookies **335**
Drunken Figs **125**

E

Eggnog Drop Cookies **350**
Eggnog Panna Cotta **388**
Embroidered Ornaments **315**
Espresso and Cacao Caramels **391**
Espresso Shortbread Cookies **291**

F

Fast Puff Pastry Dough **255**
Fig Brownies with Sour Beer
    Caramel **356**
Fig Pastry Cream **251**
Fig Preserves Cake **54**
Figgy Duff **372**
Filigree Trees **314**
Finnish Joululimppu **160**
Five-Spice Fig Soetkoekies **339**
Five-Spice Molasses Cookies **341**
Five-Spice Pomegranate Glaze **382**
Flaky Pastry Dough **229**
Flourless Peanut Butter Cookies with
    Peanut Butter Cream Cheese
    Filling **300**

Fluffy Marshmallow Cream **224**
Frangipane **187**
French Apple-Almond Cake **48**
French Silk Filing **188**
French Silk Pie **188**

G

Galette Des Rois **246**
Ganache **85, 201, 238, 385**
Ganache Filling **154, 224**
Ganache Frosting **90**
German Chocolate Pound Cake **39**
Ghee-Infused Pumpkin Bread Pudding
    with Pomegranate Molasses **378**
Ginger Cake with Mango Curd and Key
    Lime Buttercream **29**
Ginger-Lime Crumb Topping **62**
Ginger Pastry Cream **251**
Ginger Simple Syrup **29**
Ginger Sugar **248**
Ginger Syrup **394**
Gingerbread Cheesecake Bars **366**
Gingerbread Cookie Dough **312**
Gingerbread House **344**
Gingerbread Ornaments **322**
Gingerbread Thumbprint Cookies with
    Cranberry Orange Jam **303**
Gingersnap Crumb Crust **219**
Glazed Blueberries **191**
Gluten-Free Holiday Almond Rainbow
    Cookies with Matcha and Cherry **286**
Goat Cheese Crust **199**
Gold Leaf Bourbon Caramel Millionaire
    Bites **306**
Golden Syrup **134**
Grand Marnier Ganache **363**
Grand Marnier Poppy Seed Cake **69**
Granny Smith Applesauce **360, 377**
Greek Tsoureki **145**
Grilled Browned Butter Pound Cake with
    Berries **53**
Guava Cream Cheese Cookies **329**
Gumdrop Mushrooms and Leaves **347**

H

Halva and Pistachio Pinwheel
    Cookies **281**
Homemade Graham Crackers **337**
Homemade Halva **386**
Honey Butter **152**
Honey Cashew Bundt Cake **34**
Honey Filling **180**
Honey-Glazed Pecans **223**
Honey Nut Pie **216**
Honey-Orange Glaze **138**
Honey Pear Swirl Bread **165**
Honey Pie **216**
Honey Tea Loaves **131**
Horchata Buttercream **297**
Hot Cross Buns Dough **134**

I

Icing **279**
Individual Plum Lavender Tarts **237**

Italian Cream Bundt Cake **35**
Italian Cream Sheet Cake **59**
Italian Plum-and-Parmesan Scones **127**

J

Juniper, Pear, and Blueberry Breton
    Tarts **236**

K

Kahlúa Espresso Cake **68**
Key Lime Buttercream **29**
Key Lime Pie **195**
King Cake Dough **139**
Koeksisters **394**
Kulich **146**

L

Lavender Oregano Shortcrust **362**
Lavender Sandwich Cookies with Lemon
    Curd Filling **274**
Layered Meringue Terrine **374**
Lemon Blueberry Filling **236**
Lemon Cream Cheese Pecan
    Cookies **334**
Lemon Cream Glaze **54**
Lemon Curd **301, 373**
Lemon Curd Filling **274**
Lemon Icing **146**
Lemon Meringue Nests **373**
Lemon Semolina Cake **28**
Lemon Shortbread Cookies with Lemon
    Curd Filling **301**
Lemon Swiss Meringue **194**
Limoncello Meringue Cake **77**
Loaded Holiday Cookies **327**

M

Macadamia Nut Basil Topping **211**
Mango Chutney **116**
Mango Frangipane Pie **187**
Maple Butter Sauce **375**
Maple Crème Fraîche **377**
Maple Date Walnut Coffee Cake **104**
Maple Whipped Cream **215**
Marshmallow Filling **257**
Marzipan **147**
Marzipan Filling **247**
Mascarpone Cream **226**
Mascarpone Crème Fraîche Frosting **16**
Mascarpone Glaze **258**
Mascarpone Pretzel Strawberry Tart **226**
Matcha Macarons with Baileys Original
    Irish Cream Buttercream Filling **283**
McIntosh Applesauce **75, 108**
Melktertjies **340**
Melktertjies Filling **340**
Melted Chocolate **302**
Melted Snowman Sugar Cookies **323**
Meringue Cookies **374**
Mexican Chocolate Fudge Pie **217**
Mexican Chocolate Sandwich Cookies
    with Dulce de Leche Filling **304**
Meyer Lemon & Almond Madeleines
    with Avocado Oil **381**

Meyer Lemon & Blueberry Pie **191**
Meyer Lemon Curd **191**
Meyer Lemon Glaze **381**
Meyer Lemon-Olive Oil Coffee Cake **102**
Mimi's Cookies **279**
Mincemeat Braid **249**
Mincemeat Filling **249**
Mint Chocolate Biscuit Sandwich
    Cookies **307**
Miso Caramel **385**
Mulled Wine Cake **70**

N

Nanaimo Bars **363**
Natural Strawberry Cake with Browned
    Butter Frosting **19**
Norwegian Julekake **158**
Nutella and Marshmallow Strudels **257**

O

Oatmeal Cranberry Cream Pie
    Cookies **333**
One-Layer Applesauce Cake **75**
Orange and Campari Turkish
    Delight **393**
Orange and Pistachio Strawberry Tart **227**
Orange Blossom Crème Fraîche Filling **78**
Orange Blossom Filling **204**
Orange Blossom Vanilla Brown Sugar
    Pie **204**
Orange-Cardamom Loaves **56**
Orange Currant Hot Cross Buns **138**
Orange Custard Bars **359**
Orange Frosting **60**
Orange Glaze **56**
Orange Marmalade Filing **162**
Orange Molasses Filling **181**
Orange Pastry Cream **227**
Orange Spice Sheet Cake **60**
Oversized Honey Ricotta Strudel **256**

P

Paleo Magic Cookie Bars **367**
Pane Di Pasqua **148**
Pâte Brisée **216**
Pâte Sucrée **235**
PB&J Coffee Cake **103**
Peach Almond Cake **76**
Peach and Blueberry Buckwheat
    Sonker **179**
Peach and Cantaloupe Grunt **211**
Peach Mango Chutney **166**
Peach-Plum Crumble Pie **189**
Peanut Butter Cream Cheese Filling **300**
Peanut Butter Crumble **95**
Peanut Butter Filling **201**
Peanut Butter Pie **201**
Peanut Butter Waffles with Ganache,
    Curry-Banana Ice Cream,
    and Miso Caramel **385**
Peanut Butter-Nutella Coffee Cake **95**
Pear-Rosemary Bundt Cake **40**
Pear Upside-Down Loaf Cake **83**
Pear, Honey, and Lime Pie **186**

index

Pecan Butter Tarts **229**
Pecan Caramel Cinnamon Rolls **144**
Pecan Dough **231**
Pecan Ginger Linzer Cookies with Orange Marmalade **348**
Pecan-Toffee Bites **321**
Pepper Jelly Glaze **383**
Peppermint Buttercream Filling **290**
Peppermint Chocolate-Dipped Sugar Cookies **328**
Peppermint Marshmallows **288**
Peppermint S'mores with Chocolate Graham Crackers **288**
Pickled Cherries **150**
Pickled Cherry Bombs **150**
Pickled Cherry Cheese Balls **150**
Pineapple & Coconut Pie **190**
Pineapple Brown Betty **178**
Pink Grapefruit Bars **365**
Pink Grapefruit Filling **365**
Pink Peppercorn Madeleines with Five-Spice Pomegranate Glaze **382**
Pistachio Frangipane **213**
Pistachio Paste **21**
Pistachio Streusel **98**
Place Card Cookies **312**
Plum-and-Pretzel Cheesecake Pie **184**
Plum Icebox Cake **65**
Poached Pears **186**
Praline Hazelnuts **15**
Pumpkin Apple Loaf **108**
Pumpkin Bread with Concord Grape Jam and Drunken Figs **125**
Pumpkin Cake Roll with Orange Blossom Crème Fraîche and Pistachios **78**
Pumpkin Pie with Goat Cheese Crust **199**
Pumpkin Spice Shortbread Cookies **292**

Q

Queen Elizabeth Cake **47**
Quick Puff Pastry **249**

R

Rainbow Sprinkle Bread with Birthday Cake Crumb Topping **123**
Raspberry-Buttermilk Coffee Cake **93**
Raspberry Jam Coffee Cake with Pistachio Streusel **98**
Raspberry Lemon Chiffon Pie **194**
Raspberry Lemon Filling **194**
Raspberry Swirl Pistachio Meringue Cookies **395**
Rhubarb and Almond Tart **234**
Rhubarb and Browned Butter Tartlets **235**
Rhubarb Brown Sugar Cake **63**
Rhubarb Filling **213**
Rhubarb-Ginger Muffins with Rhubarb-Vanilla Bean Streusel **114**
Rhubarb Pistachio Pie **213**
Rhubarb-Vanilla Bean Streusel **114**
Ricotta Filling **256**
Right-Side Up Pineapple Crumb Cake **97**
Roasted Chestnuts **253**
Rooibos & Vanilla Biscotti **338**

Rose, White Chocolate, and Pistachio Wreath Cookies **295**
Rosemary Parmesan Soda Bread **120**
Rosemary Saltine Crumb Crust **215**
Rosemary Shortbread Linzer Cookies with Red Pepper Jelly **346**
Rose Water Glaze **295**
Royal Icing **296, 322, 339, 344**
Rum Apple Cider Rosemary Crumb Cake **73**
Rum Glaze **96, 136**
Rum Raisin Coffee Cake **96**
Rum Raisin Hot Cross Buns **136**

S

Sacher Cake Layer **90**
Sacher S'mores Torte **90**
Salted Caramel Sablè Sandwich Cookies **284**
Salted Chocolate Chip Cookies **280**
Salty Brown Sugar Swiss Meringue **81**
Salty Honey Meringue **219**
Satsuma Marmalade **176**
Satsuma Marmalade Hand Pies **176**
Scottish Fruit Slice Bars **362**
Shoofly Pie **181**
Simple Syrup **252**
Slice 'n' Bake Vanilla Bean Shortbread Sandwich Cookies with Chai Buttercream Frosting **305**
Snowflake Cookies **316**
Snowflake Sandwich Cookies with Peppermint Buttercream Filling **290**
Sour Beer Caramel **356**
Sour Cherry Shortbread Linzer Cookies **268**
Sour Cream Frosting **27**
Speculoos Cookies **296**
Spiced Buttercream **23**
Spiced Cranberry Scones **130**
Spiced Honey Caramel **65**
Spiced Persimmon Coconut Cake **23**
Spiced Pineapple Filling **308**
Spiced Pineapple Linzer Cookies **308**
Spiced Rum Raisins **96**
Spiced Simple Syrup **100**
Spiced Streusel **32**
Spicy Chocolate Sandwich Cookies with Horchata Buttercream **297**
Spicy Ganache **397**
Spicy Sweet Potato Roosterkoek **167**
Spitzbuben (Linzer) Cookies **299**
Spumoni Cake **21**
Strawberries and Cream King Cake **139**
Strawberry Cream Cheese Frosting **58**
Strawberry Cream Cheese Pound Cake Loaves **57**
Strawberry Cucumber Bread **126**
Strawberry Filling **248**
Strawberry Ginger Kouign Amann **248**
Strawberry Mascarpone Strudels **258**
Strawberry Preserves **258**
Strawberry Raspberry Cobbler **185**
Strawberry-Rhubarb Pies **192**
Strawberry Sauce **57**

Strawberry Sheet Cake **58**
Strawberry Skillet Cake **88**
Strawberry Swirl Cheesecake Pie **202**
Sugar Pie **177**
Sugar Topping **45**
Sugared Flowers and Berries **16**
Swedish Saffranskrans **162**
Sweet and Salty Monster Cookies **317**
Sweet Bread Dough **145**
Sweet Cherry and Cornmeal Upside-Down Cake **107**
Sweet Corn and Pepper Jelly Old-Fashioned Doughnuts **383**
Sweet Cream Cheese Frosting **20**
Sweet Kraut **259**
Sweet Potato Bebinca **387**
Sweet Potato Biscuits **152**
Sweet Potato Filling **259**
Sweet Potato Turnovers with Sweet Kraut & Vegan Orange Sour Cream **259**
Sweet Potato Yogurt Pie **206**
Sweetened Whipped Cream **59, 86, 87, 98**
Swiss Hefekranz **156**
Swiss Meringues **252**

T

Tahini and Milk Chocolate Chip Cookies **277**
Tahini and Cranberry Whole Wheat Skillet Cookie **276**
Tahini-Cardamom Shortbreads with Pistachios **278**
Tahini Shortcakes with Apricot Jam and Orange Blossom Whipped Cream **50**
Tangerine Glaze **130**
Tangerine Tart **239**
Tarragon Vanilla Wafers **65**
Tart Dough **230**
Tarte Tatin **230**
Tarte Tropézienne **45**
Ten-Layer Spiced Russian Honey Cake **27**
Texas Sheet Cake **61**
Thandai Powder **282**
Thandai Shortbread Cookies Dipped in White Chocolate with Pistachios and Rose Petals **282**
Thick Caramel Sauce **318**
Three-Dimensional Reindeer Cookies **324**
Toasted Chocolate Swirl Meringues **396**
Toasted Coconut Pastry Cream **190**
Toasted Coconut Sugar **308**
Toasty Brown Sugar Pastry Cream **236**
Traditional American Piecrust **209**
Traditional Roosterkoek **166**
Triple Berry Cake Doughnuts **371**
Tropical Hummingbird Layer Cake **17**
Turtle Brownies **357**

U

Upside-Down Apple Crisp Cake **87**

V

Vanilla Bean Marshmallow **91, 337**

Vanilla Bundt Cake with Bourbon-Vanilla Caramel Sauce **37**
Vanilla Buttercream **21, 350**
Vanilla Buttermilk Cake with Chocolate-Buttermilk Frosting **101**
Vanilla Caramel Filling **284**
Vanilla Custard **186**
Vanilla Glaze **122, 158**
Vanilla Meringue Topping **77**
Vanilla Royal Icing **312**
Vanilla Shortbread with Apple Pie Filling **298**
Vanilla-Almond Royal Icing **349**
Vegan Orange Sour Cream **259**

W

Walnut Golden Raisin Soda Bread **119**
Warm Chocolate Frosting **61**
Whipped Cream **205, 252**
Whipped Mascarpone **28**
White Chocolate Cream **374**
White Chocolate Honeycomb **27**
White Chocolate-Tahini Babka **154**
White Drizzle **257**
White Glaze **371**

Z

Zucchini Banana Bread **124**

CREDITS

Cover photography by Marcy Black Simpson

Photography by:
Matt Armendariz **4-5, 112, 171**
Stephen DeVries **110** (top left photo)
Joe Schmelzer **240** (top right photo), **266**
Maya Visnyei **265**

Food Styling by:
Marian Cooper Cairns **4-5, 112, 171**
Rebecca Firth **240** (top right photo), **266**
Emily Turner **265**

Photography and Food Styling by:
Maryanne Cabrera **264** (bottom left photo)
Rachel Conners **351**
Shiran Dickman **267**
Dale Gray **264** (top left photo), **368** (bottom left photo)
Amy Ho **352**